Routledge Handbook of Surveillance Studies

Surveillance is a central organizing practice. Gathering personal data and processing them in searchable databases drives administrative efficiency but also raises questions about security, governance, civil liberties and privacy. Surveillance is both globalized in cooperative schemes, such as sharing biometric data, and localized in the daily minutiae of social life. This innovative *Handbook* explores the empirical, theoretical and ethical issues around surveillance and its use in daily life.

With a collection of over forty essays from the leading names in surveillance studies, the *Handbook* takes a truly multi-disciplinary approach to the critical questions of:

- surveillance and population control;
- policing, intelligence and war;
- production and consumption;
- new media;
- security;
- identification;
- regulation and resistance.

The *Routledge Handbook of Surveillance Studies* is an international, accessible, definitive and comprehensive overview of the rapidly growing multi-disciplinary field of surveillance studies. The *Handbook*'s direct, authoritative style will appeal to a wide range of scholars and students in the social sciences, arts and humanities.

Kirstie Ball is Reader in Surveillance and Organization at The Open University Business School. Her research focuses on surveillance and global capital, and the experience of surveillance. She co-founded the journal *Surveillance & Society* and is a director of the Surveillance Studies Network.

Kevin D. Haggerty is editor of the *Canadian Journal of Sociology* and book review editor of the international journal *Surveillance & Society*. He is Professor of Sociology and Criminology at the University of Alberta and a member of the executive team for the New Transparency Major Collaborative Research Initiative.

David Lyon holds a Research Chair in Surveillance Studies, is Professor of Sociology and Director of the Surveillance Studies Centre at Queen's University, Canada.

Routledge Handbook of Surveillance Studies

Edited by Kirstie Ball, Kevin D. Haggerty and David Lyon

Routledge
Taylor & Francis Group

LONDON AND NEW YORK

First published 2012 by Routledge

Paperback published 2014
by Routledge
2 Park Square, Milton Park, Abingdon, Oxon OX14 4RN

and in the USA and Canada
711 Third Avenue, New York, NY 10017

Routledge is an imprint of the Taylor & Francis Group, an informa business

British Library Cataloguing in Publication Data
A catalogue record for this book is available from the British Library

Library of Congress Cataloging in Publication Data
Routledge handbook of surveillance studies / edited by David Lyon, Kevin Haggerty and Kirstie Ball.
    p. cm.
    Includes bibliographical references and index.
    1. Privacy, Right of. 2. Electronic surveillance–Social aspects. 3. Information technology–Social aspects.
4. Social control. I. Lyon, David, 1948- II. Haggerty, Kevin D. III. Ball, Kirstie.
    JC596.R68 2012
    363.2'32–dc23
            2011041478

ISBN 13: 978-0-415-58883-6 hbk
ISBN 13: 978-1-138-02602-5 pbk
ISBN 13: 978-0-203-81494-9 ebook

Typeset in Bembo
By Taylor & Francis Books

Contents

Contents

Contents

Illustrations

Table

Figures

Contributors

Yasmeen Abu-Laban is Professor in the Department of Political Science at the University of Alberta (Canada). She has published widely on issues relating to the comparative dimensions of gender and racialization processes, border and migration policies, and citizenship theory. She is co-editor (with David Lyon and Elia Zureik) of *Surveillance and Control in Israel/Palestine: Population, Territory and Power* (Routledge 2011).

Pete Adey is Reader in Cultural Geography at Keele University, UK and co-director of the interdisciplinary Emerging Securities Unit. His research examines the relationship between mobility, space and security with a particular interest in the cultures and contours of air-travel and, increasingly, the substance of air itself. He is author of *Mobility* (Routledge), *Aerial Life: Spaces, Mobilities, Affects* (Wiley-Blackwell), *Air* (with Reaktion's new *Earth* series), and the forthcoming co-edited volumes *Handbook of Mobilities* (Routledge) and *From Above: The Politics and Practices of the View from the Skies* (Hurst). He is just completing two major research grants on how societies prepare for and govern emergencies in the context of contemporary structures of resilience, and a historical exploration of bombing through the example of the Liverpool Blitz.

Mark Andrejevic is Associate Professor in the Department of Communication Studies at the University of Iowa. He is the author of *Reality TV: The Work of Being Watched* and *iSpy: Surveillance and Power in the Interactive Era*, as well as numerous articles and book chapters on surveillance and popular culture.

Nelson Arteaga Botello is a researcher of sociology in the Faculty of Political and Social Science at the Autonomous University of the State of Mexico, specializing in issues of violence, security and surveillance in Latin America. His most recent publications are *Vigilancia en el Sur Global* (Porrúa 2009); "Privacy and Surveillance in Mexico and Brazil: A Cross-national Analysis," in *Surveillance, Privacy and the Globalization of Personal Data* (McGill-Queen's University Press 2010); "Poverty as Space of Indetermination," in *Revista Internacional de Sociología* (2010); and "Security Metamorphosis in Latin America," in Vida Bajc and Willem de Lint (eds), *Security and Everyday Life* (Routledge 2011).

Kirstie S. Ball is Reader in Surveillance and Organization at the Open University Business School, UK. Her principal research interests are surveillance in and around organizations, surveiled subjectivities and surveiled bodies. Her publications range from scholarly articles to consultancy reports and print and broadcast media pieces. Her research has been funded by the Economic and Social Research Council, The Leverhulme Trust and the EU Framework 7 Programme. Kirstie co-founded the journal *Surveillance & Society* and is a founding director of Surveillance Studies Network.

jennifer barrigar is a doctoral candidate at the University of Ottawa, Canada (Law and Technology). Her dissertation focuses on reputation as a means of surveilling and shaping people's identities online, as well as an examination of the law's current treatment of reputation online and off. jennifer spent a summer during law school working in a national law firm and subsequently articled with the Office of the Privacy Commissioner of Canada, remaining as Legal Counsel for five years. She has enjoyed a variety of additional academic and activist experiences, including the Summer Doctoral Program at Oxford's Internet Institute, and an internship at the Electronic Privacy Information Centre in Washington, DC.

Colin J. Bennett received his Bachelor's and Master's degrees from the University of Wales, and his PhD from the University of Illinois at Urbana-Champaign. Since 1986 he has taught in the Department of Political Science at the University of Victoria, Canada. He has been a fellow at Harvard's Kennedy School of Government, a Visiting Fellow at the Center for the Study of Law and Society at University of California, Berkeley, and Visiting Professor at the School of Law, University of New South Wales, Australia. His research has focused on the comparative analysis of surveillance technologies and privacy protection policies at the domestic and international levels, and he has published extensively on these topics in published articles, policy reports and books, including *The Privacy Advocates: Resisting the Spread of Surveillance* (MIT Press 2008). Colin Bennett is currently the co-investigator of a large Major Collaborative Research Initiative grant entitled "The New Transparency: Surveillance and Social Sorting."

Didier Bigo is MCU Research Professor at Sciences-Po Paris/CERI and Professor in the Department of War Studies at King's College London. He is editor of the journals *International Political Sociology* and *Cultures et Conflits*. He has recently published (with Philippe Bonditti, Julien Jeandesboz and Francesco Ragazzi) "Border and Security: the Different Logics of Surveillance in Europe" in the volume *The Others in Europe: Legal and Social Categorization in Context,* edited by Andrea Rea, Saskia Bonjour and Dirk Jacobs (ULB Press 2011); and edited (with Sergio Carrera, Elspeth Guild and Rob Walker) *Europe's 21st Century Challenge: Delivering Liberty and Security* (Ashgate 2010). Further information can be found at www. didierbigo.com.

William Bogard is Deburgh Chair of Social Sciences at Whitman College. He is the author of *The Simulation of Surveillance: Hypercontrol in Telematic Societies* (Cambridge University Press 1996), *Distraction and Digital Culture in Life in the Wires* (CTheory 2000), "Digital Resisto(e)rs", in *Critical Studies: A Reader*, ed. Arthur and Marilouise Kroker (University of Toronto Press 2008), and other works on social control and digital culture. His current research focuses on the history of "control surfaces" as they figure into the development of digital technologies.

Simone Browne is Assistant Professor in the departments of Sociology and African Diaspora Studies at the University of Texas at Austin. She teaches and researches surveillance, biometrics, airport protocol and popular culture.

Fernanda Bruno is Associate Professor in the graduate program in Communication and Culture at the Federal University of Rio de Janeiro (UFRJ), Brazil. She has a PhD in Communication from the Federal University of Rio de Janeiro (Doctoral Research Fellow at Paris Descartes University, Sorbonne, 2000). Bruno is also a National Counsel of Technological and Scientific Development/CNPq researcher and founding member of the Latin America Surveillance Studies Network. In 2010–2011 she was a visiting researcher at Sciences Po (CERI and Médialab), Paris.

Ayse Ceyhan (PhD) is a political scientist. She is senior lecturer on Security and Technology Studies and International Relations at Sciences Po, Paris and is the director of the Programme *Security, Technology, and Society* at Maison des Sciences de l'Homme (MSH) (www.msh-paris.fr). Her research focuses on the technologization of security and its impacts on society and the securitization of borders, economy and politics. A great part of her work has been dedicated to biometrics and the securitization of borders. Currently she works on security research co-design and epistemology. She is co-editor of *Identification biométrique* (Editions Maison des Sciences de l'Homme 2011) and author of several articles on security, biometrics and technology, such as "Technologization of Security: Management of Uncertainty and Risk in the Age of Biometrics," (2008) *Surveillance & Society* 5(2): 102–23.

Jon Coaffee holds a Chair in Spatial Planning and Urban Resilience at the University of Birmingham, UK. His work has been funded by a variety of UK Research Councils as well as the UK Security Services. He has published widely on the social and economic future of cities, and especially the impact of terrorism and other security concerns. Recent publications include *Terrorism Risk and the City* (2003), *The Everyday Resilience of the City: How Cities Respond to Terrorism and Disaster* (2008), *Terrorism Risk and the Global City: Towards Urban Resilience* (2009) and *Sustaining and Securing the Olympic City* (2011).

Andrew Donaldson received a BSc in Biology before moving into the Social Sciences with his postgraduate studies. Since 2001 a major strand of his research has been the management of animal disease risk on which he has published extensively. He has acted as an expert advisor to the UK's National Audit Office on animal health policy and continues to research the everyday management of natural hazards and biological infrastructure. He lectures in environmental planning at Newcastle University in the UK, where he is a member of the Global Urban Research Unit and an associate of The Centre for Rural Economy.

Nora Draper is a PhD student at the Annenberg School for Communication at the University of Pennsylvania. Her research interests include cyber surveillance and struggles around the control of digital information. In particular, she is interested in notions of reputation in the digital age.

Greg Elmer (PhD at the University of Massachusetts Amherst) is Bell Globemedia Research Chair and Director of the Infoscape Centre for the Study of Social Media at Ryerson University, Canada. Greg's research and teaching focus on new media and politics, theories and methods in social media studies, surveillance theory, and media globalization. He was most recently Cultures of the Digital Economy research fellow at Anglia Ruskin University, senior faculty fellow at the London School of Economics, and visiting research professor at Yeungnam University, South Korea.

Pete Fussey is a Senior Lecturer in Criminology at the University of Essex, UK. Dr Fussey's main research interest focuses on surveillance, control and the city particularly in relation to crime and terrorism. He is currently researching the form and impact of the 2012 Olympic security strategy on its wider urban setting and is working on two large-scale ESRC- and EPSRC-funded research projects looking at counter-terrorism in the UK's crowded spaces and at the future urban resilience until 2050. Recent publications include *Securing and Sustaining the Olympic City* (Ashgate) and *Terrorism and the Olympics* (Routledge).

Oscar H. Gandy, Jr is Emeritus Professor of Communication at the University of Pennsylvania. His research and writing is in the area of privacy and surveillance, race and discrimination, and communication and information policy. His most recent book is *Coming to Terms with Chance* (2009), and his major contribution to the field of Surveillance Studies has been *The Panoptic Sort* (1993). His most important contributions to Communication and Information Studies are *Beyond Agenda Setting* (1982) and *Communication and Race* (1998).

Kelly Gates is Associate Professor of Communication, Science Studies, and Critical Gender Studies at University of California, San Diego. Her recent work focuses on the politics of surveillance system development in post-war United States. Her book, *Our Biometric Future: Facial Recognition Technology and the Culture of Surveillance* (NYU Press 2011), examines the effort underway since the 1960s to teach computers to "see" the human face. She is also co-editor, with Shoshana Magnet, of *The New Media of Surveillance* (Routledge 2009), and she has published articles in *Cultural Studies, Social Text, Television and New Media* and other journals.

John Gilliom is Professor of Political Science at Ohio University. His research examines the political dynamics of surveillance. He is author of *Overseers of the Poor: Surveillance, Resistance, and the Limits of Privacy* (Chicago), which explores how the words and actions of those who live under surveillance challenge prevailing thinking about surveillance and privacy. Gilliom is also the author of *Surveillance, Privacy and the Law: Employee Drug Testing and the Politics of Social Control* (Michigan), and other writings on law and the politics of surveillance. With Torin Monahan, he is currently writing *SuperVision: A Citizen's Guide to the Surveillance Society*.

Kevin D. Haggerty is editor of the *Canadian Journal of Sociology* and book review editor of the international journal *Surveillance & Society*. He is Professor of Sociology and Criminology at the University of Alberta, Canada and a member of the executive team for the *New Transparency* Major Collaborative Research Initiative. He has authored, co-authored or co-edited *Policing the Risk Society* (Oxford University Press), *Making Crime Count* (University of Toronto Press), *The New Politics of Surveillance and Visibility* (University of Toronto Press), *Surveillance & Democracy* (Routledge) and *Security Games: Surveillance and Security at Mega-Events* (Routledge).

Ben Hayes has worked with the civil liberties group Statewatch since 1996 and is a Fellow of the Transnational Institute. He has a PhD from the University of Ulster, UK. He also works as an independent consultant and researcher. He is currently involved in projects with the Transnational Institute, European Center for Constitutional and Human Rights, Cordaid and the European Commission. His recent publications include "Counter-terrorism, 'Policy Laundering' and the FATF: Legalising Surveillance, Regulating Civil Society" (forthcoming 2012), "Blacklisted: Targeted Sanctions, Pre-emptive Security and Fundamental Rights" (2010, with Gavin Sullivan) and "NeoConOpticon: The EU Security-Industrial Complex" (2009). For more information see www.tni.org/users/ben-hayes.

Richard Jenkins is Professor of Sociology at the University of Sheffield, UK. Trained originally as an anthropologist, he has done field research in Northern Ireland, England, Wales and Denmark. His theoretical interests include processes of identification, in all of their manifestations, and the modern (re)enchantment of the world. Major recent publications include *Social Identity* (Routledge, 3rd edition, 2008), *Rethinking Ethnicity* (Sage, 2nd edition, 2008) and *Being Danish* (Museum Tusculanum Press 2011). He is currently completing a long-term project about a "black magic" scare in Northern Ireland in the 1970s.

Dietmar Kammerer is a research fellow at the Institute for Media Studies, Philipps-Universität Marburg. He is author of *Bilder der Überwachung* (Images of Surveillance) (Suhrkamp, Frankfurt am Main, 2008), and has published numerous articles in German and English on the topic of culture, cinema, and aesthetics of surveillance. Other research interests include the history of video surveillance in Germany and the concept of the "control society." He also works as a freelance film critic and journalist.

Ian Kerr holds the Canada Research Chair in Ethics, Law and Technology at the University of Ottawa, Faculty of Law, with cross-appointments to Medicine, Philosophy and Information Studies. Dr Kerr has published books and articles on topics at the intersection of ethics, law and technology and is currently engaged in research on two broad themes: (i) Privacy and Surveillance; and (ii) Human-Machine Mergers. Building on his recent Oxford University Press book, *Lessons from the Identity Trail*, his ongoing privacy work focuses on the interplay between emerging public and private sector surveillance technologies, civil liberties and human rights.

Hille Koskela works as an Academy Research Fellow in the Department of Social Research, University of Helsinki, Finland. She is also an Adjunct Professor in Urban Geography. Her research interests include video surveillance and the politics of control, gender relations in surveillance practices, the emotional experience of being watched, and the responsibilization of the public to contribute in surveillance via online webcams. She has published surveillance-related articles in a wide range of multidisciplinary journals—most recently in *Surveillance & Society, Crime Media Culture* and *Theoretical Criminology*—and contributed to several international anthologies.

Inga Kroener is a Senior Research Associate at Lancaster University. Her research interests lie in the area of contemporary history of CCTV and public engagement in the UK, the history of modern science and technology, the sociology of science and public dimensions of science and technology. Her PhD was a social history of the development of CCTV in the UK. In her thesis she undertook an examination of the historical, social, political and economic factors influencing the development, usage and widespread dissemination of CCTV, in order to provide a detailed look at the question of why the UK has become so camera-surveiled. She currently works on two EU Framework 7 projects.

David Lyon is Director of the Surveillance Studies Centre, Queen's Research Chair in Surveillance Studies and Professor of Sociology at Queen's University. He is author and co-editor of many books and articles in Surveillance Studies, most recently *Identifying Citizens: ID Cards as Surveillance* (2009), *Surveillance, Privacy and the Globalization of Personal Information* (2010), *Surveillance and Control in Israel/Palestine* (2011) and *Eyes Everywhere: The Global Growth of Camera Surveillance* (2011). He is a co-founder of *Surveillance & Society* and the Surveillance Studies Network. See www.sscqueens.org/davidlyon.

Gary T. Marx is Professor Emeritus M.I.T. and an electronic and itinerant scholar—see www.garymarx.net. He has worked in the areas of race and ethnicity, collective behavior and social movements, law and society and surveillance studies. He is the author of *Protest and Prejudice, Undercover: Police Surveillance in America, Collective Behavior and Social Movements* (with Doug McAdam) and editor of *Racial Conflict, Muckraking Sociology, Undercover: Police Surveillance in Comparative Perspective* (with C. Fijnaut) *Windows in the Soul: Surveillance and Society in an Age of High Technology* (forthcoming) and other books.

Michael McCahill is a Lecturer in Criminology in the Department of Social Sciences at the University of Hull, UK. His main research interests include the social impact of "new surveillance" technologies and media representations of surveillance. He has published widely on the topic of surveillance and social control, including a book entitled *The Surveillance Web* (Willan) for which he received the British Society of Criminology book prize 2003. His most recent book (with Roy Coleman) is *Surveillance and Crime* (2011), published by Sage.

John E. McGrath is Artistic Director of National Theatre Wales, a new company founded in 2010 to bring extraordinary theatre to a wide range of spaces across Wales and beyond. Previous roles include Artistic Director of Contact, Manchester and Associate Director of Mabou Mines, New York. He has a PhD in Performance Studies from NYU, a Masters in Theatre Directing from Columbia and first class honours in English from Oxford. As well as publishing *Loving Big Brother* in 2004, he has written extensively on theatre, directed numerous productions and in 2005 was recipient of the NESTA Cultural Leadership Award.

Torin Monahan is Associate Professor of Human and Organizational Development and Associate Professor of Medicine at Vanderbilt University, TN. His book, *Surveillance in the Time of Insecurity* (2010), was the recipient of the 2011 Surveillance Studies Network book prize. Other books include *Schools under*

Surveillance: Cultures of Control in Public Education (2010), *Surveillance and Security: Technological Politics and Power in Everyday Life* (2006), and *Globalization, Technological Change, and Public Education* (2005). Monahan is an elected council member of the Sociology of Science and Technology division of the International Sociological Association and is on the editorial board for the primary academic journal on surveillance, *Surveillance & Society*.

David Murakami Wood is Canada Research Chair (Tier II) in Surveillance Studies and Associate Professor in the Department of Sociology, Queen's University, Ontario, and a member of the Surveillance Studies Centre. He is co-founder and Editor-in-Chief of *Surveillance & Society*, and co-founder and trustee of the Surveillance Studies Network. He is an interdisciplinary social scientist specializing in the study of surveillance in urban contexts worldwide, and in international cross-cultural comparative studies particularly in the UK, Japan and Brazil. He is also interested in: ubiquitous computing; resilience to disaster, war and terrorism; and science fiction literature and films.

Daniel Neyland is a Senior Lecturer at Lancaster University, UK. His research interests cover issues of governance, accountability and ethics in forms of science, technology and organization. He draws on ideas from ethnomethodology, science and technology studies (in particular forms of radical and reflexive skepticism, constructivism, Actor-Network Theory and the recent STS turn to markets and other forms of organizing) and his research is ethnographic in orientation. He has published widely, including a book entitled *Privacy, Surveillance and Public Trust* (Palgrave 2006) and an edited collection on *New Directions in Surveillance and Privacy* (Willan 2009).

Clive Norris is Professor of Sociology at the University of Sheffield, UK and Head of the Department of Sociological Studies. Since 1993 he has received several awards from the ESRC to work on projects related to the sociology of surveillance. These included exploring the police use of informers, and examining the social impact of CCTV surveillance. In 1998 he was awarded funding by the ESRC to run a series of seminars on surveillance. This brought together for the first time interdisciplinary researchers concerned with the social impact of the new surveillance technologies, and from this he co-founded the free online journal *Surveillance & Society*. Along with colleagues from six European universities, he has worked on a comparative study of the social impact of CCTV and is currently researching the legal, ethical and social implication of "smart" surveillance systems.

Jason Pridmore is the Senior Researcher with the DigIDeas project, a European Research Council-funded project at Zuyd University in the Netherlands. His work with the project focuses on the social and ethical implications of digital identities, coordinating researchers working at the intersections of e-government and security, marketing and social media, and policing and new technologies. Prior to this, Jason was a post-doctoral researcher and student at Queen's University, UK where his work focused on marketing practices as forms of surveillance, looking specifically at the development of consumer "relationships" through loyalty marketing.

Charles Raab was Professor of Government in the University of Edinburgh, and is Professor Emeritus and Honorary Professorial Fellow. He serves on boards of many research projects and academic journals, and on governmental expert groups. With the Surveillance Studies Network, he co-authored *A Report on the Surveillance Society* (2006) and an *Update Report* (2010) for the UK Information Commissioner. He has conducted research on policy and regulatory issues, including privacy, data protection, surveillance, police co-operation, identity management, data sharing and e-government. His publications include (with C. Bennett) *The Governance of Privacy* (2003; 2006), as well as reports for the European Commission, UK and Scottish government agencies, and civil society groups. He was the Specialist Adviser to the House of

Lords Select Committee on the Constitution for an Inquiry resulting in *Surveillance: Citizens and the State*, HL Paper 18, Session 2008–09. He participates in several European Union-funded research projects.

Priscilla M. Regan is Professor in the Department of Public and International Affairs at George Mason University Washington, DC. Before that, she was a Senior Analyst in the Congressional Office of Technology Assessment (1984–89) and Assistant Professor of Politics and Government at the University of Puget Sound (1979–84). From 2005 to 2007, she served as a Program Officer for the Science, Technology and Society Program at the National Science Foundation. Dr. Regan has published over 30 articles or book chapters, as well as *Legislating Privacy: Technology, Social Values, and Public Policy* (University of North Carolina Press 1995). Dr. Regan received her PhD in Government from Cornell University, NY and her BA from Mount Holyoke College, MA.

James B. Rule is Distinguished Affiliated Scholar at the Center for the Study of Law and Society, University of California, Berkeley. He is a long-time researcher and writer on privacy and personal information, beginning with his *Private Lives and Public Surveillance* (Allen Lane 1973). He has held academic appointments at Oxford University, the University of Bordeaux, Stony Brook University, the Institute for Advanced Study in Princeton, and the Center for Advanced Study in the Behavioral Sciences, Stanford. Among his more recent privacy-related works are *Privacy in Peril, How We are Sacrificing a Fundamental Right in Exchange for Security and Convenience* (Oxford University Press 2007) and *Global Privacy Protection: the First Generation*, edited with Graham Greenleaf (Edward Elgar Publishing 2008).

Evelyn Ruppert is an Open University Senior Research Fellow with the Centre for Research on Sociocultural Change (CRESC) (www.cresc.ac.uk/people/dr-evelyn-ruppert). She co-convenes The Social Life of Methods (SLOM) theme together with John Law. Her work is in the sociology of governance and explores how methods of enumeration such as censuses and transactional registers enact different kinds of subjects and populations and make different forms of power and intervention possible. More generally, her work is concerned with how the circulation and mobilization of government digital transactional data is connected to a changing relation to quantification.

Ahmad H. Sa'di is Senior Lecturer of Political Sociology in the department of Politics and Government at Ben-Gurion University of the Negev. His research has dealt with issues relating to collective memory; surveillance, political control and population management; and development and underdevelopment and ethnic relations. He has published a considerable number of articles in referee journals and chapters in collective volumes in English, Arabic, Hebrew, Japanese and German. He is co-editor (with Lila Abu-Lughod) of *Nakba: Palestine, 1948 and the Claims of Memory* (Columbia University Press 2007).

Graham Sewell (PhD University of Wales, 1994) is Professor of Organization Studies and Human Resource Management in the Department of Management and Marketing, University of Melbourne, Australia. Before taking up this position he was Professor and Chair in Organizational Behaviour at Imperial College Business School, London. Graham has published extensively on workplace surveillance in journals such as the *Administrative Science Quarterly*, the *Academy of Management Review*, and *Sociology*. He has held visiting positions at the University of California's Berkeley and Santa Cruz campuses and from 2004 to 2005 he was the Ministerio de Educación y Ciensias de España visiting professor in the Departament di Economia y Empresa at the Universitat Pompeu Fabra, Barcelona. His latest book, *Technology and Organization: Essays in Honour of Joan Woodward* (with Nelson Phillips and Dorothy Griffiths), was published by Emerald in 2010.

Gavin J. D. Smith is a Senior Lecturer in Sociology at The Australian National University and an Honorary Fellow of The Centre for Law, Justice and Journalism, City University London. Gavin is principally interested in the interplay among systems of regulation and subjects of surveillance, particularly the interpretive meanings people attribute to surveillance encounters and exchanges. He is also interested in the normative assumptions structuring the surveillance studies research field. Gavin is currently writing a monograph on the labor of surveillance work – *Opening the Black Box: Surveillance in Everyday Life* (Routledge, 2012) – and a co-authored text with Dr Martin French entitled, *Key Concepts in Social Regulation and Transparency Studies* (Sage, 2012).

Valerie Steeves is Associate Professor in the Department of Criminology at the University of Ottawa, Canada. She is the lead researcher on the Media Awareness Network's *Young Canadians in a Wired World* research project. *Young Canadians* is an ongoing project initiated in 1999 to examine children's online use patterns and social interactions. She is also the principal investigator of the eGirls Project, funded by the Social Sciences and Humanities Research Council of Canada, which explores the ways in which gender is performed by girls and young women in online spaces.

Eric Stoddart is a lecturer in the School of Divinity at the University of St Andrews in Scotland and has recently published *Theological Perspectives on a Surveillance Society: Watching and Being Watched* (Ashgate, Aldershot, UK). He is currently developing a "Surveillance and Religion" research network in his role as Associate Director of the Centre for the Study of Religion and Politics (CSRP), based at the University of St Andrews. He is editor of the journal *Practical Theology*.

Emmeline Taylor is a Lecturer in Sociology at the Australian National University. Her surveillance related research is concerned with understanding how and why some populations are subject to disproportionate levels of surveillance. This has led her to explore the growing use of surveillance in schools and its integration into pedagogical apparatus. More recently, Emmeline has explored the intensification of surveillance experienced by migrating populations. Her current research portfolio can be categorized into three key areas: social impacts of surveillance; developing offender perspectives on acquisitive crime; and examining the efficacy of alternatives to custodial sentences.

Joseph Turow is the Robert Lewis Shayon Professor of Communication at the University of Pennsylvania's Annenberg School for Communication. Much of his research focuses on the intersection of marketing, new media, and society. His most recent book is *The Daily You: How the New Advertising Industry is Defining Your Identity and Your World* (Yale University Press, late 2011).

Irma van der Ploeg holds degrees in Philosophy and Science and Technology Studies. In 2006 she was appointed Associate Professor of Infonomics and New Media at Zuyd University, Maastricht/Heerlen, Netherlands, where she heads the Infonomics and New Media Research Centre (http://infonomie.hszuyd.nl). She has published extensively on philosophical, normative, and gender aspects of medical technologies and information technologies, in particular on biometric identification technologies, and the relation between technology and the body. She is author of *The Machine-Readable Body: Essays on Biometrics and the Informatization of the Body* (Shaker, Maastricht, 2005). In 2008 she was awarded a Starting Grant for Independent Researchers from the European Research Council, for a large, five-year research project entitled 'Social and Ethical Aspects of Digital Identities: Towards a Value Sensitive Identity Management.' (www.digideas.nl).

C. William R. Webster is Director of the MBA Public Service Management programme at the University of Stirling, UK. He is the Chair of the pan-European multidisciplinary "Living in Surveillance

Societies" (LiSS) COST Action IS0807 (www.liss-cost.eu), which seeks to build a better understanding and awareness of technically mediated surveillance practices across Europe. He participates in the Surveillance Studies Network (SSN) and the European Group of Public Administration (EGPA) and is a board member of the Scottish Privacy Forum.

Toni Weller is a Visiting Research Fellow at De Montfort University, Leicester, UK. She has lectured and published extensively on the burgeoning field of information history. Most of her work focuses on the long nineteenth century in Britain, but also has links to contemporary issues around the history and origins of our own information age. She is the current editor of the international journal, *Library & Information History*. Her most recent publication is *Information History in the Modern World: Histories of the Information Age* (Palgrave 2010).

Dean Wilson is Associate Professor of Criminology and Criminal Justice in the School of Law, University of Plymouth, UK and was previously Senior Lecturer in Criminology at Monash University, Australia. Dean undertook the first nationwide study of CCTV in Australia, and has recently completed an Australia Research Council-funded project examining surveillance and plural policing in three locations. He has published widely in the area of surveillance, with specific areas of interest including biometrics, CCTV, border control, military surveillance and covert police operations. Dean is a member of the Editorial Board of the journal *Surveillance & Society*.

Preface

"Your Papers please": personal and professional encounters with surveillance

Gary T. Marx

"You ought to have some papers to show who you are,"
The police officer advised me.
"I do not need any paper. I know who I am," I said.
"Maybe so. Other people are also interested in knowing who you are."
B. Traven, *The Death Ship*

The editors of this volume invited me to write about the growth of surveillance and the importance of scholarly efforts to understand it through the prism of my half a century's involvement with the topic. Being respectful of authority, if not always power, I ambivalently accepted—unaccustomed as I am to the self-promotion and self-exegesis that often hides under the mask of academic formality and dispassion. Yet there is always a person behind the questions, methods and interpretations offered.

I will cover some sources of my initial interest in and later work on the topic; the kinds of questions surveillance developments raised for me in the latter part of the twentieth century and some efforts to conceptually rein in and organize the field's empirical richness. I conclude with a discussion of the characteristics of surveillance studies as an emerging field.

Early interest

The French poet Paul Valéry (1965) has written, "in truth there is no theory which is not a fragment of an autobiography." But can we trust the autobiographer? A little skepticism is always in order—Proust after all stressed that his recalls involved a theory not a record of the past. Kierkegaard observed that while life must be lived forward we seek to understand it by looking backwards. Our retrospective efforts involve linear stories in which discrete events are tied together in neat sense-making packages—downplaying the role of chance, memory failures, disconnection and other possible interpretations. The dots of life are there, but is the *ex post facto* pattern? To what extent does the coherence and explanation lie (but hopefully not lie too badly) in the imposed interpretation, not in the facts such as they are believed to be? The facts of course are unknowable absent a method and conceptual framework for knowing. Yet as Dmitri Shalin (2010) observes, personal characteristics and experiences can hardly be ignored in their effect on the work produced, even as we may be only vaguely aware of them.

My interest in surveillance was affected by growing up in Hollywood during the cold war when every little boy wanted to be the suspicious sheriff of the western movie with the white hat, or the square jawed

G-man with the fedora watching from the shadows of a comic book. Surveillance is likely to be of particular interest to those whose upbringing involved a stern disciplinarian who stressed the importance of liking what you see when you look in the mirror the morning after.

There are other more distant influences, or at least connections, that sparked imagination—being in a Boy Scout troop sponsored by the Los Angeles Police Department; having a relative who worked closely with the director of the CIA in the early 1970s; and a distant English relative who was George Orwell's first publisher.

With respect to young adult experiences—it was a dark and stormy day in the early 1960s at the Russian–Polish border when I first heard the words, "your papers" (there was no *please* in the gruff command). I was held for half a day's interrogation in a windowless room—without explanation or cause by persons of whom it could not be charitably said English was their second (or any) language.

My interest in surveillance was furthered on that trip (part of a year spent traveling around the world) by finding an electronic bug in my Moscow hotel, the clumsy efforts of a spy in-training assigned to our Intourist tour group. The surveillance theme was also accentuated by the difficulty in finding accurate street maps.

While all persons are experienced as subjects of surveillance, this seems more poignant when students or practitioners of the topic are themselves the targets. Consider the involuntary participant observation experiences of surveillance scholars John Gilliom (2001) and James Rule (1973). In an epilogue to his study of the surveillance of welfare recipients Gilliom details a disquieting search (complete with a black helicopter) of his rural home and land for marijuana cultivation based on an imprecisely drawn warrant (marijuana was being grown in a nearby federal forest). Rule was wrongly singled out and detained in a New York airport after a search by a drug-sniffing dog. His flight from Europe had originated in Pakistan. The previous passenger in Rule's seat had apparently left drug residue available for olfactory discovery.

With respect to my own experiences, it was easy to contrast the USSR with the presumably free society of the United States. I took a late 1950s, high school civics perspective to the Soviet encounters. I thought of surveillance in cold war and political terms as an unwelcome activity by a repressive state.

However, as a graduate student and professor in Berkeley and Cambridge in the next decade I came to appreciate surveillance as a fundamental social process characteristic of all societies—both functional and risky. The practice cut across institutions; individuals in interaction; the interaction of organizations with each other; and the public and private sectors. Surveillance was neither good nor bad, but context and comportment made it so. It was, as David Lyon (1994) has observed, Janus-headed and more.

In the classroom my studies were posing questions and presenting perspectives that involved surveillance, although the term was rarely used. In studying the creation and presentation of social reality, it was clear that things are often not as they appear, that rule breaking and rule enforcement could be intricately interwoven; that deception and covert information collection were common; and that information used by large organizations was becoming an ever more important social resource, paralleling—sometimes surpassing—and often intertwined with class, status and power. The capillaries of computerization and other new surveillance and communication tools that would rapidly expand in the next decades were beginning to be visible. At the time however, few saw information changes as being as potentially impactful as the invention of the steam engine, the railroad, the telegraph, the auto or the airplane.

My first graduate student paper written for Professor Erving Goffman was on passing among blacks. I became interested in issues of identity and in the formal records used for constructing it which ironically might also offer space for undermining official categories of identification.

Professor Erving Goffman offered an incipient sociology of personal information emphasizing the rules and contingencies around the discovery and protection of such information. Professor S. M. Lipset offered a model for understanding the social requisites and correlates of democracy and the enduring presence of inequality tied to social stratification. Professors Neil Smelser and Charles Glock illustrated how the flow of empirical events could be better understood and compared when broken into analytic dimensions.

Beyond the classroom, my perspective broadened as a result of personal experiences. I was active in CORE (Congress of Racial Equality), an organization dedicated at that time to integration through non-violence. After a major fundraising effort, an event occurred that severely damaged the group—our treasurer disappeared with the money. It turned out she was a police agent, as were several other disruptive members. I was shocked and angered that a peaceful democratic organization dedicated to ending racial discrimination could be a target of such police actions.

Within the classroom it was widely believed that some students secretly reported on their professors and fellow students. There were also police officers out of uniform in the classes I taught at Berkeley. I recall some interesting discussions with them about role conflicts, democracy and social order and how their presence in the classroom might be affecting what other students said.

In the beginning my interest was not in surveillance, or privacy or technology (especially not the latter—given sociology's party line aversion to any whiff of technological determinism), but in broader questions involving the nature of social order and in the factors associated with a democratic society. Modern society came increasingly to rely on inter-dependent, formal agencies beyond the more informal mechanisms characteristic of pre-industrial and pre-urban homogenous societies. The police as the most visible and symbolic applied agents of the state play a key institutional role in social control with their resources to support or undermine democratic ideals.

Democratic orders were indeed fragile and abusive surveillance was hardly restricted to authoritarian and totalitarian states. Yates's question ("What if the church and the state are the mob that howls at the door?") was more than rhetorical. This received greater public awareness following Watergate and the release of reports by the Church Committee (US Congress 1976) and the Rockefeller Commission (1975) (see also Donner 1980, and more recently Cunningham 2003; Earl 2011; Starr, Fernandez and Scholl forthcoming).

Initial research

I spent my first decade of research studying morally suspect and often illegal state surveillance against non-violent and generally non-criminal protest groups (Marx 1974, 1979). As the 1960s and early 1970s protest movements receded, surveillance for other uses expanded. Innovative forms were directed at white collar offences such as corruption, fencing, fraud, vice and police abuse. Because such violations are often consensual or may involve profound power inequalities they are more difficult to discover and prosecute. A congressman caught taking a bribe on a hidden video offered a strong new form of evidence.

A more equitable, science and technology-based enforcement ethos emerged for the FBI and other agencies following the death of J. Edgar Hoover and new federal funding for local police efforts (Marx 1988). This involved blending traditional undercover means with the latest in bugging, video and tracking tools; computers to identify subjects and to document their activities and networks; and emerging technical forms of forensics such as DNA and other patterns of identification and evidence. Surveillance was clearly changing in response to new social conditions and the availability of new technologies.

While hardly a flag waver for the covert arts, I increasingly came to see them as necessary in certain settings. Using surveillance against a suspected corrupt politician, fraudulent contractor, or rapist was very different from using it against nuns who were peace activists or blacks demanding the right to vote or sit at a lunch counter. Democracy could be threatened by extremist political groups. National security has always involved intelligence gathering. Surveillance by government was clearly necessary when legitimated and limited by policy, law and ethics. It could be as irresponsible not to use it, as to use it wrongly—even as the obvious risk of government abuses remained. Dastardly government deeds done in the dark hardly require sophisticated technology. However, the appearance of ever more powerful techniques offered new temptations for users and challenges for regulators.

As the year 1984 approached there was much public discussion about whether we were well on the way to George Orwell's dystopia. In a paper written for a Council of Europe conference in Strasbourg, I asked how close we were to the society Orwell had described. I examined various social indicators to assess this (Marx 1986).

Contrary to Orwell, on most conventional measures such as of social participation, social mobility, the presence of non-state voluntary organizations, literacy, access to and use of diverse communication tools, knowledge of foreign languages and attitudes toward civil liberties and minorities, society had moved in an opposite direction from the society he imagined and from the year 1948 when the book was finished.

Orwell was a better prognosticator in his treatment of language and culture (e.g. newspeak, public relations, self-inhibitions created by fear of censorship and uncertainty about being observed). Furthermore, the image of the boot on the human face and the reappearance of state violence the book described did not in general apply, something Huxley noted in a 1948 letter to his former student:

> Dear Mr. Orwell: Within the next generation I believe that the world's rulers will discover that infant conditioning and narco-hypnosis are more efficient as instruments of government, than clubs and prisons, and that the lust for power can be just as completely satisfied by suggesting people into loving their servitude as by flogging and kicking them into obedience. In other words, I feel that the nightmare of *Nineteen Eighty-Four* is destined to modulate into the nightmare of a world having more resemblance to that which I imagined in *Brave New World*.
>
> *(in Smith 1969)*

Orwell's prognostication failures would be cause for celebration were it not for the fact that new and potentially repressive (if non-violent in conventional meaning) social forms and technologies were rapidly proliferating. Softer, low-visibility, engineered, connected and embedded domestic forms were clearly in ascendance. This swept across society, far beyond criminal justice or the military where many of the tactics originated and were first used.

A great deal was going on in the mid-1980s with the arrival of ever more powerful and seemingly omniscient, omnipresent knowledge machines. Consider video cameras; drug testing; computer documentation, discoveries, predictions and networks; location and communication monitoring; DNA analysis; and the many other new forms the current volume so richly documents.

Violent and non-violent forms of social control were uncoupled, with the latter increasing in importance. Over recent decades subtle, seemingly less coercive, forms of control have emerged within societies that have not become less democratic and in which the state makes less use of domestic violence.

Threats to privacy and liberty are not limited to the use of force, or to state power, and indeed they may appear in the service of benign ends. It is important to examine control by other means, and by users other than the state—whether organizations or individuals.

Partly as a result of Orwell, the image of an all-powerful repressive state comes easily to Americans, whereas the image of powerful and repressive private groups does not. *Nineteen Eighty-Four* focused attention only on the actions of the nefarious state (which had taken over the private sector). Yet today the private sector has the same technologies as government and in many ways is subject to fewer restrictions—whether in the treatment of workers or consumers.

It was necessary to go beyond the association of surveillance only with spies, police, political abuses and the state. To do that required a comprehensive set of content-neutral concepts to rein in the rich variation and social and moral complexity, paradoxes and contradictions of the topic. Explanation and evaluation required a common language for the identification and measurement of surveillance's fundamental properties and contexts.

In analyzing this I drew from Jim Rule's work. I met Rule shortly after I began teaching at Harvard while he was working on his PhD thesis. That prescient 1969 volume published in 1973 as *Private Lives and Public Surveillance* was the first scholarly book to empirically examine the social implications of the computer databases that large organizations had started to use.

Such databases could be conceptually linked with undercover practices and other emerging tools as part of the new surveillance. With their invisibility and the absence of subject consent, computers as electronic informants are similar in some ways to police informers and infiltrators, if more passive (Marx and Reichman 1984). Yet they also went beyond the latter in their potential not only to control, but to better serve citizens—for example with respect to health and welfare services. Computer matching could identify citizens not receiving benefits they are entitled to, as well as those receiving them erroneously or fraudulently. The new information flows could weaken, blur or strengthen traditional borders of many kinds as well as create new borders of inclusion and exclusion (Marx 2005).

The forms that appeared in the later twentieth century were distinct but they also shared certain key attributes and, because they are a variant of a broader social phenomenon, they share elements with non-technological forms. The social analyst can help us see this by offering constructs that separate what appears to be connected and by connecting what appears to be separate.

In the early 1980s I began empirical studies of computer matching and profiling and location and work monitoring and wrote public policy op-ed articles on topics such as drug testing, DNA analysis, credit reports, Caller-Id, manners and new communication means, and video surveillance. While substantively distinct, these forms also shared certain characteristics.

Looking across institutions brought me away from the formal organization called police to the function called policing and back to the broader questions about modes and means of social ordering (or in current parlance, governance) that my graduate education began with.

I had an abundance of facts that called out for more systematic organization in order to locate similarities and differences. A framework that went beyond newspaper descriptions and the shoot from the lip rhetoric of those strongly favoring or opposing the new forms without detailed analysis was needed.

My goal, pursued over the next decades, became the creation of a conceptual map for the collection, analysis and application of personal data. The question was not as many people initially ask, "Is surveillance good or bad?" but rather "what concepts are needed to capture the fundamental surveillance structures and processes across diverse tools and settings in order to make better comparative statements (whether across tools, institutions or countries)?" We can then ask, "what are the facts?" "what are the values?," "where is society headed?," and "how can we differentiate appropriate from inappropriate uses?" In the appendix to an early paper on privacy and technology (http://web.mit.edu/gtmarx/www/privantt.html) I listed almost 100 related questions the topic raises. Some examples of the conceptual approach are in Marx 2002, 2006 and forthcoming.

The overarching concept of the *new surveillance* (briefly discussed below) was a first step. Viewing the separate technologies with overlapping characteristics as an ideal type offered a way to think about broad changes in society. Identifying the major dimensions of surveillance could provide a means to contrast the different tools and to actually measure where, and the extent to which, changes were (or might be) occurring in social organization and behavior and to see more clearly the implications for liberty, privacy and life chances.

Concepts

In the beginning there is the *concept*. Among areas that need to be charted are the characteristics of the *social structures* that organize the behavior; the characteristics of the *means* used; of the *kind and form* of the data collected (e.g. public, personal, private, sensitive, intimate, or as text, audio or visual); of the *goals* (e.g. management, protection, documentation, strategic planning, ritual, entertainment); of the *conditions* of collection, data security, access and use—factors significantly defined by normative or rule expectations, whether involving ethics, laws, policies, manners and of course the array of *consequences* that may result. The relative power of agents and subjects is of course a key factor in conditioning the kinds of rules and the extent to which they are followed. Finally concepts are needed that deal with *culture* as it gives meaning to the experience of being watched or a watcher. The narratives or discourses that explain surveillance vary by context and place. For example in some countries the technologies may be presented as a sign of modernization, in others as simply another tool of the benevolent welfare state or in times of crisis as a weapon against internal and external enemies.

At the most general level surveillance of humans (which is often, but need not, be synonymous with human surveillance) can be defined as regard or attendance to a person or to factors presumed to be associated with a person. This can involve *non-strategic surveillance*—the routine, auto-pilot, semi-conscious, often even instinctual awareness in which our sense receptors are at the ready, constantly receiving inputs from whatever is in perceptual range. Smelling smoke or hearing a noise that might or might not be a car's backfire are examples.

This contrasts with the *strategic surveillance* which involves a conscious strategy—often in an adversarial and inquisitorial context to gather information. Within the strategic form we can distinguish traditional from the new surveillance. The latter is at the core of contemporary concerns. *Traditional surveillance* is limited. It relies on the unaided senses and was characteristic of pre-industrial societies—information tended to stay local, compartmentalized, unshared and was often unrecorded, or if kept, difficult to retrieve and analyze in depth.

In contrast, the *new surveillance* involves scrutiny of individuals, groups and contexts through the use of technical means to extract or create information. This means the ability to go beyond what is offered to the unaided senses and minds or what is voluntarily reported. The new surveillance is central to the emergence of a *surveillance society* with its extensive and intensive (and often remote, embedded) data collection, analysis and networks.

At the ideal-typical extreme we would see *the maximum security society* (which we are far from, but perhaps moving closer to). Such a society is composed of a series of sub-societies: *a hard engineered society; a soft and seductive engineered society; a dossier society; an actuarial society; a transparent society; a self-monitored society; a suspicious society; a networked society of ambient and ubiquitous sensors in constant communication; a safe and secure society with attenuated tolerance for risk; a "who are you society?" of protean identities both asserted by, and imposed upon, individuals;* and *a "where are you, where have you been and who else is there?" society of documented mobility, activity and location.*

Regardless of whether we are dealing with traditional or the new surveillance, some common classificatory notions can be applied. In the case of surveillance social structures, for example, we can identify the *surveillance agent* (whether as watcher/observer/seeker/inspector/auditor/tester), while the person about whom information is sought or reported is the *surveillance subject*. The agent role can be further separated into the *sponsor, data collector* and *initial* or *secondary user*.

Many contemporary concerns over surveillance involve the practices of large organizations relative to employees, clients or the public. *Organizational surveillance* is distinct from the *non-organizational surveillance* carried about by individuals. At the organizational level formal surveillance involves a constituency. Organizations have varying degrees of internal and external surveillance. Erving Goffman (1961) has identified many kinds of employee or inmate monitoring, such as within "total institutions."

Within an organization *internal constituency surveillance* (scrutiny of insiders) contrasts with *external constituency surveillance* (attending to outsiders such as customers, patients, travelers). *External non-constituency surveillance* involves organizations monitoring their broader environment in watching other organizations and social trends. The rapidly growing, understudied field of business intelligence fits here.

Non-organizational surveillance, in which an individual watches another individual or an organization (whether for protection, strategic or prurient reasons) apart from a formal organizational role, is another major form. It may involve *role relationship surveillance* as with family members (parents and children, the suspicious spouse) or friends looking out for and at each other (e.g. monitoring location through a cell phone). Or it can *involve non-role relationship surveillance*—as with the free-floating activities of the voyeur whose watching is unconnected to a legitimate role.

Agent-initiated surveillance, which is particularly characteristic of compliance checks such as an inspection of a truck or a boat, can be differentiated from *subject-initiated surveillance*. The agent and subject of surveillance merge with *self-surveillance*—where individuals watch themselves (a deterrence and/or prevention goal found with many uses). Self-monitoring can be intertwined with an external surveillance agent in the form of parallel or *co-surveillance*. This is the case for example with remote health monitoring in which both the monitored person and a health agency simultaneously receive signals about the subject.

In the above case co-surveillance is *non-reciprocal* with personal data going from the watched to the watcher (e.g. employers, merchants, doctors, teachers, parents) and tends to reflect power and resource differences. In contrast, *reciprocal surveillance* is by definition bi-directional as with social networking sites. But reciprocal need not mean equal. Surveillance that is reciprocal may be *asymmetrical* or *symmetrical*. In a democratic society citizens and government engage in reciprocal but distinct and shifting forms and degrees of mutual surveillance.

These questions draw attention to who is entitled to and/or able to play the agent role and who is the subject? New tools may bring increased democratization (or a better term—equalization) as with readily available cell phone cameras and internet access or the tools may be restricted as with access to satellites, private data bases and sophisticated data mining.

A measure of democracy is the extent of restrictions on and mandatory requirements for information flows across actors and sectors. For example, what is the ratio over time of what governments and large organizations are expected to (or may) reveal about themselves (e.g. freedom of information and truth in advertising laws and policies, conflict of interest statements) and what citizens are expected to reveal about themselves to governments and large organizations? A number of dimensions of this are analyzed in Marx (2011). Contrast the extremes of a totalitarian government which must reveal nothing to citizens—who must reveal all to government, with the unrealistic case of a fully open government which must reveal all to citizens who in turn reveal only what they choose to government.

An emphasis on structure implies that the topic is static and fixed at one point in time, yet surveillance also needs to be viewed as a fluid, ongoing process involving interaction and strategic calculations over time. Among major processes are the *softening of surveillance*; efforts to create the *myth of surveillance* (which can involve generating fears supportive of turning to a technical solution and claiming that the solution is more effective than it is); and the *monitarization of personal data* so it can be sold to marketers, governments and individuals and the *commodification* of surveillance in which it (or protection from it) become products to be purchased; and various techniques of neutralization. The latter are strategic moves by which subjects of surveillance seek to subvert the collection of personal information such as *direct refusal, discovery, avoidance, switching, distorting, counter-surveillance, cooperation, blocking* and *masking*. Equivalent counter-neutralization moves by agents are also present.

Another way to think about process is to consider the links between the distinct activities covered by the umbrella term, surveillance. The most common meaning refers to some act of data collection, but in fact this must be located within a broader system of connected activities.

Once surveillance is viewed as an appropriate means, discrete units of action may be identified that implicitly answer different questions and involve distinct goals. These can be thought of as *scripts* of behavior. Seven kinds of activity conceived of as strips that follow each other in logical order can be noted. The strips are temporally, conceptually, empirically and often spatially distinct. They include: *tool selection; subject selection; collection; processing/analysis; interpretation; uses/action;* and *data fate* (e.g. secondary users, destroyed, sealed, restricted or made public). Considered together these strips constitute the *surveillance occasion* and offer a way to bound a given application.

The "career" of a particular surveillance tool may also be tracked as it emerges and then may diffuse—whether in a jagged or in a more linear direction. In the case of the latter this may be through *surveillance creep* or *gallop*, often displacing other means along the way and bringing new goals and users. There may also be *surveillance constriction* as a new, unregulated tactic becomes subject to limitations and even prohibitions. Changes in *surveillance slack*, a measure of the gap between the potential of a technology and its degree of application may also be charted.

An emerging field

The field of surveillance studies came to increased public and academic attention after 9/11 (Monaghan 2006). But the topic in its modern form has been of interest to scholars at least since the 1950s. This is related to greater awareness of the human rights abuses of colonialism, fascism, and communism, anti-democratic behavior within democratic societies, the literary work of Huxley, Orwell and Kafka, and the appearance of computers and other new technologies with their profound implications for social behavior, organization and societies.

Foucault (although writing about earlier centuries) is certainly the dominant grandfather of contemporary studies and further in the background are Taylor, Weber, Nietzsche, Marx, Bentham, Rousseau and Hobbes; and of course even further back the watchful and potentially wrathful (although also sometimes loving and protective) eye of the Biblical God of the Old Testament.

What were those interested in the topic reading at mid-century and in the following several decades? In the 1960s The Who sang "talkin' about my generation." While I cannot speak for others, neither are these observations only reflective of my experience.

I will note the kinds of literature the cohort who entered social science graduate schools from the 1960s into the 1980s were likely reading. From the 1950s to the early 1980s the ardor of the surveillance studies or privacy bibliophile could be easily and responsibly sated. That satiation was provided by journalists Barth (1951) and Packer (1964), legal scholars Samuel Dash, R. Schwartz, and K. Knowlton (1959) and Arthur Miller (1971), political scientist Alan Westin (1967), and sociologists Edward Shils (1956), Rose Coser (1961), Barry Schwartz (1968), Stanton Wheeler (1969) and Jim Rule (1973). In the early 1980s attention to the topic increased with work such as that by journalist David Burnham (1983), philosophers Sissela Bok (1978, 1982) and Fred Schoenman (1984), and sociologist Ken Laudon (1986). A small social and environmental psychology literature also existed (Altman 1975; Margulis 1977; Ingram 1978). In addition, some classic law articles reviewed cases and asserted central principles or values (Fried 1968; Bloustein 1979; Gavison 1980).

The modest amount of scholarly and media attention to the topic in that early period has been replaced by a continuing flood of attention—see summaries of recent literature in Marx and Muschert 2007, Lyon 2007 and the articles in recent edited collections such as Zureik and Salter 2005; Haggerty and Ericson 2006; Lyon 2006; Monahan 2006; Norris and Wilson 2006; Staples 2007; Hier and Greenberg 2007, 2009; Leman-Langlois 2008; Kerr *et al.* 2009; Wall 2009; Hempel *et al.* 2010; and Zureik *et al.* 2010. The growth involves many fields: philosophy, sociology, criminology, social psychology, political science, geography, law, architecture/planning, history, economics, communications, cultural studies, computer, public administration, public health, business, and science, technology and society studies.

How does the emerging field of surveillance studies compare to other fields preceded by an adjective? Social studies of surveillance start with an empirical topic—that is different from beginning with a research question, theory or method. The focus on a kind of behavior necessarily calls for breadth and crosses disciplines, institutions, methods and places. This catholicity is furthered because there is no formal organization for surveillance studies, unlike for the established disciplines and many other "studies" fields. This gives the field egalitarian openness, energy, and contemporaniety and the ability to incorporate rapid changes and new ideas. Fields with more established cultures and formal gatekeepers vigilantly patrolling their intellectual borders are more prone to ossification. This openness is a source of the field's strength and energy. Yet it can also be seen as a source of weakness—the field is diffuse, scholars lack agreement on many important issues and knowledge is not very cumulative.

The field's openness harks back to nineteenth-century generalists such as Karl Marx, Max Weber and Georg Simmel who looked broadly across areas to understand the big changes associated with modernization. They considered social change from historical, economic, social, legal and cultural perspectives. Today, specialization is hardly in danger of being replaced, nor should it be. Yet surveillance studies in focusing on substantive topics in their richness and in bringing perspectives and findings from various fields together has an important role to play.

The area is so far best characterized as multi-disciplinary rather than inter-disciplinary. In an inter-disciplinary field the distinct ideas and levels of analysis from various disciplines are integrated, rather than being applied in a parallel fashion. Illustrative of the former would be finding that workers of a particular personality type respond positively (in terms of attitude and productivity) to intensive work monitoring, while those with a different personality respond in an opposite fashion, showing how concepts from geography can inform the ethical, legal and popular culture labeling of places (whether physical or cyber) as public or private, or demonstrating how the different historical experience of Europe relative to the United States led to the former's greater concern and different policies over private sector surveillance as against that of government, while in the United States that pattern was reversed.

Surveillance studies as a growing epistemic community is unlike most other "studies" fields. It is not based on a geographical region, ethnicity, gender or life style (e.g. as with urban or women's studies). Nor is it based on a single disciplinary, theoretical or methodological perspective (e.g. sociology, postmodernism or survey research). Rather it is based on a family of behaviors all dealing in some way with information about the individual (whether uniquely identified or not) or about groups. The social significance of the activity is in crossing or failing to cross the borders of the person—factors which can be central to life chances, self-concept and democracy.

The field overlaps several related areas. It shares with technology and society studies an interest in the social impacts of (and upon) tools, but is restricted to one class of tool defined by its information function. It shares an interest in surveillance technology with many fields such as engineering and computer and forensic science, but it is concerned with the social and cultural, not the technical elements. Some of the forms studied do not even involve technical hardware (e.g. social technologies such as reading lips, facial expressions and body language).

By far the most numerous and methodologically most sophisticated studies preceded by the adjective surveillance are in the area of public health. Foucault (1977) analyzes power and the mapping of the plague in the seventeenth century as a precursor to modern surveillance. The epidemiological studies of disease and epidemics however reflect only one of many strands in surveillance studies.

The field also overlaps some of the topical interests of management information, library science and criminal justice studies, but it is decidedly not a policy, applied or managerial field. While it tends to share value concerns with civil liberties, privacy and human rights studies, most researchers begin with the values and norms of scholarship in order to advance knowledge, rather than beginning with policy, reform or activism.

Social studies of surveillance share with globalization studies an interest in the causes and consequences of increased world interdependence and cooperation; in the standardization of techniques and policies and new trans-border organizations; and in cross-border flows of data and persons. Relative to most study fields it is (and should be) more international with respect to its practitioners and its subject matter.

The journal and web resource *Surveillance & Society* has editors and advisors across Western societies. The Canadian New Transparency and the European Living in Surveillance Societies projects also have participants from many countries—although English is the dominant language which tilts toward an over-representation of Anglophone scholars and few comparative studies. Any generalizations from the English-speaking world to the world must be empirically grounded—not to mention the need to be aware of differences between (and within) English-speaking countries. More work has been done in western than in eastern Europe and little is available on other countries.

An important question is the extent to which we are moving toward a fairly uniform world surveillance society driven by a common ethos, problems, and technology developed in Western societies—as against a commonality based on convergence and amalgamation, or will we see a world of uncommonality where local differences in narratives and uses remain strong even as common technologies are adopted?

The field departs from globalization studies in the many non-global aspects it is concerned with. Much scrutinizing is at the local level and is strongly influenced by the particular cultural context—whether involving parents and children, friends, workers or shoppers and societies with democratic or authoritarian traditions. Across countries the local language used to justify or challenge a tactic may reflect different value assumptions, priorities and models of society, e.g. the welfare state, the threatened state, the religious state, the libertarian state.

Social studies of surveillance are university-based and bound by norms of scholarship involving logic, method, awareness of prior research, evidence and civility. These norms prescribe fairness and objectivity in the conduct of research; listening carefully to those we disagree with; and continually reflecting on the positions we hold. Value neutrality is necessary for reasons of principle and of strategic legitimacy.

The topic however does have great moral bite and scholars are drawn to it because they are concerned over its implications for the kind of society we are, are becoming or might become, as technology and changing life conditions alter the crossing of personal and group information borders.

Perhaps to a greater degree than for most fields, the social issues driving researchers are manifest (e.g. autonomy, fairness, privacy and transparency). These value concerns are not easily characterized in conventional terms as liberal or conservative and there are conflicting legitimate goals (e.g. between the rights of the individual and the needs of the community, the desire to be left alone and to be noticed, rights to privacy and to information).

A concern with underdogs and the negative aspects of inequality is present, but so too is awareness of the interconnected parts of the social order which brings cautiousness about social change introduced too quickly and without adequate discussion. Genuine informed consent and level playing fields are issues shared across most conflicting ideologies. An overarching value in much research is the Kantian idea of respect for the dignity of the person and the related factor of respect for the social and procedural conditions that foster fair treatment, democracy and a civil society.

After so little scholarly interest in the field for so long, the insights and sustained and focused intellectual energy reflected in this volume are most welcome! This book fills a need. While the last decade has seen many *studies of surveillance*, there has been little work seeking to define and present the broad field of *surveillance studies* and to create an empirical knowledge base. The game has many players. This comprehensive handbook by leading scholars, in offering an introduction, mapping and directions for future research provides a field for them to play on. Scholars as well as computers need platforms.

The book serves as a reminder that, while they (whether the state, commercial interests or new, expanding public-private hybrid forms) are watching us, we are watching them. Surveillance studies have an important role to play in publicizing what is happening or might happen, ways of thinking about this, and what is at stake. Making surveillance more visible and understandable hardly guarantees a just and accountable society, but it is surely a necessary condition for one.

References

Altman, I. (1975). *The Environment and Social Behavior: Privacy, Personal Space, Territory, and Crowding*, Pacific Grove, CA: Brooks/Cole Pub. Co.

Barth, A. (1951). *The Loyalty of Free Men*, New York: Viking.

Bloustein, E. J. (1979). *Individual and Group Privacy*, New Brunswick, NJ: Transaction.

Bok, S. (1978). *Lying*, New York: Pantheon.

——(1982). *Secrets*, New York: Pantheon.

Burnham, D. (1983). *The Rise of the Computer State*, New York: Random House.

Coser, R. (1961). "Insulation from Observability and Types of Social Conformity," *American Sociological Review*, 26: 26–39.

Cunningham, D. (2003). *There's Something Happening Here: The New Left, the Klan, and FBI Counterintelligence*, Berkeley: University of California Press.

Dash, S., Schwartz, R. and Knowlton, R. (1959). *Eavesdroppers*, New Brunswick, NJ: Rutgers University.

Donner, F. (1980). *The Age of Surveillance*, New York: Knopf.

Earl, J. (2011). "Political Repression: Iron Fists, Velvet Gloves, and Diffuse Control," *Annual Review of Sociology*, 37: 261–84.

Foucault, M. (1977). *Discipline and Punish: The Birth of the Prison*, New York: Vintage.

Fried, C. (1968). "Privacy," *Yale Law Journal*, 77: 475–93.

Gavison, R. (1980). "Privacy and the Limits of Law," *Yale Law Journal*, 89: 421–71.

Gilliom, J. (2001). *Overseers of the Poor*, Chicago, IL: University of Chicago Press.

Goffman, E. (1961). *Asylums*, Garden City, NJ: Anchor Books.

Haggerty, K. and Ericson, R. (2006). *The New Politics of Surveillance and Visibililty*, Toronto: University of Toronto Press.

Haggerty, K. and Samatas, M. (2010). *Surveillance and Democracy*, New York: Routledge.

Hempel, L., Krasmann, S. and Brockling, U. (2010). *Sichtbarkeitsregime*, Wiesbaden: VS Verlag.

Hier, S. and Greenberg, J. (2007). *The Surveillance Studies Reader*, New York: McGraw Hill.

——(2009). *Surveillance Power, Problems and Politics*, Vancouver: UC Press.

Ingram, R. (1978). *Privacy and Psychology*, New York: John Wiley & Sons.

Kerr, I., Steeves, V. and Lucock, C. (2009). *Lessons from the Identity Trail*, New York: Oxford University Press.

Laudon, K. C. (1986). *Dossier Society*, New York: Columbia University.

Leman-Langlois, S. (2008). *Technocrime*, London: Wilan.

Lyon, D. (1994). *The Electronic Eye: The Rise of Surveillance Society*, Cambridge: Polity Press.

——(2006). *Theorizing Surveillance: The Panopticon and Beyond*, Portland, OR: Willan Publishing.

——(2007). *Surveillance Studies: An Overview*, Cambridge: Polity Press.

Margulis, S. (1977). "Privacy as a Behavioral Phenomenon," *Journal of Social Issues*, 33(3).

Marx, G. T. (1974). "Thoughts on a Neglected Category of Social Movement Participant: The Provocateur and the Informant," *American Journal of Sociology*, 80: 402–42.

——(1979). "External Efforts to Damage or Facilitate Social Movements: Some Patterns, Explanations, Outcomes, and Complications," in M. Zald and J. McCarthy (eds), *The Dynamics of Social Movements*, pp. 94–125, Cambridge, MA: Winthrop Publishers.

——(1986). "The Iron Fist and the Velvet Glove: Totalitarian Potentials Within Democratic Structures" in J. Short (ed.), *The Social Fabric: Dimensions and Issues*, Beverly Hills, CA: Sage Publications, pp. 135–62.

——(1988). *Undercover: Police Surveillance in America*, Berkeley: University of California Press.

——(2002). "What's New About the New Surveillance? Classifying for Change and Continuity," *Surveillance and Society*, 1.

——(2005). "Some Conceptual Issues in the Study of Borders and Surveillance," in E. Zureik and M. Salter (eds), *Who and What Goes There? Global Policing and Surveillance*, Portland, OR: Willan Publishing, pp. 11–35.

——(2006). "Varieties of Personal Information as Influences on Attitudes Toward Surveillance," in K. Haggerty and R. Ericson (eds), *The New Politics of Surveillance and Visibility*, Toronto: University of Toronto Press, pp. 79–110.

——(2011). "Turtles, Firewalls, Scarlet Letters and Vacuum Cleaners: Rules about Personal Information," in W. Aspray and P. Doty (eds), *Making Privacy*, Latham, MD: Scarecrow Press.

——(forthcoming). *Windows Into the Soul: Surveillance and Society in An Age of High Technology*, Chicago, IL: University of Chicago Press.

Marx, G. T. and Muschert, G. (2007). "Personal Information, Borders, and the New Surveillance," *Annual Review of Law and Social Science*, 3: 375–95.

Marx, G. T. and Reichman, N. (1984). "Routinizing the Discovery of Secrets: Computers as Informants," *American Behavioral Scientist*, 27(4): 423–52.

Miller, A. (1971). *The Assault on Privacy*, Ann Arbor, MI: University of Michigan.

Monaghan, P. (2006). "The Watchers," *Chronicle of Higher Education*, 52(28): 18–25.

Monahan, T. (2006). *Surveillance and Security*, New York: Routledge.

Norris, C. and Wilson, D. (2006). *Surveillance, Crime and Social Control*, Burlington, VT: Ashgate.

Packer, V. (1964). *The Naked Society*, New York: Pocketbook.

Rockefeller Commission Report. (1975). *Report to the President by the Commission on CIA Activities Within the US*, Washington, DC: GPO.

Rule, J. (1973). *Private Lives, Public Surveillance*, London: Allen-Lane.

Schoenman, F. (1984). *Philosophical Dimensions of Privacy*, Cambridge: Cambridge University.

Schwartz, B. (1968). "The Social Psychology of Privacy," *American Journal of Sociology*, 73: 741–52.

Shalin, D. (2010). "Erving Goffman as a Pioneer in Self-Ethnography? 'The Insanity of Place' Revisited," Paper presented at the 2010 Annual Meeting of the American Sociological Association, Atlanta, available at www.unlv.edu/centers/cdclv/ega/articles/ds_insanity.html.

Shils, Edward. (1956). *The Torment of Secrecy*, Chicago, IL: University of Chicago Press.

Smith, G. (1969). *Letters of Aldous Huxley*, London: Chatto & Windus.

Staples, W. (2007). *Encyclopedia of Privacy*, Westport, CT: Greenwood.

Starr, A., Fernandez, L. and Scholl, C. (forthcoming). *Shutting Down the Streets: Police Violence and Social Control*, New York: New York University Press.

Traven, B. (1934). *The Death Ship: The Story of an American Sailor*, London: Chatto & Windus.

US Congress, Senate, 94th Cong., 2nd sess. Church Committeee (Select Committee to Study Government Operations with Respect to Intelligence Activities). (1976). *Supplemental Detailed Staff Report on Intelligence Activities and the Rights of Americans, Book III, Final Report*, Washington, DC: GPO.

Valéry, P. (1965). *Oeuvres*, Paris: Editions Gallimard.

Wall, D. (2009). *Crime and Deviance in Cyberspace*, Surrey: Ashgate.

Westin, A. (1967). *Privacy and Freedom*, New York: Columbia University.

Wheeler, S. (1969). *Files and Dossiers in American Society*, New York: Russell Sage Foundation.

Zureik, E. and Salter, M. (2005). *Global Policing*, Portland, OR: Willan Publishing.

Zureik, E., Stalker, L. H., Smith, E., Lyon, D. and Chan, Y. E. (2010). *Surveillance, Privacy, and the Globalization of Personal Information*, Montreal: McGill-Queen's University Press.

Introducing surveillance studies

David Lyon, Kevin D. Haggerty and Kirstie Ball

Surveillance studies today

Surveillance studies is new. That is to say, until very recently something called surveillance studies did not exist. People studied surveillance, but in isolated, piecemeal and unsystematic ways. Over the past 20 years or so, surveillance has become an increasingly important topic within both academic and public debate. Interest in surveillance studies has mushroomed, generating considerable excitement about the potential for new ways to understand human behavior. The appearance of this handbook indicates that the field has matured sufficiently for many scholars to cooperate on a joint publishing venture to map the field in at least a preliminary fashion. It does not for a moment mean that "schools" of thought have emerged in any broadly agreed upon, well defined way, or that the field has stabilized into secure and preset lines of argument. It does mean that there are some tremendously important issues to analyze and to debate that a lively community of scholars are pursuing.

Today, surveillance studies is a complex world made up of scholars who have disciplinary homes across the social sciences, arts and humanities. Through their engagement with others working on surveillance a trans-disciplinary community has emerged within which individuals work at a range of levels and in a variety of domains which we hope are reflected in the following pages. The contribution of surveillance studies is to foreground empirically, theoretically and ethically the nature, impact and effects of a fundamental social-ordering process. This process comprises the collection, usually (but not always) followed by analysis and application of information within a given domain of social, environmental, economic or political governance. Typically the process occurs through a series of interlinked, distributed and distantiated institutions, systems, bureaucracies and social connections. Consequently its effects are difficult to isolate and observe, as they are embedded within many normal aspects of daily life. Reactions and resistance to surveillance, as well as its mis- and re-appropriations, occur at grass roots, artistic and activist levels.

Surveillance is an ancient social process. It has always been a component of institutional routines and human sociality (Locke 2010), but over perhaps the past 40 years it has emerged as the dominant organizing practice of late modernity. This is the starting point for any critical understanding of surveillance. Developments in material, corporate and governmental infrastructures alongside technologies, data-handling and data manipulation have overcome historical limitations to vision (and the other senses). This has produced downstream social changes in the dynamics of power, identity, institutional practice and interpersonal relations on a scale comparable to the changes brought by industrialization, globalization or the historical rise of urbanization.

Readers of this volume will be exposed to a momentous expansion and intensification of surveillance in almost all institutional spheres of contemporary existence. Wherever one looks, one sees surveillance embedded within distinctive projects. In many workplaces employee performance is now scrutinized at a level of detail that would delight the early advocates of scientific management (Ball 2010). Warfare is undergoing a visibility "arms race," with combatants incorporating new ways to visualise, track and target the enemy, while struggling to remaining unseen themselves. Police officers now spend a good amount of their time simply collecting and processing information (Ericson and Haggerty 1997) and seeking out ways to incorporate the data collected by other institutions into police practice. The same is true in the world of international security, where the "war on terror" has embraced dataveillance, biometrics and surveillance cameras (Whitaker 1999). Commercial organizations have helped to monetize information and in the process developed a voracious appetite for fine-grained consumer data (Turow 2006). The nation state, long a significant actor in collecting data on citizens (Agar 2003; Higgs 2004), is radicalizing the scope of governmental surveillance through assorted "e-government" initiatives. Students from kindergarten through university are marked, measured and monitored and increasingly subjected to surveillance justified as a way to enhance school safety (Monahan and Torres 2009).

Such scrutiny is not only more pervasive, it is also more penetrating and consequential, playing a prominent role in decision-making about the lives of aggregate populations and individual citizens.

A number of questions arise. What is driving this transformation? How are we to understand the factors prompting change of this magnitude? There are at least two levels of explanation that we can contemplate. The first concerns the "micro/meso" level where numerous local contingencies pertaining to inter-institutional competition, local politics, specific fears/desires or even serendipity, play out in the development of any surveillance practice. Scholars studying surveillance typically investigate the convergence of many of these factors and how they help make specific surveillance practices appealing to different constituencies.

Such a focus helps foreground the local politics of surveillance, but leaves unaddressed the larger question of why surveillance appears to be proliferating so broadly. How are we to understand the growth of surveillance as a general social phenomena, one that is apparent globally—although with distinctive local inflections in different countries and contexts (Murakami Wood 2009)?

A primary candidate in trying to understand this growth of surveillance has been the new information technologies which can relatively inexpensively and easily monitor more people in more detail than was previously possible. Computers with the power to handle huge datasets, or "big data" (Manyika *et al.* 2011), detailed satellite imaging and biometrics are just some of the technologies that now allow us to watch others in greater depth, breadth and immediacy. This is not to say that the technology is determinative in any way but also does not shy away from the fact that such artifacts are a vital precondition for many of the changes that we are witnessing.

Technology, however, is not a sufficient reason to account for this change. Instead, it is better to think of a process of causal over-determination, where a confluence of factors make surveillance often appear as *the* most appealing way to advance any number of institutional agendas. Some of these factors include changing governmental rationalities, the rise of managerialism, new risks (or perceived dangers), political expediency and public opinion.

Although all of this monitoring is highly variable in terms of the projects being advanced and the practices and technologies involved, some general trends can be identified. The first entails a process of blurring boundaries, something that operates at several different levels. In the criminal justice system, for example, the boundary between the police and the public is blurred as officials seek to position citizens as the "eyes and ears" of the authorities. This is expected to operate in routine day-to-day encounters with citizens reporting on suspicious situations and informing on other citizens (Natapoff 2009). It also extends to forms of wikiveillance, where the public is encouraged to monitor internet feeds from distant surveillance cameras and inform the authorities if they see crime occurring or immigrants covertly crossing into another country (Koskela 2011).

Institutional boundaries also become more indistinct as state policing and security agencies draw upon the massive infrastructure of data collected by other governmental bureaucracies and incorporate them into security agendas. The legality of such efforts is sometimes in question, as is apparent from revelations that Chinese authorities have been hacking into private companies in the West and using open source information to conduct espionage. However, state access to other institutions is increasingly a formal legal expectation, with private organizations being positioned as a conduit or relay in an extended network of state surveillance. Examples include assorted provisions that require ISPs, banks, cell phone companies, and even libraries, to provide the authorities with routine access to data about their clientele.

A second general trend is that surveillance has become simultaneously more visible and invisible. On the one hand, as we go about our daily lives it is hard to miss the proliferating cameras, demands for official documents and public discussions about internet dataveillance. At the same time, there is a curious invisibility surrounding these practices. The actual operation of surveillance, the precise nature and depth of its penetration, along with the protocols for how one is singled out for suspicion or reward are opaque to all but a select few insiders. Also contributing to invisibility are the hidden video and audio recorders and embedded sensors which silently gather and remotely transmit data.

A third trend involves the democratization of surveillance, such that even groups that historically were largely unscrutinized are now monitored by major institutions and sometimes by other citizens (Mathiesen 1997; Goldsmith 2010). As surveillance becomes a generalized response to any number of social issues, it is hard for anyone to remain free from scrutiny. This is not to say that the democratization of surveillance has itself translated into anything approaching a leveling of social hierarchies. In fact, new asymmetries have emerged, such that the surveillance of more powerful groups is often used to further their privileged access to resources, while for more marginalized groups surveillance can reinforce and exacerbate existing inequalities.

Much of this is contingent on forms of social sorting (Lyon 2003), where data about populations are subject to institutional processing which is itself related to vastly different life chances. At the level of the individual, such social sorting is not inherently bad, as it can ideally be used to better distribute resources to a society's most vulnerable or needy. This sensibility to both the positive and negative implications of surveillance reinforces the general normative orientation of surveillance studies that surveillance is capable of being used for both desirable and detestable things. Much of the critical literature focuses on the inappropriate and often hidden uses of surveillance, with scholars often consciously positioning themselves opposite the more optimistic and often self-serving and even naïve pronouncements about the exclusively beneficial consequences of surveillance technology.

Given that many surveillance studies scholars are alarmed by some of the more disquieting instances of surveillance, a major question concerns how citizens should respond to these developments, either individually or collectively. In surveillance studies this issue of praxis often revolves around debates about the continued relevance of official privacy regimes or data protection provisions. Although there is a wide spectrum of opinion on this topic, one can crudely break these down into those who have some faith in the existing privacy structures versus those who are more suspicious or critical.

In legal terms, privacy—along with that of "data protection" in Europe especially—often seems the obvious category to wield in wars against rampant data-gathering (Reagan 1995; Bennett 1992). Advocates for a privacy approach tend to acknowledge that these regimes are limited by virtue of underfunding, scant powers of investigation and enforcement, broad exemptions and outdated assumptions about the nature of privacy. At the same time, they stress that privacy discourses and structures remain the most promising avenue for restricting surveillance and point to instances where such measures have helped thwart egregious privacy violations (Bennett 2011, 2008).

At the other end of the continuum are those who tend to accentuate the limitations of privacy as both a concept and a regime. For them, proof of the failure of privacy structures is glaringly apparent in how a surveillance society has sprung up around us, notwithstanding a large and vibrant privacy bureaucracy. In essence, the unrelenting growth of intensive surveillance measures is presented as conclusive evidence that the privacy infrastructure has proven itself to be incapable of thwarting the expansion of surveillance. Scholars in this tradition tend to focus their research more on the mundane daily practices that individuals use to try and secure a private realm, such as closing blinds, shredding documents, purchasing anti-surveillance devices, or learning how to "hide in the light" (Gilliom 2001; Nippert-Eng 2010; Whitson and Haggerty 2008; Marx 2003).

Any resistance to surveillance ultimately depends upon an informed, motivated and engaged citizenry. This points to the fact that perhaps one of the greatest surprises in the field of surveillance studies has been the comparatively muted public response to developments in surveillance that seem to be self-evident threats to personal liberties. One wants to be careful here not to discount the vital efforts by anti-surveillance activists and concerned citizens, and some of the important anti-surveillance victories that they have won. At the same time, it is clear that by and large the public has enthusiastically or resignedly accepted such technologies, accepting claims that they are viable ways to secure profit, increase security, or simply as fun devices to play with (Ellerbrok, forthcoming). This muted public response, combined with a new willingness by individuals to hand over information on assorted social media applications, has challenged many assumptions that scholars have about citizen engagement and the politics of surveillance.

These are just a smattering of the important preoccupations of scholars studying surveillance. They are themselves the culmination of an emergent process that has helped to give rise to a new and vibrant multi disciplinary field.

The rise of surveillance studies

The timing of surveillance studies' appearance is no accident, in at least two ways. First, personal information became economically, political and culturally significant in unprecedented ways during the later twentieth century. The biggest single driver of this was the shift to computerized record-keeping. What was once stored in static, fixed locations—index cards and filing cabinets—and shared with others only under strictly limited circumstances was expanded, became mobile, searchable and shareable, not only within but across organizations and even countries. This meant that surveillance capacities grew massively in several ways at once. Even as they did so, other processes, such as burgeoning global corporations, increased government outsourcing and a vast increase in the commercial use of personal data for marketing, offered new incentives for personal data-processing. Now, people not only take for granted that they have to remember their passwords or show ID but also, as social media multiply, cheerfully and voluntarily expose their data to others.

Nor is the appearance of surveillance studies an accident in social and information sciences either. In the last part of the twentieth century many social scientists queried just what model of "modernity" had dominated that century's social thought, and questions were raised about whether surveillance had been given sufficient prominence (e.g. Giddens 1987). The work of Michel Foucault (1977) catalyzed considerable controversy over the role of the "panopticon" prison plan within modernity; did this diagram for disciplinary practices mark a watershed in modernity and usher in new regimes of surveillant power? Simultaneously, in the same quarter-century, social scientists found themselves grappling with the rapid rise of new media, often seen first as information and communication technologies with "social impacts," and later as indispensable and inextricable dimensions of everyday social life.

These three major currents of thought produced a healthy debate over the realities of surveillance in the last part of the twentieth and the first part of the twenty-first centuries, marked in the latter period by the surge of surveillance developments consequent on 9/11. The attacks on America and subsequent attacks in Europe were rather specific but their surveillance repercussions have become global. At any rate, the most stimulating surveillance scholarship to emerge was not that which focused on single events, or declared that we now live in a digital panopticon or an electronic cage, but rather that which put surveillance in an historical, comparative and critical frame. The fact that "control" and "risk" had become dominant themes of politics was not a mere spin-off of cybernetics but had to do with long-term trends in political economy (e.g. Garland 2001). The fact that new technologies for personal information-handling were being adopted in many countries simultaneously did not mean that the surveillance outcomes were identical. And the fact that "surveillance" was often taken to be a loaded term—with sometimes sinister and socially negative connotations—did not mean that the quest for more "neutral" concepts would eventually succeed. Surveillance studies is not free of ethical, legal and policy dimensions, and indeed here such issues are often more readily apparent and pressing than in other fields of study.

These things are clear from some of the earliest books to appear within a recognizably—in retrospect—surveillance studies stable. James Rule's work on *Private Lives and Public Surveillance* (1973) examined the role of early computer-based administrative systems such as social security and credit cards, showing against an historical background how these were consequential new developments. The very notion of privacy, as understood in the Western world, was being challenged by the growth of automated record-keeping and the digitizing of personal data. Gary T. Marx's (1988) study of undercover policing in the United States also put such practices in an historical context and again demonstrated how new technologies were helping to change the nature of policing. The section of his book that examined "new surveillance" such as video cameras, polygraphs and computerized records became a classic. If Rule's work was in sociology and Marx's work depended on criminology, Oscar Gandy's (1993) studies in consumer surveillance—*The Panoptic Sort*—appeared within communication studies. He showed decisively how personal information is economically valuable and how the consumer playing field is far from level. Data on more and less valued customers help reproduce social inequalities.

Almost inevitably, as this research appeared in the Europe-North America axis, the question of privacy was never far from the surface. The value of personal information was becoming increasingly apparent across a range of sites. In order to try to stem the flow of such data, most people readily appealed to the concept of privacy. At the same time, other concepts within surveillance studies raised important questions about how far privacy could be conceived as the best antidote to surveillance.

The new surveillance was associated with electronic technologies and, as David Lyon (1994) pointed out in *The Electronic Eye*, several studies emphasized how this facilitated a crucial categorizing dimension in addition to the already-existing use of statistical tools in administrative surveillance. "Social sorting" (Lyon 2003) became a useful shorthand for this, which could be seen for instance in policing (Ericson and Haggerty 1997) or in public space camera surveillance (Norris and Armstrong 1999). As legal scholar Lawrence Lessig (1999) noted, the use of software code and algorithms, along with dependence on searchable and remotely accessible databases, produced new sets of problems. People were to be treated differently depending on how they were categorized.

Questions about which concepts are more helpful in understanding and, where necessary, curbing surveillance continue to be discussed and the book in your hands indicates some instructive and insightful lines of inquiry. Here are a few examples, to give the flavor of what we mean. Both "surveillance" and "privacy" are old concepts, now reapplied, filled with fresh content and used to grasp key aspects of the proliferation of personal data. Similar things might be said of "bureaucracy," "militarism" or "colonialism," each of which also hark back to long-term and consequential historical processes and link to today's practices of personal data-handling. And of course, the institutions associated with those three examples live on in various guises in the present. Today's surveillance processes simply cannot be understood without reference to their historical precedents and backgrounds.

Newer ones, like "social sorting," "surveillant assemblage," "visibility" or "exposure" are sensitizing concepts, used to alert us to new dimensions of social practice, but are still in need of further specification, empirical analysis and comparative study in different contexts. Social sorting highlights the categorizing enabled by new statistical and software practices and which tends to reproduce and amplify social divisions. The surveillant assemblage (Haggerty and Ericson 2000) draws attention to how discrete and varied surveillance systems tend to converge into flows of personal data, drawing members of any and all populations into their purview. Visibility (Brighenti 2007) prompts examination of whose data are seen by whom and with what effects, because managing visibilities is at the core of control, while exposure (Ball 2009) points more to the subjective experience of surveillance, how people actually experience being "watched" and what differences that makes to the process.

These concepts connect back, in turn, with strands of theory from various disciplinary sources. They are necessary both for explanation and also for critique and they require of anyone engaging with surveillance studies a willingness to hear what people from other "home disciplines" may have said about a particular problem. The editors of this book have each become aware of extremely productive strands of theory in disciplinary areas in which they have no training or background but that are now essential to our grasp of surveillance. While we still bring our expertise—from history, sociology, criminology and organization studies—to bear on surveillance, we must remain open to insights from disciplines such as geography, law, international relations, computer science and psychoanalysis, ethics and marketing. Surveillance studies is a multi-disciplinary field.

The concepts used in surveillance studies also indicate the need for exploration across different fields of study. Two examples are particularly important, to do with software and security. This is not to downplay the significance of other aspects of surveillance that have little or nothing to do with technology or public safety but rather to illustrate how this field of study intersects with others at some crucial points. It is hard to grasp what is going on in today's surveillance practices and processes without some informed reference to issues such as software and security.

Software, a category that until the 1960s referred to cotton or woolen fabrics, is now understood as programs and instructions that operate computers, but its intimate involvement in everyday life is less frequently recognized. Yet the codes controlling computers are crucial for data-handling and thus for most surveillance (Galloway 2004). In the world of mobile devices using social media, for instance, one is obliged to think in terms of the "techno-social." Social media are defined by the "user-generation" of content, but users may only generate that content with the available software codes. And just as users keep track of each others' activities on iPhones and Blackberries, those machines themselves are programmed to keep track of their users and the data are constantly fed back into circuits of control. This world of software code, through instructions and algorithms, not only mediates but also helps to constitute social interactions and associations (Kitchin and Dodge 2011).

Security represents another field of study with which surveillance studies has many commonalities and overlaps. They are definitely not the same as each other. Much security is defined generally, and not necessarily helpfully, in terms of "national security" and depends on surveillance (see Bigo, this volume). But at the same time, much surveillance is not directly related to security as this is commonly understood (think of social media, for instance).

Even the attacks of 9/11, which undoubtedly prompted widespread attempts to bolster security through unprecedented levels of surveillance (Lyon 2003), have to be understood in context. Those events did not produce a radical rupture in existing practices, but instead served as an important punctuation point for wider processes in the dynamics of security and surveillance that were already in play. The terrorist attacks coalesced a sense amongst security experts that surveillance might be a panacea against terrorism, and this, in turn, led to a significant expansion in the "surveillance industrial complex" as corporations rushed to sell surveillance solutions to any number of perceived security needs (ACLU 2004). At the same time, the enormity of the attacks also tended to dampen the voices of those individuals and groups who historically have been most opposed to new state surveillance practices.

These are just some of the valuable insights that surveillance studies scholars have produced about some of the most consequential phenomena of our generation. Surveillance studies will continue to intersect critically with crucial concepts from other disciplines. Indeed it is these intersections that provide the analytical leverage which follows when studying surveillance. Studies of surveillance are scattered across a wide multi-disciplinary field, one that can take the uninitiated years to begin to navigate. We hope that this handbook will offer some navigational tools to assist others in getting their bearings as well as providing many new contributions to the field.

The handbook

This handbook emerged from "The New Transparency" major collaborative research initiative. The initiative, funded by the Social Sciences and Humanities Research Council of Canada, brings together approximately 50 scholars and graduate students from Canada, North and Central America, Japan and Europe who work on surveillance issues from within their respective disciplines. The project aims to synthesize the wide array of empirical and theoretical work which is now being undertaken by surveillance scholars. It is the first, but not the only, funded research network on surveillance. In Europe, the "Living in Surveillance Societies" network has brought together academics from 21 European countries, and groups have now formed in Latin America, Australia and Asia. Many scholars from these different backgrounds have contributed to this volume.

Producing a handbook of this nature involved difficult acts of categorization and sorting not dissimilar to those with which our scholarly work is concerned. Which topics to include and exclude, how the book would be internally organized, and, crucially, who would contribute, were debated for several months. Whilst we labored to ensure that the range of genders, ethnicities and nationalities were represented, it was also impossible to include everyone we wanted to.

We were similarly conscious of the intellectual and ethical minefields that were at the heart of producing something called "Routledge Handbook of Surveillance Studies." "The" implies a definitive work; nevertheless, we had to be careful in our choice of authors and in the scope of their coverage in a subject area which has a concentration of scholars, and male scholars at that, in the global north; and "Handbook" implies that the volume would need to be useful for its readers. Critically, "of Surveillance Studies" positions this volume as the first wide-ranging multi-authored piece which attempts to constitute, delimit and represent "surveillance studies" in print. This is no small undertaking, and we do not pretend to have fully represented the range of current work within this complex field. We have tried to address some of the key concerns and to provide new scholars and those wishing to expand their horizons with a sense of what we think surveillance studies entails. Empirical and theoretical territories, ethical agendas and contexts of application are addressed, and several common themes have emerged. The concepts of identification, identity and privacy, the contextual importance of news and online media to the spread of surveillance, and theoretical foci which address the body and new combinations of the virtual and material are a few examples of these common themes.

A handbook of this nature is retrospective in focus as each chapter summarizes the current state of the art regarding its respective topic. Authors were directed to consider some of the key concepts, ongoing debates and emerging issues relating to the topic under discussion. Nevertheless the chapters also generate considerable insight into the likely agendas for surveillance scholars as the field continues to grow. The future research agendas that are to be found in this volume reflect the ongoing and problematic nature of surveillance as scholars have come to understand it. Five areas of attention for the future have been identified. The first three address empirical and ethical concerns, the fourth addresses theoretical concerns and the fifth political concerns.

First, it remains critical that surveillance scholars address the relationship of surveillance processes to different forms of governance and government which mobilize it as a mode of ordering. This is an exceptionally important question because of the capacity of government and its associated public administrations to mandate and "normalize" surveillance practices as part of the governance process. This is to say that public administration can render the surveillance practices involved in governing acceptable and uncontroversial, resulting in them becoming taken for granted by the general population. Nevertheless the configuration of surveillance practices, (particularly as these involve rule enforcement, inclusion and exclusion) convey strong messages as to which aspects of society are valued and which are not. Evidence is needed as to the transformative effects of surveillance on key social variables such as trust and the implications of requiring individuals to positively identify themselves in order to receive goods and services and to exercise democratic rights. Further evidence needs to be generated about whether and how the dynamics of surveillance practices may becoming more closely related to degrees of social stratification producing classes of surveillance "haves" and "have nots." Do privileged individuals gain access to more accurate, efficient, representative and thus more ethical surveillance which protects them and their position; whereas the less advantaged are disproportionately subject to a blunt instrument which continually disadvantages them?

A second area of concern is the internationalization of the security industry, accompanied by the massive growth in the marketing data industry and the corporate infrastructures and technologies which enable data to be shared and mined. As Ben Hayes (this volume) states:

> Research is needed to understand the process of surveillance innovation in its broadest terms. This includes analyzing the flows of public and private money into security and surveillance research, critically evaluating expenditure and effectiveness, and assessing its impact on both public policy debates and universities …
>
> He argues that research should be positioned: … within debates about corporate responsibility and accountability; by considering not just the regulation of surveillance technology but the potential regulation of the Homeland Security industry; and by drawing inspiration from the global transparency and privacy movements, from anti-lobbying initiatives and arms trade regulations, from ethical debates around science, and from the emerging United Nations business and human rights framework.
>
> *(p. 174, this volume)*

Although the globalization of surveillance and its infrastructures is aligned to corporate interests and international political economy, it remains a local issue because individual contexts become more connected, particularly through social media and participatory surveillance. This is, however, not to deny the importance of international connections which are made possible by these media (subject to the extent to which governments censor social media applications in some countries). Implications arise for government too as new forms of census-taking and national statistical measurement make use of these data sources. A key question is how any privacy or other ethical harms that arise from these practices are combated or regulated as regulators continue to struggle with problems of regulatory lag as the corporate world moves faster than they do.

A third aspect to consider is the powerful role played by print, broadcast and online media in the spread of surveillance as well as the possibilities it offers for reappropriation, resistance and artistic intervention. The news media promote many messages about surveillance which seem to reinforce beliefs about crime and social divisions by playing on fear and insecurity. Television and print media, for example, have given surveillance cameras enormous symbolic power but research has shown that such devices have had little effect on crime levels. Social media also play an important seductive role: at the same time as people are sharing details of their life online they can delight in the alternative selves they create and play with the watcher/watcher relation through visual culture, media and gaming. Research on children and young people's engagement with surveillance either through school or through their use of the internet has illuminated this tension. Further research may question the gendered and sexualized identities and emotions which operate across different populations as individuals interact with, manipulate and appropriate surveillance practices. Questions also remain over the extent to which collective action can be energized around media surveillance which is embedded to the point of its invisibility and ubiquity. What are the possibilities to resist, and to not surrender information, on a micro everyday level?

A fourth area concerns the future theoretical agenda of surveillance studies. Surveillance scholars have drawn upon a diverse theoretical body—in spite of the "Foucault obsessed" stereotypes—and have used many of the established pillars of social scientific theorizing to augment their understanding of the phenomenon. For the future, it is important to theorize surveillance as something which is spatially and temporally distributed and which has productive and constructive effects on the objects it seeks to govern. A further need is to theorize the differential roles of the state and private sectors as surveillance societies emerge. Moreover, as surveillance practice becomes embedded into everyday worlds, surveillance theory needs to take account of how lived materialities and the virtual worlds *as produced by surveillance* conjoin, co-construct and influence one another. Surveillance scholars should also reflect on the ontological, epistemological and political consequences of classifying something as being *of surveillance*. While surveillance theory de-normalizes and problematizes attempts by the powerful to amass information about populations, surveillance scholars need to be mindful about what is lost as part of that surveillance-theoretical endeavor. For example, questions of liberty, security and difference can sometimes become "flattened" in surveillance studies analyses.

A fifth and final area is the enduring issue of how to (re)politicize surveillance practices in order that they may be questioned and understood—and where appropriate—resisted, challenged and made more accountable to surveiled subjects, activists, advocates and regulators. A persistent difficulty is finding suitable entry points at which to tackle surveillance because of its ubiquity and relative normalization. Surveillance, although a normal everyday process in many contexts, is one which is inherently political: its very application constitutes polity. For example, there is an inherent political economy around surveillance which is used in response to commercial priorities and to reinforce a business's market position. Such surveillance bolsters processes of capitalist value creation and the extraction of material labor from workers and immaterial labor from consumers (Lazzarato 2004). Surveillance associated with the exercise of state power actively constitutes citizenship, political legitimacy, susceptibility to state force and violence and deception; it can redraw borders and delineate territories. Surveillance as social sorting is inherently discriminatory, yet the algorithmic criteria which divide virtual and material populations are opaque. As Colin Bennett points out in this volume, the challenge is to identify a sense of collective grievance with surveillance without engaging in a broader struggle wherein surveillance as the central issue becomes lost.

Campaigns from every point in the political spectrum have engaged with surveillance issues. The "NO2ID" single issue campaign contributed to government plans for ID cards being shelved in the UK. Statewatch, a European NGO which tracks state surveillance and its human rights infringements throughout Europe held its twentieth anniversary conference in 2011 and is as incisive as ever. The American Civil Liberties Union (ACLU) and Electronic Frontier Foundation (EFF) continue to play a leading role and provide online resources in advocacy around privacy, surveillance and human rights. "A Report on the Surveillance Society" by the Surveillance Studies Network prompted two parliamentary enquiries into the surveillance society in the UK, and the report attracted global media interest. Freedom of information requests by criminological researchers have revealed the extent to which the police are using automated license plate readers in the UK. Privacy commissioners around the world continue to work within the limitations of privacy law dictum with limited regulatory powers over broader questions of surveillance.

Although many civil society groups and privacy regulators have engaged effectively with the consequences of surveillance practice, an ongoing difficulty for challengers concerns intervention in surveillance processes before any adverse consequences occur. In surveillance assemblages, where surveillance capacity is distributed within the invisible world of algorithms, over interoperable systems, between departments of large bureaucracies and over international boundaries it is extremely difficult to pinpoint the locus of responsibility for surveillance processes. An ongoing political challenge and continuing frustration for many activists concerns developing the ability to tackle accountability for surveillance processes and their outcomes. It is at this point where theory, practice and politics intersect. With a growing body of empirical evidence outlining the dynamics of surveillance in action and the roles played by different actors, as theory begins to recast surveillance in more distributed and networked terms, points of entry and engagement will emerge where questions of politics and ethics may be meaningfully posed.

These are some of the pressing questions that need to be addressed about the dynamics of surveillance. The wide-ranging nature of these questions, grounded within the content of the chapters in this volume, indicates the extent to which surveillance has become an integral part of contemporary existence. We believe that this volume represents a solid foundation for future excursions into the complex world of surveillance. We hope that it is a useful guide and resource for those interested in learning about and building upon the excellent work done by the first generation of surveillance studies scholars.

References

ACLU. (2004). *The Surveillance Industrial Complex*, New York.

Agar, Jon. (2003). *The Government Machine: A Revolutionary History of the Computer*, Cambridge, MA: MIT.

Ball, Kirstie. (2009). "Exposure: Exposing the Subject of Surveillance," *Information, Communication & Society*, 12(5): 639–69.

——(2010). "Workplace Surveillance: An Overview," *Labor History*, 51(1): 87–106.

Bennett, Colin. (1992). *Regulating Privacy: Data Protection and Public Policy in Europe and the United States*, Ithaca, NY: Cornell University Press.

——(2008). *The Privacy Advocates: Resisting the Spread of Surveillance*, Cambridge, MA: MIT.

——(2011). "In Defence of Privacy: The Concept and the Regime," *Surveillance & Society*, 8(4): 485–46.

Brighenti, Andrea. (2007). "Visibility: A Category for the Social Sciences," *Current Sociology*, 55(3): 323–442.

Ellerbrok, Ariane. (forthcoming). "Playful Biometrics: Controversial Technology Through the Lens of Play," *The Sociological Quarterly*.

Ericson, Richard V. and Haggerty, Kevin D. (1997). *Policing the Risk Society*, Toronto: University of Toronto Press and Oxford: Oxford University Press.

Foucault, Michel. (1977). *Discipline and Punish: The Birth of the Prison*, translated by A. Sheridan. New York: Vintage.

Galloway, Alexander R. (2004). *Protocol: How Control Exists After Decentralization*, Cambridge, MA: MIT.

Gandy, Jr, Oscar. (1993). *The Panoptic Sort: A Political Economy of Personal Information*, Boulder, CO: Westview.

Garland, David. (2001). *The Culture of Control*, Chicago, IL: University of Chicago Press.

Giddens, Anthony. (1987). *The Nation-State and Violence*, Cambridge: Polity.

Gilliom, John. (2001). *Overseers of the Poor: Surveillance, Resistance, and the Limits of Privacy*, Chicago, IL: University of Chicago Press.

Goldsmith, Andrew. (2010). "Policing's New Visibility," *British Journal of Criminology*, 50: 914–34.

Haggerty, Kevin and Ericson, Richard. (2000). "The Surveillant Assemblage," *British Journal of Sociology*, 51(4): 605–22.

Higgs, Edward. (2004). *The Information State in England: The Central Collection of Information on Citizens Since 1500*, Basingstoke: Palgrave Macmillan.

Kitchin, R. and Dodge, M. (2011). *Code/Space: Software and Everyday Life*, Cambridge, MA: MIT Press.

Koskela, Hille. (2011). "Hijackers and Humble Servants: Individuals as Camwitnesses in Contemporary Control Work," *Theoretical Criminology*, 15(3): 269–82.

Lazzarato, M. (2004). "From Capital-labour to Capital-life," *Ephemera: Theory and Politics in Organizations*, 4(3): 187–208.

Lessig, Lawrence. (1999). *Code and Other Laws of Cyberspace*, New York: Basic Books.

Locke, John L. (2010). *Eavesdropping: An Intimate History*, Oxford: Oxford University Press.

Lyon, David. (1994). *The Electronic Eye: The Rise of Surveillance Society*, Minneapolis: University of Minnesota Press.

——(2003). *Surveillance After September 11*, London: Polity.

——(2003). "Surveillance as Social Sorting," in *Surveillance as Social Sorting: Privacy, Risk and Digital Discrimination*, edited by D. Lyon, London: Routledge.

——(ed.). (2003). *Surveillance as Social Sorting*, London: Routledge.

Manyika, James, Chui, Michael, Brown, Brad, Bughin, Jacques, Dobbs, Richard, Roxburgh, Charles and Hung Byers, Angela. (2011). "Big Data: The Next Frontier for Innovation, Competition, and Productivity," McKinsey Global Institute, May, available at www.mckinsey.com/mgi/publications/big_data/pdfs/MGI_big_data_full_report.pdf (accessed 14 November 2011).

Marx, Gary T. (1988). *Undercover: Police Surveillance in America*, Berkeley: University of California Press.

——(2003). "A Tack in the Shoe: Neutralizing and Resisting the New Surveillance," *Journal of Social Issues*, 59(2): 369–90.

Mathiesen, Thomas. (1997). "The Viewer Society: Michel Foucault's 'Panopticon' Revisited," *Theoretical Criminology*, 1(2): 215–34.

Monahan, Torin and Torres, Rodolfo (eds). (2009). *Schools Under Surveillance: Cultures of Control in Public Education*, New Brunswick: Rutgers University Press.

Murakami Wood, David. (2009). "The 'Surveillance Society': Questions of History, Place and Culture," *European Journal of Criminology,* 6(2): 179–94.

Natapoff, Alexandra. (2009). *Snitching: Criminal Informants and the Erosion of American Justice*, New York: New York University Press.

Nippert-Eng, Christena. (2010). *Islands of Privacy*, Chicago, IL: University of Chicago Press.

Norris, Clive and Armstrong, Gary. (1999). *The Maximum Surveillance Society: The Rise of CCTV*, Oxford: Berg.

Reagan, P. (1995). *Legislating Privacy: Technology, Social Values and Public Policy*, Chapel Hill: University of North Carolina Press.

Rule, James B. (1973). *Private Lives and Public Surveillance*, London: Allen Lane.

Turow, Joe. (2006). "Cracking the Consumer Code: Advertising, Anxiety and Surveillance in the Digital Age," in *The New Politics of Surveillance and Visibility*, edited by K. D. Haggerty and R. V. Ericson, Toronto: University of Toronto Press.

Whitaker, Reg. (1999). *The End of Privacy: How Total Surveillance is Becoming a Reality*, New York: The New Press.

Whitson, Jennifer and Haggerty, Kevin D. (2008). "Identity Theft and the Care of the Virtual Self," *Economy and Society*, 37(4): 571–93.

Part I
Understanding surveillance

Introduction

Understanding surveillance

The study of surveillance addresses some of the most significant questions of our day, often dealing with pressing issues of power, culture, identity, inequality, ethics and resistance. The first part of this handbook presents work concerned with some of those foundational themes and how they pertain to the study and operation of surveillance.

The first section focuses on theoretical debates within surveillance studies, with a particular emphasis on the influential argument by philosopher Michel Foucault about the historical rise of a distinctively modern form of "panoptic" surveillance. Following Foucault, this is itself tied to the emergence of disciplinary power that shapes behavior through a subtle form of "soul training." Many authors have subsequently identified panoptic dynamics in assorted surveillance measures, that throw some light on what is happening within the surveillance "gaze." But, as other authors show, serious questions remain about the relevance of several aspects of Foucault's model as it pertains to contemporary surveillance.

Greg Elmer's chapter addresses this question about the place of panoptic models in the study of surveillance, and the place of Foucault's work in this field more generally. Elmer concentrates on the three key themes of panopticism, discipline and control to argue for the continuing relevance of Foucault's work to the study of surveillance. He does so by returning to the works of Jeremy Bentham—the original creator of the panopticon model—in order to make a distinction between understandings of surveillance that focus on the reality of monitoring versus the more Foucauldian emphasis on the likelihood of being watched. Elmer argues that Foucault's truly unique contribution was to emphasize discipline, which entails a kind of automatic docility and self-government.

Other authors have drawn upon different components of Foucault's wider body of work to advance our theorizing of surveillance. Here, Ayse Ceyhan's contribution focuses upon Foucault's notions of "bio-power" and "governmentality," and how they relate to contemporary forms of algorithmic surveillance which involve a power over life itself. This often relies on population statistics and probability calculations. She demonstrates the relevance of Foucaldian concepts to contemporary issues, showing in particular how such surveillance is now central to neoliberal regimes, used to manage populations and reassure an often anxious public.

The French theoretical tradition contains other rich resources that can usefully advance our theorizing of surveillance. William Bogard outlines some of these works, detailing how insights from philosophers such as Jean Baudrillard and Gilles Deleuze can apply to the study of surveillance. Bogard foregrounds the model of the "surveillant assemblage" which is comprised of heterogeneous component parts which are aligned through processes of disassembling and reassembling. He also accentuates the prominence of a hyper-real form of surveillance that involves complex models of anticipatory simulation.

The second section on "difference, politics, privacy" foregrounds how surveillance, used as a device in governmental practice, can both reproduce and exacerbate different forms of disadvantage.

The state is one of the most established agents of surveillance, deploying an extensive data collection infrastructure to analyze and manage populations. Toni Weller's chapter places these state functions in a wider historical context, accentuating how processes of rationalization and the rise of bureaucracy fostered state governmental efforts. These were themselves connected to practices of warfare and welfare, as state officials gathered data to protect citizens against external threats, but also to manage populations understood as forms of human resources.

Such monitoring efforts, whether conducted by the state or other agencies, are routinely connected to structures of discrimination, as institutions make decisions about how to deal with different individuals and groups. Hille Koskela draws attention to dynamics pertaining to gender, discrimination and surveillance cameras, accentuating how such devices have often reproduced the gendered gaze, while doing little to rectify the types of harms that women experience. At the same time, however, the introduction of personal webcams has allowed women (primarily) to become involved in projects of selective exposure which complicate existing gendered dynamics of watching and being watched.

Simone Browne builds upon the theme of discriminatory surveillance, focusing on different ways that surveillance is involved in racializing populations. She accentuates historical context, stressing how seemingly disparate technologies of representation are shaded by racial factors. This includes such diverse forms of monitoring as the census, wanted posters and biometrics, all of which have at different times and in different ways been part of racializing projects.

The concept of privacy has had pride of place in attempts to limit the expansion of surveillance and mitigate its more discretionary outcomes.

James Rule notes that privacy is a highly variable concept, one that is used to serve diverse social values and purposes. At its heart, privacy entails an effort to control the flow of information about ourselves in a context of wholesale data collection conducted by large bureaucracies. Since the 1960s an international privacy movement has emerged globally, incorporating privacy regimes that often share key assumptions and principles. In essence, these amount to due process rules for how bureaucracies can and should collect and manage personal information. Such measures are often criticized for being ineffective in constraining the spread of surveillance. For Rule, the major limitation of privacy structures is that they start from an assumption that bureaucratic data collection is a legitimate practice, and as such they provide no guidelines on when surveillance is necessary and when it might be unnecessary or unwarranted.

The final section on "cultures of surveillance" emphasizes the diverse meanings, and representations of, surveillance and how surveillance can be manifest in and also shape different occupational environments.

John McGrath focuses on the day-to-day ways in which citizens have come to produce and use surveillance devices. This is manifest in artworks and cultural products where individuals perform surveillance (and occasionally perform *for* surveillance). He accentuates how surveillance can be an object of pleasure and fantasy, something that is apparent in the art world but also increasingly in mass culture.

In his contribution Mark Andrejevic concentrates on the role of political economy in the emergence of an advertising-based model of mass entertainment. This has been propounded by an information industry that celebrates interactivity while often cynically exploiting the individual data produced by that interactivity. Such manipulations are particularly important to contemplate as we move to a world of ubiquitous computing where surveillance is built into the environments where people routinely live and where digital enclosures track and collect information on everywhere you go and everything you do online. Andrejevic accentuates some of the more disquieting political implications of a world where corporations have access to a convergence of data that they use to conduct forms of predictive experiments on the public.

For many individuals their first exposure to the issues raised by surveillance occurs through popular cultural products including television, films, books and music. Dietmar Kammerer's contribution foregrounds some of the more socially significant aspects of these representations, arguing that these products can help to bridge popular and academic discussions about surveillance. In an increasingly "cinematic culture" part of the appeal of such depictions is that they can more effectively expose people to the emotional worlds of surveillance, allowing them to better see and feel the consequences of mass monitoring.

In a world permeated by surveillance large groups of people are also employed in the routine work of watching others. Gavin Smith's chapter foregrounds the occupational status of such individuals who are employed, for example, as camera operators. It is an occupational context that is frequently neglected by surveillance scholars who tend to speak in vague unspecified ways about assorted "watchers." However, the issue of who these people are and where they are situated profoundly influences the operation and functioning of surveillance. Such work is now pervasive both within state bureaucracies but also in the private sector, although it remains little seen and understood by most citizens. As Smith accentuates, however, watching in its various forms can be a trying and ambivalent form of labor. He foregrounds how human subjectivity, including assorted forms of bias, can make watching highly discriminatory. At the same time, staff employed to monitor populations can suffer from feelings of alienation and disempowerment, while also struggling to remain free from monitoring themselves. In the process they can find playful and creative uses of the surveillance devices that they operate.

Section 1.1.
Theory I: After Foucault

a. Panopticon—discipline—control

Greg Elmer

Of the three concepts in this chapter's title—*panopticon, discipline* and *control*—only *discipline* is fully and directly explicated in the work of the late French philosopher Michel Foucault, still the preeminent theoretical figure for surveillance studies scholars. The *panopticon*, which has overwhelmingly served as a common theoretical and polemical point of departure for surveillance studies, is a derivative concept stemming from the letters and architectural drawing of English social reformer Jeremy Bentham (1748–1832). And while the concept *control* is both directly and indirectly addressed in a number of Foucault's essays and books, its application in surveillance studies has typically emerged from Gilles Deleuze's (1992) brief essay "Postscript on the Societies of Control," itself an extension of the philosopher's book *Foucault* (1988).

While some surveillance scholars (Haggerty 2006; Murakami Wood 2007) have offered expansive discussions of the limits of Foucault's panoptic writings, this chapter argues that such critiques tend to attribute the theoretical contributions of such concepts to Michel Foucault alone, negating the interpretive process involved in developing these key concepts. In other words the panopticon has been largely defined by one text (Foucault's *Discipline and Punish* 1977), not as an effort by Foucault to critique Bentham, or Deleuze to likewise reassess Foucault. This chapter consequently defines *the panopticon, discipline* and *control* as *interlocutive concepts* in surveillance studies, that is as terms that together inform Foucault's panoptic surveillance (Bentham's *panopticon*), serve as the core political contribution within Foucault's panoptic writings (*discipline*) and lastly, offer forward-looking and technologically networked theories of panoptic surveillance (Deleuze's Societies of *Control*). Consequently, it is argued that reading across such key concepts may provide new interpretive frameworks for surveillance studies—ones that recognize the inability to surveil and monitor, rethink the nature of subtle yet coercive forms of governmentality, and lastly, begin to theorize future-oriented and probability-based aspects of contemporary panoptic relationships.

Following a historical—or more aptly put, archaeological—order, the chapter begins with a discussion of *the panopticon*, before turning to the concepts of *discipline* and lastly, *control*. There is a logic to this order beyond publishing history. First, as a master signifier of sorts (and notably, the only noun in this grouping of concepts), *the panopticon* for better or worse continues to serve as a key theoretical frame of surveillance studies. As we shall see, however, for Foucault the panoptic prison first and foremost served to explicate a logic that could be seen at work in the spatial design of a series of key social, medical, educational and psychological institutions. The building blocks of surveillance studies, if we can refer to these central concepts as such, thus begin with Foucault's interpretation of an architectural plan for a panoptic building. This deconstructive move calls into question the externalization of panoptic gazes at work in surveillance studies and their subsequent assumption of a panoptic theatre that assumes—at all times—a meaningful panoptic object.

The concept *discipline* as developed by Foucault, in the context of his writings about the panopticon in *Discipline and Punish: The Birth of Prison*, first published in 1975 (1977 in English), amplifies the philosopher's theory of power, as a bio-political phenomenon, an internalization of power. Curiously the notion of self-governing, or modifying one's behavior in the face of the panopticon, is perhaps one of the least developed theories in surveillance studies. As such, this section of the chapter emphasizes Foucault's theory of panoptic subjectivity, the importance of automated forms of political power and his more implicit critique of Bentham's liberalism. This section subsequently seeks to offer a more explicit discussion of the nature of coercion in the work of Bentham and Foucault, a remedy for the overly individualistic concerns—notably loss of private property—in surveillance studies scholarship.

Moving to the third concept, the chapter argues that *control*—in particular as articulated in the work of Gilles Deleuze—has tended to lend more weight to networked and immanent forms of surveillance, perspectives that highlight and otherwise question the ever-changing and ever-expanding surveillance systems, mechanisms, protocols, policies, techniques and technologies. This last section of the chapter questions why surveillance studies is far more likely to cite Deleuze's brief and sketchy postscript, than his preceding book-length manuscript—a work entirely dedicated to the work of Michel Foucault. It is argued that the postscript's explicit object of study—new technologies—has obscured or displaced the theoretical contributions that Deleuze brings to Foucault's disciplinary mechanisms, which call into question the immanent process of managing and governing the future.

Recentering the panopticon

While surveillance studies has developed a strong attachment to *the panopticon* as a guiding theoretical inspiration, the concept's genesis as both an architectural drawing and a set of letters, *as interpreted by Foucault*, is largely unexplored (see Murakami Wood 2007 for some exception to this oversight). Studies of Foucaultian panopticism often treat Bentham as an introductory footnote and fail to question how *the panopticon* has emerged from a decidedly selective translation and interpretation. Oscar Gandy (1993), for instance, in the seminal book *The Panoptic Sort: A Political Economy of Personal Information*, says only that "It is from Foucault that I derive the underlying concept of panopticism … The Panopticon is the *name* given by Jeremy Bentham to the design for a prison" (my emphasis, 9). To speak of the panopticon, in other words, is to all-too-often reference only Foucault's words, not the distinct interpretation of Bentham's panopticon plans and letters. The panopticon was not just a name or title for a building coined by Bentham, it was a sustained political project, and a schematic drawing of a reformist liberalism. It was in other words an expression of a much broader political philosophy, replete with an architectural drawing to explicate its intended effects. The core theoretical and political contributions of Foucault's *Discipline and Punish* cannot be grasped without noting the diversions, interpretations, strategic omissions and outright rejection of passages from Bentham's series of letters on the panopticon from 1787 (see Bentham 1995).

Bentham's panoptic writings were developed and subsequently published as a series of letters and an architectural drawing of a prison that invoke strong visual imagery of sightlines and architectural viewpoints. They connote a 'plan in the making,' a proposal whose components were expressed and shared in specific details, moving the reader through the exact measurements of an entire building. The first set of letters (numbers I-VI) are designed to capture the imagination of the addressee, the last two (letters V and VI) subsequently provide an overarching summary of the panopticon's architectural advantages. In conjunction with the drawings or plans of the panopticon these introductory letters form the fundamental architectural or diagrammatic components of Foucaultian panopticism—they invoke a plan that embodies a theory of power.

Focusing on these first six letters we can clearly see where Foucault in many respects inverts the governmental aspirations of Bentham's panopticon, an interpretation that places the panoptic subject at the centre of the panopticon. The distinction moves the focus away from the building as such, to the prisoners, from the act of directly watching to the probability of being watched. The role of the panopticon's tower and "inspector," to use Bentham's term, serves as a fundamental difference between the two authors' work. The second of the panopticon letters introduces the importance of the centre of the building, for Bentham much more than a tower or viewing position—the tower also doubles as a residence: "The apartment of the inspector occupies the centre; you may call it if you please the '*inspector's lodge*'" (Bentham 1995: 35). Bentham further explains that, as a familial, domestic space, the lodge plays a key role in the efficient monitoring of the inmates:

A very material point is, that room be allotted to the lodge, sufficient to adapt it to the purpose of a complete and constant habitation for the principal inspector or head keeper, and his family. The more numerous also the family, the better; since, by this means, there will in fact be as many inspectors, as the family consists of persons, though only one will be paid for it.

(Ibid.: 44)

Bentham, in short, instilled a patriarchal regime of surveillance at the center of his panopticon, one that emphasized the intransigence and immobility of the inspector and his family, as much if not more than that of the prisoners themselves.

In Bentham's panopticon the inspector and family are themselves effectively isolated, segregated or, ironically, jailed, a set of characteristics more commonly associated with Foucault's prisoners. For the family in the tower there is seemingly little else to do but watch. Watching for Bentham is automated. Foucault too agrees that the panopticon produces an automatic effect, yet with no reference to the residence and its workings at the heart of Bentham's panopticon. Foucault's panopticon emphasizes an enactment of surveillance, a subjectivation of power, as instilled in prisoners who architecturally speaking must assume ubiquitous surveillance, that they may be under inspection at any time, night or day. What distinguishes Foucault's and Bentham's definition of *the panopticon* is *perspective*, meaning that the view outward from the residence, the tower—in Bentham's terms is a site and mode of "seeing without being seen" (ibid.: 43). Conversely, for Foucault the panopticon could not be reduced or framed by a unidirectional gaze from the centre, tower or singular managerial gaze. Conceptually, for Foucault, the prisoners, not the tower, are at the centre of the panopticon. For Foucault the panopticon served as a metaphor, contra Bentham it was not to be coupled with—or reliant upon—the very act of watching, it was to be viewed as a logic and process. Foucault dubbed the panopticon a "laboratory of power," not only to highlight its experimental nature, but also to indicate its continuous search for improvement, its "gains in efficiency" (Foucault 1977: 204). But, most importantly for Foucault:

the Panopticon must not be understood as a dream building: it is the diagram of a mechanism of power reduced to its ideal form; its functioning, abstracted from any obstacle, resistance or friction, must be represented as a pure architectural and optical system: it is in fact a figure of political technology that may and *must be detached from any specific use* [my emphasis].

(Ibid.: 205)

Unlike Bentham's then, Foucault's panopticon insisted upon its figural qualities to note the productive potential of systems that constantly repeat functions. Foucault also employed a definition of surveillance that extended right to the "top" of Bentham's hierarchy with the inspector also under surveillance. In Foucault's own words:

The Panopticon may even provide an apparatus for supervising its own mechanisms. In this central tower, the director may spy on all the employees that he has under his orders: nurses, doctors, foremen, teachers, warders; he will be able to judge them continuously, alter their behaviour, impose upon them the methods he thinks best; and it will even be possible to observe the director himself … enclosed as he is in the middle of this architectural mechanism, is not the director's own fate entirely bound up with it?

(Foucault 1977: 204)

Later we discuss how conflicting notions of the surveillant gaze have informed contemporary studies of reality television and web-based forms of social networking, particularly as theorized by Mark Andrejevic (2004). However, our discussion of the panopticon unearths a remarkably divergent notion of the panopticon interpreted—and subsequently inverted—by Foucault. Foucault's inverted panopticon has, however, had only marginal influence among surveillance studies. Rather, it is Bentham's panopticon that has served as a template in that at its centre lies a *meaningful* or perhaps *valuable* panoptic object, whose actions are said to be tracked and logged, not intentionally modified. Privacy—a common theme in surveillance studies—is therefore not just a response to over-surveillance, rather it is an extension of the panopticon's tower, a coupling of Bentham's act of watching with capturing or otherwise registering a history of behavior.

But Foucault's panopticism, and his contributions for surveillance studies, have little to do with claims to personal property and privacy (information/objects that can be collected through surveillance). Rather, Foucault's inverted *panopticon* sought to establish the potential political effects of a ubiquitous form of institutional power, not an all-seeing or all-registering eye, but a landscape that could at any time impart in an individual a likelihood of surveillance. While Foucault goes to great length to emphasize the subsequent internalization of power, the self-governing effects of the *panopticon*, it is only through coupling his thoughts on disciplinary power that we can further explicate the importance of his critique of political coercion.

Discipline: subtle coercion

The distinction between watching (Bentham) and being watched (Foucault) ultimately serves to distinguish fundamental *political* differences between the two authors. While many have focused on what Foucault took from Bentham (*the panopticon*), far fewer have noted what he directly rejected—Bentham's liberalism, defined as freedom from coercion. For Bentham, the panopticon served as a form of autonomy, a new-found freedom for the prison's managers. In the panopticon the attendent need not worry about the direct intervention of judges and other superiors who might otherwise be called upon to inspect and monitor the supervision and functioning of the institution. Freed from the burden of themselves being subject to oversight (from judges and the like), Bentham argued that the transparency of the [panoptic] building "ought to be, thrown wide open to the body of the curious at large—the great *open committee* of the tribunal of the world" (Bentham 1995: 48). Bentham's prisoners were also liberated from more overtly coercive forms of institutional violence. A liberal humanism lay at the heart of Bentham's panopticon letters.

Bentham's panopticon insists upon the apparent "omnipresence" of the inspector to avoid coercive forms of punishment, yet he also continuously notes through the letters that inspection has a "*real presence*" (ibid.: 45). Building upon this fundamental difference between Foucault and Bentham, this section of the chapter notes that, relative to our other concepts, *discipline* is the only concept that can be said to be uniquely Foucaultian in inspiration and development. The concept is a pivotal one as it anchors and thus gives political weight to Foucault's definition of panoptic subjectivity discussed above. It cultivates a self-governance, an automatic subservience, without need for direct monitoring and management.

While the most persistent and explicit thoughts on *discipline* flow immediately out of Foucault's afore-mentioned analysis of Bentham's panopticon letters (with numerous direct quotes and paraphrased sections), in *Discipline and Punish*, Foucault's discussion of *discipline* reintroduces readers to his familiar archeological style of writing. The historical case studies in *Discipline and Punish* explicitly seek to move beyond a literal interpretation of the panopticon-as-institutional-prison, to a discussion of how like-minded self-governing forms of power are intensified and expanded across the social field:

> There are two images, then, of discipline. At one extreme the discipline-blockage, the enclosed institution, established on the edges of society, turned inwards towards negative functions: arresting evil, breaking communications, suspending time. At the other extreme, with panopticism, is the discipline mechanism: a functional mechanism that must improve the exercise of power by making it lighter, more rapid, more effective, a design of subtle coercion for a society to come.
>
> *(Foucault 1977: 209)*

Through the introduction of the notion of *discipline* Foucault articulates a generalizable logic of Bentham's panopticon, though importantly one that, unlike Bentham's search for individual freedom, still recognizes a coercive dynamic at play. Such is not however the case with most contemporary studies of surveillance cameras, ID systems or DNA databases, projects that typically maintain Bentham's central concern over individualized forms of coercion. Such surveillance studies posit coercive effects as flowing out of—or more aptly put, external to—the act of surveillance. Coercive effects, in other words, only result out of the misuse of data/objects collected by surveillance systems, for example by misidentifying the innocent as the guilty. For Foucault, however, the concept of *discipline* posits a range of panoptic practices. At the far end of this range—generalized and social—Foucault again turns from moral language over modifying behavior to governmental and economic metaphors and terms. Unlike Bentham, Foucault uses *discipline* to produce a new form of political subjectivity and economy, not properties, data doubles or virtual selves (Poster 1990). Reading Foucault through Bentham reintroduces a subtle form of coercion, a routinized political and economic subservience that produces docile subjects. For Foucault there can be no panopticon without such discipline, its productivity is social, expansive and governmental, not external, contingent or subsequent.

Such a "disciplinary society" thus raises important questions about the future: the subtle power/discipline of a generalized panopticism, an internalized power that seeks to pre-plan—to economize the past, present and future. That Foucault locates such mechanics and concepts at one end of the disciplinary framework, however, should not obscure the author's overall goals to highlight the process of disciplinary mechanisms, an expansionary imperative toward the social pole, an intention clearly written into one of Foucault's few concise definitions of the concept in question:

> 'Discipline' may be identified neither with an institution nor with an apparatus; it is a type of power, a modality for its exercise, comprising a whole set of instruments, techniques, procedures, levels of application, targets, it is a 'physics' or an 'anatomy' of power, a technology.
>
> *(Foucault 1977: 215)*

Foucault thus posits three criteria of disciplinary mechanism, first, its search for the "lowest possible cost," both economically and politically speaking; second, the extension and intensification of its powers and scope in an effort to avoid failure; and lastly, to link the economic growth of disciplinary power with institutional output, or in his own words "increase both the docility and the utility of all elements of the system" (ibid.: 218). Foucault's point here is that the disciplinary mechanism lies at the heart of the political economy, it both enables—and is enabled by—what he later dubs an "art of government."

In moving from the institutional or architectural to the governing of a multiplicity of subjects, and a future governmentality or art of government, Foucault's political economy in *Discipline and Punish* still rests upon a restrictive spatiality, not an incarceration but an isolation still of sorts, an *in-situ process of dividuation*. Thus while disciplinary mechanism seeks to account for human multiplicities on a distributed scale, for Foucault, they also work to "fix" or otherwise operate as an "anti-nomadic technique" (ibid.: 218). It is here, moreover, that the limits of Foucaultian panopticism and discipline begin to lose their elasticity, particularly for Gilles

Deleuze whose interpretations of Foucault's writings sought to unfix the subjects of surveillance, to enable a fluid social and individual field, while still maintaining empirical and political goals.

A diagram of control

Of the concepts under analysis herein, *control* is the most widely invoked by scholars intent on expanding Foucault's thoughts to networked computing and other digitalized forms of communication and information management. This should come as no surprise given that the concept is largely attributed to Gilles Deleuze's very brief essay "Postscript on the Societies of Control" (1992). The concept *control* itself is only briefly offered by Foucault in *Discipline and Punish*—and, ironically, only in reference to the historical epoch immediately *preceding* the disciplinary society (with the plague as social object of surveillance): "Rather than the massive, binary division between one set of people and another, it called for multiple separations, individualizing distributions, an organization of in depth of surveillance and control" (Foucault 1977: 198). In the "Postscript," however, Deleuze argues that societies of control "are in the process of replacing the disciplinary societies" (Deleuze 1992: 4). And with reference to the panopticon he makes an atypically stark distinction: "Enclosures are molds. ... but controls are a modulation" (ibid.).

Before further investigating these words from Deleuze, let us first note that the "Postscript" does not offer a wholly distinct view from Foucault, particularly with regard to the notion of time. For Deleuze, Foucault's disciplinary mechanisms laid the groundwork for the ability to infer or anticipate, since in Foucault's own words "mechanisms of power ... instead of preceding by deduction, are integrated into the productive efficiency of the apparatuses from within" (Foucault 1977: 219). In his postscript Deleuze invokes William Burrough's use of the near-future as a setting for his immanent conceptualization of control mechanisms (Deleuze 1992: 4). Similarly, Deleuze also conceived of the temporal aspects of social control through Kafka's *The Trial*, a story that witnessed an indefinite suspension of the law, or in his words "limitless postponement" (ibid.: 5). Both such perspectives however remain largely underdeveloped in "Postscript on the Societies of Control," leaving the reader wondering more about how social control is "modulated" through the near-future.

Apart from its brevity, the other obvious limitation of Deleuze's "Postscript on the Societies of Control" is that its main concept—*control*, or better still *control societies*—is rarely recognized or interpreted as a *post-script*. Written four years before the "Postscript", Deleuze's manuscript *Foucault* (1988) arguably reserves its most intensive reading, and at times its most glowing moments of admiration and appreciation, for *Discipline and Punish*. In the chapter entitled "A New Cartographer," Deleuze offers two key contributions to what he would later refer to as "societies of control." First, Deleuze does not see panopticism as a formula where one sees "without being seen"—that is assuming the position of the tower or its guard(s). Rather, in drawing upon the disciplinary sections of *Discipline and Punish*, Deleuze argues that panopticism is a mechanism that seeks "to impose a particular conduct on a particular human multiplicity" (Deleuze 1988: 34).

Deleuze's overall contributions to his later more explicit conceptualization of social control lie in the seeming contradiction at the heart of Foucault's panopticon: "Discipline and Punish is the book in which Foucault overcomes the apparent dualism of his earlier books (although even then this dualism was already moving toward a theory of multiplicities)" (ibid.: 39). While Deleuze characterizes Foucault's earlier work as engaging with questions of vision and expression, in *Discipline and Punish* he sees Foucault working his way out of the confinement of the panopticon as such, in short moving beyond the duality of *either* forms of matter (the prison itself) or forms of function (punishment) (ibid.: 33). Deleuze does not see such an equation as a contradiction in Foucault's overall argument. Panopticism is not an abstract generalization, nor an act of watching or being watched, or content and expression, rather Deleuze argues that both "forms" are in flux, the productive capacity of which (or more precisely the means through which social control is modulated) resides continuously in an "informal" space. Deleuze thus poses the question:

What can we call such a new informal dimension? On one occasion Foucault gives it its most precise name: it is a 'diagram' … The diagram is no longer an auditory or visual archive but a map, a cartography that is coextensive with the whole social field … a diagram is a map, or rather several superimposed maps. And from one diagram to the next, new maps are drawn.

(Ibid.: 34, 44)

While Deleuze's subsequent *postscript* to the diagram has helped to situate surveillant practices and processes within the context (or as enabled by) information systems, techniques of digitization and computer networks, the concept of *control* derived through a modulating set of practices and relations among social forces remains similar to Foucault, as a theorization of subjectivation, albeit as a geographically dispersed multiplicity. Alex Galloway's interpretation of internet *protocols* as diagrammatic machines (2004) likewise suggests how Foucault's biopolitical theory of subjectivity might also explain the governance of a network of things or digital objects.

Deleuze's *postscript* adds important time-based after-thoughts to his expanded concept of the Foucaultian diagram. The Deleuzian subject is embedded in a set of relationships that are increasingly fluid and in flux, and the ability to impart social norms and other forms of behavior conformity is not as easily synthesized as in Foucault's panoptic diagram. In other words, Deleuzian *control* invokes a set of informal relationships that nevertheless expand their points of contact, seek to reassign and reduce inefficiencies and spawn new cartographic mechanisms (or "machines" as Deleuze would say). The need to constantly seek out the truth suggests not only an immanent surveillant apparatus, but also one that seeks to pre-dress the near-future—to redouble past relationships so as to predict future inefficiencies. Foucault (2007) likewise foresaw disciplinary mechanisms morph into security apparatuses, the latter seeking to prescribe future relationships (what-ifs) based upon a set of "probabilities" that "works on the future … [it] will open onto a future that is not exactly controllable, not precisely measured or measurable [rather a] … plan that takes into account precisely what might happen" (ibid.: 19, 20).

What emerges is a concept of control that builds upon Foucault's interior economy, the self-governing machine that not only subtly coerces subjects into docile states, but also integrates such subjects into the machinations of wider economies, including the circulation of information and objects. Deleuze's diagram provides a more explicit rationale for expanded sites of surveillance, seeking to manage production, circulation and consumption of modern economies, with forward-looking "profiles"—simulated pictures of future demands, needs and risks. Such a networked approach, however, does make the error in assuming a meaningful object of surveillance. Rather, the diagrammatic process itself *produces or assigns a range of values to objects,* it seeks to determine the meaningfulness of surveillant objects within the context of networked economies.

Conclusions

Given the staggering amount of material, of interpretations, polemics, and indeed translations, of Foucault's panoptic writings, one can easily sympathize with authors such as Kevin Haggerty (2006) who suggest that we should "demolish the panopticon" to make way for new interpretations, theories and objects of study, namely non-human actors and forms of medical surveillance more often associated with benign regimes of care. But this is based on a common flawed assumption about Foucault's central thesis—that "Panoptic surveillance is fundamentally concerned with monitoring people" (Haggerty 2006: 30). Rather, if we bring together our interlocutive concepts discussed through this chapter, we can begin to question common assumptions of canonical texts, a practice that hopefully opens up new forms of empirical and theoretical research in surveillance studies.

It seems that Haggerty assumes a Benthamite perspective, defining panoptic surveillance as a human act of watching (or as being individually identified, as privacy scholars typically do), not the assumption of always being watched. Such a distinction has important political implications, one that speaks from the

Foucaultian-Deleuzian trajectory as critiquing non-sovereign, or better, unquestioned, forms of social and political power—a quiet conformity that is only intensified by its automation, embeddedness and modulation that *informs* the near-future. Automation is the key concept. Only through the subsumption of power, the internalization of a probable gaze, can the panopticon transform into a disciplinary society that displaces and elides the face of power.

Scholars who begin their analysis of surveillance from a panoptic gaze risk disarticulating the subject from social forms of power, leaving only individuals and their transgressed liberties. Mathiesen's (1997) inversion of such a gaze into a synopticon—from Bentham's one (tower) watching the many (cells), to the many watching the few (eg. contemporary media culture)—similarly displaces Foucault's central thesis on disciplinary power and his important critiques of liberalism. How might the synopticon shift the nature of contemporary governmentality? Taking us back to Foucault's thesis on subjectivity, Mark Andrejevic (2004) argues that such synoptic relationships—for instance on reality television—are not simply questions of personal privacy, information to be collected by surveillant gazes. Rather, focusing again on the panoptic subject, or in this case the synoptic subject (reality program contestant), Andrejevic argues that to be under the media gaze is to perform work, "the work of being watched."

More importantly, such work does not simply put one's private property at risk, but rather—predating the emergence of social networking platforms like *Facebook*—Andrejevic's synoptic example highlights the Foucaultian concern with self-governance, not a loss of privacy, but in this instance *the management of one's personal publicity*. Such a political economy of surveillance, linking the downloading of work, and the management of individual networked-identity, serves as an important update to Foucaultian-inspired critiques of contemporary forms of liberalism (or neo-liberalism), particularly in the context of a governmental regime and set of policies that have sought to "liberalize" markets, societies and individuals in an effort to increase efficiencies.

Bentham's act of watching—commonly adopted in surveillance studies—assumes a surveillant object, one that can be viewed, tracked, or monitored. The *meaningful surveillant object*, in other words, is perhaps one of the very fundamental assumptions made by surveillance scholars. This starting point however simplifies or altogether displaces typically conflictual social relationships—closely-knit communities and largely homogenous police forces, or first world nations and closed totalitarian ones such as North Korea. Such spaces and sites, however, challenge surveillance studies to integrate such panoptic-vacuums into a diagram of probability, one that increasingly monetizes or financializes "risky" social, economic and political relationships that are immune to surveillant mechanism. As I have argued elsewhere, however (Elmer and Opel 2008), such intelligence gathering is often an oxymoron, not only because it leads to uninformed actions (e.g. the preemptive invasion of Iraq, mass arrests of peaceful protestors, etc.), but moreover, because it *a priori* rejects instances where panoptic surveillance cannot be established—typically in particularly demographically tight-knit isolated communities (locally or globally).

Through the work of Deleuze, and the rejection of Bentham, conversely, surveillance studies can begin to question the economic rationalities of diagrammatic systems, the assigning of value to objects that may or may not be subject to a successful form of monitoring. The meaningfulness of networked objects of surveillance are never preconstituted, universal or equivalent, rather, as seen in the example of phone hacking by journalists in the UK in 2011, the surveillance and monitoring of individuals is subject to a broader financial and libidinal economy, one that targets valuable objects, information that can be resold and capitalized upon. Surveillance in this sense is subject to an economy that constantly seeks to rationalize relationships among people and things to better manage the future.

References

Andrejevic, Mark. (2004). *Reality TV: The Work of Being Watched*, Boulder, CO: Rowman & Littlefield.
Bentham, Jeremy. (1995). *The Panopticon Writings,* Miran Bozovic (ed.), London: Verso.

Deleuze, Gilles. (1988). *Foucault*, Minneapolis: University of Minnesota Press.

——(1992). "Postscript on the Societies of Control," *October*, 59: 3–7.

Elmer, Greg and Opel, Andy. (2008). *Preempting Dissent: The Politics of an Inevitable Future*, Winnipeg: Arbeiter Ring Press.

Foucault, Michel. (1977). *Discipline and Punish: The Birth of the Prison*, translated by A. Sheridan, New York: Vintage.

——(2007). *Security, Territory, Population: Lectures at the College de France, 1977–1978*, translated by Graham Burchell, Houndmills, Basingstoke: Palgrave.

Galloway, Alex. (2004). *Protocol: Or how Control Exists After Decentralization*, Cambridge, MA: MIT Press.

Gandy, Oscar. (1993). *The Panoptic Sort: A Political Economy of Personal Information*, Boulder, CO: Westview Press.

Haggerty, Kevin. (2006). "Tear Down the Walls: On Demolishing the Panopticon," in D. Lyon (ed.), *Theorizing Surveillance: The Panopticon and Beyond*, Cullompton: Willan Publishing, pp. 23–45.

Kafka, Franz. (2009). *The Trial*, translated by David Wyllie, original publication 1925, New York: Dover Publications.

Mathiesen, Thomas. (1997). "The Viewer Society: Michel Foucault's 'Panopticon' Revisited," *Theoretical Criminology*, 15(2): 215–34.

Murakami Wood, David. (2007). "Beyond the Panopticon: Foucault and Surveillance Studies," in J. W. Crampton and S. Elden (eds), *Space, Knowledge and Power: Foucault and Geography*, Aldershot: Ashgate, pp. 245–64.

Poster, Mark. (1990). *The Mode of Information: Poststructuralism and Social Context*, Chicago, IL: University of Chicago Press.

b. Simulation and post-panopticism

William Bogard

Panoptic and post-panoptic studies of surveillance have both drawn heavily from French post-structuralist and postmodernist philosophies. Foucault's incisive analyses of panoptic environments, particularly in *Discipline and Punish: The Birth of the Prison* (1979), provided the basis both for a disciplinary understanding of surveillance, i.e. control of visibility in confined space, and what one could call a "control model" understanding in which electronic surveillance is the norm. There has been a lively theoretical debate over the extent to which historically the disciplinary model has been abandoned in favor of the control model, and how they differ, both conceptually and in practice (cf. Lyon 2007; Hardt and Negri 2004; Haggerty and Ericson 2000) (see also McCahill, this volume).

This debate, in turn, has fostered a discussion of the limits of panoptic control as a model for surveillance in societies that must track and manage digital information. Poster (1990), for instance, coined the term "Superpanopticon" to comprehend control today as an inflated form or higher register of panoptic surveillance. Haggerty and Ericson (2000) and Mann *et al.* (2003) have questioned whether the panoptic model remains useful at all for the modern theory of surveillance, given fundamental changes in the ways societies now obtain and use information. Drawing on Deleuze and Guattari's (1987) work, Haggerty and Ericson propose the concept of "surveillance assemblages" to describe the complex assortment of machines and procedures for extracting, sorting and delivering information today. What differs from the panoptic assemblage is the machinic architecture, which is now engineered to manipulate data objects in digital networks rather than physical bodies in confined spaces. In a somewhat different vein, Mann argues that the panoptic model cannot account for all the decentralized and non-hierarchical modes of surveillance operative today, in an era when technology is making it possible for everyone to watch everyone. He calls this state of affairs "sousveillance," in which surveillance comes from "below" as much as "above" and potentially constitutes a new mode of resistance to panoptic control.

A third model, the subject of this chapter, has focused on simulation as a post-panoptic control strategy. Baudrillard's (1994) work on the subject, and Deleuze's (1992) concept of "control societies," have provided insights into how the panoptic assemblage was limited by its rigid materiality and architecture (Bogard 1996). Simulations, by contrast, are composed of digital codes and offer flexible control that can serve multiple functions, from predicting complex system behaviors, to interactive and immersive training, planning and forecasting, profiling and preemptive intervention.

Simulation is a technology of truth and reality. In this respect it does not differ from panoptic control. According to Baudrillard (1994: 1), it is the reproduction of the real according to its model. Simulations do not "represent" real events so much as manufacture hypothetical ones for specific control contexts, for example, the digital games that train soldiers in combat scenarios. Simulation, Baudrillard claims, "short-circuits" the normative relations of truth that hold between real events and their representation. In their idealized form, simulations are self-verifying, i.e. they are true and real in themselves. Baudrillard often describes simulations hyperbolically, as "truer-than-true" or "hyperreal," to draw attention to their non-representational status, as well as to the implications this has for the display and exercise of social power. We shall return to this below.

Panopticism, in contrast, is tied to a strategy of representation. According to Foucault (1979: 200–202), the goals of panoptic power are visibility and non-verifiability. Power must appear present to compel obedience, even if it is absent in fact. In Bentham's ideal prison, the architecture itself represents the reality and truth of power, irrespective of the presence of a human observer in the central guard tower. No observer is required for the machine to function, but this truth is masked. Visible and unverifiable, power is freed to expose and verify every movement within the enclosed and segmented space over which it rules. This, Foucault says, is a coercive strategy of truth—it aims to establish what is true and eliminate everything false (or abnormal, or merely apparent) and to accomplish this in populations confined in space and time and deceived as to the presence of power.

Baudrillard (1994: 6) sometimes characterizes simulation as a truth that masks an absence of truth. The panopticon, from that point of view, already functions as a complex assemblage of simulation, to the extent that power disguises itself by disappearing into its architecture. This assemblage fails, however, a failure tied to the limits of that architecture, specifically, to its model of enclosure.

We must be careful, Foucault says, not to confuse "enclosure" with "confinement" (cf. Deleuze 1992: 4). Enclosure, as a general control strategy, facilitates the accumulation of power and knowledge. It regulates flows between the inside and outside of the enclosure, for example, flows of bodies, information or contraband. But enclosure does not require material constraint. The physical interior of the panopticon may be a gentler enclosure than the dungeon, but confinement remains its technology. That technology offers an imperfect solution at best for a system that aims for the automatic function of power. Walls are permeable, they have openings, access points and exits of various sorts that are difficult to surveil. They are rigid and create hidden zones where resistance can fester. They concentrate populations and increase opportunities for collusions and intrigues. Finally, confinement cannot satisfy the expanding needs of capital for greater mobility of labor, speed of communication and risk management. All these failures have combined to produce a general crisis of panopticism.

Simulation does not confine processes to verify them. In fact, confinement becomes redundant for it, as in our example of soldiers who can be trained in virtual combat anywhere. In its ideal form, simulation reproduces truth "in advance" of its verification (Bogard 1996). This same ideal inspires the most mundane simulations to the most science fictional, from industrial process control to cloning—to control a process in advance by verifying it first in its model. This ideal or "imaginary" informs the development of all simulation technologies in use today.

What follows is a brief history of simulation from the period around the Second World War, seen as part of a more general movement from disciplinary to control societies. This is not to suggest that simulation, as a strategy of power, is recent. Its uses—to mask an absence, to verify an event in advance—extend back to the origins of military strategy. Sun Tzu, in the sixth century BC, for instance, wrote on the advantages of disguise in war, on the use of spies as simulators, whose secret lines of information could preempt battles and defeat enemies without a fight. Simulation entered philosophical discourse early. Both Platonic and non-Platonic traditions analyzed it, either as a false and dangerous imitation of truth, or as a mask that concealed truth (or its absence). It is not my purpose here to go into this long history, but to focus on the recent technical evolution of simulation that develops in response to the failure of panoptic control, a failure rooted in what has been called the crisis of the disciplines.

The crisis of the disciplines

For Foucault, disciplinary society was in crisis by the beginning of the twentieth century (Deleuze 1992: 3). In fact, the origins of the crisis were much earlier. They were present from the beginning of the disciplinary project that emerged in Europe in the seventeenth and eighteenth centuries. The disciplinary machine, Foucault writes, works like any machine, namely, by "breaking down," by failing to produce its ideal outcome—specifically, a "docile body," an "individual" that is trained, improved and made useful to the system (1979: 136). This failure is in fact manifest in the assemblage from the start, and serves a self-corrective function. In overcoming its failures by constantly reforming itself, the disciplinary apparatus expands its control over the body and the general population. Failure, in this sense, is not a negative outcome, but a productive function of the disciplines.

Deleuze (1992: 3) credits Foucault for recognizing the transience of disciplinary societies, that they "succeeded ... the *societies of sovereignty*, the goal and functions of which were quite different (to tax rather than to organize production, to rule on death rather than to administer life)." But in turn, they were to be succeeded by the societies of control, the "new monster in our immediate future." The disciplinary model of enclosure ultimately proved too inflexible, unable to adapt itself to the demands of a changing economy for modulated controls over production. The result was a "generalized crisis in relation to all the environments of enclosure—prison, hospital, factory, school, family." These environments, Deleuze writes, are "interiors," fixed containers subjected to panoptic control. Interiors, however, cannot be sites of a mode of production that today demands decentralized, dispersed and mobile administration. This requires a new model of enclosure.

Deleuze (1992: 3) has summarized the ideal project of control that Foucault laid out in his histories of disciplinary institutions, "to concentrate; to distribute in space; to order in time; to compose a productive force within the dimension of space-time whose effect will be greater than the sum of its component forces." Confinement best facilitated these ends during the nineteenth century, when technologies for tracking individuals and population movements were limited by today's standards. In the abstract, control is a force that channels flows and if or how they cross the system's boundaries. Panoptic architecture, Bentham's famous design, represented a genuine advance in the efficiency of flow-control technologies over earlier ages. The elaborate system of walls and passages insured that populations of confined individuals would move in precise and predictable ways. But this system could not last, given the rapid exteriorization of productive forces in the twentieth century and its acceleration after the Second World War by advances in computerization, networks and methods of statistical modeling.

The technical logic that organizes control societies, according to Deleuze, is "modulation." Interiors are like "molds," rigid containers that shape their objects into a fixed and final form—in the case of discipline, this form is the modern "individual." Modulation, in contrast, does not work this way. In scientific terms, modulation is variable control over the characteristics of a wave. It is not applied to individuals but to oscillations, specifically, to "trends" or "tendential" movements that have defined statistical properties (we shall return to this). One form that modulation can take is statistical control, which adjusts production frequencies and amplitudes on the basis of small samples and standard deviations. This form of control does not depend on interiors, yet nonetheless operates as a form of enclosure. New techniques of statistical tracking (e.g. data mining), combined with remote control technologies, allow certain production processes to be regulated without concentrating them behind walls or allocating them to specific institutional spaces. Such is the case, for example, with work involving quality control, inventory, risk assessment and coordination of complex component assembly lines.

What is true for space is also true for time. In disciplinary societies, interiorization is accompanied by rigid temporal controls. Linear time, Deleuze (1992: 4–5) writes, structures production both inside disciplinary institutions—for example, the work line of the factory—and between them. When one is at work, one is not at school, or the barracks, or at home, always being transported from one rigid container to the next. Linear sequencing of production, in which each phase follows its immediately preceding one, may mark an advance in control technology at the beginning of the industrial age, but it becomes a fetter in network society, which demands phasing of multiple temporal sequences simultaneously, often in non-linear ways (multi-tasking).

A mold cannot alter its form, and the object it produces is fixed. Modulation control adapts to the deterritorialization of productive forces that marks the shift from industrial to network organization in contemporary society. Rather than generate a fixed object, the individual, an enclosure that modulates can vary its structure and the product it produces in response to changing contingencies of production, for example, those generated by the speed and complexity of modern communications, or the rapid flux of global markets.

All these changes culminate in a crisis of panoptic control grounded in its inability to regulate modern productive forces. Panopticism was a limited program designed to keep watch over confined populations, not organize the mobile labor forces and financial flows of complex information economies. Simulation is a flexible response to these problems, a tendential control technology that replaces rigid controls on visibility in enclosed interiors (and their associated temporal controls) with modulated control by models, codes and new methods of social sorting. What follows traces historical developments in simulation and their connection to post-panopticism in the sociology of Jean Baudrillard, who views these developments in terms of a shift in the representational function of sign systems in the twentieth century.

A short history of simulation

Although simulation has a long history, the focus here is on how it develops as a technology and strategic model of control in the period around the Second World War, specifically as it relates to the emergence of control societies following the collapse of the confinement model. Even here, however, some historical background is necessary.

Modern simulation has its origins in statistical estimation and sampling methods devised by Leclerc and Buffon in the eighteenth century, which enabled minimal data collected on populations to generate models of their behavior. Not surprisingly, given its long history in warfare, the first modern applications of simulation were military, in the development of models to improve the accuracy of artillery and aid in logistics and combat preparation (see Wilson, this volume). In Europe, statistical estimation also supported economic production. The small samples required for simulation models served to reduce the need for surveillance of every event and allowed the control function to be positioned more squarely at the input phase of a process rather than its output. Statistically representative data substituted for blanket and often ad hoc collection of information. In these early statistical formulations, there is a harbinger of many current forms of simulation control, from risk assessment, to profiling, data-mining and financial speculation. By the end of the nineteenth century, these techniques were being applied to quality and process control problems in the field of industrial engineering. By the middle of the twentieth century, they were used to assist in the development of nuclear weapons (Stanislaw Ulam's work with Edward Teller). In applications of game theory and other statistical modeling tools, numerous lines were drawn between the commercial and military applications of modern simulation.

In locating the roots of modern simulation in statistical reason, we should not forget that it has a mechinic history as well, oriented to training functions. Early in the twentieth century, the first simulated cockpits for flight instruction appeared. The importance of simulation was recognized from the beginning of manned flight. Aircraft themselves initially served to instruct pilots, but mock cockpits reduced costs, generated efficiencies of scale and gave flexible control over training times, places and risk.

Early flight simulators used devices to make the training experience more "realistic"—to tilt cockpits, simulate turbulence, convey stalls and lifts and the feel of real controls. The Second World War accelerated these developments as the need for pilots exploded. As aircraft grew in complexity and size, so did flight simulators, and as wars grew in complexity, simulators were designed to train not just pilots, but all manner of military personnel.

Statistical reason, of course, was also embodied in these machines. To train pilots for both routine operations and emergencies, simulators were engineered to produce deviations from normal functions and allow for corrections. They had to function within parameters that specified statistically normal flight conditions, measured and responded to variances and differences in operator inputs, and so on. The technologies were only as good as the estimation models that governed their behavior.

In the 1950s and 1960s, mathematical engineers articulated the two central problems of digital simulation: the construction of the simulation and its application. Strategically, one must first design a simulation experiment, then tactically determine how to run the simulation as specified in the design. The challenge of simulation modeling is to predict the output of complicated systems. Such output is almost never independent or normally distributed. Work on statistical distribution problems in the period between the Second World War and the 1980s focused on standardized time series, initialization biases, selection, ranking and optimization problems. Application-driven simulation increasingly found its way into the manufacturing and telecommunications sectors by way of the military.

In the 1960s, general purpose simulation systems were designed to facilitate rapid modeling of tele-communication systems used, for example, in urban traffic control, telephone-call interception and switching, airline-reservation processing and steel-mill operations. Models such as these also played key strategic roles in Cold War deterrence, assisting in assessments of technical, military and political capabilities of superpower rivals. Simulation also offered a means, in conditions of limited information on a rival's specific economic plans, to predict and control flows of capital, and to manipulate labor markets and financial transactions.

In all these developments, simulation provided tools for overcoming limits of control embedded in the panoptic model, limits tied to its form of enclosure and its conceptions of truth and reality. In the 1980s and 1990s, these problems were taken up by the sociologist/philosopher Jean Baudrillard, whose work remains one of the still relatively few sources of critical reflection on the socio-cultural implications of simulation control.

Baudrillard on simulation

Simulations are types of signs, and their philosophical study draws on semiotic and post-semiotic theory. Much of Baudrillard's work contributes to this general literature, but adds some distinctive twists. His most well known analysis in *Simulacra and Simulations* (1994) relates simulation to post-panoptic control. This work has been criticized for its eclectic blend of social theory, philosophy, history, fact and fiction. But its analysis of emerging control technologies was astute for its time, and it remains the most original and cogent work we have to date on the socio-political implications of simulation control.

Typically, simulations are defined as false or deceptive signs, but Baudrillard radicalizes this view. He asserts that, as simulation ascends to a dominant position in postmodern societies, the sign's traditional function of representation, i.e. its power to "mirror reality" and separate it from false appearances, comes to an end, along with its role in the organization of society. In part, this is a consequence of technological change, in part a function of the internal logic of signs themselves, i.e. to break free from their signifieds. Panoptic space, Baudrillard argues, in contrast is *representational*, a field of relatively fixed significations, and also *perspectival*, an orientational space that organizes the way objects are displayed. Simulation replaces both. What we witness with current simulation technology is, from the point of view of sign systems, a new semiotic of control, one founded not on truth relations between a sign and the reality it purports to represent, but on the radical indeterminacy of those relations. The utopian goal of simulation, according to Baudrillard, is not to reflect reality, but to reproduce it as artifice; to "liquidate all referentials" and replace them with signs of the real. The truth of the sign henceforth is self-referential and no longer needs the measure of an independent reality for its verification. Sign systems constitute their own reality, or as Baudrillard says, they become "hyperreal."

Simulacra and Simulation was originally published in 1981, when the digital assemblages we take for granted today were just emerging—social networks, GPS, virtual and augmented reality. In one section, it uses a now dated example of the vérité experience of reality television to illustrate the demise of panopticism. In 1971, an American documentary placed the "private and unscripted" daily lives of a "real" family (the Louds) on display for seven months for all to observe. Baudrillard notes, however, that the "truth" and "reality" of the family were simulations. The Louds went about their life "as if" the cameras watching them were not there. And the viewing public watched "as if" it was secretly spying on something private. Both were complicit in the illusion. It was an illusion that nonetheless produced "real" effects. The constant presence of the cameras provoked family conflicts during the filming, even though those conflicts could not be attributed to that presence without sacrificing the illusion. Baudrillard notes that, along with principles of truth and reality, the simulation also upset clear lines and common attributions of social causality. In the final analysis, he declares, it was indeterminate whether the broadcast images of the Louds represented the real causal dynamics of the family, or merely the perverse effects of television.

Baudrillard multiplies such examples, but, for him, all point to the close of the panoptic era, which "still presupposes an objective space (that of the Renaissance) and the omnipotence of the despotic gaze" (1994: 29). Although critical of Foucault's analysis of panoptic space, which he insists reifies the concept of power, Baudrillard shares Foucault's sense that the panoptic model of enclosure and its disciplinary logic are historically finished. The discipline enforced by panoptic surveillance evolves into a general "system of deterrence," in which submission to a centralized gaze becomes a general codification of experience that allows no room for deviation from its model. In post-panoptic society, subjectivity is not produced by surveillance in the conventional sense of hierarchical observation, but by codes intended to reproduce the subject in advance. It is no coincidence that Baudrillard often draws on examples of genetic engineering and cloning to illustrate the logical, technical and human horizons of simulation control.

Baudrillard does assert that simulation entails the "end" of the panoptic model. At the same time, his conception of simulation as "hyperreality" allows for the interpretation that panoptic control has not disappeared altogether in the new information order, but in fact has shifted into a higher register. Baudrillard, for example, asserts that measures that organized the prior order of signs are reduplicated in simulation in the present order. Thus, representation does not exactly disappear as a force in control societies, but rather becomes "simulated" representation (virtual reality can be conceived in this way); power does not vanish, but becomes simulated power, no longer instantiated and invested in the real, but rather reproduced in codes and models. Extending this logic, the visible spaces organized by the panopticon become the data mines and information clouds of post-disciplinary societies, accessed not by doors, locks and keys, but by passwords, pin numbers and decryption tools. The forces of verification, far from succumbing to the general crisis of truth that marks the failure of the panoptic machine, now operate more comprehensively, antecedent rather than subsequent to events. It is in this spirit of reading Baudrillard that has led Bogard (1996) to describe postmodern control as "simulated surveillance," or surveillance as modeling. If and when simulation control becomes able to model the full range of contingencies for a predesignated range of events and control for them, surveillance will have achieved its most comprehensive expression. Every unfolding process that occurs within a defined set of parameters will be pre-screened and accounted for in advance. Such are the "dreams" of control society engineers who design virtual training systems, or who develop cloning technologies and artificial intelligence systems. It is the "reality principle" that is at stake in these changes, not reality itself. In control societies, surveillance is not governed solely by the imperative to represent reality, but to assist in the construction and application of models. What is monitored first of all is information on the performance of the model, and not the event it models.

The panopticon is a "medium" for channeling flows of information and bodies. It is a concrete assemblage consisting of lighted passageways, walls, entries and exits, and an apparatus for recording all that passes in and out of the assemblage. It is the dematerialization of this medium that Baudrillard claims is a hallmark of post-panoptic society. Hardt and Negri (2004) have theorized the dematerialization and growing abstraction of media of control in post-panoptic societies, as the information network rather than industrial production becomes the dominant model for organizing society. A parallel way of thinking about this development is through the language of "surveillance assemblages" (cf. Haggerty and Ericson 2000). Assemblages, in Deleuze and Guattari's (1987) formulation, are multiplicities of interconnected machines, some of which are concrete (e.g. surveillance hardware, bioware technology), others abstract and imma-terial (codes, models, statistical formulae, data). As it has evolved in control societies, the surveillance assemblage increasingly operates as a system of deterrence that manages the immaterial functions of net-works. Of course, the material technology of surveillance remains important—networks are still composed of interconnected computers, communication lines and information storage devices. Currently, however, developments in network technologies point to the progressive elimination of physical media, as commu-nications become wireless, as data storage becomes the function of information "clouds" and as tracking of individual and population movements no longer demands their visibility but continuous global positioning and statistical estimation. Eventually, so the science fiction scenario goes, the external medium of surveillance will dematerialize entirely with advances in genetic coding and engineering.

Finally, Baudrillard claims that the collapse of the reality principle in simulation reverses the causality of panoptic control, indeed the whole causal logic of discipline insofar as it constitutes a machinery of judg-ment. In the disciplinary machine, verification precedes judgment. Although it aims to produce automatic obedience, panoptic surveillance nonetheless reacts to events—it notices, identifies and categorizes them before passing this information on to authorities that determine its ultimate significance. In control socie-ties, however, judgment is far more proactive. The simulation model structures the event's production and meaning, and passes judgment in advance. Surveillance is relegated to a secondary function and is only there to monitor the performance of the model. It is as if the whole causal sequence of social judgment had been reversed to mirror the Queen's demands for justice in *Alice in Wonderland*:

> 'Let the jury consider their verdict,' the King said, for about the twentieth time that day.
> 'No, no!' said the Queen. 'Sentence first – verdict afterwards.'
> 'Stuff and nonsense!' said Alice loudly. 'The idea of having the sentence first!'
> 'Hold your tongue!' said the Queen, turning purple.
> 'I won't!' said Alice.
> 'Off with her head!' the Queen shouted at the top of her voice. Nobody moved.
> 'Who cares for you?' said Alice, (she had grown to her full size by this time.) 'You're nothing but a
>   pack of cards!'

If surveillance still performs a juridical function in social control today, it is more likely to be located on the side of the execution of the sentence, which ideally comes prior to the announcement of the verdict. No verification procedure is necessary to render a verdict for a judgment already made. Verification, so to speak, is complete. Reality checks that would interrupt this sequence are performed in advance and any problems are deterred in advance. Henceforth, surveillance functions to serve the application of the simulation model, to insure the model's initial conditions are correctly specified and that its run unfolds according to plan. It is not asked to extend beyond the parameters of the simulation. Thus, as it develops as a means of control in post-panoptic society, surveillance is severed from the very reality principle it was originally set up to enforce.

The future of simulation

Baudrillard's hypotheses about simulation control are deliberatively hyperbolic and speculative. The future trajectory of any technical assemblage is always uncertain. The technologies we imagine on the horizon rarely resemble or function like the ones that actually emerge. This is undoubtedly true of simulation technology in a post-panoptic world. Nonetheless, we might glean some trends from present developments.

One thread in the evolution of simulation technology is *convergence*. Historically, different uses of simulation have developed in relatively independent ways. The demand for applications that serve more than one audience and/or more than a single function has led to the merger of once distinct simulation approaches. One example of interest to the military, where many ideas for control technologies originate, is the convergence of live, virtual and constructive (LVC) simulation for training purposes. Increasingly this has come to include forms of augmented reality.

Gaming, of course, is one area of intensive development, one that also has benefitted from military applications. Computer-based games combine simulation and entertainment. They have been commercially profitable and led to the production of lower-cost information delivery platforms that have high performance computing and graphics. Trends point to the insertion of more instructional tools into game simulations, following the military example above.

Simulation aims at the replication of experience. From flight simulators to retinal laser technologies that produce images directly on the eye, the substitution of virtual for real experience has been a project of simulation research and development. *Haptic control* is perhaps one of the more fantastic applications of simulation technology. It is a means of flexible enclosure, in contrast to confinement, to return to the theme that began this chapter. Haptic simulation involves not just the simulation of touch, as its name might imply. Rather, it is a technical and social program for the replication of sensibility as a whole, including the body's proprioceptive awareness, the internal sense of its own position and movement relative to the external world. Part of this program does involve the development of technologies that reproduce or simulate the sensation of touch, but the full project of haptics is simulation control of the whole continuum of affective experience.

The term "haptics" comes from the Greek for the ability *to make contact with*. Unlike information control that requires a confined population, or a dispersed population under passive surveillance (such as CCTV), haptic technologies respond to the active body and supply it with tactile feedback. The program of haptics is straightforward: simulate the body's sense of acting in the real world.

Haptic interfaces simulate the feel of objects, their texture, surface resistance, bulk, edges and gaps. Datagloves that react with vibratory stimuli to users' handling of simulated objects, for instance, are a classic example of a haptic technology. Current applications include locomotion devices for navigating virtual worlds (updated treadmills), orthopedic equipment, touch-screen technologies, tele-operators (remotely controlled robots), diagnostic tools for measuring or producing pressure and resistance, density, heat and other intensive parameters, and, of course, computer games that provide gamers with various kinds of vibrational or positional feedback.

In all these developments of simulation control, we have moved far beyond what the panoptic model of surveillance developed in the classical age was capable of explaining.

References

Baudrillard, J. (1994). *Simulacra and Simulations,* Ann Arbor: University of Michigan Press.

Bogard, W. (1996). *The Simulation of Surveillance: Hypercontrol in Telematic Societies*, Cambridge: Cambridge University Press.

Carroll, L. (1992). *Alice in Wonderland,* Donald J. Gray (ed.), New York: W.W. Norton and Company.

Deleuze, G. (1992). "Postscript on the Societies of Control," *October* 59 (Winter): 3–7.

Deleuze, G. and Guattari, F. (1987). *A Thousand Plateaus: Capitalism and Schizophrenia, Vol. 2*, Minneapolis: University of Minnesota Press.

Foucault, M. (1979 [1975]). *Discipline and Punish: The Birth of the Prison*, New York: Vintage.

Haggerty, K. D. and Ericson, R. V. (2000). "The Surveillant Assemblage," *British Journal of Sociology,* 51(4): 605–22.

Hardt, M. and Negri, A. (2004). *Multitude: War and Democracy in the Age of Empire*, New York: The Penguin Press.

Lyon, D. (2007). *Surveillance Studies: An Overview*, Cambridge: Polity.

Mann, S., Nolan, J. and Wellman, B. (2003). "Sousveillance: Inventing and Using Wearable Computing Devices for Data Collection in Surveillance Environments," *Surveillance & Society,* 1(3): 331–55.

Poster, M. (1990). *The Mode of Information*, Chicago, IL: University of Chicago Press.

c. Surveillance as biopower

Ayse Ceyhan

This chapter explores the relevance of Michel Foucault's concepts of biopower and governmentality for understanding the rationalities of contemporary surveillance in a way that is grounded and attuned to contemporary social and political transformations.

The thesis it addresses is twofold. First, surveillance is not only a form of a liberal governmental rationality seeking maximum effectiveness and managing the market and the population by observing, classifying and sorting individuals, but is also intended to capture the contingent features of the "uncertain" (*l'aléatoire*) that characterizes our times. Uncertainty, which had been already presented by philosophers such as Thomas Hobbes as one of the main attributes of the human condition, alongside indeterminacy, represents a significant feature of the actual context. Classical modernity's aim as represented by Enlightenment thought and science was basically to remove unknowns and uncertainties. But uncertainty that has never been totally removed is still there. If in Hobbes's times it was generated by crude human characteristics like greediness and selfishness, it is now produced both by the transformations of late modernity whose main features, says Zygmunt Bauman, are being "light, liquid, mobile, slippery" and the changes occurring in security regimes by the new forms of violence and their dissemination through transnational, private and virtual networks. These dynamics impact the claims to truth, knowledge and power which no longer rely on the traditional markers of certainty like territory, hierarchy and rationality that modernity had set after the seventeenth century. In this context, the biopoliticized surveillance, that is surveillance taking the human body and its movements as the focal points, appears like a political technology of population management and a technique of reassuring populations in complex and uncertain contexts of our times where security has become a high priority.

Second, biopower understood in its Foucauldian formulation as power over life and the species' body is not the exclusive attribute of the state, but can be achieved anywhere by any organization through information gathering and data-management processes and tools. Indeed, in light of the current transformations occurring in the space of mobility as well as in the nature and the location of regulative powers, we witness a new modality of (bio)power. As societies become more dependent on information and communication technologies (ICTs) there is a change in power, intensity and scope. Becoming more and more hybrid, power deterritorializes and connects dots which are not in the first place designed to beconnected. Moreover, power is now exercised in non-traditional locations like datawarehouses, software, airline and phone companies. The actual holders of power are not exclusively states but private organizations like Google where information about billions of people is offered to everybody as material for processing and assessing without limitation, hierarchical order and precise location. Hence the emergence of a new way of managing individuals, their life and living: an electronic and digitized (bio)power which is more open-ended, flexible and embedded in domestic life as opposed to the classical territorialized biopower of the nineteenth century which was the attribute of first the sovereign and then the market.

This chapter shows how basic biological features of human beings such as their unchangeable body parts, their biometric features, behaviors and everyday life activities like moving, traveling, communicating and connecting, have become objects of surveillance. It will examine how surveillance becomes a biopolitical security and power technology and how its regulatory measures transform it into a technology of certainty (Ceyhan 2008) which is supposed to compensate for the loss of confidence generated with the transformations of late modernity. As Bauman contends in his series of books on "liquids," the transformations of modernity generated new challenges for individuals and societies and also a loss of confidence on traditional regulative forces and institutions which are no longer capable of serving as a frame of reference for human action.

The argument of the transformation of actual surveillance into a new biopolitical form of power will draw both upon Foucault's analysis of biopower that we will consider in association with the notion of the "treatment of the aleatory" (the uncertain) and the concept of governmentality developed in his lectures at the Collège de France between 1978 and 1979 (Foucault 2004 [2007] Lectures 1, 2 and 4). These concepts are still relevant for understanding the rationalities of contemporary surveillance, especially the form it took with the terrorist attacks of 9/11, and its elevation into global political technology since then. However, as aforementioned, the transformations of modernity and violence call for the adaptation of some of Foucault's arguments to the new context, especially to fluidity and digitization, significant phenomena that we intend to include in the analysis of contemporary surveillance.

Surveillance as a technology of biopoliticized security

The concept of biopower was initially introduced in the first volume of the *History of Sexuality* as a form of power over life which emerged at the end of the eighteenth century and whose vocation is to "make life alive" (Foucault 1976).

> How could power exercise its highest prerogatives by putting people to death, when its main role was to ensure and multiply life, to put this life in order [...] The object of this biopoliticized power is the 'species' body, the body imbued with the mechanisms of life and serving as the basis of the biological processes propagation, births and mortality, the level of health, life expectations and longevity.
>
> *(Foucault 1976: 138, 139)*

With this concept, Foucault reversed the emphasis on the threat of death characterizing the ancient times at the expense of the protection of life and initiated the problematic of taking life (body, health, sexuality, race) as the focal object for governing population's and individuals' self and social life which he pursued in his lectures at the Collège de France in terms of biopolitics of security and security technologies (Foucault 2004). The baseline assumption is that power focuses on the population by presupposing individuals as living subjects, and politics is essentially all about efficient techniques of estimating the fertility of territories and the health and movements of the population (ibid.).

For Foucault, security and biopower are intimately interrelated in that the biopoliticized problematic of security deals with an object that is constantly transforming and revolving around "the economy of the contingent" (Foucault 1976: 47), "the regulation of circulation and the promotion of reproductive powers and potentials of life" (ibid.: 16–20; 44; 45). The Foucauldian conception of security is broad and comprises several meanings. Different from discipline which is exercised on pre-determined individuals, security is exercised on an entire population of individuals for managing their life, health, psychology and behaviors. It refers to different meanings regarding whether it is exercised in terms of series of mobile elements and events, or in terms of milieu as the space in which circulation occurs (Foucault 2004: 22).

The notions of circulation and milieu are central to the Foucauldian analysis of liberal regimes (Foucault 2004: Lessons 1, 3, 13). Circulation is the space of the operations of human beings and defines the principle of organization of modern biopolitics. Foucault looked at circulation both in terms of town planning and the circulation of commerce, networks, goods, ideas and orders. Moreover, the problematic of circulation includes both the freeing of circulation and also more generally the suppression of the dangerous, the problem of "differentiating good circulation from bad circulation," maximizing the first one at the expense of the second (ibid.: 20). It then comprises the surveillance of dangerous populations such as "all floating populations, beggars, vagrants, delinquents, criminals, thieves, murderers" (ibid.).

Milieu is basically the regulative space of circulation. Foucault borrowed this notion from mechanics and biology after his reading of Canguilhem and Lamarck as the space in which populations are secured from death on the basis of their collective life, health and environment. It is the imaginary and real enclosure in which certain species not only are present, but can grow and prosper. Milieu is what is needed to account for action at a distance of one body on another (Foucault 2004: 20) and a set of natural givens, rivers, marshes, hills and a set of artificial givens and agglomerations of individuals' houses (ibid.: 22, 23). The milieu is the constant entanglement of a geographical, climatic and physical with human species as it has a body and a soul, a moral and physical existence (ibid.: 24). Circulation is the principle of ordering of movements and interactions which can be put in series of indefinite number of events such as the number of boats that dock at the wharf or trucks that are coming to the city, etc. These series comprise indefinite numbers of units like houses, people, goods that pile up. Security is then the management of such kinds of open series which therefore can only be controlled by an estimate of probabilities (ibid.: 22).

In *Security, Territory, Population* (2004 [2007]) Foucault examined the different meanings security is invested with. These meanings go from the sense security was given in relation to sovereignty and territoriality to the meaning it held with the advances of liberalism in the eighteenth and nineteenth centuries, He then arrived to consider security as the statistical modeling of dangerous and/or risky behavior and the normalization that this modeling generates for populations (Lectures 1, 2 and 3). In his endeavor, he also specified that security is not limited to the protection of the territory but centrifugal; widening constantly its scope to include more events such as production, psychology, behaviors, etc. (Foucault 2004: 46). This reading of security is still relevant today as we witness the broadening of security focal objects to new and unexpected objects like the body parts, personal information, biography and data. Such mutation is generated with the transformations of violence, the new forms it has taken, and also with changes in science, technology and knowledge like the discovery of DNA and the production of cutting–edge security technologies such as biometrics, face-recognition technologies, intelligent tracking systems and the whole computerization and digitization processes. These technologies are characterized by their pervasiveness as they are not just tools for security agencies but invade the daily life of individuals. Not only are they part of the public space (as with camera surveillance) but they also participate in the securitization of individuals' computers, data, luggage or houses. Moreover, some of them, like biometrics, participate in the regulation of individuals' health as they are intensively used in ophthalmology and endocrinology.

In this chapter surveillance is considered as a political technology of population management. As the vast literature produced by surveillance studies indicates surveillance is an old activity that has existed as long as humans have existed and interacted with each other (Lyon 2006). In modern times it had been intimately connected with the regulation of the capitalist society and the modernization of the army and the nation-state. According to the Foucauldian problematic of biopoliticized security, surveillance can be understood as the very form of liberal governmentality seeking maximum efficiency for the regulation of bodies and species. It is an activity undertaken both by governments and institutions and even by the subjects themselves against each other. Regarding governmental forms of governmentality, according to Foucault, the idea that government should intervene in society means that the population should be managed and even remediated or improved to ensure its members can participate productively in the market. This implies the regulation of subjects through means and diverse techniques, which are based upon the medical metaphor of body, circulation and flow. In this perspective, the biopoliticized regulation of population requires that the population has to be known both in terms of its actual behavior and with respect to the probabilities of its future behavior (what will the population probably do?). Hence the development of a whole series of systems of knowledge focusing on the identification, the tracking and the surveillance of individuals considered as dangerous for the population's health (as it was in the nineteenth century) and well-being. However, in reality, the scope of surveillance is much wider than this. As Lyon posits, surveillance is ambiguous, and is understood in its ambiguity from care to control, and the role of visibility of the surveiled is taken as seriously as the process of observing, classifying and studying (Lyon 2006). Surveillance covers all aspects of the public and private life of individuals as they are implemented in the real-time and also in terms of future intentions and projects (ibid.).

Indeed, in the aftermath of the 9/11 attacks the response was the increasing surveillance of society not in its classical state/society relations terms, but electronically and remotely within a space of fluidity and movement whose reach goes over traditional state borders. Processed across cutting-edge technologies that are becoming more and more sophisticated, surveillance is directed towards the tracking of all movements and itineraries wherever individuals go in their daily life as well as their communications and connections (Lyon 2003). But, while aiming at controlling and regulating populations' movements and preventing the emergence of risky features such as "bad circulation," which Foucault presented as the circulation of "all floating populations like beggars, vagrants, delinquents, criminals, thieves, murderers etc.," its aim is also reassuring populations in the context of fear and uncertainty created by the 9/11 terrorist attacks.

Surveillance as a means of reassurance by the treatment of the uncertain (the aleatory)

In his analysis of biopower and security apparatuses (*le dispositif*) Foucault dedicated a short but insightful portion to the question of the uncertain (the aleatory) that he considered as one of the natural processes that liberal governmentality must deal with and regulate (Foucault 2004: 32-56). Along with the space of the exercise of security, the norm and the population, the aleatory event is one of the four general features of security apparatuses (ibid.: 13, 32-56, 69-75). It is generated both by the contingent character of the event (like food scarcity which is not exactly famine but the current shortfall in the amount of grain needed to sustain a nation) (ibid.: 32) and its correlation with a variety of factors such as anti-hunger measures whose aim is to prevent the occurrence of probable events which often do not correspond to the reality (ibid.: 34).

Today these various factors are economic, environmental, biological, scientific and technological. Any incidence or change occurring on one of them may impact the biopolitical management of populations. This explains the task allocated to security apparatuses as to predicting the probable risks that may occur with the ongoing changes in environment, science, technology and health. The concept of the aleatory appears then as the explanatory variable that justifies the focus on the technologies of risk management that enable the prediction of these changes before they occur.

Foucault contended that the treatment of the uncertain (the aleatory) relies on statistics and the constitution of series of events likely to occur, such as overlaps, comparisons and calculations of costs (Foucault 2004: 11). Constituting an important dimension of the rationalization of state power, statistics were referred to in the seventeenth and eighteenth centuries as "the science of the state" or the descriptive study of the "curiosities of the state" (Deflem 1997: 155). The study of crime and diseases being one of the essential "curiosities" of the state, they were initially used in the realm of security to establish regularities. Later, by the middle of the nineteenth century, with the introduction of mathematical theories of probabilities they became more and more based on probability calculation (ibid.).

In the Foucauldian understanding, statistics and other techniques like surveillance are presented as "apparatuses (*dispositifs*) *of* security" rather than classical security means (Foucault 2004: Lectures 1-3). The concept of apparatus that Foucault borrowed from Deleuze does not refer to any single device or *techné*, but reflects an ensemble of both physical and non-physical means. Indeed, in Deleuze's understanding apparatus meant "a heterogeneous ensemble, a sort of network that includes both the said and the unsaid, that is to say discourses, laws, regulations, administrative enunciations, institutions and architectural ensembles" (Deleuze 1989: 185). Following this, Foucault envisioned security apparatuses as connecting any physical security phenomenon such as theft with a series of both measures, means, discourses and likely events (probabilities) that are expected to occur. Not only do these apparatuses calculate risks, but they also calculate their costs and foresee the reactions of power and set the optimal acceptability level by the population (Foucault 2004: 8). In consequence, security apparatuses introduce a new form of power different from classical disciplinary power, which relies mainly on coercion. Indeed, contrary to disciplinary measures, security apparatuses do not intervene directly in the game but shape the rules of the game. Instead of being straightforwardly implemented, they operate indirectly or remotely. As such, they participate in what Foucault calls "governmentality," that is the ensemble constituted by the institutions, procedures, analyses and reflections, calculations and tactics which can support "that very specific but very complex form of power whose main target is the population, major form of knowledge is the political economy and essential technical instrument are security apparatuses" (Foucault 2004: 111).

As parts of this ensemble, statistics rely on data and are concerned with the mapping of the incidence of contingent behavior considered in relation to multiple factors revolving around different spheres of life like health, sexuality, race, biology and so on. Referring to such a variety of possible domains and issues as well as to their correlations and preoccupied by their impact on behaviors, Foucault introduced the problematic of "probability and risk" without however developing them in detail as did later on scholars like Giddens and Beck. Even if the analysis of the concepts of risk, danger and probability needed in-depth developments, they however enabled Foucault to frame his problematic of security in combination with the developments of liberalism that Michel Sennelard, in his afterword to *Security, Territory, Population*, defined as "risk calculation" contending that the incitation to live dangerously implies the establishment of a variety of security mechanisms (Sennelard in Foucault 2004: 402).

The emphasis on the translation of the uncertain/aleatory into risk is relevant today for analyzing contemporary surveillance and the mobilization of the statistical knowledge for establishing probabilities about the likelihood of risky events to occur. In the aftermath of the 9/11 attacks surveillance and identification technologies have become the preferred way to manage risks and predict future dangers. Observing the emphasis put on risk-based surveillance approaches and solutions, Lyon stresses that more and more people and populations are labeled as suspicious and at the same time surveillance techniques have become increasingly intrusive and also opaque and secretive (Lyon 2003). And Deflem points out that "strategies of risk make up people not as legal-political subjects, but as statistical parameters in an equation based on objective knowledge of past and present conditions" (Deflem 1997: 152). To supply these parameters emphasis is put on the observation and analysis of behaviors as well as the tracking of movements.

The implementation of security as the assessment of probabilities is considered by political authorities as a means of reassuring populations in times of uncertainty. In the context of the adoption of precautionary measures for coping with potential dangers and risks before they occur and contending with people's emotions, this approach is widely considered as politically rewarding even if there is no such macro and micro level empirical measurements of its real efficiency. However, its reliance on sophisticated data analysis and management technologies seems for some portion of populations a scientific approach to predict insecurity while some others put emphasis on the serious privacy and freedom problems its approach generates.

Algorithmic surveillance and management of behaviors

In contemporary security and surveillance apparatuses, risk analyses are realized in computerized databases where sophisticated softwares are displayed to process data. Deploying complex algorithms for the prediction of risky behaviors and/or people, these softwares implement a "silent surveillance" that Norris et al. called "algorithmic surveillance" (Norris et al. 1998).

As exemplified by the UK implementations, surveillance systems such as Closed Circuit Television (CCTV) have been widely installed in public spaces of almost all urban areas. Related to the evolutions of crime and violence, these solutions are continuously improved in light of the top technological advances. Currently, the objective of the progress to the state-of-the-art is not only identifying criminals and violent behaviors with precision, but also predicting future risky behaviors and/or people. In this perspective several solutions such as GPS, RTLS (Real Time Locating Systems), RFID (Radio Frequency Identification) tracking devices, intelligent video cameras and selection and sorting algorithms are currently widely displayed in surveillance applications. The immediate task of these devices is both real time precise detection of dangers and risks and prediction of future risks. For instance, in videosurveillance, various systems have emerged to display the digitized model of video cameras in real time to recognize normal behavior and detect and alert on all abnormal patterns of behavior.

To realize these tasks, surveillance technologies rely heavily on algorithms. As Introna and Wood contend (2004), algorithms that form the foundation of computing have become the principal layer of contemporary surveillance apparatuses. Essential to the way computers process data, algorithms are a list of well-defined mathematical instructions for completing a task such as calculation, data processing and automated reasoning. They are introduced in computer programs by software to carry out specific tasks that computers have been programmed to understand. This process is known as coding. Software is essentially composed of many coded algorithms linked together to produce a desired output from the hardware. Algorithms can thus be deployed as event generators as they combine the understanding of the scene with the users defined criteria to trigger special programmed events (alarms, etc.) or outcomes (profiles of risky people).

Relying upon complex analysis of data, "algorithmic surveillance" (Norris et al. 1998) is thus designed to uncover relationships among widely disparate information and enable predictive analysis of behavioral patterns. Contrary to the classical panoptic form of surveillance that Foucault described, based on Bentham's model for prisons, actual surveillance is characterized by embedded, silent and hidden processes that make it difficult for individuals and society to be aware of and scrutinize it (Introna and Wood 2004). Moreover these processes threaten to replace social negotiations with technological process of judgment and generate unexpected social, ethical and juridical consequences (Lyon 2003, 2006).

One of the most distinctive features of this surveillance is that its predictive orientation is aimed at the detection of criminal acts, and at all human behavior in order to detect the risky ones. Even if this surveillance is processed through sensors, mathematical instructions and sequences of computer operations and thus appears neutral, such emphasis enhances in fact the biopolitical character of surveillance. Indeed, following the Foucauldian analysis of population management by security technologies we may then argue that through sophisticated surveillance mechanisms behavioral features of individuals and populations became an object of the political strategy of biopower. As aforementioned the principal technique of this power is the calculation of probabilities within a series of events, calculation of costs of action, normalization and correlations between different probabilities.

Towards a hybrid form of biopower

However, in current times the above-mentioned techniques and instruments are displayed slightly differently than with the nineteenth-century biopower.

As highlighted earlier, the questions of circulation and its regulation are essential for Foucault's work concerning both disciplinary power and biopower. Both powers sought to order, channel and discipline populations. In biopower Foucault developed a principle of how people are governed based upon the regulation of circulation and flows and made the health of the body the match against which the techniques of power would be measured. He thus made medical metaphors of circulation and flow as the new principles of governmentality.

Contemporary parameters of political technologies are also established in relation to movement, and the body and behaviors constitute the centerpieces of its regulation. However, the space of circulation and the nature of the regulative power have considerably changed. Not only has the space of mobility been extended outside the state borders and embraced the whole globe, but it has also become virtualized and open-ended with the display of a variety of technologies of information and communication as well as the development of huge databases where flows of information are processed and data mined. Consequently, more than a straightforward biopolitical power of the subjugation of bodies, what we witness today resembles better the politics of artefacts, which, by its very design, includes certain interests and excludes others (Lascoumes *et al.* 2001; Introna and Wood 2004). These artefacts are heterogeneous systems that function like assemblages and transform the locations of power and politics. They connect different technologies like biometrics, video cameras, GPSs and algorithms and produce an insidious form of surveillance, which impacts individuals' lives not from the outside but from the domestic and private spheres where these technologies become more and more integrated. This makes us define a new form of governmentality and regulative power that is located in non-traditional places like the Internet (Google, for instance), shopping malls, marketing services, phone companies, businesses and high-tech corporations. In these mundane, functional and dynamic locations, social negotiation is replaced by customer management, risk assessment, market analysis, and efficiency and efficacy measures (Lyon 2003, 2006).

Google for instance has become the most powerful biopolitical surveillance tool as it gathers, processes and mines large volumes of information about people and groups. Billions of people use it for information, communication, research and location purposes. Ever since these services are used, the searches always leave a mark that Google data-mining algorithms process in order to "connect the dots" of information and data which are initially unconnected. These dots concern all aspects of the past and present life of individuals and process both public, private and sensitive information. Data-mining software uses these dots and all the historical information to build a model of customer behavior which is used to predict which information would be likely to respond to further requests. Based on marketing and advertisement techniques (Lyon 2003), such an engine governs the public and private life of individuals without their consent. Moreover, Google's projects don't stay only at the level of information and search services, but also concern the field of molecular biology and genetics. As part of its further services Google has already downloaded a human genome map and is working closely with biologists on specific genetics projects that may lead to important developments in science, medicine and health. By this Google makes it clear that its aim is participating in the dream of anticipating the future and managing accordingly people's life, health, leisure and security.

This complex assemblage of silent artefacts introduces what Lascoumes *et al.* have called "hybrid" systems (Lascoumes *et al.* 2001). Hybrids are heterogeneous systems designed for multiple tasks implemented without following an overarching direction from the beginning. They represent diverse interests and values and link generic technologies, which are not *a priori* designed for being connected (ibid.: 35–36). This translates in security applications as the linkage of *a priori* autonomous tasks like identification, surveillance, marketing, tracking, risk management, systems security, etc. These tasks which are not initially all framed for providing security and managing populations are brought together for functional reasons for providing security, services and comfort.

Today we witness a new modality of power. With the politics of artefacts there is a step change in power's, intensity and scope. Biopower is not only the attribute of the state, but can be reached through digitization and assemblage of autonomous tasks and interests in unexpected locations by "friendly look-ing" organisms like search engines, software companies, airline companies and data warehouses. As such contemporary biopower is hybrid. It opens new assemblages of technologies and techniques and is no longer processed by the sole control of populations through sexuality and health, but by the tracking of individuals' body parts (biometrics) and behaviors as well as the scrutiny of their projects and thoughts. This explains its increasing focus on unchangeable body parts like fingerprints, iris and retina and on individuals' behaviors and tastes in normal life as the very sites of risk assessment and prediction.

Contemporary biopower looks to be always evolving as it runs behind the dream of the anticipation of future events and projects. This never-ending race raises however serious and crucial problems for indivi-duals as the strategic means and the basic materials of this race are their information and personal and public data. In this context, more than a problem of physical insecurity, individuals in non-conflict places face problems of data security as well as unexpected privacy issues that neither national nor federal juridical frameworks have anticipated so far.

References

Ceyhan, A. (2008). "Technologization of Security: Management of Uncertainty and Risk in the Age of Biometrics," *Surveillance & Society*, 5(2): 102–23.

Deflem, M. (1997). "Surveillance and Criminal Statistics. Historical Foundations of Governmentality," *Statistics in Law, Politics and Society*, 17: 149–84.

Deleuze, G. (1989). "Qu'est-ce qu'un Dispositif?," in *Michel Foucault Philosophe. Rencontre Internationale, Paris, 9, 10, 11 janvier 1988*, Paris: Seuil.

Foucault, M. (1976). *The History of Sexuality (Introduction: The Will to Knowledge)*, English translation 1998, London: Allen Lane.

——(2004). *Sécurité, Territoire, Population*, Paris: Gallimard/Seuil Collection "Hautes Etudes," English translation *Security, Territory, Population* (Lectures at the Collège de France) (2007), edited by M. Senellard, F. Ewald and A. Fontana, Basingstoke: Palgrave Macmillan.

Introna, L. and Wood, D. (2004). "Picturing Algorithmic Surveillance: The Politics of Facial Recognition Systems," *Surveillance & Society*, 2(2/3): 177–98.

Lascoumes, P., Callon, M., Barthe, Y. (2001). *Agir dans un Monde Incertain. Essai sur la Démocratie Technique*, Paris: Seuil.

Lyon, D. (2006). *Theorizing Surveillance: The Panopticon and Beyond*, Cullompton: Willan Publishing.

——(2003). *Surveillance After September 11*, London: Polity.

Norris, C., Moran, J., Armstrong, G. (1998). "Algorithmic Surveillance: The Future of Automatic Visual Surveillance," in C. Norris, J. Moran and G. Armstrong (eds), *Surveillance in Closed Circuit TV and Social Control*, Hampshire: Ashgate.

Section 1.2.
Theory II: Difference, politics, privacy

a. "You shouldn't wear that body"

The problematic of surveillance and gender

Hille Koskela

The ambiguities

Gender has not been the most popular research topic among surveillance scholars. Considering how well established the field of gender studies is, and how strongly surveillance studies has been embracing the study of concrete everyday issues, it is surprising that these fields have not been better integrated. The histories of (controlling) gender/sexualities and of surveillance are very much connected, and there is much to understand and discover about this topic.

Gender is embedded in a complex range of relations where power and repression are associated with the exercise of surveillance. Long before the development of contemporary surveillance technologies, gender and sexuality were intensely controlled by social and moral norms, which entailed their own forms of interpersonal monitoring, and in many places of the world this is still the case. Historically, women and sexual minorities have been pioneers in challenging and refusing to submit to such control. Today, surveillance helps to reinforce sexual norms by creating pressures for self-regulation. The operation of surveillance is also full of male assumptions and assorted gendered dynamics. Focusing on gender relations negotiated under surveillance also helps us come to terms with other forms of power and exclusion.

Early feminist scholars tended to label all sorts of things as "masculine"—technology, academic understanding, and reason—which were counterposed to the more "feminine" domains of emotion and culture. In such accounts, gender was—as we now realize—confused with sex, the biological essence of each individual being either a woman or a man. Women were claimed to be different just by virtue of being (biologically) women. It was believed that women's "softness" made a difference to how they understood the world and made decisions. Technology, among other things, was generally viewed in a negative light, as if it was something inherently masculine—a male conspiracy (Wajcman 1991). This position was also part of a larger feminist reaction to the sense that the histories produced by men reproduced the male/female dichotomy by only telling one side of any story. Unfortunately, it also inhibited the development of greater understandings of contemporary surveillance dynamics.

Feminist scholars later recognized that it is not the sexual qualities of people themselves that matter but, rather, the gendered nature of power relations. Notions of biological essence were abandoned and gender became the focal point of academic inquiry (Wilson 1991). Scholars agreed that there is no uniform category of "women," nor a single trajectory of feminist academic thinking. Mere sex as a basis for social difference was questioned and replaced by *a spectrum of multiple differently gendered identities*. This gender spectrum is significantly more complex than the male-female binary system, as it accentuates that there are sexual identities that do not fit into the normative conception of gender. Biological sex, gender and the body are connected, but not in a simple way. Rather, there is a complex range of female, male, lesbian, gay, queer, transgendered, transsexual and androgyny identities.

Additionally, gender and sexuality are constantly negotiated. Gender is not a stable quality, but is always also performed (McGrath 2004). This *performativity*, however, does not mean that gender can be escaped. Whether female, male, transgender, queer or other, the body is what is visible to others and that makes a difference in how people perceive and approach one another. This makes for a complex gendered politics of looking and being looked at. At the same time, formal surveillance systems still require people to fit into a two-gendered world. Regardless of our identities, we are treated as female or male. Thus far, only artists circulate forms asking people to tick male/female/other.

This accentuates the issue of information, as material bodies are increasingly accompanied by what has been called a "data double," or "virtual body." Visual surveillance is augmented by dataveillance, with all sorts of information being attached to bodies, creating digital shadows as bodies are turned into data (see van der Ploeg, this volume). These digital shadows are connected in various ways to actual persons, but sometimes take on surprisingly active roles of their own. Furthermore, the information is created on the basis of pre supposed categorizations, such as male/female, age, nationality, employment, neighborhood, and so on. People have little influence on how these categories are formed or into which categories they are slotted (see Jenkins, this volume). Nevertheless, such categorizations increasingly determine how people are treated, for example as welfare or health care clients, paying customers or travelers (Monahan 2009). Occasionally, such data doubles can "take over" one's material body, as in the case where a person ends up on a black list of international travel restrictions without knowing the reason why. Data enables, but also restricts, and surveillance data is very difficult, if not impossible, to correct or erase.

Gender intertwines with marginalization and practices of intense information gathering. Disciplinary power and control are linked not only with gender and sexual oppression but to the intersections of class, race, ability and the like. Surveillance data are used for social sorting, in which less privileged populations are disproportionately stigmatized, discriminated against or excluded. This also tends to sustain moral norms and cultural codes. While current academic thinking acknowledges the pluralistic nature of gender and sexuality, disciplinary practices reinforce heteronormativity: the moral and cultural pressure to fit into the male-female setting.

One of the most significant achievements of feminist studies has been to destroy the myth of the *universal subject of knowledge*. By showing that the male, white, middle-class, Western view of the world is as value laden and restricted as any other, feminists opened up the way for a serious engagement with all kinds of knowledge and viewpoints (Wilson 1991). This epistemological turn fundamentally changed academic understanding as it is now recognized that any "scientific" data are produced from particular subject positions. This does not invalidate the knowledge, but makes it vitally important to consider the specifics and omissions of each position. Moving from the simplistic female/male binary, the understanding of gendered positions has become more fine-grained, but the basic idea of politically charged, socially constructed, value-laden, gendered knowledge still applies.

When it comes to surveillance, the implications of such insights are highly ambiguous. While there is widespread understanding among academics of the subjective gendered influences on knowledge, this insight does not seem to have much influence on the *practice* of surveillance. On the contrary, many still perceive that what are captured in surveillance processes are straightforward objective data. Such understandings are problematic given that scientific data and surveillance data do not differ from each other in any crucial way. Surveillance data are no less political or value laden than any other information. Surveillance creates knowledge, based on certain assumptions, categories and technical abilities. More importantly, with surveillance the process of data construction is often purposefully concealed. While we are starting to see instances where the objectivity of video surveillance is being challenged, in many other domains—DNA and biometrics, for example—surveillance data continue to be perceived as providing objective insights into the world.

The targets

Contemporary academic understanding of surveillance targets and targeting tends to be highly critical. Following Foucault, the connection between *bodies, space, power and knowledge* is recognized to be an essential feature in conducting surveillance and maintaining control. Making the body visible is a vital element in such dynamics. By targeting the body, surveillance agents have long hoped that they could ultimately reach the mind, with the ultimate aim of having individuals internalize control.

Of all forms of surveillance, gender has gained most critical attention in the analysis of video surveillance, and as such I accentuate such visibility in this chapter. This is logical given that *vision* is an essential element of surveillance and the experience of "being watched" is highly gendered (Koskela 2002). Such video monitoring is not exclusively tied to security and crime control, but also to consumer capitalism and marketing possibilities. In such contexts gendered desires, consumption patterns and even simply the "being-looked-at-ness" of being a woman are important.

In video surveillance, vision clearly overpowers the other senses. Surveillance camera operators perceive the world in a way that is dominated by that which appears on screen, images which can be augmented by technological abilities to pan or zoom cameras. This is a highly circumscribed image of reality, where social contact is reduced to the visual. Such visual dominance is replete with gender dynamics, something that has long been accentuated in sweeping academic critiques of concealed gendered ideologies.

So, for example, in many urban settings surveillance is gendered at a very simple level: most people behind a surveillance camera are male and the people under surveillance are disproportionately female. More than men, women tend to occupy the spaces where surveillance cameras are present, such as shopping malls and public transport. At the same time, the professions responsible for conducting video surveillance, and acting on surveill images, are male dominated. Although things are changing as surveillance becomes more ubiquitous—as will be argued below in greater detail—some of the most basic surveillance settings remain gendered.

While often mediated via technology, surveillance is never purely technical. The presuppositions, experiences, emotions and attitudes of camera operators influence any surveillance practices (Norris and Armstrong 1999). Given this ongoing influence of human operatives, it is apparent that the targets of suspicion are gendered in at least three senses: (1) how *suspicion* is constructed; (2) how the need for *protection* is perceived; and (3) when and where *voyeuristic attention* occurs.

A considerable body of research has demonstrated that surveillance is used to monitor a heterogeneous assortment of "suspicious" groups, such as youths, political activists, people of color, or sexual minorities. For example, in many Western societies young black men moving in a group catch the attention of the camera operators in a control room because they are perceived as potential criminals (see Browne, this volume). An older conservatively dressed white woman, in contrast, is much less likely to be targeted as a suspect of illegal activities. She might, however, be targeted by the operators for potentially being in danger and needing protection. That is because women that tend to fit the stereotypical heteronormative female category are more likely to be considered as vulnerable, and to face protective surveillance than men or other groups considered suspicious. The same can apply to young girls. All such examples accentuate how gender is "at work" in the routine operation of surveillance.

Surveillance is also relational. What is considered appropriate behavior varies both according to time and place and in relation to personal qualities such as gender, sexuality, age, race and color. This means that what specific appearances will be regarded as "deviant" in a particular context is not a simple or straightforward matter. Moreover, people react differently to being under surveillance, something that can itself be conditioned by personal histories informed by class, race and gender dynamics.

The third point of the gendered targeting of surveillance systems concerns the voyeuristic surveillance gaze, as will be discussed in detail in the next section. However, before turning to that point it is important to reiterate that while I am accentuating visual surveillance, comparable dynamics also operate in relation to dataveillance, as new forms of control often build upon older ones. The body is not simply seen, but is now an entity onto which all sorts of information are attached (Conrad 2009). The data double influences many spheres of everyday life. Marketing is increasingly based on surveillance and consumer profiling, often reflecting gendered and sexual preferences. Health care, child care and care for the elderly are based on information systems and surveillance technologies, treating those at the margins or not fully responsible for themselves differently from those who are adult, able-bodied and more powerful. The gendered nature of surveillance also becomes apparent in situations in which one has to prove her/his (*sic*) identity. Information-based control forces people to confront the two-gendered world. In official contexts, transgender and transsexual people have to fit in either of these categories. Border security is one of the most tangible examples as these are spaces where transgendered people, for example, can find it difficult to negotiate movement across international borders.

The victims

Being under surveillance is—among other things—a subjective experience. It can evoke a variety of feelings: anger, embarrassment, guilt, shame, fear, but also a sense of security and safety. Herein lies the ambivalent nature of surveillance: it can increase a sense of security but also exacerbate feelings of mistrust (Koskela 2002). Such feelings are themselves informed by gendered and other power relations pertaining to such things as wealth and ideology, all of which combine to construct complex networks of power and interpretive frames informing how people subjectively experience surveillance.

The prominent desire to use video surveillance to increase security is complicated by the particularly pernicious tendency of the gaze to turn the body into a sexualized object *without a mutual commitment* to such sexualization. The general feminist insight that the female body is an object of a sexualized gaze in ways that are dramatically different than for male bodies also applies to women being viewed through a surveillance camera. So, for women in particular, being an object of surveillance does not necessarily or uniformly foster a reassuring sense of security.

Historically, women were policed through gendered moral norms pertaining to such things as comportment and public display. Today, unlike in the recent past, women are formally free to move about in public space at any time of the day or night without a male companion, although they often dare not do so. This is because of the increased prominence of restrictions based on *fear and insecurity*, something that accentuates a new link between surveillance and gender. Claiming that surveillance increases security implicitly means that surveillance improves women's quality of life. According to this reasoning, women are the ones for whom surveillance is particularly beneficial.

Women who rely on security camera systems to ensure their safety are ultimately forced to trust someone else to ensure their safety. In such situations that person's opportunities to influence their own destiny are also reduced. Given the gendered dynamics of looking, what one encounters here is a new form of mediated chaperoning, where male camera operators (ostensibly) look out for the security of their female charges. I say "ostensibly" here because ethnographic research on camera operators has demonstrated that the almost uniformly male camera operater often ignore or dismiss situations which most women would see as dangerous or threatening (see Norris and Armstrong 1999).

The cultural meanings of both revealing and obscuring gestures are deeply gendered. Heteronormative rules still regulate what can be revealed, and when. Constantly cautioned about dangerous unseen observers, women are advised to pay attention to their being-looked-at-ness, as if they are on constant display. Implicitly, women are criticized for straying from such rules of display: as if they should not "wear" the body they were born in. Such meanings reinforce the different ways that women are constructed as vulnerable. On one hand, surveillance equipment can be read as a sign of danger (distrust, need for control) and can thus amplify a sense of vulnerability. On the other hand, the promise of increased security generates a pressure for women to accept surveillance.

Surveillance cameras are primarily retrospective devices: more often helping to solve than prevent crimes. This means that surveillance is less beneficial in relation to violent crime than it is for property crime. The violations characteristic of property crime are often material, and surveillance cameras can help to identify criminals and perhaps retrieve stolen property. With violent crimes, however, while it is true that surveillance cameras might assist in arresting a violent offender, this does not rectify the subjective *experience* of violent victimization. In cases of sexual violence, this is a particularly crucial disadvantage, as prevention is obviously far more desirable than a retrospective response.

Indeed, it is also the case that surveillance does not necessarily erase other forms of harassment, but can open up new possibilities. Visual surveillance has a problematic relationship with sexual harassment in three ways: (1) surveillance may be *unable to spot and intervene* to stop harassment; (2) surveillance can itself be emotionally perceived as a *form of harassment*; and (3) almost all revealed cases where surveillance camera data have been *misused* are connected to gender and sexuality. Since video surveillance overaccentuates the visual, it is often of little use in situations where more sensitive contextual interpretation is required. Camera operators can identify clearly visible minor offences, but often ignore more ambivalent situations such as (verbal) sexual harassment.

Harassment involving surveillance cameras is more difficult to identify, and to thwart, than instances of interpersonal harassment. Restrictions within the visible field can mean that forms of threatening harassment that are not readily apparent can remain unaddressed, creating a sense of doubt and distrust about the operation of cameras. Surveillance cameras can be used as a means of harassment, producing deep insecurities while reinforcing women's perception that they are constantly looked at. In such cases, women are paradoxically marginalized while being at the centre (of the gaze), something that reproduces the embodiment and sexualization of women. Hence, women are justifiably worried about "Peeping Tom" voyeuristic aspects of surveillance.

It is also the case that surveillance tapes have often been misused, with gender typically playing an essential role in such cases. Security camera operators have videotaped women in intimate spaces; monitoring, recording, printing, circulating and selling these explicit images. This has included, for example, cameras placed in women's changing rooms to spy on them. Police officers have been reprimanded for such improper voyeuristic use of video cameras. Images of surreptitiously recorded intimate or sexual acts have also been recirculated for commercial purposes, shown at parties, or placed on the internet.

The perpetrators

In recent years the everydayness of surveillance has changed basic social settings. This everydayness not only refers to the fact that people are now more exposed to video surveillance, but also to the increasing public access to surveillance technologies. As surveillance devices have become smaller, less expensive and more widely available it has become possible for anyone to be an agent or object of the gaze irrespective of their gender or other forms of social positioning. One upshot of this is that *controlwork* involving cameras is more and more conducted by people other than the police and security guards—by shopkeepers, bank clerks, teachers, nurses and so on. As the practices of surveillance have become dispersed, decentralized and overlapping, they also often extend beyond the control of formal organizations. Such a democratization of surveillance also raises questions about whether the practice will remain male dominated, as women are now also increasingly surveyors.

While a digital divide still exists, the general availability of camera phones, portable video cameras, webcams and other visual recording technologies that can instantly link images to global information flows has made it easier for Western citizens to watch one another, and to widely disperse the fruits of their surveillant labor. While not all of these technologies are explicitly surveillance devices, the people who carry them can easily turn into surveying subjects. Such uses extend from random witnessing to more organized forms of political resistance. This often entails a form of *hijacking surveillance* where people use established surveillance systems for highly idiosyncratic personal monitoring projects. Among the more important of such uses is using surveillance to manage one's personal security. A practical example would be a woman who places a surveillance camera at her door and uses those tapes to prove that her abusive former partner is violating a restraining order.

The transparency fostered by surveillance no longer operates in a single direction, as people are involved in various counter-surveillance practices that can reveal official misconduct. As the differences between the authorities and the public, the controlled and the controllers, become less clear, established gender structures also become reorganized. This is apparent in relation to the recent official embrace of practices of *responsibilization* whereby citizens, both male and female, are increasingly encouraged to participate in controlwork.

The motivations of people who hijack surveillance vary considerably, something that accentuates new moral questions. Cop watchers and many video activist groups clearly seek to resist authoritarian forms of surveillance by turning the (surveillance) tools against the usual agents of surveillance (Monahan 2009). However, surveillance can also be hijacked for sexist, racist or xenophobic purposes. As such, hijacking does not necessarily challenge the emergence of a surveillance society, but can entail a simple extension and rearticulation of surveillance practices.

The players

The multiplication of surveillant agents has accentuated the fact that surveillance is not necessarily restricting and repressive. Individual citizens also *play with* various forms of surveillance equipment (Koskela 2006; Bell 2009). Recognizing this fact, scholars have sought to accentuate this "other side" of surveillance. While surveillance remains threatening in many contexts, there are also an increasing number of people who are fascinated by surveillance dynamics that extend beyond issues of social control. So, while there is voyeuristic fascination in looking, it is also important to acknowledge the exhibitionist thrill of being seen (McGrath 2004). People sometimes willingly subject themselves to a camera's gaze, turning surveillance into spectacle.

One potential reason for this development might be that people are weary of being passive targets of an ever-increasing surveillance and instead seek to play a more active role in producing, circulating and consuming visual material. In doing so they operate as surveillance subjects rather than mere objects of the gaze. Gender has been vitally important here from the very beginning as women and sexual minorities have been pioneers in performative forms of playing with surveillance (Senft 2008). Moreover, women's voluntary self-presentation can challenge the long established dynamics pertaining to the "male gaze" and "female target."

The internet and the rise of the information society more generally play crucial roles in this change. The internet provides a global forum for surveillance performances. To a certain extent, it can also liberate people from established gendered identities. The fusion of human and machine can free us from the constraining elements of the material body, as people online can play with how they represent their gender, skin color, physical abilities and mental capacities, displaying their sexual identity with less fear of stigmatization than might be possible in the real world. The virtual world, hence, helps to create "post-gender" identities. This, however, is not to be interpreted in a naively idealistic way. While people play with their online identities, the powerful dataveillance systems that operate behind the scenes of the internet to collect massive amounts of information for marketing and management purposes continue to routinely categorize and process these self-fame individuals according to established gender identities. The internet is also a forum for sexist and racist groups including assorted hate groups. Moreover, the performances that people engage in are not necessarily of their own creation, but often mimic assorted "commercial idols" as presented in reality TV shows such as Big Brother, where imitating surveillance is a key part of the appeal of such shows.

One of the more intriguing online developments that connects surveillance, gender and sexuality has been the rise of "camming" (Senft 2008). This entails "camgirls" and (often gay) "camguys" who perform a live online self-presentation. The images that they distribute range from young women turning their real-life images into "reality porn"—charging viewers for access—to gay communities building global collective identities by presenting their lives online. Mostly, however, "cammers" just continue their ordinary daily lives under the gaze of the global audience, broadcasting intimate, if often mundane, images of their private lives.

Webcams are often connected with sexuality, and are filled with flirt, strip, and tease (Bell 2009). As such, these sites also mark a move from voyeurism to exhibitionism. It is possible to see this eroticization and sexualization of surveillance as a form of resistance to the dominant gendered dynamics of monitoring. While the operator of a webcam cannot control who will see these images or how they will be interpreted, she or he still is able to control what, how and when these images are presented. Such revealing can be a form of political act which rejects the traditional understanding of objectification (Koskela 2006). And while webcams do not fit into the conventional understanding of resistance, they do suggest that resistance may be taking on new unexpected forms by being pluralized rather than homogenous, concealed rather than exposed.

Webcams exaggerate sexuality, play with voyeurism and exhibitionism and invite their viewers into various degrees of erotic commitment. The camera also "directs the eye" by inviting the viewer to interpret all kinds of activity as sexual (McGrath 2004). In this context, gender relations become even more complex. The female body is presented as something to be seen, but within a setting regulated by the person who is seen, which contrasts markedly with the normal operation of surveillance or harassing looks on the street. Emotionally, this entails resisting the dominant expectations of modesty and shame which are culturally embedded in notions of gender and sexuality.

Webcams are also interesting because they refuse to support the increased importance of security as a personal and cultural goal. Conventionally, being seen implies either being safe and secured or being threatened, depending on who is perceived as being the viewer. Webcams refuse both these interpretations, creating a need to understand the meaning(s) of being looked at in a new way. They break some fundamental boundaries between private and public, calling for new interpretations of established notions of privacy.

So, webcams are about reclaiming the body—often the naked body—and wearing it proudly. Nonetheless, we should not lose sight of the fact that most instances of surveillance remain oppressive or simply sustain unequal power relations. The internet is an arena of intense control and data gathering where individual practices of watching and presenting are tied to dominant ideologies and consumption practices.

The futures

Writing on gender risks falling into two traps: it reproduces gender as a binary system or presents women only as victims. A more careful view reveals the problematic nature of the issue: whenever you find a gendered practice, there is apt to be another element which turns the presumed gender relations upside down, or reveals how complex the multiple gendered identities are. It is precisely this complexity that makes the issue of surveillance and gender a fascinating field for scholarly research. The issues surrounding the surveillance/gender problematic are deeply ambiguous, and things are changing rapidly.

As such, there is a continuing need for more research on the connections between gender, surveillance and other forms of power on the gendered and sexualized emotions and experiences under surveillance, and on new creative forms of resistance. Thus far, there is surprisingly little empirical research on even the basic gendered elements, such as the misuse of surveillance either in traditional media or online.

Further, there is a need to rethink not only surveillance produced by the authorities but also the new amateur practices which enter the surveillance field. Paying attention to the gendered performative elements of surveillance at a minimum necessitates thinking about surveillance beyond the usual fixation on crime control and privacy rights. Nevertheless, gender is hard to escape. The mere bodily appearance makes a difference to how individuals are treated in the surveillance context. We all wear bodies and are, to a certain extent, prisoners of those gendered bodies. Even more importantly, we are judged by others on the basis of our bodies.

References

Bell, D. (2009). "Surveillance is Sexy," *Surveillance & Society,* 6(3): 203–12.

Conrad, K. (2009). "Surveillance, Gender, and the Virtual Body in the Information Age," *Surveillance & Society,* 6(4): 380–87.

Koskela, H. (2002). "Video Surveillance, Gender and the Safety of Public Urban Space: 'Peeping Tom' Goes High Tech?," *Urban Geography,* 23(3): 257–78.

——(2006). "'The Other Side of Surveillance': Webcams, Power and Agency," in David Lyon (ed.), *Theorizing Surveillance: The Panopticon and Beyond,* Cullompton: Willan Publishing.

McGrath, J. (2004). *Loving Big Brother: Performance, Privacy and Surveillance Space,* London: Routledge.

Monahan, T. (2009). *Surveillance in the Time of Insecurity,* New Brunswick, NJ: Rutgers University Press.

Norris, C. and Armstrong, G. (1999). *The Maximum Surveillance Society: The Rise of CCTV,* Oxford: Berg.

Senft, T. (2008). *Camgirls: Celebrity and Community in the Age of Social Networks,* New York: Peter Lang.

Wajcman, J. (1991). *Feminism Confronts Technology,* Cambridge: Polity Press.

Wilson, E. (1991). *The Sphinx in the City: Urban Life, the Control of Disorder and Women,* London: Virago Press.

b. The information state

An historical perspective on surveillance

Toni Weller

Spies, informers and secret agents have long been part of the history of the state, just as information gathering and intelligence have long been powerful instruments of those in government. Yet the modern idea of the information state, with its technological infrastructures, central repositories and formal procedures of surveillance, is often perceived to be something of a recent phenomenon (see also Webster, this volume). Concerns about what information might be being collected on citizens, how it is being used, how secure it is and the transparency of all these processes continue to be topical and dominant debates. Partly as a consequence of this, such debates have, in recent years, begun to come under increased historical scrutiny. Such recognition has contributed to the emergence of an "information turn" which focuses on the concept of information as a category of historical enquiry (Weller 2010). In the mid-2000s, information history work was dominated by the idea of the information state, and surveillance played an important role within this remit. This chapter explores some of the historical precedents and discourses on the emergence of the information, or surveillance, state.

The very idea of the surveillance state has become entrenched in popular and political rhetoric with some commentators suggesting that it is a defining characteristic of modernity itself, irrevocably linked with industrialization and the rise of the nation-state (Giddens 1990). Others have argued that in terms of information gathering there is more of a link between pre-industrial and modern society than scholars have conventionally believed, with the period between 1500 and 2000 witnessing a shift from local to national collection (Higgs 2004). Forms of political and social surveillance have long existed and are certainly not unique to the modern period, but from the late eighteenth century there was a shift in how this surveillance took place. Most significantly, state surveillance became more organized, formal and centralized than had previously been the case. The English *Domesday Book* of 1086 is often given as a very early example of organized state information collection on its citizens, containing over 13,000 records, which have survived some 900 years. While the Domesday Book did represent the collection of information on citizens at the request of the sovereign, it was very different from the censuses established during the nineteenth century. The former was not a regular or routine form of surveillance, it was not kept up to date and it was incomplete (Higgs 2004). An even earlier example of state surveillance was the list maintained during the Roman Republic of all adult males fit for military service, the equivalent of a modern census or military register. Censuses are also said to have taken place in ancient Egypt, and the world's oldest surviving census data dates from 2 AD in China. These collections, like the *Domesday Book*, were irregular and often localized. It was not until industrialization that states began to collect information on their citizens with any regularity, when methods became more organized, structured, rational and centralized and evolved into what we recognize as the modern bureaucratic surveillance system (see also Ruppert, this volume).

Methods of more centralized information collection and state surveillance developed out of necessity and requirement. Since the late eighteenth century, Western industrialization had a huge impact on the need for centralized information collection, most significantly in Britain, the United States and Continental Europe. Migration into new urban areas, communication and transportation revolutions, growth in the electoral franchise, and an increasingly condensed workforce, all led to societies which demanded greater response and accountability from their governments. Ultimately, this change provoked what James Beniger has termed a "control revolution" (Beniger 1986) in which new technologies and processes were operating in a society which did not have the support of an existing administrative infrastructure. Consequently, there were innovations in economic, technological and processing control in order to cope with the new demands.

Although Beniger's theory was based upon evidence from the United States, the central idea of the control revolution can be applied more generally to the West where bureaucracy emerged as a response to nineteenth-century industrialization. Bureaucracy itself was not new to the industrial period – the pre-industrial empires of Rome, China and Byzantium all had sophisticated forms of central administration – but how information was collected and ordered became much more efficient. Anthony Giddens has argued that during the nineteenth century the emergence of the industrialized nation state necessitated a change in the way the central state considered its citizens, since "no pre-modern states were able even to approach the level of administrative co-ordination developed in the nation-state" (Giddens 1990: 57). Moreover, "such administrative concentration depends in turn upon the development of *surveillance* capacities well beyond those characteristic of traditional civilisations" (Giddens 1990: 57). As with the census data, what was different about bureaucratic development following industrialization was its formality.

For Jon Agar and Edward Higgs the emergence of modern bureaucracy meant that the language of order, rationality and structure became somewhat interchangeable with state and governance (Agar 2003; Higgs 2004). By the late nineteenth century, bureaucracy had become professionalized, with government officials dedicated to the collection and management of information on citizens. In terms of administrative effort and expense alone, the surveillance state changed dramatically from its localized industrial origins to the far more centralized and formal procedures we can recognize in today's society, where questions of control of bureaucratic information are paramount. Digital technologies and the internet have made the sharing and dissemination of information instantaneous and without restriction across geographical borders. Beniger suggests that by the late nineteenth century in North America bureaucracy had become "a major new control technology" (Beniger 1986: 14). For him, the processing and rationalization of information on people was the vital aspect, which saw citizens governed less as individuals and more as "things." Although Beniger does not explicitly discuss surveillance, his argument can be seen in such terms since "the amount of information about ... [people] ... that needs to be processed is thereby greatly reduced and hence the degree of control ... is greatly enhanced" (Beniger 1986: 15). Early nineteenth-century forms of information gathering on citizens by the state are often described in terms of maintaining order and control amongst a newly emerged anonymous urban mass. Notions of control feature heavily in much surveillance discourse and these in turn have been greatly shaped by the works of the French theorist, Michel Foucault.

The Foucauldian model of power and surveillance has had a huge impact on how we, as moderns, tend to understand the notions of control, in particular social control. Foucault's *Discipline and Punish* demonstrated how "disciplined society" (Foucault 1991: 198) separated right from wrong, good from bad, sick from healthy through surveillance and regulation. An architectural manifestation of this was Jeremy Bentham's Victorian panopticon, a design in which a supervisor sits in a central position, potentially able to observe every individual, in their individual cells, but where the inmates cannot see each other, nor the central supervisor. Foucault described the panopticon as a machine which rationalizes, classifies and homogenizes—terminology which sits comfortably with the discourse of bureaucratic growth and administrative rationality.

Initially such forms of individual surveillance were discrete but, increasingly, new technologies have encouraged not only more rationalization but also the intensification of surveillance. Information that was once collected in person on paper forms is now submitted electronically and held in vast central databases. Surveillance cameras have become the contemporary panopticon. This says less about the changing technological processes *per se* and more about the increasing social, cultural and political acceptance and necessity of state information collection. More contemporary developments in the tools and technologies specifically designed to control and rationalize human activities, and indeed, to normalize such conformity, show an interesting update on Beniger's control revolution and on Foucauldian power. Homogenized forms for welfare claims, driving licenses, credit requests and job applications can arguably be seen as a way of managing modern surveillance overload. Giddens labels surveillance not only as control of information but also as "social supervision" (Giddens 1990: 59). Arguably, "social supervision" can also equate to the management of information on citizens in order to provide for their protection and wellbeing. In other words, rather than an Orwellian and sinister form of observation and monitoring, state surveillance is justified as a means which *benefits* the citizen through the application of social welfare.

This phenomenon has been described by both Jon Agar and Edward Higgs as the dual factors of welfare and warfare, unique to the modern period (Agar 2003; Higgs 2004). In Western democracies the role of the information, or surveillance, state can be argued as one of political necessity in terms both of protection of citizens against threats and also through the pastoral care of citizens' health and welfare. In countries which do not have democratic government, such as China or Cuba, the state has taken on a rather different role, although, superficially at least, with the same protection and pastoral allusions.

Traditionally, such developments can be traced back to the nineteenth century as growing urban centers, an expanding franchise and improved literacy and communications all contributed to a shift in the relations between the state and the citizen. Political reforms throughout Europe and America during the nineteenth and twentieth centuries put increasing pressure on the state to be accountable and to provide some form of social welfare for the citizens who elected them. This is the classic concept of a social contract, based on the ideas of Hobbes, Locke and Rousseau, in which citizens give up sovereignty to those who govern them in return for security, protection and welfare. However, in order for the state to offer welfare provision, those in power need to know who is eligible for payments and where they are, thus requiring some form of surveillance. As Higgs has noted, this "created huge flows of information [on citizens] and the elaboration of ever more sophisticated and anonymous systems for their storage and manipulation" (Higgs 2004: 150). Consequently, the mid-twentieth century saw the emergence of a modern information state which began routinely to develop and enforce bureaucratic, centralized surveillance for the purposes of welfare provision.

However, welfare surveillance was often a two-edged sword. The first ever state social insurance scheme, old age pensions and disability payments were introduced to Germany by Bismark during the 1880s. However, his social reforms, whilst the first of their kind in the world, were introduced primarily as a way of pacifying the growing working classes in Germany and were introduced alongside repressive legislation to tackle potential dissenters. In 1931, the first fully government-funded unemployment benefit system was introduced in Britain to cope with the impact of the Great Depression, but in order to benefit from payouts, recipients had to prove their poverty through enforced forms, questions and visits from state investigators and this proved highly unpopular. In cases such as these, state surveillance and information collection for the purposes of welfare were often precipitated by economic or political crisis and often also a desire by the state to keep a check on potential deviants. While the social contract may justify the growth of the central state, the issue of social control is also ever present.

Historically, this changing dynamic has met with mixed reactions and indeed offers something of a paradox. Whilst in the West, from the mid-nineteenth century citizens began to demand greater state assistance, accountability and reform, they also resented and often feared what was perceived as intrusive, centralized and increasingly commonplace surveillance practices. The French politician and self-styled anarchist Pierre-Joseph Proudhon summed up this resistance to the idea of a central state, particularly one associated with the idea of such intrusive surveillance, in 1851:

> To be GOVERNED is to be watched, inspected, spied upon, directed, law-driven, numbered, regulated, enrolled, indoctrinated, preached at, controlled, checked, estimated, valued, censured, commanded, by creatures who have neither the right nor the wisdom nor the virtue to do so. To be GOVERNED is to be at every operation, at every transaction noted, registered, counted, taxed, stamped, measured, numbered, assessed, licensed, authorized, admonished, prevented, forbidden, reformed, corrected, punished.
>
> *(Proudhon 1923: 293–94)*

The growth of bureaucrats and information collectors led to growing state collections of statistics and parliamentary commissions during the nineteenth century. As Oz Frankel has noted, such statistics were used by the governments of both Britain and North America to legitimate their efforts for reform (Frankel 2006). Citizen concerns over the acceptability of central information collection were matched by recognition that the information was not always accurate and often disseminated with uncorrected mistakes (Frankel 2006: 56). This issue of misrepresentation and inaccuracy has been one of the most powerful factors in the development of late twentieth-century legislation in data protection and freedom of information.

As Frankel argues, during the nineteenth century, information collection on citizens could provide evidence to legitimize state intervention or growth since "the large scale investigation was a means to extend or exceed the boundaries of the state" (Frankel 2006: 303); a lack of legibility of citizens could prevent appropriate legislation and reform. James C. Scott has also explored the idea that the state's lack of understanding of its citizens—their habits, wealth, behaviors, location and identity—has traditionally meant that state "interventions were often crude and self-defeating" (Scott 1998: 2). Consequently the early modern state began to create "a standard grid whereby it could be centrally recorded and monitored" (Scott 1998: 2), through the creation of standard forms, names, language, processes and the like, and through developments in the East and in the Third World as much as in the West. Scott's central argument is that twentieth-century attempts of the state to, as he terms it, improve the human condition, were fuelled by an ideology of "high modernism" which legitimated the "rational design of social order" (Scott 1998: 4). He suggests that such rationalization of society can be highly effective when used in liberal societies where planners had to negotiate with citizens. However, when such techniques are adopted by an authoritarian state, often alongside a fragile civil society which does not have the strength or ability to resist such structural reforms, they are much more likely to fail.

This in itself is not a new idea, and certainly has sympathy with both Beniger's idea of a crisis of control, and also with Edward Higgs's notion of a gradual shift from local to central state power. What is most interesting about Scott's argument is his suggestion that central governments attempt to force legibility on their subjects and in so doing, lose local knowledge. For social reform to succeed the state must honor this local information; he suggests that the high-modernist ideology of the twentieth century has prevented this from happening. Scott applies this theory across geographic borders and, unlike Higgs or Beniger, this includes non-Western countries. He uses Soviet collectivization under Stalin, the Maoist Great Leap Forward of 1958–61 and the city of Brasilia created *ex nihilo* in 1956 as unsuccessful examples of state efforts at legibility, coupled with high modernist ideology and authoritarian regimes. However, some critics have suggested that Scott equates the Foucauldian state with power rather too simplistically and that aspects of his argument reiterate pre-Second World War economic debates over the practicalities of central planning, and indeed other intellectual debates which have preceded him. Unlike Scott's examples of authoritarian regimes, in a democracy there is a form of social contract at work which balances increased surveillance and information collection on citizens with an expectation of state protection and paternalism. State control of information on citizens under the auspice of their welfare has long been used as a powerful justification for surveillance.

Historically, surveillance on citizens for the purposes of welfare was, and continues to be, overt; mostly citizens were asked directly for information on their finances, jobs and family situation in order to populate state statistics and, later, databases. By the end of the nineteenth century more covert surveillance was beginning to be introduced, rapidly augmented by improved surveillance technologies and techniques over the course of the twentieth century. The notion of a secret service as an organized, centralized body to monitor and collect information on dissenting citizens and potential threats to the state was a creation of the latter nineteenth century, later hugely exacerbated by the two World Wars of 1914–18 and 1939–45 and the subsequent Cold War which lasted up until the end of the 1980s. This latter point is ably illustrated by looking at the chronology of secret service creations, which cluster around the dates of the wars. The United States Secret Service was created in 1865 with an original aim of preventing counterfeiting, and the Federal Bureau of Investigation, responsible for domestic intelligence, was established in 1908. Similarly, National Secret Services were established in Britain in 1909, and in Russia and Australia during the 1950s. The South African Secret Service, established in 1995, focuses on terrorist threats and South African mercenaries in relation to domestic security.

Scott's suggestion that "high modernism" tends to fail when coupled with an authoritarian state, or fragile civil society, also notes that this combination tends to occur in times of political or economic crisis, of war or recession for example, when conditions can change the interaction and legitimacy of citizen and state (Scott 1998). The classic example of this is the rise of National Socialism in Germany during the 1930s. However, it has also been evident in more recent decades as the threat of terrorism and religious extremism have witnessed new forms of centralized surveillance, monitoring and identification, justified by the notion of warfare in this broader sense, which may not have been as acceptable to the democratic civic body in periods of lesser perceived threat. Monitoring of internet and mobile phone traffic and tighter security and surveillance at airports are now commonplace. Likewise, the United States Patriot Act, passed in October 2001 in the shadow of the 9/11 attacks, granted powers to the federal government and law enforcement agencies which were arguably much more reactionary than would have been allowed had they been legislated at a different time.

It is here that the dual notion of welfare and warfare comes to the fore. For some, such as Jon Agar, this relates more to the tools and techniques of information collection and processing which necessitated a more centralized and greater scale during times of war, most notably during the Second World War (Agar 2003). For others, warfare is not necessarily a literal war but, rather, the threat or perceived threat to a state and its citizens. This threat could come from an external force (an enemy country, overseas terrorism) or it could be internal (prisoners, law-breakers, domestic terrorism, domestic dissention) (Higgs 2004). For Beniger, the control of surveillance information relates to the control of new technologies and processes rather than to the control of people *per se*, although he recognizes that by the early twentieth century what began as information collection on citizens for the purposes of rationalizing statistics and administration, post-industrialization, had developed into something more. In North America, "government bureaucracies had begun to process information not only for the passive compilation of statistics but also for the active control of individuals: fingerprinting of federal prisoners (1904), collecting tax on personal income (1913), psychologically screening draft inductees (1919), running a national employment service (1933)" (Beniger 1986: 408). Certainly the dual influences of warfare and welfare dramatically accelerated the role, function and acceptability of state surveillance during the twentieth and early twenty-first centuries. In the West, not only were the techniques of surveillance more advanced as technologies developed, but greater media coverage of threats and moral panics in the public sphere paradoxically demanded both greater protection through increased state surveillance and, at the same time, greater liberty through legislation which allowed open access to information collections. This suggests a modern variant on the classic social contract in democratic states: citizens accept surveillance in order to ensure they are entitled to welfare and protected from threat as long as the means of such surveillance are transparent and accountable.

Giddens has suggested that, "from its inception, the collation of official statistics has been constitutive of state power and of many other modes of social organisation also" (Giddens 1990: 42). Thus, the collection of information on citizens is not limited to the role of the central state but is increasingly a function of other bodies as well. The growth of capitalist and consumer society from the late nineteenth century necessitated rationality and information collection in businesses as well as government. In its most basic form, the industrial factory clock-in and clock-out system introduced a new form of rationalized surveillance on workers. Employers began to monitor both their consumers' behavior (welfare—in order to provide the most relevant and effective service) as well as that of their employees (warfare—ensuring there was loyalty and honesty amongst staff). Equally, for Beniger, the state was not the only one with increased bureaucratic surveillance techniques: in business, monitoring consumer behavior as well as new advertising and mar keting techniques were fundamental to the emergence of modern information processing and collection (Beniger 1986). As with government civil servants, advertising and marketing became professionalized from the latter nineteenth century onwards, as information collection became increasingly routine.

There are clear links with our contemporary society, from the loyalty card which collects information about what you buy and where you shop, to the targeted pop-up ads on social networking websites based upon your selected favorites and preferences. Giddens makes the point that statistics collection is not limited to the body politic but that it also enters the social consciousness, that statistical surveillance helps inform people about the world in which they are living (Giddens 1990). He uses the example of divorce statistics influencing people's choice whether or not to marry, but there are many others. Social networking web sites offer an interesting take on social surveillance, where participants may chose what information, and how much, about them is shared online. Whilst this information is controlled by the user, it is possible for a user's friends or acquaintances to observe what they are doing without any direct interaction with them. This passive social surveillance can become, in its more extreme form, internet stalking or cyber stalking, a term recognized by the *Oxford English Dictionary* since the 1990s.

Therefore, citizens were, and continue to be, participants not just of top-down state-led surveillance, but increasingly of lateral and upwards surveillance. In the West at least, citizens are not only the subject of information gathering by the state but also the consumers of such material, reading and digesting official reports, surveys and statistics with incredible zeal. Oz Frankel has shown how during the nineteenth cen tury such exchanges introduced "a currency of explicit and tacit transactions between state and its citizens" (Frankel 2006: 2), demonstrating the complex and subtle impact of state surveillance. In democracies, such behavior can be used to call the government of the day to account, and increasingly official reports have been made publicly available in attempts to improve transparency. The WikiLeaks website, set up in 2006, claims it offers "a universal way for the revealing of suppressed and censored injustices" by inviting jour nalists to leak classified or sensitive documents for public dissemination. However, under more author itarian regimes, there can not only be state surveillance on individuals or institutions but also surveillance on individuals and institutions by other citizens. Nazi Germany and Stalinist Russia are the most oft-cited examples of such Orwellian notions of surveillance where potentially your every move is watched by someone in a form of social panopticon.

Significantly, Giddens suggests that "free speech and democratic movements ... have their origins in the arena of the surveillance operations of the modern state" (Giddens 1990: 160). Historically, calls for accountability, transparency and open access to information have tended to emerge most forcefully as a reaction to extreme social or political surveillance, or the fear of such surveillance, irrespective of whether the state is democratic or authoritarian. In other words, the history of the surveillance state is also the history of freedom of information, access and dissemination. Privacy has increasingly become, as Jon Agar suggests, a "political issue" where the dual relationship between citizen and the state has witnessed a pro found shift "from anxieties about threats to collective qualities to anxieties about threats to the individual" (Agar 2003: 343–44). Although apprehension over individual privacy has certainly previously existed (and were particularly resonant in nineteenth-century Britain with its traditions of *laissez-faire*), concerns have notably manifested in recent years through challenges to public trust in the security of centralized repositories of information. Consequently, the origins of the information, or surveillance, state have become powerful and topical areas of historical discourse which have "a role to play in ensuring that contemporary political rhetoric about the information age is balanced and accurate, situating debates within their wider historical context and creating new links between the past and present" (Weller 2010: 200).

Such historical links are vital. In today's world, governments, whether democratic or authoritarian, now control and have access to a huge amount of personal information about their citizens. Such information is used, manipulated and disseminated in an enormous variety of ways and through assorted means—most of which we now accept as part of the modern function of the state. The prevalence of surveillance issues and concerns in our contemporary society can often suggest that they are new debates, but, as this chapter has shown, the discourse of information collection, use (and mis-use), dissemination, preservation, privacy and access have long historical precedents.

In the West at least, the modern information state that we recognize today has its foundations in the late eighteenth century and the onset of industrialization when information began to be collected in more routine and centralized ways. During the nineteenth century, the state began to be transformed into a more rational, bureaucratic collector of information on its citizens for the dual purposes of warfare and welfare, with civil servants dedicated to the task. The monitoring of employees and consumers also witnessed a professionalization of business surveillance (see Sewell, Pridmore, this volume). This was exacerbated during the twentieth century following the two World Wars and international terrorism, alongside the growth of the welfare state and increasing demands to protect personal and confidential information and to ensure transparency in government. Digital technologies and the rise of the internet intensified debates and developments that had already been ongoing for two centuries, and indeed the accessibility of digital media has meant that the debates have fully entered the public consciousness, particularly in relation to social surveillance through digital technologies themselves. Whilst technology has been an important driver for change, social and cultural acceptance of the information, or surveillance, state has long been in flux as citizens have continued to debate the balance between efficiency, power and administration of state functions, against personal privacy, transparency and individual autonomy.

References

Agar, J. (2003). *The Government Machine: A Revolutionary History of the Computer*, Cambridge, MA: MIT Press.

Beniger, J. (1986). *Control Revolution: Technological and Economic Origins of the Information Society*, London: Harvard University Press.

Foucault, M. (1991). *Discipline and Punish: The Birth of the Prison*, London: Penguin.

Frankel, O. (2006). *States of Enquiry: Social Investigations and Print Culture in Nineteenth Century Britain and the United States*, Baltimore, MD: Johns Hopkins University Press.

Giddens, A. (1990). *The Consequences of Modernity*, Cambridge: Polity.

Higgs, E. (2004). *The Information State in England: The Central Collection of Information on Citizens Since 1500*, Basingstoke: Palgrave Macmillan.

Proudhon, P.-J. (1923). *General Idea of the Revolution in the Nineteenth Century*, translated by John Beverly Robinson, London: Freedom Press.

Scott, J. (1998). *Seeing Like a State: How Certain Schemes to Improve the Human Condition Have Failed*, New Haven, CT: Yale University Press.

Weller, T. (2010). *Information History in the Modern World: Histories of the Information Age*, Basingstoke: Palgrave Macmillan.

c. "Needs" for surveillance and the movement to protect privacy

James B. Rule

For many people, the term "surveillance" conjures up images of the systematic tracking of individuals' lives by distant and powerful agencies. These pop-up cartoon images are not entirely misleading. To be sure, surveillance takes many different forms. But since the middle of the twentieth century, the monitoring of ordinary people's affairs by large institutions has grown precipitously. Such direct intakes of detailed information on literally millions of people at a time—and their use by organizations to shape their dealings with the people concerned—represent one of the most far-reaching social changes of the last 50 years. These strictly *bureaucratic* forms of surveillance, and their tensions with values of privacy, are the subject of this chapter.

Surveillance

Surveillance is a ubiquitous ingredient of social life. In virtually every enduring social relationship, parties note the actions of others and seek to influence future actions in light of information thus collected. This holds as much for intimate dyads—mutually preoccupied lovers, for example, or mothers and infants—as for relations among sovereign states. Surveillance and concomitant processes of social control are as basic to the life of neighborhoods, churches, industries and professions as they are to relations between government or corporate organizations and individuals.

But whereas the ability of communities, families and local associations to track the affairs of individuals has widely declined in the world's "advanced" societies, institutional surveillance has lately made vast strides. Throughout the world's prosperous liberal societies, people have come to expect their dealings with all sorts of large organizations to be mediated by their "records." These records are ongoing products of past interactions between institutions and individuals—and of active and resourceful efforts by the institutions to gather data on individuals. The result is that all sorts of corporate and state performances that individuals expect—from allocation of consumer credit and social security benefits to the control of crime and terrorism—turn on one or another form of institutional surveillance. Perhaps needless to say, the outcomes of such surveillance make vast differences in what Max Weber would have called the "life chances" of the people involved.

No twenty-first-century society, save perhaps the very poorest, is altogether without such large-scale collection, processing and use of data on individuals' lives. Indeed, we might arguably regard the extent of penetration of large-scale institutions into the details of people's lives as one measure of modernity (if not post-modernity). The fact that these activities are so consequential—for the institutions, and for the individuals concerned—makes anxiety and opposition over their repercussions on privacy values inevitable.

Despite the slightly foreboding associations of the term, surveillance need not be unfriendly in its effects on the individuals subjected to it. In the intensive care ward at the hospital, most patients probably do not resent the intrusive and constant surveillance directed at them. Seekers of social security benefits or credit accounts will normally be quick to call attention to their recorded eligibility for these things—in effect demanding performances based on surveillance. Indeed, it is a measure of the pervasiveness of surveillance in our world that we reflexively appeal to our "records" in seeking action from large institutions.

But even relatively benevolent forms of surveillance require some tough-minded measures of institutional enforcement vis-à-vis individuals who seek services. Allocating social security payments to those who deserve them—as judged by the letter of the law—inevitably means *not* allocating such benefits to other would-be claimants. Providing medical benefits, either through government or private insurance, means distinguishing between those entitled to the benefits and others. When the good things of life are passed around, unless everyone is held to be equally entitled, the logic of surveillance demands distinctions between the deserving, and others. And this in turn sets in motion requirements for positive identification, close record-keeping, precise recording of each individual case history, and so on (see also Webster, this volume).

Privacy

Whatever the ultimate purposes of any system of institutional surveillance, its workings likely *matter* to those subjected to it. When such systems go wrong, in the eyes of the public, anguish abounds. People may find that details of their lives considered extremely intimate have been broadcast far and wide. Or they find that key decisions about themselves—on the taxes they owe, or the credit that they are entitled to, or their ability to travel without hindrance—have been based on what was expected to be private or secret information. Or they discover that data provided "in confidence" to one institution for one use has turned up as a basis for decisions by another institution, for quite different purposes. At least since the middle of the twentieth century, shock and indignation at such discoveries have triggered outcries over an array of wrongs bracketed as "invasions of privacy."

In voicing such complaints, people invoke a nebulous and diverse set of values and claims. The meanings ascribed to the rich and emotive term "privacy" have no single common denominator—but something more like Wittgenstein's "family resemblances." Sometimes we use the term to mean something akin to *personal autonomy*—as in the privacy people claim over their decisions on matters of birth control and reproduction. For purposes of this chapter, I mean by privacy something a bit different: the ability of individuals to control the flow of information about themselves—even in the face of others' demands for access to such information.

Even this restricted definition includes a variety of human motives and values. Some privacy interests might be bracketed as *consummatory*—that is, interests in privacy as an end in itself. These include desires not to be exposed in moments and situations like nudity, humiliation, extreme grief and the like. Though the rest of the world may know that such moments occur, few of us want to be subject to surveillance at such moments. Often it is not just concealment of images of ourselves that we seek in such cases: many people, for example, would go to great lengths to avoid dissemination of documentary records of embarrassing medical procedures or illnesses. In these cases, the hurt of disclosure is immediate and irreducible, regardless of its subsequent consequences.

Other privacy claims defend *strategic* interests. Here privacy matters because it represents a means to other, more distant ends. In bargaining for the purchase of a car, we do not ordinarily disclose to potential sellers the highest price we are prepared to pay. Organizers of political movements do not find it expedient to share with potential adversaries—opposing activists, for example, or state agencies—the details of the strategies they plot. Employees considering a change of jobs do not normally disclose their inclinations to their current employers until the position is in hand. In these and countless other situations, privacy represents a tool for strategic advantage.

Another crucial distinction lies between what one might call *divisible* and *holistic* privacy interests. Just as any individual might be well-fed when others are starving, one can maintain control over access to information on one's self even when others are losing such control. Here privacy is a divisible interest: one party can have it, while surrounded by others who do not. But other concerns over privacy correspond to social goods that one can only enjoy jointly with others. If we lived in a world where nearly all other citizens believed that state agencies knew everything about everyone—without cost or accountability to the state—we would all suffer, even if we did not believe our own lives were subject to such surveillance. The reason would be that we all partake of the shared benefits flowing from public confidence that not all personal information is on the public record. Here privacy is like freedom of expression: in a liberal social order, everyone loses when anyone is deterred from speaking out. Priscilla Regan's studies of privacy in US law-making are particularly acute in their analysis of such collective privacy interests (Regan 1995).

In short, the array of values flying under the inclusive flag of "privacy" is enormously rich. As the following sections show, the policy response to public anxieties over perceived invasion of privacy through institutional surveillance has addressed a selective subset of these concerns. Perhaps this should not be a surprise. It is simply not realistic to expect agreement on exactly what reasonable expectations of privacy require in any setting. Privacy in almost any sense is what philosophers call an "essentially contested concept"—meaning that people inevitably disagree over what constitute legitimate privacy claims, how much privacy is desirable, and who gets to decide these matters.

Demands for "privacy protection"

By the 1960s, the rise of large-scale institutional surveillance had begun to trigger public concern in the world's prosperous liberal societies. Civil libertarians, journalists, consumer activists and others grew alarmed at the growing power of record-keepers over the lives of those depicted in record-systems. All sorts of vital interests, from access to employment or insurance to freedom from undue attention from law-enforcement agencies, obviously turned on the workings of institutional surveillance—often without the knowledge of the people targeted, let alone their ability to assert their interests in these processes. Stories of arbitrary and destructive uses of personal data, along with historical memories of abuse of government-held personal data under repressive regimes, triggered a new social movement. This movement has been relatively low-key and heavily reliant on elite support. But like movements for environmental protection and human rights, the privacy protection movement has given rise to a still-unfolding global culture of concern over collection, sharing and use of personal information—and to the body of law and policy discussed below. The most basic premise of the movement, one might say, is that personal information is too important to be treated solely as another asset or resource at the sole discretion of the organizations that acquire and hold it (see also Bennett, this volume).

The first major national debates on the topic seem to have broken out in the United States—over the allocation of consumer credit, in some early instances, and later over government record-keeping. A major force in this *prise de conscience* was the appearance of Alan Westin's landmark *Privacy and Freedom* in 1967—surely one of the most influential works ever published on the subject. That, along with the broader rise of public alarm at repressive Nixon-era governance leading up to the Watergate Era, produced what remains America's broadest national legislation on surveillance—the Privacy Act of 1974.

At about the same time, countries in northern and western Europe began developing national legislation of their own—Sweden in 1973, for example, Germany in 1977, Denmark and Norway in 1978. By contrast to US legislation, then and now, these countries established privacy rights that applied across broad categories of different institutional settings, both public and private. Countries outside Europe—including

Australia, South Korea, and Canada—soon followed suit. By the 1990s, European Union policy-makers had come to see protection of privacy in the institutional handling of personal information as essential to its member countries' economic and social integration. The result was the European Union Data Protection Directive, requiring all current and future members of what soon became the European Union to "transpose" a core set of principles into their national laws. The European Directive has in turn exercised vast influence throughout the globe and served as a model for many national privacy codes in countries outside its borders.

At last count, at least 38 countries had adopted such codes (Rule 2007: 30). Among the more recent members of this global "privacy club" are Argentina, Japan and Hong Kong. Except in the United States, national privacy codes establish not just a body of law and policy for institutional treatment of personal information, but also a national privacy commissioner and a small staff to uphold the law and advocate privacy values in the public forum.

Despite significant differences from country to country, national privacy codes show remarkable cross-fertilization. In fact, they reflect a global culture of privacy protection lore, with principles embodied in earlier laws and policy statements heavily shaping those that have followed. It is not too much to characterize nearly all national codes as implementing global consensus principles for institutional treatment of personal data. These principles have been summarized, to take just one notable statement, in the thoughtful work by Colin Bennett and Charles Raab (2003). Privacy codes, they state, typically specify that organizations maintaining data on people:

> Must be *accountable* for all the personal information in its possession.
> Should *identify the purposes* for which the information is processed at or before the time of collection.
> Should only collect personal information with the *knowledge and consent* of the individual (except under specified circumstances).
> Should *limit the collection* of personal information to that which is necessary for pursuing the identified purposes.
> Should not use or disclose personal information for purposes other than those identified, except with the consent of the individual (the *finality* principle).
> Should *retain* information only as long as necessary.
> Should ensure the personal information is kept *accurate, complete and up-to-date*.
> Should protect personal information with appropriate *security safeguards*.
> Should be *open* about its policies and practices and maintain no secret information system.
> Should allow data subjects *access* to their personal information, with an ability to amend it if it is inaccurate, incomplete or obsolete.
>
> *(My enumeration of the principles set out in Bennett and Raab 2003: 19)*

One can find expressions of nearly all these precepts at least somewhere in the laws and policies of every national privacy code. Though stronger or weaker from country to country, both in the letter of the law and in the vigor of their enforcement, they represent prevailing global strategy for protecting individual rights over institutionally-held personal data (see also Raab, this volume).

What generalizations can we make about the aims and assumptions underlying these principles? First, they accept the essential *legitimacy* of large-scale institutional compilation of personal data, and the use of such data to shape treatments meted out to the individuals concerned. Where governments are concerned, they take it for granted that some such use may be required of citizens. Elsewhere—particularly in the private sector—they seem to view institutions and individuals as contracting parties, each of which may exercise consent over its role in the relationship. Over all, the principles aim at restricting the operation of institutional surveillance to its official purposes; at requiring that the institutions be held responsible for their uses of personal data; and at ensuring that systems be open and accountable for these uses. They represent, in short, due-process rules for channeling and adjudicating potential conflicts of interest between individuals and the institutional "consumers" of their data.

These moderate aims, let us note, scarcely address the full richness of value concerns bracketed by the term "privacy." To take just one example: they do not mitigate what some would consider the inherently dehumanizing effects of having their lives "reduced" or otherwise "sorted" by the attentions of record-keepers. Indeed, a more precise name than "privacy protection" for the practices set in train by the principles noted above is "personal data protection," a bureaucratic term of art favored by European Union officials and others.

Privacy codes: successes and failures

For some commentators, these consensus principles resolve the essential dilemmas of ethics and policy associated with institutional surveillance. By ensuring the legality and openness of personal data systems to public understanding and creating rights for individuals to challenge the lawful workings of such systems, they make it acceptable for the systems to go forward.

Other observers, less optimistic or more suspicious, see all sorts of shortcomings—not just in their application in specific national contexts, but perhaps even more in the logic of the principles themselves. Nearly everyone, at least for public purposes, agrees on the desirability of granting individuals understanding of and access to records that affect their lives and ensuring that systems work "lawfully." But the principles leave unaddressed key concerns about the larger social role played by institutional surveillance and the trajectory of its long-term development.

One obvious lacuna is that the principles are rarely held to apply to surveillance activities associated with the investigative and coercive arms of government. Law-enforcement, espionage and counter-terrorist agencies are rarely expected to make their records of ongoing tracking and other surveillance activities open or accountable to the public. No doubt most members of the public would agree that investigations of people posing authentic dangers to those around them ought to proceed in some measure of secrecy. But that is hardly to say that requirements of openness and legality should *never* apply to the activities of the agencies involved. The net result of this blackout is to leave vast swathes of institutional surveillance beyond the reach of the principles cited above.

Another serious shortcoming of the principles is the weakness of individual "consent" in relations between institutions and individuals. One of the original nightmares of privacy activists was the vision of a world where, once personal data become available to one institution for one purpose, those same data could flow seamlessly to any other institution interested in using them, for any other purpose. Thus the importance attached to the principal of "finality"—number 5 in the Bennett and Raab roster—limiting transfer of personal data from one institution to another, except where the individual agrees.

But formal "consent" is often simply not meaningful in these situations—as in many others where isolated individuals confront large organizations. In the United States, for example, taxpayers must prepare detailed summaries of their financial affairs for submission to the Internal Revenue Service, the collectors of federal income tax. The IRS in turn promises to safeguard these records. But in a world where virtually every adult is known to possess a copy of his or her own tax returns, taxpayers often find it impossible to refuse to share that information with outside institutions that demand it. Prospective employers regularly request copies of tax returns from job-seekers, regardless of whether the job in question involves financial responsibilities. The applicant can respectfully decline, but in most cases the application will probably stop there. This dilemma is repeated in countless situations: where data are known to exist under the control of the individual, inducements to share the data can be so powerful as to make "consent" to disclosure nothing more than a formality.

Perhaps more disquieting, notions of requiring individual "consent" to the sharing of personal data actually appear to run *contrary* to some of the main trends in institutional surveillance over recent decades.

Like most individuals in their daily face-to-face dealings with others, organizations prefer not to take anyone's account of himself or herself at face value. After all, people nearly always prefer to censor the flow of information about themselves. The increasingly widespread availability of computerized sources of personal data makes it easy for institutions to satisfy such preferences for personal data obtained from independent sources. Thus credit grantors prefer not to rely only on the credit references supplied by credit applicants—reasoning (correctly) that people normally prefer to supply only good news about themselves. Taxation authorities seek untainted data on taxpayers' financial situations from employers, banks, or creditors. Prospective insurers seek data on past claims by applicants for new coverage from other insurance companies. As more and more bureaucracies compile and maintain efficient systems for tracking individuals, possibilities for such symbiosis among surveillance systems grow exponentially. Whether individuals supply their *formal* consent or not for cross-checking of their records with other institutional sources, the pressures and opportunities for sharing of personal data across bureaucratic boundaries are overwhelming. It would be hard to argue that the global consensus principles summarized by Bennett and Raab have made much of a dent in the willingness of organizations to resort to such expedients.

These trends may help explain why the growth of institutional surveillance appears to be steadily accelerating. The fact that more and more personal data are computerized and centralized, fuels exchanges of information that strengthen the systems. Today, in many consumer societies, credit reporting organizations sell their reports to insurance companies, for use in screening insurance applicants. Data from banks and other financial institutions are intensely monitored by state security institutions—officially for tracking terrorists, but almost certainly to support other government aims, as well. In short, *institutional surveillance feeds on itself*. The more of it there is, the more there can be. And given the broad (if ambivalent) cultural mandate to institutions to do better by knowing more about the people they deal with, innovative forms of monitoring are constantly coming into use.

"Needs" for surveillance and pressures on privacy

This brings me to what I consider the most serious limitation of the consensus privacy principles. They simply offer no guidance on the most important of all surveillance issues—how much institutional surveillance there ought to be. What constitutes adequate justification for instituting such monitoring in the first place? When is it reasonable to judge that specific forms of it simply *go too far*, even in the service of the most estimable social purposes?

Consider the striking variety of qualitatively new forms of surveillance that have come into currency, just since the first versions of the consensus principles were conceived back in the 1960s. These new categories of personal information—those associated with the internet, for example, or with mobile telephony, or with GPS tracking, or with automated face or voice recognition—effectively render entire domains of our lives newly accessible to institutional monitoring. Asked to account for them, many people simply characterize them as "effects" of "Technology"—as though they were imposed by some impersonal agency on human affairs. One might almost think that the spread of institutional surveillance as the result of some purely natural process, like sunspots or earthquakes.

Official privacy protection policy would appear to follow the same assumptions—reacting to the existence of institutional surveillance, rather than providing a rationale for questioning its extension. If any account is given for the pervasive rise of surveillance, it is apt to be in terms of the "needs" of organizations for data on the people they deal with. In an "information society," one hears, organizations require data much as internal combustion engines require fuel. The implication is that shutting off the flow of data—on people, or anything else—would bring economic and technological progress to a grinding halt.

But matters are not this simple. Institutional "needs" for personal data are in fact extremely elastic. At one extreme, certain kinds of personal information are indeed indispensable for certain organizational performances: if someone subscribes to a publication, he or she must furnish some sort of street or electronic address for its delivery. Such requirements are what Jerry Kang calls "functionally necessary" (1998: 1290). But other so-called "needs" for personal information are not *sine qua non*, but simply add to the advantage of the organization in dealing with the people concerned.

Consider the "needs" for personal data experienced by a bank considering a married couple's application for a mortgage. The array of such information that *might*, conceivably, help predict payment is in principle virtually endless. Under present circumstances, most banks satisfy their "needs" in this respect by checking applicants' employment status, credit scores, current outstanding debts, perhaps assets and liabilities—the relevance of which are clear enough. But think of other information on applicants that might also be useful in this determination. One could administer lie detector examination or other psychological tests to weigh the prospective borrowers' deep convictions on the importance of meeting financial obligations. One could require clinical interviews to weigh the stability of applicants' marriages. One could seek DNA analysis and other inquiries into applicants' medical backgrounds to ensure that health considerations would not hinder repayment. One could even carry out electronic eavesdropping, to judge how seriously the couple were taking prospective repayment obligations.

This is hardly to say that banks today—at least, to my knowledge—claim any of this information in connection with mortgage applications. But any and all these forms of personal data *could*, under plausible circumstances, prove extremely useful in evaluating mortgage applications. Though bank planners may not recognize "needs" for such intimate data—perhaps because obtaining and analyzing such information would not now be cost-effective—such needs remain to be discovered. The *leitmotif* of the development of institutional surveillance has been discovery of new organizational needs for personal data—for cell phone records, credit scores, tax return data, etc., etc.—that often simply did not exist before.

Satisfaction of such needs is particularly difficult to resist where the information defined as needed is actually already in the public domain—information that is widely knowable at some point, but normally evanescent or "wasted." An example is people's presence in any public space at a given moment. Normally when we walk the streets, or attend a public event, or enter an airport or a library, we do so in the knowledge that anyone can observe us—and in confidence that our presence will not often matter much to anyone. But such premises of everyday information flow change drastically with creation of means that can systematically track and analyze patterns of people's movements on a large scale. These possibilities are by no means fanciful. Efforts are well underway to launch face-recognition programs that can pick out specific individuals in public places. Current sponsors of such efforts are law enforcement or anti-terrorist agencies of the state. But one can equally well imagine commercial applications of these same possibilities—for market research, insurance underwriting and the like.

As Helen Nissenbaum and others have argued, it will not do to accept the explanation that nothing essential has changed in the acceptability of such tracking, given that the personal information in question was always public (Nissenbaum 2010). Nor will it do to suggest that attempts by institutions to exploit such data must be honored, if only the data is necessary to satisfy what the organizations' proponents consider a need. If one thing about institutional surveillance is clear, it is that new needs for it continue to arise without apparent limit. This rising demand for personal data results both from strictly technological changes that bring new forms of personal data into existence, and from the sheer imagination of government and corporate planners in exploiting long-available data sources. The consensus privacy principles have posed little effective barrier to the resulting extension of institutional surveillance.

Indeed, looking back over the roughly 40 years since passage of the first national privacy codes, a skeptic might observe that the world has more privacy protection laws, but less privacy.

Conclusion

It would be comforting to believe that deep-going privacy values will ultimately force some limits to indiscriminate extension of institutional surveillance. At some point, many imagine, attempts to extend institutional surveillance over yet further domains of private life will finally go "too far," provoking grass-roots revolt.

But from all evidence, public sensibilities in these matters are as elastic as the "needs" of organizations for more personal data. Demands for personal information held intolerable at one moment can be redefined as inevitable, if irksome, a few years or decades later. As I write, air travelers in the USA are coming to accept airport security screenings that include inspection of images of their naked bodies, through the use of ultrasound-like devices that penetrate clothing. When such "naked machines" were first proposed for this purpose in the early years of the new millennium, I thought that surveillance proponents had overplayed their hand: surely the inevitable public revulsion at such total exposure would produce a backlash. But relentless official reminders of terrorist threats—and at least one near-disaster allegedly involving a would-be terrorist with explosives attached to his thighs—appear to have disarmed public objections, at least among Americans. Thus we stand to become inured to routine, government-sanctioned collection of images of ourselves in our original condition. One has to wonder what new and compelling needs for such images will be discovered, once their availability is established.

The global consensus principles discussed here do not provide much defense against such practices. They inveigh, I have argued, against uses of personal data that are capricious, illegal or inconsistent with the avowed purposes of surveillance systems. But the supposedly legitimate purposes to which such systems are increasingly put, by resourceful government and private organizations, are multifarious and ever-expanding. As managerial ingenuity and technological sophistication make it possible to know more about individuals, and to link such knowledge to new techniques for shaping the lives of the people concerned, new demands for institutional surveillance continue to arise.

Think 50 years ahead—roughly the stretch of time since institutional surveillance first became politicized in the 1960s. What new domains of life will fall under the sweep of such activities over this period? What new forms of exchange among organizations, including sharing of personal data between government and private institutions, will come to serve needs perhaps not even imagined at this point? Will the second half of the twenty-first century bring a world where, as early privacy advocates feared, all personal data provided at any point for any purpose will become available everywhere, for any purpose?

It would be rash to reject this possibility. And such developments might indeed help usher in a world that would be more law-abiding, more productive, less dangerous, more orderly—perhaps even ultimately more just. But it would certainly be a less private world, in many senses of that term. If such an outcome is to be avoided, publics and policy-makers will have to be willing to advocate restriction on institutional surveillance as a bad thing in itself, even when mobilized for ends—like efficiency, safety and order—that nearly everyone endorses.

Such a categorical *prise de position* does not appear on the immediate horizon, in any of the world's surveillance-intensive countries.

References

Bennett, Colin and Raab, Charles. (2003). *The Governance of Privacy: Policy Instruments in Global Perspective*, Aldershot: Ashgate.

Kang, Jerry. (1998). "Information Privacy in Cyberspace Transactions," *Stanford Law Review*, 50(4): 1195–294.

Nissenbaum, Helen. (2010). *Privacy in Context: Technology, Policy and the Integrity of Social Life*, Stanford, CA: Stanford University Press.

Regan, Priscilla M. (1995). *Legislating Privacy: Technology, Social Values and Public Policy*, Chapel Hill: University of North Carolina Press.

Rule, James B. (2007). *Privacy in Peril: How We are Sacrificing a Fundamental Right in Exchange for Security and Convenience*, New York: Oxford University Press.

Westin, Alan F. (1967). *Privacy and Freedom*, New York: Atheneum.

d. Race and surveillance

Simone Browne

Introduction

Starting with John Fiske's assertion that surveillance "is a way of imposing norms" where "those who have been othered into the 'abnormal' have [surveillance] focused more intensely upon them," (1998: 81) this chapter considers certain moments, both historical and contemporary, where surveillance reifies the social construct of race. The four sections that make up this chapter (the slave pass, the rogues' gallery, the census, the biometric body) examine extraordinary acts of surveillance, as well as those of the everyday, that are racializing in their effects. I focus on racializing surveillance as a technology of social control. Racializing surveillance is that where surveillance practices, policies and performances concern the production of norms pertaining to race and exercise a "power to define what is in or out of place" (Fiske 1998: 81). Mindful of David Theo Goldberg's caution that the term "racialization" should be used precisely, and not merely to ascribe "racial meanings or values to social conditions or arrangements" (Goldberg 2002: 12), my use of the term "racializing surveillance" signals those moments when enactments of surveillance reify boundaries and borders along racial lines, and where the outcome is often discriminatory treatment. In his discussion of black masculinities and video surveillance in the public sphere, Fiske argues that "surveillance is a technology of whiteness that racially zones city space by drawing lines that Blacks cannot cross and whites cannot see" (1998: 69). Drawing from Fiske's claim and situating race as socially constructed rather than biologically fixed, this chapter explores surveillance and the work it does to zone spaces, draw lines and shape looking relations.

What follows is a discussion of race and surveillance that begins in the past, as our past reveals a great deal about contemporary practices. For example, the zoning of black mobilities in city spaces is not limited to the contemporary era. Consider the eighteenth-century lantern laws passed by the Common Council of New York City that stipulated that "no Negro or Indian slave above the age of fourteen years do presume to be or appear in any of the streets" of New York City "one hour after sunset without a lantern or a lit candle." As Fiske tells us, "power needs to be able to see what it has categorized as the abnormal" (82). In New York City and other spaces that zoned black and Indian mobilities in the early 1700s, it was the lantern that aided in this surveillant seeing. Candlelight was used to "Other" some into the abnormal and to uphold racial categories.

To say that racializing surveillance is a technology of social control is not to take this form of surveillance as involving a very specific set of social practices that maintain a fixed racial order of things. Rather it suggests that how things get ordered racially by way of surveillance depends on space, time and is subject to change, but most often upholds "Othering" practices that first accompanied European colonial expansion and that sought to structure social relations and institutions in ways that privilege whiteness. Racializing surveillance is not static or applied only to particular human groupings. It relies on techniques, some of which are discussed below, to reify boundaries along racial lines, and in so doing, it reifies race. While the focus here is on race and surveillance and how they are coupled, race must be understood as operating in an interlocking fashion with class, gender, sexuality, location and other markers of identity. Although the examples cited are mainly from the United States, the techniques and technologies discussed have been and are applied to other spaces and at other times to order things racially, for instance census taking as a means of racial classification, or identification documents with biometric identifiers used for "negatively discriminatory practices" (Lyon 2003).

This chapter is organized into four parts, with each discussing theoretical concepts that allow us to think deeply about racializing surveillance, its past and its present. These include: Michel Foucault's "disciplinary power" (1979) and the regulation of slave life; rogues' galleries and what Torin Monahan calls "marginalizing surveillance" (2010); the census and the business of racial classification; and biometric technology and the notion of prototypical whiteness.

The slave pass

According to Christian Parenti, the history of surveillance in America can be traced to the "simple accounts" of slave owners (2003: 15). Of course, the accounting practices of transatlantic slavery were also present outside of the Americas. These simple accounts included slave vessel manifests listing human cargo, plantation inventories, diaries which contained observations about plantation life and instructions for governing slaves. One example involved the "General Rules" recorded by Charles Tait for his Columbus, Texas plantation: "4th In giving orders always do it in a mild tone, and try to leave the impression on the mind of the negro that what you say is the result of reflection." The detailed cataloguing of slave life was a mechanism of disciplinary power, where disciplinary power, as Michel Foucault tells us, is "exercised through its invisibility," while imposing a "compulsory visibility" on its targets (1979: 187). Disciplinary power, then, operated on the enslaved as a racializing surveillance that individuals were at once subjected to and that produced them as racial, and therefore enslavable, subjects. Such a racializing surveillance was apparent in the plantation security system, a system that relied on, as Parenti lays out, three "information technologies: the written slave pass, organized slave patrols, and wanted posters for runaways" (2003: 15). Here, surveillance and literacy were closely articulated as slaves and indentured servants who could read and write could also forge passes and manumission papers or alter existing ones by replacing dates, names and other unique identifiers, in this way functioning as "antebellum hackers" able to "crack the code of the planters' security system" (20). These forged passes were used for unauthorized travel outside of the plantation and were produced by fugitives upon demand by slave patrollers, or "pattie rollers," who were often non-property owning but armed white men who policed slave mobilities. Sometimes producing a forged pass was not necessary. Any piece of printed text would do given that fugitive slaves were aware that many of these pattie rollers were illiterate, so they would hand over these "passes" when apprehended. This security system, then, relied on the "racially defined contours of (white) literacy and (Black) illiteracy," a dichotomy that was not so readily upheld (18). Less easily counterfeited passes were later fashioned out of metal.

The compulsory visibility of the racial subject can be seen in the circulation of newspaper advertisements and wanted posters for runaway slaves and truant servants. These texts were primarily aimed at a white public that was assumed to be literate and free, and who in consuming these texts became part of the apparatus of surveillance, the eyes and ears of face-to-face watching and regulating. In detailing physical descriptions, the surveillance technology of the fugitive slave advertisement made the already hypervisible racial subject legible as "out of place." For instance, a March 15 1783 advertisement in *The Royal Gazette* offering a "Two Dollars reward" for "a Mulatto, or Quadroon Girl, about 14 years of age, named Seth, but calls herself Sall," attests to the role of fugitive slave notices, and similarly wanted posters, in upholding racial categorization. This notice went on to state: "sometimes says she is white and often paints her face to cover that deception." Seth's, or Sall's, duplicity is not limited to her use of an alias, as this notice tells us, but also to her racial ambiguity, witness her apparent choosing to self-identify or pass as white, rather than as "a Mulatto" (one black parent and one white parent) or a "Quadroon Girl" (one black grandparent) as per the racial nomenclature that arose out of slavery. Later such classifications as a form of population management were made official with the first US federal census in 1790. I will return to the census as a technology that formalized racial categorization later. For now, the wanted notice for fugitive slaves as an information technology demonstrates that then as now race was a social construct that required constant policing and oversight. However, the format of the fugitive notice was repurposed in the form of handbills that functioned as a means of counter-surveillance. An 1851 handbill produced by abolitionist Theodore Parker attests to this as it cautioned "colored people of Boston" to steer clear of "watchmen and police officers" and to "keep a sharp look out for kidnappers, and have top eye open." "Top eye" here was a directive to look out and about with keen intent as police officers were empowered to act as slave catchers under fugitive slave laws. Black spectatorship, along with the gazes of white abolitionists and other allies, functioned as a form of oppositional looking back at racializing surveillance.

In her discussion of black spectatorship, the gaze and looking relations during slavery and the racial apartheid of Jim Crow in the southern United States, bell hooks tells us that black people often "cultivated the habit of casting the gaze downward so as not to appear uppity. To look directly was an assertion of subjectivity, equality" (1992: 168). hooks suggests that the often violent ways in which blacks were denied the right to look back—think of the gruesome beating and murder of 14-year-old Emmett Till in Mississippi in 1955, allegedly for looking at a white woman—"had produced in us an overwhelming longing to look, a rebellious desire, an oppositional gaze" (116). Such politicized and oppositional looking were agential acts and can be seen, for example, in a June 14th 1783 runaway slave notice printed in the *Royal Gazette* for 16-year-old Sam, who is described in the notice as "five feet high" and "remarkable in turning up the whites of his eyes when spoken to." This notice records Sam's oppositional gaze, his looking back, and shows us that resistance can be found even in the simple act of rolling one's eyes. Black looks have the power to trouble surveillance as a "technology of whiteness" (Fiske: 1998: 69).

The rogues' gallery

In the mid-nineteenth century the public would visit rogues' galleries to look at the booking photographs of arrested individuals. Viewing the mug shots displayed at the rogues' gallery constituted the visitor "as an official 'insider' opposed to the state's enemies" (Parenti 2003: 38). These police galleries went portable via mug books linked with dossiers detailing arrest histories, known associates and physical descriptions that, as Parenti outlines in his discussion of the Chinese Mug Book and its use by San Francisco Police Department Detective Delos Woodruff, would be employed for "both technical and moral purposes" (39). Mug books "helped construct 'insider' and 'outsider' identities and in effect recruited rank-and-file citizens into the state's project of surveillance and control" (Parenti 2003: 39).

Today, such practices find their contemporary incarnation in the weekly editions of *Busted!*, *Charged* and *Mugly!* shame rags and the online collection of mug shots at www.bustedmugshots.com. The for-profit mug books of *Busted!* and its ilk are now sold locally at gas stations and convenience stores for around $1. They involve their buyers and those that browse the accompanying websites in a practice of shaming the "busted" as part of a wider project of surveillance. In each issue ads for legal representation appear between mug shots that are sectioned off under headings such as "Busted Beauties" and "Old Farts." On some pages readers are incited to play a game of "whodunit?" by matching criminal charges to unmarked mug shots. The people depicted in the photographs of such mug shot magazines have been arrested for various offences, but mainly public intoxication or possession of a controlled substance. Many of the photographed display the telltale signs of alcohol and drug use: disheveled hair, droopy eyelids and sometimes the tooth decay associated with methamphetamine use, more commonly known as "meth mouth." While the publisher of *Mugly!*, for example, insists that a proprietary formula is used to randomly choose which photos to publish to reflect "the disparity of race in the [general] population, not necessarily the population of those arrested" (*Dallas Observer* 21 June 2010), such mug shot magazines offer us a voyeuristic look into a whiteness marked as grotesque and subject to police intervention and public shaming in the figure of the "meth head."

The "meth head" has become an increasingly visible form of embodied deviance displayed in the public domain through drug awareness and prevention programs, such as the Faces of Meth™ website of the Multnomah County Sheriff's Office in Portland, Oregon. Torin Monahan's (2010) work on identity theft as socially constructed moral panic reveals how representations of methamphetamine use shifted from being "feminized and racialized as white (*vis-à-vis* crack cocaine)," and somewhat valorized from the 1980s through the early 1990s as a drug capable of generating the power to multitask in ways that were productive to capital accumulation (i.e. efficient household management and mothering) to a "dangerous, homemade narcotic manufactured and used predominantly by people in low-income white rural communities" (2010: 58). Making important links between postindustrialization and the condemned rural spaces "where community-sustaining industries have been downsized or eliminated, such as the towns of the Midwest that have historically relied on farming, truck driving, factory work, and coal mining for reliable jobs," (58) or what many have termed national sacrifice zones, Monahan reveals how the "war on drugs" and neoliberal social policy work to uphold certain class distinctions and socio-spatial inequalities by othering some whites into the category of abnormal. Such abject whiteness can be seen in the Montana Meth Project's graphic print and television campaign, depicting addicted teens in various acts of meth-induced psychosis, prostitution, picking at scabs and open sores, and meth mouth. What Monahan calls "marginalizing surveillance" is important for understanding these campaigns as not only about raising awareness of social problems and drug-use reduction, but also about policing a whiteness rendered abnormal. Marginalizing surveillance, Monahan states, is "an explicit power relationship of enhanced control of populations considered to be risky, dangerous, or untrustworthy" and that "affixes those characteristics to the objects of surveillance, thereby reifying identities of suspicion and legitimizing the ongoing selective deployment of surveillance" (10). The Montana Meth Project, Faces of Meth™, and even *Busted!*, reify "identities of suspicion" by visually framing a whiteness that is negatively racialized as contagion and polluting. Such hygienic surveillance has its history in the public health campaigns of the late nineteenth and early twentieth centuries mounted by organizations such as the American Social Hygiene Association that sought to educate the young white population about the importance of cleanliness, self-mastery, managing class anxieties and racial regeneration. Campaigns such as The Montana Meth Project use a hypervisible whiteness and mark it (*or market it*) as the "shameful class," (Foucault 1979: 182). In so doing they demarcate the "good" from the "bad" white subject without necessarily making links to state curtailments on social services or reduced access to suitable health care.

The census

Having its roots in the Latin *censere*—to assess or judge—the census is used by the state to manage its residents by way of formalized categories. Census enumeration fixes individuals within a particular time, and renders a population legible in racializing, as well as gendering and spatial ways. This "state stocktaking," as Goldberg puts it, makes known "population size, shape, distribution, quality and flow of labor supply, taxation and conscription pools, political representation, voter predictability, and the necessities of population reproduction" (2002: 189). While such "state stocktaking" that sees the census informant provide the enumerator with answers to a series of questions regarding biographical data might seem benign and everyday, this involves a form of racializing surveillance not only through its reinscription of racial categories but also when the collected data is used for discriminatory outcomes, like drawing voting districts along racial lines. For example, some of the statistical knowledge generated by census taking has been controversially used in the state of Texas to realign congressional and legislative districts in a manner that ensures that the voting population remain majority white, regardless of growth in the Hispanic and African-American populations. This move has been reproduced in other states in such a way that it may violate the 1965 Voting Rights Act that outlawed discriminatory voting practices.

One constant has remained in terms of racial categories and the US census form: an unspecified "whiteness." "White" has always been listed first among the boxes from which to choose in order to answer the question "what is your race?" The current proliferation of racial categories was first reserved for the management of blackness, and then later for other groupings to reflect changing immigration patterns. For example, in the 1890 census "Mulatto," "Quadroon," and "Octoroon" appeared as subcategories of "Black" "only to be collapsed into the singularity of an unqualified blackness" by the 1900 census, reflecting the one-drop rule of hypodescent (Goldberg 2002: 189). "Mulatto" was reintroduced in 1910 and was replaced with "Negro" by the 1930 census, a category that fell in and out of favor, depending on each subsequent decennial enumeration. For the 2010 census "Black, African-Am or Negro" were subsumed under one box. As Goldberg notes, when the category "Mexican" was introduced it was understood to mean not white unless the census informant "explicitly and accurately claimed white descent" (2002: 190). Thus, it was left to the enumerator to judge whether the census informant's claim to whiteness was valid, rather than accepting at *face value* the informant's self-identification as white. It was not until 1940 when both the Mexican government and the US State Department intervened that the category "Mexican" became formalized as white. The category was later replaced with the new subcategory "Hispanic" in 1980.

The market research industry relied at its outset on information culled from the US Census that was then correlated with other data, such as credit scores and retail loyalty card transactions, to profile through patterns (or by "lifestyle segments") and for direct marketing strategies (Parenti 2003: 103). For Oscar H. Gandy, Jr, data mining and internet "cookie" technologies of the sorts now used for consumer profiling and market segmentation raise concerns around privacy and the possibilities of "computer-enhanced discriminatory techniques," when, for example, information brokers profile an individual's web browsing activity and this information is then used to provide (or deny) e-commerce services and transactions in a discriminatory manor (Gandy, Jr 2006: 363). This practice falls under the rubric of what David Lyon calls "digital discrimination," marking the differential application of surveillance technologies where "flows of personal data—abstracted information—are sifted and channeled in the process of risk assessment, to privilege some and disadvantage others, to accept some as legitimately present and to reject others" (2003: 674). This sifting of data flows to render some segments of populations as legitimate while rejecting other demographic groupings as illegitimate along racial lines was apparent in 2001 when inaccurate voter registration lists for certain county election boards in the state of Florida were generated by a subsidiary of the data-mining company ChoicePoint and were used to disenfranchise "an estimated eight thousand potential voters, many of them African Americans" who, as Gandy points out, were "far less likely to have supported George W. Bush" in the US Presidential election (2006: 373). In other instances, zip codes and credit scores might be used to restrict the products and services available to certain consumers, or to target specific consumers for predatory lending services like payday loans, pawn shops and "high cost" subprime mortgages that contribute to the higher foreclosure rates in segregated black and Latino neighborhoods.

The biometric body

A key area from which to understand the role of surveillance in the cultural production of race is that of biometrics. Biometrics is a technology of measuring the body that is put to work for verification and identification purposes, enabling the body to function as evidence (see van der Ploeg, this volume). This is the idea that the body will reveal a "truth" about a subject despite the subject's claims. This seems simple enough. However, how such technology is researched, developed and deployed sometimes reveals itself to be racializing. This is not to say that biometric technology is inherently racist, but that it is sometimes used to draw and uphold racial lines. A look at the history of such practices is helpful here.

The metal outside caliper, a device used to compare the outside linear dimensions of objects with those measurements made with other tools, such as a ruler, was the instrument of choice for Alphonse Bertillon, creator of anthropometry. Anthropometry, or Bertillonage, was a system of measuring and cataloguing the human body for purposes of identification and crime solving, and as such it anticipates contemporary biometric technologies, such as fingerprint analysis, hand geometry and facial recognition technologies. This early biometric system was put to work as a "scientific method," alongside the pseudo-sciences of craniometry and phrenology, to classify many as criminal. As for craniometry, its measurements were used to support polygenism and other theories around racial difference in matters such as intelligence, classifying some as more primitive than others and therefore outside of the category of rights-bearing human beings. Bertillonage used a series of measurements of the torso, head and limbs obtained through a choreographed routine that saw the subject sit, stand on stools and extend limbs so that they could be measured. Once recorded, these measurements were indexed on a database that amounted to the first ostensible link between body measurements and identity. Although Bertillonage later gave way to the fingerprint as the standard criminal justice biometric, it continued to be used as a means of administrative surveillance directed at particular racialized populations. For example, in 1912 the French republican government passed a law aimed at controlling the mobility of France's itinerant Roma population that required individuals without fixed addresses to be issued identity cards. These cards listed name, place and date of birth, and included photographs as well as anthropometric measurements such as head size, length of cubit (left forearm from the elbow to the tip of the middle finger), length of the right ear and other measurements first developed by Bertillon.

Current biometric technology converts measurements of the human body into digitized code, making for unique templates that computers can sort by relying on a searchable database (on-line or one-to-many identification), or use to verify the identity of the bearer of a document, like a passport, within which the unique biometric is encoded. The latter use is termed one-to-one or off-line authentification. Popular biometric surveillance technologies include iris and retinal scans, facial and vascular patterns, and fingerprint data. One feature that this technology shares with earlier biometric technologies like craniometry is that in some instances it is inscribed in classificatory schemes that see particular biometric systems privileging whiteness, or lightness, in how certain bodies are lit and measured in the enrolment process. Some racial groupings have higher fail to enroll (FTE) rates than others. For finger-scan technologies these groups that often FTE are the elderly, workers who come in contact with caustic chemicals and heavy hand-washing like hospital workers, and those referred to as of Pacific Rim/Asian descent. On this point, Joseph Pugliese writes, "the Social Darwinian resonances of 'lower quality' fingerprints must not be ignored, as they paradigmatically situate Asian bodies on a lower position on that racial hierarchy, constituted, respectively, by Caucasian, Mongoloid (Asians), and Negroid races" (2005: 8). It is rarely acknowledged that this notion that certain racialized bodies "fail to enroll" only makes sense when whiteness provides the unspoken standard against which such groups are compared. Hence, a logic of prototypical whiteness informs such research, development and practice, digitally segregating racialized populations. A 2009 publication on "Face Gender Classification on Consumer Images in a Multiethnic Environment," basically a study that examined how face detection technology could be employed, for example, in shopping mall settings or for digital photosharing applications, makes use of archaic racial terminology. In the end, this study found that when programmed generically for "all ethnicities" the gender classifier "is inclined to classify Africans as males and Mongloids as females" (Gao and Ai 2009: 175). The idea of feminized Asian males and masculinized African females has its roots in the same classificatory schemes introduced by proponents of polygenism and craniometry.

Although these reports are troubling, it must be noted that biometric technology can also be used in ways that challenge racializing surveillance. This is apparent in the complicated 2009 case of Suaad Hagi Mohamud which I will briefly present here as it hints at both the limitations and liberatory potential of biometrics. On 21 May 2009, Somali-born Canadian citizen Suaad Hagi Mohamud attempted to board a KLM Royal Dutch Airlines flight out of Jomo Kenyatta International Airport in Nairobi to return home to Toronto, after a three-week visit to Kenya. Upon inspecting her passport, airline authorities claimed that her lips looked different than those observed in her four-year-old passport photo. They branded her an imposter and not the rightful holder of the passport that she presented and detained her overnight in the airport. Two Canadian High Commission officials met with her the following morning, told her "you are not Suaad" and confiscated her passport. Mohamud was held in the airport for four days until she was released on a bond, tasked with proving her identity within two weeks. To prove her identity to officials at the Canadian High Commission in Nairobi Mohamud bared the contents of her wallet, showing them her Canadian citizenship card, driver's license, health card and other identity documents. The officials did not accept Mohamud's ID cards and she was charged with using a false passport, impersonating a Canadian and with being in Kenya illegally. Canadian authorities turned over her passport to Kenyan officials to aid in their charges against her. She was subsequently jailed by Kenyan authorities, and faced possible deportation to Somalia. While Mohamud was in limbo in Kenya, the Canadian Minister of Foreign Affairs Lawrence Cannon was quoted as saying, "there is no tangible proof" that Mohamud is Canadian and that "all Canadians who hold passports generally have a picture that is identical in their passport to what they claim to be."[1] Cannon made this statement after Mohamud submitted her fingerprints to Canadian officials in Kenya, and after an officer from the Canadian Border Services Agency visited her place of employment in Toronto so that her co-workers could identify a photo of her. It was later revealed that there were no fingerprints on file with the Canadian government with which to make a comparison to those taken from Mohamud in Kenya.

In yet another attempt to establish her identity Mohamud requested to be DNA tested. It was not until 10 August that a DNA test conducted on Mohamud in comparison to a test conducted on her Canadian-born son confirmed Mohamud's identity, with a probability of 99.99%. Charges against her were dropped, she was issued an emergency passport and she boarded a plane to Amsterdam to make her way home to Toronto arriving on 15 August. This DNA verification not only proved who she said she was, but apparently determined her citizenship status as well.

This case—or the lips case, as it was termed in the Kenyan media—reveals the workings of discretionary power exercised by the customs inspector, and increasingly by the airline official as proxy customs inspector, and it also raises a series of concerns regarding what proof of identity state officials will accept from a stranded and detained citizen abroad, and who can be abandoned by the state at international border crossings (or denied access to them) and by what technological means. The answer as to whether Mohamud's ordeal was racially charged or not is found in an interview that took place after her return to Canada where she stated that she felt that she would not have been detained at the Kenyan airport if she were white, and further argued that "the Canadian High Commission wouldn't be treating me the way they treat me. If I'm a white person, I wouldn't be there in one day. I wouldn't have missed the flight."[2] While some of the research and development of biometric technology, as discussed above, is informed by the classificatory schemes that categorize many as less than fully human and that replicate existing social inequalities, the Mohamud case demonstrates that in some instances biometric identifiers can put forth a challenge to the materialities of race and surveillance at the border when customs agents seemingly determine who is in or out of place at the border in racially specific ways. It is not surprising that since Mohamud established her right to return to her country of citizenship by way of DNA when government functionaries challenged the integrity of her documents that there are now some who use this case to argue for DNA-encoded travel documents.

Conclusion

The major point of this chapter has been to accentuate how surveillance at various moments and by particular means reifies the social construct that is race, especially for those practices that lead to negatively racializing outcomes for some groups and individuals. The idea of "racializing surveillance" was presented here as a way to categorize both historical and contemporary practices where surveillance shapes boundaries, bodies and borders along racial lines. Importantly, this chapter offers some insight into moments when people challenge racializing surveillance whether through oppositional gazes, forged passes and having "top eye open" or by other agential acts.

Notes

1 Minister Cannon's statement to the press on 24 July 2009: www.cbc.ca/world/story/2009/08/12/f-haji-mohamud-timeline.html (downloaded from the world wide web 23 June 2011).
2 "Skin colour a factor in Kenya ordeal: Mohamud," CBC News: www.cbc.ca/canada/toronto/story/2009/08/21/mohamud-interview.html?ref=rss&loomia_si=t0:a16:g2:r3:c0.0647694:b27126294 (downloaded from the world wide web 7 July 2011).

References

Fiske, J. (1998). "Surveilling the City: Whiteness, the Black Man and Democratic Totalitarianism," *Theory, Culture & Society*, 15(2): 67–88.

Foucault, M. (1979). *Discipline and Punish: The Birth of the Prison*, Harmondsworth: Penguin.

Gandy, O. H., Jr (2006). "Data Mining, Surveillance, and Discrimination in the Post-9/11 Environment" in K. D. Haggerty and R. V. Ericson (eds), *The New Politics of Surveillance and Visibility*, pp. 363–84, Toronto: University of Toronto Press.

Gao, W. and Ai, H. (2009). "Face Gender Classification on Consumer Images in a Multiethnic Environment," in M. Tistarelli and M. S. Nixon (eds), *Advances in Biometrics: Third International Conference on Biometrics* (Proceedings), pp. 169–78, Berlin: Springer-Verlag Berlin Heidelberg.

Goldberg, D. T. (2002). *The Racial State*, New York: Blackwell Publishers.

hooks, b. (1992). *Black Looks: Race and Representation*, Toronto: Between the Lines.

Lyon, D. (2003). "Technology vs. 'Terrorism': Circuits of City Surveillance Since September 11th," *International Journal of Urban and Regional Research*, 27(3): 666–78.

Monahan, T. (2010). *Surveillance in the Time of Insecurity*, New Brunswick, NJ: Rutgers University Press.

Parenti, C. (2003). *The Soft Cage: Surveillance in America From Slave Passes to the War on Terror*, New York: Basic Books.

Pugliese, J. (2005). "In Silico Race and the Heteronomy of Biometric Proxies: Biometrics in the Context of Civilian Life, Border Security and Counter-Terrorism Laws," *Australian Feminist Law Journal*, Volume 23: 1–32.

Section 1.3.
Cultures of surveillance

a. Performing surveillance

John McGrath

The first decade of the twenty-first century could, with some justification, be described as the decade of universal surveillance—the decade in which the prospect of continuous, comprehensive surveillance was accepted as a likelihood in most societies and a reality in many.

To a great extent this development had long been predicted. From the dsytopias of Orwell, Huxley and many a Hollywood screenwriter, to the growing prominence of privacy campaigns, we had long been warned that it was only a matter of time and technology before we were all under the eye of Big Brother. And so, in technological terms at least, it proved to be. However, the ways in which surveillance, and responses to surveillance, manifested in society were neither as consistent nor predictable as the many prophets had suggested. Indeed, at the end of the decade public acceptance of and, more importantly, engagement with, surveillance has never been greater. Big Brother, in the form of a central, state-controlled surveillance system, has proven, in his periodic manifestations, to be dependant not so much on technology as on the age-old structures of totalitarian state control (where secrecy is a more defining characteristic than visibility). The innumerable Little Brothers—police systems, private security firms, shop-owners—who created most of the network of surveillance through much of the decade—have only fitfully joined up into anything like a comprehensive system (usually in high-profile crime cases) and in most Western societies the average citizen has remained remarkably sanguine about the prospect of being viewed and recorded.

At the end of the decade though, a universal system is more or less effectively in place—the product not of a government plan, but of the semi-chaotic interplay of Google's mapping ambitions and the wide-spread embrace of social networking—whereby an extraordinary amount of public and private activity is recorded, uploaded and shared online.

So, in the space of ten years we have gone from a dystopic fantasy-fear of universal surveillance, through chaotic manifestation involving multiple, largely non-centralized, viewing systems, to a new reality whereby surveillance is becoming primarily a citizen (or consumer) activity, standing alongside the comparatively sluggish state systems that seek to monitor or control us.

How did this transformation from deep-seated fear of surveillance, to a largely apathetic acceptance, to an apparent ecstasy of engagement, occur? The story of surveillance has turned out, it could be argued, to be less one of technology, government, law or rights, than one of cultural practice. It is the way in which we have come to produce and exchange surveillance of ourselves that is defining the experience of surveillance going into the second decade of the twenty-first century.

This entry is a journey through a series of cultural artefacts relating to surveillance. Some are artworks responding to surveillance, some are media and corporate products engaging with and exploiting shifting public perceptions, and some are cultural practices in the sense of surveillance-based activities by members of the public revealing prevalent attitudes and shifting norms. The unifying characteristic of all the examples explored is that they, in some way, perform surveillance—make of it not just a subject for commentary, but a practice through which subjects reimagine themselves. The entry will explore these performances of surveillance in relation to the three periods broadly suggested above. (It is worth reading alongside Kammerer's parallel survey of surveillance in Literature, Film and Television.)

The warning period

Whereas the great dystopic visions of surveillance society largely dealt with technology that was at that point only a fantasy, in the 1970s video recording became sufficiently available for many visual and performance artists to start exploring the artistic potential of the technologies. One of the figures who engaged most rigorously with the potentialities of video surveillance in art was Bruce Nauman. Two pieces of work by Nauman demonstrate the range and impact of his artistic enquiry.

Going Around the Corner Piece (1970) consists of four video cameras and four monitors placed at the corners of a large square of wooden walls. The cameras and monitors are arranged in such a way that, as viewers turn the corner around the outer edge of the wooden square, they see a rear view of their own body in the monitor ahead. As they complete the movement around the corner, the image of the body turns around the corner on the monitor ahead, and disappears from sight. The piece creates the effect of pursuing one's own image around the corners of the square. The effect is produced simply by having a camera send an image to a monitor diagonally opposite. Viewers can only see themselves in the monitor as they are turning the corner because only then are they both in view of the camera behind them and able to see the monitor around the corner in front. Inevitably the viewer speeds up, hoping to catch up. Equally inevitably, the image speeds up too. Despite understanding the logic of the piece quite quickly, viewers often stay with it for a while, circulating at different speeds, tantalized by the impossible possibility of catching their own images. As this impossibility of encountering one's own image, mirror-like, is established, the desirability of such an encounter grows. Seeing one's self perpetually disappearing around the corner, glanced from behind, the longing for a meeting with this particular self-image intensifies.

In this deceptively simple, brilliantly conceptualized art work, Nauman warned us not that Big Brother was out to get us, but that our engagement with surveillance over the coming years was likely to be far more complex than generally prophesied. Going Around the Corner Piece indicated that, among many other things, narcissistic desire, and our fascination with the borders of the image, were likely to impact substantially on our lives under surveillance.

A second piece by Nauman, Learned Helplessness in Rats (Rock and Roll Drummer) (1988), seems, on the surface, a more direct commentary on the politics of surveillance. The installation is usually shown in a partially walled-off gallery area where a rotating surveillance camera watches an empty Plexiglas maze about nine inches high. The live image of the maze is transmitted on a monitor, but it is alternated with recorded footage of the same maze with rats running inside. Meanwhile a video projector shows a rock drummer, while the sound of the drums plays loudly over speakers. It is a disorienting piece to view—the doubling of the empty maze with the rat-filled maze plus the movements of the camera and the high volume drumming lead to an initial confusion. There seems to be a lot happening in the maze, though in fact nothing is happening. The space is restructured by the surveillance doubling; empty Plexiglas easily viewed from above becomes an anxiety-ridden labyrinth in which terrifying animals may be lurking.

Nauman's use of rats, of course, refers us to the closing scenes of Orwell's Big Brother, where Winston Smith's phobia of rats is the thing that is finally used to break his resistance to the state. The rock and roll drummer also seems to predict the use of extreme noise in US counter-insurgency practice. However, once again, the piece does far more than warn us that we are being treated like rats in an experiment.

Learned Helplessness … suggests that, rather than guarding us against crime and unpleasantness, surveillance imagery may introduce demons into the spaces we inhabit. The rat introduced in this piece does not disappear once we realize the emptiness of the maze. Under the auditory stress of the high volume drumming, we worry about the rat, about why it has been introduced, about the way in which it separates the maze from its images, the images from each other. The present meaning of the work becomes dependent upon the surveillance insertion of what has been removed.

Nauman is exploring the ways in which the constant presence of the watching camera, rather than fixing reality, starts to multiply and complexify it.

Another visual/conceptual artist who embraced the possibilities of surveillance at an early stage was Sophie Calle. Unlike Nauman, Calle was not particularly engaged with the ways in which emerging video technologies impacted upon the artist's studio or the gallery space, or in making artefacts incorporating these technologies. Rather Calle focused on the ways in which the personal practice of surveillance impacted upon the self, the psyche, and the prospect of any relationship with another.

Among many artworks in which Calle has acted sometimes as surveyor and sometimes at the subject of surveillance, one emblematic piece is The Shadow (1981) in which Calle hired a private detective, through an intermediary, to place her under surveillance for a day (the detective did not know that his employer was also the subject). The resulting artwork includes passages written by Calle in which she describes her experience of being followed, her attempts to identify the detective and her decisions about what places and parts of her life to show her follower. Alongside these beautifully written journal entries run the detective's records of Calle's movements, both written and photographic. The difference between the records—between Calle's construction of herself in the detective's eyes, and the detective's actual experience and judgments—alongside the simple exposure of inevitable inaccuracy (the detective finishes work early, claiming Calle has gone to bed when she has actually gone to a party)—demonstrate that surveillance is far better at opening gaps and creating new vectors of desire than it is at fixing facts.

In other work, Calle has, rather more controversially, inhabited the position of the spy. In Suite Venitienne (1979), she followed and photographed a man she had met randomly at a party—publishing the photographs and her notes as an artwork. In another piece, Address Book (1983), she used a lost address book that she had discovered by accident as a starting point—calling numbers in the address book and talking to the people who answered in an attempt to establish a picture of the owner. As well as being fascinating artworks that tell us much about the ways in which surveillance activity would come to structure our psyches, the controversies surrounding these early works by Calle reveal a lot about the nature of the public discourse about surveillance in this early period. The artist's more controversial projects have tended to involve Calle exposing details about the lives of middle-class men, presenting them as objects of desire or fascination, and presenting to the world, without their knowledge, elements of their lives which, while not exactly private, were assumed to have gone unnoticed. Calle introduces us to the prospect that, in a society where surveillance becomes common currency, the socially accepted vectors of visibility and desire may be turned on their heads, and warns us that the loudest claims for privacy are likely to be made by those who feel their privileges are endangered.

The gendered nature of surveillance is heightened further in work by Mona Hatoum. In Corps Etranger (1994) and Deep Throat (1996), the artist uses an endoscopic camera inserted inside the orifices and passages of her own body to create footage of spaces rarely seen. The reference to the famous porn film Deep Throat reminds us that the voyeuristic need to penetrate the unseen is neither neutral nor innocent, but Hatoum creates artistic environments from her footage of her own throat and intestines that are very different from any sexual fantasies. In Corps Etranger we stand in a booth surrounded by the footage of Hatoum's innards. In Deep Throat the footage is projected on a plate, and we are invited to sit at the table to consume it. Hatoum reminds us that beyond the street cameras there are numerous other disciplines, from the medical to the military, where the new capacity to see and record is having impact, and that our deepest psychological fears and fantasies will resonate through all of these surveillance phenomena.

Performance art and theatre were also fertile territories for the early exploration of surveillance and video technologies in this "warning period." Downtown New York artists from the 1970s to the 1990s were particularly advanced in their explorations of the potentials for video technologies in live performance (not least no doubt because of the close relationships between these companies and the visual arts scene in New York). Key avant-garde company Mabou Mines developed one of the first combinations of both live and recorded video with live performance in Haj (1983), significantly staging this work as a solo performance by a woman seated at a three-mirrored dressing table (the video monitors were concealed in the mirrors and the audience sat facing the monitor-mirrors). From its first use onstage, the exploration of live video was intimately tied up with the questions of self-reflection: "vanity."

If Mabou Mines delved consciously into the psychology and politics of newly available video technologies in performance, it was another downtown New York company, The Wooster Group, which, in the 1980s and 1990s, made the integration of video into live performance the signature of a new kind of theatre. In a series of landmark productions during those decades, the company explored how the three "tracks" of live performance, recorded video and live video could work to complicate and enrich the theatrical space and the relationship of the audience to the performance. TV monitors were a staple of these Wooster Group performances, often pushed around the stage by the performers. Live video cameras would transmit hidden action to the monitors—echoing Nauman's instinct that it is the edges of the image that fascinate us in surveillance. In one of the company's greatest performances, Brace Up (1991) (based on Chekhov's Three Sisters), much of the action that is most center stage in the original play—the family meal for example—was performed at the edges of the stage, largely obscured from the audience, but transmitted via live cameras and microphones. One of the characters, Anfisa, the aging nanny, was played by an actress who couldn't leave her nursing home and so was presented as a recording, and other actors were sometimes presented on video if they couldn't make the show that night. The Wooster Group seemed to be proposing that we were entering a world where the nature of presence itself was changing. All of this came to a disturbing and moving head with the death of Ron Vawter, one of their founding members and a performer central to most of the company's work. Through the multiple video recordings of Vawter that had been developed for current and upcoming projects, he continued to have a real and complex presence in much of the company's work, highlighting questions of presence and absence all the more, and introducing the idea that, in a surveyed society, we might come to experience death in a very different way.

On a general social level, the proliferation of surveillance technology during this period was largely experienced through the prism of crime prevention, and the process went at very different speeds in different countries, as a result of differing legal frameworks and political contexts. The UK was widely considered to be the country where the deployment of surveillance cameras (usually called CCTV or Closed Circuit Television at that time in the UK) in public spaces happened most rapidly. TV programs such as Crimewatch UK supported the political discourse in favor of this deployment by engaging the public in a weekly ritual of surveillance viewing. Watching a carefully selected range of imagery, TV audiences were encouraged to believe that they could help solve crimes through their response to footage from the CCTV cameras which had, within a decade, become endemic in Britain's streets and shops. (See McCahill in this volume for a wider discussion of Crimewatch and similar programs.)

Crimewatch UK and its equivalents worldwide were probably the emblematic mass media products of surveillance technology during this "warning period." Like the avant garde art works of Nauman and The Wooster Group, the TV show demonstrated the addictive appeal of never quite seeing enough. The premise of Crimewatch UK, after all, was that this CCTV footage had not so far provided sufficient evidence to solve the crimes under consideration—it demanded our obsessive engagement to fill its seductive gaps (see also Norris, this volume).

The emerging complexity of the public's response to surveillance was demonstrated forcefully in one of the most famous and most tragic cases of CCTV crime recording—the James Bulger murder (see McCahill, this volume). Not unlike Ron Vawter for The Wooster Group, James Bulger became a newly present figure in his death. We saw images of a small child being led away by two not much bigger children, and this seemingly naïve image became horrific in retrospect. Through the proliferation of surveillance, we had learned something that we might not have wanted to know, but that we could not afford to forget. The inherent ambivalence of the Bulger case continued to haunt discourse around CCTV in the UK and beyond. There was a skepticism around the effectiveness of the technology in relation to the crime-prevention claims made for it, and yet there was a hunger for its implementation, for its capacity to show us more about ourselves and society than, perhaps, we had previously imagined we wanted to know.

However, the idea that surveillance might be a source of pleasure, something actively pursued, was left to a few artists to explore: a situation that was all about to change entirely.

The Little Brothers period

The TV show Big Brother first premiered in the Netherlands in 1999, and had soon been franchised across much of the globe. The essential format, where a group of "housemates" compete to stay in a house under 24-hour surveillance has stayed remarkably consistent in all of the programme's incarnations. While Big Brother was by no means the first example of what became known as "reality TV," it was the first to centralize the concept of 24-hour surveillance as the key organizing principle. Viewers often became obsessed with watching the most uneventful of broadcasts—staying awake to watch the housemates sleep. The seemingly counter-intuitive fascination of surveillance explored by Nauman and others—the idea that it is the edges, the not quite seen, that seduce us—turned out to have a mass-market application. And the psychologies of narcissism and reflection explored in early artworks like Haj turned out to be rich sources of public pleasure.

The public response to Big Brother was complex (McGrath, 2004), but one element worth focusing on here is the attitude of the contestants. Though widely seen as naïve and in search of some form of easy celebrity, participants in the program would, when interviewed, usually talk about their reasons for taking part in terms of the challenge of the show itself, focusing on what they might learn about themselves, or simply on their love of the format. Rather than being naïve, it could be argued that Big Brother contestants were instinctively engaging with one of the most significant shifts in behavior and identity of their lifetimes. They were exploring who they would become under 24-hour surveillance—and discovering a difference between those surveiled selves and their former "private" identities. They were enjoying the thrill of surveillance living, and the disruption of the top-down viewing structures of traditional media.

During this same decade a number of artists explored the proliferation of surveillance in enlightening ways. At this point digital video and audio technology had advanced massively, and surveillance had become a more prominent social concern. Key artists often chose to explore the social structures surrounding surveillance.

Perhaps the most thorough investigation of surveillance practice in the context of visual arts has been undertaken by Julia Scher. In a series of installations and web-based projects, Scher has played very productively both with the actual mechanics and technology of setting up surveillance systems, and with the semantics and iconography surrounding these systems. Scher's gallery installations are usually fully functioning surveillance environments, but imagery will be distorted and presented back in unexpected ways, and the trappings of the system will be playfully deconstructed. In a series of installations under the group title of Security by Julia, Scher has interrogated both the human and the technological aspects of these systems, often using humour to make her point. One exhibition was staffed by old ladies dressed as security guards in pink uniforms. In another, American Fibroids (1996), young male security guards, again in pink, supervised tables of the "bits and pieces" of the security trade: badges, hats, old hard drives, pass cards, ropes, cameras, T-shirts, arranged as though for sale—"a cross between a security fleamarket and a sex shop," in Timothy Druckrey's description (Druckrey, *Art and Text*, May 1996). Scher's giddy, camp engagement in the stuff of surveillance (other highlights include the Children's Guard Station (1998)—a full, child-size guard's security desk in Fisher-Price colors)—demonstrates an art whose creator desires not only auto-reproduction, but the systems of security themselves, and who imagines the surveillance machine desiring back: "I offer distinguished and ambient space. I am full and waiting for you," announces the soundtrack to American Fibroids. "It's who you play, not who you are. Come into my area now. Please loosen my access control." Scher often highlights the fact that, far from a powerful Big Brother figure, security systems are usually staffed by poorly paid, poorly trained workers, given the trappings of a police-like uniform, but with little real institutional status. The power dynamics of surveillance are not straightforward.

Scher's artworks also disrupt the perceived neutrality of surveillance systems by talking back to us, and establishing their own personalities. Her website Wonderland (1997) asks us to enter the following data:

Are you afraid of the Future? Yes/No

Do you abuse yourself? Yes/No

What advances in technology frighten you?

Once we have entered our replies and clicked, the page changes and a voice comes through our computer speakers:

Your data has been downloaded. You are no longer important to us.

Another version of us—a surveillance version—has, Scher implies, been created, and has become more important than our original selves.

The ways in which the multiple Little Brothers of corporate surveillance systems were coming to affect our very sense of self, and particularly the ways in which our data might be part of this transformation, was a key concern of "surveillance art" in this period. While the narcissistic fascinations of visual surveillance were publicly embraced and examined on TV, several artists started to explore the ways in which the non-visual realms of surveillance were starting to assert themselves. In their theatre piece Super Vision (2005) multi-media New York company The Builders Association developed a digital stage environment where they could imagine the "data bodies" developed by a series of characters in multiple, interweaving narratives. In one story, for example, a father uses his young son's data to create a new credit-worthy self, borrowing and trading on the basis of his son's unsullied records. The production imagines this data-son, growing up far more quickly than his flesh-and-blood equivalent, using digital modeling to bring a projection of the data-body into the stage world. In another story, a frequent flier is pursued by the information gathered about him at various immigration points. We are, the production suggests, no longer solely, or perhaps even primarily, our real-world selves. The data that flows through cyber-space about us sometimes has a far more significant impact on our lives than our actual actions.

Whereas The Builders Association chose to create an extraordinary visual representation of the unseeable aspects of surveillance, other companies have tried to take us into the datasphere in a more immersive way. UK company Blast Theory have the longest and arguably the most successful track record in this area. Their investigation into the seductiveness of surveillance began in a fairly low-tech way with Kidnap (1998). For this piece the company recruited volunteers for a potential kidnap. Of the people who wrote in to apply, a number were put under surveillance by the company—recording their daily movements from a camera-packed, blacked out van. Eventually two "victims" were actually kidnapped, and placed in a "safe house" where their movements were videoed and broadcast on the web. The piece demonstrated our fascinated pleasure in the narratives of surveillance, just the moment before Big Brother was launched upon the TV-viewing world.

In future work Blast Theory became far more engaged with technology, and particularly the relationship between online and "real-world." In Uncle Roy All Around You (2003), the company mapped the streets in the area where the piece was to be performed/played, and created an infrastructure where audience-participants could choose whether to play online or on the real streets (real world players carried small devices allowing them to communicate with online players and to interact with the virtual map of the space they were navigating). Both groups needed to develop negotiation and navigation skills partly dependent on their relationship with the figures in the other sphere, as they searched for the mysterious "Uncle Roy." Ultimately the piece explored the notion of trust online, asking participants the question "When can you begin to trust a stranger?" Success in the game depended on forming a trusting relationship with a player on the other side of the digital divide. At the end of the game, successful street and online players were invited to extend the commitment of trust:

> Somewhere in the game there is a stranger who is also answering these questions. Are you willing to make a commitment to that person that you will be available for them if they have a crisis? The commitment will last for 12 months and, in return, they will commit to you for the same period.

Of course acting on this invitation, or dismissing it as the rhetoric of the game, was a choice for the players, but the possibility of a dramatic commitment to a stranger who was only known across the digital divide was real.

Blast Theory introduce a complexity, a sensuality and an emotional resonance, to the world of digital identities. They emphasize the separateness of the bodily and digital worlds, but also their capacity to affect each other in ways that have little to do with statistical information.

In the "Little Brothers" period of our developing surveillance culture, the key discovery was, perhaps, that just as there were multiple, often contradictory systems observing us, so there were multiple, contradictory selves produced by this surveillance. From Big Brother contestants, to Blast Theory game players, we were starting to perform and play with these multiple selves. And we were seeing the possibility that such performances might be more effective responses to the controlling impulses of surveillance systems than any amount of privacy protection.

The social surveillance period

I recently attended a performance by a student comedian aged around 20. It was close to Halloween and he was wondering what it might be like to be a ghost. "If I died and became a ghost," he pondered, "the first thing I'd do is … " He paused. "Well, the first thing I'd do of course is update my Facebook status."

In the second decade of the twenty-first century we have entered a world in which letting the maximum possible number of people know our moods, our whereabouts, our opinions, our plans, and even our relationship to the afterlife has become, for many of us, a social necessity. With the development of Web 2.0 applications that depend on networking and interactivity as opposed to simply information retrieval we have embraced a reality where the amount of information we share online has gone from the simple data of credit checks and government records to a vast wealth of constantly updated narrative, imagery and emotional content. (See Bruno in this volume for a comprehensive overview of Web 2.0 participatory surveillance.)

As predicted by artists such as Julia Scher and Blast Theory, the surveillance-data-sphere leads not to a fixing of identity, but to an eternal multiplication of selves, some of them in our control, some of them very much not.

This network of surveillance selves is driven by a complexity of emotions, obsessions, desires. As Bruce Nauman predicted, we are quick to engage in the pursuit of our surveillance selves, and to imagine doubles and ghosts just around the corner. One thing we seem to have no desire to do is to limit the proliferation.

A more somber version of our student comedian's concerns is evidenced in the many memorial sites that now populate Facebook and other profile-based networks. When an individual dies, their profile often becomes the location of a continuing dialogue, not only about, but often with the deceased person, where friends, acquaintances and strangers express their thoughts, and engage in a one-way conversation with the dead. On these memorial sites the personality of the individual can seem to mutate—often into a kind of contemporary sainthood, and parties and hook-ups are still planned—in the afterlife or some distant digital equivalent. Such sites are a particularly stark example of the realities of digital identity. Once sufficient data is circulating about us, it may be able to live on without our involvement.

The art that is growing out of social networks often lacks the kind of curiosity about technology that characterized the early instances of surveillance art. With technologies of surveillance so omnipresent, artists are often more interested in the emerging forms of human relationship that these technologies have helped give birth to. So, there is an increasing instance of performance-based work that takes its structures from interactive gaming, but without employing any gaming technology at all (companies such as Hide and Seek, Coney and Punchdrunk in the UK). This work is often focused on the creation of social relationships and structures among the "players," and on the taking on and losing of identities.

The exploration of what in our lives can make a claim to "reality," is another key theme. German company Rimini Protokoll are among the leaders of a theatre movement which often puts "real" people on stage to explore a subject in which they are, in some way, "specialists." For Call Cutta (2005), the company wanted to explore the relationship we have with call centers and the ways in which call centers approach us and deal with our data. Starting with an investigation of the "reality" under question, Rimini Protokoll developed the performance by setting up a fully-functioning call center in Calcutta, which audiences in Berlin could call to experience the performance. The call center operators were trained at length in the details of customer service and manipulation, but rather than having the normal goal of making a sale, or imparting a piece of information in the minimum time possible, these operators were attempting to take the audience members on an emotional journey which might include everything from surrendering to childhood memories to falling in love over the phone. The performers had scripts which drew on the kinds of options and routes that guide the calls made by call center sales teams, but their scripts drew attention to exactly the kind of things that call center calls are usually structured to hide—distance, history, geography and the personality of the call center operator.

Call Cutta introduced emotion and personal relations into what is usually a banal exchange of data. However, the piece did not create a hierarchy of realities—claiming that the emotional relationships explored in the piece were in any way more or less real than other tele-encounters. Rather, the piece demonstrated how, in our networked world, distant data selves can form relationships as emotionally intimate and economically difficult as our encounters in the family or on the street.

Art works such as Call Cutta are helping us to engage with the new reality of what might be called a post-surveillance society, a reality where the question is no longer how much of our life is seen and recorded, but how many versions of our life or self are generated. Within this world of selves we will be living with a new set of connections and consequences, from the economic to the emotional. Our post-surveillance performances will help us discover how.

References

Druckrey, T. (1996). "Julia Scher: Telephobic Modernity and the Ecologies of Surveillance," *Art and Text*, May: 50–53.
McGrath, J. (2004). *Loving Big Brother*, London: Routledge.

b. Ubiquitous surveillance

Mark Andrejevic

One of the indisputable facts of the digital era is that we are living in a time when more information is gathered, collected, sorted and stored about the everyday activities of more people in the world than at any other time in human history. This is in part a result of the technological possibilities created by digital interactivity—that networked devices can record how (and when and where) they are used—but it is also the result of economic choices about how to support the information infrastructure upon which growing numbers of people are becoming increasingly reliant. The global privatization of the network infrastructure and the commercialization of the applications that rely upon it have led to the development of an advertising-based model that exploits the interactive capacity of digital media to enable more sophisticated and detailed forms of consumer monitoring in the service of increasingly targeted advertising and marketing appeals (see Turow and Draper, this volume).

This commercial model is not the sole economic model for networked digital media, which rely upon a range of funding schemes, including subscription-based services, one-time purchases, and, in some nations, state support. However, the economic model that spans a growing range of networked applications, from Google to Facebook to a wide assortment of mobile applications, is based on interactive advertising which in turn depends upon the collection of detailed information about user behavior, background, and preferences. One result has been the multiplication of outlets, applications, and platforms that gather information about users. Even the code that runs the world wide web is being updated to allow applications of all kinds to view much more detailed information about user activity and behavior.

The digital realm is by no means the only one in which monitoring takes place, nor are commercial ends the only ones served by surveillance technologies and practices. However, digital technology has augmented the scope and range of surveillance systems new and old. Networked devices like mobile phones and laptops facilitate the collection of detailed information about user behavior while older databases move into digital form that can be more readily searched, sorted, and mined. Even audio and visual forms of surveillance can be digitized to make storage cheaper and easier and to enhance search and data recognition technology. Digital technology is, for example, crucial to the development of cameras that can recognize faces and compare them with stored databases of images. In addition to commercial entities, security and policing organizations, both public and private, are becoming increasingly reliant upon digitized surveillance equipment and the copious amounts of data collected by the private sector, finding ways to piggy-back on existing databases or to subcontract data collection and sorting.

Broadly construed, then, the notion of ubiquitous surveillance refers to the prospect of a world in which it becomes increasingly difficult to escape the proliferating technologies for data collection, storage, and sorting—the fact that, as David Lyon puts it, "our whole way of life in the contemporary world is suffused with surveillance" (2007: 25). As he notes, the notion of ubiquitous surveillance can be related in certain respects to the development of ubiquitous computing. To the extent that networked forms of interactive communication become pervasive, they enhance and extend the monitoring process because they can gather information about user activity. There is, necessarily, a spatial component to the notion of ubiquity: as interactivity migrates into new spaces, the capability for monitoring arrives with it. The prospect of so-called ubiquitous computing is frequently portrayed as a projection upon the physical world of the capability of networked interactivity to "recognize" users and register their traces.

This version of interactivity might be considered the ultimate digital rejoinder to the anonymity of the modern urban environment: the creation of spaces that will recognize us wherever we go, responding to our presence in ways that incorporate information about our histories, desires, needs, and wants. For example, South Korean and US developers envision literalizing this vision of an interactive city in sub-urban Seoul with their plans for New Songdo City, which will be equipped not just with wireless networking, but with haptic technology and ubiquitous radio-frequency ID tagging that lets residents know whether they have placed their recyclables in the right bin and sounds an alarm if someone falls and is unable to get up. These are spaces of convenience, assistance, and efficiency, but they are also spaces equipped with an unprecedented potential for repression.

So-called "smart" spaces that recognize us and play our favorite music, respond to our queries, provide us with recommendations, or let us enter and exit restricted spaces to which we have been granted access need to know who we are, the details of our personal preferences, our movements, perhaps even our background histories and our desires, hopes, and dreams. If the goal of ubiquitous computing is, as MIT's Project Oxygen initiative puts it, to bring "abundant computation and communication, as pervasive and free as air, naturally into people's lives," it does the same thing for surveillance (MIT Project Oxygen 2004).

Embedding computer chips into the surrounding environment is not the only way to make it interactive and thus subject to monitoring. The development of portable mobile devices renders any space covered by the wireless networks that support them interactive—to varying degrees. Mobile phones, for example, can gather information about users' time-space path during the course of the day—and have been used by police to locate suspects' whereabouts and to monitor traffic flow. Applications that run on those phones and other portable networked devices can provide more detailed information about user activity, as can applications running on laptop computers. Interactive digital television recorders like TiVo also capture detailed information about user behavior—with an eye to using it for target marketing. The use of radio frequency identification (RFID) tags on items ranging from consumer goods to delivery trucks creates another level of interactivity: information about the movement and the properties of these items can be remotely scanned and stored via radio waves. Similarly, as a range of digital interactive devices go mobile, they become more individualized, following users throughout the course of the day and providing enhanced addressability: a mobile phone is associated with an individual user in a way that household land line phones or shared desktop computers are not.

We might describe the spaces "covered" by various communication networks that render them interactive (for applications ranging from internet access and television viewing to mobile telephony, GPS devices, eBooks, and so on) as spaces that have been enclosed by information architectures that make monitoring possible. Such networks can be wired, as in the case of fiber-optic internet connections, or wireless, as in the case of mobile phone networks and RFID scanners. We might specify the coverage range of any surveillance technology as the space (or spaces), virtual or physical, which it "encloses." Digital enclosures are those created by the interactive and data storage capabilities of digital media technologies (Andrejevic 2007). An RFID enclosure would be created by the range of the device that is able to scan RFID tags as they move through space. The virtue of this type of description is that it traces the relationship between a material, spatial process—the interactive overlay of physical space—and the capture of information. Moreover it highlights one of the historical resonances of the notion of "enclosure"—the separation of users from the product of their activity enabled by the capture of control over the productive resources they use. When interactive resources are owned or controlled by one group of people but used by others—as in the case of online platforms like Facebook or applications like Google—some of the productive activity of users can be captured and put to work by those who control the infrastructure. Monitoring, in this context, refers to the collection of information—with or without the knowledge of users—that has actual or speculative value for economic or policing purposes. The notion of a digital enclosure suggests that ubiquitous interactivity also has the potential to facilitate unprecedented commodification of previously non-proprietary information as well as to enable centralized control over a range of information resources. Information that previously went uncaptured—about people's time-space paths through the course of the day, the details of when and where they chat with their friends, even the random queries that drift through their minds (to the extent that these are transformed into Google searches) can be cheaply captured, stored, and sorted.

The internet itself can serve as a form of interactive enclosure—both wired and wireless—as evidenced, for example, by the ability to monitor and control remote applications. As anyone who pays attention to customized ads or online news feeds knows, many online applications already "know" where a user is located thanks to the machine's IP address. The metaphor of a digital enclosure makes it possible to describe different levels and kinds of monitoring. Not only are enclosures owned and controlled by different entities, but their technological capabilities and the scope of data collection vary widely. Access to interactive resources is non-uniform in several respects—not all regions and areas are equally equipped and different areas may have very different capabilities for information gathering and different objectives for its use. We can thus talk about different types of overlapping, intersecting, and embedded interactive enclosures—mobile phone networks, wireless internet networks, smart card readers, credit card systems, ATM networks, and so on. Each has a differing ability to provide access to information and other resources and to collect different types of information under different circumstances. We might include other types of surveillance and tracking technologies—RFID tag readers, CCTV networks, and so on, as tracing their own monitored spaces, some circumscribed by visibility, others by the reach of electromagnetic signals or sound waves.

Rather than a uniformly monitored space, then, we could map how a particular space is overlaid with varying (sometimes overlapping) surveillance capabilities. At one extreme we might envision a space that is entirely "off the grid"—beyond the embrace of monitoring and recording devices—if not beyond the reach of the human gaze or ear; at the other, a fully monitored space, permeated by available surveillance technologies, able not simply to observe, but to record and store, aggregate and sort a variety of information. Both extremes are ideal types rather than existing spaces: there is no endpoint of total surveillance; new dimensions for monitoring develop along with the uses of information and the creation of new technologies. The claim of accounts of ubiquitous surveillance is that spaces of the former type are becoming increasingly rare—and that there is a convergence of a range of technologies and applications toward the latter.

However, the notion of a fully-monitored space can be misleading insofar as it suggests centralized control and access to captured information by a digital-era Big Brother. The model of overlapping surveillance enclosures describes more accurately a world characterized by a proliferation of different monitoring networks with varying capabilities for information capture under the control of different entities. This is not to rule out the possibility that data might be aggregated under centralized control under certain circumstances. The ability of authorities in some jurisdictions to access commercial databases, for example, would make it possible to collect under one umbrella a range of data originally captured by different entities for varying purposes. Also, to the extent that certain platforms devised by companies like Google or Facebook might serve as the basis for a range of different activities, commercial entities have the ability to aggregate large swathes of data under their control.

The notion of multiple, overlapping monitored enclosures, with different capabilities and purposes, is captured by Haggerty and Ericson's description of a "surveillant assemblage" comprising interlinked technologies and practices that serve a range of desires, including those for "control, governance, security, profit and entertainment" (2000: 509). Not only is such an assemblage composed of different types of surveillance with varying degrees and types of interconnection, it also enables the migration of information collected for one purpose across a range of other, sometimes unanticipated functions. Thus, for example, cell phones seeking the nearest tower also supply information that can be used to track traffic flow. Similarly, information posted to a website for one purpose can be "scraped" by automated applications for a range of other purposes, from marketing to policing to background checking. By the same token, different groups of people are subject to different components of the surveillant assemblage. Those without access to some of the interactive technologies that capture detailed personal information might nevertheless be subject to restrictions on their ability to travel, thanks to their inclusion on a no-fly list, or they might find themselves captured by webcams installed at border crossings. Whereas monitoring can facilitate access to goods and services for some, it can also be used to exclude others. Surveillance, as Oscar Gandy (1993) has noted, is not just a form of oversight, it is also the power to sort and differentially target individuals for everything from further investigation to access to special commercial offers. Typically, relatively affluent groups and places are subject to more comprehensive forms of commercial monitoring, whereas less affluent groups and places are targeted by policing and security-oriented forms of monitoring.

Convergence and ubiquitous surveillance go hand in hand, undermining clear-cut boundaries between state and commercial surveillance, policing and marketing. The CIA's investment arm, for example, has purchased an interest in so-called "sentiment analysis" start-ups that scour blogs, social networking sites, and online chats to provide a real-time analysis of conversations about brands, policies, public figures, and anything else that people might be writing about. Conversely, private data companies tap into public databases—where available—of property records, criminal records, automobile registrations, court filings, and so on—in order to build comprehensive profiles that can be used for marketing, background checking, and security contracting. In the USA and elsewhere, post-9/11 security regimes have engaged in extensive subcontracting with commercial database companies. Commercial databases of all kinds become tempting information troves for law enforcement agencies seeking data about individual suspects or about patterns of what counts as suspicious behavior. In one notorious case, for example, the US Federal Bureau of Investigation sought information from supermarkets about the sales of Middle Eastern food in the San Francisco area as part of a plan to track down Iranian spies. State authorities often have the power to pressure private applications or networks not just to gather data but also to restrict access to resources or information.

The FBI's use of supermarket records highlights a telling shift in how data is thought about and used in an era of ubiquitous surveillance. When data is cheap and plentiful the temptation is to accumulate the data first and find uses for it later. Targeted surveillance is supplanted (or supplemented) by the monitoring of entire populations. Instead of first identifying a suspect or a target and then researching it, the development of ubiquitous surveillance envisions the prospect of obtaining an overview of populations that will allow potential targets (for marketing or policing) to emerge from the data itself thanks to algorithms that search for "suspicious" behavior. In the case of marketing, data collection at the level of the population as a whole makes it possible to search for unanticipated correlations with predictive power (that, say, people who buy a particular brand of car are more likely to vote for a particular political party, and so on). Both forms of surveillance depend upon the capture of as complete a portrait of the population as possible. To put it in slightly different terms, ubiquitous surveillance technology goes hand in hand with surveillance practices that rely upon comprehensive population monitoring. When such practices prove inaccurate or flawed, the proposed remedy is often more detailed surveillance. There is no logical endpoint to the amount of data required by such systems—no clear point at which marketers or the police can draw the line and say no more information is needed. *All* information is potentially relevant because it helps reveal patterns and correlations.

At least three strategies peculiar to the forms of population-level monitoring facilitated by ubiquitous surveillance in digital enclosures have become central to emerging forms of data-driven commerce and security: predictive analytics, sentiment analysis, and controlled experimentation. Predictive analytics relies upon mining behavioral patterns, demographic information, and any other relevant or available data in order to predict future actions. For marketers, the goal of predictive analytics is, in a sense, both pre-emptive and productive: to manage risks before they emerge or become serious while at the same time maximizing sales. For security purposes, predictive analytics serves the purpose of the psychic "precogs" in the film *Minority Report*: as a means of anticipating and averting future crimes, threats, or risks. The difference, however, is that predictive analytics is actuarial in the sense that it does not make definitive claims about the future acts of particular individuals, rather it traffics in probabilities, parsing groups and individuals according to how well they fit patterns that can be predicted with known levels of accuracy. Predictive analytics relies on the collection of as much information as possible, not to drill down into individual activities, but to unearth new patterns, linkages, and correlations.

Sentiment analysis also relies on strategies for monitoring a population in its entirety. The goal is to take the emotional pulse of the internet as a whole—in real time. It is a strategy directly linked to the rise of the so-called "social web"—the popularity of a range of applications that facilitate various kinds of communicative networks, from blogging and social networking sites to comment and feedback pages to messaging utilities like Twitter. Sentiment analysis is based on the notion that such sites provide a real-time glimpse into the feelings of millions of people on myriad topics. It is a monitoring strategy that takes advantage of the fact that the content of online conversations—often intended only for those involved in the discussion—can be captured, aggregated and sorted once posted online.

Highlighting the convergence between media monitoring old and new, the Nielsen Company—well known for its ratings service—has developed online applications that automatically cut and paste comments from online discussions in order to track what is being said about products and services online. So called "data scrapers" downplay the threat to privacy by saying they are not interested in tracking specific comments back to particular users—rather they are interested in an aggregate picture, a kind of real-time spot poll. Hence the imperative to accumulate as much data as possible. Sentiment analysis and "mood analysis" applications troll through twitter feeds, blogs, social networking sites, online forums, bulletin boards, and chat rooms, probing the emotional pulse of the internet. The goal is not comprehension, but instantaneous and ongoing mechanized monitoring of aggregate flows.

Such applications frequently invoke the language of "listening" with its overtones of attentiveness, dialogism, and response. But it is a particular kind of listening in which no one individual message is being heard. What takes place instead is an ongoing search for patterns. Thus the rhetoric of listening readily slips into that of visibility, with its connotations of monitoring and oversight. Companies talk about the ability of their applications to peer into online venues and get a glimpse of what people are saying. These are formulations that invoke the familiar equation (in the age of reality TV) of eavesdropping with authenticity. Unlike opinion polls, sentiment analysis relies on "real" conversations insofar as people are not aware their comments are being monitored by interested parties. The goal, for example, is for drug companies to hear how their products are being described in health forums, for car companies to learn what people like or dislike about their new designs, for politicians to learn what people *really* think about their proposed policies—or slightly more nefariously, what people say about controversial issues when they are not aware that outsiders may be listening in. The goal is a version of transparency enabled by the combination of the ability to capture a range of interactions that become "visible"—or at least recordable—once they migrate into a monitored enclosure.

Sentiment analysis represents the commercial embrace and reconfiguration of the role of feedback in so-called "convergence culture" (Jenkins 2006): the ability for consumers to make their voices heard via interactive technologies. It creates ad hoc brand or issue communities, built not by consumers with shared interests but by search algorithms that assemble conversations or posts about particular brands and topics. In combination with predictive analytics, the goal of sentiment analysis is both pre-emptive and productive: to minimize negative sentiment and maximize emotional investment and engagement; not merely to record sentiment as a given but to modulate it as a variable. Modulation means constant adjustment designed to bring the anticipated consequences of a modeled future into the present so as to account for these in ways that might, in turn, reshape that future. If, for example, sentiment analysis reveals resistance to a particular policy or concerns about a brand or issue, the goal is to manage these sentiments in ways that accord with the interests of those who control, capture, and track the data. The goal is not just the monitoring of populations but also their management.

Such forms of management require more than monitoring and recording a population—they also subject it to ongoing experimentation. This is the form that predictive analytics takes in the age of what Ian Ayres (2007) calls super-crunching: not simply the attempt to get at an underlying demographic or emotional "truth"; not even the ongoing search for useful correlations, but also the ongoing *generation* of such correlations. In the realm of marketing, for example, data researchers use interactive environments to subject consumers to an ongoing series of randomized, controlled experiments. Thanks to the interactive infrastructure and the forms of ubiquitous surveillance it enables, the activities of daily life can be captured in virtual laboratories in which variables can be systematically adjusted to answer questions devised by the researchers: what makes a particular advertising campaign more effective?; what types of political appeals are most likely to generate a response?; what behaviors are easiest to influence?; which locations are the most conducive to desired responses on the part of consumers?; and so on.

The infrastructure for ubiquitous interactivity and thus ubiquitous surveillance transforms the media experiences of daily life into a large laboratory. As Ayres puts it, "Academics have been running randomized experiments inside and outside medicine for years. But the big change is that businesses are relying on them to reshape corporate policy. They can see what works and immediately change their corporate strategy" (Ayres 2007: 50). The goal of such experiments is to generate what various start-ups and marketers call "actionable intelligence" based on the largest sample possible. Such experiments can take place on an unprecedented scale—in real time. They rely upon the imperative of ubiquity: as much information about as many people as possible.

The migration of an increasing range of the activities of daily life, from socializing to shopping, media consumption, personal correspondence, and work, into interactive enclosures facilitates the further development of these monitoring-driven strategies for managing citizens and consumers.

Taken together, the technology that captures more and more of the details of daily life and the strategies that take advantage of this technology lead to a shift in the way those who use data think about it. Chris Anderson argues that the dramatic increase in the size of databases results in the replacement of data's descriptive power by its practical efficacy. The notion of data as referential information that describes a world is replaced by a focus on correlation. As Anderson (2008) puts it in his manifesto on "The End of Theory":

> This is a world where massive amounts of data and applied mathematics replace every other tool that might be brought to bear. Out with every theory of human behavior, from linguistics to sociology … Who knows why people do what they do? The point is they do it, and we can track and measure it with unprecedented fidelity. With enough data, the numbers speak for themselves.

This is a data philosophy for an era of information glut: it does not matter *why* a particular correlation has predictive power; only that it does. It is also a modality of information usage that privileges those with access to and control over large databases, and, consequently, it provides further incentive for more pervasive and comprehensive monitoring.

This incentive is at work in the ongoing attempts by commercial and state entities to extend the reach and depth of their monitoring capacities. Consider, for example, Facebook's ongoing modifications to its privacy policy—designed to make it possible to gather and use more information about users. The company's goal is to replace web browsers like Google as the platform that people use to find information on the world wide web—and in so doing to be able to capture increasingly detailed information about user behavior. As for the public sector, post-9/11 security culture has provided a ready pretext for extending the reach of state surveillance via new media technologies. Shortly after the 9/11 attacks in the United States, for example, the US Department of Defense revealed a plan to create a "database of databases" that would aggregate the information stored in both public and private databases so that it could be sorted to look for patterns of suspicious activity.

As mobile technology becomes cheaper, more readily available and continues to run on applications developed by commercial entities, it seems fair to predict that the tendency toward more comprehensive forms of ubiquitous surveillance will continue. This development will not be uniform; in some regions, states will likely take more aggressive stances toward monitoring user behavior and communications, whereas in others the commercial sector will be the ones most actively exploiting interactively generated data. Different regions will also continue to have widely different forms of privacy protection and regimes of state regulation regarding the collection and use of personal information.

Many of these differences will be framed in terms of the tradeoff between convenience and security on the one hand and privacy on the other: as if privacy is the digital-era capital we must spend in order to attain the benefits of the online economy and to avoid the perils posed by the terrorist (or subversive) threat. In both cases, we should be wary of the forms of political and economic blackmail that serve the interests of those seeking to extend the reach of monitoring technologies or their control over and access to databases. This framing is deceptive insofar as it naturalizes economic and political decisions that ought to be the subject of political debate and contestation. The decision to privatize and commercialize the internet underlies the emerging surveillance-based economic model of customized advertising and target marketing. Similarly, the attempt to centralize or consolidate political power underwrites attempts to increase security without similarly bolstering accountability. When the US government, for example, exempts surveillance provisions in the USA Patriot Act from the accountability provided by the Freedom of Information Act, it is sacrificing accountability in the name of security—a decision that may, in the long term, threaten both. Threats by countries including India and the United Arab Emirates to ban Blackberry messaging devices unless the company provides the state with the ability to access encrypted information further exemplify state efforts to gain access to data generated in yet another type of digital enclosure.

Privacy-based critiques of the advance toward ubiquitous surveillance tend to assume a non-existent uniformity in cultural values. The notion of privacy is a highly variable one across space and time, which makes it ill-suited for dealing with issues that are often trans-national and future-oriented in scope, given the international reach of many interactive enclosures. As Gandy (1993) argues, issues of surveillance relate directly to questions of power, and this means considering how access to and control over both databases and the infrastructures that generate them impact power relations. If interactivity promises convenience, it can also result in alienation: a loss of control over the fruits of one's own activity. In the realms of commercial and state surveillance, all of our captured and recorded actions (and the ways in which they are aggregated and sorted) are systematically turned back upon us by those with access to the databases. Every message we write, every video we post, every item we buy or view, our time-space paths and patterns of social interaction all become data points in algorithms for sorting, predicting, and managing our behavior. Some of these data points are spontaneous—the result of the intentional action of consumers; others are induced, the result of ongoing, randomized experiments.

The complexity of the algorithm and the opacity of correlation render it all but impossible for those without access to the databases to determine why they may have been denied a loan, targeted for a particular political campaign message, or saturated with ads at a particular time and place when they have been revealed to be most vulnerable to marketing. This is not so much an argument against the forms of convenience and security associated with surveillance as it is an argument for accountability and transparency.

Much will hinge on whether the power to predict can be translated into the ability to manage behavior, but this is the bet that marketers—and those state agencies that adopt their strategies—are making. Perhaps more accurately, this is the bet that a society makes when it turns to a monitoring-based system of data-mining and predictive analytics as a means for supporting its information and communication infra-structure. Given an unconstrained choice, individuals may likely choose not to have their information collected, mined, and turned back upon them for screening, sorting, and marketing or propaganda pur-poses. The question of ubiquity is not simply an issue of the multiplication of monitoring devices and the attendant growth in the reach and depth of surveillance, but also of the social relations that shape who uses the information and for what ends.

References

Anderson, C. (2008). "The End of Theory: The Data Deluge Makes the Scientific Method Obsolete," *Wired Magazine*, 16, 23 June, available at www.wired.com/science/discoveries/magazine/16–07/pb_theory (accessed 30 August 2008).

Andrejevic, M. (2007). "Surveillance in the Digital Enclosure," *Communication Review*, 10(4): 295–317.

Ayres, I. (2007). *Super Crunchers: How Anything Can be Predicted*, London: John Murray.

Gandy, O. H. (1993). *The Panoptic Sort: A Political Economy of Personal Information*, Boulder, CO: Westview Press.

Haggerty, K. D. and R. V. Ericson. (2000). "The Surveillant Assemblage," *British Journal of Sociology*, 51(4): 605–22.

Jenkins, H. (2006). *Convergence Culture: Where Old and New Media Collide*, New York: New York University Press.

Lyon, D. (2007). *Surveillance Studies: An Overview*, Cambridge: Polity.

MIT Project Oxygen. (2004). "Project Overview," available at www.oxygen.lcs.mit.edu/Overview.html (accessed 20 May 2007).

c. Surveillance in literature, film and television

Dietmar Kammerer

Video in Latin literally means "I see." Thus, the term "video surveillance" could be translated as "I see surveillance." If we take etymology as our guide, the question is: What constitutes the visibility of surveillance? Even though most surveillance cameras are publicly visible, only few members of the public have actually been inside a control room, let alone know about the complex operations and procedures that take place there. If, nevertheless, many people believe that they know how surveillance "works," it is probably because they are drawing on representations of surveillance in popular culture. Many sociologists have pointed out this fact. David Lyon remarks that "we know about surveillance because we have read about it in a classic novel" or "have seen a film depicting surveillance" (Lyon 2007: 139). Gary T. Marx draws our attention to "the close links between surveillance and culture, and control and entertainment" (Marx 2009: 377). In his view, sociologists should not diminish or ignore artistic offerings, since these "can bring us the big picture and push conventional boundaries of thought and image" (ibid.: 390).

Images of surveillance abound in popular culture and mass media (see also McCahill, Taylor, Norris, McGrath, this volume). Film scholar Thomas Y. Levin even discerns a "rhetorics of surveillance" in contemporary cinema (Levin 2002: 578). Still, the relation between "surveillance" and the "spectacle" is not unidirectional. The surveillant imaginary finds its way into novels, films, song lyrics and other media but, on the other hand, surveillance is itself influenced by popular culture, as the media can shape our attitudes and actions towards surveillance (Lyon 2007: 142; Marks 2005: 236).

This chapter discusses surveillance in literature, film and television. In its first section, it will identify several prominent as well as lesser known examples of popular culture products that relate thematically or structurally to surveillance. Far from being exhaustive, this section offers a starting point for further empirical research. The second section introduces four key concepts in this field. First, the notion that narrations of surveillance offer readers and viewers possible future (dystopic) scenarios of our society. Second, these popular narratives provide scholars with metaphors and models for thinking about and explaining surveillance in general (Orwell's "Big Brother"). They also offer bridges between academic discussions and popular, non-academic debates. Third, it will be argued that representations of surveillance are essential to the functioning of surveillance in general. Fourth, claims that we live in a "cinematic society" will be discussed critically. The last section concludes this chapter with suggestions for further empirical research and theoretical study.

I Representations

Surveillance in literature

When discussing surveillance in literature, George Orwell's *Nineteen Eighty-Four* almost inevitably springs to mind. Yet there are many more novels that deal with aspects and issues of surveillance. Mike Nellis lists numerous instances of what he calls the "surveillance novel": within science fiction, in spy novels, in police procedurals, technothrillers and in the literary novel (Nellis 2009). And while identifying *Nineteen Eighty-Four* as an "Ur-Surveillance Novel," he identifies two more literary works under this label that date long before Orwell's classic account of a dystopic totalitarian state, namely, Yevgeny Zamyatin's *We* (1924) and Franz Kafka's *The Castle* (1922).

We by Zamyatin (1884–1937) is told as a series of diary entries in which the main protagonist, a high-ranking mathematician called "D-503," reflects upon the totalitarian society he lives in, which is strictly based on scientific and Taylorist principles, and the disturbing events that unfold when he unexpectedly encounters a mysterious woman who introduces him to the world beyond the closely guarded city walls. In the beginning, D-503 gladly contributes his knowledge to his "algebraic world," in which all life is calculated by algorithms and emotions are "only a matter of technique." Spontaneity and imagination are quelled by the authorities using neurosurgery. Liberty is condemned since it undermines the operations of the "United State." "[I]f human liberty is equal to zero, man does not commit any crime. That is clear." In order to maintain total control, flying vehicles equipped with "spying tubes" and mechanical "ears" are employed in public space. There is no privacy, since the walls, floors and ceilings of every building are made of glass.

In sharp contrast to the painful transparency and logic of Zamyatin's dystopic world, Franz Kafka's *The Castle* depicts a world dominated by uncertainty, opacity and inefficiency. Everything in the novel is ambiguous. The nameless protagonist arrives in a village where he has perhaps been summoned to work as a land surveyor. The villagers seem to be expecting him and not to be expecting him, and there seems to be a job and to be no job. Governing the village is a castle from which officials, who sometimes can and cannot be spoken to, give contradicting orders. Even though the castle's bureaucracy seems arbitrary or incompetent at best, the inhabitants of the village hold the officials and the castle in the highest esteem, while completely and blissfully ignoring the reasons behind any of the officials' decisions. Speculations and assumptions abound.

Though *The Castle* does not feature any surveillance technology—and it is unclear if the bureaucracy of the officials is efficient in any way—the novel's general atmosphere of mistrust, paranoia and despotism is commonly associated with a surveillance society. The castle represents a self-sufficient system totally neglects the consequences it imposes on its outside world while it immunizes itself against any form of critique by consciously obscuring its inner procedures and decisions.

Another of Kafka's novels, *The Trial* (1925), deals even more directly with what is commonly feared in a surveillance society. It tells the story of a man arrested and prosecuted by an authority that never reveals itself. Despite his efforts to find out the nature of his alleged crimes, he is never presented before a court nor is he told what he is accused of.

George Orwell's *Nineteen Eighty-Four* (1949) is undoubtedly the most famous cultural expression of the fear of surveillance and a powerful premonition of the "totalitarian potentials of any modern bureaucratic state" (Lyon 2007: 143). Evocations of a menacing "Big Brother" have become commonplace in discussions about surveillance and control, and so have debates about whether or not Orwell was "right" in his predictions. Indeed, many of the elements that characterize life in Oceania seem familiar today: the ubiquity of surveillance cameras in public space, at the workplace or in shopping malls remind us of the "telescreens" and hidden microphones Winston Smith encounters every day. Social division and exclusion is fostered; privacy and human dignity is eroded, or abolished altogether, with reference to an ongoing war (on terror).

On the other hand, as has often been noted, surveillance today comes not in the shape of a centralized and threatening state, but as manifold "Little Brothers" who do not affect us so much as citizens, but as consumers. Private commercial companies hold potentially more information on their customers than any state institution. The data is often given voluntarily. On these grounds, the usefulness of the "Big Brother" metaphor for understanding contemporary surveillance regimes has variously been contested (Lyon 2007; Nellis 2009).

Even so, one should not dismiss Orwell too hastily. As a literary novel, *Nineteen Eighty-Four* is not so much interested in the outer appearance of surveillance society, but in the psychology of surviving in it. "Doublethink" or "newspeak" might be more important instruments for control than telescreens and the face of Big Brother. Essentially, the novel is not so much about a society, but rather about individuals, their emotions and their mutual betrayal. The pressing question is not: "Are telescreens everywhere?," but: "What does O'Brien look like today? (How) would we recognize him?"

As Nellis has shown, surveillance as a literary motif is found mostly within popular genres like science fiction or the spy novel. Only few (self-defined) "serious" literary novels deal with issues of surveillance and control in our contemporary society. Most of them were published in the years after 9/11, without necessarily making explicit reference to the attacks. In Tim Lott's *The Seymour Tapes* (2005) a voyeuristic family father covertly installs miniature surveillance cameras in his home. *What Was Lost* (2007) by Catherine O'Flynn alternates between the present and events that happened 20 years earlier, when a little girl went missing in a shopping mall. *Surveillance* (2005) by Jonathan Raban opens with a feigned terrorist attack on the city of Seattle, orchestrated by the federal authorities in order to test civil defense procedures. Raban vividly describes "the permeation of surveillance technologies and mentalities into the everyday lives" of ordinary people (Nellis 2009). Quoting from the novel, Nellis calls *Surveillance* "an ambitiously inconclusive piece […] for these inconclusive times." Aimed at teenagers and young adults, Cory Doctorow's *Little Brother* (2008) takes an outright decisive approach. The book portrays a group of teenagers who defy the near-totalitarian emergency rules imposed by the Department of Homeland Security in their city after a terrorist bombing. Methods on how to evade state surveillance are delineated at length. In all the novels discussed above, surveillance technologies are presented as part of the problem, not the solution. All of them are pervaded by a feeling that this could be—or even is—happening not tomorrow, but today.

Surveillance in film

It is easy to see how surveillance and cinema relate to each other. Technologically, both rely on apparatuses of (acoustic and visual) recording. Structurally, both create situations where one side is watching and the other is being watched. It is no wonder that surveillance also plays an important thematic role in many films. John S. Turner calls surveillance "ubiquitous" in popular cinema. He even goes further, stating that "the very medium of cinema itself can be understood as hypersurveillant" (Turner 1998: 94). This statement rightfully calls our attention to the similarities between the Foucauldian "panopticon" and mass media. But its sweeping character should not make us oblivious to the multitude of possible connections between "surveillance" (which is itself not a homogeneous concept) and "film" (or any other cultural expression).

Even though surveillance is commonly associated with the advanced technologies of the late twentieth century, representations of surveillance in cinema can be said to be as old as the medium itself. The detective, the spy, the voyeur or the policeman are prominent figures in the cinema around 1900. Thomas Y. Levin reminds us that early cinema is "replete with micro-dramas of surveillance in which people are followed and recorded using both visual (photographic/cinematic) and acoustic (gramophonic) means" (Levin 2002: 581). In these plots, the viewers' pleasure of looking is reflected back to them by what they are shown on the screen.

Sometimes, the new recording instruments could even take on the role of lead characters themselves. In films like *The Story the Biograph told* (1904), *Falsely Accused* (1908) or *The Evidence of the Film* (1913) photographic or cinematic cameras accidentally record the mischievous or criminal act, thus providing "automatic" evidence that, at the end of the film, vindicates the wrongly incriminated heroine or hero. Film historian Tom Gunning states, "The camera recording the very act of malefaction appears in drama, literature and early film before it was really an important process of criminal detection […] fascination with photographic evidence seems to predate considerably its widespread application in reality" (cited in: Kammerer 2008: 276). Today, computerized surveillance technology is deployed in the hope of automatically spotting crimes.

Decades before cameras were used for workplace surveillance, the Soviet film *Aelita: Queen of Mars* (1924) was one of the first to depict future television as an instrument of the powerful to oversee the working class, an idea that was taken up by Fritz Lang for his dystopic *Metropolis* (1927) and, in a comical way, by Charlie Chaplin in *Modern Times* (1933). In the German production *World Without a Mask* (1934) an engineer accidentally invents a television apparatus that can see through walls. In this film, it is the criminal underworld that wants to profit from the new technology.

In the 1950s, surveillance in the movies shifted from merely being a thematic concern to also being a topos of "intermedially-displaced cinematic reflexivity" (Levin 2002: 581). In *Rear Window* (1954) and in *Peeping Tom* (1960) the audience finds itself on the side of the voyeuristic, surveilling subject. The former pleasure of looking becomes inextricably intertwined with (or replaced by) guilty feelings of voyeurism and an atmosphere of paranoia. In Michelangelo Antonioni's *Blow Up* (1966), the central character dramatically experiences the loss of his seemingly secure position of distant observer as well as the breakdown of the assumed objectivity of the photographic medium.

With the spread of surveillance cameras in public space, as well as the spread of computers and databases in the late 1960s, more and more movies became concerned with the prospect of living in a world of pervasive surveillance. *The Anderson Tapes* (1971) portrays a group of burglars who use the security camera system of a luxury apartment building in order to execute their coup, but at the same time are oblivious to the fact that they are constantly under surveillance themselves from different sides. Released in the year before the Watergate scandal, the film also depicts illegal surveillance by federal agents. Also in 1971, George Lucas directed *THX 1138*, a remake of his own short film *Electronic Labyrinth: THX 1138 4EB* (1967). Both films present a dystopian futuristic scenario in which total control over society is exercised by computers, surveillance cameras and android police officers.

Arguably the most classic surveillance movie is Francis Ford Coppola's *The Conversation* (1973). What is remarkable about the film is most of all the ambivalent role it assigns its central character. Even though Harry Caul (Gene Hackman) is portrayed as a leading audio surveillance expert, he literally fails to understand the meaning of his secret recordings and consequently ends up trapped in a net of surveillance and deception. In the last scene of the film, Caul destroys his apartment in a frustrated and unsuccessful attempt to locate the bug that was planted in his home. Levin suggests that *The Conversation* indicates "the move away from a *thematic* to a *structural* engagement of surveillance" in movies (Levin 2002: 582). Lyon accents the "subtle interplay between the role of the surveilor as detached technical expert and the role of the uncertain, unnerved subject who realizes he is under surveillance" (Lyon 2007: 145).

These two poles can be taken to describe most, if not all, surveillance movies: on the one hand, the plot-driven spectacle of high-tech and the display of external events; on the other, the inner drama of the protagonists, which subtly explores the psychology and personal ethics of surveillance. *Blue Thunder* (1983) and *The Osterman Weekend* (1983) fall into the first category; Michael Radford's adaptation of Orwell's novel *Nineteen Eighty-Four* (1984) as well as its parody *Brazil* (1985) into the second.

Even though surveillance was not a major topic on movie theatre screens during the 1990s, surveillance cameras and issues of data protection are featured prominently in films such as *Thelma and Louise* (1991), *Demolition Man* (1993), *Fortress* (1993), *Menace II Society* (1993), *Sliver* (1993), *The Net* (1995) and *Snake Eyes* (1998) (Turner 1998; Levin 2002). In Wim Wenders' *The End of Violence* (1997), a cynical movie producer and a disillusioned surveillance technician become involved in a complex conspiracy with a fatal ending. In 1998, the nexus between media and surveillance became the focus of *The Truman Show*. In this film, surveillance is carried out not for reasons of security, policing or control, but for entertainment, even if—or, to the contrary, precisely because—the life under observation is nothing but ordinary (Marks 2005). Although ingeniously realized, Peter Weir's movie was not the first to couple surveillance and the media. Decades earlier, *The Secret Cinema* (1967), *Hi, Mom!* (1970) or *Death Watch* (1979) already exploited the premise of someone being unwittingly the subject of media entertainment.

In addressing the role of the media in a surveillance society, these movies reveal a blind spot in Foucault's thinking about surveillance. As Thomas Mathiesen argues, we not only live in a panoptical society, where the few watch the many, we also live in a "viewer society," in which the many watch the few (cf. Mathiesen 1997). In this way, the importance of the spectacle for surveillance—which Foucault famously denied—is established.

Whereas in *The Truman Show* surveillance was hiding behind the veneer of an idealized 1950s dream world, in *Enemy of the State*, also released in 1998, surveillance technologies were at the centre of a high-tech spectacle featuring, among others, miniature cameras, audio bugs, face recognition software and surveillance satellites. In *Enemy*, surveillance is not so much something one should fear, but a technology one should know how to use. Since there is no way of evading surveillance, the main character must learn how to use the technologies and "hack" the system in order to outsmart his persecutors. Similarly, albeit in a more science-fictional setting, in *Gattaca* (1997) and *Minority Report* (2002) the survival of the central characters rests on their ability to manipulate surveillance technologies in order to defeat them. Their message seems to be that you cannot eschew or abandon the all-seeing eyes, you can only try to use them to your advantage.

In the past decade, surveillance has been "normalized" and is now a regular feature on the movie screen. Films are "about" or informed by surveillance in manifold ways. *Timecode* (2000) and *Caché* (2005) address surveillance in a structural way by undermining audience's expectations of what a "surveillance image" looks like and how it differs (dramaturgically or aesthetically) from what we expect of a diegetic filmic image (cf. Levin 2002). Other films like *Panic Room* (2002) and *Freeze Frame* (2004) probe the double-faced nature of surveillance between care and control, protection and paranoia. In these films, the protagonists feel protected by surveillance at the same time as they are threatened or terrorized by it. In *Red Road* (2006) and *Gigante* (2009) security guards use surveillance cameras in order to pursue their own agendas. In both films, surveillance is a mere backdrop to a dramatic story about personal issues of the protagonists and it can be contested whether they are "about" surveillance at all (Lyon 2007: 151–52).

Surveillance on television

Since the 1990s, more and more television formats employ footage of non-scripted or "authentic" events. These formats are generally subsumed under the heading "reality television." "Reality" or "factual television" promises to present "life, as it is," to be based on non-fictitious characters, emotions or events. Even though reality television seems to be the outcome of filming in a documentary style, of exercising less artifice and hence less control, it can regularly be associated with surveillance in many ways (cf. Andrejevic 2004). For Lyon, reality television is driven by "the desire to be watched" (Lyon 2007: 152). While this may be true of television formats of the *Big Brother*-type, "reality television" as a genre comprises more variants than only exhibitionist game shows. From a surveillance studies perspective, at least four types are important: hidden cameras, real life, real crime footage and reality game shows. All types could be exemplified by various television shows, and some shows share characteristics of more than one type. For reasons of space and clarity, each type will be discussed by one example.

The US series *Candid Camera* used hidden cameras in order to film unsuspecting people reacting to staged situations or pranks. Originally devised by Allen Funt in 1948, the show prompted many imitations and variations. In all of them, people are led to believe that they are accidentally in a "real" situation, which is most often out of the ordinary, awkward, embarrassing or sometimes even hazardous. While the circumstances are fabricated and the other participants are actors, the reactions and emotions of the person filmed are deemed to be "true." The movie *The Truman Show* satirizes this principle.

An American Family, first aired in the United States in 1973, chronicled the experiences of the Louds, a US-American family, over a period of several months. During the filming, the parents decided to file for divorce, and their eldest son decided to come out as a homosexual. As Andrejevic notes, the show triggered many of the responses which still today dominate debates on reality television: "laments over the decline of the private sphere […], an inordinate fascination with celebrity, as well as musing on the educational – indeed anthropological – character of the show" (Andrejevic 2004: 66). For Andrejevic, *An American Family* is also an exemplification of the problem of all documentary film-making: "How does the artifice of filmmaking impact the 'reality' of what it seeks to portray?" (ibid.).

Beginning in 1984, *Crimewatch* reconstructed unsolved crimes for a British television audience in the hope of gaining information from the public. The show relies on filmic re-enactments of crimes, often followed by interviews with police detectives. It also broadcasts footage from surveillance cameras and photos of wanted criminals. Even though the ostensible purpose of *Crimewatch* and other similar real crime shows is education and law enforcement, it is safe to assume that a great part of the audience tune in for entertainment. By using real surveillance material, the producers not only add another "case" to their show, they also explicitly advertize surveillance as a useful technology for crime prevention. As a *Crimewatch* moderator noted, "If you needed *proof* of how effective CCTV cameras *can* be, have a look at these clips" (cf. Kammerer 2008: 272).

Big Brother has internationally become the most successful of a variety of game shows that put their candidates under permanent observation. Unlike in *Candid Camera*, participants are fully aware of the cameras. Instead of being put in a temporary situation, they are voluntarily put in an enclosed space. Avoiding eviction from this confinement is the objective of this and similar game shows. Taking its name from George Orwell's *Nineteen Eighty-Four*, *Big Brother* explicitly evokes surveillance as its central theme while ironically denying the novel's dystopian undertones. *Big Brother* aims to be entertainment, not political commentary. The show has been heavily criticized for its apparent affirmation of surveillance as well as the use of surveillance for the production of entertainment.

But as important as *Big Brother* may be for an analysis of our contemporary culture, the difference between television entertainment and social reality must not be forgotten. Neither *Candid Camera* nor *Big Brother* show "real" life. Instead, both create highly fictional settings, either by using actors or by confining people in a separate, laboratory-like space. The dispositifs of the "test" and the "experiment" are as important for these shows as Bentham's panopticon. No "reality show" shows reality "as it is"; all edit and select their material, all rely on the staging and framing of people and situations.

II Key concepts and debates

The following will discuss major concepts in the debate around popular culture and surveillance.

Novels, films—and indeed popular culture in general—offer ways to publicly debate the consequences of surveillance in an academic as well as non-academic discourse. Peter Marks notes that "fictional works provide stimulating points of reference for surveillance scholars" (Marks 2005: 222). Surveillance, by its very nature, is hard to describe. We may spot the camera on the wall, but we do not see dataveillance or wiretapping. We may have read about data mining and Echelon, but we cannot estimate the actual impact these instruments have on our individual lives.

Even taken as an academic concept, surveillance is notoriously difficult to define. Bereft of any reasonable assessment of the overall consequences of surveillance, it is no wonder that many either choose to ignore them altogether or to overreact in paranoid fashion. Popular culture can help us shape our imagination by providing metaphors, images and references for discussing and theorizing surveillance. Furthermore, works of popular culture offer bridges between academic discussions and popular perception. The public is far more likely to gain its understanding of surveillance from fiction than from academic studies. As Marks puts it, "Many more people read Orwell than read Foucault" (ibid.: 236).

Second, fictional narratives of surveillance can help us understand our present society by comparison. By presenting alternative worlds, novels and films aid us in the reflection of our own situation: (How) does our society differ from what is represented? Can we discern elements of the dystopian world in our world? How are we better (or worse) off than the society portrayed? In this perspective, popular narratives are similar to the scenarios and ideal type situations of scientific methodology, which also serve as models to measure our own situation against.

But literary or filmic narratives are not meant to be analyzed methodically, they must be heard, seen or read. As Gary T. Marx argues, unlike scientific theories, artistic statements "can convey the experience of being watched or of being a watcher" (Marx 2009: 390). They can help us to get "inside" a world which we do not (yet) know. Marx also promotes comparing works of popular culture over time and across different settings in order to "reveal the archaeological stratum of a culture as it influences, and is influenced by, social and technological change" (ibid.: 391).

Third, as David Lyon notes, not only is our understanding of surveillance in part shaped by popular media, but those media also "affect in turn the surveillance that they depict, as consumers of media are also subjects of surveillance" (Lyon 2007: 155). We not only find our present culture and media heavily saturated with the aesthetics and rhetorics of surveillance (cf. Levin 2002). We also have to look at how surveillance itself is shaped and influenced by popular representations and public perception.

Generally speaking, the relation between popular culture and surveillance is not a one-way street. In this view, surveillance as technology and practice, and the images of surveillance represented in culture and media, are two sides of the same coin. Taking the example of video surveillance, Dietmar Kammerer examines how the production of surveillant images is related to and dependent on the production of images *about* video surveillance, including not only movie or television images, but also signage, news reports and advertising (cf. Kammerer 2008). The surveillant imaginary is not external to the working of surveillance, but intrinsically linked to its functioning. Analyzing the affective, aesthetic and entertainment elements of the "cultures of surveillance" can help us avoid the traps of techno-determinism and counter the belief that surveillance simply "works." Kammerer finds that the debate about video surveillance is as much about its "mythology" (in Roland Barthes's sense of the term) as it is about its reality (ibid.: 253). Though it is essential to recognize the cultural aspects of surveillance, the role of the media should not be overestimated. In Mathiesen's "viewer society," the "panopticon" is complemented by the "synopticon" of electronic media, and any understanding of the effects of the "viewer society" must consider panoptic as well as synoptic aspects (see also McCahill, this volume). But while Mathiesen rightly calls our attention to parallels in the historical development of the disciplinary society and mass media, his argument risks losing balance when he claims that television "controls or disciplines our *consciousness*" (ibid.: 230). In Mathiesens's "viewer society," mass media effectively impede alternative thinking.

Similarly, Norman Denzin argues that in our "cinematic society" the voyeuristic gaze has become ubiquitous through television, cinema and video. "The voyeur is the iconic, postmodern self […], we find ourselves, voyeurs all, products of the cinematic gaze" (Denzin 1995: 1). His argument however not only rests on a conflation of (pathological) voyeurism and (cultural) scopophilia, it also wrongly reduces the historical variety of cultural expressions and viewers' responses to a predetermined relation of cause and effect. But, as Marks reminds us, films and novels (or indeed any other medium) are not monolithic entities commanding us to obey blindly. "Rather than reducing their audiences to passivity and pessimism, such texts have a built-in counter narrative that can inspire us to question and resist the negative trends while critically assessing any changes presented as positive" (Marks 2005: 236).

III Emerging issues

If we want to advance the discussion on the cultural aspects of surveillance, these questions must be addressed: first, the field of research must be expanded to include not only cinema, literature or television, but all forms of (popular) cultural expressions, such as pop songs, computer games, music videos and advertising campaigns (cf. Kammerer 2008; Marx 2009). However, caution is called for when assessing whether a cultural product or a fictional work is really "about" surveillance or not.

Second, the discussion must abandon simplistic arguments that the "surveillance culture" conveniently couples pathological voyeurs with eager narcissists and television solely promotes a joyous affirmation of surveillance. The situation is much more complex and contradictory.

Third, multidisciplinarity is essential. Surveillance studies must embrace disciplines like art studies, visual culture or cultural studies. Not only do they provide the instruments to analyze cultural products, their methods and concepts should be applied to phenomena outside the cultural sphere in a strict sense, such as the discourse on security. In a risk society, surveillance technologies and laws are routinely defended and legitimized by narratives about what *could* happen and must be prevented. Such narratives are by definition fictional. Advocates of surveillance routinely appeal to our imagination and construct speculations about possible futures. As Stanley Cohen rightly notes, "social-control ideology is deeply embedded in […] general predictions, fantasies, visions and expectations" (cited in Marks 2005: 223). Scholars of cultural sciences could examine the constitutive role of fiction and imagination in security discourse. This way, thinking about the "cultures of surveillance" can criticize and counterbalance the alleged "rationality" of the security and surveillance dispositif as well as expose the techno-fetishism that dominates much of the debate.

References

Andrejevic, M. (2004). *Reality TV: The Work of Being Watched*, Lanham, MD: Rowman & Littlefield.

Denzin, N. K. (1995). *The Cinematic Society: The Voyeur's Gaze*, London: Sage.

Kammerer, D. (2008). *Bilder der Überwachung*, Frankfurt am Main: Suhrkamp.

Levin, T. Y. (2002). "Rhetoric of the Temporal Index: Surveillant Narration and the Cinema of 'Real Time'," in T. Y. Levin, U. Frohne and P. Weibel (eds), *CTRL [Space]: Rhetorics of Surveillance from Bentham to Big Brother*, Karlsruhe: ZKM.

Lyon, D. (2007). *Surveillance Studies. An Overview*, Cambridge: Polity.

Marks, P. (2005). "Imagining Surveillance: Utopian Visions and Surveillance Studies," *Surveillance & Society*, 3(2/3): 222–39.

Marx, G. T. (2009). "Soul Train: The New Surveillance in Popular Music," in I. Kerr, V. Steeves, and C. Lucock (eds), *Lessons from the Identity Trail: Anonymity, Privacy and Identity in a Networked Society*, Oxford: Oxford University Press.

Mathiesen, T. (1997). "The Viewer Society: Michel Foucault's 'Panopticon' Revisited," *Theoretical Criminology*, 1(2): 215–34.

Nellis, M. (2009). "Since 'Nineteen Eighty Four': Representations of Surveillance in Literary Fiction," in B. J. Goold and D. Neyland (eds), *New Directions in Surveillance and Privacy*, Cullompton: Willan Publishing.

Turner, J. S. (1998). "Collapsing the Interior/Exterior Distinction: Surveillance, Spectacle, and Suspense in Popular Cinema," *Wide Angle*, 20(4): 93–123.

d. Surveillance work(ers)

Gavin J. D. Smith

Introduction

This chapter focuses on a significant group of people who have all-too-often remained in the shadows of surveillance studies: those responsible for the daily operation of surveillance. Surveillance work is a complex and diverse activity, being invariably situated within tortuous socio-technical and multi-actor entanglements, and subject to an array of cultural forces, organizational goals and bureaucratic rules. Thus, considering the role played by surveillance workers in the daily production of surveillance illuminates both the social constitution of surveillance systems and the intricate forms of communicative, symbolic and embodied interactivity fashioning everyday labor relations. It enables one to discern the dependence of surveillance systems on the artful practices of their custodial overseers, a diverse group of data-deciphering "optometrists" who bring such regulatory *dispositifs* to life, who attribute both the products of their labor and the wider manufacturing process with classificatory codes and meaning and who contribute their interpretive energies in exchange for the accumulation of tacit knowledge, emotional stimulation and a salary.

The chapter is in four parts. Part one situates surveillance work both as a routine, everyday practice and as a strategic organizational activity. Part two considers why surveillance workers, despite having a pivotal position in the production of surveillance, are a relatively unknown and neglected entity in scholarly inquiry. Part three draws attention to the empirical and theoretical significance of surveillance work by illustrating the influence of workers and their associated occupational cultures on circulations of surveillance. Findings from ethnographic research on video surveillance operation is utilized to: (a) reveal the key dimension of surveillance work; and (b) make the case for surveillance work as a trying, ambivalent and unique form of labor. Part four presents a short manifesto requesting a much greater assortment and variety of surveillance work anthropologies.

The ubiquity of surveillance work(ers)

To a greater or lesser degree, we are all surveillance workers, complicit in the art of monitoring, interpreting and making sense of social reality. Our will to biological survival and social acceptability requires that we routinely and unremittingly observe, analyze and organize all manner of everyday social phenomena, e.g. television programs, human/animal behaviors, commodity circulation, weather patterns and information flows. Western popular culture further helps cultivate the surveillance sensibility, naturalizing the act of watching and positioning the audience as voyeuristic surveillance agents. Nevertheless, there are clearly many varieties and degrees of surveillance work: that which is conducted for social development, participation, pleasure and proficiency, and that which is conducted by professional laborers to accomplish organizational imperatives and to acquire income. The contextualized objectives, social relations and rationalities underpinning and influencing these forms of surveillance are clearly very different. Thus, surveillance work is both a *mundane activity* performed by social actors in their bid to identify and become aware of cultural conventions, rules, norms and customs, and an *organizational activity* performed by professionals in their bid to meet a variety of bureaucratic ends and ideals.

While there are clear and important overlaps between the practices and categories of surveillance work(ers), our concern is with organizationally situated surveillance work(ers), and specifically, with reviewing how such labor is practiced and experienced by those responsible for the regulation and management of social reality, the mitigation of social arbitrariness and the anticipation of unknown futures. What will also be made evident is the broad diversity of surveillance work and its centrality in the wider surveillance studies narrative. Indeed, scholars interested in this research field need pay greater attention to surveillance-in-action: as a participatory mode of being-in-the-world (in terms of socialization, pedagogy and the interaction order) and as an organizationally based mode of work (in terms of the prioritization and expansion of information collection techniques and corollary emergence of a specialized human/non-human labor force tasked with "reading," categorizing and deciphering this data such that it becomes expert and institutionally-relevant knowledge).

Surveillance work is constituted by countless observational strategies and calculation techniques (varying greatly in their sophistication) and is an activity at the very heart of the social relations spawned by modern bureaucratic organizations. Almost every public vocation depends upon some form of surveillance work. Medical practitioners, for example, routinely employ scanners and body probes to identify and monitor disease as it pervades and seizes the bodies of patients. Teachers observe and assess the pedagogical progress and behavioral conduct of their students. Social workers use home visits, medical/police files and external reports to detect individuals at risk of abuse or neglect, or in need of welfare services. Tax inspectors collect and examine the income and expenditure records of workers/organizations and formulate appropriate rates and thresholds. Citizens (sometimes unknowingly) "volunteer" footage captured on a range of mobile devices to a plethora of observers. Soldiers employ satellite technology and infrared sensors to locate enemy forces, landmines and the storage of weapons. Police officers gather all manner of information derived from daily mobilities and crime scenes in order to direct their enquiries and identify and apprehend suspects. Police informants use insider status and knowledge and a range of presentational strategies to acquire information on peers. Camera controllers monitor public behavior in a bid to identify risky bodies and activities. Electronic monitoring officers administer tags and review whether or not offenders have obeyed their ascribed curfews or detention orders.

Surveillance work, however, is by no means limited to state sponsored/administered professions. The private sector has also bureaucratic and commercial interests in the systematic accumulation and analysis of information. Energy firms, for instance, exploit the services of probes, robots and artificial intelligence to discover oil and gas supplies. Surveyors apply visualization technologies and modeling platforms to determine and evaluate the adequacy and safety of critical infrastructure. Consumer loyalty programmers strategically record the buying habits of their customers in order to hone marketing techniques. Corporations hire security consultants to conduct industrial espionage and gather/relay critical business intelligence on rival companies. Private investigators shadow spouses suspected of adultery and citizens suspected of benefit fraud. Investigative journalists obtain information through phone taps, email interception, bugs and covert cameras to expose the practices of organizations, high profile celebrities and public servants. Social researchers administer surveys and/or conduct participant observation in their bid to comprehend the attitudes of societal members and/or document their situated social practices.

Thus, any occupation or trade requiring an employee to collect, assess and process information—and action particular responses based on that data—is in effect asking that individual to conduct surveillance work. Naturally, this work varies markedly in type and intensity depending on the precise aim and function of the observation; specifically, whether it does or does not involve the systematic monitoring of human beings and processing of personal information, and whether such practices have significant implications for the subject's mobility or well being. Yet despite the centrality and importance of watching in the everyday production and application of surveillance (and social relations) and the diversity of forms this observation takes depending on organizational imperatives and context, few studies have examined how this labor is situationaly enacted, performed, managed, regulated, experienced and understood. Indeed, while the organizational objectives, protocols and logics underpinning surveillance have received significant analytical attention, surveillance workers—with some notable exceptions—are noticeably invisible, their role and significance either presupposed or overlooked by a scholarly collective more concerned with excavating the power relations and socio-political implications associated with new envisioning technologies.

The invisibility of surveillance work(ers)

Two dominant theoretical suppositions in the surveillance studies field presently restrict the number of applied research projects on surveillance work(ers). The first presumption relates to the framing and privileging of the "system" as a structurally coherent technical and mechanical enterprise which defines, produces and administers social reality through the systematic exploitation of its sophisticated organizational configuration, resources, techniques and legitimizing capacity to both draw upon and procure expert knowledge. This focus tends to abstract and valorize systemic processes, effectively removing them from their political-economic context and socio-cultural (or "lived") anchoring. The second presumption relates to the association of surveillance operation/production with systemic functionalism and autonomization. This interpretation overly (and unproblematicaly) exaggerates the agency and bureaucratic rationality of the *system*, while simultaneously stripping away the agency and value/affective rationality of the *actor*. Surveillance systems, from this point of view, are assumed to achieve in a relatively deterministic and unproblematic fashion the formal ends imagined and desired by their creators and overseers. Functionality and proficiency are simply (and non-empirically) "read off" organizational materials (e.g. official documents/paraphernalia which detail technical composition/specifications) derived from the system under observation, with the socially complex and transformative structure-agency interplays, either simplified or overlooked.

Methodological factors are also responsible for the relative invisibility of surveillance workers' experiences within surveillance studies. Most varieties of surveillance operation are governed by stringent secrecy directives, companies seemingly as keen to extract and capture informational flows as they are to prevent and prohibit everyday work practices from being directly inspected and made transparent. Data protection legislation is ironically appropriated by system gatekeepers to impede the independent scrutiny and analysis of daily operations. As such, placing under observation the social and cultural activities of surveillance workers is both methodologically challenging and pragmatically difficult (see Smith 2012). Even when a social researcher secures entry, project viability demands that rapport with participants is swiftly established and maintained. Cultural politics, however, ensure that this is far from a straightforward process (Smith 2012). Organizations, then, have a monopoly over information gathering/processing *and* access control, a situation effectively ensuring that bureaucratic virtues such as fairness and accountability are left more to trust than direct inspection.

The cultural situation and complexity of surveillance work: the labor of watching

The steady increase and diffusion of surveillance work as a key occupational task has been recently identified in an assortment of biomedical, psychological, organizational, sociological and criminological studies. This research indirectly investigates and evaluates the social and ergonomic impact of envisioning technologies on decision-making practices, commodity manufacturing, service provision, labor relations and subjectivity in a multitude of work-related arenas. Although proffering important insights on integration politics, specifically how such innovations are incorporated and appropriated by existing occupational cultures and organizational configurations, limited empirical attention is paid to the situational experiences, narratives and actions of those administering surveillance devices.

Studies of surveillance work(ers) have been predominantly global north centric and have principally considered state applications of surveillance, specifically as they relate to criminal justice and/or the exercise of social control. In particular, ethnographic research on the frames of reference drawn upon by UK-based video surveillance controllers in their inspection and assessment of citizenry behavior has dominated this area of inquiry, with the surveillance camera, at least from a popular cultural perspective, still the allegorical object most commonly aligned to what might be termed the "surveillance imaginary." A number of recent research initiatives, however, have begun the task of extending horizons of understanding in this area of inquiry; the surveillance practices of social workers, electronic tagging officers, customer relations employees, call centre workers, private investigators, corporate spies, investigative journalists, and citizens— as they engage with Web 2.0 applications and utilize a variety of portable recording devices—coming under much greater empirical scrutiny and figuring more prominently in subsequent accounts.

A major strand of the qualitative research on surveillance work has shown how laborers both embody and then effectively reify dominant cultural values, stereotypes and goals in their classificatory arrangement of social reality. In particular, ethnographers have paid attention to the role of subjectivity in orientating the gaze and in the categorization and sorting of social groups according to their ascribed identities, motivations and propensity to consume. Norris and Armstrong's (1999) pioneering observational study of three public space video surveillance systems in the UK is a case in point. The two authors sought to establish the interpretive frameworks or "working rules"—effectively, "value prejudices"—operators drew upon to determine camera positioning. The researchers show persuasively that suspicion is not an innate or discernible behavioral quality but rather a socially constructed phenomenon, a classificatory mechanism engendering the values and prejudices, positioning and ideology, of dominant social groups. It was racist, sexist, fascist and classist ideas, beliefs and stereotypes, rather than behavioral forms, which largely determined where and at whom cameras were pointed, the operators predominantly associating criminality with young working-class males, minority and marginalized populations and forms of immobility/non-consumption. Of the targeted observations witnessed by Norris and Armstrong, 93 percent were directed toward males, 85 percent of whom were in their teens or twenties and wearing clothing and accessories conventionally associated with discredited or unruly subcultural collectives. The authors claim that such targeting practices reflected the operators' distrust of and disdain for working-class male youth in general, and black youth in particular. They also illustrate the operators' generalized dislike for social groups with low consumption propensities or capacities, beggars, prostitutes, drunks, street traders, youth gangs and the homeless not only acquiring a derisive label but also a greater intensity of surveillance than other "conventional" consumers.

These findings emphasize the categorical or labeling power surveillance workers wield in both the symbolic construction of social reality and concomitant decision-making protocol. The socially and culturally grounded nature of "categorical sorting" is also discernible in McCahill's (2002) research on shopping mall security officers. Like Norris and Armstrong, he also found that young males were overwhelmingly demonized and stigmatized by the situated essentialism that these workers projected onto the mediated realities encountered. It was not law breaking or criminality which dictated their visibility but rather the social category under which they were deterministically grouped. Acquisition of this institutionally derived and ascribed label effectively ensured for some a punitive subjection to dispersal/banning orders and other types of social exclusion. Clearly, therefore, *appearance*, *group membership* and *non-consumption* are influential variables determining one's degree of visibility and the variety of intervention consequently administered.

This research illustrates the extent to which surveillance workers impose their own subjective conceptions and interpretational schemata upon that which is remotely observed, and the consequences for those duly—often involuntarily—exposed; such categorizations impinging on and exercising constraint over the mobilities, self-definitions and life chances of individuals occupying particular social positions. Indeed, whilst this unique form of social constructionism and anonymous unilateral monitoring equips the observers with significant "definitional capital" and thus symbolic power, it simultaneously places the observed—who can neither challenge nor identify their overseer—in an asymmetrical power relation. So, while camera operators can freely choose to scrutinize who and what they like, they themselves remain invisible and relatively unaccountable for the gaze that they project. Indeed, this occupational activity is bounded by an exceedingly limited set of legal rules and regulatory jurisprudence. From this perspective, then, the watched are rendered passive objects, the watchers empowered voyeurs, the latter group afforded inimitable and exclusive capacities to access social life and relations in a privileged and intimate fashion, and exploit the knowledge acquired to regulate populations and order social reality. Whether these processes in law enforcement and social control share similar features with the other types of surveillance work previously discussed, and how such processes might vary in and across differing cultural contexts, are issues for further research.

Another way of understanding the complex and negotiated world of surveillance work has been developed in my own ethnographic research on camera operators (Smith 2007). I found these individuals to be creatively involved in the social construction (or perhaps, "consumption") of reality, deriving tacit understandings of human behavior and reflecting on scenes vicariously encountered with anecdotal narratives. These occupational tales effectively become working protocols, helping the operators: a) personalize what is otherwise an often impersonal cityscape; b) derive pleasure and meaning from an occupational lifeworld defined by routine and alienation; and c) produce informed responses to the mediated situations encountered. In other words and adopting the classic "if men [sic] define situations as real, they are real in their consequences" Thomas theorem, the banal stories and characters invented by the operators exercise a considerable influence on what is "visualized" (or searched for) and what intervention (if any) is actioned.

Surveillance workers' musings as biographically reflexive "hermeneuticians" (interpreters) comprise a mix of imagination and memory, and this interchange between the fictional and the real not only constitutes the cultural circulation of the occupational lifeworld, but makes the trying work of watching both pedagogically and professionally meaningful, and socially entertaining and pleasurable. Surveillance technologies "become" social platforms the moment they are integrated into lived forms of social practice, this research illustrating the entanglement of watchers and watched in complex, distanciated (though virtually intimate) relational interplays, interactivity which both recreates and extends conventional norms and modes of social interaction. An example of this is illustrated in a research respondent's commentary: "If they [known shoplifters] see us looking at them [through the cameras], they'll often wave back at us or gesticulate … It's all in good humour. Sometimes when they're pissed off that we've spotted them, we'll deliberately follow them from camera to camera until they see the funny side and cheer up! Passes the time, you know." In other words, technology as a socially situated and facilitative medium is adapted and appropriated by both groups in their everyday experiential arrangement and navigation of the metropolis.

Conducting research on surveillance workers necessitates engagement with the wider occupational culture within which everyday social relations are ingrained, and awareness of how such situated and normative "grammars" (or traditions) both mediate and shape the everyday experience and production of surveillance (Smith 2012). It involves excavation and exploration of the various socio-cultural factors and operating rules prompting staff either to embrace or sabotage/neglect the systems of surveillance that they are tasked to oversee, and critical consideration of the interrelated structural processes influencing whether or not systems of surveillance accomplish their formal objectives. Hucklesby (2011), for example, discovered that occupationally derived insecurity and discontent influenced the working practices of electronic monitoring officers, employees often adopting informal methods to either accomplish or evade organizational goals. Norris and Armstrong (1999) found distrust and poor institutional integration between local authority-employed operators and the police to be a crucial determinant of low video surveillance prosecution rates and restricted police deployment to operator-located incidents.

A further social process affecting the success or otherwise of surveillance work can be seen in McCahill's (2002) research on how managerial use of surveillance technology to monitor and control employees was undermined and resisted by security staff and lower level workers due to shared class loyalties and solidarity. Security personnel, culturally, had more in common with and greater sympathy for their working colleagues and their informal practices, than they had with the goals and actuarial controlling strategies implemented by their superiors. Consequently, the unofficial, often illicit, workplace activities in which certain workers engaged were ignored. This is an important theme in the current literature on surveillance workers—the fact that these individuals, as organizational employees, are often as much the subjects—as the agents—of surveillance (Ball and Wilson 2000; Ball 2003; Thompson 2003). My study (2004) of college campus security officers also shows that strained social relations between employers and employees, combined with boredom and monotony arising from watching televisual images for hours on end with limited financial and psychological gain, can result in resistance, sabotage and system reappropriation.

This research on surveillance work, then, illustrates the influence of the workers' embodied subjectivities in determining and fashioning lines of sight. Operators effectively filter the bodies, behaviors, actions and environmental conditions they encounter according to a classificatory calculus largely powered by personalized values and biographical knowledge. What shocks or bores one watcher can entertain and stimulate another. It would seem that the surveillance worker accrues symbolic empowerment through her/his anonymous positionality, access to information portals and definitional capacity to produce and consume social reality in particular ways. Yet these studies also draw attention to the wider sets of relations constituting surveillance as a distinctive social process and form. Organizational directives and workplace cultures are shown to be pivotal in determining exactly what becomes subject to forms of observational and interpretive scrutiny and what, by the same token, remains unseen. Surveillance work, therefore, is contextually situated and the result of multi-dimensional negotiations among numerous actors: organizational goals are sometimes unproblematicaly internalized and enacted, and other times rejected, the degree of systemic integration being entirely contingent upon the extent of social integration and cohesion.

It is easy to imagine and perceive "the gaze" projected by surveillance workers as inevitably engendering and facilitating forms of organizational and disciplinary domination, and the work of watching as invariably empowering and authoritarian in nature. Yet recent research (Smith 2008, 2012; Hucklesby 2011) on the everyday nature of surveillance work challenges this reading. By reflecting on the affective and exploitative dimensions of surveillance work, these studies illustrate the role of feeling (specifically excitement, pleasure, apathy, stress, monotony and fear) in shaping social experience and action. Analyzing the commentaries and practices of camera operators as they reflect on a) the situational complexity and occupational ambivalence of their organizational role as passive—but compelled—watchers of an external social world over which they have privileged access but no direct physical control nor organizational authority, and b) the unrealistic performance targets and associated accountability governing and dictating their daily activities, helps exemplify the multi-dimensional power structures and emotionality constituting surveillance regimes.

Understanding surveillance from this perspective fosters an appreciation of discipline as a property which is both dispersed and operational at multiple levels: from the identification and exclusion of "non-belonging" behaviors and bodies, to the paradoxical self-disciplining practices cameras operators adopt as a result of being recurrently exposed to the darker sides of human nature and to vistas depicting social disorder and suffering. Indeed, camera operators, as risk assessors, bio-mechanics analysts and behavioral inspectors, are required to vicariously identify those social situations or motions posing a threat or challenge to the everyday normative order, and respond to such events in an emotionally detached and professional manner. They must dispassionately film people attempting suicide and being beaten unconscious, the latter scene an all too common feature of alcohol-fuelled and hedonistically driven night-time economies. As one camera operator remarked to me: "It's one of those jobs where you're always looking at the nastier sides of life. It's the nature of the job. You just never know quite what you are going to face next." Proactively searching for danger and disorderly potential means that camera operators are, by way of a self-fulfilling prophecy, repeatedly and graphically subjected to an overwhelming variety of violent incidents and traumatic spectacles. Over time, the negative social realities encountered are subconsciously absorbed and internalized, cultivating what I have term "the damaged subjectivity," that is, a set of experientially derived interpretive beliefs and assumptions about human behavior and social life based on profound distrust, malaise, fear and apathy (Smith 2012). As a result of the labor that they practice, operators come to perceive and frame the social world as chaotic, disorderly, unruly, precarious and dangerous. They start fashioning and modifying their behavior accordingly, one camera controller informing me that: "Nowadays I don't go out at night in case I bump into the wrong person in a bar or taxi queue, 'cos I've seen what happens to unlucky people. You can get a beating just from being in the wrong place at the wrong time."

In effect, camera controllers both define and are defined by the spatial realities they habitually confront, with occupationally derived memory clearly not a phenomenon that is easily managed or erasable. The operators' estrangement from both the commodity that they are trying to produce (i.e. social order) and the manufacturing process more generally (i.e. the means of production) prompts adoption of multiple coping strategies. Informal deployment of the cameras, for example, serves a re-enchantment function, helping operators to escape (albeit temporarily) from their recurrent encountering of both mediated banality and social disorder/ harm, and to re-establish a sense of ontological trust in the harmonic patterns and balance of the "natural order," as symbolized in a variety of everyday vistas e.g. cobwebs, cloudscapes, rivers and sunrises/sunsets (Smith 2012). The operators also partake in individualized and collective forms of emotional management, the function of which is stress relief and relaxation. The application of black humor, bullying and emotional detachment—and appropriating cameras for voyeuristic ends, for instance, allows potentially pathological (and health degenerative) feelings and conditions (e.g. insecurity, anxiety, trauma, boredom, frustration, uncertainty, cynicism and discord) to be channeled and mitigated (often being projected onto others). The success or otherwise of such ingenious, if routinized, fractures, is contingent on a variety of contextual factors. Surveillance workers are also situated within and stratified according to wider occupational hierarchies, and often find themselves subject to intra and extra organizational constraints. They are increasingly embroiled in struggles over camera positioning/control and continually receive quasi-indictments requiring them to publicly defend their assembled footage in a court of law (Smith 2008).

By focusing attention on the everyday experience—or "labour"—of watching, surveillance work may be discerned as far from a straightforward mechanical or technical exercise performed by a collective of rule-following, dispassionate and detached bureaucratic officials. On the contrary, engagement with operational lifeworlds illustrates that these individuals are emotionally invested in the labor that they produce and routinely endure situational ambivalence regarding their multiple roles and identities as embodied subjects, citizens, professionals, informational conduits, creative hermeneuticians, expert risk assessors and film directors (Smith 2008). As such, far from being simply empowered agents of control, these surveillance workers often find themselves experiencing and needing to manage profound feelings of alienation, frustration, exploitation, stress and anxiety, emotions emerging as a consequence of the labor that they are required—and under-subsidized—to perform and the concomitant scarcity of support services proffered. Again, this research illuminates the extent to which surveillance workers are as much the *subjects* of surveillance as the *agents*; watchers repeatedly exposed to a simulacrum—or compressed representation of the world—over which they have little direct influence. Consuming disorder, albeit from the physical safety of a darkened room, has real consequences. Visibility, it would seem, can be an *un*intended trap.

The necessity for active engagement: lifeworlds and laboring codes

Scholars researching surveillance have tended to either disregard the daily operational realities of surveillance or ascribe an organizational rationality to the form of such social relations. Yet, by placing too much emphasis on the "system," it is easy to unwittingly attribute the everyday production of surveillance with a misplaced post-human and mechanical determinism, to exaggerate, elevate and autonomize surveillance as a reality/practice seemingly above and beyond human mediation and intervention. This can generate an abstracted, overly technical and structurally derived surveillance cognition, a dehumanized perspective that neglects the empirical diversities and complexities inherent within surveillance work and which fixates on assumed power differentials. Accounts based on these premises tend to overlook the transformative capacity of agency, and the significance of individual values, emotional drives, symbolic meanings and occupational cultures in shaping interplays between and among spatially and socially dispersed actors and actants.

Focusing attention on the pivotal—albeit ambiguous—role of surveillance workers, and on the rampant interactivity occurring within and across surveillance "enmeshments," illuminates the intricate social relations underpinning and determining this unique form of social practice. Far from being dispassionate and detached robots or technological "plug-ins," surveillance workers are, in reality, reflexive and knowledgeable social actors, involved in a variety of sense and decision making activities. The tacit knowledge they acquire and then subsequently deploy informs societal organization and understanding, and the cultures that they actively assemble—and social hierarchies in which they are positioned—influence systemic integration and functionality. It is the interpretative encounter occurring between surveillance workers and the commodities and "social texts" that they are in the business of manufacturing, and the resultant circulation of meanings, feelings and relational collectives, that need become a central feature of future surveillance studies analysis (Smith 2012). Further comparative research is required to explore the types of physical and emotional labor performed by surveillance workers in a greater diversity of organizational arenas and cultural contexts. Such studies need better understand: a) how biography, memory and organizational positioning influence surveillance worker decision making; b) the intricate and multi-dimensional social relations in which surveillance workers are situated; and c) the social realities that surveillance workers produce, consume and inhabit, and the embodied consequences associated with human-technology interactivity in general, and the "labour" of watching in particular. Attention could also be directed to analysis of the people, processes and activities which tend to escape attention, as existing literature overwhelmingly focuses on exactly whom and what is rendered visible.

This research, however, demands the introduction of particular theoretical and methodological tools. Insights from phenomenological and ethnomethodological traditions, symbolic interactionism and hermeneutics, and social psychology, could be strategically adopted to extend the horizons of understanding with respect to lifeworld organization and constitution. Recognizing that surveillance-*of*-phenomena and surveillance-*as*-work are elective affinities, intermeshed in an iterative social exchange, helps one to discern the processual nature and dynamic of surveillance systems. Indeed, interpreting surveillance production non-dualistically as a dialectical social process, entrenched within culturally specific circuitries, facilitates an ontological understanding of such systems as being always "in transition"; social realities defined by negotiation, struggle and complexity (Smith 2012).

Using a broad definition of surveillance work is now necessary to incorporate the diverse panoply of occupational practices, technologies and activities comprising its contemporary composition. Computerized "codes" and mechanized protocols are, for example, increasingly replacing human operatives as the key laboring devices for data collection, scanning, analysis and classification. Such algorithmic (that is, automated, disembodied and computer-generated monitoring)—and essentially invisible—surveillance offers an increasingly rational, cost-effective and efficient solution to human irrationality (and associated failures), with a multitude of software programs now firmly embedded in an array of contemporary security industry applications. Whilst researching these codes demands the acquisition of new languages and skills, the employment of experimental methodological approaches and the formulation of research questions which reflect interdisciplinary logics, such innovations remain firmly entrenched in social relations involving computer scientists, organizational technicians and security practitioners.

The sheer diversity and prevalence of embodied surveillance work, the continued priority given to information gathering/processing and the dependence ultimately placed on human beings to make conclusive arbitrations about risk, proportionality and direction means that surveillance work is set to continue, albeit in a technologically facilitated and hybridized format. Indeed, the issues highlighted through the chapter are unlikely to diminish in their significance, specifically the subjectively defined nature of the codes employed to categorize and organize acquired information, the influence of occupational culture in shaping the rules of engagement (or disengagement as the case may be), and the transformative capacity of human emotionality in determining the watcher's value orientation, organizational commitment and embodied subjectivity. Surveillance work is a truly foundational everyday practice, and scholars interested in the ambivalent work of watching need begin disentangling entanglements of surveillance-as-labor, surveillance-as-commodity, surveillance-as-symbolic property, surveillance-as-pedagogical-resource and surveillance-as-social-relation.

References

Ball, K. (2003). "Editorial. The Labours of Surveillance," *Surveillance & Society*, 1(2): 125–37.

Ball, K. S. and Wilson, D. C. (2000). "Power, Control and Computer Based Performance Monitoring: Repertoires, Subjectivities and Resistance," *Organization Studies,* 21(3): 536–65.

Hucklesby, A. (2011). "The Working Life of Electronic Monitoring Officers," *Criminology and Criminal Justice*, 11(1): 59–76.

McCahill, M. (2002). *The Surveillance Web: The Rise of Visual Surveillance in an English City*, Cullompton: Willan Publishing.

Norris, C. and Armstrong, G. (1999). *The Maximum Surveillance Society: The Rise of CCTV*, Oxford: Berg.

Smith, G. J. D. (2004). "Behind the Screens: Examining Constructions of Deviance and Informal Practices among CCTV Control Room Operators in the UK," *Surveillance & Society*, 2(2/3): 376–95.

——(2007). "Exploring Relations Between Watchers and Watched in Control(led) Systems: Strategies and Tactics," *Surveillance & Society*, 4(4): 280–313.

——(2008). "Empowered Watchers or Disempowered Workers? The Ambiguities of Power Within Technologies of Security," in K. F. Franco Aas, H. O. Gundhus, and H. M. Lomell, (eds), *Technologies of Insecurity: The Surveillance of Everyday Life*, London: Routledge–Cavendish.

——(2012). *Opening the Black Box: The Everyday Life of Surveillance*, London: Routledge.

Thompson, P. (2003). "Fantasy Island: A Labour Process Critique of 'the Age of Surveillance'," *Surveillance & Society*, 1(2): 138–51.

Part II
Surveillance as sorting

Introduction
Surveillance as sorting

Introduction

How do population groups become divided, such that one group receives different treatment and has different experiences and expectations from others? This question has fascinated and concerned people for centuries. In the social sciences, it has often been answered with theories of class, race and gender, each of which also has its own history and cultural variations. During the later part of the twentieth century, however, as neoliberal political doctrines became ascendant and as new electronic technologies were entrenched as the organizational infrastructures of late modern societies, a fresh feature of social structuring became apparent. Summed up in the concept of "social sorting," it is facilitated by surveillance.

This is not to say that sorting mechanisms are new. They are not. There are ancient examples and, of course, modern bureaucracies were designed to sort between different categories of the population to ensure, for instance, that claimants obtained the correct care or employees received the right wages. Rather, a more recent confluence of political ideology and technological development helped to produce a situation in which the means of sorting themselves became decisive and generalized through several once-distinct social spheres. Whether one considers police use of surveillance cameras, marketing use of geode-mographic databases, the ways that electronic ID systems distinguish between would-be entrants, the filtering processes of security measures at airports—they all express and embody social sorting techniques.

As David Lyon observed in what is often taken as a classic version of the basic argument, social sorting points to a world well beyond nightmare fears of the Big Brother state. It is one in which surveillance is diffused throughout society, whether at work or play, in worship or performance, whether web-surfing or purchasing. All kinds of data are "manipulated to produce files and risk categories in a liquid, networked system" (Lyon 2003: 13). In all its ambiguity and complexity, surveillance is rationalized and automated through searchable databases and statistical techniques and the resulting classifications directly and indirectly affect people's choices and life-chances. And they do so, not merely in fixed ways but as we proceed through the paths of everyday life. Our highly mobile bodies are traced and tracked unceasingly by com-puter codes with which simultaneously we interact both to display our data and to determine directions we take in response to the process.

But how exactly does this work? A fine literature on surveillance as social sorting developed in the first decade of the twenty-first century and this volume adds several significant pieces to that. Focusing first on the techniques involved, Oscar Gandy indicates that not only "who you are" but also "what you are" has become a vital element of "actionable intelligence" through which people are evaluated and rated for various purposes. Markets are segmented and targeted in ways that often evade privacy or data protection law and may contain errors, but that have the effect of amplifying negative assessments. His forceful conclusion is that such software-supported statistical discrimination should be labeled and treated as dangerous, requiring responsible control.

To understand further how this operates in a consumer context, Joseph Turow and Nora Draper focus on what they call media buying, a phenomenon that has expanded tremendously in recent decades. Starting with banner, interactive links and cookies, web users are now followed by tracking pixels (called "web beacons") and related means, to produce complex and highly valuable data that is used and traded within a plethora of organizations. The consequences for what was once called reputation and even for how consumers decide between options is far-reaching. And the connections between this and Gandy's work on the "cumulative disadvantage" produced by "rational discrimination" are easily made, both in the sphere of consumption and in what follows, the sphere of "security."

It was once safe to assume that assessments and judgments made by marketing corporations could be considered "soft surveillance" with little direct connection to policing or security arrangements. No more. The flows of personal data and of profiles from one organization to another, courtesy of intermediary agencies such as data brokers, ensures that what is done on shopping trips or online becomes part of that "actionable intelligence" of which Gandy writes. Homeland Security makes extensive use of Facebook. So Inga Kroener and Daniel Neyland argue that in the case of camera surveillance—also a source of personal data and social sorting—further things can be said. Systems set up for "security" purposes tend to have the perverse effect of creating further insecurities. And, as Franko Aas *et al.* (2009) show, such insecurities are also unequally distributed.

Another way in which social sorting occurs is through the operation of older mechanisms of structuring a society, now reinforced using new technologies. Colonialism provides a well-documented example and Ahmad Sa'di discusses various permutations of this theme. However, his key point is that even after classic colonial systems have been officially dismantled, some resilient features of colonialism may persist into the present. In his cogent argument, surveillance is the very means whereby two parallel but conflicting forces are reconciled. The constantly shifting boundaries of the world capitalist system are articulated with fixed racial and moral orders through experimental forms of "scientific" or rational surveillance. Key examples of this appear in North African countries especially.

But whether in Egypt or Algeria, India or Argentina, colonizing forces had frequent resort to identification systems as a means of maintaining order, as they saw it. As identification is basic to much surveillance, analyzing how it is achieved and established also teaches much about sorting mechanisms. And while colonialism might have been the test bed for identification systems, successful models often made their way back to their countries of origin, too. Thus, as Richard Jenkins demonstrates, the question of "who you are" is frequently answered today with passports, identity cards and social security numbers. He also shows that surveillance, that is "a means to an end, one-sided, increasingly impersonal, intrusive and yet distant, routine and banal," is what today frames identification. Thus, "categorization may be on its way to achieving dominance in identification."

This does not happen on its own. Specific pressures push towards certain kinds of surveillance "solutions" for perceived security problems. Since 9/11 especially, the trend towards government outsourcing has accelerated. At first geared towards determining who was a likely terrorism suspect, the social sorting net has widened to include in particular migrant groups at borders and in airports as well as political dissidents and protesters. This is fostered by what Ben Hayes calls the "surveillance-industrial complex" with its corporate-governmental revolving doors, security lobbyists and agencies devoted to showing why technical solutions are superior to—or can pass as—democratic and political ones. This is a sobering analysis of one of the most powerful drivers of surveillance that underscores again the urgency of investigating and confronting social sorting.

Downstream from such globalized drivers, of course, are the ordinary people whose lives are sorted for better or for worse as their data are scrutinized. Not only at border and airports, but also in medical facilities, laboratories and elsewhere, the body is as it were on display. For as Irma van der Ploeg shows, not only is the body implicated in obvious ways as biometrics or full-body scanners are installed for "security" purposes, but how we understand the body is also up for grabs. When information about the body in part constitutes what we understand *as* the body, telling the difference between the one and the other becomes increasingly hard. Those data are used for social sorting, which for Van der Ploeg underscores again how singularly important it is to know what is done with those data.

References

Franko Aas, K., Oppen Gundhus, H., Mork Lomell, H. (eds). (2009). *Technologies of Insecurity*, London and New York: Routledge.

Lyon, D. (ed.). (2003). *Surveillance as Social Sorting: Privacy, Risk and Digital Discrimination*, London and New York: Routledge.

Section 2.1.
Surveillance techniques

a. Statistical surveillance

Remote sensing in the digital age

Oscar H. Gandy, Jr

Roger Clarke's insights with regard to the nature of "dataveillance" (Clarke 1988) marked a critical turning point in our understanding of the role that computer analysis of statistical data would come to play in the constant, routine, and largely automated surveillance of people, places and things. By extending Michel Foucault's arguments regarding the role of data and statistical analysis in the identification, classification and representation of social reality in terms of what we have come to acknowledge as "data doubles," profiles or shadows, Clarke and those who followed his lead have dramatically altered the meaning and significance of remote sensing, or surveillance from afar.

By reviewing the development of statistical techniques and their application in a myriad of attempts to manage the governance of relations between citizens, consumers, corporations and the multidimensional state, this chapter emphasizes the consequences that flow from institutionalized reliance on a continually changing matrix of classifications (see also Ruppert, this volume). After establishing the essential character of these classificatory systems as technologies of discrimination, it reveals how the consequences of their fundamental limitations are experienced as cumulative disadvantage by large segments of society.

Identification, classification, evaluation and discrimination

Statistical surveillance (SS) is an increasingly dominant means of making sense of the complexity in our rapidly changing environments. It is best understood in terms of the functions it serves for the actors within the institutions of business and government (Gigerenzer *et al.* 1989). For them, the surveillance that is most highly valued is that which provides "actionable intelligence." Actionable intelligence allows goal-directed, knowledgeable actors to choose between the alternatives that have been presented to them as reasonable. For the most part, these are choices about the kinds of relationships to pursue, establish, or maintain with an entity or object of interest. From the perspective of the critical technology assessment that this chapter is intended to provide, the choices that matter the most are those that affect the life chances of individuals within society (Gandy 2009: 19-34).

The actionable intelligence that is derived from the statistical analyses of data is used primarily to place individuals within a dynamic multidimensional matrix of identities. The character of these identities reflects the interests of the institutional actors seeking to influence how individuals understand and respond to the options that are set before them. The strategic presentation of options is designed to maximize the benefits and minimize the risks that are associated with managing the behavior of these individuals.

Identification is the term we use for the process that separates out and reliably marks a single, unique individual. Identification determines "who you are," in terms of an absolute and reliable distinction that can be drawn between you and anyone else. The ability of identification systems to link names and other unique identifiers to markers or traces from individuals who would otherwise be anonymous is a highly valued capacity of modern surveillance systems. Statistical analyses are dramatically increasing the scope, accuracy and reliability of these determinations.

It is important to keep in mind that the "identification" being discussed here is not the same as self-identification, or "who you think you are." We are referring only to the kinds of identification that are produced by institutional others. This is a process that generally reflects the exercise of power. Identification or misidentification by others is immaterial to the extent that it is purely informational; however, in its use, it has a material force. It can literally change the quality and duration of a person's life.

Classification involves a different kind of determination. Here the goal of surveillance is a more precise determination of "what you are." Rather than being governed primarily by the pursuit of distinction or uniqueness, the goal of classification is achieved through the simultaneous maximization of similarities and differences within and between analytically determined groups. Thus, classification involves a determination of to which, among a variety of strategically defined "groups," an individual can be said to belong.

Again, as with identification, group membership is not determined by the individual, but by an institutional other. While voluntary membership in some formally recognized organization or social group might in fact be data that help to determine the group to which individuals may be assigned, such personal, and occasionally autonomous, choices do not control those assignments. It is primarily a kind of "strategic essentialism" that leads us to treat some groups as something other than the social constructions that they actually are. These abstractions bear no necessary relationship to the groups with which individuals voluntarily and actively identify. Indeed, individuals may never know the names, or even the existence of the groups to which they have been assigned.

Geoffrey Bowker and Susan Star invite us to think about classification as a technology for segmenting the world. By placing "things" into "boxes" we increase our ability to do particular kinds of work (Bowker and Star 1999: 10). As they suggest: "assigning things, people, or their actions to categories is a ubiquitous part of work in the modern bureaucratic state" (Bowker and Star 1999: 295), and it is no less true in the modern corporate and public spheres.

Evaluation is not strictly an assessment of an individual, as in determining whether he or she is a good or bad person. Evaluations tend to be relational and predictive, as in assessing whether the relationship between the individual and an identifiable other would be expected to be harmful or beneficial in the future. An evaluative assessment is increasingly expressed in terms of the probability that a particular benefit or loss would be realized. Even though a particular score or rating may be used to represent an individual's evaluative status, these determinations are based in large part on a characterization of the group, or category to which the individual has been assigned.

Discrimination is best understood as a choice between individuals or groups that is made on the basis of a distinction that involves an evaluative assessment. In those cases where the choice is beneficial for the one chosen, it is reasonable to assume that those not chosen are comparatively disadvantaged as a result. Discrimination involves a choice by a powerful actor. Often, operationalizing that choice involves imposing a requirement to choose that ultimately disadvantages the reluctant chooser.

Statistical discrimination (SD) is the term being used to characterize a decision to exclude or deny opportunity to an individual on the basis of the attributes of the group to which he or she is assumed to belong. For example, SD occurs when an employer refuses to hire an African American male because he is assumed to be ignorant, dishonest, lazy, or criminally inclined on the basis of generally held, and perhaps statistically validated, estimates of the distribution of those traits among African Americans. As a result, what would otherwise be treated as illegal racial discrimination is routinely justified as a legitimate and inherently rational act (Gandy 2009: 69-72).

Although it varies across nations, it is generally illegal to base discriminatory decisions on membership in groups defined on the basis of "protected traits," such as race, gender, national origin, age, or sexual preference. At the same time, it is important to understand that no one escapes the expanding web of SD. Our continually adjustable matrices of identification may vary to some extent reflecting differential advantages of class, position and status. Yet, virtually all of our interactions with the institutions of commerce and government generate data that will be used to enhance the scope and impact of our statistical constructions.

Segmentation and targeting

SD is generally accomplished on a massive scale through two closely related, but independent activities identified as segmentation and targeting (S&t). *Segmentation* refers to the reclassification of the objects of analysis into distinct categories on the basis of their relative status as objects of interest, as well on the basis of their statistically determined linkages or associations with costs, benefits and risks.

For example, in contemporary credit markets, some consumers are valued primarily because of their tendency to incur late payment costs or other penalties that result in higher average profits than would be derived from other more resourceful customers. From the perspective of organizations marketing other goods and services, it is recognized that different population segments have characteristic tastes, preferences, needs and tendencies to respond to particular offers, opportunities and appeals. Knowledge of these attributes facilitates the development of specialized communications designed to take advantage of these opportunities. *Targeting* refers to the delivery of specialized communications to the appropriate segment through an appropriate communications channel.

The same techniques that help to identify these more precisely defined segments are then used to design promotional messages that have been optimized to increase the probability of obtaining the desired responses from an individual. They are also used to determine which media placements provide the greatest net benefit from the investment in the capture of the targets' attention.

Future developments in this area are likely to involve the use of intelligent agents that individuals may encounter as anthropomorphic avatars. Advances in persuasive computing, or "captology persuasive," suggest that in the near future these interactive systems will be capable of sustaining highly realistic online interactions. These interactive systems are being designed to create the impression that a personalized recommendation or appeal from a respected member of the target's community or reference group has just been received.

Success in S&T and SD more generally will depend to a large extent upon unfettered access to information about the status and activity of individuals. This access will be acquired through a variety of remote-sensing technologies and service providers that will rely upon a continually expanded stream of data, and an ever more powerful set of analytical tools.

Statistical surveillance as remote sensing

Because of the relatively narrow framing of privacy law and regulation in terms of interactions with idealized "reasonable" human beings (Nissenbaum 2010), it is important to understand how SS differs from direct or even indirect visual or auditory surveillance. SS is remote in distance, time and manner. The sensory inputs to decision systems that are derived from the analysis of transaction-generated information (TGI) are likely to be combined with still other digitally encoded information. Included among these data are assessments derived from the analysis of electronic transcriptions of text and speech captured from a variety of network-enabled interactions. Not only will this surveillance be panoptic in the sense of its inclusive "field of view," but also very little of this sensing will take place under the active control of human agents.

SS is unlike traditional surveillance that depends upon technological enhancements to visual, auditory and other sensory capabilities that allow observation or eavesdropping from a distance through the capture and amplification of signals or information that would otherwise be lost in background noise. The sensory infrastructure of SS is no longer primarily oriented toward the production of an accurate impression or representation of the present or the recent past. Its lens is increasingly being focused on a strategic representation of the future. It is this distinction that makes all the difference between old and new forms of surveillance.

It is of course true that this magical window into the future depends upon the analysis of data gathered in the comparatively recent past. Initially, dataveillance was limited to some fairly routine methods of identification as aids to the screening, authentication and verification of transactions. However, Clarke (1988) accurately predicted that the comparison of acquired data against existing norms and standards would come to support the development of profiling, or "multifactor file analysis," as a means of further identification and classification.

These profiling techniques were thought to "hold great promise because they can detect hidden cases amid large populations" (Clarke 1988: 504). In addition, Clarke suggested that profiling also "purports to offer the possibility of detecting undesirable classes of people before they commit an offense" (Clarke 1988: 507). It is this promise of enhanced predictability and anticipatory segmentation that generated both sustained interest and heightened concern about the dangers of dataveillance as a novel form of remote sensing that we understand as apprehension through analysis, rather than through observation.

Analytical tools

Thomas Davenport and Jeanne Harris (2007: 168-73) identified a variety of analytical technologies or software tools that the organizations of business and government were acquiring and putting to use in their pursuit of actionable intelligence. Many of the statistical packages or algorithms that are being developed in a highly competitive marketplace have been specialized for the generation of predictive models and simulations that help organizations plan for an uncertain future (Wilkinson 2008). An important set of management resources are the "rule engines" or "expert systems" that generate recommendations and rationales about what kind of relationship, if any, the organization should pursue with a given individual in the future.

Data-mining tools rely upon still other analytic approaches to identify patterns in data sets that have not been anticipated, and may not be well understood once they have been described (Hand 2006). A rather specialized set of data-mining resources has been optimized for the analysis of texts and audiovisual materials. These systems generate descriptive summaries, comparisons, and increasingly, alerts about problems, threats or dangers on the horizon. One of the most widely known link-based data-mining algorithms is *PageRank* as developed by Sergey Brin and Larry Page and implemented in their highly successful Google search engine. The algorithm assigns ranks to individual web pages on the basis of the number and ranking of the pages that provide a hyperlink to it.

What all these systems have in common is their ability to transform mountains of data, almost without regard to their forms, into statements and graphic representations that can support a critical decision, or in the case of automated systems, generate a rationale for the decisions that have just been implemented.

Organizations that are most concerned with the generation of actionable intelligence tend to be less interested in explanation than they are in reliable prediction. Whether their focus is consumer behavior, criminal activity, or political choices at election time, the ability to predict the choices that target populations will make within acceptable margins of error is more important than understanding precisely why those choices will be made.

It should be understood that the more sophisticated analytical models require powerful computers, specialized software and highly trained analysts. As a result, the most powerful tools are actually being used by a relatively small segment of the population.

The developers of software packages and analytical services continually struggle to find ways to expand this highly profitable market. Many of these firms are developing intelligent systems that provide users with a form of computerized "hand-holding." Online resources provide users with step-by-step suggestions and explanations regarding decisions to be made, as well as guidance to interpreting the results of steps that have been taken. In one sense, these new intelligent systems are engaged in an ongoing attempt to discover the goals, interests and intentions of their users in the same way that their corporate clients are trying to understand and anticipate the goal-oriented behaviors of their customers, competitors or adversaries (Hand 2006; Wilkinson 2008).

Depending upon the kinds of decisions for which a model or algorithm is being acquired, different standards of performance may be applied. Obviously, a 100 percent success rate, or complete accuracy is an unreasonable goal for any decision-support system, whereas 65 percent may be a highly competitive standard of performance. It is also true, however, that the success achieved by a given system with an existing data set is unlikely to be achieved when it is applied to a new population, or at a different point in time.

Because system training and performance testing is necessarily retrospective, in the sense that a model in development is being evaluated on the basis of its ability to predict what an individual or entity did in the past, it is a somewhat more difficult challenge to predict what it will do in the future. This is true because influential factors or circumstances are likely to have changed for any given individual. Differences are also likely to be observed among individuals who were not part of the original training set. This is especially true where the training set was acquired through non-random convenience samples.

Additional problems arise because of the fact that the data about individuals are necessarily abstract, and simplified representations of the complexity that defines human beings and the circumstances in which they make their lives. Some of those data may also be in error because of irregularities in the systems and routines that capture information about individuals. They may also be in error because of biases inherent in the selection of measures, and the standards used to characterize differences between them as meaningful.

This all means that the accuracy, precision and reliablity of the predictions being made necessarily depend upon the quality and character of the data being used, and this quality depends in part on the sources from which they are acquired.

Sources of data

A relatively recent shift toward the digital capture, processing, storage and transmission of data that is being accomplished with the assistance of networked computers has exponentially increased the power and scope of surveillance. Financial incentives, combined with the greater ease and reliability of computers, are often amplified by the authoritative compulsion of government regulations.

Sensors within the environment that are capable of producing status location, and relational information interact routinely with devices worn by, or implanted in, individuals. These interactions generate data that are routinely integrated into the networked data stream.

In addition, the ability to search across record systems and files with the assistance of advertiser-supported search engines, means that massive amounts of TGI can be identified and then delivered in the specific forms required for analysis (Andrejevic 2007). Increasingly, with the power and intelligence being provided through remote servers, rapidly expanding "cloud computing" resources mean that instantaneous access to data and preliminary analysis will be provided through hand-held terminals that also serve as mobile phones and recreational media.

We are reminded by Davenport and Harris (2007) that corporations have dramatically increased the amount of data that they personally collect about their clients, customers, and suppliers. Much of that information is derived from computer-mediated transactions with individuals, including those accomplished online. Yet, the most consequential analyses of personal information rely on data that have been acquired from profit-seeking consolidators of information extracted from public and private systems of records.

These "omnibus information providers" have "carved out a distinctive marketplace in personal information and information products" (Nissenbaum 2010: 46), that bears only a passing resemblance to the database-marketing firms that once dominated the field. Robert O'Harrow (2005), an investigative journalist, provided an early assessment of this rapidly developing field. He emphasized the way that government agencies in the USA were using these firms as strategic gateways that allowed them to bypass the limitations on data gathering and information sharing imposed by privacy regulations.

Uses and abuses of statistical surveillance

Critics of SD have distinguished between the harms derived from surveillance that befall individuals and those that affect society more generally. Impacts on individuals that derive from discriminatory actions are understood as occurring to "groups" or segments of a larger social unit. Individuals are subjected to differential treatment, or suffer disparate outcomes as a result of their treatment as member of a disfavored group. Higher order impacts can be observed at the societal level, for example, as a result of the relations between groups that result from their classification as criminals, terrorists, or other groups deemed less worthy of respect (for other examples of the marginalizing effect of surveillance, see Fussey and Coaffee, McCahill and Arteaga Botello, this volume). It is also possible to identify threats to the status of a social system that result from the loss of interpersonal or institutional trust generated by the accumulated experience of statistical discrimination (SD).

It is not clear how these system level impacts of SD will vary as a function of relations between individuals and bureaucratic institutions. There is a tendency to treat discrimination by private or commercial providers of goods and services to consumers as less problematic than similar forms of discrimination by government agencies or their representatives, despite the fact that the actual services may be indistinguishable in form or substance. Indeed, in an era of increasing privatization, government services may actually be provided by the same private organizations, but under more profitable terms.

We generally observe a high level of discomfort on the part of consumers with the idea that the same goods and services are being sold at different prices to different individuals at the same time on the basis of particular characteristics of those consumers. Although there are specific economic rationales that are offered in support of different forms of price discrimination, the market conditions and organizational behaviors that might actually work to the advantage of resource-constrained consumers are rarely encountered. Instead, the objective reality we usually face is one in which those with limited resources pay higher prices for lower quality goods and services.

The same set of concerns are at the base of discomfort regarding the use of SD in the management of electoral campaigns or in mobilizing support or opposition to public policy proposals. Mark Andrejevic argues that the collection and analysis of TGI from within the "digital enclosure" he associates with networked interactive media "facilitates social Taylorism rather than fostering more democratic forms of shared control and participation" (Andrejevic 2007: 257).

Idealized notions of democracy assume a level of equality in the participation of individuals in the production of influence over decisions taken on their behalf by legislators, judges, and bureaucrats. Those assumptions are largely unwarranted in an environment in which carefully crafted messages, or information subsidies, are delivered to precisely targeted audiences that have been identified and located by intelligent systems (Gandy 2009: 151-4).

Identifying and assigning the costs of errors

As a critical technology assessment, this chapter is concerned primarily with the identification of the *externalities*, or the unintended negative consequences for society that are produced as a result of SS in support of SD. There are many examples of the intentional delivery of harms: such as those we associate with predatory lending and the marketing of dangerous products to vulnerable consumers (Gandy 2009). Yet, we set those impacts aside because there are already laws and advocates who are mobilized to press for their enforcement.

It has become something of a commonplace for discussions of external costs to make use of the example of pollution as a way to present the meaning and importance of these collateral harms. Contemporary debates about climate change and the consequences that flow from reliance upon carbon-based energy underscore the negative impacts that affect all life on the planet now and into the foreseeable future. In some of these discussions, a special emphasis is placed on the differential impacts of these insults that affect some regions, communities, people and life forms more than others. These discussions are often framed in terms of environmental justice.

Identifying the errors

Because SD involves making decisions about individuals on the basis of their membership in groups, it is important to recognize that there will always be some degree of error in the assignment of those individuals to groups. We have suggested that these errors are unlikely to be random, or equitably distributed across all relevant populations. The non-random distribution of harm is made more likely because past negative decisions tend to affect future assessments of individuals who are members of groups that have historically been disadvantaged. A clear example can be seen with regard to what is often discussed as "the neighborhood effect" (Gandy 2009).

Forms of discrimination that result in African Americans living and growing up in racially segregated neighborhoods generally result in the cumulation of disadvantages associated with education, health and employment and in their interactions with the criminal justice system. These deviation-amplifying systems operate through their reliance on available statistical indicators in the same way that the ready availability of negative stereotypes influences the decisions made by employers, government officials and those who provide goods and services in the marketplace. The effects of negative assessments expand exponentially over time and across numerous behavioral domains.

Consider the cumulative disadvantages that emerge from reliance on crime statistics as evidence of criminality within populations. We know, or should know, that not all criminal behaviors generate an accessible digital record. This is in part determined by the fact that some kinds of criminal activity are more likely to go undetected than others. It is also true that, over time, some kinds of crime become more salient as parts of the public agenda as they become subjects of specialized, and highly publicized, "wars" on crime.

White-collar crimes, and therefore white-collar criminals, including those committing financial crimes, are less likely to arouse the attention of police. Certainly crimes committed electronically are not as likely to lead to arrest and conviction as are the street-based drug and property crimes that are more likely to be committed by the poor. As a result of these factors, poor people of color are more likely to have criminal records. In addition, the race-linked statistics that have been generated as a result of targeted crime control efforts will frequently be used to justify even more intensive surveillance of these populations (Gandy 2009: 135).

Assigning their costs

As we have suggested with regard to the comparative evaluation of data-mining algorithms or classificatory systems, there are no readily available or reliable approaches to assigning appropriate values to the costs of the errors that will undoubtedly be made.

The problem of identifying the social and individual costs associated with classification errors is quite substantial, and not well appreciated by those who develop, compare and evaluate these tools. Understandably, formal evaluations seek to have a common standard of performance, such as an error rate. However an error rate is essentially meaningless if the rates vary as a function of the classification problems to which they have been applied.

We generally draw a distinction between Type I and Type II errors. We make a *Type I* error when we conclude that there is a difference, or a meaningful pattern, when there in fact is none, such as identifying an ordinary tourist as a terrorist. We might also label this as a "false positive." We make a *Type II* error by concluding that there is no difference, or no pattern or signature in the data before us, and we therefore fail to identify the terrorist boarding the plane. The willingness of security forces to detain large numbers of individuals is based on a determination that it is far worse to miss a single terrorist, than to inconvenience a large number of passengers. The fact that most passengers tolerate this inconvenience suggests that they accept the implicit assignment of relative values.

Still, it is actually quite difficult to estimate the true costs to individuals and to the groups that are differentially burdened by the use of SD. In part this difficulty is based in the fact that there are often no markets, and no economic data from which the value of the harms can be derived. It is also difficult to assign appropriate weights to specific instances of harm when the impacts are cumulative and multiplicative, rather than discrete.

There is also no easy way to assign value to the loss in autonomy, or individual freedom that results from a self-imposed set of barriers to opportunity that fear of SD tends to invite.

Bringing statistical surveillance under control

For a host of reasons, including traditional limitations in the laws designed to protect privacy (Nissenbaum 2010), the most promising opportunities for reducing the cumulative impact of SD on the most vulnerable members of our communities are likely to be found in the realm of product liability and safety and performance standards. SS and SD systems will have to be classified and then regulated as "inherently dangerous technologies." Assignments of responsibility for their use will have to be broad, reaching from the designers of software to the managers who authorize their use.

Efforts to internalize the costs of the harms associated with the use of these discriminatory technologies may require imposing personal information (PI) taxes at the point of its production or secondary use. The political challenges involved in establishing a PI tax will probably be even more difficult than those we have seen in the campaigns that have designed to introduce a carbon tax at the point of extraction or transformation of raw materials into fuel.

Because there don't appear to be any more promising alternatives on the horizon, our efforts to bring these technologies under socially responsible control should not be any further delayed.

References

Andrejevic, M. (2007). *iSpy: Surveillance and Power in the Interactive Era*, Lawrence, KS: University Press of Kansas.

Bowker, G. C. and Star, S. L. (1999). *Sorting Things Out: Classification and its Consequences*, Cambridge, MA: The MIT Press.

Clarke, R. A. (1988). "Information Technology and Dataveillance," *Communications of the ACM*, 31: 498-512.

Davenport, T. and Harris, J. (2007). *Competing on Analytics: The New Science of Winning*, Boston, MA: Harvard Business School Press.

Gandy, Jr, O. H. (2009). *Coming to Terms with Chance: Engaging Rational Discrimination and Cumulative Disadvantage*, Burlington, VT: Ashgate.

Gigerenzer, G., Swijtink, Z., Porter, T., Daston, L., Beatty, J. and Krüger, L. (1989). *The Empire of Chance: How Probability Changed Science and Everyday Life*, New York: Cambridge University Press.

Hand, D. J. (2006). "Classifier Technology and the Illusion of Progress," *Statistical Science*, 21: 1-15.

Nissenbaum, H. (2010). *Privacy in Context: Technology, Policy, and the Integrity of Social Links*, Stanford, CA: Stanford University Press.

O'Harrow, Jr, R. (2005). *No Place to Hide*, New York: The Free Press.

Wilkinson, L. (2008). "The Future of Statistical Computing," *Technometrics*, 50(4): 418-35.

b. Advertising's new surveillance ecosystem

Joseph Turow and Nora Draper

Profound transformations in the advertising industry are cultivating new "industry logics" that are shaping individual profiles in the digital media world. It is a complex, quick-changing system. It is also a system that has not received the attention of communication researchers, sociologists, or other academics interested in the fundamental forces shaping people's views of themselves and the world around them. In the public policy arena, especially in the USA, the concerns around data mining of this sort come from the notion that individuals can be identified and harmed using data that has been collected about them. Less attention has been given to the practice of constructing personae or "reputations" of individuals that determine the information, consumer deals and surveillance attention that a person receives. Types of firms that did not exist a decade and a half ago have as their core aims assembling data about the audience, trading the data, trading access to the audience members, and/or evaluating the success of those activities. The new media-buying system is increasingly affecting more than just the commercial messages individuals receive. It has created the technologies and logics to personalize price, information, news and entertainment based on audience categorizations that the individuals being described do not know about and with which they might not agree. The advertising system's increasing ability to define individual reputations raises new versions of concerns about the system's power over the opportunities people receive as well as the visions of themselves and the world that they are presented with (see also Gandy, this volume).

The transformation of media buying

Advertising lies at the core of much of the media, and it is the force that sustains much of the content on the web, including many—if not most—bloggers. At base, advertising involves payment for media attempts to persuade people to purchase or otherwise support a product or service. Most people likely think of advertising in terms of its most visible manifestation, the persuasive message. Yet the definition suggests two sets of activities in addition to the creation of the ad. One, part of marketing research, entails evaluating whether and how the message worked. The other, traditionally called media planning and buying, revolves around providing funds to pay for placement of the notice. Before the 1980s, advertising practitioners considered media buying and planning as rather straightforward, unexciting components of a standard ("full-service") agency's offerings to clients. During the 1980s and 1990s, however, that sector of the advertising industry went through enormous transformation. A number of factors were involved, but many of them centered on the fragmentation of media channels due to cable television (Turow 1997). A clutch of new agency holding companies with international footprints (WPP of the UK, Omnicom and Interpublic from the USA, and Publicis from France) established freestanding media-buying operations that claimed to be able to quantitatively sort through the best ways to reach increasingly dispersed audiences in the most efficient and accountable ways possible. In addition to these were two firms holding a particular claim to fame as buying authorities: Aegis, based in London, and Havas, based in Suresnes, France. These six companies were eventually quite successful at dominating the territory. According to a research firm that keeps track of buying-firm developments, they spent $224 billion on advertising worldwide in 2009 (RECMA 2010). That year the six firms controlled about 45 percent of purchasing in the US advertising market; in most European countries the share reached 80 percent (RECMA 2010).

The 2000s marked a period when the major buying firms began to earnestly exploit the rise of the commercial internet with their quantitative audience-targeting models as a testing ground for the coming age of ubiquitous digital media. Although advertising "online" appeared during the 1980s on computer dial-up services such as Prodigy, the business was marginal and ad agencies did not consider that it had mainstream possibilities. The growth of commercial advertising on the World Wide Web with the introduction of the Netscape browser in 1994 pointed to a venue for marketers to reach millions of audience members. The second half of the 1990s marked a transition period during which publishers and various partners refined three technologies that would become the basis for the audience-marketing logic that took flight in the next decade: the banner, the interactive link, and the cookie. The banner and the advertising-oriented link seem to have emerged together on 26 October 1994, when the popular online technology magazine *Wired* began to sell pictorial banners in large quantities on its new website Hotwired. Soon thereafter Netscape employees Lou Montulli and John Giannadrea revolutionized advertising by creating the cookie, a small text file that a website could place on a visitor's computer. They were responding to online retailers' complaints that they could not handle customers' multiple purchasing requests (Schwartz 2001). Every click to put an item in a virtual shopping cart would appear to the online store as if had been placed there by a different individual. Consequently, a person would not be able to buy more than one thing at a time. Montulli and Giannadrea made the cookie with an identification code for the visitor and codes detailing the clicks that the person had carried out during the visit. The next time the person's computer accessed the website, tags on the browser would recognize the cookie. Importantly, the cookie could not by itself distinguish between two separate people using the same computer. That was the result of Montulli and Giannadrea's decision to have the cookie work without asking the computer user to accept or contribute information to it. There was an ominous downside to that seamless approach: by not making the computer user's permission a requirement for dropping the cookie, the two programmers were building a lack of openness into the center of the consumer's digital transactions with marketers.

During the 1990s and into the 2000s marketing technologists developed other methods for following individuals through the digital environment. A web beacon (or tracking pixel) is a graphic on a web page or in an email message that often activates a program to monitor the activity of visitors—for example, what they read and for how long. A Flash cookie is a collection of cookie-like data stored as a file in a user's Adobe Flash computer software; marketers sometime use it so that the data will not be lost when standard cookies are deleted. The development of the banner ad, the link, the cookie, the web beacon, and the Flash cookie helped digital divisions of media-buying firms and their technology partners to refine their digital trade through the 2000s to make it central to marketers considering advertising online. In parrying criticism of these and related activities, marketers and technologists would make much of the point that the identifying data that many websites place in cookies are "anonymous"—that is, not linked at the moment of use to the person's name, postal address, or email address. Yet if a company can follow an individual's behavior in the digital environment—and that includes the mobile phone and potentially the television set—its claim that the person is anonymous is meaningless. That is particularly true when firms intermittently add offline information to the online data and then simply strip the name and address to make it anonymous. Moreover, firms are often confident that they can encourage users to give up information at a later point in the online interaction.

The essential importance of some cookie-like way to trace people's actions in the digital environment relates to a state that marketers increasingly value in the competitive and fractionalized media world: accountability. Those who celebrate the possibilities of the internet and its mobile and televisual offshoots emphasize that the new media allow for the quantitative measurability of audience activities in ways that would represent a much more accurate understanding of a client's return on investment (ROI) yielded by its ad monies than had been possible with analog advertising vehicles such as newspapers, magazines, radio, television, and outdoor boards. Moreover, media buyers contended, it was now possible to go beyond measuring the responses of panels or samples of audiences, as had been the norm in the analog world. Now, they say, it is possible to note and store the responses of individuals via their click-like behaviors— for example, using the mouse to activate a link, moving a mouse to activate tracking pixels on an ad, or pressing a button to change a channel or choose a product on a television screen.

The emphasis on quantitative measurement initially served a direct-marketing model of advertising. The goal was to provoke a sale or an action that would conceivably lead to a sale. The rapid rise of Google search as an advertising powerhouse beginning around 2001 was a result of an auction-based pay-per-click (PPC) revenue system that reflected this approach. Google initially carried its PPC model to the contextual advertising system that it established with sites throughout the web and in its Gmail service. In a contextual advertising network, when an advertiser bids for a keyword, the network's computer finds a web page from its roster of sites that reflects the keyword. Based on the relevant context, the network serves the ad. If the visitor to the site clicks on the ad, the advertiser pays the agreed-upon amount and the network shares it with the website. In both the advertising search and contextual advertising businesses the percentage of the visitors who click might be one percent or less. But with hundreds of millions of visits, a search engine such as Google could still make significant amounts of money with the PPC model.

While Google executives extolled this direct-selling approach as the purest example of web results in action, many web content providers did not have nearly the numbers of visits enjoyed by a search engine such as Google or a "portal" such as Yahoo. These smaller publishers preferred to sell display advertising on a cost-per-thousand-impressions (CPM) basis that paralleled the tradition of newspapers, magazines, television, and other analog media. The logic was that ads for companies that sell cars, financial services, and movies may not need to yield a direct response to have an impact on a person's image of the product and future purchase decisions. But foregoing the direct-click payment model of advertising sales did not mean that media buyers were giving up on their insistence that the web was a more measurable platform than traditional media. Instead, media buyers and publishers advanced new ideas of how to think of the success of image ads that could be measurable even as they paid on a CPM basis. Some of the notions centered on "engagement"—time spent on, or interest in, the page with the ad as an indication of the opportunity to see it. A different way to think of the measurability of an image ad's success was to look at whether viewing an advertisement at one point led to the purchase of a product at another point—either on the web or off. This definition of success—call it *the long click*—became an important reason for following individuals' activities across media, and ultimately from online media to offline retailers such as supermarkets and car dealers.

In all these cases, fierce competition for dollars led publishers to garner visitors' characteristics and sell that information along with their engagement possibilities. Often keeping people's names and email addresses off-limits (and calling it anonymity), some sold segments with demographic information such as age, sex, geographic area, income, and employment status they got from registration or bought from data firms. The ability to use cookies and web beacons to tag audience members and track what they viewed allowed publishers to create and offer up segments of inferred interests to advertisers who might draw conclusions about purchasing interests from that information. Advertising networks were doing the same thing, though across websites, and they and data-collection firms often "matched" their cookies with the cookies of other tracking firms to enhance the ability of advertisers to target very specific types of individuals—and often even very specific (though still anonymous) individuals. By the late 2000s, audience-data exchanges owned by Google, Yahoo, Microsoft, Interpublic and other major players facilitated the auction of individuals with particular characteristics, often in real time. That is, it is now possible to buy the right to deliver an ad to a person with a specific profile at the precise moment that person loads a web page. In fact, through cookie-matching activities, an advertiser can actually buy the right to reach someone on an exchange whom the advertiser knew from previous contacts and was now tracking around the web.

Through these processes the audience became a focus of deconstruction by marketers and content firms. A variety of organizations emerged to help marketers find the specific audiences and audience members they want at the lowest prices possible, while a variety of others emerged to help publishers provide those audiences but keep prices relatively high. Media-buying firms struggled to find their place as advertising sales networks and exchanges threatened to usurp buyers' key functions of planning the best roster on which to advertise and bargain for the best price. The ecosystem became denser as the amount of money advertisers spent online expanded dramatically from around $9 billion in 2003 to around $34 billion in 2008 (Stevenson 2009). A chart circulating within the trade during 2010 depicted 22 types of organizations between advertisers and publishers. In addition to *agencies* with media-buying divisions (for example, WPP, Publicis, Havas), it listed categories such as *ad exchanges* (e.g. Doubleclick, AdECN*), ad networks* (AOL, Google, Microsoft), *yield optimizers* (Rubicon, PubMatic), *ad servers* (DoubleClick, Atlas), *data qualifiers* (DoubleVerify), *analytic specialists* (Omniture, Coremerics), and *research operations* (comScore, Nielsen, Quantcast) (Kawaja and Savvian 2010). One category the scheme omitted was publishers—the firms that create and distribute content on the web. They as well as all the companies represented in the chart have as their core aims some portion of five activities: assembling data about the audience (or *consumers, visitors, targets* or *users*, as audience members are variously called), trading the data about them, trading access to the audience members, creating specialized display ads and videos for the targets, serving specialized ads to the targets, and/or evaluating the success of those activities.

Targets or waste

These converging surveillance activities point toward a broadening future for social discrimination. It is one where individuals receive advertisements, discounts, and even news and entertainment agendas based upon ideas that advertisers, data firms, and publishers circulate about their audiences often without their knowledge and permission. To begin to get an idea of how this surveillance ecosystem operates, consider a Powerpoint deck that Publicis's MediaVest buying operation presented to its clients during 2010. Headlined "Why We Are Betting on Ad Exchanges," the first slide offered the basic explanation for MediaVest's decision to put its energies into the new approach to advertising spending: "Key benefit: Buy only the impressions that match." Two columns of text then elaborated the point illustrated by a series of pictures descending with them. One set of text highlighted the key chain of thinking about ad exchanges: "Insight / Media / Technology / No Waste." The other column of text elaborated the flow of reasoning in the following way: "Leverage our own data to create audience segments → Access millions of consumers through open ad impressions → Exchange allows all impressions to be 'filtered' → Buy only the impressions that match our segment." The slide suggested that marketers would be able to reach only the people who count to them. MediaVest would create target segments based on its clients' data about the best customers. It would then bid in the exchanges for the right to reach people who fit those profiles. They would get the client's messages, and the audience reached would be free of waste—the term for the population the client did not care to reach. Importantly, Oscar Gandy, Jr notes that the same techniques that allow marketers to separate the 20 percent of consumers who account for 80 percent of purchases from the rest are similar to the risk calculations used to predict behavior in other arenas, including the identification of potential terrorists for the purposes of homeland security (Gandy, Jr 2006: 364).

The approach is by no means relegated to MediaVest. It is becoming standard operating procedure among media buyers in the big-six firms as well as many of their smaller competitors. Marketers are increasingly using databases to predict whether they should consider particular Americans as targets or waste. Those considered waste are ignored or shunted to other products the marketers deem more relevant. Those considered targets are further evaluated according to demographics, beliefs, and lifestyle that companies store and trade about them. They receive different messages and possibly discounts depending on their profiles. Increasingly, the goal of marketers is to present people with different information about a product depending on the conclusions marketers have made regarding an individual's character, lifestyle, and spending habits (Turow 2006). To get an idea of the specificity that this individual-oriented surveillance takes, here are brief sketches of firms that MediaVest and other agencies rely on in attempts to reach the right individuals for their clients:

Acxiom, a top US marketing-communication agency, which, according to its website, helps clients "acquire, retain, and grow loyal (and profitable) relationships" in digital media, especially via email, banner, search, website optimization, and mobile. Acxiom's cross-advertiser reach is prodigious. The client list on Acxiom's website includes nine of the top ten automotive companies, 12 of the top 15 credit card issuers, seven of the top ten retail banks, nine of the top ten telecom/media companies, seven of the top ten retailers, nine of the top ten automotive manufacturers, six of the top eight brokerage firms, three of the top five pharmaceutical manufacturers, two of the top five life/ health insurance providers, eight of the top ten property and casualty insurers, two of the top three lodging companies, and two of the top three gaming companies. Acxiom's use and analysis of customer data is central in serving these clients. A goal the company repeats throughout its website involves helping a client decide which consumers are *not* worth targeting. It is called "contact suppression," a practice based on making assessments of the "risk profile" of individuals for certain industries. The firm's Senior VP of Consulting Services described Acxiom's contributions this way at a shareholders meeting:

Should I continue to target people who are in fact going to default on their loans? Or, take, for example, a telecom industry where they're constantly flipping cell phones. I want to understand those characteristics and to say, is that a customer I really want to target? … Once we have that fundamental building block in place now, we can then enhance that with external information that we keep in our knowledge bases about every purchasing consumer across the country. And we can then use that to now start doing strategic segmentation, so we can break your customer base into each one of those strategic segments, from high value to low value.

(Acxiom Investor Day – Final 2008)

eXelate is a leading targeting exchange with the motto "data anywhere. audience everywhere." It determines a consumer's age, sex, ethnicity, marital status, and profession by partnering with websites to scour website registration data. It also tracks consumer activities online to note, for example, which consumers are in the market to buy a car or are fitness buffs, based on their internet searches and the sites they frequent. It sells these packages of information about individuals as cookie data so advertisers can target them.

Rapleaf is a firm that says it helps marketers "customize your customers' experience." To do that, it gleans data from individual users of blogs, internet forums, and social networks such as Facebook and Twitter. It uses ad exchanges to sell the ability to reach those individual cookies. The company website says it has "data on 900+ million records, 400+ million consumers, [and] 52+ billion friend connections." Beyond simply providing the data that a marketer can link to other data about individuals through common cookie-matching procedures, Rapleaf also makes inferences that marketers can apply in deciding whether or not to pursue an individual as a customer. So, for example, it claims that if your friends are not likely to make timely mortgage payments you may also be a likely candidate to default.

33across analyzes people's comments, activities, backgrounds, and connections on social networks to pull out those who fit profiles advertisers want to reach. The firm finds people who directly fit all the advertisers' criteria. It also carries out statistical analyses of those people, and of the firms' customers, to find "lookalikes" who would seem to be good prospects. In addition, 33across offers its clients "high degree interest" connections. These are individuals who are attractive because they have friends or friends-of-friends who are active shoppers (and so might already be influenced) as well as having many friends themselves (so they may influence others). People who fall into different attractive profiles would see different campaigns with potentially different products and offers.

Lotame deals with a "multitude of social networks" and other publisher sites that according to its website allow it to collect "over 240 billion monthly … interests, actions and attributes" in order to "create precise audiences and derive insights from our superior knowledge of human behavior." For the individuals it comes across, the firm monitors and stores information about demographics (age, gender, geography, household income, and education level), interests (declared to the site and undeclared), actions (what people create, rate, send, share, upload, comment, edit, watch, "and more"), media use (online, which can include videos, widgets, music, forums, blogs, and photos), recency and frequency (how often and when individuals express interests and/or actions), interactions (how people interact with content and ads, including clicks, time spent, and videos completed), and sentiment and exposure (what individuals say, what they read, when and how they say and read it). This interrogation of people's creative activities in the digital realm leads the company to interact with particular individuals "based on what they talk about, the sentiment they've expressed in discussions, or the content or conversations they've read or participated in." It also leads Lotame to tailor display ads and commercials for the targeted individuals. In turn, as the firm's website suggests, Lotame monitors the results and adds its analysis to the data to further "learn what demographics, interests, attributes, and actions drive a campaign's success based on goals." This process continues with new data, new people, and new advertisers.

These firms represent merely the tip of an iceberg of minute-by-minute activities that aim to analyze billions of bits of information about individuals, create profiles about them, and turn those profiles into reputations—that is, attributions of their value to certain marketers and therefore to certain media firms. The territory for these activities is broadening quickly beyond the web. It is reaching out of the home into brick-and-mortar stores through various forms of mobile items that include smart phones, tablets, and devices that supermarkets and other stores offer customers as they shop. It is even extending to the central audiovisual medium in the home, the large television set, via attempts by cable-industry giants to create "addressable" advertising and programming (most notably in Project Canoe) as well as attempts by Google, Apple, Microsoft, and other firms to bring the internet and its tracking, targeting, and tailoring technologies to the home set.

The future of reputation

Google CEO Eric Schmidt suggested the trajectory these activities are taking in an interview with James Holman, Jr of the *Wall Street Journal* in 2010. "Let us say you are walking down the street," he said. Because of the information Google has collected about you, "we know roughly who you are, roughly what you care about, roughly who your friends are." As the *Journal*'s interviewer noted, Google also knows, to a meter, where you are.

> Mr. Schmidt leaves it to a listener to imagine the possibilities: if you need milk and there's a place nearby to get milk, Google will remind you to get milk. It will tell you a store ahead has a collection of horse-racing posters, that a 19th-century murder you have been reading about took place on the next block. Says Mr. Schmidt, a generation of powerful handheld devices is just around the corner that will be adept at surprising you with information that you didn't know you wanted to know.

Holman then quotes Schmidt directly:

> The power of individual targeting—the targeting will be so good it will be very hard for people to watch or consume something that has not in some sense been tailored for them. … As you go from the search box [to the next stage of Google], you really want to go from syntax to semantics, from what you typed to what you meant.
>
> *(Jenkins, Jr 2010)*

Schmidt went further: "I actually think most people don't want Google to answer their questions. They want Google to tell them what they should be doing next" (Jenkins, Jr 2010).

By stressing the trust implied in letting Google tell them what they should be doing next, Schmidt was also implying that his firm would have their trust in using their data to assess their future interests, friendships and activities. Doing that, Google will be turning profiles into reputations for marketers. That is, Google will help them decide that certain demographic, lifestyle, friendship, and personality markers make certain people valuable and others not valuable targets for particular types of businesses (see also Pridmore, this volume).

All this will take place under an umbrella of industry exhortations that individuals and households are receiving the most relevant, and therefore interesting, materials possible. Personalized customer relationship marketing by marketers and media firms will reach out to people to assure them of the benefits of tailored content. Research suggests that, despite marketers' claims, many Americans do not want marketers to tailor advertisements to their personal interests, particularly when the information required for such tailoring is gleaned through online tracking (Turow *et al.* 2009). Lobbyists will similarly assure government officials, whom they will surround with the most desirable streams of marketing and media available in order to gain their favor. Individual clicks will still be key technologies in measuring results. They will indicate your activities online, measure your responses, determine what content environment promotes the buying of particular products, and help determine where you belong in the schemes of value concocted by advertisers and publishers. But the click will less and less be defined as a finger on a mouse or a remote control. Your voice will register your interest, particularly in the mobile space and on home televisions, as voice recognition takes off. Your role in the long click that links ads and content with purchases will also be traced by whatever replaces the credit-card swipe—a near-field-communication chip in a mobile device, a voiceprint, or something that is not even in the laboratory yet.

What are the social costs of a world in which discrimination through digital surveillance becomes the norm? One way to answer is to ask what a society needs from its media. We suggest that a good society should have a balance between what might be called society-making media and segment-making media. Segment-making media are those that encourage small slices of society to talk to themselves, while society-making media are those that have the potential to get all those segments to talk to each other. A hallmark of the twentieth century was the growth of both types in the USA. A huge number of ad-supported vehicles—mostly magazines and newspapers—served as a way to reinforce, even create, identities for an impressive array of segments that advertisers cared about, from immigrant Czechs to luxury-car owners to Knights of Columbus and far more. At the same time, some ad-sponsored newspapers, radio networks and television networks—especially the latter—were able to reach across these groups. Through entertainment, news, and information, society-making media acted out concerns and connections that people ought to share in a larger national community.

For those who hope for a caring society, each level of media had, and continues to have, its problems. Segment-making media have sometimes offered their audiences narrow, prejudiced views of other social segments. Similarly, society-making media have marginalized certain groups, perpetuated stereotypes of many others, and generally presented a portrayal of the world that is more the ideal vision of the corporate establishment sponsoring them than a reflection of competing visions of various publics. Nevertheless, the existence of both forms of media has meant that the potential has existed for an equilibrium between healthy social segments and a healthy collectivity. In the ideal scenario segment-making media strengthen the identities of interest groups while society-making media allow those groups to move out of their parochial scenes to talk with, argue against, and entertain one another. The result is a rich and diverse sense of overarching connectedness: what a vibrant society is all about.

The past three decades have marked a steady movement away from even the potential of a balance between these two functions of media. The reason has directly to do with the profound shift in the long-term strategies of major advertisers and their agencies away from society-making media and toward media which have allowed them to search out and exploit differences between consumers. This is a slow process that will evolve through the twenty-first century. We can already see stages, however. During the 1980s and early 1990s, with cable TV splintering channels to the home, advertisers' focus was on identifying segment-making vehicles. They encouraged the growth of electronic and print channels that reached the slices of society that marketers found valuable. The past decade has seen the rise of a new mini-industry within advertising that is upending not only traditional marketing practices but traditional media practices as well. The emerging media-planning and-buying system is predicated neither on the primacy of society-making nor segment-making advertising media channels. Rather, it is built on the primacy of the chosen person: on sorting audiences to find and track valued individuals and serve them personalized ads and other content anywhere they show up.

Contemporary concerns among government officials and advocates tend to focus on aspects of these activities that might lead to financial theft or the spread of private health information. Critics tend to treat other kinds of marketing surveillance—the kinds that Rapleaf and Acxiom carry out, and the kind Eric Schmidt described—as a kind of residual category that is bad because it is creepy and sneaky. The perspective described in this chapter aims to suggest that these practices represent a far greater area of concern, one that runs to the heart of the opportunities people receive and the options they have to see themselves and their world. The marketing ecosystem and its relation to the media deserve far more critical attention than they have as yet received.

References

Acxiom Investor Day—Final. (2008). Fair Disclosure Wire, available through LexisNexis Academic (accessed 16 May 2010).

Gandy, Jr, O. (2006). "Data Mining, Surveillance, and Discrimination in the Post-9/11 Environment," in K. D. Haggerty and R. V. Ericson (eds), *The New Politics of Surveillance and Visibility,* pp. 363–84, Toronto: University of Toronto Press.

Jenkins, Jr, H. W. (2010). "Google and the Search for the Future," *Wall Street Journal,* 14 August.

Kawaja, T. and Savvian, G. C. A. (2010). "Display Advertising Technology Landscape," *AdExchanger.com,* 3 May, available at www.adexchanger.com/events/kawaja-on-value-chain-at-iabs-networks-and-exchanges-marketplace (accessed on 16 August 2010).

The RECMA Global Reports. (2010). *RECMA,* available at www.recma.com (accessed 16 August 2010).

Schwartz, J. (2001). "Giving the Web a Memory Cost Its Users Privacy," *New York Times,* 4 September.

Stevenson, V. S. (2009). *Communications Industry Forecast, 2009–2013,* New York: VSS.

Turow, J. (1997). *Breaking up America: Advertisers and the New Media World,* Chicago, IL: The University of Chicago Press.

——(2006). *Niche Envy: Marketing Discrimination in the Digital Age,* Cambridge, MA: MIT Press.

Turow, J., King, J., Hoofnagle, C. J., Bleakley, A. and Hennessy, M. (2009). *Americans Reject Tailored Advertising and Three Activities that Enable It,* SSRN, available at http://ssrn.com/paper=1478214 (accessed 13 January 2011).

c. New technologies, security and surveillance

Inga Kroener and Daniel Neyland

The introduction of new technologies often forms a focal point for drawing together questions, concerns and fears regarding how those technologies might be used. In the case of security-focused technologies with surveillance capabilities, we find numerous technologies introduced on a rapidly evolving basis, from ever more sophisticated surveillance cameras, to biometric identification and verification systems, full body scanners to motion detection systems. Some of these technologies attract questions which retain a stubborn prevalence (such as: How should this technology be regulated?) and others attract further technology-specific concerns (such as: Can security body scanners see me naked?). Such technological developments and associated questions intersect with further tensions regarding, for example, clashes between the need to regulate new technology and the needs of intelligence-led policing operations or between new technologies and legacy systems. Furthermore the extent to which technologies offer a means to address fears of terror, or are themselves to be feared, veer in and out of prominence, raising questions of security or insecurity for whom, in what location and with what consequences?

The central question for this chapter will be: In what ways and with what consequences do new security-focused surveillance technologies usher in both notions of security and insecurity? We recognize that there are now a plethora of different surveillance-related technologies, but in order to present a manageable analysis we focus on one prominent security technology: surveillance cameras. It should be remembered, however, that many of the issues we raise about surveillance cameras are also applicable to other security devices. After a brief introduction to surveillance cameras and related security issues, we present three contemporary social science perspectives: the literature on risk; Foucauldian notions of disciplinary power; and science and technology studies. The merits and possibilities offered by these alternative approaches for understanding the security/insecurity nexus are examined.

Digital surveillance cameras and security

There are assorted difficulties in trying to define "security." Traditionally defined as military security for nation states, the concept has been broadened to include personal and individual security and safety. To take the example of the UK, the term "national security" is used with regard to the protection of the nation state. MI5 is formally responsible for national security in the UK, which is defined as "threats to national security from espionage, terrorism and sabotage, from the activities of agents of foreign powers, and from actions intended to overthrow or undermine parliamentary democracy, by political, industrial or violent means."

However, responsibility for counterterrorism and national security also falls under the remit of other governmental departments, committees, and individuals (such as the Home Office, MI6, the Government Communications Headquarters, and the Security and Intelligence Coordinator in the Cabinet Office, to provide a few examples). "Domestic security" is not used in reference to national security (protection of the nation state), rather it refers to protecting and securing domestic premises (in contrast to the USA and some European countries). "Internal security" is used in place of "domestic security" to refer to the protection of civil society and the public. In this context, the definition of security becomes blurred—the UK does not have a single government department responsible for national security (protection of the nation state from external threats and terrorism), so this falls under the remit of a number of organizations (some of which are outlined above). For government departments such as the Home Office, security therefore takes on a double meaning—it refers not only to public security in terms of counterterrorism, but also public security in terms of combating crime and ensuring public safety.

Surveillance cameras have emerged as a key technology for handling both senses of security over the last 25 years. It is difficult to judge the number of surveillance cameras in any one country due to the large number of privately owned cameras and, often, the absence of any register of publicly owned cameras. It is even more difficult to pin down precise articulations of the security justification for surveillance camera systems (with a variety of justifications offered from a need to deal with petty crime issues, through local area investments, to the threat posed by international terrorists). The oft-quoted figure that the UK contains 4.2m. cameras is no more than an estimate, but feeds into claims that the UK is the most surveiled nation with the least privacy protection. This number of cameras does not seem to contribute to any clear sense that the UK is the most secure country in the world. The UK's largest police force, London's Metropolitan Police, on the frontline of anti-terror activities, has access to thousands of surveillance cameras from its control room. However, these are used for a range of purposes from traffic monitoring to interventions in suspected drug dealing. In the 7 July 2005 London terror attacks, surveillance cameras did not facilitate preventive intervention, but merely enabled a history of the day to be replayed, aiding in identifying suspects.

Across EU member states there is great variation in surveillance camera numbers, the purpose to which systems are put, and the extent to which such systems are regulated. In Germany, for example, the deployment of surveillance cameras in public space is repeatedly challenged, and there are fewer than 100 cameras in public areas. Belgium and Austria have a larger number of surveillance camera systems than Germany (although far fewer than the UK), but these are mostly used for traffic management and minor offences. Video surveillance is also used to protect government and ministerial buildings; however the images are not recorded, as the cameras are used for immediate interventions only, ruling out any opportunity to reconstruct history in the manner of the UK Metropolitan Police. The Czech Republic, Denmark, the Netherlands, Lithuania, Poland, Italy, and Slovenia have all seen increases in the number of surveillance cameras deployed in recent years. Strong regulation in Denmark seems to have restricted the number of cameras, while the exact opposite is the case in the Netherlands, where camera use has expanded in areas that range from traffic management to school monitoring, notwithstanding ostensibly strong privacy regulations.

In the USA, the deployment of surveillance cameras appears to be combined with a more distinct security articulation. For example, surveillance cameras with facial recognition software have been used in public space, after having first been installed for the 2001 Superbowl. The Lower Manhattan Security initiative was also launched in 2005, combining a network of (perhaps eventually, 3,000) surveillance cameras with increased police presence and counterterrorism technologies. In Washington, surveillance cameras have been installed in commercial districts and in residential areas. The Department of Homeland Security (DHS) provided funding for surveillance cameras as part of a $2 billion program to finance homeland security needs across the country. This financed, among other things, a network of 2,250 cameras in Chicago and a "Watch Center" and network of cameras across the city of Baltimore.

Conversely, although Canada began installing surveillance cameras in public spaces in 1992, these have mostly been used in settings such as banks, restaurants, shops, and transport hubs; not security-focused operations. Video surveillance in Canada remains less intensive than in the UK, partly due to the active involvement of the Privacy Commissioner in campaigning against their overuse. Although cameras in spaces such as transport hubs and banks have been met with seemingly little resistance in Canada, the installation of cameras to surveil public space has been widely debated and in turn resisted by privacy campaigners and privacy commissioners.

From this brief opening introduction to video surveillance, it is clear that to think of surveillance cameras as primarily a security technology or even an anti-terror technology, requires prioritizing one particular use of these systems over others. To imagine surveillance cameras being used to intervene in terror attacks (rather than providing a history to be replayed after an event), also requires a selective focus. Surveillance camera systems are used to monitor traffic, maintain order in schools, and watch the flow of pedestrians in transport hubs far more frequently than they are used for security or anti-terror operations. Yet such systems are often funded through anti-terror budgets, made available to anti-terror operations and gain the kind of publicity required to justify their budgets in moments of terror. In the following sections, three social science approaches will be drawn on to investigate how surveillance cameras, terror, security, and insecurity might be understood.

Risk

Social scientists have provided a variety of ways of understanding risk. Lupton (1999) argues that "the contemporary obsession with the concept of risk has its roots in the changes inherent in the transformation of societies from pre-modern to modern and then to late modern or post-modern, as some theorists prefer to describe the contemporary era." Late or post-modernity generally refers to the widespread and broad socioeconomic and political changes that occurred in Western societies since the Second World War. Due to these changes, it is argued, an increasing sense of insecurity has emerged, pushing notions such as risk to the fore (Lupton 1999). This growing sense of insecurity and awareness of risk has led some commentators to describe post-modern or late modern society as being a "risk society." Beck suggests the risk society "is increasingly occupied with debating, preventing and managing risks that it itself has produced" (Beck 1992). It is concerned with future events, which produce feelings of anxiety. The move to a risk society is also coupled with a move away from an understanding of science and technology as progress, to one where risks produced by science and technology need to be anticipated and managed.

Such an approach enables us to think of surveillance technologies and issues of security and insecurity in broad terms, raising questions such as to what extent are video surveillance systems involved in managing risks that surveillance cameras have helped to introduce and what kinds of risks are anticipated and built into video surveillance systems?

Technological development may also have brought with it an expectation that risks and problems can be solved via technology. Advancements in technology may now give us hope that any problems that arise can be solved by more technological developments. The notion of managing security–insecurity through risk can be seen in, for example, the introduction of the DNA Database in the UK in 1995 and the widespread use of video surveillance and the emergence of biometrics.

However, for some social scientists, technological interventions in security–insecurity carry their own risks. For example, Norris and Armstrong (1999) argue that motifs of the "stranger society" are invoked to justify surveillance systems. Security in this instance is not solely focused on, for example, terror attacks, but more broadly oriented toward ideas of the decline of communities and communication. The loss of face-to-face communication is said to lead to a decline in intimate knowledge of others, resulting in less predictability in others' behavior. The "stranger society," rather than being managed through new technologies, becomes intensified by developments such as gated communities, the privatization of public space, and the widespread use of remote video surveillance cameras. Although these developments are implemented in order to manage risk, and in the case of surveillance cameras to reduce the public's fear of crime, they may instead have the opposite effect. Although in the UK the political rhetoric surrounding cameras has been that "cameras make the public feel safer," international studies have suggested that surveillance cameras may, in fact, heighten individuals' feelings of insecurity. Technological developments can draw attention to the risks that surround us. For example, surveillance cameras may not positively impact on an individual's perception of public space, but reinforce existing negative feelings. Alternatively a lack of control over our own security, and our reliance on surveillance products rather than other people to keep us safe, may contribute to a growing sense of insecurity.

To return to the central question—How do surveillance cameras usher in notions of security and insecurity?—the literature on risk enables us to look at this question in light of issues such as: how are surveillance camera systems co-opted into risk management strategies, to what extent do video surveillance systems exacerbate the risks they are introduced to manage, and does video surveillance enhance a sense of security or insecurity?

Foucault, governmentality and disciplinary power

Foucault's work has broad resonance across the social sciences. His writings on governmentality suggest a particular approach to the subject of order. Foucault refers to 'epistemes' as periods of time characterized by specific practices of knowledge and order. Each of these epistemes focuses on a different object, machine or architecture. For Foucault, the modern project of ordering which runs from the eighteenth century onwards "was the dream of a transparent society, visible and legible in each of its own parts, the dream of there no longer existing any zones of darkness, zones established by the privilege of royal power or the prerogative of some corporation. It was the dream that each individual, whatever position he occupied, might be able to see the whole of society" (Foucault 1980: 152). The primary architecture and disciplinary mechanism of this modern episteme was provided by the panopticon which was characterized by "An inspecting gaze, a gaze which each individual under its weight will end by interiorising to the point that he is his own overseer, each individual thus experiencing this surveillance over and against himself. A superb formula: power exercised continuously and for what turned out to be a minimal cost" (1980: 158). For Rose and Miller governmentality should thus be understood as "the complex of mundane programmes, calculations, techniques, apparatuses, documents and procedures through which authorities seek to embody and give effect to government ambitions" (Rose and Miller 1992). In short, they advocate studying the conduct of conduct.

In terms of surveillance specifically, Foucault's work concentrates on the dynamics of disciplinary power. Foucault's interest lay in the disciplinary power of administration, through which activity is reorganized in order to make it more visible and more amenable to observation. Surveillance is increasingly rationalized as it extends into more areas of society. Foucault used Bentham's panopticon as a metaphor for modern society (as he sees it a carceral society, reminiscent of Weber's "iron cage") in order to depict what he termed the "formation of a disciplinary society." The formation of this disciplinary society entailed three broad historical processes; the first being economic, the second juridico-political, and the third scientific. Alongside these historical processes he identified several reasons for its formation: "the large demographic thrust of the eighteenth century; an increase in the floating population … ; a change of quantitative scale in the groups to be supervised or manipulated … the growth in the apparatus of production" (Foucault 1977).

Foucault's focus on power and discipline accentuates individual processes of subjectification and subjugation, whereby the body becomes the site for the enactment of power. Bentham's concept of the panopticon is used to present surveillance as an instrument through which people conduct their actions while aware of their own constant visibility. The idea of being constantly observed: "Constrain[s] the convict to good behaviour … the worker to work … the patient to the observation of the regulations … he who is subjected to a field of visibility … becomes the principle of his own subjection" (Foucault 1977).

In the literature on video surveillance, those who follow a Foucauldian line of thought argue that the increasing number and sophistication of cameras acts as an example of the expansion of disciplinary mechanisms. This follows from a literal translation of Bentham's panopticon to convey an "all-seeing" architecture. However, a counter-argument can be made that panoptic metaphors are limited in their utility for understanding surveillance cameras due to the selectivity of video surveillance, with camera operators often deciding what counts as an appropriate focus. Perhaps surveillance cameras do not therefore make all subjects equally visible.

Using a Foucauldian perspective necessitates thinking about surveillance and surveillance technologies as means to monitor and control a populace. This leads to further questions regarding the extent to which a surveillance technology could match a literal version of the panopticon (seeing all, recording all). In practice, surveillance camera systems tend to be partial in their real-time visibility, monitoring, and recording. However, Foucault's work introduces a rich array of ideas pertaining to history, relations of governing, rationales of government, and the possibility of resistance, which might help think through complex notions of security and insecurity.

For our central question, Foucault's work enables us to think about security and insecurity in terms of governmentality and the conduct of conduct. What are the specific disciplinary architectures envisaged in the design and implementation of video surveillance systems? How is the conduct of conduct shifted through the introduction of surveillance cameras (for those operating systems and those subject to its gaze)? How do disciplinary architectures and particular techniques developed through surveillance cameras for understanding conduct establish expectations regarding security and insecurity and with what consequences?

Science and technology studies

Science and technology studies (STS) focuses closely on technology and its operation. This is not to suggest that using STS ideas enables straightforward and definitive statements to be made regarding what video surveillance does, can do, or will do in the future. STS moves away from any suggestion that technology straightforwardly determines social or political outcomes and instead focuses on, for example, hybrids of people, technology, objects, and information. It treats change as an on-going accomplishment and takes seriously the need to get inside the technical detail to analyse such matters as the design, development, and working order of technologies. This has enabled STS to develop a sophisticated vocabulary for talking about and engaging with technologies. It has also facilitated the study of interactions between humans and non-humans. Furthermore, STS has enriched research on technology by elaborating sensibilities for engaging with the day-to-day activities which constitute and maintain a variety of modes of technology-in-action. STS is useful for engaging with surveillance cameras-in-action precisely because questions regarding what surveillance cameras might do, how they might work, whether they induce security or insecurity, for whom and with what consequences, remain open.

Four sensibilities in particular are useful for engaging the study of surveillance cameras, security, and insecurity. These sensibilities should not be understood as factual statements about the nature of technology. Instead, they are designed as principles for orienting research. The first sensibility is that *technology does not determine outcome* (Mackenzie and Wajcman 1999). In this sense, technologies are always involved in a range of what we might term social, political, and technical relations which contribute to any experience of that technology. It is only through an understanding of these relations that we can generate a detailed sense of the nature of a technology, its history and so on.

The second sensibility is that *attempts to produce, make sense of, utilize and mobilize forms of information (in this case footage from surveillance cameras) and retain the integrity of that information are always complex*. For Latour (1990) this is a challenge of immutable mobility: the work required to move information and get that information to perform in the same way in many different times and places. Often information turns out to be mutable or not very mobile. Although Latour uses this concept to explore the immutable mobility of scientific data, the same questions can be applied to surveillance camera footage. In the latter case, this raises questions of who or what narrates surveillance camera images on behalf of whom or what, in what situations, and toward what kinds of consequences.

The third sensibility is that *technology can be conceived of as congealed social and political relations* (Winner 1980). That is, the end product of technology development, although open to numerous interpretations, also embodies the social-political arguments that went into its development. However, drawing on the first sensibility, the imperative should not be to straightforwardly read off from any set of political relations how a technology should be understood, but instead to utilize an understanding of social and political relations as one means to engage with, assess, explore, and research the deployment of any particular device. Social and political relations are not to be understood as determining how a technology operates, but instead provide one possible condition of being.

The fourth sensibility is that technology, people, information, and objects can be thought of as ontologically multiple (Mol 2002). That is, the nature (ontology) of something is not just open to question, but can be understood as multiple and distinct. This is not an argument for pluralism, suggesting one thing can be seen from several perspectives. It is instead an argument for multiplicity; the simultaneous co-existence of distinct natures. For surveillance cameras, systems, operatives, and images, this sensibility suggests the possibility of opening up for question the multiple natures of the entities involved.

Drawing on these four sensibilities enables a particular kind of engagement with security–insecurity. The first sensibility draws to our attention the indeterminacy of, for example, surveillance camera systems. Although it would be possible to make assumptions regarding the impact, use, and wider consequences of installing a surveillance camera system, this sensibility operates as a precautionary principle. As the first section of this chapter demonstrated, even assuming that video surveillance is primarily a security or even crime-focused technology requires careful scrutiny.

The second sensibility draws attention to the complexity of information that flows through technological systems. It warns against any assumption that surveillance camera footage simply speaks for itself (a claim often made by proponents of video surveillance in relation to, for example, the use of surveillance camera footage in legal proceedings). Instead, the sensibility advocates getting close to the action to figure out how surveillance camera footage is narrated, and by whom, in what kinds of demonstrations it is used, to what ends, and drawing on what further support mechanisms. This approach suggests that, when surveillance camera footage is mobilized, it is not sent out into the world alone, but rather is supported by a range of what Latour would term allies.

The third sensibility suggests that surveillance camera systems can be researched on the basis of the social and political relations they come to embody as a result of their design, development, installation, and use. Any particular surveillance camera system can thus be researched for its social and political history and how this might continue to shape the operation of the system. The local politics of: relations between operators, managers, and funders of systems; relations between political authorities and the police; and relations between distinct publics (such as residents, shoppers, retailers, and so on) close to surveillance camera systems can all be taken into account in developing an understanding of the politics of video surveillance.

Taken together, these first three sensibilities provide a basis for engaging with security–insecurity and the development of new technologies. They set out an approach to research which suggests getting close to the action of how particular systems in specific locations are installed and used, how surveillance footage is understood, narrated, and mobilized and recognizes, that the social and political relations of surveillance cameras require careful handling in research. Security and insecurity, utilizing these sensibilities, comes to be seen as a local and situated accomplishment.

The fourth sensibility, focused on multiplicity and ontology, suggests thinking about deep uncertainties regarding security–insecurity. Following this line of argument, objects, for example, could become the focal point for questions of their ontological security. A prominent recent example of this was provided by the water bottle scare at international airports in 2006. Liquid containers and their owners had previously been considered ordinary, pervasive, mundane, and a feature of the retail sales of airport departure lounges. Suddenly, following a terror alert, they were shifted into ontological multiplicity and insecurity. Were water bottles a drink, a bomb, a surveillance target, a reason to question owners and/or a new sales opportunity? Although seemingly a philosophical question—What is/are the nature/s of water bottles?—the organizational (for airports), personal (for passengers with bottles) and business (for travel companies) consequences of this new ontological insecurity were for a time stark. Ontological security was re-established via the dislocation of all landside water bottles from passengers, with security checks used to confirm this separation. Surveillance camera systems could be drawn into consideration to enhance both ontological security (tracking any deviant bottles and their owners, reaffirming the singular ontology for airside bottles) and insecurity (as the threat and security measures seemed to enhance feelings of being unsafe—Who is carrying what kind of bottle, and where are they doing so?).

For our central question—of surveillance technologies and notions of security and insecurity—an STS approach enables us to ask particular kinds of questions. If we move away from assumptions that technology straightforwardly determines outcomes, then what are the range of entities that need to be incorporated into research in order to understand security–insecurity? How do these entities combine to narrate surveillance camera footage, rendering its contents meaningful and secure? Furthermore, what are the contemporary and historical political and social relations which shape how these entities are assembled and in turn shape the operation of video surveillance? Finally, how does video surveillance generate both ontological security and insecurity?

Conclusion

In sum, this chapter suggests that security technologies with surveillance capabilities such as surveillance cameras usher in notions of both security and insecurity. Security–insecurity can be analysed through distinct social science perspectives. We have provided three such perspectives: risk, the work of Foucault, and STS. While it would still be possible to draw in other approaches, each of the perspectives considered here allows for different kinds of questions and different modes of engagement with questions to be brought to the fore.

The literature on risk enables us to look at security–insecurity in relation to surveillance technologies through consideration of what are sometimes termed 'risk management strategies'. However, this literature also draws our attention to broader notions of risk, that the introduction of new technologies can heighten awareness of risks, that technologies can generate more of the uncertainty, they were installed to address than and that very particular notions of who or what is a risk can be designed into security technologies with significant consequences (particularly for those who may now find themselves defined as risky).

Foucault's work, conversely, provides a means to engage with security–insecurity in terms of rich social and political histories within which specific disciplinary architectures are envisaged, designed, and implemented. Drawing on Foucault's work offers us opportunities to study the conduct of conduct and how this might alter in relation to the introduction of new security technologies. Foucault's work (on visibility and the gaze, disciplinary power and epistemes) also suggests means to assess the establishment of security expectations and their consequences.

STS work re-orients the contours of these investigations by bringing technology to the fore. STS suggests moving away from any counter-expectation that technologies straightforwardly determine outcomes, to instead focusing on the range of entities (for example, people, technology, objects, information, and policies) that contribute to accomplishing notions of security and insecurity. STS also draws our attention to complex questions regarding the nature of information at the heart of security systems (for example, how is surveillance footage narrated, by whom, and for whom, rendering its contents meaningful and secure) and the contemporary and historical political and social relations which might shape how security technologies are assembled and operated. Finally, adopting an STS approach also suggests accentuating ontological matters, bringing to center-stage the question of how people, things, spaces, and information might be understood as ontologically secure or insecure.

References

Beck, U. (1992). *Risk Society: Towards a New Modernity*, London: Sage.

Foucault, M. (1977). *Discipline and Punish: The Birth of the Prison*, Harmondsworth: Penguin Books.

——(1980). *Power/Knowledge*, New York: Pantheon.

Latour, B. (1990). "Drawing Things Together," in M. Lynch and S. Woolgar (eds), *Representation in Scientific Practice*, Cambridge, MA: MIT Press, pp. 19–68.

Lupton, D. (1999). *Risk*, London: Routledge.

Mackenzie, D. and Wajcman, J. (1999). *The Social Shaping of Technology*, 2nd edition, Buckingham and Philadelphia, PA: Open University Press.

Mol, A. (2002). *The Body Multiple: Ontology in Medical Practice*, Durham, NC: Duke UP.

Norris, C. and Armstrong, G. (1999). *The Maximum Surveillance Society: The Rise of CCTV*, Oxford: Berg.

Rose, N. and Miller, P. (1992). "Political Power Beyond the State: Problematics of Government," *British Journal of Sociology,* 43: 173–205.

Winner, L. (1980). "Do Artefacts have Politics?," *Daedalus,* 109(1): 121–36.

Section 2.2.
Social divisions of surveillance

a. Colonialism and surveillance

Ahmad H. Sa'di

If Western colonialism is to be defined by its effect—that is by its ability to essentially shape large non-Western populations' modes of life rather than by some of its manifestations such as Western rule, Western cultural or ideological hegemony—it would be reasonable to argue that colonialism has not ended. Western powers and Western-dominated international organizations continue to vigorously pursue efforts to have non-Western populations change their modes of living to embrace the principles of governable and rational economic individualism within an international hierarchical division of labor, which was at the heart of colonialism. Such an understanding would yield interpretations of colonialism that might radically depart from prevailing official histories and their periodization (which usually follow a linear narrative of causes for colonialism, occupation, colonial rule, national awakening and de-colonization).

This essay is limited to the period between 1492, when Columbus discovered the New World, and the late 1950s, when Western-directed domination (mainly by the UK and France) waned. As such, I leave outside the discussion both the phenomena of neocolonialism and postmodern modes of governance. Analytically, I treat colonialism as a gigantic two-tier machine. The first component refers to the expanded reach of the World Capitalist System (WCS) to areas which had historically been beyond its purview. This was accomplished through various methods, including direct occupation, indirect rule, unequal trade treaties, imposing financial trusteeship, or through removing (annihilating or expelling) native populations and replacing them with European immigrants. The second component aims to create a new social order that would absorb, sustain and reproduce modes of life compatible with the WCS. It required altering the structures of cognition, consciousness, emotions and behaviors of the newly incorporated populations as well as disciplining their bodies. The expansion of the WCS has been exhaustively explored by sociologists, historians and economists, mainly those broadly associated with the dependency/world system perspective. Meanwhile, the modes through which the populations in the colonies were incorporated into this system have been discussed in the literature pertaining to colonial governance and surveillance, though these works have remained largely inchoate and under-theorized. This short essay aims to sketch the main methods used to convert the large and varied colonized populations into governable colonial subjects, through power/knowledge discourses. Such discourses should not be seen as separate from the wider changes which engulfed Europe. Rather colonialism played a transformative role, though in divergent ways, with regard to both the colonizers and the colonized.

After the discovery of the New World, it seemed that Europe's old powers, Spain and Portugal, were following in the footsteps of ancient empires in exploiting the populations of the newly discovered

Ahmad H. Sa'di

territories. Yet, the large quantities of gold and silver that were transferred to Europe from the New World, a good part of which was used to import luxurious commodities from Asia and Africa, along with the discovery of short and direct maritime routes to India and Africa, invigorated a worldwide commerce and led to more frequent and intensive encounters between Europeans and other peoples. This process began with Europe as inferior to some cultures which then flourished in terms of sciences and the commodities they could offer. Only since the late eighteenth century, following various European developments at the cognitive, cultural, economic and scientific levels, which we now broadly refer to as the Enlightenment and industrial revolution, did Europe take the lead in steering the world economy. These developments were accentuated in the nineteenth century following the second industrial revolution, which gave Europe great technological advantage over the other parts of the world and solidified an international division of labor. Alongside the considerable increase in Europe's coercive power, economic forces led to Western domination of a large part of the globe, which, by 1914, extended to 85 percent of the earth's surface. Its expanding industries needed cheap raw materials from the colonies, new markets for its outputs and new venues for high-return investments.

While Western expansion was achieved by the actual or threatened use of force (e.g. gunboat diplomacy), maintaining the acquired colonies and protectorates was accomplished with the aid of various surveillance and control methods which aimed to alter the colonizeds' modes of living. These methods were derived from Enlightenment principles premised on the belief in science, progress and humanity's mastery over nature. It is not surprising, thus, that philosopher Immanuel Kant (1724–1804), who was among the first to define the term Enlightenment, was also the first to offer a scientific definition to the concept "race"; a key category in colonial ideology, governance and science. Indeed, the association between ideas which stem from the Enlightenment and colonialism prevailed as the colonies became laboratories for experimenting with Western ideas, including practices of population management and control. Thus, for example, the panopticon, Bentham's ultimate disciplinary device, which Foucault described as an epitome of Europe's modern disciplinary power, was built in India rather than Europe (Kaplan 1995). Colonial administrator William J. Herschel also first introduced fingerprinting as an identification method in India in 1858, in an effort to determine the identity of prisoners, government pensioners and contractors. Only later was fingerprinting employed in England.

The expansion of Western colonialism during the nineteenth century, and the domination over what seemed to those engaged in colonialism (politicians, administrators, diplomats, military commanders, scholars and populists) to be a mixture of strange populations, habits, rituals, religions, languages, bodily reactions, etc., required a scientific knowledge of these peoples in order to rule them and alter their modes of living. Moreover, given its magnitude and complexity, the world could neither be comprehended nor managed directly. Rather, it had to be summarized, represented in miniature, segmented and translated through various scientific methods, symbols and forms into two-dimensional representational objects. Maps, tables, records and photographs skipped over the hurdles of time, space and complexity, and made colonial peoples and contexts submissive to Western knowledge-driven domination.

The first step towards effectively ruling the new populations was to divide and sub-divide them into small governable units. This process was reflected in the transformation of the concept "race" from a wide and largely descriptive term which denoted physical differences among four or five groups of humanity into eighty groups, and then into something that was used in lieu of groups' terms as small as nation or even tribe. More important, however, was its essentialization, with the emergence of "racial types" (which were quite often attributed to ethnicities, classes or castes) as sub-categories, whereby physical characteristics were associated with various mental, behavioral and temperamental attributes. These "racial types," following the Darwinist approach, were hierarchically arranged on the scale of evolution. The exploration and mapping of racial types was institutionalized through the establishment of professional societies, such as the Aborigines Protection Society 1837, the Ethnological Society of London 1843 and the Royal Anthropological Society 1863. The scientific knowledge produced by members of these societies composed the bulk of colonial knowledge, which shaped the dominant discourse employed not only by colonial officials but also by the wider public in the West. Beside, scholars, explorers, missionaries and colonial officials helped to produce this knowledge, such as Harry H. Johnston (1858–1927), who while serving as Commissioner for British Central Africa in the 1890s conducted an ethnographic survey along with his aid W.G. Doggett of the "marked types of African Man" from "the low ape-like types of the Elgon and Semliki forests" to the "Apollo-like Masai." These types were positioned both in space and on an evolutionary scale. His illustrated publications, such as *British Central Africa* (1897), embodied the theory of the Negro race's low intellectual, moral and cultural status and provided "evidence" for its improvement under British colonial rule (Ryan 1997: 158–61).

Such categorizations were frequently objectified and reintroduced as valid categories in colonial population surveys and guided the official approaches towards indigenous populations. Although some of these categorizations rested on local knowledge, the new meanings attributed to them were colonial in nature (Guha 2003). Moreover, the colonial administrations introduced a significant change in the methods of analysis which increased the usefulness of the data gathered via censuses which used these categories, by introducing political arithmetic and statistics. Along with developments in the sciences of statistics and demography, the unit of analysis was decreased, and the individual became the surveyed unit instead of the household (ibid.: 156–58).

Following two great rebellions in the colonies, the Indian in 1857 and the Jamaican in 1865, categorization of the indigenous populations became to be seen as an insufficient tool of governance, and a need emerged to render the various categories of the local population, particularly those inimical to colonial rule, visible and easily identifiable to the colonial gaze. Towards that end they employed photography, something which was being widely used by ethnographers as a tool which supposedly yielded objective and verifiable images and captured the minuteness and exactitude of the subject as well as enabling the seizure in a single shot of a group of persons who were considered representative of their "racial types." Thus, for example, the missionary-explorer David Livingstone instructed his brother, Charles, to take photographs of the racial types as follows:

> Secure characteristic specimens of the different tribes … for the purpose of Ethnography. Do not choose the ugliest but (as among ourselves) the better class of natives who are believed to be characteristic of the race. … and if possible, get men, women and children grouped together.
>
> *(Quoted in Ryan 1997: 146)*

Following the Indian rebellion the Political and Secret Department at the Indian Office undertook a photographic survey of *The Peoples of India*, which was composed of eight volumes, with 468 photographs in each set. Despite inaccuracies in the use of concepts denoting various groups, such as tribe, caste, race, etc., this represented the colonial desire for panoptic control, where photographs were placed on maps that located the "racial types" in geographical locations and physiognomic hierarchies. Similar books were produced on other peoples and the wildlife in the colonies, thus giving the Westerner—whether a colonial official, an officer, a missionary, a traveler, or a businessman—the illusion that the natives and their natural environment are visible and controllable (see e.g. Ryan 1997).

Such categorizations and the stereotypes attached to them were frequently internalized and objectified by the colonized, thus blurring the colonizer/colonized division. Moreover, given the hierarchical order of the various groups, the benefits that some gained from the colonial regime and the allocation of some groups to certain functions in the colonial system—such as the Gurkhas in India who were considered a friendly warrior race and consequently incorporated into the security apparatus and frequently used against subversive tribes—distrust among different groups scaled up as the indigenous population were made to participate in colonial rule. Yet, this was not always the case. The French in Algeria, in line with their universal approach, instead confronted the Muslim population with a choice between two alternative identities of Muslim and French. Since adopting the second identity meant renouncing the first, only very few thousands among Algeria's small Westernized elite adopted the French identity. The prerequisite of dominating a large, undifferentiated and largely unfriendly indigenous population led the French to use harsh surveillance measures, which included issuing internal passports, limiting the movement of certain populations to specific areas and eventually creating camps where landless peasants were concentrated. Such harsh measured were only used by British colonial authorities in periods of conflict or against groups that defied the colonial system of surveillance, such as the "criminal/notorious tribes" in India, that were resettled, quarantined, subjected to harsh control methods including registration with local police, fingerprinting and separating children from their parents (Major 1999).

Along with locating the colonial subject in a group which was assumed to possess certain socio-psychological and moral characteristics and whose size was periodically assessed through censuses, subjects were also localized spatially. In tandem with the inauguration of colonial rule, borders defining political entities were drawn, thus converting him or her to a subject of a specific administration. Moreover, a person's locality and land were made to appear on various maps produced by the survey department that the colonial administrations established soon after assuming control. Indeed the colonial administrations used cartography as a tool of governance, where settlements, even remote ones, building plots, roads, railways, mineral areas, etc. were defined in unprecedented precision on cadastral maps. Moreover, land surveys and registration were conducted in order to convert the land into a commodity, thus undermining non-capitalist relations, and to assess the quality of the soil for purposes of taxation or modifying land use. These acts of surveillance have had a tremendous impact on indigenous populations, particularly in colonies with settler populations (e.g. Akerman 2009 especially Chapters 4–6) such as Algeria—where the settlers controlled 75 percent of the agricultural irrigated land in the coastal area—and Palestine, where such surveys assisted settlers in acquiring land. In the case of Palestine the results were far-reaching.

Since the colonial system rested, in the final analysis, on the use of force, the British government lobbied colonial administrators to prioritize the production of standard topographical maps (of 1:250,000), which were required to defend the empire. The absence of such maps, as during the second Boer War and the first stages of the Palestinian revolt of 1936–39, hindered the British war effort. However, with developments in aerial photography and reconnaissance, the indigenous population became more visible than ever to the colonial gaze. British maps which were based on aerial photographs of Palestinian localities, for example, were acquired by the Zionists before the 1948 War and had significant impact on their war performance.

While surveying and map drawing allowed the colonized populations to be summed up and presented on maps, charts, tables and records as object of surveillance and reform, Western colonialism also endeavored to constitute colonized subjects through various additional methods of surveillance and self-monitoring. The first of these is taxation. Normally, colonial authorities managed the budget of each colony independently, and becoming self-sufficient was considered an important benchmark in assessing the administrative efficiency and progress in the general conditions of the colony. Therefore, taxation became the main indicator of colonial success. While revenues were used for administration as well as to carry out socio-economic projects (schools, hospitals, roads, railways, etc.), their significance lies in how they drew the colonized population into the market economy. To pay their taxes colonized peoples not only had to change their economic activities to market-oriented ones—including commoditizing the land, growing cash crops, and working as wage laborers—but also to modify the details of their lives as individuals (and in this way colonialism was different from other forms of rule, see e.g. Kaplan 1995). It is not surprising thus that taxation was frequently articulated in the colonial discourse in moralistic terms as improving the "lazy" (or careless) natives by prompting them to become industrious, thrifty and accountable. Such an improvement was monitored through accountancy, a "scientific" technique on which bases, rewards and sanctions were decided. Moreover, through taxation and accountancy, the colonized people were compelled to monitor their own economic activities (Bush and Matby 2004).

Probably the most effective form through which various colonial practices of surveillance and self-surveillances were propagated was missionary work. While it is misguided to portray missionaries as agents of colonialism, yet as Europeans through their various engagements: imparting Western education, providing Western medical care, and above all spreading the European version of Christianity, missionaries helped inculcate large indigenous populations with Western notions of surveillance and self-monitoring. Not only is Christianity the utmost form of self-surveillance—where the believer's actions, thoughts and desires are supposedly visible and that for which s/he is accountable—but it also enforces other behaviors such as tax-paying and obedience. Moreover, some missionaries lent religious support, regardless of how disingenuous, to the racial order. The Rev. David Livingstone, for example, expressed his views in his book: *Missionary Travels and Researchers in South Africa* (1870). The mere hierarchy of those who imparted Christianity over new converts also found expression in the hierarchy of the churches. Moreover, as Europeans, their perception of order and civility became a yardstick for assessing the natives' self-improvement. Therefore when the European powers forced the local leaders through gunboat diplomacy to open their countries to commerce and missionaries, it seems that they greatly appreciated the role that missionaries played in "normalizing" the others.

Beside religion, education was considered the main venue for inculcating colonial discourse and practices of individual governance among the indigenous population. This was particularly the case in elite colleges, such as Victoria College in Egypt and The Gordon Memorial College in the Sudan. The colonizer/colonized hierarchy was manifest in all aspects of the educational system: the hierarchy of the personnel—where the high positions were always filled by Europeans—the Eurocentric curricula, the educational messages, the language of instruction which was the language of the colonizer, etc. Moreover, the objective of "character building" that these schools promoted tended to cultivate a governable, productive individual capable of self-mastery and self-surveillance. This included strict schedules and an emphasis on sportsmanship, (healthy) competition in the classroom and on the sports field, (physical) punishment and rewards, an ethos of self-sufficiency and group spirit, imparting debating skills, and instilling the virtues of manliness and obedience in young men through the scouts' activities. These were to affect the conduct and the consciousness of the students. Even after graduation such schools maintained their influence through a variety of rituals and annual reunions. Graduates of these colleges who were educated to become compradorian elites—an intermediary class between the mass of the colonized population and colonial power—were also to constitute a role model in their countries. Yet it was always important for colonial authorities to keep the Westernized local elite aware of their roots, such that they would not be too alienated from the mass of the native population. Such awareness would make the assignment of the colonial officials who advocated for direct rule easier and spared members of this elite the agony of their sealed fate as being members of an inferior race. While they might model European habits and style, they could never be Europeans. Indeed the cultural and intellectual achievements of indigenous individuals were assessed by colonial administrators and more generally by Europeans as mimicry rather than mastery.

The racial boundaries upon which colonialism was established were under constant threat by the movement of population and the daily, mundane and prolonged encounter between Europeans and indigenous populations. Therefore policing the racial boundaries became a vital worry of colonial administrations. The dangers of interracial sex and the birth of mixed-blood children loomed ominously. Those living in faraway countries, whether British soldiers or Indian or Chinese workers, were often single and healthy young men, whose sexual energies, according to nineteenth-century theories, had to be discharged. Accordingly, the questions of who bedded and who bred with whom became a main concern of colonial authorities. Policing racial boundaries developed in two directions. The first revolved around regulating and licensing brothels and the surveillance of both customers and inmates. In cities where foreign workers, sailors or soldiers were present, public brothels were geographically clustered, according to the ethnicity of the workers and their clientele in a way which reinforced the racial hierarchy. Only White men were allowed to visit all brothels. In order to prevent the spread of venereal diseases, which in various cases presented a serious threat to the British army's readiness or to the health of the general population in international trade hubs, the British authorities imposed harsh disciplinary measures on non-White prostitutes who catered to White customers. Such measures included occasional compulsory medical examinations. Those suspected of having contagious diseases were locked in government-run hospitals and forced to undergo treatment.

Prostitution was conceived as upholding the racial order in another way. Since it was financially impossible for British soldiers to bring their wives with them, the colonial system arranged prostitutes for them. The dire alternative, it was thought, would be for the soldier's masculinity to be compromised. Widespread homosexuality among soldiers would lead some to become effeminate, a characteristic that was attributed to men of lower races (Bryder 1998: 814).

The second strategy through which the racial order was upheld was maintaining the homogeneity of racial groups despite the bio-power imperatives of the WCS. At first, the colonial administration sought to achieve this by including women among the workers who were sent to plantation colonies. Even though they comprised a small fraction of such workers, through their sexual roles as wives or prostitutes, they were perceived as maintaining racial boundaries. However, following developments in public health in the early twentieth century, and the consequent decrease in the mortality rate among children, the colonial authorities found that it was preferable financially and racially to encourage high birth rates among the local population, rather than import foreign workers. Thus surveillance efforts shifted from regulating prostitution to enforcing public health practices (e.g. Manderson 2002). Moreover, at around the same period the number of British women who were allowed to live with their partners in the colonies increased.

Yet, the most serious challenge to the racial hierarchy was posed by the presence of single White women in the colonies. The idea that such women could be dominated by non-White males as prostitutes, concubines or even as wives was seen as chastening Europeans' sense of superiority and undermining colonial rule. Therefore considerable efforts were made to avert such developments including imposing harsh penalties on indigenous men who were convicted of raping White females. In some cases—such as *The White Women's Protection Ordinance, 1926* in New Guinea—the death penalty was institutionalized, although such acts were rare (Bryder 1998: 808). Yet, deterring indigenous men was not enough. The British authorities in some colonies, such as Hong Kong, occasionally deported White prostitutes back to Europe, as their presence was too embarrassing to Europeans' and Americans' racial pride. And while it was not always possible to prevent poor European women from arriving in the colonies, the British authorities were relieved that White prostitutes in India, for example, were Roman Catholic and Jewish émigrés from central Europe rather than protestant (ibid.: 809).

Other challenges to the racial order that demanded continuous surveillance had broadly to do with the inclusion/exclusion of new ambiguous groups. The first such category were Europeans who were not citizens of the colonizing power, but tried to become so, such as Italian, Spanish and Maltese who strived to acquire French citizenship and be part of the French colonial project. This group, despite being European, lacked the qualities attributed to the French "national character." The discourse of national character, in France and England, was in fact a fine-tuning of the racial discourse. Not only was the nation conceived of as a distinct race, and the two concepts of race and nation were frequently interchangeable, but European nations were also ranked hierarchically. Thus including such groups, in addition to the collective assimilation of over 100,000 Algerian Jews under the *Cremieux Decree*, raised anxieties about internal strangers and pseudo-compatriots (Stoler 1992: 518).

The second category where inclusion was problematic concerned mixed-blood children. In such cases the external features attributable to race might be particularly misleading. Therefore a need emerged for a basis by which such persons could be screened and included or excluded from the nation. Both the Dutch and the French had to wrestle with this issue. European education and living in a European milieu was thought to indicate the degree of European-ness of mixed-race children. In 1928 the French issued a formal guideline to be used in cases of doubt regarding the identity of the French parent (almost always the father). The "French-ness" of the child was to be determined according to the child's "physical features or race" by a "medico-legal expert" and a "moral certainty" derived from the fact that the child "has a French name, lived in a European milieu and was considered by all as being of French descent" (ibid.: 532–33). Even those whose identity was confirmed tended to stay behind, and were assigned functions in the system of colonial bio-power which White men of good stock would not do. The Hanoi society, whose aim was to raise such children as French citizens, stated that its objective was "to inculcate them with our sense of honor and integrity, while only suggesting to them modest tastes and humble aspirations" (ibid.: 533).

The anxiety regarding such "internal strangers," underscores the inaccuracy of the "racial types" and the "national character" as screening devices, something that was apparent even to those who used them. Yet, even when the screening results were precise, it was not always possible to associate the colonized people's categorization with certain emotions or behaviors. The Chinese, for example, were considered enigmatic. The explorer and photographer, John Thomson, whose work *Illustrations of China and Its People* (1973–74) followed the racial types paradigm, illustrates the point, in his reference to a picture of a Chinese boy:

> [Although] a fine, attractive-looking little fellow, his full hazel eyes beaming with kindliness and intelligence … [as he grows older, however] The softness of the eyes is then frequently replaced by a cold, calculating expression, the result of their peculiar training, and the countenance assumes an air of apathetic indifference which is so necessary to veil the inner feelings of a polished Chinese gentleman.
>
> *(Quoted in Ryan 1997: 161)*

The answer to such anxieties seemed to rest on identifying a grammar of conduct unique to the colonial race (the English or the French). It could neither be copied nor learnt, and would maintain racial boundaries, despite the intensity of the encounter between colonizers and colonized and the emergence of internal strangers. One of these codes, which particularly prevailed under the Raj, was the idea of honor and ruling others honorably. For example in his work, *Lectures on Colonization* (1861) Herman Merivale, a senior official in the Colonial Office, argued that what made the British an imperial people is their "sense of national honour, pride of blood, tenacious spirit of self-defence, the sympathies of kindred communities, the instinct of a dominant race, the vague but generous desire to spread our civilization and our religion over the world" (quoted in Patterson 2009: 211). The sense of honor was considered a key variable for understanding empires' rise and decline. Therefore, dishonorable acts by the British officials or members of the British communities in the colonies, particularly women, were seen as damaging colonial prestige. While honor could be acquired or lost, as the history of the rise and decline of empires shows, it was associated, in the British colonial discourse, with race. Overall, the natives were perceived as either having a flawed and diminished sense of honor, which the notorious and effeminate Indian clerk, the *babu*, who aped English customs epitomized or the martial races whose rigid and exaggerated sense of honor could easily lead to bloodshed and mayhem. In both cases they could not be trusted as rulers who would bring about progress. Only the British possess a balanced approach of decisiveness and self-mastery along with kindness, fairness, honesty and integrity in one's beliefs and action, gentlemanly conduct, devotion and a deep sense of duty. While these characteristics could be identified they cannot be taught as they are part of the sensitivities, which book knowledge cannot impart (Patterson 2009).

To sum up, through various practices of surveillance colonial powers tried to reconcile two antithetical forces: the WCS which is premised on fluidity, constant shifting of boundaries, the movement of peoples, etc. and colonialism which is founded on a notion of rigid racial and moral order. Moreover, as a form of governance, colonialism was interesting in fixing the population socially and spatially, and surveying and documenting the changes in their lives. This contradiction called for various strategies of policing the racial order. Yet, deploying these surveillance strategies has had immense and varied implication on the lives of the indigenous populations until the present. This includes, for example, the creation of new nations, the struggle for de-colonization, the incorporation of the ex-colonies in the world economy, civil wars, ethnic cleansing and genocide which were prompted by the racial categorizations that the colonizing powers established. Such practices also led to the emergence of new elites and hard-to-change borders and administrative practices.

References

Akerman, J. (ed.) (2009). *The Imperial Map: Cartography and the Mastery of Empire*, Chicago, IL: The University of Chicago Press.

Bryder, L. (1998). "Sex, Race and Colonialism: A Historiographical Review," *The International History Review*, 20(4): 791–1072.

Bush, B. and Matby, J. (2004). "Taxation in West Africa: Transforming the Colonial Subject into the 'Governable Person'," *Critical Perspectives on Accounting*, 15: 5–34.

Guha, S. (2003). "The Politics of Identity and Enumeration in India c. 1600–1990," *Comparative Studies in Society and History*, 45(1): 148–67.

Kaplan, M. (1995). "Panopticon in Poona: An Essay on Foucault and Colonialism," *Cultural Anthropology*, 10(1): 85–98.

Major, A. J. (1999). "State and Criminal Tribes in Colonial Punjab: Surveillance, Control and Reclamation of the 'Dangerous Classes'," *Modern Asian Studies*, 33(3): 657–88.

Manderson, L. (2002). *Sickness and the State: Health and Illness in Colonial Malaya, 1870–1940*, Cambridge: Cambridge University Press.

Patterson, S. (2009). *The Cult of Imperial Honor in British India*, New York: Palgrave Macmillan.

Ryan, J. (1997). *Picturing Empire: Photography and the Visualisation of the British Empire*, London: Reaktion.

Stoler, A. (1992). "Sexual Affront and Racial Frontiers: European Identities and the Cultural Politics of Exclusion in Colonial Southeast Asia," *Comparative Studies in Society and History*, 34(3): 514–51.

b. Identity, surveillance and modernity

Sorting out who's who

Richard Jenkins

Identity is a matter of knowing "who's who," and if we didn't know *that* we wouldn't know "what's what" either. A sophisticated classificatory ability to identify others and ourselves is what makes the human world, the largely taken-for-granted environment within which we live our everyday lives, possible. Human beings, on the basis of a relatively small number of cues, are able to identify the finest of collective and individual similarities and differences between people, identifying themselves and others as individuals and as members of collectivities. This entails registering, inferring and interpreting a variety of verbal and non-verbal information. Whether or not these identifications are "accurate," the process of identification contributes to a more or less stable sense of predictability during interaction, which allows behavior to be adjusted in a spirit of conflict avoidance or provocation, and in a host of other ways produces and reproduces everyday life as a navigable environment (Goffman 1969). Identification is absolutely central to "knowing what we are doing" as competent human beings.

Identity

The perspective on identity that I have outlined above draws its original inspiration from interactionist sociology, on the one hand, and post-functionalist anthropology, on the other (Jenkins 2008). Before exploring its relevance to the study of surveillance, a number of themes and arguments need to be made explicit and explored in more detail.

The first of these is that identity is not a thing or an essence; it is not something that we *have*. It is, rather, something that we *do*, a process of identification. In that process, there is always at least the possibility of change, no matter how modest or potentially awkward. Identification is always, in principle, open-ended. To use the word "identity," which is a noun, is therefore somewhat misleading. It is, however, such a long-established usage in everyday common sense and the social sciences that it is unlikely to be discarded. And, indeed, I shall sometimes use the word in this way here, if only in the interests of stylistic variety. Nonetheless, we should always remember that when we talk about "identity" we are actually talking about processes of *identification*.

Second, although identifications are in principle changeable—and many, such as occupation or marital status, are actually routinely changeable—not all identities are as mutable as others. For example, identifications that are internalized during early primary socialization—"primary" or "basic" identities (Jenkins 2008: 69–72)—are likely to be robust. These include individuality, kin group membership, gender, and in

159

some contexts ethnicity and/or "race." What is more, identifications that are rooted in physiological embodiment—some of which I have just mentioned—are also likely to be particularly difficult to change. Gender reassignment, for example, is possible, but in a number of respects it is not easy. Even age, which might seem to be forever changing, can only be manipulated in very limited ways; its perpetual motion is actually the essence of its irresistibility.

The other broad constraint on identity change is the authority or power of persons and/or institutions that are responsible for identifying individuals or collectivities in particular respects. For example, if a court of law finds an individual guilty of, say, downloading and exchanging child pornography and, as happens in several jurisdictions, places his or her name on an official register of sex offenders, that should prove to be an unbending and unforgiving identification. Similarly, to return to the example of gender reassignment, the imprimateur of an authorized "identifier"—a medical doctor or a panel of doctors—is required before identity change can be effected legally. In this case, the point can be extended. The sex of a newborn infant is not necessarily self-evident; in the industrialized world at least, individual sex is, in the first place, officially assigned and registered by an authorized medical professional.

Which brings me directly to the third point. Despite the thrust of a social science literature that has recently focused disproportionately on assertions of selfhood, collective mobilization and demands for recognition, there is more to identity than "I," "me," "us" and "we." "You," "them" and "they" are also part of the equation. Identification is a dialectical interplay between internal *self-identification*—which can be individual or collective—and external *categorization* by others. Practical identifications emerge out of interactions between these "sides" of the process, with each influencing the other. In principle, neither the internal nor the external are paramount, although in any specific situation one or the other may be more influential; this, however, is a matter for empirical discovery rather than theoretical presumption.

Thus categorization of a person or group from "outside," by others, is integral to the process of identification, and to knowing "who's who" and "what's what" in the human world. However, identification—and therefore categorization—involves more than "just" knowing. Knowing is never neutral or disinterested. Categorizing others necessarily contributes to how we treat them. On a broader canvas, classification—the allocation of individuals to collective categories—is fundamental to *social sorting* (Lyon 2007: 94–117), the identification and ordering of individuals in order to "put them in their place" within local, national and global "institutional orders" (Jenkins 2008: 43–45). Practices of social sorting are ubiquitous and far-reaching in modern societies, having gradually come to occupy a role at the heart of modern bureaucratic governance that is all the more potent because their taken-for-grantedness renders them almost invisible, part of the furniture of the state and business. Social sorting is central to the formation and shaping of actors as particular kinds of people, with particular life chances, subject to particular constraints and permitted access to particular opportunities, and to the historical emergence of institutional and demographic macro-patterns.

In other words, categorization, classification and social sorting have consequences (Bowker and Starr 2000), in particular through the allocation of rewards or punishments. Punishments are perhaps more visible and better documented. For example, in ethnic profiling by the police, street-level law enforcement is informed by presumptions about the individual likelihood of guilt according to visible ethnicity or "race"; this has been called "categorical suspicion" (Marx 1988). Immigration rules, although there is considerable scope in their operation for individual discretion, are more formal, defining who must be interrogated at the border, and who is forbidden to enter under any circumstances. Medicine is also in the business of classifying and categorizing: the *Diagnostic and Statistical Manual* (DSM) of the American Psychiatric Association, for example, is a compendium of classifications (diagnoses) and their rewards and penalties, which range from treatments that may transform upset and disordered lives for the better, to involuntary institutional confinement and intrusive interventions. Policing practices and immigration rules also involve rewards, for those who are lightly policed or ignored, or who may be admitted as of right. Penalties and benefits are, in fact, inseparable in practical processes of categorization and classification; they may also encourage the internalization of external categorization, as argued by the "labelling" or "social reaction" perspective in the sociology of deviance (Jenkins 2008: 95–99).

The next point, once again against the grain of recent social science orthodoxy—in this case an emphasis on diversity—is that identification is a matter of similarity as well as difference. They are complementary sides of the same coin. It is, for example, a basic classificatory principle that difference makes no sense without similarity, and *vice versa*: to allocate an individual example of anything to a category is to make a judgment about what it differs from *and* what it resembles. It cannot be otherwise. The logic of classification aside, the realities of everyday life point in the same direction. Pursued to its extreme end point, the argument that difference is the key element in identification would leave us adrift in a world of unconnected alienated individuals, in which the best we could ever hope to know about anyone is who he or she is *not*; who they *are* would be a mystery. In fact, the notion of who someone *is* might not even make any sense. Fortunately, this is not the real human world. In that world, affiliation and belonging to families, organizations and other groups is an important dimension of identification, and similarity and difference go hand in hand with each other.

Finally, "identification" and "identity" are among the very few social science concepts that make as much sense individually as collectively. Individuals identify others and are in turn identified; collectivities are identifiable and collective decision-making processes may generate identification (immigration rules, for example, or medical diagnostic categories). How we understand the relationship between the collective and the individual, the macro and the micro, structure and action, public issues and private concerns, or history and biography—there are many ways to formulate the issue—is among the persistent key themes of social theory. It gets to the heart of the sociological enterprise: politically, in terms of why sociology matters, conceptually, in terms of our theories, and operationally, in terms of the methods that we employ to gather data. Thus any concept that works at both "levels" is of strategic importance to the discipline (which may be one reason for the recent ubiquity of identity as a topic).

This issue also gets to the heart of how identification works. For example, despite the emphasis on individuality in twentieth-century popular and academic discourses, the uniqueness of personal identification— that there is only one of you, and only one of me—is completely bound up with collective identification. Our individuality is, among other things, a matter of the idiosyncratic portfolio of collective categorical memberships—for example: male, middle-aged, balding, grey-haired, father, Northern Irish, social anthropologist, sociology professor, guitarist, Sheffield resident, Danish speaker, Dylan fan, Guinness drinker—that characterizes each of us. In this way, our difference from others is constructed in large part— perhaps even totally—out of our similarities to others. What is more, these are *public* collective identifications, there is nothing ineffably private or personal about them; they are available to others.

Approaching this from the other end of the spectrum, it is clear that collectivity and collective identification, if they are to be anything other than abstractions, unanchored in the real human world, have to relate in some way to actual individual members, present or past. An ethnic group with no current self-identifying members, for example, is not an existing ethnic group; it is either extinct or imaginary. However, it is possible to imagine a realistic collective category that, although it has no current members, is a "category in waiting": one might think here of a nation-state that has ceased to exist as such, that is still known about as an entity that once existed, having perhaps been absorbed into another polity, and which might well reappear given changed circumstances (as in the Balkans, post-Yugoslavia, or the post-Soviet eastern Baltic).

More intriguingly, however, the members of a category do not necessarily have to know about either its existence or their membership of it, in order for it to have effects. For example, many teachers, at all levels of education, routinely classify their pupils and students into different categories, according to behavior, achievement and possibly home background: "troublemakers," "hard workers," "non-academic," "good family," and so on. The children and young people concerned do not have to know about these categorizations for them to shape their experience of education. The classic study of this effect is Rosenthal and

Jacobsen's experiment (1968). Contemporary research ethics would almost certainly not permit such a study today: following a bogus testing procedure, pupils were allocated to "improving" and "non-improving" categories. Although the allocation was actually done randomly, those placed in the former category did better than those in the second, because teacher expectations and behavior towards the members of each category changed. This study illustrates that the act of categorizing, in addition to its impact on the identification and experience of the categorized, is likely to have consequences for the categorizers, too.

To sum up, I have outlined the bare bones of a theory of identification, and of categorization in particular, along the following lines:

- identification is a process, rather than a thing or an essence;
- in principle at least, identification is an open-ended process, permitting of change;
- external categorization is at least as important in that process as internal self-identification;
- self-identification and categorization are likely to be closely related;
- categorization has consequences, for categorizer(s) as well as categorized;
- power and authority are significant when it comes to categorization, and its consequences;
- identification—and certainly categorization—depends on perceptions of similarity as well as difference; and
- identification, and categorization, can be individual or collective.

Stated this baldly, the emphasis on categorization that I have developed throughout this section is clear. Why I have chosen this emphasis when, according to my own argument, categorization and self-identification are equally central to identification, will, I hope, become clear in the next section.

Surveillance

In order to proceed to that clarification we need, first, a working definition of surveillance. The following is simple, to the point and more than adequate for research purposes: "surveillance refers to processes in which special note is taken of certain human behaviours that go[es] well beyond idle curiosity" (Lyon 2007: 13). To turn to the word's French root, surveillance is the business of watching over people. This can be either well- or ill-intended; if it were disinterested, it would merely be "idle curiosity." In order to be *surveillance*, watching must have a point, an objective. It is not, or at least it should not be, an end in itself: it is a means to an end.

The ends and purposes of surveillance are worth lingering on briefly. The following are some common reasons for engaging in surveillance: the defense of the state and the "homeland," the prevention and active policing of crime, traffic and transport management, immigration management, public order management, child protection, public health oversight, rubbish disposal management, private property protection, customer relations management and marketing. Looking at this short list, there appear to be two basic reasons for surveillance: the *protection* or the *management* of people, whether the population-at-large or specific, smaller sets of people. The line between protection and management is, of course, fine and imprecise—control and care have always been intimate bedfellows—and each is central to modern governmentality, in the private sector as well as the public domain of the state and local government.

Another characteristic of surveillance is that it is *one-sided*; it is an ethological rather than ethnographic approach to information gathering, observational rather than interactive. It may involve the physical co-presence of the surveiled and the surveiler, there may even be situations in which it is embedded within ongoing interaction, but the watcher does not share the data gathered or their interpretation with the watched, and does not ask questions or reveal that surveillance is taking place. If that does happen, something other than surveillance—an exchange or negotiation of some sort, often about the terms and content of identification—is taking place. Even in a bureaucratic interview the surveillance is generally tacit and implicit. In this sense, Bentham's remote panopticon, particularly as interpreted by Foucault (1979), may be the archetype, if not the prototype, of surveillance.

The final point to note here is that surveillance is not only a means to an end and one-sided, it is also increasingly *impersonal*; by this I mean generic watching of the population-at-large, rather than the focused observation of targeted individuals. Much contemporary surveillance is a trawling exercise, undertaken in the hope or expectation that something noteworthy will show up on the screens. It can only be differentiated from "idle curiosity" by virtue of the plausibility of its objectives (traffic management, crime prevention, public safety, "homeland security," for example) and the fit between the means and the end.

Surveillance makes very little sense if the people being watched cannot be identified. If, as I have argued, surveillance is one-sided and increasingly impersonal, how do the watchers approach the task of identifying the watched? Setting to one side the surveillance of already-identified individuals—whether they are known bad guys, as in television's *The Wire*, or innocent civilians, as in Tony Scott's movie, *Enemy of the State*—the impersonal, generic nature of much contemporary surveillance poses a problem.

The problem presents itself most immediately to the watchers: How are the people on the screens, on the tapes, or in the internet chat rooms to be identified? "Who's who" needs to be established if surveillance material is to realize its full value as intelligence. As I have argued, identification is an emergent property of an interaction between self-identification and categorization by others. However, in most scenarios impersonal generic surveillance necessarily denies itself one, very important, side of that interaction, self-identification: there is no dialogue between watcher and watched and categorization has become the dominant mode of identification.

The consequences of this become clear if we think about what we do when we meet someone who is hitherto unknown to us, but about whom we want to know more. We begin by attempting to identify them and, in addition to all of the visually obvious non-verbal sources of information, such as embodiment, clothes and other expressions of style, a whole spectrum of vital information becomes accessible through talking to each other. Some of this is non-verbal, too: paralinguistic behaviors such as tone of voice, accent, and so on. But the main focus is linguistic and conversational: we introduce each other, we pay attention to language use, and, perhaps most important of all, we ask questions. These encounters are informal interviews of a sort, and usually reciprocal.

Language-based information is either only available in an impoverished form during surveillance, as on audio recordings, the quality of which is likely to be less than high-fidelity, or it is not available at all. It is possible, of course, to use lip-reading to make out what people are saying on video, but this is very unusual. So, how are watchers to deal with this deficiency? Although this is an under-researched topic, if Lyon's recent overview of surveillance studies (2007) can be taken as a guide, some things can be said about it with reasonable confidence.

First, and here we return to ethnic profiling and categorical suspicion, watchers will rely disproportionately on appearances. This raises an issue of everyday epistemology, neatly summarized in common-sense aphorisms such as "appearances are deceptive" and "you can't judge a book by its cover." It is notoriously difficult to make valid judgments about people on the basis of appearances alone: appearance is readily manipulated, may legitimately change from one situation to another, and without adequate knowledge of cultural, local and context may be enigmatic or unreadable. So on the one hand, it is easy to deceive watchers, appearance-wise; on the other, a considerable amount of prior knowledge is necessary if appearance is to be interpreted with any likelihood of accuracy.

Prior knowledge is, however, problematic in its own right. The ubiquity in everyday thought of stereotypes, labels that classify human social groups, of whatever kind, in a partial fashion, is well-known, although there is debate about whether they are a neutral aspect of human cognition, necessary to simplify complex and rich information—which is how language and categories in general work—or are necessarily bound up with group identification, boundary maintenance and the exclusion of Others. Regardless of which position one adopts in that debate, prior knowledge, for all of us, is, by definition, incomplete, and is also likely to be bundled up with stereotypes of others (and Others) that are, at best, superficial and partial and, at worst, wrong.

Given this, it is not surprising that the other thing that watchers can do in order to compensate for the qualitative information deficit that is endemic to surveillance—despite, or perhaps even because of, the quantitative information glut generated by IT-based surveillance—is to index and interpret what little they have in the light of other, apparently objective, "factual" sources of information. Some of this information is a product of modern communication systems: computers sending e-mails can be identified, phone calls can be traced, passports are now electronically registered, and vehicle registrations are readable by CCTV. In addition, modern states have sponsored and developed an array of techniques for fixing the fluidity of identification and registering it within the archives and projects of government (Caplan and Torpey 2001). Passports, identity cards, driving licenses, central personal registers, criminal records, fingerprints, DNA analysis and iris-recognition are some of the contemporary options. All of these information sources offer some scope for correlating the fuzzy data derived from personal surveillance with "hard facts," and may be brought into play to resolve the "problem of appearances."

They do not, however, necessarily solve that problem. Prior knowledge is still important, because unless there is already some pre-existing idea of "who's who" and "what's what"—intelligence in policing parlance—the task is either a search for a needle in a haystack or a version of the "run crosstabs" approach to statistical analysis, which produces lots of patterns but cannot tell you which are meaningful. There are particular problems with intelligence: it may be inaccurate, it tends to be historical rather than forward looking, individuals may over-invest in it to the exclusion of all else, and the "bad guys" can manipulate it.

To sum up, the watchers' capacity to interpret surveillance data is likely to be compromised because they: (a) lack one of the most important sources of information that we routinely use to identify people, i.e. language and, specifically, conversational inquiry; (b) rely on their individual and cultural prior knowledge, with all of its inadequacies, not least its stereotypical nature, to interpret appearances; and (c) also depend on a different kind of prior knowledge, intelligence, with all of its shortcomings. As a result, their capacity to know "who's who," and consequently "what's what" is likely to be problematic, at best.

This means that the watched have a problem, as well as the watchers: the validity of surveillance data is, in fact, a worry for everyone. Generic surveillance, in particular, is a controversial civil liberties and human rights issue, not least with respect to its implications for legal presumptions of innocence. There are privacy issues that are not easily resolvable. Finally, surveillance is also problematic if, for example, it involves the diversion of resources from other, more interactive, kinds of policing and further exacerbates that gulf which separates the police from many of the communities that they are supposed to serve.

Modernity

Surveillance has many faces. In the small-scale, face-to-face local worlds that characterized the pre-modern human world, social life was monitored and regulated by informal community surveillance. This is the gossip and twitching curtains that anyone who has ever lived in a village knows very well. One of the defining characteristics of modernity, however, has been the emergence of formal, bureaucratic organization, as the standard way of organizing collective activities and enterprises. While these organizations have their face-to-face everyday worlds, they have also formalized procedures of surveillance, registration and management. These are crucial to the allocation of resources and penalties in the modern world, and typically involve formal encounters—the interview, in one form or another—that combine elements of surveillance with supervision, categorization and allocation. These formal organizational processes combine in complicated ways with everyday informal surveillance, to produce real and systematically patterned consequences in individual lives (Gubrium and Holstein 2001; Jenkins 2008: 169–99).

As I have already suggested, there is more to be said about modernity and surveillance than this. The study of surveillance has a great deal to offer social science debates about identification in the modern world. There is, in particular, an influential conventional wisdom about the nature of modern identity, the most eminent and influential proponent of which is perhaps Giddens (1991). This point of view argues that self-aware, reflexive self-identity: (1) only became possible under conditions of modernity (individualism, literacy and mass education, affluence, leisure, etc.); and (2) is the characteristic mode of modern identity. Regardless of what one might think of the first part of this thesis—which is *at best* a fine example of argument by definition: everything depends on the meaning of "reflexive self-identity"—the second is almost certainly wrong.

This is for two reasons. First, as I have argued earlier, internal self-identification works hand-in-glove with external categorization in the identification process: practical everyday identity, "who's who," emerges out of the interaction of both. Self-identity without categorization is unthinkable. Second, it is arguably categorization, if anything, that characterizes the modern human world, as surveillance and monitoring have taken advantage of technological development to bring under their impersonal purview many hitherto private areas of life, and the categorizing procedures of formal organizations have become increasingly influential in the allocation of rewards and penalties.

Technology is not in itself determinate, however. The increasing impersonality of surveillance has undoubtedly been encouraged by the exponential development of information technology over the last few decades and the opportunities that it offers for monitoring, recording and data management and analysis. Some of the expansion of surveillance has happened simply because it became technically possible. There are, however, factors other than the imperatives of technological development at play here. At the risk of oversimplifying a complex history, at least four other twentieth-century social developments—the formal organization of business and government, increasing social mass and scale, the notion of preventative policing, and the politics of external and internal threat—must be added into the mix.

I have already discussed formal organizations. Suffice it to add here that Weberian "iron cage" bureaucracy is no more imperative than technology. There are many ways to run a large organization: impersonal surveillance and monitoring is only one. The growth of populous, sprawling, complex cities and the development of mass transport systems and infrastructures—everything from airports to motorways—has created teeming public spaces that seem to invite, even to require, micromanagement if they are to function efficiently. Preventative policing, which is pre-emptive rather than reactive, has increasingly turned to overt surveillance technology in order to deter crime and disorder, as one response to social mass and scale: large areas can, in principle, be "patrolled" without the presence of officers on the ground. At a time of declining urban tax bases this has an attractive economic logic. Politically, the increasing grasp on daily life of the state under siege—whether that is the Soviet state of the 1930s and 1940s or the US state of the 2000s—is legitimated by appeal to the threat of invisible, almost spectral, enemies such as "counter-revolutionaries" and "terrorists."

Taking all these factors together, the scope and scale of surveillance have inexorably expanded. From NKVD informers and postal intercepts to wiretaps, internet monitoring, spy satellites and unmanned drones, and from traffic cops to vehicle registration recognition technology and CCTV monitored by centralized traffic management centers, surveillance has expanded to fill the spaces and means available to it, becoming simultaneously more intrusive and more distant. It has also become more routine and banal: routine in that surveillance is now a taken-for-granted feature of everyday life in most modern nation-states, and certainly in most modern cities, and banal in that the most trivial aspects of our lives—credit card records, for example, even rubbish disposal—have become subject to official oversight.

In the process, surveillance, the systematic watching of people—a means to an end, one-sided, increasingly impersonal, intrusive and yet distant, routine and banal—has come to frame individual and collective identification in the modern human world. "Who's who?" is increasingly a question that, individually, is answered, even *must* be answered, in terms of the formalities of passports, identity cards and social security numbers. The management of public spaces is increasingly a matter of the visual categorization of the public by invisible watchers. Travel is governed by a combination of both of these. Categorization may be on its way to achieving dominance in identification; in which case there will be, eventually, a new sociology of identity to be written.

References

Bowker, G. C. and Starr, S. L. (2000). *Sorting Things Out: Classification and its Consequences*, Cambridge, MA: MIT Press.

Caplan, J. and Torpey, J. (eds). (2001). *Documenting Individual Identity: The Development of State Practices in the Modern World*, Princeton, NJ: Princeton University Press.

Foucault, M. (1979). *Discipline and Punish: The Birth of the Prison*, Harmondsworth: Peregrine.

Giddens, A. (1991). *Modernity and Self-Identity: Self and Society in the Late Modern Age*, Cambridge: Polity.

Goffman, E. (1969). *The Presentation of Self in Everyday Life*, London: Allen Lane.

Gubrium, J. F. and Holstein, J. A. (eds). (2001). *Institutional Selves: Troubled Identities in a Postmodern World*, New York: Oxford University Press.

Jenkins, R. (2008). *Social Identity*, 3rd edition, London: Routledge.

Lyon, D. (2007). *Surveillance Studies: An Overview*, Cambridge: Polity.

Marx, G. T. (1988). *Undercover: Police Surveillance in America*, Berkeley: University of California Press.

Rosenthal, R. and Jacobsen, L. (1968). *Pygmalion in the Classroom*, New York: Holt, Rhinehart and Winston.

c. The surveillance-industrial complex

Ben Hayes

This chapter examines the relationship between the private sector and the state in developing and implementing surveillance systems for law enforcement and security purposes, the confluence of political, economic and social relations that constitute the "surveillance-industrial complex." In the post-9/11, security-focused world, surveillance is big business. Commercial suppliers of surveillance technologies, applications and services of every kind have fuelled the growth of a huge, global market. The surveillance-industrial complex provides a framework for analyzing this market and the wider implications of the burgeoning relationship between the state and the surveillance industry for governance and democracy.

The power of the private sector to influence government surveillance agendas is embodied in the surveillance-industrial complex. The consolidation of surveillance into one of the dominant organizational paradigms of contemporary governance, economies and societies does not mean that those surveillance mechanisms most closely linked with state power, control and coercion have simply developed in an *ad hoc* fashion as societies have reoriented themselves around the potentially infinite power of information technology to record, analyze and shape human activity. On the contrary, the surveillance-industrial complex is at the heart of many of the transformations in population control, policing and intelligence gathering described in this volume (Sections 3.1, 3.2 and 3.3, in particular); it is the entity in which the practical and political steps needed to transform an information technology into a system for surveillance and control are inevitably embodied.

The surveillance-industrial complex does not amount to a comprehensive theory of surveillance. It nevertheless contains several important theoretical assumptions about the corrosive nature of the state-corporate nexus on political culture, democratic governance and social control. First, the surveillance-industrial complex intimates the links between governments, state agencies and corporations: the "revolving door" between those officially tasked with protecting us and those private actors engaged in the race to supply the new methods of surveillance and control that will enable them to do so. This is an undesirable relationship within which political decisions are shaped not just by democratic concern for the "public good" but by profitable courses of action for private entities. Second, the surveillance-industrial complex highlights the somewhat perverse political and economic model that underpins these social relations: one in which governments outsource key aspects of security and surveillance policy and practice to the private sector, subsidize private innovation in surveillance capacities and techniques, and procure the resulting technologies and expertise—all of which is to the dubious benefit of both untrammeled state power and those private corporations and actors best placed to profit from this relationship. Third,

167

like the concept of the "military-industrial complex" that inspired it, the very idea of the surveillance-industrial complex warns of a nexus so entrenched that it promises to deliver ever more pervasive, intrusive and effective surveillance technologies *in perpetuity*, just as its military counterpart continues to provide ever more high-tech means to "shock-and-awe," to target and neutralize the enemy.

Crucially, these links, between the new apparatuses of state-surveillance and the military-industrial complex, are of more than conceptual significance. The defense sector has rapidly diversified into all things "homeland security," bringing military logic, technology and experience squarely into the realm of policing and civil security. They are joined in the surveillance-industrial complex by multinational information technology (hereafter: IT) companies supplying the latest in identity management and "dataveillance" to an increasingly networked (or "interoperable") world of security checkpoints and rapid reaction forces. This scared new world is as much the result of the relationship between coercion and profit—"a merger of shopping mall and the secret prison" (Klein 2007: 306)—as it is the marriage of technology and security. The "techno-security paradigm" has also been described as a "war without end" (Mattelart 2010: 137–61). It is in these senses that the very content of democratic and political culture is at stake.

This chapter sketches the contours of the surveillance-industrial complex. It begins by situating the role of surveillance and surveillance technology in the post-9/11 security landscape. It then looks at the key players and markets in the surveillance industry and the techniques and pressures brought to bear on governments in respect to procurement. This is followed by a discussion of the state-sponsored process of innovation in surveillance technology and the broader implications of the securitization of research. A final section considers issues, methods and challenges for those wishing to engage with the surveillance-industrial complex. Three caveats should be kept in mind. First, while the chapter focuses primarily on those aspects of surveillance most closely associated with state security, it is suggested that the reach of the surveillance-industrial complex extends throughout the "surveillance society," from the workplace to the world wide web. Second, while the chapter necessarily focuses on the dark side of surveillance, the point at which it threatens the fabric of democracy or civil liberty, this should not be taken to mean that all state surveillance is bad or unwarranted. Third, where concrete information is provided, the chapter focuses almost exclusively on Europe and North America and not other parts of the world, though does so with the firm belief that the trends emerging in the democratic, capitalist heartlands are likely to be replicated elsewhere (see Arteaga Botello, this volume).

Conceptual frameworks: security and surveillance, security as surveillance

For the purposes of this discussion the terms "surveillance-industrial complex" and "security-industrial complex" appear largely interchangeable. More intuitive is to perceive the former as a sub-component of the latter, taking its place alongside the "prison-industrial complex," the "disaster-industrial complex" (Klein 2007) and other concepts inspired by Eisenhower's 50-year-old concerns about the threat posed to democracy by the fusion of state power and corporate interests.

Crucial to this discussion is the changing nature of "security" and the increasingly central role of surveillance in its practice. The perception, privatization, pro-activity and pervasiveness of and the apparently unflinching preoccupation with security both shape and are being shaped by the surveillance-industrial complex. In the English-speaking world, and within many other languages, "security" has acquired the status of a modern day "weasel word": so ubiquitous that it defies full comprehension, so reified that it appears beyond criticism. Post-9/11, the concept of "security" has become so broad as to encapsulate the entire policy spectrum of the coercive state apparatus, including any government policy or practice that could conceivably prevent something bad from happening, from policing and counter-terrorism to critical infrastructure protection and crisis management. In many languages, this new national security blanket is a far cry from the social security cushion the word once signified. Non-coercive elements of public policy such as food, energy, transport, information and communications technology, health and the environment are also being "securitized" and recast into new paradigms of food security, energy security, transport security and so on, in turn reshaping how these issues are framed and approached by policymakers. Surveillance, one again, is at the heart of this reconfiguration of state practice and public policy intervention.

By definition, the security-industrial complex recognizes that the state—while retaining its monopoly over the "legitimate" use of violence—has entered into a partnership with the private sector in order to exercise that power. In the words of a former European Commissioner for Justice and Home Affairs: "Security is no longer a monopoly that belongs to public administrations, but a common good, for which responsibility and implementation should be shared by public and private bodies." This privatization of security calls into question fundamental assumptions about the social contract between the state and the citizen (Krahmann 2010), providing fertile ground for state theorists, surveillance scholars and political economists alike (see Bigo, this volume).

Another crucial trend shaping the new security landscape is the shift from reactive to proactive security. Governments and state agencies no longer just respond to crimes, instead they try to pre-empt them by identifying and neutralizing risks before threats to security can be realized. Consequently, policing and criminal justice is now as much about managing and mitigating danger as it is about crime and punishment. A new *logic of security* is supplanting the criminal law as a primary principle from which the use of physical force and other coercive measures can proceed (Hörnqvist 2004). This trend, which relies implicitly on new and established forms of surveillance, emerged long before the events of 9/11 and was widely anticipated within the literature on risk, policing and actuarial justice. What no-one could have foreseen, however, was the rapid expansion of corresponding executive powers under the so-called "war on terror," including security detention (often without the prospect of trial), control orders, discretionary expulsion, "rendition" and even the outsourcing of torture, all underpinned by a plethora of public and private blacklists and databases. This has led some to argue that we are now witnessing the emergence of a new "securitarian order" predicated on the globalization of surveillance; a new means of "managing mass society" through the "religion of national security," counter-insurgency and the "lessons of total war" (Mattelart 2010).

The reorientation of coercive state forces around the doctrines of national security has other practical effects, fostering a blurring of the boundaries between what was traditionally seen as (internal) security and what was traditionally seen as (external) defense. This convergence is visible on many levels: the territorial, the political, the strategic, the technological and "on the ground." National borders now matter much less to police, security and intelligence agencies whose investigative powers reach across newly constructed international surveillance and enforcement regimes. The rationale for military forces is now as much about proactive intervention as traditional defense, with increasing deployment on global policing and counter-insurgency (or "peacekeeping" and "crisis management") missions. *Integrated* national security and defense strategies comprising "mission areas" such as counterterrorism, border control and infrastructure protection are in turn supplanting once-distinct police, security and military doctrines (see for example the defense and security strategies of the European Union, USA, Britain, France and Germany). This blurring of boundaries has fostered a transfer of military logics and technologies into the realm of policing and security, a process that is driven increasingly by the security-industrial complex. Tactics developed in foreign counter-insurgency operations, for example, have helped hone domestic public order policy.

A holistic dimension to security can also be observed in the construction of new, networked, "interoperable" or "joined-up" security systems (some are going so far as to describe them as "security ecologies"). In practical terms this means enhanced cooperation between police, intelligence, military and other government bodies; the exchange of information among myriad public and private bodies and across borders; and the use of a whole range of benign apparatuses for security purposes, from travel records to traffic controls. It appears that as far as surveillance is central to the (re)organization of our late modern societies, "interoperability" is emerging as its ultimate goal: seamlessly integrated, computer-aided systems designed to maximize the utility and security of local, national and international productivity and resources.

The idea of so-called "smart cities," which is steadily being embraced by technology and security companies as well as urban planners and environmentalists, is also built around the idea of interoperability.

Amid the hype it is increasingly difficult to reconcile these new, networked systems of law enforcement and control with the principle of the "separation of powers" in the liberal democratic model. Investing power and control in surveillance and detection mechanisms and executive-led, interagency hierarchies renders traditional "checks and balances"—judicial control, accountability mechanisms, data protection, etc.—inherently more difficult to achieve. Left unchecked, these trends could ultimately facilitate the transfer of the "full spectrum dominance" model, developed by US military strategists to assert complete control over the "battlespace" into the internal security sphere, manifesting itself in a world of red zones and green zones (Klein 2007; Hayes 2010).

The surveillance business: key players and markets

The international market for surveillance technologies now provides at least as useful a barometer for the likely trajectory of state policy and practice as the strategy documents of governments and security agencies. Estimates as to the value of relevant global markets should, however, be taken with a proverbial "pinch of salt" since many originate from market intelligence specialists that seek to "talk up" markets in order to sell their analyses and secure investment, both public and private. Regardless, they are demonstrative of a booming, global industry. *Visiongain*, for example, suggests that global government spending on homeland security in 2010 topped $178 billion and forecasts that the cumulative value of the homeland security market will total nearly $2.7 trillion over the next decade.[1] An expected annual growth rate of 7 percent suggests that this market will defy the current global recession. Sub-components of the global homeland security market correspond closely with the security "mission areas" in contemporary national security strategies. Examples include border security, with the global market in perimeter surveillance and unmanned ground an aerial vehicles estimated at $15.8 billion in 2010,[2] identification management, with the global market in biometrics forecast to reach $11.2 billion in 2015,[3] and "cyberwarfare," with the cyber-security market forecast to reach $12.5 billion in 2011.[4]

As noted above, the extent of defense sector dominance, and the role of large multinational defense contractors in particular, is a key feature of the rapidly developing homeland security industry. *Visiongain* describes homeland security as "the defence industry's newest and most promising sector" (ibid.), while the Vice President of *Thales*, one of Europe's largest defense companies, has described "a shift in emphasis" and an increasing balance between what we see as defense and homeland security: "security" is a more politically acceptable way of describing what was traditionally "defence" (cited in Hayes 2009: 72). The trend of defense sector diversification into all things "security" is borne out by their homeland security revenues. In Europe, the "big five" defense sector contractors (*EADS, BAE Systems, Finmeccanica, SAFRAN* and *Thales*) have recorded rapid year-on-year growth in their security businesses, as have their counterparts in the USA (*Boeing, Lockheed Martin, General Dynamics, Northrop Grumman* and *Raytheon*). While these companies may indeed be best placed to deliver the new high-tech security infrastructures demanded by national governments, they also bring with them methods and techniques "that correspond more closely to military logic: neutralising, knocking out and destroying the enemy" (Hörnqvist 2004: 35).

The other major players in the security and surveillance business are IT conglomerates and dedicated security companies. *L3 Communications, Hewlett Packard, Dell, Verizon* and *IBM* all feature in the top 20 contractors retained by the USA's Department of Homeland Security (hereafter: DHS),[5] while *Ericsson, Indra, Siemens, Diehl* and *Sagem* feature prominently in Europe. Dedicated security contractors like *Booz Allen, G4S, Securitas* and *Smiths Detection* have also enjoyed sustained growth as more and more functions are outsourced to private companies. The role of insurance actuaries in promoting security and surveillance technologies should also be considered: just as we pay a premium if we park our cars on the street rather than in a garage, so states and corporations invite favorable premiums by maximizing the security of their infrastructures.

The security-industrial complex is already having a big impact on state practice, politics and culture. A two-year study by investigative journalists at the *Washington Post* entitled "Top Secret America," unprecedented in terms of its scope and detail, found that there were 1,931 intelligence contracting firms doing work classified as "top secret" for 1,271 government organizations at over 10,000 sites around the USA. The research also found that contractors make up nearly 30 percent of the workforce of America's intelligence agencies, with a 50:50 ratio of contractors to permanent staff at the DHS. Of 854,000 people in the USA with top-secret clearances, it is estimated that 265,000 are contractors. Government organizations were found to be contracting scores of private companies to conduct psychological operations, "special military operations" (e.g. SWAT teams and unconventional warfare), top-secret conventional military operations and counter-drug operations.[6] *Lockheed Martin*, which received more than $36 billion in government contracts in 2008 alone, has worked for more than two dozen government agencies including surveillance and information processing for the CIA, the FBI, the Internal Revenue Service (IRS), the National Security Agency (NSA), the Pentagon, the Census Bureau and the Postal Service.[7] "What started as a temporary fix in response to the terrorist attacks," suggests the authors of "Top Secret America," "has turned into a dependency that calls into question whether the federal workforce includes too many people obligated to shareholders rather than the public interest—and whether the government is still in control of its most sensitive activities" (*Washington Post* 2010).

Research revealing the extent of expenditure and outsourcing in the USA (see also Klein 2007: 389–407) raises important global issues. First, as suggested above, considerable importance can and should be attached to the relationship between securitization, privatization and globalization (Klein 2007; Mattelart 2010). Second, the global reach of many security and surveillance contractors raises complex jurisdictional problems in terms of holding them and their employers to account. One only has to look at the host of allegations surrounding the conduct of private security companies in Iraq and Afghanistan to put this problem in context. Third, and perhaps most importantly, the apparatuses for border control, population surveillance and the interception of telecommunications that are now available on the international market can be extremely repressive in the hands of authoritarian governments. At the time of writing, the case against *Nokia-Siemens Networks* (*NSN*) for providing Iranian security agencies with the surveillance technology used to round up activists and protestors in 2009 is pending at a District Court in the United States, raising searching questions about corporate complicity in torture and the reach of the absolute prohibition against torture in international law. It also points toward the need for the same kind of regulation of the homeland security sector that governs the sale of arms, torture devices and dual-use goods.

Whereas the homeland security industry appears a more than willing partner of the state, the private sector can also become embroiled in surveillance through the imposition of legal obligations, for example those placed on telecommunications companies, financial institutions and travel carriers to facilitate surveillance and data retention. Indeed, *NSN* submits that the technology it supplied to Iran simply follows the standard international "lawful interception" requirements, the very same standards drawn up by Western governments in the early 1990s.

The business of surveillance: political economies and practices

The correlation between the growth of the private security industry and the increasing privatization of security may appear as the natural order in capitalist society, but it is imperative to question how these processes are unleashed and sustained. It is certainly the case, as noted above, that the demand for increased security following 9/11 coupled with a relative lack of state capacity resulted in the pursuit of both new security and surveillance technologies and the outsourcing of security activities. But as 9/11 inevitably loses its impact with the passage of time, and governments even begin to talk about returning their counter-terrorism strategies from a "war to law" footing, the legacy is a surveillance-industrial complex that appears almost self-sustaining. Four factors contribute to this assessment.

First, as suggested above, state agencies and public bodies have increasingly embraced the techno-security paradigm. Second, the structure of the global market in surveillance technology is a very long way from economists' Holy Grail of "perfect competition." It is a market dictated not by the demands of "rational" and informed consumers, but by the policy choices of governments and state agencies. It is a market skewed by generous security "research" subsidies on the one hand (see following section) and the public procurement of security on the other. Although Western government procurement processes are ostensibly guided and regulated by international conventions drawn up by organizations like the OECD, they are in practice subject to various techniques designed to influence officials and civil servants. The development of the surveillance industry and privatization of surveillance has instituted a "revolving door" between government officials, civil servants, the corporations they deal with and the lobbyists who represent their interests. The revolving door can exert a tremendous influence on expenditure, policy and practice *vis-à-vis* security and surveillance (Klein 2007: 308–22). The first two US Secretaries of State for Homeland Security are among the most eminent personalities to further their careers through successful consultancy practices (see *Ridge Associates* and the *Chertoff Group*). While both governments and industry can cite obvious advantages in recruiting from the private and public sector respectively, the revolving door inevitably sees personal and corporate interests intervene to shape the national interest. At the same time, the secrecy that shrouds the influence brought to bear on state policy and acquisition decisions means the revolving door is extremely difficult to detect and remedy. Yet in the week that this chapter was being finalized, the UK government cancelled the £6 billion privatization of the UK's search-and-rescue capabilities at the last minute following a report that the successful bidder had recruited a former government official in possession of "commercially sensitive" material.[8]

Third is the rapid growth in national and international security industry lobbyists, "think-tanks," "BONGOs" (Business-oriented NGOs), "GONGOS" (Government-oriented NGOs) and other enterprises that directly and indirectly promote surveillance, technology and industry-led solutions. Just as the military sector does its business at arms fairs, exhibitions, demonstrations, gala dinners, conferences and through the pages of glossy magazines and pseudo-academic journals, so private security networking across government, industry and academia now provides a fertile and normalizing environment in which technology options can be showcased and policy options influenced. This powerful lobby is a key stakeholder in implementing surveillance policies that actively seek to influence both individual procurement decisions and the direction of the broader security agenda.

Fourth, those involved in the business of selling surveillance and security are inevitably embroiled in the politics of fear that sustains their bottom line: the "powerful impetus to perpetuate the sense of peril that created the industry in the first place" (Klein 2007: 306). This momentum chimes ominously with how both democratic and authoritarian governments have long used "enemies within," "moral panics" and external threats to maintain and extend their grip on power. These profoundly negative political forces are accompanied by a disingenuous faith in state-corporate security methods: if an incident occurs, it is a reason for spending more on security; if no incident occurs, it justifies what is already being spent. This *argumentum ad ignorantiam* threatens to entrench security expenditure *ad infinitum*. Olympic security is a case in point.

Innovation and the securitization of research

To observe the rapid diffusion of state surveillance technologies accompanied by the excitement and fascination with the endless profusion of future applications—drones, smart CCTV, behavioral analysis, tracking and identification systems, nanotech applications, virtual fences, earth observation, automated targeting systems and less-lethal weapons, to name but a few—feels not unlike a new kind of arms race, albeit one in which all the high-tech weaponry is pointing inwards. Although not yet on anything like the same scale, governments are ploughing money into security research and development (hereafter, R&D) in the name of enhancing both public safety and the global competitiveness of their industrial base (Hayes 2009; 2010). This relationship suits both the potential end-users of the new technologies and systems, who can influence their design, and the private sector, which gets both an early buy-in from government and a *de facto* subsidy to bring their products to market.

The United States' DHS spends over $1 billion per year on R&D. The European Union is midway through a seven-year, €1.4 billion security research program (hereafter: ESRP), with significant additional funding allocated to the security aspects of the other themes in its €51 billion framework research program. The design of the ESRP was largely outsourced to the major players in the nascent European homeland security industry, instituting an apparent conflict of interests within which large multinationals have been able to shape the security research agenda, apply for the subsequent R&D funds on offer, and then sell the resulting technologies and systems back to the governments that funded their development (Hayes 2009; 2010). According to a report commissioned by the European Parliament, "it is mostly large defence companies, the very same who have participated in the definition of EU-sponsored security research which are the main beneficiaries of [ESRP] funds" (Jeandesboz and Ragazzi 2010: 25).

The design of science and technology agendas is important because it dictates both the direction of research and academic conduct. In the financial year 2006/07, approximately 30 percent of the total UK government spend on R&D went to the military sector. The presence of "soldiers in the laboratory" is problematic because it contributes to "a narrow interpretation of security issues" which "drives a largely weapons-based R&D agenda—critically dependent on the expertise of scientists and technologists—and a corresponding 'defence' posture" (Langley 2005: 73). The ESRP, which brings together industry, academia, public bodies and NGOs, has been similarly "framed by the concerns of the defence and security industry and national and European security agencies and services" (Jeandesboz and Ragazzi 2010: 10). A large proportion of the budget has been "dedicated to developing technologies of surveillance, to the detriment of a broader reflection on the impact of such technologies for citizens and persons concerned with the EU's security policies" (ibid.). Non-coercive means of dealing with threats such as social policy, peace-building, mediation, dialogue, conflict resolution and rights-based approaches to security may also be sidelined in the promotion of high-tech surveillance and interdiction strategies.

The growing influence of the defense and security sectors in universities also raises important concerns about academic freedom, couched as it is in a cloak of secrecy and intellectual property restrictions and hidden away in corporate-sponsored science parks and R&D institutes (Langley 2005). These centers are "havens for 'spin-out' activities which facilitate technology transfer between universities and commercial companies"; they promote a "culture of individualism and high status, of long hours of work and the absence of trade unionism—a set of values enshrined in the Thatcher view of the industrialized university, driven by 'economic advancement' (ibid.: 20). In this context the corporate support of research raises serious ethical and practical concerns, "especially where weapons, human behavioral control technology and surveillance systems are concerned, in particular where they 'spill' over into everyday life" (ibid.: 15). Dissent and ethical concerns are, however, "stifled or at best difficult to articulate" because of the widespread presence of military interests within science, engineering and technology (ibid.: 35).

Should we worry about the growing influence of "spooks in the laboratory"? At a time when academic budgets face pressure from the cuts engendered by the global recession, increased funding for security R&D encourages universities to enter into partnership with state agencies and security companies. Universities have certainly responded to the demand for academic partners in developing homeland security strategies and technologies. In the USA the DHS works with 12 centers of excellence dealing with every kind of security mission area, from the Center for Border Security and Immigration (University of Arizona) to the Center of Excellence in Command, Control and Interoperability (Purdue and Rutgers Universities). Similar institutes are emerging all over the insecure world. It would be quite wrong to suggest that they inevitably promote hard security technologies or operate in some kind of ethical vacuum, but it is important to consider how the innovation process breaks the science, technology and politics behind the development of new security and surveillance systems and policies into composite parts, putting moral distance between those involved and the end product. The people behind surveillance science—the engineers, mathematicians, computer programmers and so forth—are not driven by any particular desire to improve the surveillance society but by the dual imperatives of securing funds to advance their research and applying it in the "real world." This is not to say that personal goals cannot subsequently become intertwined with institutional goals. Those involved can and do:

> become part and parcel of their systems, they find colleagues, and even emotional attachments in their systems, they define their particular system as something they should foster, feeling great satisfaction when they manage to make the system function still better. These are entirely common-place processes; this is how we all become more or less enveloped by the systems we are working in.
>
> *(Mathiesen 2006: 41)*

Researching the surveillance-industrial complex: issues and challenges

This chapter has made the case for further research into the nature and influence of the surveillance-industrial complex. In-depth study into the influence of defense, homeland security and IT companies on the development of state surveillance systems is imperative if we are to fully understand how the coercive elements of the surveillance society are being constructed. The activities of key multinationals, the growth of surveillance markets and how they are influencing government strategy, policy and practice warrant further attention.

To fully grasp the significance of the state-corporate surveillance nexus, research should focus on the impacts of those areas in which it is, or threatens to become, most deeply entrenched. Many of these areas are discussed elsewhere in this book. They include border control apparatuses, identification systems, smart cameras and mobile surveillance devices (e.g. drones), critical infrastructure protection, crisis management, command-and-control centers, public surveillance, "megavents," nano-surveillance, interception technology, dataveillance and open-source intelligence gathering. Freedom of Information requests, corporate literature, technology exhibitions and the reconstruction of public-private security dialogues from the conference presentations of think-tanks, lobbyists, security agencies and civil servants provide a wealth of material on the convergence of state-corporate and techno-security agendas (e.g. Hayes 2009).

The roll-out of high-tech surveillance systems implicitly threatens privacy and civil liberties, yet the democratic structures we rely on to protect those rights and freedoms appear to have been marginalized by a creeping technological determinism. Research that examines the implementation of new surveillance technologies needs to include more qualitative consideration of the relationship between states and corporations and its implications for governance, regulation and accountability. Such research should also be situated in a broader social and political context, within the wider (perhaps global) processes of "securitization" that are embodied in the narratives of the state, the media, academia, corporations and the fears of ordinary people. Research is needed to understand the process of surveillance innovation in its broadest terms. This includes analyzing the flows of public and private money into security and surveillance research, critically evaluating expenditure and effectiveness, and assessing its impact on both public policy debates and universities. Does your university accept military and security funding?

To uncover how certain policies have been shaped by corporate interests and demonstrate the techniques and pressures brought to bear on public policy is to pose a direct challenge to corporate power. That challenge can only be strengthened by positioning research into the surveillance-industrial complex within debates about corporate responsibility and accountability; by considering not just the regulation of surveillance technology but the potential regulation of the homeland security industry; and by drawing inspiration from the global transparency and privacy movements, from anti-lobbying initiatives and arms trade regulations, from ethical debates around science, and from the emerging United Nations business and human rights framework.

Notes

1 www.visiongain.com/Press_Release/23/'Global-market-for-homeland-security-will-amount-to-178–2bn-in-2010' -says-visiongain-report.
2 www.visiongain.com/Report/549/The-Border-Security-Market-2010-2020-UAVs-UGVs-Perimeter-Surveillance -Systems.
3 www.businesswire.com/news/home/20110125005931/en/Research-Markets-Global-Biometrics-Technology-Mar ket–2010–15.
4 www.visiongain.com/Report/561/The-Cyberwarfare-Market-2011-2021.
5 www.flightglobal.com/assets/getAsset.aspx?ItemID=35942&tracked=1.
6 http://projects.washingtonpost.com/top-secret-america/articles/national-security-inc.
7 www.tomdispatch.com/blog/175339/tomgram:_william_hartung,_lockheed_martin%27s_shadow_government.
8 www.bbc.co.uk/new/uk-england-devon-12390758.

References

Hayes, B. (2009). *Neoconopticon: The EU Security-Industrial Complex*, Amsterdam: Transnational Institute/Statewatch.
——(2010). "Full Spectrum Dominance as European Union Security Policy: On the Trail of the Neoconopticon," in K. D. Haggerty and M. Samatas (eds), *Surveillance and Democracy*, London: Routledge, pp 148–70.
Hörnqvist, M. (2004). "The Birth of Public Order Policy," *Race & Class*, 46(1): 30–52.
Jeandesboz, J. and Ragazzi, F. (2010). *Review of Security Measures in the Research Framework Programme*, Brussels: European Parliament Directorate General for Internal Policies.
Klein, N. (2007). *The Shock Doctrine*, London: Penguin.
Krahmann, E. (2010). *States, Citizens and the Privatization of Security*, Cambridge: Cambridge University Press.
Langley, C. (2005). *Soldiers in the Laboratory: Military Involvement in Science and Technology – And Some Alternatives*, Folkestone: Scientists for Global Responsibility.
Mathiesen, T. (2006). "'Lex Vigilitoria'—Towards a Control System Without a State?," in T. Bunyan (ed.), *The War on Freedom and Democracy: Essays on Civil Liberties in Europe*, London: Spokesman, pp. 38–42.
Mattelart, A. (2010). *The Globalisation of Surveillance*, Cambridge: Polity.
Washington Post. (2010). "National Security Inc.," D. Priest and W. M. Arkin, *"Top Secret America" Series*, available at http://projects.washingtonpost.com/top-secret-america/articles/national-security-inc (accessed 20 January 2011).

d. The body as data in the age of information

Irma van der Ploeg

Imagine a large international European airport. At the immigration service booth, a man claiming to come from Afghanistan asks for political asylum. He is taken away to be interviewed and his fingerprints are scanned with an electronic device. The data are sent to be checked against a database and a match is found: the person in question is known to the system as having applied for asylum before in another EU country. The man is taken into custody, has a facial photograph and an iris scan taken, and will be evicted as soon as possible to the country of his first application. Elsewhere in the airport, a long queue of passengers stands in line at a security checkpoint. One by one, they pass through a gate, and a narrow corridor. Behind the walls an officer looks at a set of monitors. An alert flashes: based on pupil dilation, heart rate, skin temperature and facial expression, a woman has been classified as a person of interest. She is quickly taken to a back office and subjected to thorough inspection and interrogation. Meanwhile, a group of smartly dressed, briefcased men walk past the entire line, up to a small booth. They each look briefly into what looks like a small camera, put their hand flat on a designated surface, and after just a few seconds, the gate opens, allowing them to pass through without further checking.

On an ordinary morning in the middle of the week, a woman somewhere in a northern European country picks up the mail from the doormat. One of the letters is from the clinical genetics center in the capital. She opens it and reads: "Dear Ms Björk, Hereby we inform you that, resulting from our analyses of the central genetic database, it has come to our attention that your genetic profile indicates an elevated risk for breast cancer. We strongly suggest that you present yourself to the radiology department of your local hospital at your earliest convenience, and/or see your physician for further advice and guidance."

Elsewhere in a laboratory of the molecular immunology department of a medical faculty, a researcher starts her working day. She works on a project that, in collaboration with the theoretical informatics department, aims to gain a better understanding of a particular type of leukemia in children. She has at her disposal a database containing DNA microarray data on 500 children suffering from this disease. She will mine these data, searching for prognostic markers that could help improve diagnosis and therapy. Understanding the determinants of therapy response and resistance could make patient-tailored therapy possible. This way, it is hoped that her work will result in more successful treatment with fewer adverse side effects.

Looking back, it may now seem overly optimistic, or even somewhat naïve. The sense of revolution that came with the amazing pace of developments in information technology (IT) and digital technology in the final decade of the twentieth century, and the few years beyond that, inspired a highly optimistic belief in a new kind of freedom. Back then, social scientific attempts to make sense of the amazing pace of integration of computer technology in ever more domains of public and private life were often framed in oppositional terms. The information revolution signaled a movement away from the physical to the immaterial, a shift in importance, e.g. from material production to a service economy and information trade; from congested freeways and polluting transportation systems to the lightness of glassfiber communication networks and the mobility of frictionless electronic data flow. At the level of personal identity, from the gravity of a needy, overdetermined bodily existence to the weightless mode of multiple virtual personae. The fast growing popularity of immersion in online social spaces, then usually referred to as "cyberspace" or "virtual reality," called forth a discourse that emphasized play and experimentation, allowing free construction of multiple identities, unhindered by the limits of embodiment "in real life."

Fortunately, new forms of freedom, in particular of information and communication, did materialize, as regularly demonstrated by political events in countries all over the world. But this, of course, is only half the story.

Had one looked at this information revolution more in terms of an equally revolutionary increase in surveillance capacity, there might have been more anticipation of a few other characteristics of today's information society: the obsolescence of the idea that digital technology creates a sort of double, "virtual" reality existing free from ordinary, material reality, and—the central topic of this book—the immense increases in surveillance of people in a vast range of domains of our digitized society. A surveillance, moreover, that quite pervasively, and indeed to an ever increasing extent focuses on people's bodies. The analysis of surveillance, indebted to Michel Foucault in a way that can hardly be overstated, has always revealed the body as a focal point of surveillance practices, and the detailed monitoring and registration of its movements, states and behaviors as one of the primary mechanisms of disciplinary power. The digitization processes occurring all through society now, however, have brought forth an unequalled pervasiveness and intensity, an unprecedented number of ways in which bodies can be monitored, assessed, analyzed, categorized, and, ultimately, managed.

The stories at the beginning of this chapter illustrate, each in their own way, how intimate and important aspects of our personal lives are affected by the registration and processing of various types of data generated from bodies. In each example information technologies are involved in assessing futures, risks and life chances, whether it concerns the freedom to enter or leave a particular country, the odds of getting a life-threatening disease, or an estimation of individual response to life-saving treatment. In each example information technologies are in effect scrutinizing, identifying, and assessing *bodies*.

What the examples highlight, is that in a rapidly growing variety of practices, bodies and information technologies are interconnected in a way that gives us a new perception of what bodies are and what they comprise: in all three cases aspects of physical bodies are translated into digital code and information. Over the course of several decades, and in tandem with developments in information technologies, a new body has been emerging. It is a body that is defined in terms of information. Who you are, how you are, and how you are going to be treated in various situations, is increasingly known to various agents and agencies through information deriving from your own body; information that is processed elsewhere, through the networks, databases, and algorithms of the information society.

This has opened up tremendous possibilities for intensified surveillance practices. Once translations of bodily characteristics into digitally processable data have been made, these bodies become amenable to forms of analysis and categorization in ways not possible before. The biometrically authenticated and profiled bodies at the airport are automatically classified as either known or unknown, legal or illegal, wanted or unwanted, low or high security risk—assessments with concrete consequences for the immediate futures of the persons concerned. Similarly, the body defined in terms of its genetic profile, nicotine or medication intake, disease history, etc., becomes a body that is assessed as either normal or abnormal, as healthy or pathological, as low or high risk. Particular profiles can be produced from large amounts of data, and social/digital identities affixed to persons behind their backs, whether they actually fit the category in question or not. With the growing interconnection of networks, cross-matching of databases, and sharing of information between agencies and institutions, both in the public and private sectors, such attributed identities can become like a person's shadow: hard to fight, impossible to shake.

To most people, the precise topography and mechanisms of information systems and networks are highly opaque. And even though some of us live in times and places where a general trust in authorities and those in positions of trust may be warranted, satisfactory democratic controls and regulations adequate to the information age are still in large part yet to be installed.

The body in historical change

What we, at any given historical period, think of as "the body" is subject to change. How we think and speak of the body, even how we experience it, is in large part a function of the knowledges and languages available to us. And not only are the cognitive and linguistic involved here. It is as much a matter of the material and practical ways that we handle and treat the body that tells us what kind of an entity we consider "the body" to be. For this reason it is not only science but also technology and its many ways of shaping daily practices that, together, constitute what a human body is. And because these practices, both on a scientific level and in daily life, are subject to change over time, the body itself may be said to change as well. So, we may need to consider how the translation of (aspects of) our physical existence into digital code and information, and the new uses of bodies this subsequently allows, amounts to a change on the level of ontology, instead of merely that of representation. As Katherine Hayles writes:

> When changes in incorporating practices take place, they are often linked with new technologies that affect how people use their bodies and experience space and time. Formed by technology at the same time that it creates technology, embodiment mediates between technology and discourse by creating new experiential frameworks that serve as boundary markers for the creation of corresponding discursive systems. In the feedback loop between technological innovations and discursive practices, incorporation is a crucial link.
>
> *(Hayles 1992)*

Instead of the standard dual picture of the body as an ahistorical, natural entity, the representations of which change over time (due to scientific and technological innovations), we may need to consider how all three terms are caught in a process of co-evolution: with technological and discursive practices converging towards an ontology of information, it is unlikely that their mediating link, embodiment—even while acknowledging its constraining and limiting power—will remain unaffected. And because embodiment concerns our most basic experience of the body and of being in the world, these developments carry profound normative and moral implications we ought to attempt to uncover.

This historicization of the body does not apply exclusively to our age of digitization and informatization; on the contrary. When, for example, under the banner of the scientific revolution and the age of Enlightenment the taboo on dissecting corpses was lifted, an experience of the body in anatomical and physiological terms gradually evolved. This new perception of the body was mediated through many new medical procedures and techniques, and their concomitant representational practices such as the anatomical atlas. From then on, these techniques, such as for example surgical ones, grew to incredible levels of sophistication and perfection, impacting immensely on the collective experience of our bodies, how they work, and what can be done to them when something is wrong. Crucial to our contemporary bodily self-understanding were also the later developments in endocrinology, immunology and neurology. Our hormones, immune and nervous systems, and, of course, our brain, and the various practices in which they have become objects of management and treatment, all changed our conception of what our bodies are made of.

Again, the significance of this is not merely that of a new perception, or definition, that is, of *representations* of the body (with "the thing itself" remaining the same), but, more fundamentally, a change on the level of *ontology*: it is our very bodies, and our subjective forms of embodiment that are caught in this historical process of change.

Today, we are once more living in times of far-ranging technological change, a process in which information technologies are pivotal. These changes are affecting almost every part of society and daily life, up to our very bodily existence. With our bodies gradually becoming entities consisting of information—the body as data—the boundary between the body *itself* and information *about* that body cannot be taken for granted anymore (van der Ploeg 2002).

Body data: examples and practices

The most obvious domain where this change takes place is, of course, medicine. New medical technologies range from genetic analysis to diagnostic imaging, from electronic record keeping to epidemiological research on large databases. The number of often amazing ways in which various ITs are involved in rendering bodies visible, knowable, and searchable, even treatable, are proliferating, it appears, on a daily basis. Within these new technological practices, diagnosing and treating ailing material bodies has become indistinguishable from generating and analyzing electronic data; caring and curing becoming a matter of information management.

But it is not just in medicine where the various new uses of IT are redefining the body. The IT-mediated monitoring and surveilling of bodies that is rapidly becoming a hallmark of modern medicine, has also—boosted tremendously in the wake of September 11th 2001—become part of domains like public security, law enforcement, policing, and forensics.

Fingerprinting has been around for quite some time, but its usefulness has increased infinitely with the development of automated pattern recognition systems that, within seconds, can retrieve a matching print from a database containing millions. Well known too are the more recent DNA databases with genetic profiles of convicted criminals. The criteria for inclusion into these databases differs from one country to another, but the general trend is a steady lowering of the threshold. Another related use of this technique involves sampling entire sections of a population in a particular area, when traditional methods fail to generate a suspect. Usually in such cases, the information gathered is destroyed after it serves its specific purpose, but this does not prevent some law enforcement officials dreaming of, and sometimes publicly advocating for, building databases that will include the entire population.

Less well known perhaps are the databases with digitized images of faces. When a watchlist is coupled to video images from surveillance cameras and face recognition systems, it becomes possible to search crowds and streets for specific persons. Social media like Facebook and Youtube with their millions of uploaded personal images are themselves the biggest databases of facial images of all, a fact astutely recognized by software developers and law enforcement agencies of various kinds.

But beyond mere recognition of individuals, faces have been turned into a source of data for recognizing gender, ethnicity, age, and emotional states; information quite profitable for marketers and useful to security agents. So-called second generation biometrics involves integrating a number of developments into complex "multimodal" systems combining a range of body data. These systems include new sensor technologies, among which most notably are those that work from a distance, and those able to pick up with growing precision new types of body data like pupil dilation, galvanic skin response, electro-cardiograms and electroencephalograms. Also, a new set of traits and behaviors are now used for biometric profiling such as gait, posture, activities and movements such as how one sits on a chair, or how one moves through an office while executing daily tasks. Add to this the development of so-called soft biometrics, i.e. automatic classification systems based on non-identifying traits such as height, weight, gender, age, ethnicity (see below), and a picture emerges that makes the surveillance potential of "classic" biometric authentication schemes we have only just come to accept as an inevitable part of modern life pale in comparison.

Body boundaries and integrity

There is no doubt that most of these practices have been designed to serve useful purposes, and they often do so. The complicated medical interventions and ever more complex treatment protocols made possible by the clever use of information technologies are impressive and mostly beneficial; likewise it is hard to object to pooling and analyzing medical data from patient records to advance medical science, or rationalize policy and healthcare funding. Similarly, it is hard to be anything but in favor of improved security in public space, or increasing the chances of solving heinous crimes. And even though all these purported advantages need constant critical assessment and civic watchfulness, grand evaluations in generally positive or negative terms serve little realistic purpose.

The point here, then, is first to indicate the prolific and ubiquitous nature of the generation and processing of "body data," and second, to identify a fundamental philosophical and normative challenge posed by this informatization of the body. This challenge can be formulated thus: how do we maintain the distinction between the body itself and information about that body, if the body itself, in a way, now consists of information? For example, in the chain of biological sample, isolated DNA, DNA records, STR profiles, complete genetic profiles, (what are today believed to be) medically non-coding polymorphisms, and (what are today known as) "health-related loci"....where exactly is the transition from bodily matter to bodily data? Does it really still make sense to try to make the distinction?

Issues like this are not just academic philosophical puzzles, but have practical and normative relevance. They are comparable to the legal and ethical debates concerning the status of prostheses, implants, (donated) organs, gametes, or blood: here too, questions arise on how to define the body's boundaries. In the case of the body-as-information, the problem is that we have very different regimes for protecting bodies and for protecting information from unjustified access and intrusion, however "personal" that information may be. Whereas in the first case the very integrity of the body and issues of self determination are at stake, in the second, the far weaker concepts of informational privacy and personal data protection apply. But this task division presumes that it is self-evident what belongs to "the body itself," and where information about the body begins—in other words, this task division runs into trouble exactly because this crucial distinction has lost its self-evidence.

An interesting case in point is biobanking. Regulation of the use of these collections of biological samples is an issue generating much debate, controversy and jurisprudence. In his interesting analysis of current regulatory discourse on this matter, Lee Bygrave (2010) traces ambiguities concerning the question of how such samples relate to the concepts of information and personal data, and hence, to what extent data protection and privacy rights are applicable and mobilized in this context. He thus takes the argument in the opposite direction than the one taken here so far. Instead of arguing that the informatization of the body may indicate some sort of extension of what counts as the body proper, and therefore require stronger protective regimes than merely that of data protection, he investigates the question to what extent the body and its parts and material derivatives are to be conceived as data and information to be protected under data protection law. To some extent, acknowledging the privacy aspects of biobanks would actually amount to an improvement and strengthening of protection for individuals concerned. Either way, the fact that Bygrave is able to trace the increasing ambiguity of the distinction between the body itself and information about the body in a number of recent key documents issued by EU regulatory bodies is indeed significant.

This issue is particularly relevant to a curious aspect of this new body, also highlighted by the examples, namely that it has become (re-)searchable at a distance. The digitized body can be transported to places far removed, both in time and space, from the person belonging to the body concerned. Databases can be remotely accessed through network connections; they are built to save information and allow retrieval over extended periods of time. A bodily search or examination used to require the presence of the person involved—a premise so self-evident that to question it would be ridiculous. Today, however, this is not so obvious any more.

Take again the example of forensic DNA-typing. Lawyers and legal scholars have been keen to point out the seriousness of the breach of bodily integrity at stake in taking DNA samples from suspects. Stringent legal rules have been installed to safeguard the rights of those suspected, and, although far less, of those convicted of crimes. But of course, it can hardly be the saliva swab taken from the inner lining of the mouth, or the hair pulled from a sleeve that constitutes such a compromising of bodily integrity. It is not the *generation* of the body data per se, but the information about the body thus gathered, and all the analyses, processing, and knowledge about the person this information makes possible, that is of concern. Moreover, the storage of this information allows researching suspects' bodies over indefinite periods of time. With new analytic techniques becoming available time and again, it is tempting to reopen old and unsolved cases, and search the data anew. Under our current normative framework, such a search would merely count as a privacy-sensitive data search, whereas we may have to come to acknowledge that it actually amounts to a (new kind of) body search.

In a medical context it is also easy to imagine how, for example, an internal examination of someone's body can be executed by a "third party" located elsewhere, by remotely accessing digital diagnostic images and data—possibly without the patient being aware of this. Again, under current regulations, this would merely count as (confidential) data sharing between professionals, whereas it may be better regarded as a virtual physical examination of the patient's body.

Issues of similarity and difference

Whenever we talk about the human body, we are all aware that "the human body" does not exist as such. People come in a variety of shapes, colors, genders, and ages, sharing, of course, most of their physiology and anatomy with most of humanity, but never all. Moreover, these differences between people are commonly used to categorize people as belonging to specific groups defined in terms of age, gender, ethnicity, (dis-)ability, and so on, and hence are of great ethical, legal and political significance (Lacqueur 1990; Schiebinger 1993). In the context of surveillance practices with their social sorting effects, these issues are of particular concern, for social sorting based on bodily differences may easily slip into the pernicious forms of exclusion and discrimination that were at the centre of the great emancipatory struggles of the previous century.

Illustrative of these problems are the set of technologies emblematic of the use of bodies in surveillance: biometrics. Here, issues of similarity and difference emerge in at least two different ways (van der Ploeg 2010). On the one hand there is the matter of *exclusion* of certain categories of "different" people from system use, because the systems can only cope with difference to a limited extent. In biometric discourse the set of problems connected with this issue is referred to with a number of concepts, such as, for example, "usability," "accessibility," "failure to enroll," "exception handling," and "template aging." In the context of biometric technologies, "accessibility" refers to the problem that many people, often specific categories of people like the elderly, children, people with a particular ethnic or professional background, are unable to enroll in a biometric system because they do not possess the required bodily feature or a sufficiently "machine-readable" one.

Almost all biometric techniques present, for example, an age range in which the biometric data can be optimally acquired and processed. The elderly, as well as infants and children, have a problem being enrolled by many existing fingerprint scanners because of the particularities of the height of their papillary relief. In the very young, the height of the papillary relief is still underdeveloped, whereas in the elderly it often shows a wearing down. In the discourses of social theory and politics, these matters invoke considerations in terms of normalization and social exclusion (Foucault 1979; Star 1991). Normalization here refers to the production and enactment of norms, through which the very distinction between what counts as normal and what as exception or deviancy is performed within and through technological practices. When a biometric system fails to cope with variations in human features falling outside a certain range, it thereby categorizes and excludes, with more or less serious consequences to the people concerned.

On the other hand, the issue of bodily differences emerges in relation to biometric technologies that *use* the differences mentioned, trying, e.g., to *automatically classify* people in gender, age, and ethnic categories. So-called "soft biometrics" is a set of experimental biometric applications aiming at using "partial identities," and recognizing general body characteristics such as body weight, gender, age, or ethnicity. Here, questions about the *black-boxing* of contingent and contestable *constructions* of those categories arise (Bowker and Star 1999).

Even in the 1990s, the then still relatively unknown biometric technologies had some people worrying about the possibility that collecting a biometric identifier would conflict with race, gender, or other anti-discrimination laws. This was then seen by many biometrics advocates as being based on unfounded and ill-informed beliefs about biometrics, saying that from any biometric it was impossible to infer such sensitive category information. Despite such reassurances, however, a growing line of research today is concerned with the above mentioned "soft biometrics." They are called "soft," because, unlike biometric *identification* technologies, they focus on traits that do not single out one individual from all others, but on ones that are shared by large numbers of people. From an identification perspective, however, that can be useful as supporting information or as a "secondary mechanism," which, when used in conjunction with identifying biometric traits, can substantially improve the success rates of identification technologies. Also, they can be used to establish membership of a category (e.g. establishing adulthood) without actually identifying, for which reason a certain privacy-protective potential is sometimes attributed to these technologies. For example, one could thus classify subjects in broad age categories, in order to determine legal competence to apply for certain services, or buy certain products, while preserving anonymity. On the other hand, there are all too many situations imaginable in which filtering people out on the basis of their gender, age, or ethnic/racial background constitutes illegal discrimination, and developing systems to automate this process could therefore be considered inherently risky.

Also, and contrary to what their apparent self-evident reference in ordinary language and everyday life may lead one to believe, the reification of these categories and distinctions, as the history and philosophy of science have made abundantly clear, is essentially contestable and unstable (Lacqueur 1990; Schiebinger 1993). For example, the distinction between the male and female gender on a genetic level does not always match the one made on an endocrinological, anatomical, psychological, or socio-cultural level; and even when birth-registered gender is taken as a reference point, a problem exists where even this is amenable to change during an individual's lifetime. In an exacerbated form, and notoriously so, similar problems exist with ethnicity and race classifications, all of which have been proven to lack any indisputable basis in "nature" (Harding 1993). Unfortunately, the signs are that such insights from the more critical humanities will not easily find their way into high tech R&D, so that, despite all efforts at their deconstruction, the new realities concerning these categories may follow the dictum "*If technology defines a situation as real, it is real in its consequences.*"

Conclusion

New technological configurations often come with new economic, social or cultural realities, and ICTs appear particularly powerful in reshaping our world. But contrary to the de-physicalization predicted at the close of the previous century by many commentators on the information revolution, it appears that we may have to take a subtle but highly consequential reconfiguration of the very materiality of our bodies and embodiment into account as well.

References

Bowker, G.C. and Star, S. L. (1999). *Sorting Things Out: Classification and Its Consequences*, Cambridge, MA and London: MIT Press.

Bygrave, L. A. (2010). "The Body as Data? Biobank Regulation via the 'Back Door' of Data Protection Law," *Law, Innovation and Technology,* 2(1): 1–25.

Foucault, M. (1979). *Discipline and Punish: The Birth of the Prison,* New York: Vintage/Random House.

Harding, S. (ed.) (1993). *The "Racial" Economy of Science,* Indianapolis: Indiana University Press.

Hayles, K. N. (1992). "The Materiality of Informatics," *Configurations,* 1(2): 147–70.

Lacqueur, T. (1990). *Making Sex: Body and Gender from the Greeks to Freud,* Cambridge, MA and London: Harvard University Press.

Schiebinger, L. (1993). *Nature's Body: Gender in the Making of Modern Science,* Boston, MA: Beacon Press.

Star, S. L. (1991). "Power, Technology and the Phenomenology of Conventions: On Being Allergic to Onions," in J. Law (ed.) *A Sociology of Monsters: Essays on Power, Technology, and Domination,* Oxford: Basil Blackwell, pp. 26–56.

van der Ploeg, I. (2002). "Biometrics and the Body as Information: Normative Issues in the Socio-technical Coding of the Body," in D. Lyon (ed.), *Surveillance as Social Sorting: Privacy, Risk, and Automated Discrimination,* New York: Routledge, pp. 57–73.

——(2010). "Normative Assumptions in Biometrics: On Bodily Differences, In-built Norms, and Automated Classifications," in S. Van der Hof and M. Groothuis (eds), *Innovating Government—Normative, Policy and Technological Dimensions of Modern Government,* The Hague: TMC Asser Press, pp. 29–40.

Part III
Surveillance contexts

Introduction

Contexts of surveillance

This section introduces readers to some of the contexts where surveillance operates as a mode of ordering, governance and organization. As well as demonstrating the different empirical findings generated by studies of surveillance within these contexts, it points to some of the key dimensions along with how surveillance processes and their consequences vary.

It is important to acknowledge that "surveillance" and "the surveillance society" are not singularities. In order to understand them at an empirical level it is helpful to think of the surveillance society as made up of "domains of surveillance." This section of the handbook contains work on key surveillance domains, featuring surveillance which, alongside some similar features, has very different dynamics. They are made up of similar types and levels of actor: institutions, business organizations, governments, regulators, individuals and groups of individuals working alone, collaboratively or counter-productively towards particular strategies and goals. Nevertheless, they have different origins and some would argue different trajectories, although a powerful counter-argument is that some domains of surveillance, particularly the military and the commercial, are converging. Concomitantly the span of surveillance over populations and its consequences also vary. Different norms and belief systems about surveillance, different types of power relations and degrees of inclusion, exclusion, normativity and exception emerge. These factors simultaneously point back to surveillance as an ordering process as well as to its relative contextualization. When seeking to understand surveillance in context the key questions are: Which domain of surveillance are we investigating? What are the organizations involved? At what level of analysis are we working? Which practices, systems and social networks are implicated? Whose consequences are being investigated and how are these negotiated or resisted by those affected?

This is not uncharted territory in surveillance theory. Michaelis Lianos (2004: 414–415) warns:

> it is a simplification to attribute as a matter of course specific intentions to all acts of mechanisms of control without taking the trouble to carry out an analysis of the complexity that causes their birth, survival and proliferation.

Lianos (2003) outlines the function of different institutional *dispositifs* of surveillance—translated to mean "socio-technical systems." He notes that different *dispositifs* promulgate control as necessarily planned and integral to bureaucracy, but because of the myriad of goals and strategies which exist therein, simultaneously they are fragmented, decentralized, atomized and impersonal. More recently Helen Nissenbaum (2009), in a discussion of privacy violations made the important observation that whether a violation of privacy had occurred in any one context depended upon whether the norms of information appropriation and distribution already operant within that context had been violated. Her extensive description and analysis of contrasting scenarios reinforces the idea that surveillance practices are profoundly embedded within local contexts.

In the first subsection, "population control," we see three examples of how surveillance is used to govern human and non-human populations as they enter into and move around the spatial territories of political jurisdictions. In the case of border control, census and non-human surveillance, surveillance is closely integrated with the primary goals of their respective authorities. In the case of cities and schools, surveillance features in a milieu of agendas broadly designed to promote a more secure, resilient and appropriate environment which is "fit for purpose." The chapters in this section highlight how surveillance is applied to form, regulate and stratify populations and spaces, resulting in varying entitlements for citizens and the (re)production of space as a function of the surveillance embedded within it. Peter Adey focuses on surveillance and the international border, outlining the challenges of identifying and authenticating bodies, and the consequences for bodies as information about them becomes mobile, creating new borders within and without nation states. Pete Fussey and Jon Coaffee then discuss how the application of video surveillance in the city became routinely used by planning departments and is a sought-after response to terrorist attacks. The result is an internally divided cityscape with security and surveillance built in to protect areas generating high levels of economic value. Evelyn Ruppert then charts the history of the census as a way of knowing, constituting and governing populations. She highlights how inclusion in a surveillance regime becomes politicized as state recognition of hitherto marginalized communities. Some groups have campaigned to have their ethnicities represented within census categories. New moves to constitute censuses from government administrative data and not just through questionnaires imply that the population as a whole will be more closely tracked as its characteristics change over time. Andrew Donaldson outlines how the food chain has become an object of surveillance as authorities tried to regulate the threat posed to humans by low-quality and diseased animal products through the tracking of animals from birth to death. Donaldson calls for a more robust theorization of the productive and distributed nature of the food chain as a surveiled object. Finally Emmeline Taylor outlines the increased presence of surveillance in schools, the lack of evidence as to its effects, and suggests that it may have a powerful formative effect on young people's expectations of the presence of surveillance throughout their lives.

The second subsection, "crime and policing," is perhaps familiar intellectual territory for many readers of this volume. Surveillance studies initially grew out of a concern with public order control methods used by law enforcement agencies which featured overt and covert data gathering. Policing is another example of how powerful public authorities directly use surveillance in order to meet their goals. Kevin Haggerty begins by discussing how the police have become information workers, and outlines the different ways in which they gather and use information in order to detect crime and prosecute offenders. As there are questions over the ability of the police to use and manage such data, concern is expressed over recent access by police to external databases about the population. Michael McCahill then highlights how media reporting of crime creates a synoptic effect where the attention of society as a whole is disproportionately focused on working-class crime as reported by the media. This, he argues, reinforces existing social divisions and fuels further public investment in panoptic crime-fighting measures which target already-disadvantaged populations. The growth in video surveillance and its questionable effectiveness as a tool to prevent and detect crime is then discussed by Clive Norris. Reinforcing McCahill's arguments, Norris underlines the symbolic power of CCTV. He suggests that it represents not only the ability of governments to be seen to do something about crime and terror, but also the capacity to maintain the status quo through the deployment of technological "solutions." The relationship of surveillance deployment to modes of government goes far beyond mere symbolism in Nelson Arteaga Botello's account of surveillance in Latin America. In a profound contrast to Norris, he suggests the combination of high violent crime rates with extreme inequalities in newly formed democracies excludes certain sections of the population from the protection of surveillance and exposes them to state violence as their living conditions form "infra-surveilled" zones in Latin American cities.

The sub-section entitled "security, intelligence, war" illustrates how surveillance and the intelligence it generates are used fundamentally to exert statehood and sovereignty. Inclusion and exclusion are reproduced at a grand scale as surveillance embeds political ideologies to reinforce notions of citizen and alien, friend and foe, and determines and constitutes the deployment of military force. The chapters in this section highlight the long history of surveillance and the military, demonstrating that the current state of affairs is the product of technological, political and ideological trajectories. Dean Wilson tracks the development of military surveillance from notions of a drilled military machine to full spectrum dominance and the Revolution in Military Affairs. A blurring of boundaries between internal and external security and the militarization of all kinds of threat (drugs, terror, crime, pollution) has resulted in militarized surveillance techniques being turned on domestic populations across the globe. Didier Bigo notes these trends as he discusses how the fields of security studies and surveillance studies have emerged. In particular he suggests that we consider the consequences for democracy when security infrastructures are now focused on the pre-emption of threat, based on a future already known through the use of simulation and databases. Torin Monahan similarly argues that surveillance studies has been catalyzed by the response to 9/11 which catalyzed many of the developments discussed by both Wilson and Bigo. Monahan argues that relations between individuals, private companies and the state have been transformed in the post 9/11 era, as new bordering practices, data fusion and unprecedented connections between systems cement surveillance into critical infrastructure and reduce the means for challenge by civil society organizations. He points out how the US government has given the population responsibility to identify potential suspects, thus promoting an enduring politics of fear and acceptance of increased security and diminished privacy. Finally, Gates discusses the legacy of 9/11 for the rest of the world, highlighting how the USA has utilized forces of neo-liberal economic globalization to enroll as many corporations and states as possible to protect "the homeland." A renewed "security-industrial complex" has emerged which spans international boundaries.

The fourth sub-section concerns the everyday worlds of "production, consumption, administration". In each chapter it is difficult to distinguish surveillance practices from the everyday organizing practices of state administration and private enterprise. Unlike the issues discussed in the previous two sub-sections, surveillance features as a bi-product of the mass information processing required in the modern bureaucracy. Identifying practices *as surveillant* in these contexts is less easily accomplished *a priori* and is more a matter of perspective-taking on different forms of economic activity. Of particular importance is the observation that everyday workers, consumers and citizens are fundamentally implicated in the production of surveillance practices by organizations and are enticed and rewarded for doing so. Graham Sewell introduces a framework of contrasting lenses through which surveillance in the employment relationship can be understood. Surveillance is seen as something which is multi-directional and multi-level, interpellating and mediated by a wide array of social and economic relationships embedded within the workplace. Jason Pridmore introduces a variety of perspectives on consumer surveillance. Of particular importance is his observation that social media have produced a vast stream of data for marketers to use, locating the consumer as a "pro-sumer": consumers who by their participation in social media actively produce consumer categories that are at the heart of consumer surveillance. Finally William Webster, in contrast to earlier chapters, outlines the sometimes contradictory roles taken by public administrations in relation to surveillance. As well as promoting surveillance for security, public administrations are involved in the regulation of surveillance and, crucially, its normalization as vast databases of personal details are used to help administer the health, welfare and social care policies of the modern state.

In the final sub-section, "digital spaces of surveillance", new phenomena and insights that have emerged from developments in online applications and internet infrastructure are introduced. Contradiction and ambivalence abound as surveillance imperatives butt up against opportunities for participation and inclusion from state to individual levels, creating multiple sight-lines and tensions. David Murakami Wood addresses globalization and observes how it constitutes new objects of surveillance to reinforce first world dominance: failed or problematic developing states, environmental systems and global flows of communication. Fernanda Bruno offers a detailed examination of participatory surveillance stemming from Web 2.0. Even though Web 2.0 has opened up new opportunities for expression and community building it also has resulted in the same being cemented into a surveillance web. Bruno observes surveillance is often a secondary function in such activities and a new form of function creep, so typical of the spread of surveillance, is illustrated. She outlines the potential for online communities to "watch back," and to create synoptic effects on the corporations that gather online data. Finally Valerie Steeves outlines the experience of young people and internet surveillance. She demonstrates a growing sense of privacy and surveillance awareness in young internet users. Young people's negotiation of identities, both online and in relation to their parents and friends are sources of tension which makes this a particularly rich area to study.

A broad consideration of the different contexts of surveillance thus begins to illuminate its complex and multi-layered nature. Institutions such as the military, national and local state government and private enterprise in its various guises as an employer, service provider and technological innovator practice surveillance as a central pillar, supplement to or bi-product of their strategies. Effects of these practices are felt, assimilated or resisted by entire societies, urban populations, formally and informally organized groups and individuals. For example, increased internal security post 9/11 has seen the stigmatization of certain ethnic groups by their being subject to disproportionate levels of scrutiny. Other minority communities campaign for fair treatment by being included in surveillance regimes. Consumers and workers find themselves complicit in surveillance and having to negotiate the different moral positions inherent in community participation and data generation. Children and young people find new tensions in parental relationships as they engage in social media. The permutations are endless. For the surveillance scholar, it becomes critical to draw clear boundaries around the object of one's scholarship and to define the terms of one's engagement with surveillance as a phenomenon.

Bibliography

Lianos, M. (2003). "Social Control after Foucault," *Surveillance and Society*, 1(3): 412–430.
——(2004). *Risk and Power: The Challenge of Depoliticizing*, Naples: Centro di Ricerca sulle Istituzioni Europee & Elio Selino.
Nissenbaum, Helen. (2009). *Privacy in Context: Technology, Policy, and the Integrity of Social Life*, Palo Alto, CA: Stanford University Press.

Section 3.1.
Population control

a. Borders, identification and surveillance

New regimes of border control

Peter Adey

Introduction

Borders are the key sites in the distinction of territories. As places of the sorting and effective differentiation of the (global) mobilities of people and things, borders are married to the practice and evolution of surveillance. This chapter is concerned with such processes of border-making or bordering which act to instate or reinforce existing regimes of regulation and governance over mobilities by way of a manifold array of surveillance techniques and technologies. Perhaps borders are the focus of such intense practices of monitoring, surveillance and sorting because they are "pinch points," the filters in a hydraulic system of flows of movement that circulate and move between and *within* national state and supra-national state boundaries. Constituting the contact zones between populations, borders are the site of political exertion, of decisions over who gets in, who leaves and who doesn't, moments of the sovereign decision over who or what is inside or outside the regime of their care. If critical decisions like this are to be made, then critically they require surveillance measures in order to provide the basis upon which decisions may be taken, although we will complicate this later.

Surveillance has gone hand in hand with the border's development as ever increasing modes of seeing and monitoring have evolved in response to the border's role; borders have been long deemed the blueprints for our surveillance futures—or surveillance societies. Sites of highly contentious and visible forms of screening and scrutiny, borders are now the exemplar of futuristic and high-tech security fantasies that equally open up security practices to increasingly concerned activists, civil rights groups and the oversight of a public increasingly worried about the fortunes of their privacy and how susceptible they might be to discrimination. The border's visibility even works both ways. Borders are subjected to the focus of high-profile political action, from the activities of terrorists to the occupation of airports from protest movements. It is because resistance to the skein of regulations and measures which overlay borders is so politically and culturally volatile that such action is particularly visible and potent.

Peoples and things cross, flow and butt up against borders which are no longer found at the edges of states. Borders might even be located within and now outside territorial containers as bodies too are stretched, made informational and pulled and pushed within and across national boundaries. Surveillance seems to disrespect the traditional jurisdictional limits of nation-states by transborder supranational and interoperable surveillance systems in order to, paradoxically, reinforce their borders. The chapter will show how both the location of the border as well as its functionality are being undone along three interrelated lines. These will move from the increasing focus upon the body and its information, to how surveillance is requiring this information to be ever more mobile, making the location of the border increasingly unclear.

It is also important to note that other sorts of surveillance measures inhabit borders which are not directly related to the scrutiny of subjects who are about to cross them, but the wider securitization of the border zone. Within ports and airports, staff or private areas will be regulated as secure or clean zones, which will be managed through identification access schemes. Public areas will be controlled by video surveillance systems, and car parks may be monitored and managed by Automatic Number Plate Recognition systems (ANPR). Perimeter fencing and surveillance will most likely police the border of the border. Surveillance must therefore also monitor the security or integrity of the border space itself. The concern of border surveillance is, therefore, not only for the literal border crossing. Moreover, we see similarly sophisticated systems in place to identify passenger flow throughputs in order to target appropriate staff rostering and timetabling to the correct rhythms of business throughout the day, or to even encourage further consumer spending. In short, the surveillance of the border is complex. It operates according to an often contradictory layering of national and international jurisdictions, regulations and concerns. It responds to and coexists with more localized imperatives which reflect the overlapping modes of interest and authority such as the border's commercial business and multi-modal purposes.

First, the chapter outlines how borders are increasingly involved in capturing bodies. Second, borders must work even harder to sort and differentiate one person from the next and one proportion of the population from the other(s) by fluctuating assessments of risk and trust based upon interlocking systems of surveillance. Finally, research is suggesting that borders are increasingly pulling out and unsettling established notions of territory and boundary, inside and outside, as borders are both proliferating and extending themselves beyond their usual location and jurisdiction (see Gates, Monahan, this volume).

Borders and bodies

The border has long been a site of visibility. It is a point at which individuals must be made recognizable from diverse and intermingled populations and thus borders have often required processes of identification. In order to track and monitor the movements of groups of populations across and within borders according to the administrative or management techniques born within modern liberal governments, the border reinforces the territorial sanctity of the nation-state and the populations moving between them. Individuals need to be distinguished from populations in order to assess the rights of the individual to move. Border monitoring and surveillance therefore place considerable scrutiny over the performance of one's rights as a citizen of the state. With the formal development of the passport, the photograph was instituted as an enhanced measure of the document which could *individuate* the citizen by presenting distinguishable detail in order to identify one individual from another. The passport photo cemented the identity of the citizen— they were who they said they were—with the rights of mobility bestowed upon them. As we will explore later, however, this is not a guarantee of mobility.

Today's borders are animated by similar concerns for the identification of individuals as well as other sorts of documents, objects and temporary permissions such as the visa. Biometric technologies turn bodily characteristics into patterns of data recognizable from systems of records in order to "verify" or "identify" one's identity and therefore their suitability to cross a border. The difference between these two different functions—verification versus identification—is key. A verification technique is when biometrics are used in order for a traveler/passenger to prove their identity, matching up the body at the border with the identification documents they may own and the identity stored within an electronic database. In contrast, an identification technique will use biometric technology in order to "identify" someone from a wider system of records. This is a more targeted system which is used to identify someone in order to ascertain, for instance, their migrant status, as seen in the Eurodac system which identifies asylum applications and persons who have been apprehended when crossing an external border of the European Union. The use of fingerprints, facial and other iris recognition systems have augmented the passport's link to its owner's face with other bodily characteristics held within biometric documents such as the "smart" or biometric passport. What's more, today's techniques of border surveillance and identification have created a whole new raft of social practices and habits we are asked to perform—and are perhaps getting used to performing— in the crossing of borders. From the placing of finger tips on a scanner to looking directly at a camera, to taking off our belts and our shoes, the analysis of border surveillance should not lose sight of how the techniques and technologies it examines are experienced in entirely socially embodied and culturally embedded ways. Of course this sort of issue has provoked inflammatory discussion over the wearing of Muslim head coverings such as the Niqab in airports and other public spaces.

Border surveillance comprehends mobile subjects as encumbered or prosthetically tied to a large amount of stuff, personal belongings and objects. They are also concerned with a related issue, that of the passenger's potentiality: what it is a traveler might do. Within both foci the organization of border surveillance has turned with even more interest to the body. Other surveillance measures have become increasingly sophisticated in their ability to penetrate the body's boundaries. These are not necessarily for the purposes of identifying identity, which is no longer a simple marker of trust via citizenship. Highlighted by privacy groups such as Electronic Privacy Information Center (EPIC) and fascinating academic studies (see Amoore and Hall 2009), backscatter and wave millimeter technologies are able to see through the body's surface in order to visualize concealed weapons, explosives or drugs and other contraband, with troubling implications for privacy and passenger rights. Questions arise as to how these techniques unsettle the body's essential "integrity," as its gaze penetrates through normal boundaries of vision. Others show concern with the abuses this sort of technology may be enabling, with reports of security screeners ogling a desiring and humiliating gaze at women passengers from a separate room. At the airport, full-body x-ray scanners are now becoming commonplace since the attempted Christmas bombing of 2009 on a flight from Schiphol to Detroit. At ferry and cargo ports, the boundaries of containers and lorries too may be opened up by other surveillance devices. Some technologies are able to see through walls, picking up the body-heat or the particle signatures of hiding illegal migrants or of taxable and illegal goods.

At the same time as bodies are more carefully visioned in order to monitor the hiding of illicit objects, the border is continuing to narrow its gaze upon travelers in order to ascertain their hidden intentions and deceptions. Seen across new border initiatives in airports within the USA and the UK, screeners are becoming increasingly anxious to consider passenger body language, mood and expressive relations in order to identify "hostile" or "terrorist intent" (Adey 2009). Undoubtedly such techniques are not unusual for the border as drug enforcement agencies have persistently tried to detect and decipher suspicious and nervous-looking border crossers for a long time. Within the USA and under the Behavior Detection program, surveillance has gone somatic. Following the direction of Israeli security techniques combined with scientific expertise from neuro-psychology, the spotting of deception through facial ticks and revealing frowns is happening in parallel with efforts to make the border zone a more calming, relaxing and less stressful experience. Together with a more fleeting and sliding touch of distant technology, the employment of human factors and ergonomics to the redesign of border spaces is rationalized in several ways. More obliquely, border agencies are concerned to simply improve the passenger experience of borders which has been historically relatively poor. Improving relations with security staff and authorities may well provide greater public trust in their abilities. However, the enhancement of the passenger experience also comes with another payoff; working on the assumption that the border can be more calm and relaxed, an improved border is premised on the notion that it will cause those with something to hide to rise to the surface of the visible. Border screening in the US Transport Security Administration's "Checkpoint Evolution" aims to be "unpredictable," layered and more comfortable. Composure and re-composure benches adorn these sites, giving passengers more time and comfort to gather their belongings together after having them all screened through the x-ray machine. Tempered by the ambience of moody paneling and cool blue lighting, if you are willing to be subjected to the airport-border's new enhanced screening measures an improved passenger experience may await your movement through the border. If not, passengers may be subjected to intense forms of scrutiny that include more invasive "pat-down" and body searches.

Filter

At the border the body is not assumed to end at the skin. Border surveillance goes beyond the body-corporeal to its abstractions or "data doubles." These are spectral bodies of information which allow more complex and disaggregated decisions over mobile populations to be passed between disparate networks. As we will see in the following section this sees an undoing of the border as a simple geographical site. What is clear, however, is the way in which borders require these abstractions in order to make decisions over who may or who may not pass. Displaced onto what Judith Butler describes as "petty sovereigns," the sovereign decision is repeatedly performed and re-performed in the remaking of the border by distributed border agents and personnel from agencies such as the UK's Border Agency (UKBA). The border agent-bureaucrat delegates the sovereign decision to allow one entrance to a state and to make the routine distinctions between citizen/foreign. The decision is made over who to admit or to expel, defining the limits of the state in that very moment (Vaughan-Williams 2010).

Making these decisions over entry and denial sees surveillance playing a constitutive role in sorting out or weeding "high" from "low" risk, the "good guys" from the "bad guys." Indeed, the concern over increasingly sophisticated border surveillance practices is how these decisional moments of sorting are becoming deferred onto code and software which has the capacity to "decide" or discriminate auto-matically. Particularly evident of this trend are the controversies over so called profiling, found especially within the airport security screening systems such as the United States' Computer Assisted Passenger Pre-screening System (CAPPS I and II) and the subsequent Electronic System for Travel Authorization (ESTA system) now in place. These systems work by gathering information on passengers recorded within Flight Reservation data such as Personal Name Records (PNR), Advanced Passenger Information (API) electronic data transfer protocols and more diverse and distributed interconnected databases which record more detailed travel preferences and behaviors (Bennett 2005). The concerns over the earlier CAPPS systems and today's US Customs and Border Protection Agency's ESTA system is that they may sort passengers according to racial, ethnic and other social differences. This may happen in orders of risk and they may do this without the agency, deferred or otherwise, of a human. Debates over the required submission and transfer over this information have also occurred in Europe, particularly in response to the EU's agreement with the USA over ESTA, which has seen all passengers travelling to the USA required to submit and pay for an ESTA application whilst all airlines are required to submit and transfer PNR and API data.

Surveillance may not only sort out one person from the rest or another, but play a critical role in people's life chances by profiling; flying "while Arab" has become a popular way to describe these practices of passenger profiling. What happens to those deemed high risk, for those placed on no-fly watch lists, for those denied entry? Even within the apparently more permeable boundaries of the European Schengen area, border surveillance aims to maintain the "fortress" frontiers of its member states by actively managing trajectories or vectors of movement that extend lines of securitization within and beyond the Schengen area. Schengen works by both ring-fencing its area from outside travel, whilst it intensively differentiates the mobilities and immobilities of certain travelers within and without its borders—a trend creating a status of insider. Borders must be continuously rewritten or retraced to sustain the permanence of their presence. The patrolling of the 3,000-km US-Mexican border by state officials and, most concerning, vigilante groups intent on defending the homeland (Rumford 2006) acts to reinforce the border's existence. In Israel's division of the West Bank by its imposing eight-meter-tall wall, the maintaining acts of border agents engaged in a cat and mouse game with illegal border crossers seen elsewhere, is literally made concrete. Borders like these are often vast and inhospitable frontier-like geographies, with very real and hard implications for the life of the border crosser and their future survival. Likewise, the external borders of the European Union are similarly patrolled and maintained by Frontex, the European Border Agency charged with policing the outer boundaries of the European frontier through inter-state cooperation promoting "Integrated Border Management."

This redrawing of boundaries is happening continuously. Between Canada and the United States, pre-clearance (discussed in the following section) is increasingly unbundled and uneven through agreements designed in order to facilitate "trusted," "low risk" and economically productive mobility. NEXUS, for example, elicits movement between a regional zone of space that crosses both the United States and Canada. Movement, for those belonging to this scheme, is made frictionless by expedited security lines and enhanced immigration queues. Members pre-cleared by submitting their details in order to join up to the scheme effectively purchase their post-national citizenship which affords them their faster mobility through dual belonging. Concerns have been raised over these kind of premium, "smart," or "trusted" traveler schemes that potentially stream travelers into differential flows of trust or risk, and therefore subject those who either cannot afford to, or may not possess the right "trusted" characteristics, or who are unprepared to deliver certain levels of information about themselves, to unfair levels forms of scrutiny.

As these systems appear ever more integrated into airline frequent flyer programs and other elite and priority passenger schemes, the sorts of authority we see performed through border surveillance is complicated by the involvement of both public state security providers, licensed operators, private security firms and other businesses. Within this context, expediting a passenger through a border may have less to do with their assumed risk and more to do with the pressures of commercial interests and the need for efficient passenger throughput. Within target driven environments and contractual arrangements, the political economy of border surveillance is an important contributor to unease over its practices. Furthermore, given the involvement of a distributed series of actors involved in the decisions or judgments over expulsion or entry, citizen or foreigner, high or low risk, the decentralization and deferral of the border decision through the complex assembly of expertise and information should be questioned.

The question on the US-Mexican border for Roxanne Lynn Doty is related to just this issue of deferral. For how can we ever really know where a decision is made in a long and difficult chain of uncertainty and contingency? This constitutes a barely visible yet violent action in its concealment and blurring (2007: 116). Indeed it is this propensity to defer, to push to an arm's length, that we will see aptly characterizes the direction in which border surveillance and security is travelling.

Exporting the border

Controlling the movement of EU peoples increasingly takes place away from the border and before "undesirables" reach EU Member States through much wider and distributed forms of surveillance. A wide range of airport, airline and civil personnel are "urged to reach deep into societies to uncover undocumented foreigners, deter asylum-seekers and prevent the exit of the 'huddled masses'" (Lahav and Guiardion cited in Walters 2006: 194). Protecting the integrity of the EU involves penetrating within societies both inside and outside the Schengen area. The result is a form of management that is based on trajectories and vectors of threat. As the Schengen Information System (SIS) moves from its first generation system of "reporting" to one of reporting and "investigation" in SIS II, border agencies and national police forces will be able to perform checks on a plethora of information, including alerts for firearms and criminal records, missing and wanted persons, stolen vehicles and witnesses. This includes the UK who is not a Schengen member; it also demonstrates, relatively precisely, the propensity for surveillance to creep beyond the function of its initial purpose.

The European Commission's agreement with the United States over ESTA mentioned above has created a similar transatlantic architecture of trajectories of information flow crossing the ocean before passengers do. The arrangement sees data "pulled" from European carriers "pre-emptively," extending the function of the airline check-in desk as the initial gateway of territorial access. The globalizing of information has clearly surfaced in this coordination of resources, as even within Europe members of the European Civil Aviation Conference (ECAC) security audit program have begun harmonizing their national security practices. Port border and marine surveillance security systems (Cowen 2009) exhibit similar tendencies in the securing of supply chains where each object or container may well possess an electronic signature required for approval well before that object reaches the shores of its country of destination. Creating consistency over supply chain surveillance and security practices is critical in evolving models of container shipping, enacted through emerging trusted or approved chains of custody intended to ensure adequate security along an object's path of movement. Containers themselves are also becoming increasingly smart. Not only locatable, containers are now able to tell officials whether they have been tampered with, and even report on changes to their internal temperature should they be hijacked or stowaways find their way in.

Bearing witness to the contemporary assembling of all of these distributed systems of data capture, distribution and decision-making, border surveillance is best described by Mark Salter as delocalized—the border is moved off-center and off-shore. The state's affinity for "remote control" (Lahav and Guiraidion in Walters 2006) is particularly evident in border pre-clearance programs. Focusing on Britain's policy towards borders post the July bombings in 2005 and the 2007 attack on Glasgow airport, we see new ideas about the border being proposed through an enhanced language of border security which has less and less to do with container-like territorial control but rather the management of population flows. As Vaughan-Williams (2010) explains, the UK Home Office has argued for a wholesale change in how we think of the border, animated by a raft of structural and ideological changes within UK government following 9/11, and several major disruptions or "emergencies." Within the focus of the UKBA e-borders program, there is a shift away from the position of "a single, staffed physical frontier, where travelers show paper-based identity documents to pass through," to one that will respond to alterations in the structure and function of society. Across a raft of UK legislation, networks, interdependencies and complexities appear to be characterized by "the step change in mobility that globalization has brought" (Vaughan-Williams 2010: 1072). Alongside the UK Anti-Terrorism Act (2002), Civil Contingencies Act (2004) and others, for the border "a new doctrine is demanded" (Home Office in Vaughan-Williams 2010). No longer "a fixed line on a map," the border must evolve with its mobile agents, evolving into a "new offshore line of defence" (Home Office in Vaughan-Williams 2010).

The emphasis of all these re-imaginings is to distance or dislocate the border from territory, to push the surveillance and securitization of individuals to arm's length. "Exporting" (Rumford 2006) the border means risky individuals can be checked at a distance so it is not "too late" when they reach the UK's shores. Such a process is constituted by airport security officials stationed in other airport borders, or decisions over one's ability to travel taken way before one's journey begins. The subsequent requirements of the UKBA's e-borders program have since been challenged within the Parliamentary Home Affairs Select Committee as well as the European Commission, both questioning whether the scheme would actually contravene freedom of movement within Europe. The system had also proposed the enormous capture of data sent from foreign border agencies and carriers prior to travel which would be analyzed at the UK's Joint e-borders Operation Centre (J-BOC). Whether this would conflict with data protection laws has been another stumbling block to the system.

What we are seeing is thus a continuation of the informational delocation of bordering practices, with an added physical dimension. Off-shore borders are predicated on the sophisticated "technological" fixes of information sharing and biometric technologies as well as an ideological push to off-set threats to the outside of the homeland. These practices should not be divorced from wider efforts to disentangle the policing of borders from the necessity of propinquity. Proximity is no longer a compulsion in this regard. Unmanned Aerial Vehicle (UAV) surveillance of the US-Mexican border is a prime example of the distanciation of this process as borders are not only monitored but maintained by the *projection* of power.

Off-shore and delocalized borders are unsurprisingly not immune from contestation. Racial and ethnic discrimination was leveled at the British government's border agencies in a 2002 claim to the British high court, due to the agreement that gave British immigration officers permission to undertake immigration scrutiny at Prague Airport in the Czech Republic, in order to "pre-clear" passengers before they boarded flights for the UK. Czech *Roma* passengers were denied express permission to visit the UK or were treated unfavorably. The evidence of the European Roma Rights Center indicated that a Roma passenger was 400 times more likely to be refused pre-entry clearance to the UK than an individual non-Roma. Not only that, the Roma were subjected to longer questioning by immigration officials than the non-Roma, and 80 percent of Roma were subjected to a second interview as compared with less than 1 percent of non-Roma.

Although the appellants were successful in their second appeal charge of racial discrimination their first appeal failed. This first charge argued that the UK had a domestic and international obligation to the principle of non-refoulement—in other words, that one who has left their first state on the grounds of persecution should not be rejected and returned without appropriate enquiry into their fear of persecution (Kesby 2006). Their argument rested on whether the Romani passengers had actually left the territory of the Czech Republic. The implication of this position was this: had the location of the UK borders moved to Prague Airport, albeit in a very ad hoc way given the temporary operation of the UK pre-clearance program? And if so, did the UK and International obligations to non-refoulment apply extra-territorially? What is so crucial and interesting for our purposes is the way the border is imagined. Although their claim was rejected, the court had to decide *where* the Roma passengers were placed in relation to their own country's borders and those of the United Kingdom. Whether they were located inside or outside a particular territory made a dramatic difference to their ability to claim asylum or international human rights. Whilst Lord Bingham drew upon a difference between an actual and metaphorical border, legal scholar Alison Kesby suggests that:

> it is arguable that the Roma were confronted with the "UK border" while still in Prague. There was a disjuncture between the location of the "geographical" border and the place at which the border was experienced. Immigration rules which otherwise would have operated at UK ports were to apply extra-territorially.
>
> *(Kesby 2006: 8)*

Questions over the status of the exported border are not necessarily new. Since 1952, the international airport system permits the extension of sovereignty through pre-clearance programs in Canada that literally moves the US border to Canadian space. Formalized in the 1974 Canada–United States Air Transport Preclearance Agreement, travelers to the United States may be "cleared by American authorities while still inside the Canadian terminal" (cited in Salter 2006: 56). In this sense, the borders of the United States do not remain at its geographical limits, but are extended over "variegated authority and overlapping sovereignties" (Salter 2006: 56). Whilst border agencies work to maintain the power and sovereignty of the Canadian state to set and define the laws of the national territory, Salter argues how such a rendering is simply "shattered by a purpose built American border post" within Ottawa's airport and through others such as Calgary, Edmonton, Vancouver and Montreal. In what Salter describes as the "up-streaming of international borders" we see a "concrete example of the deterritorialization of sovereignty, where a state enjoys authority and legal precedence outside of its national territory" (2006: 56).

Conclusion

Border surveillance has clearly moved on in all kinds of ways. It would be difficult to see border surveillance as always operating in a closed and static field of isolation; rather, it is responding to the changing forms and structures of governance, different senses of threat and risk, and very different kinds of technological development.

Just as the border has crept and evolved beyond anything recognizing the first border checks, border surveillance works across boundaries and frontiers drawing upon the resources of information networks between states. It pushes and pulls at these flows just as it modulates the mixtures of people and things. Some are sent packing and others eased through. Bodies are touched, made informational, but nevertheless subjected to sometimes unpleasant and very unequal forms of treatment as some travelers are slowed and distressed with far longer consequences for their life chances. But perhaps surveillance is helping to ship the border elsewhere, now that we see the border's impact, its practices and its exceptions proliferating the texture of everyday life?

References

Adey, P. (2009). "Facing Airport Security: Affect, Biopolitics, and the Preemptive Securitisation of the Mobile Body," *Environment and Planning D: Society and Space,* 27: 274–95.

Amoore, L. and Hall, A. (2009). "Taking Bodies Apart: Digitised Dissection and the Body at the Border," *Environment and Planning D: Society and Space,* 27(3): 444–64.

Bennett, C. J. (2005). "What Happens When You Book an Airline Ticket? The Collection and Processing of Passenger Data Post-9/11," in *Global Surveillance and Policing,* edited by E. Zureik and M. B. Salter, Portland, OR: Willan Publishing, pp. 113–38.

Cowen, D. (2009). "Containing Insecurity: US Port Cities and the 'War on Terror'," in *Disrupted Cities: When Infrastructure Fails,* edited by S. Graham, New York and London: Routledge.

Doty, R. L. (2007). "States of Exception on the Mexico/US Border: Exceptions, Enemies, and Decisions on Undocumented Immigration," *International Political Sociology,* 1(1): 113–37.

Kesby, A. (2006). "The Shifting and Multiple Border and International Law," *Oxford Journal of Legal Studies,* 27(1): 101–19.

Rumford, C. (2006). "Theorizing Borders," *European Journal of Social Theory,* 9(2): 155–70.

Salter, M. B. (2006). "The Global Visa Regime and the Political Technologies of the International Self: Borders, Bodies, Biopolitics," *Alternatives,* 31: 167–89.

Vaughan-Williams, N. (2010). "The UK Border Security Continuum: Virtual Biopolitics and the Simulation of the Sovereign Ban," *Environment and Planning D: Society and Space,* 10(2): 1071–83.

Walters, W. (2006). "Border/Control," *European Journal of Social Theory,* 9: 187–203.

b. Urban spaces of surveillance

Pete Fussey and Jon Coaffee

Introduction

Surveillance has always been a part of urban life. Yet despite such antecedents, stretching back to antiquity, a number of changes in both city life and the means of observing it have animated significant changes in the scope and techniques of urban surveillance. Principal among these is the tension between the increase in scale and simultaneous decrease in the "knowability" of cities. As cities dramatically expanded during the industrial revolution, generating uncharted spaces populated by shifting demographic configurations, they risked becoming less intelligible. This expansion, normally driven by the centripetal migration of the underprivileged, led to epithets of degeneracy, disorder and disease being applied across entire geographies, affording prominence to the ecological heuristic of "dangerous spaces."

Such developments led the grand projects of urbanization and industrialization to accent another modernist goal: that of rendering, translating, cataloguing and ordering the apparent chaos of urban life. These broader processes of understanding, observing or, more forcibly, monitoring the city are perceptible across a breadth of intellectual disciplines. These range from literary and cultural critiques—apparent in Dickensian London and the immersion of Baudelaire's flâneur in the crowded multitudes of Paris—to, perhaps most famously, Foucault's critiques of the ordering and repressive features of modernity.

Whilst surveillance gained centrality amid aspirations for conceptually deciphering and ordering the urban sphere, in more recent years it has also incorporated greater technological sophistication. In turn, this has culminated in new and shifting interactions between surveillance technology and urban society.

Amid this broad temporal and thematic context, this chapter focuses on the last 25 years where urban spaces have been increasingly configured around both overt and subtle forms of security featuring the use of video surveillance. This process has significantly impacted on urban life in myriad ways, including the technological demarcation of "high-status" areas, heightened scrutiny of particular sub-populations, and the continual shift—or creep—of urban surveillance. Further corollaries include contestations over the governance and selective "ordering" of the late-modern city. In examining these rapid developments, the chapter is organized over three broad areas of discussion: key concepts, ongoing debates and emerging trends as they apply to video surveillance of the late-modern city.

Key concepts: the rise of contemporary urban surveillance

Of all urban surveillance mechanisms used to patrol the late-modern city, the use of video surveillance has attracted the most commentary, with greatest attention perhaps focused on the UK. Widely viewed as holding the dubious accolade of the planet's most surveiled nation (a claim that is probably outdated given China's unparalleled mega-event-driven developments in this area in more recent years), the UK experienced an unprecedented and accelerated deployment of video surveillance across its urban spaces during the 1990s. Stemming from a modest distribution in a handful of towns and cities around 1990, by the end of the millennium, almost all of Britain's 61 cities had a degree of surveillance camera coverage.

Whilst there is broad consensus that rapid expansion of camera surveillance occurred around this time, there is less agreement over why this took place. From an administrative practice-oriented perspective, surveillance cameras are portrayed as a rational evidence-based response to crime and disorder problems. By contrast, critical sociological conceptualizations present a wider range of explanations. These include: theorizations of surveillance cameras as a coercive tool of a malign state, commercial or other interests; as an exemplar of embedded disciplinary technologies; as part of a wider shift towards societies of control; and as a component of a converging "surveillant assemblage"; and notions of technological perfection and "hypercontrol." Although these accounts have much to say about the functionality of surveillance cameras once operational, less attention has been placed on the way those interests may be mediated and transmitted through the processes of installing cameras in the first instance.

Among those studies that have centered on the dissemination of cameras across urban spaces a central argument has been that specific configurations of crime and disorder policy environments have proved crucial in propelling the expansion of surveillance camera networks (Fussey 2007). Indeed, in the UK, as the then Conservative government's flagship "tough" law and order agenda of the 1980s and early 1990s was matched by spiraling crime rates, seemingly novel technological responses to crime became more desirable.

From the 1990s onwards in the UK, surveillance cameras held privileged status amongst the assortment of Home Office crime prevention strategies. Public articulations of their effectiveness, belief in rising crime, high rates of the fear of crime and the coalescence of video surveillance into existing dominant administrative discourses of crime control influenced its popularity in policy circles. Despite the contemporaneous popularity of Orwellian, Foucauldian or malign interest-based explanations of surveillance camera deployment across the UK, the rapid development of this strategy can be seen as a product of eight years of government largess in the form of unparalleled statutory funding for camera installation. These initiatives alongside the preceding policy context can be viewed as the principle reasons why Britain's urban spaces were more closely observed by surveillance cameras than those of other countries.

Application

Whilst crime control, particularly in terms of pre-event prevention, constitutes one of the key attractions for those deploying surveillance cameras, public and policy discourses have increasingly centered on the utility of urban surveillance cameras in the fight against terrorism. For decades, surveillance has been a central feature of counter-terrorism work. In more recent years, surveillance strategies have extended beyond intelligence (widely regarded as the most effective form of counter-terrorism) and targeted surveillance applications to encompass urban space surveillance cameras. Surveillance camera footage monitoring 9/11, the 2004 Atocha bombings, the 7th and (failed) 21st July 2005 London urban attacks have become iconic. This continual replaying and, hence, re-articulation of the spectacle of barbarism has enabled the creation of a dubious fact by repetition: that surveillance cameras are central to the amelioration of such atrocities.

There are many points of debate here. In the wake of 9/11, surveillance cameras along with other advanced technologies of urban surveillance have significantly advanced, with the UK often seen as a "model" for the implementation of urban security. However, as many have noted, 9/11 did not necessarily change the shape of surveillance strategies but did significantly affect their intensity. As Lyon articulated:

9/11 may be viewed as both revealing and actually constituting major social change. The attack brought to the surface a number of surveillance trends that had been developing quietly, and largely unnoticed for the previous decade and earlier.

(Lyon 2003: 4)

The utilization of surveillance cameras for counter-terrorism purposes is of course not a new phenomenon. Indeed, one of the first uses of urban space surveillance cameras for this purpose in mainland Britain was in assisting the identification of two English-born members of the Provisional IRA (PIRA) who planted a bomb outside Harrods in Knightsbridge, London during March 1983. Despite the seeming prominence of urban surveillance cameras in terrorist investigations their actual involvement is however a more complex issue. With the notable exception of "Operation Marathon," the investigation that led to the arrest and conviction of racist nailbomber David Copeland in 1999, surveillance cameras consistently play a more ancillary role than traditional policing and intelligence strategies in counter-terrorism operations. This particularly applies to the much-publicized violent jihadi extremist attacks listed above, irrespective of the iconic nature of their associated camera footage. As the impotence of the surveillance cameras that tracked Hani Hanjour and Hasib Hussein on their respective ways to execute atrocities in New York and London demonstrates, it is not necessarily the establishment of identity that is important in such cases, but the establishment of intention.

Mirroring similar developments in the realms of policing and jurisprudence, the post-9/11 period has seen increasing convergence of surveillance strategies aimed at tackling both crime and terrorism. This process is multi-directional. Urban surveillance strategies originally conceived to tackle crime are increasingly used to counter terrorism. At the same time, formerly anti-terrorist measures, such as Automatic Number Plate Recognition (ANPR) (Automatic License Plate Recognition or ALPR in North America), have become applied to more routine criminal and civil infractions. Together, such processes point to a coalescence of crime control and security, and raise considerable concerns over "surveillance creep," the retention of legitimacy and issues of governance (see below). Added to these socio-ethical concerns are practical operational considerations. Crime and terrorism are distinct phenomena and the utility of urban surveillance cameras varies across these differing applications. Proponents of surveillance cameras have consistently cited their utility in stopping a criminal act before its commission via its deterrence effects—an argument with some evidential basis with regard to preventing property and vehicle crime, although not more serious interpersonal crimes. With reference to terrorism, this utility often shifts to the post-event context. It is thus unlikely in the extreme that cameras patrol urban spaces with equal efficacy across these divergent tasks.

The penetration of surveillance cameras into British towns and cities was not entirely due to the fear of crime or terrorism. The neo-liberal relaxation of planning laws and expansion of out-of-town shopping had stimulated a decline in traditional town centre spaces of consumption. Crucial to this process was the role of the state in providing funding and limiting regulation. Thus whilst camera networks were expanding they were also normalized as an expected feature of public space. Other specific legislative and policy climates also drove the dissemination of urban surveillance cameras, particularly in relation to residential spaces. In the UK, amid the exorbitant amount of crime and disorder-related legislation introduced during the former Labour government's last term in office (1997–2010), one has arguably had greatest influence on the expansion of surveillance cameras in England and Wales: Section 17 of the Crime and Disorder Act, 1998. This provision placed a statutory duty on local government agencies in England and Wales to foreground crime and disorder issues as part of their daily operations.

The effect of this Act was to require all local government agencies to incorporate security concerns into their core business wherever possible. The impact was felt particularly strongly amongst local authority housing agencies. In such times of uncertainty, old orthodoxies prevailed. When confronted with new and daunting tasks, planners appeared to find succor in long-standing (yet highly contested) staples of "administrative criminology"—rational choice-informed models that sought to reduce the opportunities for offending and increase "capable guardianship" or the observation of a specific geography as a means of deterrence. Unsurprisingly, surveillance cameras (and their assumed deterrence capabilities) became a central theme of this approach. Globally, the role of these more localized policy environments is crucial to the spread of urban surveillance and provides a caveat to many of the macro-based coercive or interest-based explanations of surveillance cameras. For example, in their study of surveillance camera diffusion in Australia, Sutton and Wilson (2004) identify resistance amongst those from "welfarist" working cultures within local crime control practitioner networks which, ultimately, prevented surveillance camera implementation in many areas.

Ongoing debates: cameras for controlling, cleansing and regenerating

The rise and application of urban surveillance cameras is not only connected to the goals of direct enforcement. More diffuse, abstract and symbolic applications—such as the removal of fear or enticement to use particular spaces or reside in formerly "dangerous" parts of the city—are also common. Of central importance is the embedding of surveillance cameras within urban regeneration projects.

In the 1990s, the response of urban authorities to perceived insecurity was dramatic, especially in North America, and in particular Los Angeles (LA). LA assumed a theoretical primacy within urban studies with strong academic emphasis on its militarization, portraying the city as an urban laboratory for anti-crime and surveillance measures. This reflected a process of "fortress urbanism" where, stimulated by middle-class paranoia and the desire to "protect" pockets of economic vibrancy, a profusion of security features had become immersed within the urban landscape (see also Arteaga Botello and Wilson, this volume). As Mike Davis noted in *City of Quartz* "in cities like Los Angeles on the hard edge of postmodernity, one observes an unprecedented tendency to merge urban design, architecture and the police apparatus into a single comprehensive security effort" (1990: 203). Here, the boundaries between the two traditional methods of crime prevention—law enforcement and fortification—have become blurred. Defensible space and technological surveillance, once used at a micro-level, were being rolled out across the city.

In *Ecologies of Fear* (1998), Davis further extrapolated current social, economic and political trends to create a vision for the future city (in the year 2019), technologically and physically segmented into zones of protection and surveillance, incorporating high-security financial districts and gated communities. In this vision economic disparities created a "spatial apartheid," an urban landscape of cages covered by a "scanscape" of omnipresent surveillance.

In the 1990s, despite "Fortress LA" becoming a powerful symbol of the post-modern city, many critics argued that Davis had portrayed a partial and dystopian image of the city; one shackled with terror, fear and anxiety and under the constant gaze of surveillance cameras. That said, the broad trend of parachuting accommodation for the affluent into the formerly "dangerous spaces" and the attendant shepherding of intensified urban surveillance regimes into specific urban geographies has undoubtedly spread internationally (see Arteaga Botello, this volume). There are many reasons for this, operating simultaneously at the macro-market and micro-social levels.

Although the criminological literature is saturated with debate over the deterrence value of such visible security measures with no definitive consensus, one clear function is to patrol the spatial and moral borders of these geographies. In addition to excluding those who do not belong, repeated experience relates how the inhabitants of new and gentrified "padded bunkers" demand protection from the heavily stereotyped incumbent populations. Surveillance is emblematic that these security concerns are being addressed and thus enhances the attractiveness and commercial value of such developments. In such geographies, surveillance-based security is highly symbolic. Such principles and processes extend far beyond the global North to become a globalized lingua franca of security planning. Of the abundant potential candidates, it is perhaps the gated Alphaville development, São Paulo, that most closely resembles the apotheosis of this approach.

In the UK the most high-profile massing of surveillance technologies occurs within the central financial zones of London as a direct response to fears of terrorist attack. Following the Provisional Irish Republican Army (PIRA) bombings of London's financial heart in 1992 and 1993 a so-called "Ring of Steel" was created to foment a technologically delineated securitized zone predicated on monitoring and restricting access (Coaffee 2009). Whilst target-hardening measures (such as security bollards and barriers) altered the urban landscape, it was camera surveillance that police considered the most important feature. An additional phase of expansion, intensification and "hardening" subsequently occurred during the late 1990s with the introduction of ANPR and further camera network upgrades, rendering the "Square Mile" area the most intensely monitored space in the UK (Coaffee 2009), and, at that time, Europe.

This template has since been applied more broadly both domestically within the UK and internationally. Given heightened security fears surrounding the development of London's second corporate centre at Canary Wharf since the late 1980s, and particularly following the PIRA bombing of February 1996, a fortified "Iron Collar" (Coaffee 2009) was developed. This was designed along similar security principles as the "Ring of Steel" for analogous reasons of reassurance and resilience. Increasingly this "Ring of Steel" model is applied internationally as a component of the global war on terror. In New York a ring of steel for Lower Manhattan is currently being developed comprising the strategic deployment of hundreds of cameras, many with an array of functionality which extends to the detection of radioactive material. This security system—officially called the Lower Manhattan Security Initiative—aims to throw a surveillance cloak over the area so that terrorists can be tracked, monitored and ultimately deterred (Coaffee 2009).

In London, such initiatives have crept into new territories and new roles. ANPR cameras, once the cutting edge of surveillance camera technology, have since become a routine part of traffic surveillance across the UK, particularly within densely populated urban municipalities. Of course, ANPR is just one of a growing suite of video-analytic approaches, designed to augment and overcome human fallibilities in interpreting video feeds from the cameras.

In the UK three major urban sites have been repeatedly selected for such experimentation: Belfast (particularly prior to the 1998 "Good Friday Agreement"), East London and, to a lesser extent, Birmingham. Among these, during the 1990s, the East London borough of Newham was one of the first public spaces in the world to apply Face Recognition cameras, and the area has continued the tradition of deploying novel technological forms of control. Subsequent initiatives include Intelligent Passenger Surveillance, deployed to automatically alert surveillance camera operators to unattended luggage or lingering passengers in London Underground stations, private sector microphone-equipped cameras in Shoreditch (Hackney) and the development of "behaviour analytics." Most recently, the UK has also become an importer of urban surveillance strategies. Among other notable examples is the recent application of gunshot sensor technology (essentially microphones attenuated to the specific frequency ranges of gunshot sounds and linked to GPS technologies in order to help establish the location of firearms discharges), currently deployed to tackle gang violence across numerous US cities, and now Birmingham, UK.

Although this chapter draws heavily on the UK and London models of urban surveillance, extreme versions of these approaches are now emerging globally. In the global powerhouse of consumer goods production, the Chinese city of Shenzhen—labeled Police state 2.0—the latest tracking technologies are reported to be watching the 12.4 million inhabitants with a massive network of surveillance cameras which will, over a short time, rise to 2 million in number, rendering it the most camera-surveiled city on the planet (Klein 2008).

Aside from headline-catching discussion on the scale and sophistication of surveillance technologies, another major area of debate has centered on the type of order imposed by such measures. UK Research, in particular, has highlighted how new policies on anti-social behavior use surveillance cameras to gaze selectively on the conduct of specific groups of people to keep city centers free of visible, less affluent and/ or "non-desirable" users. Indeed, surveillance cameras increasingly became a key part of a wider narrative of urban renaissance and of systematically and routinely embedded within city centre regeneration schemes (see Coleman 2004). Some have referred to this as a broader strategy of new forms of governmentality where responsibility for safety and security is decentralized to co-opted institutions to embed risk management features into everyday life.

It is important to note, however, that despite the prominence of neo-liberal models of regeneration that reinforce structural inequalities and "manage out" the urban poor or "undesirables," surveillance applications are not always coercive, nor always for the benefit of the wealthy against the poor. In some circumstances, this symbolic application of surveillance cameras may operate to reassure local businesses to remain in an area in an attempt to retain infrastructure, basic amenities and, hence, community cohesion rather than solely functioning to persecute particular sub-populations. This signifies a potentially paradoxical role of urban surveillance, which threatens urban diversity through social sorting whilst simultaneously, by forming part of a strategy to counter community transition and disorganization through retaining community amenities, aiming to ground disparate groups in a particular area (Fussey 2007). Similar to Lyon's (1994) repressing and protecting "Janus-faces" of surveillance, here surveillance cameras operate in a simultaneously fragmenting and consolidating capacity.

Emerging issues?

In a public speech during May 2010, Barack Obama joked that he had the ultimate weapon to protect his daughters from the amorous intentions of American boy band the Jonas Brothers: predator drones. Although the subsequent media "fallout" followed a predictable pattern, these comments resonate with a broader process of deep social consequence, public importance and newsworthy value: the increasing use of "drones" (properly called Unmanned Aerial Vehicles (UAVs)) and other military technologies to patrol urban civil spaces (see Wilson, this volume).

Such applications are becoming widespread. In the UK, their proposed use gained prominent publicity from an investigation by *The Guardian* newspaper. A subsequent Freedom of Information (FOI) request to Kent Police revealed that the police have considered a number of options, ranging from military "High Endurance Rapid Technology Insertion" (HERTI) vehicles, similar to those currently deployed in Afghanistan, to more lightweight "mini-airship" machines. To date, police deployments have utilized BAE Systems' GA22 owing to its diminutive size, attendant portability and, crucially, its immunity from statutory oversight from the Civil Aviation Authority (CAA) (the body that regulates the use of UK airspace and aircraft over 7 kg). Although small, the GA22's surveillance capabilities are significant and current specifications include 25x optical zoom cameras equipped with thermal imaging and automatic camera targeting capacities. Despite these developments, the current legal landscape surrounding UAVs is contested: the CAA is currently investigating the illegal use of UK airspace by the Merseyside Police when deploying similar technology to chase a suspected car thief. Other ethical debates surrounding the emerging use of this surveillance technology concerns the governance of law enforcement. Most prescient here is the incursion of the private sector into the state's delivery of social control, both in terms of the commercial influences upon security policy and the impetus to generate "cost neutrality" by using government surveillance infrastructures to undertake commercial work.

Such military-metropolitan convergence of surveillance technology is, of course, not confined to the UK. As Graham (2010) identifies, in addition to the contested geographies of Israel-Palestine, UAVs are also utilized to define and assert territorial governance at the US border. Here the US Department of Homeland Security uses the technology to patrol its southern- and northern-most extremities to identify unauthorized incursions from Mexico and Canada. For Graham, such developments constitute a broader trend of "new military urbanism," where the urban sphere—now home to the majority of the global population—is the site of experimentation and application of martial techniques and technologies of control:

Western security and military doctrine is being rapidly reimagined in ways that dramatically blur the juridical and operational separation between policing, intelligence and the military ... [a]t the same time, state power centres increasingly expend resources trying to separate bodies deemed malign and threatening from those deemed valuable and threatened within the everyday spaces of cities.

(2010: xv)

Elsewhere, across public, political, media and academic debate, much has been made of the potentiality of new technologies when deployed in urban spaces, whether this be with regard to utopian ideals of crime reduction or dystopian visions of social control. Among these, the role of "extra-spatial" surveillance technologies, such as "dataveillance," miniaturization and "nano-surveillance," and techniques that harness online social media, have gained particular attention.

In spite of these developments, and the valuable critiques they have stimulated, surveillance technologies do not operate in a vacuum. Many novel technological measures are extensions of existing practices. Rarely do mechanisms of tackling crime and terrorism, for example, incur a genuinely transformative approach. Instead, the old wine of existing processes and practices is normally presented via the new bottles of technological delivery. As such, innovations in technological surveillance often adopt the well-worn approaches of capacity, connectivity and categorization. In such circumstances, "emerging issues" are often "old issues"; only, they become reasserted in new ways.

The senescence of these debates does not subordinate their importance, however. New technologies of urban surveillance may serve to reanimate and reinvigorate critical arguments over the governance, control and selective visions of order that strive to organize the urban realm. The aforementioned technologies, for example, raise a breadth of issues—including the merger of military and civilian forms of control, the role of private sector security in the public realm and the categorization of urban sub-populations—that are as important today as they ever have been (see Hayes, this volume).

The histories of law enforcement and of security provision are littered with hard lessons that are not easily remembered. In the UK, one recent and highly controversial "anti-terrorist" initiative illustrates these issues: Project Champion. Project Champion was conceived in the wake of the attempted terrorist attacks in London and Glasgow during 2007, and several high profile cases in Birmingham. Within this specific geography, these included the alleged first attempted UK al Qaeda plot during 2000, a violent jihadi extremist plot to kidnap and dismember Muslim soldiers serving in the British Army and the arrest of a suspected Taliban "commander." The initiative comprised an attempt to develop a ring of ANPR, public and covert surveillance cameras around Sparkbrook and Washwood Heath, two predominantly Muslim areas of Birmingham. Crucially, it was funded by the Association of Chief Police Officers (Terrorism and Allied Matters), mobilized by the West Midlands Police Counter Terrorism Unit and delivered under the auspices of (and largely without consultation with) the civic Safer Birmingham Partnership. What is more, Project Champion was designed as a "parallel system"—surveillance cameras would operate in isolation from Birmingham's existing surveillance infrastructure and feed into a separate control room monitored solely by anti-terrorist police officers. Perhaps unsurprisingly, the application of £3.3 million of anti-terrorist operational funding to encircle densely Muslim-populated areas of the city with minimal consultation and little public or judicial oversight was deemed somewhat inflammatory. In a rare display of mobilized opposition to surveillance cameras, substantial community-generated pressure led the Project to become suspended and, ultimately, cancelled.

Through these events, many of the dominant issues surrounding the surveillance of urban spaces are visible. Here, the cordoning off and splintering of high-value urban areas, in common with the commercial and affluent areas of London and Los Angeles described above, is apparent. However, the use of surveillance cameras to demarcate and encircle spatially defined suspect communities represents an additional and highly controversial development of this theme. Common to other forms of control that contribute to the over-policing of particular sub-populations, such strategies have significant practical, operational and social costs. They risk the further erosion of trust between enforcement agencies and the populace—thus undermining the extensive (and expensive) community engagement programs that have been simulta-neously deployed—and, ultimately, undermine the legitimacy of the police and the consent of the policed. At the same time, highly symbolic messages challenging the ideals of citizenship, inclusion and the genuine pluralism of multi-cultural society are articulated.

Interesting additions to the debate over the convergence of surveillance assemblages may also be offered by analysis of these events. Whilst both urban counter-terrorism and crime control initiatives may increasingly rely on surveillance cameras, they do so in different ways. In turn, this affects the specification and application of cameras. As discussed above, crime and terrorism are generally different forms of activity and place different requirements on surveillance cameras. As a result, many Project Champion cameras held different specifications and positions to those installed in Birmingham for more routine crime prevention and community safety ends. These reasons, in addition to the aspiration to conduct counter-terrorist investigations in secrecy, away from external observation or oversight, drove the attempt to establish a parallel surveillance camera network isolated from Birmingham's extant surveillance infrastructure. Whilst, in many respects and across many geographies, there is a tendency for surveillance networks to integrate into more potent ensembles, or assemblages, it is important to note that the growth of surveillance initiatives is not always uni-directionally shifting towards convergence.

The final point concerns the impact of global recession on the expansion of urban video surveillance net-works. In the UK, as elsewhere, at a time when children's playgrounds and schools are not being repaired, public sector jobs are melting away and trade unions are drawing up their battle plans, spending finite public resources on surveillance cameras requires greater justification than before. This new era of justifications has significant implications for its scale, integration, and operation. One common response to this has been the integration of erstwhile fragmented extant networks, in order to operate with greater efficiency on economies of scale. At the same time, the municipalities that run many of Britain's urban surveillance camera networks are facing unprecedented cuts in funding, particularly those in the poorest and crime-ridden areas. System upgrades are being suspended, the majority of which are long-term conversions from analogue to digital data storage. As the availability of analogue tapes and other hardware reduces and their costs increase, difficult times lie ahead for those charged with monitoring the urban realm. Whether such reductions in funding lead to the decommissioning of urban surveillance cameras or abandoning them to atrophy and fall into disuse remains to be seen. More likely, however, is a reduction of staffing overheads, thus limiting the prevalence of 24/7 monitoring and stimulating growth of sub-contracted and distanciated monitoring regimes. Less capacity for observation also means less capacity for reflexivity and evaluation of existing practices. In these circumstances, existing orthodoxies and unexamined "common-sense" approaches are likely to gain greater prominence. As such, the use of urban surveillance cameras to patrol borders of order, entitlement and suspicion is likely to continue for the foreseeable future.

References

Coaffee, J. (2009). *Terrorism, Risk and the Global City – Towards Urban Resilience*, Aldershot: Ashgate.

Coleman, R. (2004). "Watching the Degenerate: Street Camera Surveillance and Urban Regeneration," *Local Economy*, 19(3): 199–211.

Davis, M. (1990). *City of Quartz – Excavating the Future of Los Angeles*, London: Verso.

——(1998). *Ecology of Fear: Los Angeles and the Imagination of Disaster*, New York: Metropolitan Books.

Fussey, P. (2007). "An Interrupted Transmission? Processes of CCTV Implementation and the Impact of Human Agency," in *Surveillance & Society*, 4(3): 229–56.

Graham, S. (2010). *Cities Under Siege: The New Military Urbanism*, London: Verso.

Klein, N. (2008). "Police State 2.0," *The Guardian* (g2), 3 June, pp. 4–9.

Lyon, D. (1994). *The Electronic Eye: The Rise of the Surveillance Society*, Cambridge: Polity.

——(2003). *Surveillance after September 11*, Cambridge: Polity.

Sutton, A. and Wilson, D. (2004). "Open-Street CCTV in Australia: Politics & Expansion," *Surveillance & Society*, 2(2/3): 310–22.

c. Seeing population

Census and surveillance by numbers

Evelyn Ruppert

Introduction

On 1 November 2010, Chinese officials, backed by a team of 6.5 million census takers, began a 10-day enumeration of more than 400 million households and 1.3 billion people in the People's Republic of China. The undertaking is the sixth decennial census of China (founded in 1949), the largest-ever census in history. On 1 April 2010, India began the first stage of its 15th national census, the seventh since partition, of over 1.2 billion people. The process involves census enumerators visiting each household twice: the first time to list all houses and households and the second, immediately after the census reference date of 1 March 2011, to record individual sociodemographic data. Alongside the census, India is also planning to prepare a National Population Register (NPR) which will include photograph and fingerprint biometrics. The NPR might usher in the era of register-based censuses in the country and could provide population counts on a real time basis when combined with the system of birth and death registration. In 2011, Germany was due to undertake a complete register-based census of over 82 million people, which would mark the first census to be conducted since the 1987 enumeration of the former Federal Republic of Germany (FDR) and the 1981 enumeration of the former German Democratic Republic (GDR). Rather than a door-to-door canvass as in the case of India and China, the census will be based mainly on the administrative data of population registration offices and the Federal Employment Agency. The Nordic countries have adopted population registers as a source of statistics since the 1970s (Denmark, Finland, Sweden, Norway). In 1981, Denmark was the first country in the world to conduct a totally register-based census and Finland followed in 1990. Since 1980, the censuses in Norway and Sweden have been partly register-based and these countries were planning for their first register-based censuses in 2011. In July 2010, a cross-country campaign was mounted against the Canadian government's decision to scale back the 2011 census to a mandatory short eight-question form coupled with a longer voluntary survey of about 4.5 million households. Critics argued that this will possibly lead to a register-based system in Canada. Frances Maude, the Cabinet Minister responsible for the UK census recently affirmed that his government is examining different ways to count the population more regularly such as using existing public and private databases in order to provide better, quicker information, more frequently and cheaply. Previous studies and inquiries in the UK have recommended that the 2011 enumeration be the last census.

As these examples illustrate, a census is only one of many methods states use to numerically constitute, know and govern populations. While the population census has been a key method and continues to be so, it is considered to have a number of shortcomings: it is too expensive, cannot deliver data sufficiently fast and at sufficient levels of locality and detail, and cannot be integrated with other data sources. Consequently, population registers and joined-up government administrative databases are being investigated or implemented as alternatives.

Do all of these methods constitute surveillance? Yes and no. The reason is that rather than simply being different perspectives on a population that is "out there" each method identifies and makes up different populations. This is because they constitute their population objects (what) and subjects (who) differently. A census surveils populations while other methods "watch over" *both* individuals and populations. It is because of this dual "watching" that the move to alternative methods has raised concerns about their surveillant consequences for individuals.

To be sure, censuses have always raised concerns about privacy, confidentiality and surveillance due to the volumes of personal data compiled, from that on income and ethnicity to housing and living arrangements. In China, growing wealth has made some people suspicious of questions on property ownership, as have questions on family size since the reporting of unregistered births are punishable under China's one-child family planning policy, and on residence for rural migrants whose house registration (hukou) is not in order. There are indeed examples of governmental uses of census data to persecute individuals, with the most extreme being Hitler's use of the census to track minorities for extermination during the NAZI regime (Higgs 2004). The American government also used 1940 US Census data to intern Japanese, German and Italian Americans. Yet, such uses have been rare. This is because the object of concern of censuses is the whole population and the categories that make it up. This was well expressed by one commentator amongst many opposing the Canadian government's scaling back of the census:

> The focus of interest is not you, but 'us': statistical categories of people just like you – the people who live in your neighborhood, who are in your age group, with your level of education, in your ethno-racial group. Census shows how we compare to our peers and how one group compares to another. These data don't track you, they accurately map what is changing in Canadian society. Then it's up to Canadian society to decide what needs to change. Neighborhood by neighborhood, region by region, and nationally.
>
> *(The Progressive Economics Forum 2010)*

What this commentator is pointing to is what I will call the surveillance of populations. It is a form of power/knowledge concerned with managing, regulating and maximizing the potential of a population as measured in categories and their quantities, rates, patterns, and probabilities. It is an entity which is more than merely the sum of its parts. Censuses are connected to a problem of population, which is to know the whole in order then to govern the individual, a relationship most fully elaborated by Foucault (2007). The subject of the census is the individual only insofar as he/she can be categorized, known and governed as a member of a population.

By investigating this aspect of censuses I bring to the fore the politics of surveilling populations. I then argue that questions of individual privacy arise more in relation to alternatives such as population registers and administrative databases which surveil both individuals and populations. Given that the genealogy of censuses is diverse, this chapter focuses on the United Kingdom to shed light on how censuses constitute and surveil a population and the consequences for how individuals are known and governed.

Seeing population: surveillance of the whole

It is common to liken a census to a photograph of a population at one moment in time. From it one gains a recognition of who people are and where they are. It is not a collection of dry statistics but a reflection of a society, complete with its problems and preoccupations. This has not always been so in the past. Early countings equated people to things, as units of potential tax revenue and/or the means to fill military ranks. The modern population census has certain features, especially universality and individual enumeration, which illustrate the more humanistic motivation behind these censuses in contrast to the purely mercenary motivation typical of the very early censuses.

(Domschke and Goyer 1986: 3)

The standard handbook of national population censuses, in three volumes of over 1,000 pages each, itemizes the contents and the approximately 200-year history of censuses for every state in the world. Importantly, it naturalizes the census as a reflection of an entity that exists "out there." However, as even the handbook attests in its many thousand pages, states have defined their populations and the categories that make them up in various ways. These practices are part of a long genealogy of census making that has been organized by states in relation to different governing objectives and rationalities.

Prior to modern censuses, counting people was not so much a means of producing knowledge than of registering people and property, usually for the purposes of tax assessment and military conscription. Such was the purpose of the *Domesday Book* of 1086, which consisted of a detailed inventory of land and property prepared for William the Conqueror. It is commonly identified as the first count of people in England and the single most exhaustive exercise in information collection by the English central state (Higgs 2004). But it was not until the seventeenth century that the English state originated systematic techniques of recording and calculating populations that came to be called "political arithmetic" (Desrosières 1998). Theorized first by William Petty, political arithmetic involved keeping written records of baptisms, marriages and burials and then assembling them into numbers to provide objective knowledge and a social measurement of society. Desrosières (1998) argues that the English liberal tradition fuelled opposition to the conduct of direct surveys or censuses of population, which meant that political arithmeticians had to resort to this indirect method and calculation of population. However, population surveys and censuses were being undertaken by other states at the time (e.g. in Sweden and the Netherlands), and most notably France had organized vast surveys including its 1666 enumeration of its colony New France (part of which was to later become Canada). This enumeration is recognized as the first population census in North America. The United States undertook its first enumeration in 1790, prescribed in the Constitution of 1787 as a means of apportioning seats in the House of Representatives. It was not until the early nineteenth century that England did the same in part due to the growing concern that the population was increasing more rapidly than the means of subsistence, a view advanced in Thomas Malthus's now famous work, *The Principles of Population* (1798) (Higgs 2004). In 1800 "An act for taking an Account of the Population of Great Britain, and the Increase or Diminution thereof" was passed directing the taking of a census of England and Wales in 1801. However, from 1801–31 the censuses were not nominal (i.e. they did not list individuals) but instead provided simple head counts (numbers of men, women, families and houses) and information about characteristics such as occupations and ages. The schedules were also completed by officers of the established church or of the poor law system who calculated totals from parish registers. The first nominal census was conducted in 1841 by the newly established General Register Office (GRO), which initiated "the practice of instructing enumerators to hand out schedules to household heads for them to supply details of the members of their households on Census night" (Higgs 2004: 72). While census schedules were always checked by an enumerator, since 1841 individuals have been expected to complete forms for themselves and other members of their households.

Several features defined and still define what is referred to as the modern census, a practice that is now conducted by most Western states:

Universality: every person within a defined territory is included.
Individuality: every person (not households and not just males) and his/her characteristics are categorized.

Simultaneity: everyone is enumerated at the same point in time.

Periodicity: enumeration is conducted at regular intervals (e.g. every ten years) (Domschke and Goyer 1986: 4).

It is on the basis of all of these features that the 1841 UK census is declared "modern." The census replaced early modern counting and information gathering about people through dispersed and in many respects intrusive administrative practices that often involved face-to-face scrutiny (Higgs 2004). Numerous local and central institutions and officials linked to the central state, such as ecclesiastical courts, justices of the peace and overseers of the poor, regularly collected information about people in their jurisdictions, especially about people who were migrants or poor. The introduction of the census introduced the systematic and centralized collection of information on households and individuals. Its purpose was also different: instead of producing knowledge for the purposes of tax revenues and military needs, the objective was to produce knowledge about how individual inhabitants of a territory make up a population. Such centralization went beyond the census and included practices of civil registration to replace that which had been largely carried out by local admin-istrations and dispersed across thousands of archives (parish chests, diocesan registers, estate papers) (Higgs 2004). The centralization of administrative practices is also connected to the documenting of individual identity as a legal and bureaucratic category in systems of registration and identification developed by government, police and public institutions that began in the nineteenth century (Caplan and Torpey 2001). Through practices such as birth, death and marriage registrations to passports, drivers' licenses, national insurance or social security numbers, individual identity has been inscribed, codified, verified and documented by official institutions of the modern state. The practices have been used not only to verify or authenticate identities but also to anchor and connect identity to transactions and interactions with governments.

Higgs (2004) contends that the centralization of knowledge production especially in relation to the census constitutes a less intrusive process in part because people are called upon to identify and account for themselves. The subject of interest is the self-attesting individual who self-identifies with biographical categories such as gender, income, occupation and ethnicity (and in some cases is identified by or identifies other members of his/her household). But there is another reason: the object of interest of a census is the population not the individual. Foucault (2007) defined population as the "final objective," where indivi-duals "are no longer pertinent as the objective, but simply as the instrument, relay, or condition for obtaining something at the level of population" (42). The level that is pertinent for a government's economic-political action is that of the population, whereas the multiplicity of individuals is pertinent insofar as, when properly managed, will make possible what is desired to be attained for the whole. In this light the population is a collective political object towards which policies, programs and interventions are directed in order to produce effects.

Foucault (1994) conceived of technologies such as the census as a political technology of individuals through which people come to see themselves as part of a larger entity. He connected a technology of individuals to three particular rationalities or reasons of state. One is the necessity of political knowledge—a specific knowledge or political arithmetic of the state and its forces. It is a knowledge that seeks to reveal the nature of the state, which has to be governed. A second is the understanding that the true nature of the state consists of a set of forces and strengths that can be increased or weakened according to the policies followed by governments. A third reason is the concern with individuals in relation to how they reinforce the state's strength: how they live, work, produce, consume and die. His question then is what political technologies of government have been developed as part of the reason of state that have made the indi-vidual a significant element for the state? What are the techniques that give a concrete form to this new kind of relationship between the social entity and the individual, the techniques through which the individual could be integrated into the social entity?

Foucault called such technologies biopolitical because the focus is on the "species body," a multiple body that is not exactly society. It is a collective entity that is not simply a collection of living human beings but a living entity imbued with biological processes such as births and mortality. The objective of biopolitics is to manage, regulate and maximize the potential of a population. It is a form of power/knowledge that recast the relationship between the individual and power by understanding population as a machine for producing wealth, goods and other individuals. In this way, biopolitics is not a politics of individual identity but of the collective and the purpose is to intervene in individual lives at the level of their generality. To do so requires a form of power/knowledge that can surveil through totalizing procedures that assemble individuals into one.

However, while Foucault described population as the object of biopower and connected to the three rationalities of political government, he did not investigate the development of specific practices of observation that made it possible to know and then act upon population. To the contrary, he tended to over-emphasize population as an object on which power can act and as a thing that follows natural processes and laws (Curtis 2001). Biopolitics require specific totalizing procedures, that is, techniques that can constitute an entity out of various individual parts to make up the whole. Population is not a thing that can be observed. It is a theoretical entity because it is a particular way of organizing social observations and configuring social relations. Rather than a thing waiting to be discovered, practices are necessary to render the population an object of knowledge. Biopolitics thus requires specific totalizing and collectivizing procedures including statistical methods and an administrative infrastructure to "translate the imaginings of state officials about social relations into practical observations and measures of the 'population' and its activities" (Curtis 2001: 32).

In the eighteenth and nineteenth century censuses constituted a key technology for knowing population in this way. It involved two kinds of statistical work that are necessary to produce numerical facts (Desrosières 1998). One requires the establishment of general forms, categories of equivalence, norms and standards that transcend singularities. Categories (a word which is derived from the Greek term *kategoria* and refers to a judgment rendered in a public arena) are "conventions of equivalence, encoding, and classification [which] precede statistical objectification" and are the "bonds that make the whole of things and people hold together" (Desrosières 1998: 236). In relation to censuses, the most basic equivalence is to be a member of a population, an undifferentiated abstract essence that effaces individual variation (Curtis 2001). However, this general equivalence is not the basis on which the census is taken. Generalizing the individual into the population involves identifying her difference and resemblance to categories. The population is understood as an entity divided and differentiated into numerous categories (genders, conjugal status, ethnicity, religion, etc.) and each individual is encoded in relation to those categories. It is through such operations that different people can be "held together" and numerical descriptions of a population can be generated.

The second operation involved in statistical work is made possible by the first. This is a cognitive operation that involves mathematical tools that summarize categories into averages and correlations (Desrosières 1998). It is an operation that reveals statistical constants and regularities that Foucault (2007) argued made it possible to see and understand population as an entity. While a population is of course made up of individuals who are different and whose individual behaviour cannot be predicted, through the operation of statistics a population can be seen as an entity possessing regularities in death rates, incidence of disease, accidents, and so on. It is through statistics that the population, its processes and its aggregate effects can be seen and which are not reducible to the individual. It was because of such state investment in statistics for evaluating wellbeing and relative prosperity that the etymology of statistics is connected with state building and administration and has rendered statistical information persuasive because of the double reference to science and the state (Desrosières 1998). It is an investment that was also made possible by what Ian Hacking (1990) has argued was one of the most decisive events of the nineteenth century: the shift from discerning truth from natural law to probabilistic law. Instead of determinism this shift led to techniques for the "taming of chance." In relation to the governmental objective of normalization this was expressed in the classification and regulation of deviations from the norm through an intensive mapping of people and making up of populations through practices such as censuses.

The census is thus a totalizing procedure that involves establishing equivalences between bodies (categories) and statistical operations to make up and see populations, watch their patterns and regularities and identify their probable trajectories. It is a form of "watching over" a population. But beyond seeing populations, censuses also organize how states can intervene at the level of the individual, to calibrate and channel their desires, behaviors and conduct towards producing effects at the level of the whole and thus become surveillant. It is as members of populations that such channeling and calibration can be made possible. If the politics of individual surveillance are concerned with questions of liberty, privacy and confidentiality then the politics of surveilling and knowing the whole concerns how people are known and then governed. This is not to deny the importance of concerns about privacy but to suggest that they obscure the politics of population and the totalizing effects of practices such as censuses. The politics of population is not about us as individuals but how we are constituted as members of governable populations. As such, it is a politics that brings into question the populations that methods conjure up and legitimize.

Politics of surveilling population

As previously noted the census has sometimes been understood as an instrument of state power, surveillance and control. At the same time it has been upheld as essential for evaluating the wealth, progress and well-being of populations, ensuring equity in public service provision and resource allocation, identifying discrimination, and apportioning political representation (Kertzer and Arel 2002; Higgs 2004). As the quote at the beginning of this chapter stated, "The focus of interest is not you, but 'us': statistical categories of people." However, as argued above, "we"—or population—is not a natural, already and always there entity, but made up through specific practices such as the census which involve numerous decisions such as who to count, what categories to include and how to count. That is, how the whole is surveiled and known is not given.

Becoming aware of the consequences of counting and the recognition of identity in censuses has led to many groups taking part in the census and sometimes mobilizing to change and influence it. These movements are not only about claims to rights and resources but to truth about themselves. There are many examples in the twentieth century that illustrate how subjects have constituted themselves as citizens by engaging in census making and how census making is inherently a political practice. A collection compiled by Kertzer and Arel (2002) documents a number of examples of how censuses involve a range of actors and agencies that interact and influence census making: racial categorization in the US and Brazilian censuses, ethnic categorization in the censuses of Israel, Canada and the United States and debates in France over the use of ethnic categories in the census. For example, Melissa Nobles documents how prior to the 2000 census of the United States, individuals who identified with more than one racial group could only do so by selecting the "other" category. Subjects could only maintain and assert their difference by identifying as "other." Their identification as "other" was a challenge to the census categories as revealed in the lobbying efforts of civil rights organizations, including a march on Washington by people demanding multiple race identification. When the ability to select multiple racial categories was introduced for the first time in the 2000 census, many African American and Hispanic civil rights groups protested that this was a "whitewash" against which ethnic and policy-related distinctions would be lost while others argued for the category "multi-racial." Since the identification with census categories is the basis on which certain rights are conferred (such as political representation and resource allocation), the census classification was thus a struggle over citizenship rights. Indeed, all of the examples in the collection illustrate how interest groups and non-state organizations have successfully influenced and altered census questions and categories. These are struggles over citizenship rights as recognition in categories is connected to entitlements such as group differentiated social programs and resources.

As such, practices like censuses also come to influence the definition and organization of programs for intervening and directing individual lives. For Foucault, this is the relay and correlation between individualization and totalization where people are governed as members of a population and in relation to the management of population. Indeed, it is first through the identification of populations—of migrants, families or homeowners—that governing interventions are defined. The objective is that every individual function well as a member and reinforce the wellbeing of the totality and that to govern in this way requires surveilling and monitoring the whole.

Surveilling the population and the individual

In the opening of this chapter I noted how population registers, joined up government registration and administrative databases are being adopted in some states and investigated as alternatives to censuses in others. In the early nineteenth century such centralized registration systems were partial and distributed across different and disconnected state offices. While numerical knowledge of populations has been and can be constructed out of identification registers such as birth and death rates, individually, no one register can account for the changing and dynamic characteristics of the whole population. Now, that may be changing. New information and communication technologies (ICTs) enable the storage, maintenance, searching and linking of government databases and incorporate new techniques such as biometrics and machine-readable microchips in citizenship and identity documentation. These administrative systems regularly compile and track individuals over time and across space. They are used to not only verify or authenticate identities but also to record transactions and interactions with governments. Legitimized and verifiable identifications are essential to the validity of these administrative systems: subjects must ensure that their identification corresponds to the authoritative categories of a state classification system (e.g. gender, nationality, age). Some states are now able to join up different administrative databases while others are developing technical infrastructures to do so.

What happens when the object of biopolitics—the population—is constituted on a different basis, as an aggregate of individuals recorded in administrative databases that track authoritative identifications and transactions (activities, movements) with governments? One consequence could be the doubling of the object and subject of surveillance, such that both the individual and population are simultaneously observed and calibrated. Rather than captured at one moment in time and understood as relatively stable and fixed categories, populations and people, the total and the individual, are conceived of as modulating and changing entities that require constant tracking, surveilling and calibrating. Some commentators refer to this as "real-time population estimates based on administrative records" and statisticians argue that this method can improve accuracy, timeliness and fairness in the detection of social needs and inequalities, and at the same time illegal activities and movements. But alongside such evaluations are also concerns that real-time tracking involves increased surveillance of individuals and is far more intrusive than early modern practices. Ironically, in the Canadian case, one of the arguments advanced by the government for doing away with the mandatory long-form census is that the questions represent an intrusion into personal privacy. These are some of the controversies and matters of concern that are emerging as states develop and advance alternative methods of surveilling populations.

Conclusion

There are many methods that states have used and are developing as means of numerically constituting, knowing and governing populations. Each constitutes population objects and subjects differently and thus makes up different populations. A census involves people self-identifying with categories that, when assembled, make up the population. Rather than a politics of individual identity the practice involves struggles over how people are categorized and constituted as members of governable populations. Emerging methods such as population registers and joined up administrative data involve different procedures. Population is an aggregation of multiple authoritative identifications and transactions recorded in administrative databases. The population is thus a by-product of the transactions of people who must ensure that their identification corresponds to authoritative state categories. For both methods, a population is a collective political object towards which policies, programs and interventions are directed in order to produce effects. However, they have different surveillant and governing consequences. While the population is the object surveiled by censuses, administrative data doubles the object of surveillance, such that both the individual and population are simultaneously "watched over." Governing then becomes a matter of tracing, tracking and calibrating both entities. These differences give rise not only to a politics of privacy but of how people are known and governed as members of populations.

References

Caplan, J., and Torpey, J. (eds). (2001). *Documenting Individual Identity: The Development of State Practices in the Modern World*, Princeton, NJ: Princeton University Press.

Curtis, B. (2001). *The Politics of Population: State Formation, Statistics, and the Census of Canada, 1840–75*, Toronto: University of Toronto Press.

Desrosières, A. (1998). *The Politics of Large Numbers: A History of Statistical Reasoning*, translated by C. Naish, Cambridge, MA: Harvard University Press.

Domschke, E. A. and Goyer, D. S. (1986). *The Handbook of National Population Censuses: Africa and Asia*, New York: Greenwood Press.

Foucault, M. (1994). "The Political Technology of Individuals," in J. Faubion (ed.), *Power: Essential Works of Foucault 1954–1984*, New York: The New Press.

——(2007). *Security, Territory, Population*, translated by G. Burchell, edited by A. Davidson, Lectures at the Collège de France: Palgrave Macmillan.

Hacking, I. (1990). *The Taming of Chance*, New York: Cambridge University Press.

Higgs, E. (2004). *The Information State in England: The Central Collection of Information on Citizens since 1500*, Basingstoke: Palgrave MacMillan.

Kertzer, D. I. and Arel, D. (eds). (2002). *Census and Identity: The Politics of Race, Ethnicity, and Language in National Censuses*, Cambridge/New York: Cambridge University Press.

Progressive Economics Forum. (2010). "Privacy and the Census: It's Really Not All About You," 30 July 2010, available at www.progressive-economics.ca/2010/07/30/privacy-and-the-census-its-really-not-all-about-you/ (accessed 1 Feb 2011).

d. Surveillance and non-humans

Andrew Donaldson

Introduction

Much of the work outlined in this volume focuses on the direct or indirect surveillance of people, considered as subjects. Yet significant amounts of surveillance are directed towards animals other than human beings, driven by logics of both care and control. The surveillance of non-human life is a routine and everyday feature of contemporary societies that goes unnoticed or unrecognized. In part this may be because it is difficult to conceive of non-humans as being subjects (i.e. as possessing subjectivity) under surveillance in the same way as humans. Non-humans are rarely granted the same reflexive agency as humans and often occupy tightly bracketed, and relatively uncontested, socio-economic niches as material resources or health threats. From this point of view, "disease surveillance," "veterinary surveillance" and "foodchain surveillance" might be seen as related to the more pernicious forms of surveillance dealt with in surveillance studies by terminology only. The division is compounded by the fact that little of the literature that deals with the surveillance of non-humans actually uses the term "surveillance." Nevertheless, it does detail processes of monitoring, categorization and intervention that parallel other forms of surveillance. Surveillance is not passive observation and so the root concerns of surveillance studies are questions of agency: what prescribes, what enables and what motivates?; what specifically makes surveillance in practice? This chapter provides an overview of several forms of surveillance of non-humans with the aims of introducing the reader to areas they may be unfamiliar with, unsettling notions of the agencies involved and examining the possible ways in which surveillance might be analyzed if we remove our preconceptions about its subjects.

Borders, biosecurity and trade

Biosecurity is a relatively recent addition to "public" discourse and, prior to 2001, was little used even as a term of art. In 2001 an unprecedented outbreak of foot and mouth disease (FMD—a disease of hoofed mammals including livestock species such as sheep, cattle and pigs) in the UK brought the term out into the open as a cornerstone of efforts to combat animal disease, and revealed it as a fundamentally surveillant process (Donaldson and Wood 2004). The escalating concerns over international terrorism following the 9/11 attacks on the USA cemented further connotations of biosecurity in the political lexicon. A deliberate animal disease epidemic could cause significant disruption (FMD cost the UK £8 billion and caused the postponement of a general election; H5N1 bird flu cost Asian farmers an estimated US$10 billion in 2004) and a zoonotic disease (transferable to humans) or human disease used as a method of attack could have severe consequences. At its root, biosecurity is about the management not of disease, but of disease risk (Donaldson 2008), and it involves multiple regimes of monitoring and intervention. Regardless of what we now call this process, it has been occurring on an organized global scale for some time.

In 1920 a devastating outbreak of the cattle disease, rinderpest, in Belgium was traced to zebus from India being transported to Brazil via Antwerp. The rinderpest outbreak led to the formation, in 1924, of the OIE (Office International des Epizooties) the global animal disease surveillance body. The OIE is now known as the World Organization for Animal Health, in reference to the WHO (the World Health Organization), which performs the same function for human diseases. Notably, the OIE predates the WHO, hinting at a period where the movement of non-human animals was of greater magnitude and importance than the movement of humans. In 1998 the OIE became the official health and sanitary standards body for animals and animal products in international trade after an agreement with the WTO, finally cementing the centrality of global trade to animal disease in the emerging structures of global governance.

The OIE develops and regularly updates standards for the animal health services of its members. These are collected in the Terrestrial Animal Health Code and the Aquatic Animal Health Code, each of which has an accompanying manual of diagnostics and vaccines for the diseases specified in the code. The Terrestrial Animal Health Code lists over 80 types of animal disease. A condition of OIE membership is that any member country's Veterinary Authority must report any new incidence or change in the behavior of a listed disease within the member country to the OIE. By following the standards of practice set out within the Codes, OIE members can regulate trade in animals and animal products among themselves with a reduced risk of spreading animal disease. Diseases specified by the OIE, and in turn by state laws, are termed "notifiable"; anyone detecting symptoms of a notifiable disease is required to pass that information up the disease surveillance hierarchy. At a local level this may result in the quarantine and slaughter of the diseased animals, as well as bans on the movement of livestock until potential dangerous contacts can be traced and a transmission route established. At an international level, other countries can ban imports from the effected country. This process is dependent on a system of classifying countries as disease free or not, in accordance with continual monitoring of disease incidence.

In 2001, these local and international measures were in force, preventing the UK from exporting livestock or animal products until the territory could be confirmed as disease free. Standard containment measures for FMD at the time were the slaughter and destruction of all infected livestock, and this was extended to dangerous contacts and contiguous premises in an attempt to prevent spread. When this approach did not seem to be working quickly enough, attention turned towards enforcing basic biosecurity practices within disease hotspots. Known as "blue boxes" these areas were patrolled by police and local government officers, who oversaw the disinfecting of vehicles, machinery and people and the monitoring of all movements within the blue boxes. Continued spread of the disease was blamed on "poor biosecurity" in government rhetoric. Control was sought over people as proxies for disease.

Another disease event that brought biosecurity back into the public eye was an outbreak of bird flu at a turkey production unit in Norfolk, UK. The unit belonged to a British company, Bernard Matthews, which had a wholesome corporate image and which was quick to issue statements that it had the highest biosecurity standards. These included rigorous clothing disinfection and assigning workers to specific turkey sheds so that cross contamination did not occur in the event of a disease outbreak. The well-monitored schedule collapsed during the event and workers who were drafted in to other sheds to help deal with the clean-up were likely to have spread the disease when they returned to their normal assignment. The more pronounced presence of bird flu in Southeast Asia—which gained widespread international coverage as a result of human deaths in 2004–05—has resulted in a transformation of poultry production in the region towards large-scale closed production units and even more stringent control of workers (involving stripping naked to be sprayed in disinfectant before entering the facilities). The agency of disease is always a hybrid one and controlling animal disease in production is always going to involve controlling humans as long as they are part of the system.

Biosecurity in practice, politics and rhetoric serves a function of control over spaces, borders and behaviors. It has been argued that biosecurity represents a geopolitical response to the insecurity and unpredictability of biology that is laid bare by the continued "molecularization of life"—the view of all life, and the properties of living organisms, as a molecular scale process that has accompanied progress in the biological and biomedical sciences (Braun 2007). In this view, biosecurity is a form of imperialism by which the West (through organizations such as the OIE and WHO) seeks to secure life through interventions in parts of the world that present biological risks. This position focuses on biosecurity for exotic zoonotic diseases patrolling both international borders and species boundaries—SARS from Civet Cats in China in 2002, H5N1 from wildfowl to poultry to humans in Southeast Asia in 2004, Swine flu in Mexico in 2009 (although the transition from pig to human is thought to have occurred earlier in China, rather than in factory farms in Mexico as first presumed).

The geopolitical view is complicated by two other distinctive analytical positions on biosecurity. The first points to the mundane materialities of farming practices where biosecurity is enacted, debated and contested on a routine basis in the West (Donaldson 2008; Enticott 2008; Law and Mol 2006). The "blue box" tactics used in the 2001 FMD crisis in the UK stand as a clear example that "surveillance biosecurity" is not simply a strategy employed by the West on "the rest." The second position is not explicitly about biosecurity, but rather counters the notion that contemporary biosciences are really pushing towards an ever more reductive molecular biological reality, with all its associated insecurity. Rather, we are witnessing a re-biologization of life, a view in which systems are becoming more important than molecules, and in which the techniques of collecting and processing molecular data are embedded in wider, and thoroughly routine, relationships of risk reduction (Donaldson 2007). These ideas will be discussed further, later in the chapter.

The systemic view is an essential one when considering the main element of the surveillance of non-humans. Livestock diseases represent a complex and hybrid form of agency; they cause problems not just through the relationship of a pathogen and a host animal, but also through the very systems in which that animal is embedded. The increased mobility of livestock and the complex logistics of modern food production introduce many new routes for infection and for the subsequent spread of disease. However, the surveillant techniques developed for regulating the flows of biological materials involved in animal disease have borne fruit. In an interesting footnote to this section, at the time of writing it seems that rinderpest has been eradicated. If this does indeed prove to be the case, it will be only the second viral infection, and the first to affect animals, ever to be rendered extinct by deliberate intervention (the first was smallpox). The surveillance work of the OIE has, in just under a century, removed the very disease that prompted the organization's founding.

Behaving like pigs

In direct interactions, people seem to have little problem in imagining animals as sentient others, with individual subjectivities full of personality, desires and intrinsic rights. However, these notions do not carry through comfortably into the scientific, economic, legal and political institutions of the modern state. Animals that live within human societies have economic value, they are owned, and have no legal status in and of themselves. They are not held responsible for their actions, and any negative behavior is considered a product of the environment created by their human owners. This constructed position is a comparatively recent one. The criminal prosecution of animals and subsequent judicial trial in a courtroom was a well-documented occurrence in medieval Europe from the thirteenth to the fifteenth centuries. A 1906 work by EP Evans entitled *The Criminal Prosecution and Capital Punishment of Animals* has as its frontispiece an illustration of the execution of an "infanticidal sow" in the Norman city of Falaise in 1386, based on a fresco from a local church. In a judgment given in 1457 in Savigny, not only was a sow executed for infanticide, but her six piglets were also charged with complicity in her crime. In most of the world, non-human animals are no longer put on trial as they are considered to lack moral agency. They lack a capacity to rationalize right from wrong. In fact, by comparison to many human models of agency and subjectivity, based around the conscious will to act, to overcome constraints and determine one's own fate, non-human animals do not possess agency at all. Recent research claims to show that dogs, as hierarchical social animals, have co-evolved behaviors which enable them to live within human social groups. They can feel and display guilt and contrition in meaningful ways. Yet dogs that commit infanticide are now destroyed by lethal injection without trial and their owners are blamed by the popular media and prosecuted by the state. These vignettes are presented not as the opening to a discussion of animal ethics. They stand as examples that might cause us to question the ways in which we conceive of non-human agency. Our contemporary view is informed by scientific studies of animal behavior and cognition that have construed non-human animals as more-or-less complex input/output systems—behaving machines. This model lies at the centre of a common form of surveillance: animal welfare monitoring.

For some time now it has not been enough for wealthy nations to simply enjoy the benefits of reliable mass-produced meat. We expect that the livestock that provide our steaks, rashers and chops should have had a pain- and stress-free life right up until the point of slaughter. Livestock welfare regulation arose as a response to the perceived and documented conditions of industrial livestock farming. Now, in Europe, basic standards of animal welfare are enforced under cross-compliance—they have to be met for farmers to receive subsidy payments—and under national law. Similar conditions pertain elsewhere and are gradually being suggested for newly emerging global economies such as China. Various voluntary "farm assurance" schemes operate which can hold livestock producers to higher standards and permit the meat to be marketed under a scheme's brand, as a means to increase consumer confidence and add value to the end product. For these various regulations to have any impact, animal welfare has to be measured and monitored. The standard means for assessing animal welfare is the ethogram, a catalogue of typical discrete behaviors for a species, based on multiple observations over space and time. These are essentially stereotyped movements and postures, seen as innate, and are described in neutral terms with no reference to what drives the behavior. The length of time spent enacting each discrete behavior can be recorded and certain combinations of behaviors and timings can then be classified as normal. Normal behavior is associated with good welfare and animals can be measured against this scale.

The ethogram is the standard evaluative tool of animal behavior, but there is an approach developed in studies of pig production that differs starkly in its philosophical basis from the mainstream one. The whole animal approach of Qualitative Behavioral Assessment (QBA)—associated with the animal behaviorist Francoise Wemelsfelder—"psychologizes movement," positing an emotional agency behind the animal's interaction with its environment, and relies on people to interpret this and describe it in human terms, offering up such subjective statements as, "this pig is happy." Statistical analysis has revealed considerable agreement amongst different observers about a particular animal's state of well-being. It is an approach offered up as being less reliant on trained "expert" evaluators and more on those with day-to-day experience of animals. If the ethogram approach is mechanistic in its mathematical calculation of welfare based on the different behavioral sub-systems of an animal, the QBA approach is a holistic or integrative method. The radical perspective (in animal science terms) adopted by QBA to define a more thorough and ethical approach is actually to make the observed animal a subject. It is also an approach that purports to rely on the relational subjectivity that exists between humans and non-humans living together in particular contexts. What QBA offers is a web of formalization that stabilizes such subjectivity as meaningful in the context of established science and animal husbandry.

The determination of animal welfare is a form of surveillance, or at least a component of a surveillant system of monitoring and intervening. When we think of an individual human as the subject of certain forms of surveillance, they are the one subjected to monitoring and intervention. The intervention impacts directly on them. This can be the case with some forms of animal welfare monitoring (in much the same way as child welfare monitoring) and this seems to be the underlying form of relationship that allows QBA to operate. Yet even as a more empathetic approach, QBA is tied to a logic of large-scale food production (it was developed in an agricultural college) and so in practice it is part of an extensive regulatory framework which is not necessarily designed to act in the welfare interests of individual animals but of whole populations. Intervention is not on the level of the animal even if it is conceptualized as a subject; it often takes the form of reward or censure of the animal owner. Monitoring and intervention are connected and yet distanced. Change happens within a wider system, such that when we apply the model of an individual subject of surveillance to the surveillance of non-human animals, we reveal a dislocated agency.

In light of this particular dislocation, we might question the extent to which surveillant practice can modify animal behavior—in the way that is it often said to alter human behavior—through the subject's conscious or unconscious awareness of being surveiled. However, other forms of surveillance are in use in animal production, especially within pig production, which is frequently carried out indoors in large semi-automated units. Food and water consumption can be monitored remotely as proxy indicators for animal health, or more direct control of each individual animal's life can be engineered into the system. In 2009, widely circulated footage from the BBC showed pigs demonstrating an interesting awareness of the surveillant system in which they were embedded. Sows in breeder units were fitted with RFID collars that, coupled with an automated feeding stall, permitted only one nutritionally balanced meal a day. The feeding stall would not dispense food to pigs returning for second helpings. However, some sows did not like wearing their collars and soon learnt how to remove them. This prevented them from receiving food. Some enterprising animals then learnt that if they picked up discarded collars and carried them into the feeding stall, they could receive another pig's share of food. An undeniably disruptive agency, but how to classify it: resistance or identity theft? Or is it just—to borrow a phrase I have heard used by animal scientists to value an animal's actions without moralizing them—a "behaving pig"?

Production and consumption

The automated monitoring of food and water intake in animal production, noted above, is a population level of surveillance that is becoming increasingly common in animal health. Veterinarians involved in livestock production have long filled the role of engineer, monitoring a production system rather than just individual animals, but now they need not visit the production unit. Large-scale automated data collection, plus recorded information on milk and meat yields, means data can be viewed from a distance for clues they offer as to herd health and possible modifications to production efficiency. In the case of food and water monitoring, the system can automatically alert stock managers or vets when intake moves out of normal parameters, potentially indicating ill health. This approach parallels the "syndromic surveillance" techniques utilized in human public health. In human populations this systemic approach is used in attempts to pre-empt clinical diagnosis by monitoring trends in "health related" data, which can include: absenteeism from work or school, purchases of over-the-counter drugs and internet searches for particular terms. It does not target individuals, but looks for trends in an area that might indicate an oncoming epidemic or, in recent years, an act of bioterrorism (Fearnley 2008). In monitoring livestock, however, more direct forms of mass surveillance can be employed. This section deals with an example that monitors animals through the transition from livestock to deadstock and beyond: "from farm to fork" as the European Union catchphrase states.

The term foodchain surveillance is usually used to describe the routine monitoring and removal of zoonotic pathogens from materials intended as human foodstuffs. The foodchain in this common usage is an arena for surveillance activity that is necessary to protect human health. National and international standards for contaminants and pathogens are agreed and monitored through regulatory mechanisms aimed at reducing risk, in much the same way as with the veterinary standards noted above. However, the meaning of the term should perhaps be extended to take in other forms of activity that cast the foodchain less as an arena and more as an outcome of action. The example I will relate in this section is more concerned with the co-effectuation of the foodchain and forms of surveillance. That is, the ways in which particular socio-technical forms of food supply management and surveillance are literally put into effect together and co-determine each other.

DNA TraceBack is a beef traceability technology developed and marketed by the company Identigen, which was formed in the Republic of Ireland and now operates throughout Europe and North America (with offices in Kansas, USA). TraceBack is the main product of the company and emerged from PhD research being done into cattle breed identification via novel genomic techniques. At the time of this work, BSE and vCJD were high on media and policy agendas, with bans on beef imports from countries with a disease problem resulting in large losses to the sector. Identigen's founders, then working at Trinity College in Dublin, developed genetic techniques for verifying the source of meat products. Since this time, "traceability" has become a highly desired (and in some cases, legally required) property of specific foodchains; essentially, it refers to the capability to reliably track food products from production to consumption and is a key organizing concept in European food safety regulation.

The DNA TraceBack product consists of DNA sampling tools, a proprietary DNA analysis platform (the ID-GENerator) and IT system. Cattle are sampled shortly after birth, at the same time as they are ear-tagged, and/or at slaughter. A particular DNA profile (based on the biomarkers that are the core of the patent) for each animal is recorded in the system along with associated data, such as birth, movement and health statistics. In a supply chain that implements the technology, any meat product can be traced through the chain back to its origins, meaning that should a food safety issue arise its source can be quickly identified and isolated from the rest of the supply chain. The use of the DNA technology removes the reliance on problematic external labeling for traceability: the product carries its own "label" internally at all times. The final element of the system is the TraceBack logo, which can be used on final food product to indicate to consumers that a reliable monitoring system is in place. In this, TraceBack shares common ground with the farm assurance schemes noted in the previous section that offer their logo as a symbol of good animal welfare standards.

In practice, the extent to which consumers actually pay attention to the information or branding provided by assurance schemes remains questionable. TraceBack differs from welfare assurance schemes because it offers other capabilities to the retailers using it. The supermarket retailers who first adopted the technology in Ireland (Superquinn and Tesco) use the technology to carry out supply-chain audit. Regular sampling is an essential part of assuring the correct functioning of the TraceBack system itself, but this also allows the retailers to check that the flows of meat from producer through slaughter, cutting, packaging and distribution are operating as they should. As with welfare monitoring, and some forms of biosecurity, there is a dislocation—or distribution—of agency apparent here. Intervention is not carried out directly on the supposed principal object of surveillance. In biosecurity practice and welfare assurance it is the animal keeper who bears the brunt; with traceability technologies used as an audit tool, it is the components of the supply chain that do so.

Unlike in the QBA welfare tool discussed in the previous section, there is no sense here of anybody wanting the animal to be a subject, to be sentient. Animal identity in this case is purely a DNA barcode, purely a material feature. But the animal body here is a complex object and the monitoring of meat acknowledges it is a key component that ties together production, supply and consumption. The reconstruction of animal identity through TraceBack is a means of reconstructing the process of the foodchain in a manner similar to the work which is carried out in post-outbreak disease surveillance epidemiology to reconstruct the disease event that connects places (Donaldson and Murakami Wood 2008). This is usually hard (and often lengthy) detective work. Hinchliffe (2001) provides a masterful account of the problems inherent in attempting to pin down and engage with non-human agency on the molecular scale in the UK's handling of BSE. TraceBack consists of a constant monitoring that is aimed at rendering reconstructive snapshots of the system as simple routine.

The concept of "informed materials" can be used as a way of thinking about the type of object the animal body becomes in TraceBack (Donaldson 2007). Simply put, this means not considering a particular object or substance in isolation, but rather considering the very concrete connections it has to its context. A cut of beef is not the same thing without the informational environment (generated by TraceBack) that surrounds it, adds to it and makes it useful—to consumers and to retailers in this case. Once an animal is tagged and sampled, its body becomes an informed material—becomes something more. And it becomes an integral link in a system that seeks to align the goals and practices of producers, retailers and consumers. Welfare monitoring and other assurance schemes will also add their information and their influence to the system. Part of what defines a foodchain as an idea is its integrity, the reliable coupling of production and consumption. So the foodchain is at least partly made up out of different surveillant agencies that constitute that reliability in various forms.

Conclusion

In bringing this chapter to a close there are four observations I would like to make based on the overview of surveillance of food animals, their welfare and their diseases. First, our critical understanding of these activities as surveillance is neither sufficiently international nor broad enough in its scope. A focus on zoonotic diseases and incidents with a high media profile (SARS, bird flu, BSE) often excludes those mundane infectious agents which claim more lives globally, such as E. coli and Campylobacter.

Second, there often seems to be a dislocation of agency in the apparent separation of the moment of monitoring and the moment of intervention. The reflexive individual subjected to scrutiny, singled out, acted upon or acting in response to surveillance is not always apparent. My assertion is that a more complex, distributed entity is what is under surveillance. In this case, that entity might be the foodchain itself.

Third, the surveillance of non-humans is carried out for the benefit of humans. Surveillance is a part of food production—it is in fact essential to the just-in-time logistics of modern food production. Considering processes of monitoring and intervention in terms of animals in the foodchain can negate the immediate kneejerk reaction of "surveillance = bad" and permit a more nuanced description of the agencies at play, without engaging a critical dimension based on the moral position of individual rights. This demonstrates the productive dimension of surveillance which is often submerged in other accounts as the "product" is viewed as unwelcome. The combination of welfare monitoring and traceability creates a new virtuous foodstuff, produced from animals that have led as good as life as possible, that are well fed and disease free. This is an inventive process, information rich and embedded in an impressively resilient materiality. The idea of an informational material environment, producing an informed material, is surely a transferrable notion to other fields of surveillance studies. It is also a concept that can help us to engage with the real and traceable linkages between human and non-human subjects of surveillance, which brings me to my final point.

Barker (2010) has recently identified a "biosecure citizenship" emerging in New Zealand that focuses state attention not just on the human body, but on that body's "symbiotic associations" with other living things, be they pathogens or invasive species. This is occurring in ways that are distinct from the forms of surveillance that have been involved in public health in that it aims to scrutinize the wider, tacit ecological relationships that humans have to other species and environments, rather than formally target specific pathogens. At present this form of citizenship is prescriptive, bringing into play regulation and self-discipline through normative pressures, and defining the kinds of relationships between species and spaces that are deemed appropriate and biosecure. As surveillant processes, under the rubric of biosecurity, begin to focus more consciously on the full breadth of human/non-human interactions they raise significant questions for the social sciences: what does it mean to be human in the world today and what new forms will our societies take?

References

Barker, K. (2010). "Biosecure Citizenship: Politicising Symbiotic Associations and the Construction of Biological Threat," *Transactions of the Institute of British Geographers*, 35: 350–63.

Braun, B. (2007). "Biopolitics and the Molecularization of Life," *Cultural Geographies*, 14: 6–28.

Donaldson, A. (2007). "Socialising Animal Disease Risk: Inventing TraceBack and Reinventing Animals," *Genomics, Policy and Society*, 3: 57–69.

——(2008). "Biosecurity After the Event: Risk Politics and Animal Disease," *Environment and Planning A*, 40: 1552–67.

Donaldson, A. and Wood, D. (2004). "Surveilling Strange Materialities: Categorization in the Evolving Geographies of FMD Biosecurity," *Environment and Planning D: Society and Space*, 22: 373–91.

Donaldson, A. and Murakami Wood, D. (2008). "Avian Influenza and Events in Political Biogeography," *Area*, 40: 128–30.

Enticott, G. (2008). "The Spaces of Biosecurity: Prescribing and Negotiating Solutions to Bovine Tuberculosis," *Environment and Planning A*, 40: 1568–82.

Fearnley, L. (2008). "Signals Come and Go: Syndromic Surveillance and Styles of Biosecurity," *Environment and Planning A*, 40: 1615–32.

Hinchliffe, S. (2001). "Indeterminacy In-decisions – Science, Policy and Politics in the BSE (Bovine Spongiform Encephalopathy) Crisis," *Transactions of the Institute of British Geographers*, 26: 182–204.

Law, J. and Mol, A. (2006). "Globalisation in Practice: On the Politics of Boiling Pigswill," *Geoforum*, 39: 133–43.

e. The rise of the surveillance school

Emmeline Taylor

Schools have always been sites of surveillance. Registration verifies attendance, reports compound and adjudge activity, continual examination and assessment monitor progress, and the spatial containment of pupils enables the observation and scrutiny of behavior. In contemporary society the routine use of a suite of surveillance technologies in schools is superseding that of any other institution, including prisons, and pupils are emerging as the most heavily surveiled populace in countries such as the United Kingdom and North America. Whilst at the present time these technologies are being used for fairly innocuous purposes, such as the automation of library book lending, the potential impact is massive. Upcoming generations will emerge from surveillance schools desensitized to, and expectant of, intense scrutiny and objectification. They will have no experience or comprehension of a world without invasive surveillance for even the most mundane of activities

There are many issues raised by the use of surveillance in schools, and these vary over time, by country, by technology, objectives, location, and so on. This chapter focuses on three principal strands of investigation. First, it provides a brief overview of the technological surveillance practices that are currently being employed in schools, and second, it explores why and how these surveillance practices have flourished in the school environment. In doing so it will be argued that the cultivation of fear by the media, the inadequate regulation of surveillance technologies and the criminalization of youth have served to escalate, legitimate and proliferate surveillance practices in educational institutions. Drawing upon the limited number of empirical studies to date, the third section attempts to elucidate the potential impact that these surveillance practices have upon pupils. It examines the impact on privacy and trust and explores the potential for surveillance in schools to habituate and normalize intense scrutiny amongst young people, shaping the way for a new societal order (see also Bruno, this volume).

Introducing the surveillance school

Visual surveillance devices such as closed circuit television (CCTV) currently represent the most common manifestation of surveillance in schools internationally. In the UK it is estimated that 85 percent of secondary schools have some form of CCTV system, whereas in US high schools this has been estimated to be two-thirds. Asian countries such as the Philippines, China and South Korea are rapidly expanding the use of CCTV in schools, as is Australia. Systems vary, with some schools utilizing a handful of strategically placed cameras in limited locations around the campus; whereas others have scores of cameras monitoring virtually every area including corridors, classrooms, the canteen and sports hall. Although less common, some schools have installed fully operative CCTV cameras in sensitive locations such as pupils' toilets, and some have generated alarm (as well as police intervention) by inadvertently filming schoolchildren changing clothing for sports activities. These developments represent substantive challenges to expectations of privacy. There is also a growing trend for schools and nurseries to utilize webcams to enable parents to observe their children in the classroom. Some schools install covert cameras, whilst others have equipped their CCTV cameras with microphones enabling audio monitoring to accompany visual footage. In 2009, four schools in Greater Manchester, UK equipped classrooms with surveillance cameras and microphones to monitor teachers' performance for development purposes.

Biometric surveillance technologies, in particular Automated Fingerprint Identification Systems (AFIS), but also facial recognition, palm vein scanners and iris scanners have been used to verify the identity of pupils. The first reported use of AFIS in a school was in Minnesota, United States in 1999. Just over a decade later, it has materialized in schools all over the world, primarily used for purposes such as registration, library book loans and cashless catering. AFIS is becoming more common in many European countries such as Belgium and Sweden. However, some countries have taken steps to outlaw its use in schools, such as China and Hong Kong, as a result of privacy concerns. First used in 2001 in the UK, the routine fingerprinting of pupils has become increasingly common with recent estimates stating that a third of UK schools are routinely fingerprinting pupils from the age of four.

Facial recognition systems are emerging in schools. In 2009, ten UK schools began trialing the faceREGISTER system developed by Aurora Computer Services. Cameras take 3D photos of students to identify them, and pupils then confirm their identity by entering in a four-digit code (arguably rendering the need for the facial recognition technology obsolete). It is reported that the systems have been installed to tackle lateness and truancy. There are also sporadic reports of facial recognition technology being installed on school buses in the United States. Volpe Industries Inc. has developed a facial recognition system that can display profile information such as a child's special medical needs or who is allowed to pick up the child to drivers, alongside GPS tracking, constant video recording and optional audio recording.

Some schools have implemented radio–frequency identification (RFID) microchips in school uniforms or ID cards to track the movements of pupils. School uniforms embedded with RFID transmitters have been trialed in Japan, California and the United Kingdom to allow parents and staff to track children as they move around the school campus. In the Philippines, some schools use RFID in school passes for library book lending, purchasing items, and to monitor attendance. Primary schools in the Japanese city of Osaka use RFID microchips placed in pupils' clothing, backpacks and student ID cards to monitor their movements. Whereas in California, InCom Corporation prematurely ended a pilot program that required students to wear RFID badges following pressure from parents and civil liberties groups. A number of nebulous benefits have been attributed to RFID in schools, including increasing the speed and accuracy of registration, heightened security, enabling the visual confirmation of attendance, and to ease data input for schools' behavior monitoring systems. However, there has been no independent research to substantiate or refute these assertions.

"Cashless catering," usually underpinned by a form of biometric identification such as AFIS, is used in school canteens to monitor and control pupils' purchases. Some systems are programmed to "flag" when pupils attempt to buy items that their parents have specified as being unsuitable due to special diets, allergies, or preference. Some systems such as *My Nutrikids*, enables schools to send a weekly report to parents informing them of everything their child has bought to eat at the school.

Other surveillance technologies are used in schools such as internet tracking, the remote blocking of websites, and transparent equipment such as lockers and book bags. Globally, many schools request that pupils pass through security arches upon entering the school premises or use hand-held metal detector wands to perform random searches without requiring consent. The array of devices, whilst certainly not present in all schools, represent a shift from human-centered strategies of discipline and control to technological mechanisms.

The overarching reasons cited for the implementation of surveillance in schools are to detect and prevent crime and to increase efficiency whilst reducing financial expenditure. There is a multitude of other objectives which surveillance technologies are claimed to fulfill. Amongst these are to tackle bullying, truancy and smoking, to monitor pupil behavior, to encourage healthy eating, to provide evidence if a complaint is made about a pupil or teacher, to reduce lunchtime queues, to assist in the invigilation of exams, to remove the stigma attached to having free school dinner tokens, and to monitor staff performance. These technologies purportedly have numerous benefits but there is no independent evidence to suggest that it can deliver them.

Explaining the rise of the "surveillance school"

There are many reasons why schools have emerged as sites of technological surveillance. Various features of the school have facilitated its expansion. For example, pupils are relatively powerless compared to other members of society and so they are limited in their capacity to resist surveillance. Another reason is the need for a "guardian of truth" in a growing "litigation culture" where surveillance is actively sought out as a neutral observer to verify events and elicit the *truth* (Taylor 2010b). The following section focuses on two tangible processes underpinning and enabling the burgeoning of surveillance schools. First, it explores the increasing perception of schools as dangerous and risky based in part on the cultivation of fear by the media, and second, the alacrity with which technology develops and takes root, making it difficult for regulation and law to keep apace.

Schools as sites of violence and risk

Just as terrorism provided a fertile ground on which surveillance could propagate in the metropolis, moral panic about endemic school violence has provided a veneer of acceptability, even reverence, for the increased surveillance of pupils and their environment. Fear is amplified by the media which enables the transformation of random acts of violence into a continuous narrative depicting a universal and imminent threat to (and from) pupils (see also McCahill, Kammerer, Bruno, Norris and McGrath, this volume). Idiosyncratic events, such as school shootings, are transmitted to a global audience as further evidence of school campuses becoming increasingly dangerous territories. As the perceived problem acquires momentum, policy makers and law enforcers are required to act swiftly so as not to be held accountable for any future incidents. The supposed "knife crime epidemic" in UK schools clearly underpins the powers granted to school staff to search pupils without consent, and screen all pupils coming on site. Similarly, the justification for facial recognition technology has been rooted in the need to prevent "another Dunblane." School shootings are used to present the "need" for surveillance. For example, in reference to the Columbine High School massacre, Monahan (2006: 109) asserts that despite the failings of CCTV to prevent the atrocity "the terrifying shooting has become a key reference point in justifying increased surveillance and security systems in schools throughout the United States."

The cultivation of fear is played upon by manufacturers and suppliers of surveillance equipment. For example, in 2005, just days after a schoolboy was murdered in the UK, Anteon UK Ltd sent an email to 340 local authorities referring to the murder to promote its "VeriCool" school registration software (BBC News 2005). The email stated "Like everyone else, we were shocked and saddened by the apparent murder of the young schoolboy … We believe that we can help reduce the possibility of such future tragedies and so wish to bring to your attention our new anti-truancy and first day contact system." The Advertising Standards Authority (ASA) described the advertising campaign as "offensive and distressing." As some schools begin to develop strategies to counter the perceived risks (often assisted by seemingly benevolent security companies who donate equipment to run "pilot programmes"), other schools quickly follow suit through fear of being regarded as negligent of their responsibility *in loco parentis* if they didn't.

This symbiotic process results in the perception that all schools "need" ever more sophisticated technologies to "safeguard" pupils.

Expensive and disproportionate responses are recast as "necessary interventions, worth any cost, inconvenience, or more profound alteration of educational environments" (Monahan 2006: 113). But what if these measures do very little to safeguard young people? Is a false sense of security worse than having none at all? It has been claimed that, despite high-profile violent events, schools continue to be one of the safest places for young people, with a "one in two million chance of dying a violent death in school" (Monahan 2006: 109). In the USA, statistically "students are safer at school than they are in their own communities, in cars and even in their own homes" (American Civil Liberties Union 2001, cited in Monahan 2006: 109–10).

Law, regulation and enforcement

Globally the regulation of surveillance is diverse. However, it is commonly acknowledged that, as new ways of observing, scrutinizing, recording and analyzing individuals and their data emerge with ever increasing frequency, legal systems worldwide are unable to keep apace. The dearth and inadequacy of legislation permits ever more invasive surveillance practices to be introduced in schools.

Drawing upon the UK as an example of a country with a proliferation of "surveillance schools," it is clear that a lack of legal regulation has contributed towards their profusion. The European Union Data Protection Directive 1995 requires that members protect citizens' "right to privacy with respect to the processing of personal data." EU member states have implemented this in different ways. In the UK, the Directive manifested itself in the Data Protection Act 1998 (DPA 98). In applying the DPA 98 decree to the widespread introduction of AFIS (Taylor 2010a) and CCTV (Taylor 2011) in schools it has been argued that the various elements of statute are impractical or inappropriate in the school setting. Headteachers are vested with the autonomy to implement any technology they desire, and they are not legally obliged to gain the consent of parents, or even inform them. The ill-defined and vague legislation presented in the DPA 98 provides very little protection to the pupils as "data subjects." In addition, the ubiquity of CCTV and AFIS far surpasses the enforcement capabilities of the Information Commissioner's Office (ICO), tasked with ensuring compliance with the DPA 98, and as such any contravention of the scant provisions of the Act is likely to go unidentified and under-enforced.

In the United States, constitutional interpretation has evolved in the courts, materializing in a number of laws and executive orders dealing specifically with the concept of data protection. However, two developments of significance, the Privacy Act 1974 and the Computer Matching and Privacy Act 1988, are only applicable to personal information held by the federal government and do not have any authority over the collection and use of personal information held by other private and public sector entities, including schools. The American Civil Liberties Union asserts that schools using CCTV are "unconstitutionally intruding on the legitimate expectation of privacy of students, faculty, staff, and visitors," and are in effect "engaging in unreasonable search without a warrant and without probable cause or reasonable suspicion" (ACLU–Colorado, 2001 cited in Warnick 2010: 320). Irrespective of this declaration, it is unlikely that CCTV in schools will be ruled as unconstitutional in the US courts. The main reason compounding the issue is that, historically, under the Fourth Amendment, young people are denied liberty rights because these rights presuppose the capacity to make informed choices, whereas the limited cognitive and emotional capacities of young children do not necessarily provide for this (Warnick 2010).

The impact of surveillance in schools

There has been very little empirical research on the impact that surveillance technologies have upon individuals in the school. This has enabled a common assumption to prevail: that technological surveillance merely automates school processes and in doing so enhances security and relieves resource. However, the findings from the handful of studies that have been conducted suggests that surveillance in schools potentially undermines privacy, erodes trust, makes pupils feel criminalized and can have a "chilling effect" on creativity and interaction.

Privacy

Empirical research on the impact of surveillance on privacy has focused almost exclusively on CCTV. Perceived invasions of privacy by CCTV have been found to rely upon a complex of factors such as location of the cameras, their rationale and whether they were being monitored continuously. Direct and in-depth discussion of privacy in empirical research has mainly focused on the installation of CCTV in the pupils' toilets. Research illustrates that the toilet is representative of a private domain for pupils in which they can, in Goffmanesque fashion, discard their public performance and reside backstage (Taylor 2010b; McCahill and Finn 2010). Some pupils have been particularly expressive about their need for (relative) privacy in the school environment and attributed a number of values to it, such as the ability to express emotions that they did not want to be publicly observed. The presence of CCTV in the toilets made pupils feel uncomfortable and spied upon, thereby eradicating its function as a private realm in which to rejuvenate the psyche and accumulate the moral and emotional capital needed for the next emergence into public.

Mistrust and the criminalization of youth

Pupils have asserted that the use of surveillance, in particular CCTV and AFIS, was symptomatic of an underlying mistrust of them and were incensed about the lack of trust that they were afforded by schools and society (Taylor 2010b). In relation to the depiction of schools as sites of violence outlined above, young people felt they were being increasingly criminalized whereby the growing use of surveillance technologies is perceived as requisite to contain an increasingly savage youth spawned from the generic moral decay apparent in wider society. In a classic exposition of Becker's labeling theory, surveillance as a manifestation of suspicion and mistrust were perceived to breed misbehavior amongst some of the pupils in my own research study (2010b). Some pupils described a rational decision to engage in deviant or criminal behavior because they were "being treated like they are doing anyway" (Pupil, cited in Taylor 2010b: 391). For these individuals, to demonstrate trust is not to surveil and the very presence of CCTV as a symbol of mistrust was enough to galvanize "a self-fulfilling prophecy."

Social interaction and "distanciation"

Visual surveillance can have a detrimental impact on associational activity, curtailing creativity, innovation and experimental modes of expression. This is of particular importance when it is used in institutions such as schools where creativity and intellectual exploration are central to education. Furthermore, surveillance has initiated a process of "distanciation" whereby pupils are increasingly denied the opportunity for social interaction. Surveillance, whether it is facial recognition replacing registration, or fingerprinting to borrow library books, interrupts pupils' traditional patterns of "sociation" or "face-to-face" interaction with parents, teachers and their peers. McCahill and Finn (2010: 287) found that there was "no negotiation," for example, with teachers for "late arrivals"; pupils could no longer buy their friends dinner due to cashless catering systems; and the "automated text messages" impacted on dialogue with parents.

Habituation and the normalization of surveillance

The rise of the surveillance school could represent a process whereby intense technological surveillance is normalized through habituation. In a global media age where data profiles are increasingly used to verify and authenticate identity, young people need to be taught the importance of their personal data and the potential repercussions of providing it, and not to be casual about sharing it for increasingly mundane activities. Rather than simply automating existent processes, the use of technological surveillance introduces a myriad of issues that require further investigation by surveillance scholars. Bacard laments that if one wanted to develop a surveillance society they should "start by creating dossiers on kindergarten children so the next generation couldn't comprehend a world without surveillance" (Bacard 1995: 173). Examining the normalization and appropriation of surveillance by those that are subjected to it is paramount in assessing whether surveillance practices in schools are part of an offensive to subjugate the fears of society about "surveillance creep" by teaching the next generation to accept increasing scrutiny.

Encouraging conformity is a key aspect of the school and is identifiable in numerous mechanisms and rituals. The school uniform depersonalizes and embodies conformity, the school bell signals when to start things and when to end, the timetable regulates the passing of time, and the subject offerings reinforce the notion that pupils are passive recipients of others' ontologies. Foucault argues that the school as *institution disciplinaire* functions to create "subjected and practiced bodies" that are required for the successful operation of society (1977: 138, 211). In this respect, Foucault's theorizing is not dissimilar to the functionalist perspective that sees education as a means to socialize society's members to adhere to the dominant norms and values that underpin it. The school operates as "a pedagogical machine" producing the "useful individuals" required by society (Foucault 1977: 211). Technological surveillance practices in schools reinforce mechanisms of social control and the contemporary power dynamics of the neoliberal state whilst disciplining the future workforce. By locating intensive surveillance in schools, young people are normalized to its use and arguably will not object to enhanced scrutiny in later ife.

Avoidance, resistance and subversion of surveillance in schools

The "Surveillance Camera Players" have found infamy by challenging and undermining the gaze of the cameras through performance, and similarly it has been found that pupils have developed their own tactics of resistance to the use of surveillance in their schools. Schoolchildren have resisted the gaze of CCTV cameras in three main ways: avoidance of areas monitored by CCTV cameras; restricting the ability of the CCTV cameras to identify individuals; and third, by repositioning the cameras so they were no longer monitoring their behavior (Taylor 2010b; McCahill and Finn 2010). However, avoidance of, or interference with the cameras has been taken to be harmless and humorous subversions of the operation of the CCTV within the school. Rather than a product of malice or criminal intention, it has been considered as a playful expression of rebellion that is common amongst young people. It can be likened to relatively trivial activities performed by a boisterous minority in schools such as scrawling a name on a desk or experimenting with the boundaries of the school uniform.

Pupils in Australia have subverted the fingerprinting technology at their school through the use of "Gummy fingers" which are gelatinous moulds that can be used to replicate the fingerprint, often made from sweets. The artificial fingers complete with fingerprints can be used to register absent classmates. With the publication of step-by-step guides on the internet, it is probable that these techniques to circumvent the technology will become more commonplace.

There are more earnest examples of pupils mobilizing themselves collectively against the use of surveillance in their schools. Some pupils have protested against the installation of CCTV cameras in their classrooms. For example, pupils at a school in Waltham Forest, UK walked out of their school following the introduction of CCTV because they felt it threatened their civil liberties. The pupils refused to return until they had received assurances that it had been turned off. Furthermore, upon their return to the school, the pupils wore masks to continue their protest. In other cases individuals have refused to return to their school until CCTV cameras have been removed from pupils' toilet areas.

Although the avoidance and resistance of the surveillance techniques found in schools are not regarded as serious attempts to defy the surveillance practices and rules of the school, they do represent a clear challenge to surveillance. As such these acts cannot be ignored, irrespective of whether they represent a rejection of the CCTV or AFIS per se, or the authority of the school more widely. It is possible that they are indicative of an underlying rejection of the disciplinary function of the school. Several theorists have identified a general opposition to school authority amongst working-class adolescents in an attempt to maintain their own values and resist attempts by the dominant culture to impose theirs.

Conclusion

There has been very little exploration of the impact surveillance has upon pupils but recent empirical findings suggest that often the technologies do little to safeguard young people, do not represent financial savings or increased efficiency, but yet they strip pupils of their privacy, undermine their trust in others and create an atmosphere of suspicion. Importantly, the incessant use of omnipresent technological surveillance has the ability to displace the very building blocks of democratic society. Social attributes such as trust, privacy, anonymity and freedom of expression and movement are being displaced by surveillance, paving the way for a new regime of social ordering. Schools as microcosms of society can permit us a prophetic glimpse into the future, and as such it is a crucial time for surveillance scholars to study the phenomena of the "surveillance school." After all, the normalization of surveillance through pedagogical apparatus and instruction could potentially render the discipline of "surveillance studies" itself obsolete.

References

Bacard, A. (1995). *The Computer Privacy Handbook: A Practical Guide to Email Encryption, Data Protection and PGP Privacy Software*, New York: Peachpit Press.
BBC News. (16 November 2005). "Murder E-Mail Advert Criticised," available at http://news.bbc.co.uk/2/hi/uk_news/scotland/4440808.stm (accessed 27 May 2011).
Foucault, M. (1977). *Discipline and Punishment*, New York: Pantheon.
McCahill, M. and Finn, R. (2010). "The Social Impact of Surveillance in Three UK Schools: 'Angels', 'Devils', and 'Teen Mums'," *Surveillance & Society*, 7(3/4): 273–89.
Monahan, T. (2006). "The Surveillance Curriculum: Risk Management and Social Control in the Neoliberal School," in T. Monahan (ed.), *Surveillance and Security: Technological Politics and Power in Everyday Life*, London: Routledge.
Taylor, E. (2010a). "From Finger-painting to Fingerprinting," *Education Law Journal* 4: 276–88.
——(2010b). "I Spy with My Little Eye: the Use of CCTV in Schools and the Impact on Privacy," *The Sociological Review*, 58(3): 381–405.
——(2011). "UK schools, CCTV and the Data Protection Act 1998," *Journal of Education Policy*, 26 (1): 1–15.
Warnick, R. (2010). "Surveillance Cameras in Schools: An Ethical Analysis," *Harvard Educational Review*, 77(3), Fall: 317–343.

Section 3.2.
Crime and policing

a. Surveillance, crime and the police

Kevin D. Haggerty

Popular depictions of the police tend to portray an action-packed and often violent profession. In the routine operation of policing, however, a considerable volume of an officer's time is consumed with filing, not fighting. The police are information workers, concerned with collecting, analyzing and communicating a diverse array of intelligence within and outside of the police's formal institutional boundaries (Ericson and Haggerty 1997). Indeed, the police are remarkably enthusiastic collectors of information, displaying a desire to amass and secure access to volumes of data that can far surpass their ability to make it pragmatically useful.

That the police conduct surveillance is not a particularly startling insight. Surveillance, in its various forms, is now the preferred institutional response for dealing with any number of social problems. The police, who have an extremely wide organizational remit, are called upon to deal with a bewildering range of issues (some of which are criminalized, while others are not), so it seems appropriate that they might engage in different forms of surveillance and have access to specialized surveillance technologies and databases (Coleman and McCahill 2011).

Despite this long-standing affinity between the police and surveillance, there is much that is new in the scope and operation of police surveillance, something that can be attributed to such things as new organizational models, information technologies, political ideologies, public fears, developments in crime politics, trends in criminal behavior, and so on. Combined, such factors have significantly strengthened and expanded the police's surveillance mandate across the globe.

Concerns about police surveillance sit at the fulcrum of two of modernity's great nightmares. On the one hand is the fear of routine victimization, with crime becoming an endemic part of daily life. Here, police surveillance is understood to be a necessity, as a bulwark against the prospect of descending into an anarchic world of failed states run by criminal gangs. At the other extreme sits the prospect of a totally controlled society, something that was foreshadowed in several totalitarian regimes during the course of the twentieth century. Here police surveillance is positioned as a more sinister tool that always risks being used to regulate the minutia of human conduct in a manner reminiscent of Orwell's dystopic vision of total control (Cohen 1985).

This chapter details some of the issues pertaining to surveillance undertaken by the police for purposes of crime control. In doing so I draw attention to the considerable variability in the police's anti-crime surveillance measures. At the outset, however, it is worth noting that the police are themselves a highly variable institution. Despite many similarities between police forces internationally, policing is not standardized; it displays considerable variation related to local cultures, legal regimes, national histories and political structures, among other things. Organizational units even within the same police force can operate quite differently, as is apparent in the distinction between uniformed constables and detectives working in civilian clothing. Policing units can themselves often be distinguished one from the other on the basis of the primary (but not necessarily exclusive) forms of surveillance they conduct, with constables relying on informants, detectives on undercover work, cyber police units conducting dataveillance, aerial units combining cameras with forward-looking infrared radar (FLIR), while traffic units use radar and increasingly rely on automated license-plate readers. Such variability means we should be cautious about drawing broad conclusions about surveillance in policing.

In what follows I concentrate primarily on the public police. It should be stressed, however, that policing occurs in a range of institutions, including insurance companies, securities regulators, intelligence agencies, taxation departments, welfare offices and immigration services, to name just a few, with each conducting their own forms of surveillance. The private police (often called "security guards") are also significant players in the dynamics of anti-crime surveillance, and often greatly outnumber state police employees as is the case, for example, in Brazil, South Africa, the United States and many other countries. In the aftermath of the September 11th 2001 terrorist attacks the line which traditionally separated policing from national security has also become blurred in many Western jurisdictions. On top of all of this, officials encourage individual citizens to conduct their own anti-crime surveillance. This includes such things as trying to reduce the risk of home break-ins by maximizing the sight lines around their homes, installing personal surveillance cameras and participating in assorted "crime watch" programs.

The fact that the police exist in a wider institutional matrix is particularly important for understanding police surveillance, as the police increasingly rely on forms of monitoring that are conducted by other government, security and commercial actors, a point I return to below.

A key starting point for understanding the wider politics of police surveillance follows from the social constructionist insight that crime is not a naturally given phenomenon, but that certain acts *become* crimes through highly variable institutional practices of categorization, monitoring and processing. Consequently, the police do not so much detect crime, but deploy assorted measures that selectively draw attention to the behaviors of certain categories and classes of people that *could be*—depending upon a host of contextual factors—processed as crimes. In societies deeply split by race, class and gender divisions, such selective monitoring often gives rise to accusations that the police are discriminatory; that police surveillance is being used to control and criminalize certain groups—something that may result from the police's actions even if it is not their specific intention (see Browne, this volume).

Another analytical issue pertaining to police surveillance concerns the dynamics of "surveillance creep," the process whereby surveillance measures (both "low-tech" and "high tech") introduced for one defined purpose can quickly develop new uses, expanding to focus on new places and populations. This is now a general tendency in the dynamics of surveillance, but the police play a particularly important role here by alternatively reconfiguring surveillance measures used in other domains for police purposes or serving as a launching-off point for the movement of surveillance practices into wider society.

In what follows I introduce some of the different forms of surveillance conducted by the police. I start with the police's more established "low-tech" surveillance practices of snitching and undercover policing, and move to a discussion of some newer and more technological forms of police surveillance. I dedicate one section to surveillance camera technology given how important such devices have become in many urban policing contexts. The concluding substantive section accentuates how the police are not just watchers, but are also themselves monitored.

This is necessarily a selective overview, but the general points about the aims, challenges and political concerns pertaining to specific surveillance measures often generalize to other instances. It is also the case that while I treat these measures separately, one of the most important trends in policing concerns how different surveillance practices are increasingly being aligned and used in concert, something that will undoubtedly only increase in the future.

Snitching

A common expression in policing is that a police officer is only as good as her informants, something that accentuates the centrality of "snitching" in police work. Snitching involves someone trying to gain personal advantage from informing the officials about other's crimes (Natapoff 2009). Or, viewed from a different angle, it involves the authorities positioning a person such that they feel compelled to turn on their criminal collaborators. The typical snitching scenario involves an apprehended (not necessarily charged) suspect providing information about the crimes of their associates. It can also involve informants who have a long-standing relationship with the police, and who are paid for information. The level of snitching in most jurisdictions is impossible to quantify, but it is often pervasive.

Snitching is essentially officially sanctioned punishment bartering. For any barter system to work, both parties must stand to gain from the exchange. For the police, informants can provide access to criminal organizations that they otherwise could not infiltrate. Police also use snitches to try and work up the criminal hierarchy, using an informant's testimony to build cases against more serious offenders. For prosecutors, snitching lubricates the court's wheels, making criminal prosecutions faster and more certain. Indeed, if snitching were eliminated, the courts in many jurisdictions would lurch to a halt, as no snitching would translate into little plea bargaining. For suspects, snitching presents an opportunity to catch a break. This could mean, for example, that in exchange for cooperating they might not be charged, that they will be prosecuted for less serious crimes, that their sentence will be reduced, or that they are incarcerated in a comparatively desirable institution, and so on.

While snitching might not be something that immediately comes to mind when thinking about police surveillance, snitches remain one of the most important ways that the police routinely keep tabs on individual offenders and criminal organizations, as citizens are alternately enticed or coerced to detail the actions of their friends and collaborators. Official reliance on snitches also produces a host of harms. These include how snitching tends to result in a form of secret justice, and produces vastly different outcomes for people charged with the same crimes. Snitching corrodes already strained police/community relations and results in criminals intimidating or punishing informants. To cultivate snitches police will let crimes go unpunished and sometimes even turn a blind eye to serious offences that they know their valuable snitches continue to commit. Perhaps most disastrously, snitching has been a conspicuous factor in many false convictions, as informants with little to lose have indicted innocent individuals in hopes of striking a deal.

Undercover policing

Besides snitching, another long-standing low-tech police surveillance practice involves undercover operations, with officers surreptitiously assuming a host of different roles in hopes of catching criminals. Today this is recognized as a routine and perhaps necessary part of police work, but in the early emergence of the modern Western police institution the prospect that the state would deploy undercover operatives was highly controversial, raising fears of despotic forms of state control. Despite our contemporary familiarity with the general existence of undercover policing, it continues to be plagued by legal and ethical concerns (Marx 1988).

At the most basic level, undercover policing can be unsettling because it involves sometimes extreme levels of deceit and public manipulation. In hopes of collecting intelligence the police have pretended to be, for example, inmates, vagrants, journalists, pornographic book sellers, prostitutes, lawyers, census enumerators, lovers, priests, assorted forms of criminals and many, many more roles. The police will also fake entire social gatherings in attempts to lure reclusive criminals into the open. A classic example of such an operation involves mailing suspects a notice informing them that they have won a prize, or that their social security benefits have been suspended. When the suspect arrives at the appointed "social event" or "welfare office" they are immediately arrested. While such tactics are justified as being necessary, having police officers collect intelligence by posing as journalists or priests also obviously risks undermining public trust.

The internet has created new possibilities for undercover police surveillance, as officers assume virtual identities in hopes of learning about illegal activity. Contemporary revelations that the police and immigration authorities are "friending" people on Facebook in order to access their personal data is an obvious example. Another involves ongoing concerns about sexual predators on the internet, with police organizations across the globe responding to such anxieties by pretending to be paedophiles in order to communicate online with real paedophiles. Alternatively, officers pose as children in youth-oriented chat rooms to entice potential child molesters. As early as 1999 Shari Steele of the Electronic Frontier Foundation estimated that "at least half of the 13-year-old girls in chat rooms are probably policemen." This is undoubtedly a gross overestimation, but it does raise the question of what percentage of the panic-inducing paedophile-related communications on the internet are created entirely by one police officer for eventual consumption by another police officer. How would we know one way or the other?

Such a scenario also points to a recurring problem that undercover work poses for the police; the prospect of "blue on blue" crime. This occurs when a police officer or police organization unaware of a specific undercover operation will swoop in and arrest police officers posing as criminals. Tragically, such mistakes have occasionally resulted in officers shooting other officers who they did not know were working undercover. At a more prosaic level, undercover policing can also put officers in highly stressful situations, breaking up friendships and families and occasionally resulting in emotional collapse. Ethically, undercover policing can straddle a line between catching legitimate criminals and entrapment, where citizens are induced or coerced by the police to engage in criminal acts that they otherwise would not commit.

Police surveillance technologies

As noted, the preceding examples of police surveillance were notably "low tech." Consequently, they contrast with much of what is interesting and occasionally unsettling about contemporary surveillance which involves more "high-tech" surveillance options. The police are now positioned as potential users of almost any new surveillance device. This is particularly apparent when surveillance devices originally produced for military applications are transferred to civilian policing settings, technologies which include satellites, helicopters, drones and sensors (Haggerty and Ericson 2001). Rather than such technologies being a rational response to the practical demands of crime control, they can amount to a form of technological solution in search of a problem, with the police serving as a convenient site for justifying the expanded uses of such devices. Such developments are part of the more general emergence of a surveillance industrial complex (see Hayes, this volume). This general intensification of police surveillance, when combined with the fact that the police's adoption of surveillance technologies can desensitize citizens to the eventual expansion of these devices to other non-policing contexts, gives police surveillance technologies a political significance that extends well beyond issues of detecting or deterring criminals.

While many surveillance technologies have been introduced into policing in recent years it is worth remembering that the police have long sought to rationalize their practices by embracing different technological systems. One of the most important classes of such devices are those that seek to identify people. The early embrace of such practices occurred in the nineteenth century in the context of the rise of a "society of strangers," as rural populations moving to urban centers encountered a litany of unknown others. Such strangers posed a dilemma for the police who sought to keep track of suspect populations and identify known criminals.

A notable early police attempt to address this problem was the Bertillon system. Introduced in France in the 1880s, "Bertillonage" as it was called, combined the emerging archive of police photographic "mug shots" with a series of standardized measurements of several ostensibly unchanging physical attributes of a person's body, storing those details in a coded filing system. Bertillonage was ultimately abandoned with the increasing popularity of fingerprinting, which identifies people by the unique patterns on their fingertips. More accurate than its predecessors, fingerprinting also had the distinct forensic advantage of being able to position suspects at crime scenes by virtue of the latent prints that they leave behind. Fingerprinting, combined with police "mug shots," remained at the core of police identification practices for approximately a century (Cole 2001), although both saw significant advances during that period which made the data easier to collect, search and distribute.

Efforts to identify criminals (and others) were radically expanded in the 1990s with the emergence of DNA typing, something that allows the authorities to identify unique individuals from trace DNA elements found in saliva, semen, blood, hair, and so on. This gave rise to new investigative practices and also new organizational sections, most notably the "cold case" units that sought to re-examine unsolved cases that might benefit from new forensic techniques.

While DNA testing marks a major scientific advance, to be an effective policing technology DNA systems ultimately require a matched sample. Consequently, there have been recurring calls from the police to expand DNA databases such that they would include ever-larger population groups. DNA identification therefore stands as a clear example of surveillance creep (Nelkin and Andrews 1999), as early proposals for DNA databases came with recurrent reassurances that DNA would only ever be collected from the worst of the worst criminals. Instead, in countries such as Norway, Canada and the United States we have seen a progressive expansion such that more and more classes of offenders are required to submit a DNA sample to be stored on the database. In the UK, one now only has to be a suspect (not even charged with a crime) to have your DNA collected and stored. In other countries the security establishment routinely lobbies for the state to collect DNA from every citizen and all visitors.

Police surveillance is also now being transformed by developments in information technology. Networked computing has allowed for an exponential increase in the amount of information that many institutions collect, analyze and disseminate. While the police collect their own data about myriad phenomena, they are also eagerly eyeing the data amassed by other institutions, recognizing the policing potentials inherent in the data collected by banks, libraries, airlines, telecommunications companies, internet service providers, and others.

To date much of the police's access to and use of such data has been somewhat haphazard and idiosyncratic. Efforts are now underway to change that situation, to find ways for the police to secure regular access to the data collected by other government, police, security and corporate institutions. This is typically referred to as "breaking down information silos," a practice that promises to expand significantly, giving the police more regular access to reams of ever more fine-grained data on citizen's travels, interests, habits, contacts, physical location, and so on. So, the United States, for example, has seen large commercial data brokers such as ChoicePoint prospectively formatting the vast amounts of data they collect on individual American citizens (but also citizens in countries such as Argentina, Brazil and Mexico) and selling it to American law enforcement agencies. This provides the police with "one-stop information shopping" for detailed data about individuals—information that the state is often legally prohibited from collecting itself. In the European Union a spate of "data retention" legislation now mandates that private companies maintain data on their customer's communications (cell phone and internet use) so that it can be made available to the police if deemed necessary.

Such information-sharing efforts became particularly popular after the terrorist attacks of 2001 when the authorities in many countries passed legislation that compelled various organizations to provide the police access to at least some of their data. Ultimately, any success that the police will have in this regard is contingent on a series of local legal and political factors, but there is no denying that the police see accessing such data as a major step forward in their attempt to identify criminals—and people who might become criminals.

This greater ability to link information across institutions for policing purposes promises to dramatically alter people's lived experiences. Marginalized and criminalized populations are most likely to feel the hard end of such initiatives. As information systems become ever more tightly linked we can envision a future where criminalized populations must find alternatives outside of mainstream institutions. One can gain a glimpse of such a world in Alice Goffman's (2009) excellent ethnography of wanted men living in a Philadelphia ghetto. Almost all of these men have various warrants out for their arrest, usually for non-payment of fines. They are vulnerable to arrest each time they have dealings with state and an increasing number of private institutions as they can only access those services after their personal details are searched on linked databases. The upshot is that they cannot get welfare or travel internationally, and in order to work or acquire medical assistance they must do so in the alternative "grey economy."

Police efforts to access the data collected by other institutions are also subtly changing the dynamics of criminal suspicion. Previously, individuals became suspects or known to the police because of what they did—or were presumed to have done. The police might then initiate formal surveillance measures if they deemed it appropriate. Today, the emergence of policing focused on databases means that the data system itself can generate suspicious populations. Aggregate data can be analyzed using sophisticated data algorithms (see Gandy, Jr, this volume) to single out people with profiles that authorities have deemed "risky"—the classic example involves the work of immigration authorities who use profiles to flag individual travelers as security threats because they are travelling alone, on a one-way ticket bought with cash, have no luggage and are arriving from any number of "high risk" countries. In such instances the data system effectively constructs suspicion on the basis of a combination of weighted data points, serving up "risky" individuals for greater levels of police scrutiny.

In terms of the official response to crime, such dataveillance gives a greater forward-looking dimension to policing. Historically, the crime control apparatus was primarily concerned with events that occurred in the past, punishing offenders for acts that they had already committed. What little consideration of the future there was in crime control came from justifying such measures as potentially preventing or deterring crime. Today, greater attention to potential criminal risk factors for various populations is starting to focus crime control more on reducing risks such that crime might not occur—something that often goes by the name of "pre-emption." This operates by analyzing data for indicators that someone with a specific constellation of attributes is statistically likely to commit crime in the future, and intervening today to try and reduce those risk factors. While we are still in the very early days of such pre-emption efforts, they raise ethical issues about whether the state should be singling out people on the basis of crimes that they have not yet committed—and might never commit.

As noted, many other surveillance devices are rapidly finding uses in policing including helicopters, wiretaps, drones and the like. All such devices are justified as a way for the police to better identify suspects and detect crimes. They can also come with a cost that is difficult to calculate. In particular, such devices can further distance the police from the communities they are supposed to serve, something that is routinely held out as a major dilemma for the prospects of consensual policing.

Surveillance cameras

One of the more significant recent "high-tech" developments in policing has been the introduction of surveillance cameras. These are also often referred to as "closed circuit television" (CCTV), although that terminology is increasingly inappropriate as the cameras no longer use "closed circuit" technology, nor are the images displayed on a television. Whatever they are called, the embrace of these devices marks a notable transformation in police practice and public attitudes.

Surveillance cameras were originally introduced in private settings such as corner stores and retail outlets. Any footage that the police received from those cameras was handed to them at the discretion of the camera owners. It was only in the early 1990s, particularly in the United Kingdom, where public surveillance cameras controlled and operated by public authorities truly took off. Again, it was not the police who installed and operated these devices, but they were and continue to be regularly provided with the images and intelligence they produce. The reasons for this expansion are complex (see Norris in this volume) having been justified for several reasons beyond any ability to catch criminals, including the belief that they might reassure the public, manage traffic, and be a key element in urban regeneration programs more generally. The exact number of cameras in most countries is debatable, but the unassailable truth is that there are many cameras, their numbers grow daily, they are increasingly integrated, and their technological abilities to see are becoming more sophisticated.

The introduction and expansion of cameras signifies a rather remarkable change in public attitudes. One generation ago the idea that the state would install video cameras to watch its own citizens stood as perhaps the iconic symbol of a totalitarian society. Today, such devices are widely supported.

There remains, however, the vexatious issue of whether the routine use of such cameras actually reduces crime. While most police officers have anecdotal evidence of cameras helping to catch a particular criminal, at the more aggregate level even the most rigorous and comprehensive evaluations typically conclude that any evidence for the camera's crime-fighting power is ambiguous, at best (Gill and Spriggs 2005). The crime-reducing ability of public cameras is blunted by the fact that criminals modify their behavior in order to operate notwithstanding the presence of cameras. Cameras sometimes displace criminal behavior to neighboring areas, something that the camera-equipped community might applaud, but at a broader societal level hardly counts as a progressive development.

There are serious methodological challenges in trying to discern any effect of surveillance cameras. At the most basic level, it can be difficult or impossible to know what the crime rate would have been if the cameras were not installed, making before-and-after comparisons problematic. There is also wide variability in the abilities of such cameras with some being stand-alone systems that provide little more than grainy images of the flow of humanity. More sophisticated systems can digitally scrutinize people with the aid of pan, tilt, zoom and now audio capabilities. Still others are dummies, installed in hopes of deterring unwanted behavior, but which record nothing. Some systems are unmonitored, others are monitored by security guards and still others by police officers. The number of people staffing the cameras, their training and level of professionalism can vary dramatically. The physical location and density of the cameras and the degree to which they are publicized can also distinguish one system from another. These different configurations suggest that there is a world of difference in the operational dynamics of systems, making comparisons of their effects difficult. It seems fair to say, however, that the cameras have not lived up to the early optimistic claims of those who believed that cameras would significantly reduce crime and ease public anxieties about victimization.

In many contexts surveillance cameras also represent another clear example of "surveillance creep." Most cameras were initially justified as a means to counter high-level crimes such as child abductions and terrorism. Once installed, the camera's ability to monitor the minutia of public behavior has encouraged authorities to use them to address a host of low-level regulatory matters. In the UK, for example, local authorities have used cameras that were legally authorized to counter terrorism to regulate such prosaic misdeeds as people putting their garbage out on the wrong day, not cleaning up after their dog, urinating in public, littering, delivering newspapers without a license, smoking under-age, posting flyers and driving in an anti-social manner.

Policing under surveillance

The police are often referred to as a "low-visibility" profession, one where officers work outside of the limelight of public scrutiny and away from the direct oversight of supervisors. It is clear, however, that this image has been inaccurate for some time. Officers are monitored by practices that operate both internally and externally to the police organizations.

Internally, the police are monitored in a range of different ways, from the polygraph tests that they must often take as part of the recruitment process, medical testing and regular re-certification for firearms proficiency. The day-to-day police work of line officers is also scrutinized in detail by supervisors to ensure that they adhere to regulations pertaining to the bureaucratic formatting and dissemination of police-generated information—something that can entail intensive and extensive forms of oversight

(Ericson and Haggerty 1997). Officers are also policed by internal units specializing in investigating police wrongdoing. While questions remain about the efficacy of such internal investigations, officers are always cognisant that their actions might be scrutinized by such units. Occasionally, internal affairs will go to considerable lengths to detect police wrongdoing, as was the case in New York where officials sought to test the integrity of their officers by hiding illegal drugs where police officers would find them and also reporting fictitious instances of drug dealing to test whether officers would respond appropriately.

In a society characterized by a greater prevalence of monitoring devices the police also increasingly find themselves scrutinized by citizens and external institutions. Sometimes this involves instances where inappropriate police actions have been captured by cameras designed by contrast to catch criminals or protect officers, such as those installed in holding cells or on police vehicles. Internationally, officers also find that they are now routinely filmed at public protests, with both sides of any confrontation recording the encounter. On a day-to-day basis, the increasing ubiquity of camera-equipped cellular telephones means that citizens commonly have their actions photographed or recorded. Usually this occurs haphazardly but it can also be a conscious policy of groups concerned about police violence, such as "cop watch" organizations who seek out and record police behavior.

This increasing prevalence of policing in front of the camera poses a host of challenges for the police. For example, it can elevate non-routine and perhaps unrepresentative encounters to the status of highly symbolic political events. This, in turn, makes it increasingly difficult for the police to control the stories that they tell about their actions and ultimately reduces their relative power (Goldsmith 2010). In the process, the issue of "spin control" becomes ever more important for the police, who must be increasingly attuned to how to advance their preferred interpretations of often unflattering or disturbing videos of police behavior. So, surveillance technologies are not only used by the police, but are increasingly directed at police officers by different constituencies, changing the day-to-day practices of policing while increasing the risk of scandal.

Conclusion

The police have long been agents of surveillance, and the consequences of their monitoring are particularly significant given the high value we place on security but also because of how police actions can fundamentally alter an individual's life course or serve to cumulatively marginalize certain populations.

The expansion of new surveillance options is fundamentally altering what it means to do police work, with officers becoming ever more focused on collecting and analyzing reams of data and using assorted surveillance devices that range from DNA to license-plate readers to in-car cameras to wiretaps. None of these developments, however, necessarily works in a seamless fashion. There are always hiccups and localized forms of resistance and failure when new police surveillance measures are introduced. This is particularly apparent in relation to the ongoing calls for the police to share intelligence with other security organizations. As has long been known, the police are eager to collect information and acquire data collected by others, but they are much more reticent about divulging their own data. Questions also remain about the police's ability to effectively manage and use the surveillance data that is now available to them.

We appear to be in the midst of a major recalibration in the public's fears of police surveillance, with citizens and politicians alike being more willing to empower the police with surveillance and dismiss lingering anxieties about the inherently repressive potential of such practices. It remains to be seen how this transformation will shape the scope and operation of police surveillance into the future.

Note

Special thanks to Ariane Ellerbrok for her extensive comments on this chapter and to my co-editors Kirstie Ball and David Lyon for their valuable feedback.

References

Cohen, Stanley. (1985). *Visions of Social Control: Crime Punishment and Classification*, Cambridge: Polity.

Cole, Simon A. (2001). *Suspect Identities: A History of Fingerprinting and Criminal Identification*, Cambridge, MA: Harvard University Press.

Coleman, Roy and McCahill, Mike. (2011). *Surveillance and Crime*, London: Sage.

Ericson, Richard V. and Haggerty, Kevin D. (1997). *Policing the Risk Society*, Toronto: University of Toronto Press and Oxford: Oxford University Press.

Gill, Martin and Spriggs, Angela. (2005). *Assessing the Impact of CCTV*, London: Home Office Research, Development and Statistics Directorate.

Goffman, Alice. (2009). "On the Run: Wanted Men in a Philadelphia Ghetto," *American Sociological Review*, 74: 339–57.

Goldsmith, Andrew. (2010). "Policing's New Visibility," *British Journal of Criminology*, 50: 914–34.

Haggerty, Kevin D. and Ericson, Richard V. (2001). "The Military Technostructures of Policing," in *Militarizing the American Criminal Justice System: The Changing Roles of the Armed Forces and the Police*, edited by P. Kraska, Boston, MA: Northeastern University Press.

Marx, Gary T. (1988). *Undercover: Police Surveillance in America*, Berkeley: University of California Press.

Natapoff, Alexandra. (2009). *Snitching: Criminal Informants and the Erosion of American Justice*, New York: New York University Press.

Nelkin, Dorothy and Andrews, Lori. (1999). "DNA Identification and Surveillance Creep," *Sociology of Health and Illness*, 21(5): 689–706.

b. Crime, surveillance and media

Michael McCahill

Introduction

As Thomas Mathiesen (1997: 219) says, "it is, to put it mildly, puzzling that Michel Foucault, in a large volume which explicitly or implicitly sensitizes us inter alia to surveillance in modern society, does not mention television—or any other mass media—with a single word." For Mathiesen this was a crucial omission in Foucault's work because with the development of mass media the Benthamite project of the panopticon (where the few see the many) has been accompanied by the synopticon, where the many observe the few (see also Kammerer, this volume). As several writers have argued, these developments can have a significant democratizing impact on surveillance processes. A brief perusal of the newspapers at the time of writing provides ample evidence of the democratizing potential of the "viewer society." The release by Wikileaks of secret US Embassy cables or the launch of Justspotted.com which will scan social media to provide information on the whereabouts of thousands of celebrities both clearly illustrate how new media allow the "many" to watch the "few."

However, as Mathiesen clearly states in his paper, the rise of the "viewer society" does not mean that "panoptic" surveillance disappears or is no longer relevant (see also Bogard, this volume). Instead he explains how panopticism and synopticism *"have developed in intimate interaction, even fusion, with each other"* (Mathiesen 1997: 223, original emphasis). To illustrate this point, Mathiesen refers to the functioning of the Catholic Church which utilizes the confession to allow the "few" to see the "many," but at the same time has "enormous cathedrals intentionally placed in very visible locations" which allows the "many" to see and admire the "few" (1997: 223). This chapter draws upon Mathiesen's notion of panoptic-synoptic fusion to explore the mutually reinforcing discourses of "crime," "surveillance" and "mass media." While the synopticon may have democratizing potential, as it enables the many to watch the few, this chapter argues that in the context of media, crime and criminal justice the fusion of panoptic-synoptic regimes continues to reinforce "asymmetrical power relations" (Coleman and McCahill 2011: 170). Focusing mainly on developments in the UK, the USA and Canada, the chapter aims to support this argument by drawing upon the literature on mass media, crime and surveillance in news reporting (television and newspapers) and "Reality TV." The chapter begins by arguing that the fusion of panopticism and synopticism reinforces long-established trends whereby the mass media focus disproportionately on "working-class" street crime while under emphasizing white-collar crime and non-violent crime (Reiner 2007). Next the chapter reviews some of the literature on "media effects" (see also Taylor, Kammerer, Bruno, Norris and McGrath, this volume) which suggests that synoptic representations of crime generate an impetus for the introduction of further "panoptic" regimes which in turn fall disproportionately on marginalized populations (see also Arteaga Botello, Fussey, Wilson and Gandy, this volume). The chapter then shifts focus by examining the relationship between policing, surveillance and the mass media. This section looks critically at the claims that have been made for the "democratizing" potential of "new media" by pointing to some of the structural limitations that restrict "bottom-up" scrutiny of powerful groups. The concluding section identifies some emerging issues in the literature and makes one or two suggestions for further research on surveillance, crime and the mass media.

"Us" and "them"—news from the panopticon

Crime is a topic that has always featured prominently in news reporting in the mass media (Reiner 2007). As Mathiesen (1997: 231) says, "news from … [the] panopticon—news about prisoners, escapes, robberies, murder—are the best pieces of news which the synopticon … can find." However, as Mathiesen's quotation clearly indicates, not all crimes or criminals are considered as equally "newsworthy." In Victorian England, synoptic representations of crime in newspapers tended to focus predominantly on crimes of the working class and relied upon stereotypical accounts of the "great unwashed" (Jermyn 2003; Coleman and McCahill 2011). In contrast, crimes committed by relatively powerful groups (state violence, deaths at work, income tax evasion, corporate criminality, domestic violence) remained hidden from both panoptic and synoptic regimes (Coleman and McCahill 2011: 172). As research in many jurisdictions has shown, the focus on violent, interpersonal street crimes continues to dominate media-reporting on this issue (Reiner 2007). But what happens when we add "new surveillance" technologies to the "crime-media" nexus?

As Chris Greer (2010: 227) has pointed out, recent years have witnessed a shift towards "a more explicitly visual culture" in which "the availability of an image may determine whether or not a story is run." In this respect, the proliferation of visual surveillance technologies in many countries means that news from the panopticon travels directly to the synopticon. This chimes neatly with the key "professional imperatives" of news reporters who tend to prioritize dramatic and violent crimes through the use of "spectacle" and "graphic imagery." Some of the most iconic images in news reporting in recent years have featured images captured by panoptic visual surveillance systems which are then displayed synoptically to the watching millions. These images include the visual obituaries captured by CCTV cameras of James Bulger being led to his death from a shopping mall, Jill Dando shopping in Hammersmith and Damilola Taylor skipping across a paved square in Peckham. Panoptic-synoptic fusion is also evident in the video recordings of criminal events in process, such as the terrorist bomb explosion in Ealing, or the images of offenders shortly before they commit crimes as in the case of the "7/7 bombers" in London. Other highly mediatized crimes reach the mass media through decisions made by those committing the crimes who aim to achieve maximum synoptic coverage. The attack on the Twin Towers in New York on September 11 provides perhaps the most dramatic example of a crime committed "in a way calculated to achieve the maximum possible media impact" (Reiner 2007: 328). Meanwhile, convicted Oklahoma City bomber, Timothy McVeigh, urged all Americans to watch his execution and victims and relatives were allocated tickets for a CCTV showing.

While the images provided by visual surveillance systems from the panoptic are readily consumed by the synopticon, media representations of surveillance in general are not uniformly supportive of "new surveillance technologies." Critical press coverage has been reported in relation to speed cameras, Electronic Monitoring (EM), and the DNA database (Finn and McCahill 2010). However, this critical discourse in the press does not necessarily undermine the broader ideological impact of media reporting which continues to be presented in a way that reinforces existing social divisions. News reporting on visual surveillance technologies, for example, has revolved around a binary opposition between "Us" and "Them." In short, CCTV cameras that target "Them" (e.g. thieves, robbers, muggers) are good, while speed cameras that monitor "Us" ("law-abiding" motorists) are bad. Similarly, the press coverage on Electronic Monitoring has suggested that "They" ("thugs" and "criminals") are offending with impunity whilst on tag and putting "Us" ("law-abiding citizens") at risk (Finn and McCahill 2010). In their analysis of media representations of "data subjects" in three UK newspapers between 2000 and 2010, Finn and McCahill (2010) also found a clear distinction between "Us" and "Them." In short, they found that "good" data subjects ("innocents on the database," "speeding motorists," "international travellers") were described in "neutral" language and offered advice on "how to avoid surveillance," while "bad" data subjects ("criminals," "yobs," "prostitutes") were described in "emotive" language and not offered any advice on "how to avoid surveillance" (Finn and McCahill 2010).

Crime, surveillance and infotainment

Images captured by "panoptic" surveillance appear not only in the news but also in Reality TV programmes such as *Crimewatch UK*, *Crime Beat*, *Eye Spy*, *Police Camera Action!*, and *World's Wildest Police Videos*. *Crimewatch UK* includes reconstructions of crimes, interviews with police officers and victims, and CCTV footage of suspects designed to encourage the public to telephone and provide the authorities with the details of suspects (Jermyn 2003). Not all social groups of course are equally represented in the images used for "citizen informer" campaigns mainly because "working-class street crimes" take place in public spaces, many of which have CCTV cameras in operation. In many areas in the UK, local newspapers have teamed up with programs like *Crimestoppers* in an attempt to encourage citizen involvement in crime prevention activity. With these developments panoptic-synoptic fusion becomes complete when images captured by panoptic systems are displayed synoptically in local newspapers so that the culprits can be identified, arrested and subject to further panoptic regimes. One local newspaper in the UK had a "Caught on Camera" campaign which between 2000 and 2009 synoptically displayed 278 separate photos from CCTV footage (Finn and McCahill 2010). A trawl through the photos shows that young working-class men dressed in tracksuits and baseball caps are the "face" of CCTV crime prevention (Finn and McCahill 2010). These "citizen informer" campaigns have been rolled out nationally in the UK with the launch of "Internet Eyes" which allows registered on-line viewers to monitor live CCTV footage from commercial systems so that they can notify the authorities "the instant a crime is observed." From January 2011 meanwhile this campaign will go "global" when Internet Eyes is launched in Canada (interneteyes.co.uk).

As Jermyn (2003) points out, "images of victims" in Reality TV shows "fulfil a rather different set of curiosities and cultural uses than those of the criminal" (2003: 175). In her analysis of *Crimewatch UK*, Jermyn says that unlike criminals who are filmed often "unawares in public spaces by an impersonal surveillance camera … pictures of the victims are personal and private, taken from family functions, celebrations, in homes and on holidays" (2003: 181). Here video footage and photographs are used "to underline victims' familial ties" (2003: 175). In fact it would be "difficult to imagine a *Crimewatch* victim outside of the parameters of the family: to not be in the family would be to not be a proper victim" (2003: 185). These representations have broader ideological implications in terms of the construction of "victimhood." To begin with these familiar images of victims at family occasions confirm that they are like "us" ("ordinary" people with families) and not like "them" (criminals). These media representations can also have implications for female victims in general. As Jermyn points out, the literature on "female victims of sexual crime has shown how their place as 'deserving' or 'undeserving' victims is recurrently constructed by the British press in terms of whether or not they adhere to conventional familial structures or not" (2003: 188). These observations are supported by Finn and McCahill (2010) in their media analysis of three UK newspapers including an article in one British newspaper which commented on the CCTV footage that had captured the "last known images" of one of the women murdered in Ipswich. The newspaper refers to the "haunting images" of the woman but then immediately goes on to say that the CCTV footage showed "her preening herself and preparing for the evening ahead as a street walker" (cited in Finn and McCahill

2010: 24). Thus, while some victims who have their final moments captured by "panoptic" surveillance are represented as "typical teenagers" or innocent children "skipping along the pavement," others are referred to as "prostitutes" and presented in negative and stereotypical language (Finn and McCahill 2010).

Media "effects"—surveillance and moral panics

In his paper on the "viewer society," Mathiesen (1997) hints at the likely effects of "synoptic" representations of crime when he says that in mass media reporting on this issue "the material is hurled back into the open society as stereotypes and panic-like, terrifying stories about individual cases" (1997: 231). Mathiesen goes on to suggest that these synoptic representations of crime, which exaggerate potential threats and generate public anxieties, establish the basis for the introduction of further panoptic measures such as "computerized registration and surveillance systems" (1997: 231). The idea that synoptic representations of crime create public anxiety and generate public support for further panoptic measures is nothing new. For instance, media responses to the minor disturbances of spectacular youth subcultures in the late 1960s were quickly followed by decisions to take the fingerprints from juveniles and to publish their names in the local press (Coleman and McCahill 2011: 125). In relation to the introduction of "new surveillance" technologies, similar observations have been made in many countries. For instance, the 1999 Columbine High School tragedy in the United States was immediately followed by the introduction of surveillance cameras and student ID cards in many US schools. Similarly in the UK CCTV images of the abduction of James Bulger in a shopping centre in Liverpool are considered to have provided one of the main catalysts for the introduction of open-street CCTV surveillance cameras during the early 1990s. The images captured by the surveillance cameras in this case did not prevent the death of James Bulger, but as Mathiesen (1997) notes, even when the new "panoptic" measures fail to have any impact on crime, these failures "are taken as a sign that still more resources are needed" (1997: 231).

The fusion of panoptic-synoptic regimes was evident on a global scale following the terrorist attacks of September 11 in the United States. For many writers, the media-induced outrage and panic that followed the events of September 11 facilitated the introduction of further "panoptic" measures (CCTV, biometrics, message interception, data mining, etc.) that previously would not have been regarded as publicly acceptable. In an era of "globalization" media-induced fear campaigns also send messages to those beyond the confines of national borders. Thus, following the events of September 11 and the lead shown by the United States in introducing the USA PATRIOT Act, anti-terror bills were introduced in Indonesia, China, Russia, Pakistan, Jordan, Mauritius, Uganda and Zimbabwe (Coleman and McCahill 2011). For other writers, the events following September 11 have led to the blurring of "fact" and "fiction" as portrayals of "terrorism" on television are said to have shaped public and political discourse. In his analysis of the television series *24*, starring Kiefer Sutherland as counterterrorism agent Jack Bauer, Torin Monahan (2010: 33) explains how the "ticking time bomb" scenario in the television program "was invoked repeatedly in the U.S. presidential primary debates in 2007." He goes on to argue that *24* also "played an active role in reshaping public perceptions and political discourses about terrorism ... especially by normalizing practises of torture" (Monahan 2010: 26). Once again, the new panoptic measures (racial profiling, stop and search, citizen informer campaigns) introduced following synoptic displays of the threat of terrorism have fallen disproportionately on marginalized groups including young Muslim males in the United States and a number of European countries (Coleman and McCahill 2011: 117–19).

Surveillance and policing—the rise of the citizen journalist

One of the key issues in recent publications on surveillance, crime and the media concerns the extent to which the proliferation of "new media" has transformed hierarchies of surveillance by facilitating "bottom-up"

247

scrutiny of powerful actors such as the police. As many media theorists have argued, historically powerful actors like the police came to act as "primary definers" who could use their position of dominance in relation to the media to "patrol the facts." Mathiesen (1997) also worked with a "hegemonic model" of "primary definers" to explain police-media relations arguing that those "who are allowed to enter the media from the outside to express their views" are primarily the "institutional elites" including the police who employ "informational professionals" who "are trained to filter information, and to present images which are favourable to the institution" (1997: 227). However, as a number of highly "mediatized" events from around the world have demonstrated—from Rodney King in Los Angeles in 1991 to the G20 protests in London in 2009—the news is no longer a commodity over which the police enjoy outright ownership. A combination of increased ownership of new technologies, such as video cameras and mobile phones with cameras, along with the emergence of video-sharing platforms like YouTube, have led some to argue that the "viewer society" has been accompanied by the "media producer society" (Goldsmith 2010). These developments potentially have a profound impact on "police image management" because the police can no longer rely on "trusted local news outlets to shape what is reported publicly about them" (Goldsmith 2010: 918). But the rise of the "media producer society" refers not only to the proliferation of new technologies which allow images to be rapidly disseminated. It also involves groups of "professional" and "citizen journalists" using information technologies as part of an explicit strategy designed to hold the "powerful" to account (Goldsmith 2010; Greer and McLaughlin 2010). Examples from around the globe include the Cop Watch program in Vancouver and the Fitwatch program in the UK which was established "to monitor and evade the surveillance activities of police Forward Intelligence Teams (FIT)" (Coleman and McCahill 2011: 152). Meanwhile, video-evidence of police misconduct collected during the 2004 Republican National Convention in New York by the radical collective I-Witness led to 400 cases against protesters being dropped by the prosecution (Greer 2010: 536).

Many of these developments culminated at the G20 protests held in London in 2009 following the death of the newspaper vendor Ian Tomlinson. As Greer and McLaughlin (2010) have shown in their media analysis of the events surrounding Tomlinson's death, the G20 protests were originally organized around a news frame of "protester violence." However, when video footage was handed to the press on 9 April 2009 by an American fund manager providing "clear evidence of police violence against Tomlinson minutes before he collapsed," the news frame of "protester violence" collapsed and was replaced with the theme of "police violence" (Greer and McLaughlin 2010: 1050). The news frame of "police violence" was consolidated the day after Tomlinson's death when video footage began to circulate on video-sharing platforms showing a police officer striking Nicola Fisher on the legs with a baton whilst hiding his police identification number (Greer and McLaughlin 2010: 1052). The importance of "citizen journalism" at the G20 protests cannot be underestimated. Like the Christopher Report conducted in Los Angeles after the Rodney King case, which stated that it was unlikely that a police investigation would have taken place without the existence of the George Holliday videotape, the Inquest stated that the Ian Tomlinson case "could have been swept under the carpet and the cause of his death dismissed as being from 'natural causes' without the benefit of the video footage and photographs that entered the public domain to challenge directly the police version of events" (in Coleman and McCahill 2011: 136).

The events surrounding the G20 protests raised a whole series of questions on public order policing in the UK. Soon afterwards a number of official inquiries were announced and several official reports appeared that were highly critical of the police. These reports raised questions concerning the use of "kettling" (a containment strategy used by the police to control large crowds during political demonstrations), the use of tasers, the concealment of police identification numbers and the deployment of untrained officers (Greer and McLaughlin 2010; Goldsmith 2010). For some this intense critical media scrutiny presents "a direct challenge to previous research findings that the police are superordinate commentators in the 'hierarchy of credibility' and foregrounds the rise of the citizen journalist as a key definitional force in the production of news" (Greer and McLaughlin 2010: 1053). Questions remain however over whether or not these developments are likely to have any lasting impact on the policing of demonstrations and on the extent to which these developments may be said to have transformed "hierarchies of surveillance." Thus, while videotapes of police misconduct may circulate from time to time in the electronic media, generally speaking everyday news reporting and Reality TV continues to portray the police as "crime-fighting" heroes. Thus while the release of images by citizen journalists may generate "periodic legitimacy crises" which opens up the political space for "bottom-up" scrutiny, these cases are often exceptional and may have a limited impact on the reversal of "hierarchies of surveillance" (Coleman and McCahill 2011: 180).

These developments however need situating in a wider political context. As Greer and McLaughlin (2010: 1041) point out, the rise of the "citizen journalist" is driven not only by the availability of new technologies which allow "bottom-up" scrutiny of the powerful; instead these developments are partly a product of the current "information-communications marketplace that sustains the commodification and mass consumption of adversarial, anti-establishment news" (Greer and McLaughlin 2010: 1041). But even in a climate of escalating "news media adversarialism" (Greer and McLaughlin 2010: 1055), there are still structural limitations to counter-surveillance. For instance, there have been many reports in recent years of the police using the powers enshrined in new "anti-terror" laws to confiscate the video-recorders and mobile phones of "citizen journalists" (Coleman and McCahill 2011: 165; Goldsmith 2010: 929). Also, the everyday capture and storage of data does not necessarily lead to authoritative interventions against the perpetrators of police violence. As Monahan (2010: 140) has argued, while the beating of Rodney King in Los Angeles was captured on video camera and then displayed synoptically to the watching millions, this "did not necessarily catalyze correctives to actions of police brutality, nor did it motivate greater police engagement with urban communities." Similarly, despite 296 complaints about police behavior during the G20 in London (with similar difficulties at G20 in Toronto) there have been no successful prosecutions at the time of writing.

Conclusion

Media representations play an important role in shaping public perceptions of crime and the subsequent response to crime by the authorities. The use of images from panoptic surveillance in the news media provides the "spectacle" and "graphic imagery" beloved of news journalists and leads to an over emphasis on crimes such as robbery, murder and terrorism and an under emphasis on other "serious" harms that result, for instance, from workplace injury, corporate crime or domestic violence (Coleman and McCahill 2011). In this respect, the inclusion of "surveillance" into the "crime-media" equation reinforces long-established trends where the vast majority of research has shown that the media focus disproportionately on interpersonal, violent and sexual crimes and under emphasize white-collar crime and non-violent crime (Reiner 2007). These media representations in turn generate support for the introduction of further panoptic surveillance and the fusion of panoptic-synoptic surveillance becomes complete when these panoptic regimes are used to disproportionately target marginalized populations, reinforcing existing divisions along the lines of age, gender, ethnicity and class.

One potential criticism of this view of panoptic-synoptic fusion centers on how "media effects" are often assumed by media researchers rather than explored empirically (Greer 2010). In this respect it would be useful for "surveillance studies" scholars to explore a number of issues which to date have received very little attention. For instance, empirical research could examine the audience reception of synoptic representations of "crime" and "surveillance." Because "new surveillance" technologies operate discreetly, often in a covert fashion, it is very likely that public perceptions of panoptic surveillance will be shaped by the synoptic representations of these technologies that they have witnessed through the mass media. We also know very little about how those on the receiving end of panoptic-synoptic regimes experience and respond to surveillance. As we have seen in this chapter, images from "panoptic" surveillance displayed on "Reality TV" shows and in newspapers are often dominated by images of young working-class males who have become the "face" of CCTV (Finn and McCahill 2010). However, these individuals are "mute witnesses" whose stories have yet to be heard (Jermyn 2003: 176). The "democratizing" impact of "citizen journalism" also requires further research. For instance, some have spoken of the "new visibility" of policing whereby "the capacity to photograph and film" the police has become "widely available in the hands of ordinary people" (Goldsmith 2010: 919). These arguments are clearly important but require some qualification and critical scrutiny. As the events surrounding the G20 protests demonstrated, a crucial factor in the increase in police visibility was the capacity not only to take pictures on mobile phones with cameras, but also to disseminate images rapidly via video-sharing platforms. But as research in the UK has shown, access to video-sharing platforms and social-networking sites is not equally distributed throughout the population. The persistence of a "digital divide" in the UK means that up to "thirty per cent of the population" do not have "internet access in the home" (Chadwick and Stanyer 2010: 12). This means that "those that take advantage of new technologies … remain a minority and still tend to be wealthy, well educated and younger" (Chadwick and Stanyer 2010: 37). Thus while journalists can now access stories and images circulating on the internet, it could be argued that the democratizing potential of these developments is limited because this information has been placed there by relatively privileged social groups who have the "economic" and "cultural" capital required to use the "new media" of the "post-broadcasting age."

References

Chadwick, A. and Stanyer, J. (2010). "Political Communication in Transition: Mediated Politics in New Media Environment," paper delivered at the American Political Science Association Annual Meeting, Washington, DC, September 2–5, 2010.

Coleman, R. and McCahill, M. (2011). *Surveillance and Crime*, London: Sage.

Finn, R. and McCahill, M. (2010). "Representing the Surveilled: Media Representation and Political Discourse in Three UK Newspapers," paper presented at 60th Political Studies Association Annual Conference, Edinburgh, 29 March–1 April 2010.

Goldsmith, A. J. (2010). "Policing's New Visibility," *British Journal of Criminology*, 50: 914–34.

Greer, C. (2010). *Crime and Media: A Reader*, London: Routledge.

Greer, C. and McLaughlin, E. (2010). "We Predict a Riot?: Public Order Policing, New Media Environments and the Rise of the Citizen Journalist," *British Journal of Criminology*, 50: 1041–59.

Jermyn, D. (2003). "Photo Stories and Family Albums: Imaging Criminals and Victims on *Crimewatch UK*," in P. Mason. (ed.) *Criminal Visions: Media Representations of Crime and Justice*, Cullompton: Willan Publishing.

Mathiesen, T. (1997). "The Viewer Society: Michel Foucault's 'Panopticon' Revisited," *Theoretical Criminology*, 1: 215–34.

Monahan, T. (2010). *Surveillance in the Time of Insecurity*, New Brunswick, NJ: Rutgers University Press.

Reiner, R. (2007). "Media Made Criminality: The Representation of Crime in the Mass Media," in M. Maguire, R. Moran and R. Reiner, (eds), *The Oxford Handbook of Criminology*, (4th edition), Oxford: Clarendon Press.

c. The success of failure

Accounting for the global growth of CCTV

Clive Norris

In 1999 in an article entitled "The eyes have it: CCTV as the 'fifth utility'," Stephen Graham predicted that the development of CCTV was likely to mirror that of the major public utilities of water, gas, electricity and telecommunications that had emerged during the nineteenth century. The rapid rise of the traditional utilities was fuelled by demands for improved public health through the provision of clean water and reliable sewage management and of lighting in both city streets and the domestic home, and the commercial advantages and instantaneous communications afforded by the telephone and telegraph. In the nineteenth century, once the utilities were in place in one town or suburb, neighboring areas, fuelled by civic pride or the need for competitive advantage, soon followed suit. However economies of scale dictated that the initial plethora of local providers rapidly combined, through merger and takeover, to provide city wide, regional and even national coverage.

In the late twentieth century, the demand for CCTV was primarily fuelled by fears of rising crime and public safety, made particularly acute in the UK by the public outrage over the tragic abduction and killing of a two–year-old toddler by two ten–year-old old boys. On the basis of the initial, but rapid, development of a patchwork of local CCTV systems and the media-fuelled clamor for such systems, Graham speculated that, within 20 years, CCTV coverage would be ubiquitous and approaching universality. It was unlikely, he argued, that there would be a single centrally controlled monolithic system but, as pressure mounted to provide more universal coverage, there would be a push towards sharing images from smaller systems with larger configurations, enabling the monitoring of a wider area from one central location. Economies of scale would dictate that the expensive task of building, managing and staffing control rooms would lead to progressive delocalization and the growth of large-scale centralized control rooms.

Futurology is a notoriously unreliable science, but Graham's prediction has proved surprisingly accurate, as a brief review of the development of CCTV in the UK will show. In the UK, the use of CCTV for a variety of crime prevention purposes emerged gradually throughout the 1960s and 1970s. These systems were introduced piecemeal and largely confined to public transport and the retail sector, where CCTV was seen as useful in deterring and apprehending shoplifters. It was not until 1985, however, that CCTV was permanently deployed to monitor public space. The system was introduced in Bournemouth, a seaside town on the south coast of England, ostensibly to counter vandalism on the sea-front, but was given added impetus by the presence of the Conservative Party Annual Conference which, the previous year, had suffered a massive explosion caused by an Irish Republican Army bomb, very nearly killing the Prime Minister. Over the next two decades the twin concerns of crime control and anti-terrorism provided the primary rationale for a massive investment of public funds first in the UK and then around the world.

In what follows we will outline the exponential global growth of CCTV. We will then review the evidence of evaluations from around the world as to its effectiveness in preventing and detecting crime and reducing fear of crime. Finally, we will explore the reasons for the apparent failure of CCTV and why this has not undermined its continued, world wide, appeal.

The first major impetus for a government-backed expansion of CCTV in the UK came in 1993 when two ten-year-old boys were caught on CCTV in a shopping mall abducting a toddler whom they subsequently killed. Amidst high levels of public anxiety about rising crime, CCTV was placed in the national spotlight and, in reaction, the government announced a "City Challenge Competition" to allocate £2 million of central government money for open street CCTV. A total of 480 bids were received and 106 schemes funded from an increased allocation of £5 million. The competition was repeated between 1995 and 1998 and in total they secured £85 million for the capital funding of 580 CCTV systems. In 1999, the new Labour administration, as part of its ambitious crime reduction program, set aside £153 million to support the expansion of CCTV. The two rounds of the competition received 1,550 bids and around 450 of these were funded (Norris et al. 2004).

There was also substantial government investment in the CCTV surveillance of schools, hospitals and transport facilities, and it has been estimated that, by 2005, over £500 million of central and local government funds had been allocated to CCTV. In addition, during the same period, it was estimated that around £4.5 billion of private funds were spent on the installation of CCTV and maintenance of CCTV systems in the UK, and this excludes the monitoring costs associated with these systems (Norris et al. 2004).

How many cameras or systems this translates to is impossible to measure accurately, although in 1999 it was estimated that in the UK in an urban environment, on a busy day, a person could have their image captured by over 300 cameras on thirty separate CCTV systems. Norris and McCahill "guestimated," on the basis of a survey in one London borough, that there may be as many as 4.2 million publicly and privately operated cameras in the UK or one for every 14 of the population (Norris et al. 2004), although more recent and, possibly, more reliable estimates suggest the figure may be only 1.85 million cameras, a figure that still equates to one camera for every 32 citizens (*The Guardian* 2/3/2011).

What is incontestable is that, during the course of the last two decades, CCTV has become a "normalized" feature of British urban life. Within urban areas, CCTV has become ubiquitous, and not just on city streets. It is now routinely found in parks, commons and cemeteries; on buses, trains and taxis; on the roads and at sea or at airports; in restaurants, bars and cafes; in kindergartens, schools and universities; in factories, offices and warehouses; in hospitals, health centers and maternity clinics. Citizens of urban Britain are watched over from cradle to grave.

Although the depth and breadth of CCTV surveillance is unique to Britain, a similar development is emerging worldwide, albeit at different rates in different counties. In countries where strong privacy and data protection regimes have prevailed, such as Denmark or Canada, this has, at times, enabled resistance. In Germany where the state was captured by the totalitarian regime of the German National Socialist party, there has been a public mistrust of the state's power to surveil its citizens, recognized by constitutional protection, and this has limited the diffusion of CCTV. Similarly in Norway, occupied by Germany during the Second World War, and displaying a strong data protection regime, there are few cameras. In the UK, the lack of a legal right to privacy, a weak data protection regime, and the absence of constitutional protection were all important in allowing the rapid rise of CCTV in the 1990s but the most significant factor was the provision of hundreds of millions of pounds of central government money to develop the infrastructure of local schemes, a pattern which is being repeated in other countries (Hempel and Toepfer 2004).

The 2003 UrbanEye survey (Hempel and Toepfer 2004) of six European capital cities showed just how unusual the UK was at the time. Denmark and Austria had no open street systems, there was only one in Norway (consisting of six cameras), 14 systems in Budapest and 15 in Germany. In the UK there were already over 500 systems. But in other European countries not included in the UrbanEye survey, there was also sustained growth in open street CCTV before 2004. In France, after a central government initiative, by 1999 more than 200 French towns planned to install CCTV in high-risk locations. Similarly, in the Netherlands between 1997 and 2003 more than 80 of the country's 550 municipalities were using CCTV in public places (Norris *et al.* 2004). In the Republic of Ireland, the first CCTV system was installed in Dublin in the mid 1990s and expanded in 1997. In 2004, the government announced funding to extend CCTV to 21 different areas. In Italy, in response to public anxiety about rising crime, the Ministry of the Interior announced plans to install CCTV in 50 Italian cities (Norris 2011).

The terrorist attacks of 9/11 on the twin towers in New York and the subsequent "War on Terror" gave a massive funding impetus for the introduction of CCTV around the globe and this was further boosted by the Madrid and London terrorist bombings in 2004 and 2005. Since then, there has been a major expansion of CCTV deployed to monitor critical infrastructures, particularly airports, railways, metro systems and power stations. The "War on Terror" has also provided the context for the massive expansion of open street surveillance of the general population.

By 2007, France planned to increase its estimated 340,000 CCTV cameras threefold, Germany had doubled the number of cities with CCTV from 15 to 30, the Republic of Ireland had increased the number of cities with CCTV system from 21 to 49 and the Polish capital of Warsaw had introduced a major city wide system with 515 cameras (Hempel and Toepfer 2004). By 2008, despite the long-standing reluctance to embrace public area CCTV in Nordic countries, Finland and Denmark both announced open street schemes for their capital cities. By 2009, Austria, Belgium, Bulgaria, Croatia, the Czech Republic, Denmark, Finland, France, Germany, Greece, Hungary, Ireland, Italy, Lithuania, Netherlands, Norway, Poland, Portugal, Spain, Sweden, Switzerland and the UK all boasted CCTV systems operating in public space for the purposes of crime prevention (Norris 2011).

Outside of Europe, a similar pattern emerges. In the USA, the first national survey of CCTV carried out in 1997 found only 13 police departments using CCTV to monitor public space and by 2001 this had increased to 25. However, since 2001 and the terrorist attack on the World Trade Centre, billions of dollars of federal money have become available for domestic security projects and this has fuelled a massive expansion of public area CCTV. Major cities such as Baltimore, Chicago, New Orleans, Philadelphia, San Francisco and Washington DC have now installed extensive systems. Chicago boasts an integrated network of around 15,000 cameras, linked to a $43 million operations centre. In California alone, 37 out of 131 jurisdictions now operate public space video surveillance programs. In Canada, in 2009, the SCAN study reported that 30 cities had installed, or were considering installing, public space CCTV systems. Similarly, in Australia, it was reported that over 30 mainland cities had installed public area CCTV systems (Norris 2011).

There are no systematic surveys of the deployment of CCTV in Africa, Asia or South America, however the inter-continental spread of CCTV can be gleaned by a brief look at some of the capital cities around the world. In Asia, the Japanese capital of Tokyo has experienced a rapid expansion over the last decade, with CCTV being deployed on the transit system and extensively at the neighborhood level. The Chinese capital, Beijing, was reported to have 263,000 surveillance cameras by 2006, and was planning a massive expansion in preparation for the 2008 Olympic Games. In contrast, Delhi, the capital city of India, has only a limited police-operated CCTV network consisting of several hundred cameras (Norris 2011).

On the African sub-continent, in 2009, Kenya launched a scheme to cover the central business district of Nairobi. In Lagos, the capital city of Nigeria and one of the largest cities in the world with a population of 18 million people, there are plans to install 10,000 solar-powered CCTV cameras as part of the Lagos Safe City Project. In the Middle East, Tehran, the capital of Iran, has an extensive network of police-controlled CCTV (Norris, Wood and McCahill 2004). More recently in the capital city of Saudi Arabia, Riyadh, CCTV has become a routine feature of the urban landscape, being deployed in shopping malls, on the railways and as part of the traffic management system. In South America, Rio de Janeiro, the capital of Brazil, and host to the football World Cup in 2014 and Olympic Games in 2016, is set to see a major expansion of its CCTV network in 26 city districts, with over US$ 500 million set aside for developing security in the run-up to the Games (Norris 2011).

Public space CCTV is now truly a global phenomenon. In less than two decades, it has expanded from a local initiative in a few small towns in the UK to become the international crime prevention "success" story of the new Millennium, set to penetrate every major city, in every country, on every continent. Just as Graham predicted, like electricity and gas, it appears that video-surveillance will become a central part of the global urban infrastructure across the planet. But how can we explain this? Such a rapid and universal take up would suggest that the benefits in preventing and detecting crime and promoting public safety and security (the main justifications given for its deployment in any setting) are unequivocal. Let us review the evidence.

The evaluation of CCTV

In Britain, in the early 1990s, the mass expansion of state-funded CCTV occurred before any systematic evaluation as to its effectiveness for preventing and detecting crime was carried out. The absence of evaluation seems not to be just a British malady. In the USA and Australia, for example, the massive expansion of CCTV post 9/11 was conducted without any local evidence to suggest that it would be effective in either reducing crime or preventing terrorism.

The reduction of crime

In the absence of systematic evaluation in the UK before widespread public funding was made available for CCTV, politicians relied on the self-interested claims of practitioners and system promoters to justify its crime-reduction potential. While a number of small-scale evaluations had been conducted during the 1990s, the results of these studies came up with mixed and often contradictory findings (Norris *et al.* 2004).

A similar pattern emerges when we review the more recent evaluations from around the world. In Los Angeles the evaluators reported that neither camera systems they studied had "any significant effect in reducing violent or property crime rates within the target areas" (Cameron *et al.* 2008: 29). Studies in Philadelphia and San Francisco both found an overall 13 percent reduction in crime but this was largely made up of a reduction in less serious disorder or property crime. For serious or violent crime, neither study found evidence that cameras had an impact[1] (Ratcliffe and Taniguchi 2008: 12).

An evaluation funded by the Australian Research Council on the impact of CCTV in two Gold Coast suburbs and the Queensland City Train Network concluded that overall:

> The effectiveness of CCTV as a crime prevention measure is questionable. From this research it appears CCTV is effective at detecting violent crime and/or may result in increased reporting as opposed to preventing any type of crime.
>
> *(Wells* et al. *2006: iii)*

The UK Home Office-funded evaluation of 14 CCTV systems, one of the largest and most systematic ever conducted, found:

> That the CCTV schemes that have been assessed had little overall effect on crime levels. Even where changes have been noted, with the exception of those relating to car parks, very few are larger than could have been due to chance alone and all could in fact represent either a chance variation or confounding factors.
>
> *(Gill and Spriggs 2005: 43)*

The findings of individual evaluation studies have, over the last decade, been systematically reviewed by a number of researchers for and on behalf of national or regional government agencies. In particular, Welsh and Farrington (2007) conducted a meta-evaluation of 44 worldwide evaluations and concluded:

The results suggest that CCTV caused a small (16%) but significant decrease in crime in experimental areas compared with controlled areas. However, this overall result was largely driven by the effectiveness of CCTV schemes in car parks, which caused a 51% decrease in crime. Schemes in most other settings had small and non-significant effects on crime: a 7% decrease in city and town centers and in public housing.

(2007: 8)

Similarly, in 2008 Cameron *et al.,* using a similar methodology, and drawing on a slightly different selection of studies reported:

Of the 44 evaluations included in our analysis, 43% reported the cameras had no or an uncertain effect on reducing crime, 41% reported statistically significant reduction in crime, and 15.9% reported some undesirable effect ... Within the 19 evaluations that found no statistically significant effect on crime or were uncertain as to CCTV's effect, 36.8% (7) reported a reduction in crime, 52.6% (10) reported an increase in crime, and 10.5% (2) reported no change or a very small change in crime.

(2008: 4)

Apart from in the limited domain of car parks the best available evidence suggests that CCTV is at best an unproven technology for reducing crime and at worst an ineffective and costly distraction from finding more suitable strategies.

Detecting crime and gathering evidence

There has been little systematic evidence as to the effectiveness of CCTV in helping increase detection rates. However, limited evidence can be derived from various studies. In their Australian evaluation, Wells *et al.* found that, in the course of 100 hours of observation of the control rooms, 181 incidents were surveiled by the camera operators, which led to 51 arrests. However, as they go on to note, only seven of the 51 arrests could be directly attributed to the cameras (Wells *et al.* 2006: ii). In the San Francisco evaluation, the system had assisted the police department in charging a suspect with a crime in six cases.[2] In the UK, a senior Metropolitan Police Officer revealed that CCTV had only contributed evidence in 3 percent of street robberies (*The Guardian* 6/5/2008).

CCTV and fear of crime

It is often claimed that, regardless of its preventative effect or contribution to criminal arrest and prosecution, the presence of CCTV provides reassurance to the public and makes people less fearful about becoming a victim of crime, and attitude surveys have shown that people report that they would feel safer if CCTV were installed. However, while the public believes that, in general, people will feel safer when the cameras are introduced, when people are asked whether it will make them personally feel safer, far fewer think it would. It has also been found that knowledge of the camera watching over them had no effect on respondents' levels of fear of crime, seemingly repudiating the idea that CCTV can be justified as a measure to reduce the fear of crime.

The 2005 British Home Office evaluation reported:

CCTV was found to have played no part in reducing fear of crime; indeed those who were aware of the cameras admitted higher levels of fear than those who were unaware of them.

(Gill and Spriggs 2005:60)

255

This finding is supported by studies that have attempted to explore people's behavior rather than just their attitudes. These show that CCTV has a limited impact in getting people to use their town centers and high streets more. As the Home Office 2005 evaluation found:

> On the whole, these findings suggest that there is no connection between worries about being a victim of crime and avoidance behaviour. They also indicate that respondents believed CCTV would have an impact on their avoidance behaviour (encouraging them to visit places they previously avoided) but in practice this rarely occurred.
>
> *(2005: 54–55)*

The problem of the rational offender

Regardless of the empirical evidence above, perhaps the continued belief in the efficacy of CCTV is due to our common-sense understanding of the role of cameras in promoting deterrence and detection. Advocates of CCTV generally argue that CCTV will reduce crime because it provides a visible deterrent to crime. This speaks easily to our common sense. If we are tempted to offend we will be less likely to do so if we think we will get caught. There are four fallacious assumptions here.

First it assumes that we are aware of the presence of the cameras and we believe them to be looking at us. Early evaluations of CCTV in the UK and Germany found that up to 60 per cent of people in city centers that had installed CCTV were unaware of its presence. Second, it assumes that, even if the offender is aware of the cameras, they have factored them in to a rational calculation. Much criminal behavior, however, is sub-rational, committed by those who have been drinking or taking drugs, which we know will seriously impair their judgment. Third, advocates downplay the issue of displacement, suggesting that, while the rational offender is deterred, the same offender appears not rational enough merely to commit the crime in a different place, or choose to commit a different type of crime less susceptible to camera surveillance. Finally, it assumes that, if the offender is aware of the cameras, they will be deterred, but this appears not to be the case. Research with street robbers, burglars, shop thieves and card fraudsters has revealed that few indicated that the presence of cameras made any difference as to whether they would commit a crime or not (Gill and Loveday 2003).

The problem of the all-seeing eye

The presence of CCTV cameras in an area does not guarantee that the incident will be captured by the CCTV system. It is highly contingent on the interaction of the technical, organizational and environmental features of the system. Even if an incident is seen by the cameras, this does not guarantee it will be noticed by the operatives and, if it is noticed, that a deployment will result. Nor does deployment mean that the officers will be able to locate the suspect when they arrive.

If the officers fail to find someone at the scene, the system should, it might be assumed, have captured evidence of the crime being committed and recorded images of the offenders so that they can be identified at a later time. However, whether a criminal incident that is captured on CCTV results in a crime being detected and an offender arrested and successfully prosecuted relies on much more than just the presence of cameras. It requires, for example, the cameras to be serviced and working properly, to have not become obstructed by foliage and to be capable of operating in different lighting conditions, from bright sunlight to the dark of the night. This, in turn, will be contingent upon a set of political decisions about funding which determined the quality and capacity of the cameras that were installed and the extent of funds set aside to perform routine maintenance.

Even where the cameras are working and do focus on a crime taking place, this does not guarantee it will be noticed by an operative. The costs of monitoring systems with dedicated CCTV operatives, twenty-four hours a day, is extremely expensive, and a luxury few systems can actually afford. It cannot be assumed that the images are being monitored. The typical situation in European countries reported in the UrbanEye study was that: "Monitoring of images occurs only on an irregular basis by one observer who often has to fulfill other parallel tasks" (Hempel and Toepfer 2004:7). Operatives often have tasks other than merely monitoring the screens, such as changing tapes and filling in logbooks, all of which distract their eyes from the monitors. But in large-scale systems with multiple camera feeds, the problem is one of information overload. Since not all images can be displayed on the bank of monitors, they have to be shown in sequence or the feeds from particular cameras given priority.

If it is not possible for each camera to be monitored, it has also not proved possible, in analogue systems, for all the images to be continuously recorded. The sheer volume of tape required to capture the images of, for example, a 40-camera system recording in real time, in full quality would be overwhelming. If each camera were connected to a video recorder using three-hour tapes this would generate 6,000 tapes per month and would require a team of operatives just to manage the video recorders. The solution has typically been to "multiplex" the monitoring and recording so that images from four or more cameras are displayed on each screen and captured on a single tape. However, it still requires the tapes to be changed every three hours. To overcome this, time-lapse recording is often used, whereby not every frame of video stream is recorded. In a five-camera system the picture rate would be updated every 0.2 seconds rather than 25 times per second. What this means is that 80 percent of the information (images) from each camera is lost. Multiplexing and time-lapsing substantially reduce the number of tapes required, but at a considerable cost in terms of their value as evidence. It means that crucial frames, clearly identifying a person's face or the crime taking place, are missing. While it is certainly true that, at times, the cameras and recorders do capture the perfect image for use in identification and evidence, it still requires someone to identify the suspect and, while a few of the most notorious and serious cases may generate national media attention, the vast majority of images remain unidentified. It is also true that, in major cases, CCTV footage can provide the vital evidence. But locating the footage from the hundreds of cameras in an area, on separate and often incompatible systems can, in itself, be a major police operation, taking hundreds of officers to locate, log and review the evidence.

Conclusion

If CCTV has been such a failure why has it become such a globally widespread phenomenon? We can highlight three primary reasons. First, over the last four decades there has been a general disillusionment with the ability of governments and their criminal justice systems to respond to crime. In particular, traditional methods of policing, punishment and rehabilitation were largely seen to have failed. Crime has continued to rise, and even where crime rates fell, the intensity of sensationalist media reporting about crime meant that the public still believed crime to be rising (see also McCahill, Taylor, this volume). Add to this the worldwide specter of terrorist attacks, induced by the destruction of the twin towers on 9/11 and subsequent bombings in Europe and Asia, which mean that governments believe that they must be seen to be doing something. CCTV may not be a solution to the problem of crime or terrorism but it is a solution to the problem of governments being seen to do something about the problem of crime and terrorism. The fact that suicide bombers are not deterred, and may even be spurred on, by the presence of cameras is then beside the point.

Second, where CCTV is funded by local police budgets, there has tended to be reluctance for the widespread introduction of CCTV. In general, police officers are only too aware that CCTV is not a panacea to the crime problem. Only when central governments facilitate its introduction, through the provision of generous capital grants, do we see widespread up-take. The Al-Qaeda terrorist threat has provided the impetus for governments to provide these funds, but so have other sensational crimes, such as brutal child murders, which periodically occur in all countries and lead to a sustained outcry that "something must be done." And why would a municipality or police force *not* want to have CCTV if someone else is paying for it?

Third, CCTV represents much more than just the ability to prevent and detect crime. It is about the power to watch, to deploy, to intervene, to identify and to regulate, often through exclusion. It is a mistake to view policing, either public or private, as primarily about law enforcement and crime control. It concerns the reproduction of order. It is essentially conservative and focused on the maintenance of the status quo. The status quo always serves dominant interests: the old over the young, the rich over the poor, the indigenous over the immigrant, the commercial over the citizenry. As numerous studies of CCTV control rooms have found, the primary target of CCTV is the young male, often from an ethnic minority, displaying the visible symbols of working-class or youth subculture who, through passivity or activity, is deemed out of place in the consumption-orientated high streets and malls of the global urban landscape.

Notes

1 King, J., Mulligan, D. and Raphael, S. (2008). *Citris Report: The San Francisco Community Safety Camera Program*, California: Berkeley School of Law, available at www.citris-uc.org/files/CITRIS%20SF%20CSC%20Study%20Final%20Dec%202008.pdf.
2 Ibid.: p. 13.

References

Cameron, A., Kolodinski, E., May, H. and Williams, N. (2008). *Measuring the Effects of Video Surveillance on Crime in Los Angeles*, Prepared for the Californian Research Bureau, University of Southern California: School of Policy Planning and Development.

Gill, M. and Loveday, M. (2003). "What do Offenders Think About CCTV?" in M. Gill (ed.), *CCTV*, Leicester: Perpetuity Press.

Gill, M. and Spriggs, A. (2005). *Assessing the Impact of CCTV*, London: Home Office Research, Development and Statistics Directorate.

Graham, S. (1999). "The Eyes Have It: CCTV as the 'Fifth utility'," *Environment and Planning B: Planning and Design*, 26(5): 639–42.

Hempel, L. and Toepfer, E. (2004). *Urban Eye: Final Report to the European Commission, 5th Framework Programme*, Berlin: Technical University of Berlin, available at www.urbaneye.net/results/ue_wp15.pdf.

Norris C. (2011). There's No Success like Failure and Failure's No Success at all: Some Critical Reflections on Understanding the Global Growth of CCTV Surveillance," in A. Doyle, R. Lippert, and D. Lyon (eds), *Eyes Everywhere: The Global Growth of Camera Surveillance*, London: Routledge.

Norris, C., Wood, D. and McCahill, M. (2004). "The Growth of CCTV: A Global Perspective on the International Diffusion of Video Surveillance in Publicly Accessible Space," *Surveillance & Society*, 2(2/3): 110–35.

Ratcliffe, J. and Taniguchi, T. (2008). *CCTV Camera Evaluation: The Crime Reduction Effects of Public CCTV Cameras in the City of Philadelphia, PA Installed during 2006*, Philadelphia, PA: Temple University.

Wells, H., Allard, T. and Wilson P. (2006). *Crime and CCTV in Australia: Understanding the Relationship*, Centre for Applied Psychology and Criminology, Australia: Bond University.

Welsh, B. and Farrington, D. (2007). *Closed Circuit Television Surveillance and Crime Prevention: A Systematic Review*, Report prepared for the Swedish National Council for Crime Prevention, Stockholm: Swedish Council for Crime Prevention.

d. Surveillance and urban violence in Latin America

Mega-cities, social division, security and surveillance

Nelson Arteaga Botello

In Latin America, the increased presence of electronic surveillance devices in urban space is underpinned by "zero tolerance" public security policies introduced in the last ten years. The goal of such policies has been to reduce the incidence of crime and violence in the mega-cities of the region, and to reduce feelings of insecurity in large sections of the population. The most commonly used surveillance techniques include video surveillance in public and private spaces and national biometric identity card schemes. This has had a profound impact upon the configuration of cities in Latin America, in that an urban logic has developed which distinguishes between supposed "secured" and "dangerous" spaces.

In "secure zones" distinct surveillance devices are used which control access to and movement around residential areas, corporate buildings, public offices, banks, commercial centers, financial districts and avenues or streets that have high levels of movement of people, automobiles and merchandise. Surveillance in these spaces is not only directed toward guaranteeing security, but also towards enabling the population to feel "protected." Outside these "secure zones" are spaces where high levels of marginalization and poverty occur together with high rates of violent crime and with inter-family violence. They are places where racism and police violence mark everyday life, spaces in which electronic surveillance devices are scarce if not non-existent. Cities become differentiated according to whether they are hyper-surveiled or infra-surveiled urban spaces.

Although these phenomena are also seen in Global-Northern cities, the Latin American context, particularly when its public security policies are considered, is significant. The development of "zero tolerance" security policies coincided with a rise of inequality and urban poverty. The latter, in particular, has been identified as a possible outcome of the policies of free political change which happened in the 1990s, and processes of "democratic transition" which occurred at the same time. Electronic surveillance devices in Latin America have thus been introduced under "zero tolerance" public security policies in a context of inequality and poverty, are maintained by democratically weak institutions, and occasionally reflect the practices of previously authoritarian governance regimes. This chapter has two objectives. First, to describe the principal axes which configure this scenario and second, to develop a framework of reference for the analysis of surveillance in the Global South in general, and in Latin America in particular.

The chapter proceeds as follows. First the characteristics of urban violence and the conditions of social exclusion in cities are discussed. Then, the logic of the security policies which have been established to counter such violence is described, which generally tends to see the excluded, marginalized or poor as potential delinquents. Subsequently, it will be shown how surveillance develops as part of this security policy dynamic. Such development is not limited to the installation of electronic devices; it reflects logics of governance and of social organization. Finally, a reflection on the implications of the security logic and surveillance in the social context of Latin America will be presented. Latin America is a diverse region, and even when the countries that are part of it share a similar history and similar societies, each one of them also has unique social and economic dynamics and social structures (Cardoso 2010). In this sense, this chapter shows the general tendencies of surveillance, inequality and security in Latin America. As surveillance emerges as a feature of modern social organization its everyday impact will vary according to how political and social governance is enacted in different regions and countries of the world.

Urban violence and social exclusion

Towards the end of the 1980s Latin America experienced a significant increase in criminal violence, notably between 1990 and 1995, when 60 percent of its population had been victimized by some type of criminal offence. For example, the Ministry of Justice, Security and Human Rights, Argentina, reports that the number of offenders doubled between 1990 and 1999, while the rate of delinquent acts for each 10,000 inhabitants in 2004 reached 343.0, and 332.0 in 2005. The United Nations Office on Drugs and Crime, Division for Policy Analysis and Public Affairs states that in Mexico, the crime rate totaled 1,000 crimes per 100,000 inhabitants in 1990 and reached 2,500 crimes per 100,000 inhabitants in 1998; the crime rate per 100,000 inhabitants increased to 1,391.5 in 2000. It also states that in Guatemala criminal offences rose almost 100% percent between 1995 and 1998, reaching 239.63 recorded crimes per 100,000 inhabitants in the year 2000. In Nicaragua, crime against people and property doubled between 1992 and 1996. In 2005 the perception of crime levels (an indicator which measures fear of crime and insecurity, and the modification of personal habits to protect oneself) in Latin American countries increased to 82.68 percent. During the same year the Inter-American Development Bank points out that this indicator rose to 84.75 percent in Argentina; in Mexico, it reached 77.76 percent; and in Nicaragua it reached 92.49 percent.

Even in Central American countries, which lived in a state of armed conflict during the Cold War, recent death rates caused by criminal activity are higher than during periods of armed conflict. It is significant that during 2006 the main cause of death in El Salvador was "aggression with the firing of another weapon," causing a total of 2,793 deaths. In this region the patterns of violence preceding internal conflicts have multiplied due to drugs and arms trafficking, youth gangs, kidnappings, money laundering and homicide. In Central America, according to the Geneva Declaration Secretariat, in 2004 the homicide rate rose to 20 per 100,000 people, 77 percent of these offences being committed with firearms. In this region of America, until 2005, the most violent countries were as follows: El Salvador with 3,778 homicides, 11.5 per 100,000; Guatemala, with 5,338 homicides, 8.0 per 100,000; Honduras, with 2,417 homicides, 5.0 per 100,000; and Nicaragua, with 729 homicides, 2.2 per 100,000.

Towards the middle of the 1990s, when criminal violence in the region had reached its peak, the homicide rate reached 28.4 per 100,000 people, second only to Sub-Saharan Africa, which reached a rate of 40.1. For 2004, the rate for Central and South America varied between 25 and 30 homicides per 100,000 people, while in South Africa, the rate reached close to 35 (Geneva Declaration Secretariat 2008). Accordingly, the five countries of Latin America with the highest rates of homicide are Colombia, Venezuela, Bolivia, Ecuador and Brazil; the three with the lowest rates of homicide are Chile, Peru and Panama. The data on victimization are only a sample of the increased levels of criminal violence and offer—in a majority of cases—valuable information that could allow a reduction in these high levels of criminality. According to the most recent data from the region, all Latin American countries showed rates of victimization above 20 percent, a majority above 30 percent and 40 percent, and five of those between 40 percent and 60 percent: Guatemala, El Salvador, Venezuela, Mexico and Ecuador. As indicated by the report of Latinobarómetro of 2008, the rate of victimization in the region is 33 percent.

This significant increase in criminal acts coincides with the economic changes which have occurred since economic policy was reoriented toward trade liberalization, especially since the 1980s. This ended a period of economic growth in the region brought about by "import substitution industrialization," established shortly after the Second World War. The subsequent economic crises of the 1980s and 1990s, brought about to a large extent by policies of economic adjustment, produced a corresponding increase in inequality and poverty. This can be clearly observed in Latin American urban spaces.

Some data indicate that 65 percent of the total poor population in Latin America inhabit urban zones. In fact, it is estimated that 50 million people are living in extreme poverty in these areas. Davis (2006), in a worldwide study of marginal urban populations, shows that the five largest centers of extreme poverty are located in Latin America (Mexico City, Caracas, Bogota, Rio de Janeiro, and Lima). In a majority of the cities, armed violence—as perpetrated for example, by armed groups and gangs—has occurred where political institutions and public security providers suffer from weak governance, where alternative forms of political authority and security delivery are in abundance, where there is a sense of social crisis or malaise, macroeconomic distortions, political disorder and inequity, and where the urban population is growing.

As Wacquant (2008) points out, the conjunction of abysmal inequality with grossly inefficient or sometimes nonexistent public services and massive unemployment in the context of a polarized urban economy is the scourge of countries and cities in Latin America. It is a condition that only exacerbates delinquency. However, poverty in and of itself does not generate delinquency; rather its increase is also related to at least two other factors. The first is a dynamic expansion of the forms of urban life and a secularization of values, along with rules which regularly accompany this process. This is linked with the emergence of a series of new cultural and symbolic forms, as well as with the construction of new subjectivities in regards to crime and violence. In certain locations this factor has been connected with very concrete cultural expressions—through music such as funk or samba in the case of Brazil, music known as "narcocorridos" in Mexico, the cumbia "villera" in Argentina, rap in some other Latin American cities, and punk or *ska* in almost all of the countries of the region.

The second factor deals with the processes of political change as characterized by scenarios of "democratic transition." Authoritarian systems, which, in some cases were military dictatorships such as Argentina, or were single party governments as in Mexico, prevailed until they were formed into democratic institutions. However, this transition has created institutional "emptiness," where old authoritarian practices have not disappeared and the new democratic ones have not quite consolidated. This has had a direct impact upon the regulation and control of crime. Democracy, paradoxically, appears to take away the state's capacity for coercion, often leading to a scenario in which a "firm hand" is needed to end the high rates of criminal activity, typically achieved through the use of military-style policing and "zero tolerance" policies (see Wilson, this volume). Violence thus occurs against the backdrop of weak institutions which resort to firm measures—exclusion and urban marginalization—as well as the consolidation of new cultural values. The cities of Latin America thus exhibit a particular morphology characterized by the fragmentation and fracture of the urban spaces. Closed residential zones which can be considered to be islands of well-being keep away the so-called "dangerous classes," thereby marginalizing them in the economic globalization processes of Latin American cities (Koonings and Kruijt 2007).

These dangerous groups are exactly the ones who live in what Buck-Morss (2003) calls "wild power zones," characterized by the junction of violence and poverty, where the most violent crimes are registered, alongside high rates of infant death, inter-family violence and malnutrition. This occurs in a climate of profound racism where police violence prevails, and where acquiring a weapon is the best option of security. In both areas of the city—the bunkers of the middle and upper classes, as well as in the wild power zones where social fragmentation is reflected—a culture of fear is constructed day by day. Internal borders are constructed which limit, surround and contain what is considered to represent the danger: crime.

Security

The urban violence which has developed in Latin America in the last two decades has established a form of government in which security has turned into a ruling principle. With security as the government priority, resources for health, education and urban development have been redirected to support public security policies. In many of the region's countries, speeches about security are articulated under a military narrative which highlights the need to drive a "war against insecurity" or "a war against crime." In countries such as Brazil, Mexico, Colombia, Ecuador, Peru, El Salvador and Guatemala, public security policies are not exclusive to the police: the armed forces are also involved. On many occasions, the army is used to intervene in neighborhoods considered dangerous—usually shanties, "lost cities" (ciudades perdidas) and "barrios"—to dismantle presumed gangs of delinquents who are believed to live there. In general these actions are supported by the more affluent sections of society and, with the "war speeches" of government authorities, the policies become established as the only acceptable way to re-establish the supposed lost order.

These high income sectors have also developed their own security strategies characterized by the isolation of large urban centers in fortress cities (Caldeira 2000). Neighborhood spaces such as the "residential zones" in Mexico or the so called "countryside" in Argentina, are enclosed and have mechanisms of access control, such as video surveillance systems, fingerprint-reading technology and identification cards. The architecture of the houses is also homogenous and reflects the design of North American suburbs. Those members of the middle class who do not have access to this type of housing have opted to close their neighborhood streets to traffic, even though this contravenes the laws of traffic flow in many cities. The closure of neighborhood streets is a political act, one intended to defend a position of privilege which is being threatened not only by the increase of delinquency, but also by the economic transformations that began to occur during the 1980s and the first half of the 1990s.

In addition, securitized exclusionary mechanisms have been established along the commercial and business districts within the globalized nodes of Latin American cities. Zones such as Santa Fe in Mexico City (Mexico), Puerto Madero in Buenos Aires (Argentina), Miraflores in La Paz (Bolivia), Centro Comercial Leste Aricanduva in Sao Paolo (Brazil), Larcomar in Lima (Peru), and *Sanhattan* in Santiago (Chile) are examples of spaces whose objective is to organize services, the construction of buildings, streets and avenues in a way that guarantees the optimum development of business and commercial operations carried out by the middle- and upper-class sectors. These spaces are protected by private police: there are more than 1,630,000 private security guards in Latin America and the majority of private security businesses are managed by active or retired police officers. The reality is that those who directly provide security services work in low-skilled, low-paid jobs. Even police work as private agents at certain times during their working day. Even though this is sanctioned in some countries—such as in Uruguay—in other countries sanctions do not exist, even though the security industry is regulated—as in Brazil. In Central America, providing personal police to private security firms is only allowed in El Salvador and Panama (Dammert 2007).

Thus, the meaning of security in Latin America must, out of necessity, be anchored in the idea of control, specifically as it relates to delinquency and violent crime. This belief has led to the formation of a variety of spaces where fear is managed: neighborhoods, commercial centers, private and government buildings, parks, business districts, streets and avenues. This is in addition to the implementation of security policies in zones considered "dangerous," typically shanties and marginal neighborhoods. Here, policies are established to reduce the apparent risk of being a victim of any kind of offence or crime. Although a group of countries in Latin America appear to have consolidated policies and reforms to the political and judicial system, it is still possible to observe neighborhoods and communities which have established and perfected their own security mechanisms. In general, the problems of inequality, poverty and social exclusion are considered the causes of offences and criminal violence. However, governments are under political pressure to control, contain and punish criminality immediately and expeditiously. Security strategies appear as a new form of government applied to social insecurity, in the context of the turbulence of economic deregulation, unstable employment, marginalization and urban exclusion (Wacquant 2008).

Surveillance

In the past ten years, public security has become a central element of public discourse in Latin America, which has seen a concomitant rise in the use of distinct and diverse electronic surveillance devices. The walls that enclose the residential zones of the region have effectively been reinforced with the installation of surveillance technologies to control the entrance to these neighborhoods. Such technologies range from video surveillance, to the use of electronic access cards and even biometric recognition systems such as fingerprint and retinal scans, as are used in some Brazilian, Colombian and Costa Rican cities. Public and private buildings have extended their use of electronic surveillance devices, which allow access control to these buildings, such as electronic lock keypads, biometric hand readers, proximity detectors, cards with magnetic bands, iris and fingerprint readers and movement detectors. Urban space is left divided by electronic walls of protection, identifying those who, from a process of stigmatization and categorization by their visible economic and racial characteristics, are considered as possible instigators of crime and violence.

Surveillance has gradually expanded to include the main roads and avenues within cities, especially through the installation of video surveillance, but also with checkpoints set up by local and national police, including the army as seen, for example, in Mexico, Colombia, Peru, Bolivia and Brazil (Arteaga Botello 2011). Checkpoints serve several purposes: to find possible suspects, wanted criminals, drunk drivers or drug users (particularly in Brazil, Ecuador, Guatemala, Honduras and Chile); to check the legal status of automobiles; as well as to detain adolescents or youngsters under the legal age to drive. The intention is to legitimize and normalize the notion that human traffic is required to be surveiled, thereby guaranteeing that those who enter any closed place or other area (such as a commercial centre, school, or neighborhood) can travel safely. In this sense, the roads and avenues have turned into spaces of surveillance which connect closed residential zones and business or commercial centre districts, as well as work places.

Beyond the electronic walls and the surveiled transit spaces that connect them, the spaces beyond, such as shanties, *villas miseria*, lost cities or marginalized zones, are zones of savage power. The latter are not protected by electronic surveillance technologies: they are infra-surveillance spaces. It seems that groups in these areas do not warrant security nor protection. Instead they are watched when they, as "risky bodies," cross the electronic borders of commercial centers, residential zones or financial districts. Moreover, it is expensive and complex to surveil a shanty, *villas miseria* or a lost city. The labyrinthine layout of the streets, irregular topography, the density of their construction and the disorder of their growth make these spaces very complicated to surveil in a consistent way. Enormous quantities of cameras would be needed to observe the population. In this sense they are spaces that can be considered *inpanoptical*. Once outside these zones, individuals are subject to intense police observation, but if they remain inside individuals are excluded from the protection and care that surveillance can provide, and left to face the conditions of "savage power" that tend to prevail there. If we then consider that these zones suffer from economic and urban services shortages, a complex and difficult intersection of economic and social exclusion coupled with diminished citizenship rights emerges (see also McCahill, Fussey and Coaffee, Gandy, this volume).

However, it is important to note that there is a high degree of variation, both in terms of the form of surveillance used within and between Latin American countries. This variation depends on the extent to which government and private organizations have the economic capacity to invest in surveillance systems. Nevertheless, in those countries where surveillance devices are not used extensively there are larger transformations and reforms in their police and judicial institutions, for example in Jamaica, El Salvador,

Honduras, Nicaragua, Panama and Paraguay. The largest expansion in the use of software, computers and electronic surveillance devices is found in countries with the greatest lag in institutional reform and transformation of police and judicial systems. This can be seen clearly in the cases of Mexico, Brazil, Argentina and Venezuela, where electronic surveillance has been introduced in institutional contexts inherited from authoritarian regimes.

Thus states with police and judicial organizations that have a long tradition of authoritarian practices have a greater use of electronic surveillance technologies. Furthermore, they also use actuarial language and statistical practices to identify and control dangerous or risky groups. The use of population and crime data facilitates the detection of behaviors and the identification of social spaces to be placed under police and judicial control (Dammert 2007). New forms of discrimination are applied to the individuals to whom these data relate and over whom authority can be exercised. For example in Chile, Argentina, Mexico, Brazil and Peru, electronic surveillance systems were used for political ends, where social movements have attempted to claim access to better urban services, better life conditions and a more democratic administration of the city. For example, in the urban protests in Argentina in 2001, following government measures which froze all bank accounts, video surveillance was used to detect the protest's leaders, and when the protests turned violent, to help determine the administration of arrest warrants. In December of the same year, video surveillance was used to film food riots. A similar situation was observed in student protests against the increase of urban transport costs in Chile in 2006. Systematic surveillance was also used against the Mapuche indigenous movement in Chile, a sector of the population considered "dangerous." The Mapuche indigenous movement is classified as a terrorist group by the Chilean government, and the people who, because of their ethnicity, are connected to that group have been subject to systematic and overt surveillance. Police have used the information collected to break into these communities, bearing military arms, without judicial warrants. Furthermore, paramilitary commandos make night raids, firing their weapons, while they install surveillance cameras and devices that interfere with cellular phones in the Mapuche zones. In the same way, indigenous communities in Peru in 2009, who were protesting against the invasion of their lands by oil companies, were recorded by surveillance cameras, which led to the arrest of many indigenous leaders. A similar situation was seen in Mexico during the peasant protest against the construction of a new airport in Mexico City in October 2001. By definition, this weakens democratic institutions in some Latin American states.

Surveillance is converted, then, into a form of population governance which in the first instance connects Latin America to the logic of public security management, but also establishes new forms of social sorting in the organization of urban space, in which police and judicial institutions participate equally. Therefore, surveillance strengthens these new governmental capabilities, aligned with the logic of public security, which establishes a new way of governing in a context of economic degradation, unemployment, marginalization and exclusion. But above all, surveillance acquires a central position in organizational practices that are not totally modern, generating negative effects in the processes of democratic consolidation in the region.

Conclusion

This chapter has suggested a three-point framework within which surveillance in the Global South in general, and in Latin America in particular, can be understood. The first point refers to the violence and insecurity in which surveillance technologies have been installed. The installation of electronic walls of protection, especially in upper-class sectors, and the transit spaces under surveillance that connect them, contrasts with the presence of infra-surveillance spaces. Surveillance has consolidated security within the region, both as a logic of social organization in the Global South, and as a way in which particular forms of governance are exercised.

The second point refers to the conditions of inequality and poverty which mark the region. Surveillance, as it "looks after" the population, is distributed unequally according to income level. It is a privilege from which a large part of the population is excluded. This reconfigures divisions between public and private in that different sections of society do not have access to surveillance devices to ensure their security and privacy (Zureik 2010). Therefore the expansion of surveillance devices tends to reproduce, and in some cases amplifies, social inequality and poverty. Future research must ask how the processes of economic policies are linked to the logic of surveillance.

The third point refers to the logic of institutional policies in the Global South, and particularly in Latin America, where old authoritarian forms prevail. It is certain that in the region, authoritarianism which characterized the political regimes until the middle of the 1990s is not present. During that period, the authoritarian use of such technologies was directed toward groups which were considered to be subversive and revolutionary. However, the authoritarian use of surveillance technologies toward groups who are still considered a threat to social peace and order, through their demands and actions, still prevails. Such groups are regularly considered incapable of following institutionally hegemonic, democratic models, and their interests are not seen to represent the general interests of society. In this way, surveillance may seem to be generating authoritarian political uses over social movements outside projects of democratic transition in the region.

These three elements can be applied to understand the social and political institutions of each country, in the Global South and Latin America in particular. However, it is also important to know that this takes place within a particular cultural context. Latin America tends to exhibit low levels of individualism, low levels of trust, and high tolerance for both social inequalities and the concentration of power within the state.

This chapter has tried to show some of the elements of the framework for the understanding of surveillance in the context of Latin America, as part of the Global South. The idea is made clear that by considering surveillance in Latin America it is possible to observe how, on different levels and in different social and institutional spheres, surveillance issues are transformed from public policies pushed by the state into policies that offer assurance in everyday life. Public, residential and commercial spaces are securitized through the use of population surveillance systems. Electronic surveillance is constituted as a particular form of government, in order to contain marginalized and excluded groups within and between neighborhood, business and consumer spaces, who are considered the source of criminal violence in Latin American societies. This has generated a group of "security archipelagos" that further fragment the mega-cities of the region. In these archipelagos, different forms of accessing and living in the city for groups and diverse individuals are established. The installation of large surveillance systems that feed enormous and costly data bases established new forms of organization and sorting which directly impact in the way in which the citizenry is structured and lives (Lyon 2007). In a context of democratic construction such as that lived in the region, this can represent, in some cases, a backward step towards the authoritarian regimes which ruled for decades in Latin America. This is especially so if information production accelerates through the systematic surveillance of cities, with little challenge or resistance to the installation of such devices.

References

Arteaga Botello, N. (2011). "Security Metamorphosis in Latin America," in V. Bajc and W. de Lint (eds), *Security and Everyday Life*, New York: Routledge.

Buck-Morss, S. (2003). *Thinking Past Terror: Islamism and Critical Theory on the Left*, London: Verso.

Caldeira, T. (2000). *City of Walls: Crime, Segregation, and Citizenship in São Paulo*, Berkeley: University of California Press.

Cardoso, F. (2010). "Novos Caminhos na América Latina?," in F. Cardoso (ed.), *Xadrez Internacional e Social-democracia*, Sao Paulo: Paz e Terra.

Dammert, L. (2007). *Report on the Security Sector in Latin America and Caribbean*, Santiago: FLACSO.

Davis, M. (2006). *Le Pire des Mondes Possibles*, Paris: La Découverte.

Koonings, K. and Kruijt, D. (2007). "Fractured Cities, Second-class Citizenship and Urban Violence," in K. Koonings and D. Kruijt (eds), *Fractured Cities: Social Exclusion, Urban Violence & Contested Spaces in Latin America*, London: Zed Books.

Lyon, D. (2007). "Surveillance, security and social sorting: emerging research priorities," *International Criminal Justice Review*, 17: 161–71.

Wacquant, L. (2008). "The Militarization of Urban Marginality: Lessons from the Brazilian Metropolis," in *International Political Sociology*, 2: 56–74.

Zureik, E. (2010). "Cross-cultural Study of Surveillance and Privacy: Theoretical and Empirical Observations," in E. Zureik, L. Harling, E. Smith, D. Lyon and Y. Chan (eds), *Surveillance, Privacy and the Globalization of Personal Information: International Comparisons*, Montreal and Kingston: McGill-Queen's University Press.

Section 3.3.
Security, intelligence, war

a. Military surveillance

Dean Wilson

Introduction

While numerous authors have indicated the foundational importance of military surveillance it remains an area that has to date received only scant attention from surveillance scholars. Nevertheless, military surveillance has had a major impact upon the development of surveillance practices. The monitoring of soldiers and training such as drill were intended to produce "machine-like" armed forces that were highly disciplined and controlled. As Dandeker (1990, 2006) suggests, techniques of discipline and control originating in the armed forces subsequently migrated to bureaucratic administration in civilian spheres. Mobilization for war also entailed the advent of surveillance techniques that encompassed whole societies rather than just the military. Personal, health and security checks scrutinizing large segments of the population in terms of fitness for service informed large-scale identification schemes later mobilized by welfare states in the post-war period.

The quest for information and intelligence to provide strategic advantage has also provided a catalyst for the development of surveillance technologies ranging from the utilization of aerial balloon reconnaissance in the nineteenth century through to the development of radar and signal interception, global positioning systems, thermal sensors, unmanned aerial vehicles and satellites. Reliance on information technologies for warfare has been a defining feature of the Revolution in Military Affairs (RMA) that applies informational systems of control to military engagement. Theorists such as Paul Virilio have also argued that post-industrial societies have moved into a state of perpetual war preparedness, whereby the agendas of politics and science are channeled into military goals. In such a scenario new surveillance technologies are continually developed and trialed in an ongoing simulation of war. The transference of technologies and techniques of surveillance developed for military objectives, particularly subsequent to the "War on Terror," to the civilian sector continues apace, and is evident in police work, border control, the labor market, medical and legal institutions and in terms of entertainment and communications (see also Hayes, this volume). Nevertheless, the relationship between military and civilian surveillance remains dialectical, with civilian innovations increasingly being investigated for potential military application.

Soldiers, discipline and surveillance

By the end of the seventeenth century, European states had accumulated sufficient control over their territorial resources to maintain standing armies that could engage in prolonged campaigns. Dandeker (1990: 69) suggests that this laid the material basis for the development of the modern state as a "surveillance machine." An important series of reforms are thus associated with Maurice of Nassau, who from 1585 until his death in 1625 was Captain-General of Holland and Zeeland. Prince Maurice faced the problem of fighting the Spaniards in the Low Countries, and looked to Roman precedents for military models. An important innovation initiated by Maurice was the introduction of systematic military drill for soldiers. While armies had always needed to train recruits, previous assumptions had been that once soldiers were trained to use their weapons, the task of the drill master was complete. Nassau analyzed the complex actions required to load and fire matchlock guns, divided them into a series of 42 separate moves, each accompanied by a name and a specific command. Soldiers could then be taught to make each move in unison responding to shouted orders. Moreover, military drill was to be conducted day-in and day-out, fashioning the individual solider into a kind of automaton responsive to orders and commands, and acting in a rationally calculable manner.

Surveillance and control were also intrinsic to new forms of military organization. A crucial development in this was the advent of smaller sub-units trained to co-operate in more complex patterns of organization, as opposed to the more rudimentary organization of pike squares with protective sections of muskets. Battalions of 550 were further divided into companies and platoons whereby a single voice could control the movements of all soldiers. The division of soldiers into smaller units and the practice of drill rendered individual soldiers increasingly visible to their superiors, a visibility heightened by military uniforms and insignia allowing battlefield commanders to distinguish regiments and ranks at a glance. However, gunpowder rendered such personal observation of battles problematic. Furthermore, by the First World War the deployment of the breech-loading rifle and machine gun meant bright colorful formations of neatly ordered soldiers were suicidal, giving rise to attempts to conceal visibility through camouflage.

The spatial layout of military encampments was also to have significant influence on surveillance architectures. Foucault argued that the military camp served as a model for the panoptic society. In the military camp, tents and huts were spatially distributed to replicate the hierarchical authority and supervisory structure of the army. Officers' tents oversaw the main gate and the arms depot while captains' tents overlooked rows of company tents. The military camp was, according to Foucault, "the diagram of power that acts by means of general visibility" (Foucault 1977: 171). The spatial construction of the temporary military camp formed a template for other constructions that would utilize its supervisory potential in other spheres—all manner of buildings from asylums, prisons, factories, schools, housing estates and even shopping malls (Foucault 1977: 171).

Production, security and total war

If the architectural template of the military camp diffused throughout broader society through a range of institutions, so did innovations in manufacturing that had military origins. The micro-movements and corporeal discipline inherent in the practice of drill invented by Maurice of Nassau were important precursors of industrial discipline. In the late eighteenth and early nineteenth centuries, French and American armories began to produce military equipment with fully standardized components. The demand for the interchangeability of parts led to more systematic means of monitoring compliance with uniform routines and recording deviations. In addition, individual aspects of the manufacturing process were to be broken down and deskilled, with the result that identical movements could be performed ceaselessly by a multitude of workers. In America such innovations were transferred to the civilian sector as contracts for arms production were granted to outside firms, on the basis of their degree of conformity with the uniform system of production. By the late 1850s, basic components of this system of manufacture were evident in the production of various products ranging from pocket watches and sewing machines to typewriters and bicycles. Although the link to Taylorism and techniques of "scientific management" in industrial manufacturing and military discipline has been disputed (see Dandeker 1990), the synergy between military drill and industrial discipline is evident. Military requirements were also crucial in fundamentally extending the surveillance capacities of modern nation states. If military organization and training diffused surveillance techniques throughout society, so too did war-time mobilization. The extension of the surveillance power of the state for military objectives was perhaps first evident in the compulsory military service of the French Revolution in the late eighteenth century, which required the marshalling of a vast bureaucratic machinery to mobilize the population as a resource of war. Along with the novel idea that everyone owed military service to the nation-state in time of war, this heralded the extension of the surveillance capacities of states most evident in the conflicts of the twentieth century. Many European states began to calculate military potential in terms of population size, a perspective which required assembling an intimate knowledge of the number and distribution of their citizens. Conscription was thus closely intertwined with systems of taxation and national census taking (see also Ruppert, this volume). From the mid- to late nineteenth century most European states introduced some form of conscription, and attendant with this was the registration of citizens. While Britain and the USA did not maintain conscript armies prior to the First World War, such a situation did not extend beyond the conflict. In Britain the 1915 National Registration Act authorized the creation of a register of all men and women aged 15 to 65 who were not members of the armed forces or resident in certain institutions. The General Register Office (GRO) oversaw military recruitment data gathering, while also collating files on potential munitions, mining, railway and agricultural workers who could be mobilized for the war effort.

If war offered opportunities to develop the surveillance apparatus of the state to monitor its people, it also permitted distinctions to be drawn between those categorized as loyal citizens and those suspected of being hostile aliens intent on subverting the state from within. In Britain the GRO maintained a Central Register of War Refugees in part to monitor those who it was suspected might side with the German Army should they invade. The GRO supplied information to MI5 on enemy aliens throughout the period. Following wartime, although internal registration was suspended, the control of movement from other states was intensified. In Britain the first passports were issued in 1915, following the 1914 Status of Aliens Act. Wartime restrictions were extended with the passing of the 1920 Aliens Order which stipulated that anyone wanting to leave or enter the country had to carry a passport indicating their nationality and identity. Similar surveillance of "enemy aliens" was undertaken in the USA. In Britain such registration schemes were revived in 1939. The priorities of "total war" thus involved two crucial developments in state surveillance—the development of the international passport system and mass registration systems within nation-states that would continue to inform subsequent identity schemes.

Speed, calculation and science

From the time of Maurice of Nassau many tactical innovations in military organization had been founded to enhance the precision and speed of military maneuvers. The speed of war increased dramatically in the mid-nineteenth century, in no small part due to the railways and the electric telegraph. Railways had a dramatic impact on the speed and logistics of war, increasing the size of armies and facilitating their movement and control. They increased the speed of war, with military power increasingly defined in terms of mobilization times, and led to attempts to accelerate mobilization in the second half of the nineteenth century. The emergent war machine, dependent on railways, was also dependent upon the electric telegraph. Appearing in the 1840s, the electric telegraph was particularly useful for coordinating movements of men and materials through the rail system and in connecting HQ with units in the field (Dandeker 1990: 86).

If military surveillance has to some extent been driven by the pragmatics of disciplining, coordinating and mobilizing arms and soldiers with maximum tempo, it has also been fuelled by enduring dreams of attaining a cosmic vision with the capacity to render enemy territories calculable and knowable. In the fifth century BC Sun Tzu noted that the key to rapid military victory was foreknowledge (Bogard 1996: 85). Although initially used for scientific investigations into topography and weather, balloons were engaged in military surveillance operations from the eighteenth century. The armies of Napoleon used balloons in

Figure 3.3.1 An RQ-1 Predator Drone preparing for a mission over Iraq

1797 at the siege of Mantua and other armies soon followed this lead. Balloons were used for aerial reconnaissance during the American Civil War and the Franco-Prussian War of 1870–71. At this time the production of interpretable images relied on the human eye and a sketch pad. Aerial reconnaissance assumed greater significance in the First World War when it was combined with photography, not only to produce short-term tactical information before an artillery attack, but also to gather long-term strategic information about enemy intentions and movements. During the Second World War developments in aerial surveillance continued apace, with the creation of high-resolution color film and lenses that compensated for air temperature and atmospheric pressure. The quest for commanding God-like vision of territory has continued to fuel technological advancements in aeronautics and space technology from U2 spy planes to satellites and Unmanned Aerial Vehicles.

By the Second World War a defining feature of military surveillance was also the incorporation of science and the accelerated pace of weapons development. While scientific advice had been sought previously, military leaders increasingly believed the deployment of a new secret weapon might decisively tip the balance of fighting. As a result, scientists, technologists, design engineers and efficiency experts were drafted into the task of refining existing weaponry and inventing new weapons on a scale hitherto unseen (McNeill 1983: 357). One significant innovation in surveillance technology emerging from the Second World War was radar, where British scientists and engineers discovered how to use short radio waves to locate aircraft at distances sufficient to allow their interception by fighter pilots during the Battle of Britain. Radar technology continued to advance, rapidly finding new uses in gun laying and navigation. Also emerging from the Second World War was the concept of a complete weapons system in which each constituent part fitted seamlessly with others. Standardized package sizes consequently fitted standardized cargo spaces in railway cars, airplanes and trucks. This was a process that transferred the techniques of business corporations to the industrialization of war, with the effect of reducing costs and increasing output. As the historian William McNeill suggests "war, in short, became well and truly industrialized as industry became no less well and truly militarized" (1983: 358–59). In the post-war period, a grouping of military strategies known as C3I (command, control, communications and information) would also transfer to organizational, marketing and consumer contexts, illustrating the continuing interchange between commercial and military strategy (Graham 2010: 64).

Technophilia and militarization

The significance of surveillance technology in warfare has accelerated considerably in the past half century. Since the Cold War, the US military particularly has been searching for more flexible structures to meet uncertain crises that are difficult to predict in advance. In the period following the Second World War, politicians and military strategists recognized that any future wars would be fought with the weapons and troops available at the outbreak of hostilities. As the time it would take to transform a peace economy onto a war footing was simply too long, Americans decided to place the nation in a constant state of military preparedness (Haggerty 2006: 252). This military preparedness included a harnessing of scientific expertise directed towards military goals. In the post-war period a multitude of technologies now familiar in daily civilian life were initially developed for military application, including microwaves, closed-circuit TV, satellite surveillance, wireless communications, remote control, virtual reality, data-mining and the internet (Graham 2010: 65). Thus a significant military-industrial complex has emerged, shaped by military priorities.

This unremitting condition of military preparedness has been accompanied by the so-called "Revolution in Military Affairs" (RMA). The subject of considerable debate amongst US military theorists and commanders, the RMA considers how new technologies of surveillance, communications and "stealth" or "precision" targeting through "smart" weapons can be harnessed to sustain global US military dominance based on "network-centric" warfare (Graham 2010: 28). RMA theorists also conceive of US military operations as colossal network enterprises, drawing on the flexible organizational structures and processes of the civilian business sector. As Stephen Graham has noted, RMA was envisaged as "a `just-in-time' system of post human, cyborganized warriors that utilize many of the principles of logistics chain management and new-technology based tracking that are so dominant within contemporary management models" (Graham 2006: 250). The rhetoric of RMA is riven with technophilic fantasies on a global scale of informational and digital interactions that provide real-time situational awareness to usher in "full spectrum dominance." This is what Haggerty terms "information war" by which information achieves prominence of place as a tactical and strategic resource. Also contained within the vision of RMA is the idea of war without casualties (at least for aggressors) in which superior information, communications and technological artefacts, often with remote capabilities, render the battlespace calculable and amenable to precision-calculated targeting. Such technological fetishism also has its origins in the collapse of the Soviet Union, and the subsequent uncertainties about the dimension and character of future conflicts.

Surveillance technologies have long been mobilized in warfare. As already detailed in this chapter, aerial reconnaissance, radar, computing and railways all had military origins pre-dating the Cold War. Nevertheless, the second half of the twentieth century witnessed the vigorous advance of visualizing technologies. For the US military, Vietnam became a laboratory for testing a plethora of surveillance technologies. The list of devices includes reconnaissance aircraft, communication devices and an elaborate reporting structure alongside more curious excursions such as helicopter-mounted "people sniffers" to detect ammonia left by human urine and sensors fashioned like twigs, plants and animal droppings dotted along the Ho Chi Minh trail to identify vehicle noise and body heat (Haggerty 2006: 254).

In contemporary warfare the immense range of surveillance equipment deployed has transformed the battlefield into a surveillant assemblage of visualization technologies. The coordination of technology, communication and command is thus intended to create a totally transparent battlespace spread across air, land, sea and space. Some sense of what Haggerty describes as "a military cartographic frenzy" (2006: 255) is provided by moving vertically from the subterranean mapping of caves, bunkers, pipelines and cables through to military satellites circling the globe providing continuous surveillance from the stratosphere. On the ground interactive maps informed by geographical positioning systems facilitate precise situational awareness. Military vehicles and weapons systems are equipped with night vision and video facilities that facilitate combat being monitored in real time and for the remote guidance of munitions. Sensors, monitoring and constant surveillance-also generate vast fields of data to be analyzed by commanders and analysts, often situated in locations far distant from the cross-hairs of action. In the airspace above helicopters, aircraft and unmanned drones instantaneously feed yet more visual and statistical data into the dispersed grid of information through radar, night vision equipment, video and reconnaissance cameras, while spy planes intercept radar, telephone and microwave communications (Haggerty 2006: 255).

Within such scenarios rests the imagined vision of RMA as a seamless information web rendering battlespaces transparent while providing maximum strategic advantage through data flows. The immense importance placed upon informational superiority is intended to operate as a synchronized assemblage, allowing the coordination of all actors within a network who can gain access to a common picture. The promise of surveillance-imaging technologies is therefore that they will lift the "fog of war" providing precise and instantaneous visual and statistical data that finely calibrates the movements of the enemy and facilitates the control, coordination and dispatch of a formidable array of high-tech precision weaponry. This advanced informatization of warfare has been envisaged as offering "full dimension protection"—enabling the avoidance of close combat and minimalizing operational risk through overpowering adversaries in the field via superior speed and the application of superior firepower from a distance (Dandeker 2006: 231).

The technological blanket of surveillance technologies across the field of battle has accelerated the pace of combat to an unprecedented level. Nevertheless, while such technology may reduce the fog of war it cannot completely erase it. One possible unintended consequence of this is that the increased speed of data flows strains human fallibility, causing an increase in incidents of friendly and "blue on blue" incidents, such as have been witnessed in recent conflicts in Iraq and Afghanistan (Dandeker 2006). Moreover, the complexity of such systems, and the sheer volume of visual and statistical data generated, can inspire information overload that incapacitates and even retards action rather than accelerating it. This was particularly evident in Vietnam, where the sheer volume of information spawned precipitated a form of command paralysis. In the Gulf War also, satellite systems produced such enormous volumes of data that information systems were overwhelmed (Haggerty 2006: 258). Furthermore, the sheer extent of data available in remote as well as proximate locations led to the micromanagement of battles from afar. With such remote command and control, field officers may prove reluctant to make immediate decisions without the approval of commanders located in distant control rooms.

The military techno-fantasy of RMA has also been undermined by growing cognizance of its blindness to specific geographical contexts. Consequently a growing strand of US military thought now envisages future wars as asymmetrical conflicts fought within the three-dimensional complexity of the urban centers of the Global South. Such urban centers are argued to be great levelers between the high-tech surveillance and communications systems of US forces and low-tech and often informally and poorly equipped adversaries on the ground. The physical structure of such environments—with dead spots, noise and signal absorption and the limited efficacy of GPS in urban contexts—are considered to nullify the previously much vaunted strategic advantage of technoscience wielded by the US military (Graham 2006). As Stephen Graham has documented (2006, 2010) this has inspired a new raft of innovation aimed at rendering complex three-dimensional cityscapes transparent through surveillance technology. An example of such a project is entitled "Combat Zones that See" (CTS). Initiated by the US Defence Advanced Research Agency (DARPA) at the commencement of the Iraq insurgency in 2003, the project envisages Global South cities with total CCTV with motion pattern analysis capacity and linked to the tracking of whole populations through number plate recognition and facial recognition technology. Urban contexts are configured as yet more intelligent via the ubiquitous positioning of micro-scale and nano-scale sensors. In the military dream, as Graham notes, such military surveillance systems are disturbingly coupled with robotic automated weapons controlled at a distance to instigate what he chillingly describes as "potentially endless streams of state killing" (2006: 256).

While such visions of an automated surveillance-military killing machine may appear fanciful, such schemes have nevertheless attracted considerable research and development finance. Additionally, the long-standing tendency of military technologies to migrate into civilian application should alert us to the possibility of such technophiliac dreams taking root in domestic contexts. In the 1990s, the end of the Cold War stimulated questioning of the US military's vast technoscience infrastructure. In 1994, the US Attorney General and the Deputy Assistant Secretary for Defense signed a memorandum of understanding on "operations other than war" in which they agreed to the development of advanced technologies and systems terms that could be used for both law enforcement and military application. This idea of "dual use" technologies was particularly influential in the development of "sub-lethal" weapons. It is also evident in the utilization of Unmanned Aerial Vehicles (UAV), developed in military contexts and now increasingly deployed in policing contexts such as drug law enforcement, border control and even traffic policing.

The drift of military technologies into domestic application is of considerable importance given the oft-noted convergence of internal and external security, a process markedly accelerated since the "War on Terror." This indicates some of the complexities of examining contemporary military surveillance exclusively in terms of the armed military forces of nation-states. Traditional Westphalian notions of the modern liberal state envisaged a military power projected out at external enemies in times of war, and an internal policing apparatus mobilizing criminal law to maintain social order internally. However in contemporary times such neat distinctions—external and internal, police and military—have become increasingly blurred. Some scholars suggest that policing, civil enforcement and security services are merging into a continuum of security forces that function both within and without national boundaries (Graham 2010). Moreover, a raft of "wars" against such diverse threats as drugs, crime, terror, biological contagion and illegal immigration, indicate new and dispersed forms of warfare that meld with the fabric of civilian life. In waging these various wars, a militarized surveillance and security infrastructure is increasingly focused both within and without national borders. These new open-ended wars intersect with the writings of contemporary military strategists who have coined such terms as "irregular war" and "fourth generation war" to describe envisaged future conflicts, comprising deterritorialized threats that can be either supranational or domestic, and which dissolve traditional battlefield distinctions between soldiers and civilians. Visions of contemporary conflict as open-ended, deterritorialized and waged against an enemy diffused within the civilian population have been powerful in stimulating a security economy internally—one that militarizes domestic spaces through surveillance techniques and hardware.

The dictates of information war and the proliferation of visual surveillance technologies across battle-space have also had synoptic implications, with the field of combat being rendered more transparent than ever before. While the accelerated mediatization of conflict has caused military authorities to carefully control images in order to remain "on message," the proliferation of civilian devices such as camcorders, mobile phone cameras and digital cameras within combat zones can destabilize the stage management of conflicts. Images of Abu Ghraib prison in Baghdad, and private soldiers engaged by the Blackwater Corporation firing on civilians, exposed that war in Iraq was not the bloodless exercise in precision that the military public relations machine intended to project. Despite such counter-surveillant intrusions into virtual space, the mediatization of military operations has overwhelming functioned to showcase high-tech weaponry and a form of "wartainment," whereby the brutal realities of death are distanced and erased. Since the Gulf War of 1990, with its spectacular images of precision-guided weapons, war has increasingly been enacted as a vast media spectacle channeled through the circuits of commercial media. This was again evident in Iraq in 2003 where the campaign of "shock and awe" also functioned as a showcase of US high-tech weaponry broadcast through the circuits of civilian media (Graham 2010).

Conclusion

It is fitting in conclusion to revisit some of the key themes outlined here. Underpinning developments in military surveillance from the time of Maurice of Nassau have been fantasies of military power embedded in notions of temporal and spatial mastery. Developments in military surveillance have persistently accelerated the tempo of combat, while generating increasing reams of data aimed at making battle calculable and predictable. On a purely technical level, the demand for control of time and space in military operations has migrated into civilian spheres, with a multitude of innovations from containerization to Global Positioning Systems redeployed for civilian application. Moreover, militaries continue to scrutinize civilian innovations in communications and surveillance for potential military application. For some theorists, there is far more at stake in military surveillance. Drawing on the work of Virilio, Bogard argues that a perpetual state of war preparedness has evolved, evidenced through incessant gaming, mock-ups and simulations and the migration of military technology into the civilian sphere. These, he argues, indicate a general militarization of society whereby "the more blurred the conventional distinctions between peacetime and wartime, civilian and soldier, enemy and friend become" (Bogard 1996: 96, see also Bogard, this volume). Der Derian (2001) also indicates the melding of entertainment, military and technology into what he terms the "military-industrial-media-entertainment network" that promotes a concept of "virtuous war." The "virtuous war," capable of actualizing violence at a distance with no or minimal casualties, is represented through real-time surveillance and instant media communications as "bloodless, humanitarian and hygienic" (2001: xv).

The implications of these developments should continue to be interrogated by surveillance scholars. As Graham has noted, one consequence of the mediatized sanitation of conflict has been the construction of Global South cities, and their inhabitants, as "little more than receiving points for US military tech-noscience and ordnance" (2006: 265). Thus simulated and mediated surveillance images of conflict efface the significant body count of contemporary conflict, while rendering the victims of such technology and information barrages as little more than "bare life." Moreover, the blurring of border control, policing and military power may well mean that military fantasies of techno-control are destined to re-emerge in domestic settings with ever greater rapidity, and may increasingly emerge from within these settings (see Arteaga Botello, this volume).

References

Bogard, W. (1996). *The Simulation of Surveillance: Hypercontrol in Telematic Societies*, Cambridge: Cambridge University Press.
Dandeker, C. (1990). *Surveillance, Power and Modernity*, London: Polity.
——(2006). "Surveillance and Military Transformation: Organizational Trends in Twenty-First Century Armed Services," in K. D. Haggerty and R. V. Ericson (eds), *The New Politics of Surveillance and Visibility*, Toronto: University of Toronto Press, pp. 225–49.
Der Derian, J. (2001). *Virtuous War: Mapping the Military-Industrial-Media-Entertainment Network*, Boulder, CO: Westview Press.
Foucault, M. (1977). *Discipline and Punish: The Birth of the Prison*, London: Penguin.
Graham, S. (2006). "Surveillance, Urbanization and the US "Revolution in Military Affairs," in D. Lyon (ed.), *Theorizing Surveillance: The Panopticon and Beyond*, Cullompton: Willan Publishing, pp. 247–69.
——(2010). *Cities Under Siege: The New Military Urbanism*, London: Verso.
Haggerty, K. D. (2006). "Visible War: Surveillance, Speed, and Information War," in K. D. Haggerty and R. V. Ericson (eds), *The New Politics of Surveillance and Visibility*, Toronto: University of Toronto Press, pp. 250–68.
McNeill, W. (1983). *The Pursuit of Power: Technology, Armed Force, and Society since A.D. 1000*, Oxford: Basil Blackwell.

b. Security, surveillance and democracy

Didier Bigo

Introduction

This chapter explores the relationship between security, surveillance and democracy. A simple view is that security protects democracy. If democracy is attacked, its political systems take exceptional and emergency measures to ensure its survival. Another view is that this rhetoric is even more dangerous than the danger it deems to combat. Security, when it forms exceptional measures beyond the realm of normal politics and the rule of law, paves the way for the destruction of democracy and its perversion into a permanent state of emergency, and everyday state of exception without end. Difficult political questions arise concerning the relationship between violence, danger, political community and action. Careful political judgments are required, which are too often transformed into an evaluation of the positive and negative aspects of security and freedom. A debilitating metaphor of "balance" emerges between two equal and necessary values that the government in charge has to "calculate" in order to find the right equilibrium (Bigo *et al.* 2010).

In a context in which, according to these narratives, violence arises and becomes global, taking radically new forms, the balance always moves in favor of more security because of the new dangers to come. Security measures are raised and some individual freedoms are sacrificed in the name of the "right" balance. Individuals, the city, the nation, the planet, depending on the scale of the danger, need to be protected by security measures in order to survive. Moreover, the state's duty to protect implies that it must act efficiently, not only to detect those responsible after an act of violence, but also to respond at the time, and more importantly, beforehand, so that violence may be prevented. In order to act in this way, the state and its agencies need to gather, store, analyze and apply as much information as possible. This dominant narrative assumes also that the more information is gathered by the state, and in a timely way, the greater the level of security is offered to it and its citizens. Versus global insecurity, the answer is global security.

Security is thus a joint venture between timely information, surveillance and intelligence capacity, and preventative and protective actions. The assumption is that citizens will happily give information in order that they enjoy the pleasure of being securitized, to be protected by a group of professionals in charge of security. It is difficult to imagine who would not want to be protected in the face of violence, and who would not be seduced by promises of enhanced security, especially when democracy is at stake. This reasoning, and its repetition through time, by different governments, private actors, or international organizations, shows only two things. First, that it is difficult to learn lessons from the past. Second, that it is easy to claim that a situation is radically new, that rules have to be changed to cope with the present and future situation, and to be obeyed. But this story of novelty is an old story. Historians show this repetitive pattern of political arguments emphasizing a new period of danger in order to justify more power for the ruler. They find it in many narratives, from the thirteenth century to now, even if the creativity within discourses of unease and fear makes each incidence seem original.

One should therefore question the assertion that the contemporary situation is more dangerous because of the threat of nuclear terrorism, the existence of databases, the globalization of mobility, of markets, of networks of states, of technology and so on. This assertion reflects how the transnational guilds of professional security compete to define, classify and prioritize major risks and threats. But their priorities do not always reflect the views of those outside their guilds. Democratizing security supposes then to examine how these professionals deliver their different truth(s) about the danger in the world, and to put them in context. Further, the voices of the "undesirables," that they have excluded through security-based social sorting, need to be heard and sometimes listened to in order to change notions of danger, security, and normal activity, as a form of freedom. Both security studies and surveillance studies have attempted this in different ways, but come from very different starting points.

Security studies and surveillance studies: where do we come from?

Philosophers and historians have been active in this debate. Some of them, quite obscure for years, have become routinely cited, even if they were not always read carefully: the names of Schmitt, Benjamin, and even Agamben, Badiou or Foucault have been mobilized. Social sciences specialists (psychologists, geopoliticians, politists), although initially silenced, as if the twin towers explosion left them without a voice or explanation, have actively participated in an orgy of explanations which appear to be new, but in fact repeat old paradigms. To make this argument, this chapter will focus on security studies in international relations and surveillance studies in sociology.

Security studies in international relations

The terminology of security studies emerged as recently as the late 1970s, even if it claims to be the depositary of a long tradition. Security studies had long been considered as a sub-field of international relations (IR). It differentiated itself when international relations began to focus more on behaviorism, world economy, international organizations and collaboration between states. The dominance of the realist school from IR became less so in security studies, which also became known as strategic studies, defence studies, or war studies. The key element was to define security as "national security," and national security as the security of the state (as an apparatus and as a collectivity of citizens). By adopting this position, the field focused its analysis on the oppositionality of different state interests surrounding their national security in the international realm, and retained the inter-war narrative of the possible death of one state by another one (but only by another one). Issues of internal turmoil, riots and revolution were excluded from IR and war was always seen as a "clash of nations." Security has been defined as "survival," and mainly in military terms.

By the mid 1980s, the field had attracted its critics. Some voices from the realist school insisted that the concept of international security had to be enlarged in order to cope with changes in the wider world. Barry Buzan pleaded for an extension of the security agenda to political, economic, environmental and societal—rather than just military—sectors. He argued that each area had its own form of security, and that in some cases the state was not the main actor, but he maintained the unity of the notion of security by claiming that all forms of security were related with a specific "existential threat" and that survival was at stake (Buzan 1983). Although this book was not really discussed beyond a narrow circle of specialists, it became, after the end of bipolarity, a mantra for many security professionals who were afraid that the peace dividend narrative was diminishing both their budget and their legitimacy. The agencies insisted that the military were more than fighters: as soldiers, they were disciplined and thus useful in emergency situations.

They agreed with the idea of an enlarged security encompassing many risks coming from policing, but also from any form of natural catastrophes. The academic field of security studies then became divided between the "classics," who continued to focus on deterrence and major war between states, and "neo moderns," who extended the security role to any risk management in need of speed and discipline (the so-called qualities of the army). This extension included all the "small wars"—counter-insurgency and fighting terrorism, "pacifying" so-called failed states—and international policing. The latter included the surveillance of the international trade routes of drug dealers, organized crime, and illegal migrants; obliging the military forces to work more with intelligence services; developing private forms of engagement; and, if absolutely necessary, collaborating with police organizations or even with NGOs. As a result, competitive networks of transnational guilds associating these diverse experts were formed (Bigo and Tsoukala 2008). Even if some networks tied to the "classic" view were not supportive of UN international policing, the argument that security was defined in broader terms than military traditional fights was finally accepted. Civilian protection became a key word to justify intervention against natural catastrophes (and the environment) or against war lords, criminals at the head of "failed" states in order to rebuild their societies, and to introduce freedom. This enlargement of the terms of reference for security created emotional discussion about the boundaries of international relations. It obliged IR to think again about the state's inside/outside relation; of domestic law and order and international security. In a context where police agencies were going abroad, and military agencies were involved at home, security studies could no longer be monopolized by international relations, a paradox that the neomodern promoters of enlargement had not anticipated. Security studies, with its new focus on policing, crime, justice, social order and surveillance began working in a trans-disciplinary way with sociology, politics, linguistics and criminology, but with two different models.

The neomodern security studies specialists reintroduced a number of ideas to the mainstream IR community, but they were often stereotypes. Those ideas concerned the importance of rising crime, positing that cities were dangerous places, that migrants were more violent and more likely to be criminals, that transversal threats were permeating states, that identity and otherness were at stake, that internal order was transformed into internal disorder, and that security had to be globalized in order to stay civilized. In this logic, security was transmuted into a global common good, more important than peace or freedom. It was a "security first" argument.

To the contrary, for a minority of IR academics, often located on the margins, this encounter with other disciplines was central and worked both ways. It transformed the way in which they discussed security in IR in three important ways. The first was the emergence of the idea of "human security." This stemmed from a renewed focus on the subject of security if it was not the state, in contrast to previous analyses. The second was the criticism of the idea of security as a thing, or a value, or even a perception. Instead security became understood as the result of a securitization process coming from a speech act accepted by a certain audience, which transformed any "object" or "target" into a "security" realm, different from normal politics, and implying exceptional means, often coercive ones (Waever et al. 1993). This linguistic turn, associated with a more constructivist approach, questioned the positive value of security and enabled a focus of research on securitization and desecuritization processes. The third puts this linguistic turn into a more sociological and political context, integrating (in)securitization processes not only into political processes but also into the everyday practices of public and private bureaucracies and their use of traditional and new technologies to govern their specific populations (C.A.S.E. 2007). It is the engagement of this minority with surveillance studies, which is likely to produce a very rich encounter.

Surveillance studies in sociology

Surveillance studies as such is quite a new "brand." The roots of surveillance studies are linked with the sociology of policing, with criminology and the sociology of technology. Its network of researchers is different to IR and encounters between the two fields are rare. Different assumptions concerning security are held in surveillance studies, and the very choice of terminology gives a different picture of the relationship between the state and its population. The grammar of protection is analyzed in more detail and not repeated as the doxa of state legitimization, as is often the case in international relations.

At the core of surveillance studies lies the idea that the state may endanger its own citizens. The source of that danger is seen as emanating from both external, international threats, and internal threats concerning population controls. Coercion is taken seriously, as is policing. State practices in surveillance studies are conceptualized very differently from the "natural contract" so often referred to by philosophers when they describe the historical practices of the liberal state in both realist and liberal versions of IR. Surveillance studies examines the effectiveness of surveillance and control practices inside the nation. One of its concerns is with how liberal states always try to exonerate themselves from accountability, transparency and general democratic practices in relation to their use of high policing, intelligence services and national security. The sociology of policing and its search for the enemy within, the study of surveillance techniques and their impact on privacy and other key issues sheds new light on the way citizens in general and specific population groups are governed. The history of civil liberties and of civil rights struggles against the governants (a terminology so difficult to find in IR and which is replaced by the one of leadership) lies at its core with security appearing as a pretext, a justification for domination rather than a "necessity," or a condition of possibility for freedom to exist. The network of early researchers in surveillance studies was heavily influenced by Gary Marx's work on undercover policing (Marx 1971). By analyzing the policing techniques used against civil rights movements in America he connected political sociology with the sociology of policing (very often seen in the USA through functionalist lenses). He developed the idea of a surveillant gaze whose distribution was larger than any form of police organization, and was well spread in liberal societies. He has been, among others, both skeptical about the rise of databases in the bureaucratic realm, and cynical about their so-called efficiency. Haggerty and Ericson similarly analyze how police organizations are but a node in a network of risk assessment, by the way they certify and authenticate truth about violence, theft and crime and connect the individuals not only to the state but to the "social security" and the "insurance" technologies which distribute protection (Haggerty and Ericson 2000). Theoretical connections have been made with the works of Michel Foucault and François Ewald. Foucault's *Surveiller et Punir* has also given surveillance studies a position which has once again challenged the assumptions of security in a liberal–realist narrative. It should be noted, however, that the title has been mistranslated as *Discipline and Punish*, which has then created many erroneous interpretations of Foucault, particularly of the difference between "surveiller" and "discipliner." The Benthamian notion of panopticon that Michel Foucault has elevated to the truth of the program of the disciplinary societies has been largely discussed, and sometimes overused (Lyon 2006). At the same moment, few researchers have understood the difference between the truth of the program of the dispositif and its diagrammatic logic, thus criticizing Foucault as if Foucault were Bentham! Nevertheless, this influence of a critical discourse neutralizing the "essentialization" of security as a need or a value has enabled the notion of surveillance as a key concept to develop, while the notion of security was left fallow and was redirected towards governmentality and risk. David Lyon, among others, has been central in focalizing attention towards the terminology of surveillance, as opposed to security, control, or policing. His early works explained that electronic surveillance, dataveillance, was a widespread phenomenon in "liberal" societies and that this surveillance was not or not only an instrument reinforcing domination and verticalization of power relations. He tried to give a more Christian ethical perspective in a field dominated by Marxist and Foucaldian approaches and to understand how a hermeneutic of love and care was compatible with the government of subjects, a discussion which is still ongoing.

This interest in the government of populations, and on the techniques which construct and delineate them (for example statistics), developed in the same period as governmentality studies, but surveillance studies has developed its own path by focusing more on new technologies. As summarized by David Murakami Wood, from the late 1970s and into the 1980s the study of surveillance remained an occasional thing, a sideline of those studying media, policing or prisons. But this expanded after "the computer (and therefore the database) had shrunk to a size where it could fit on a desktop, and the neoliberal economic revolution of Thatcherism and Reaganomics saw a surge in financial, workplace, consumer management and in entertainment that both necessitated and exploited the newly available computing power" (Murakami Wood 2009: 54), the impact of databases in everyday life has been a key concern for sociologists and economists, as well as business management specialists. With Oscar Gandy Jr. and others, David Lyon has shown how surveillance has become horizontally widespread and rhizomatic, invested in many different sites through old and new technologies. It was "liquid," circulating, connecting and reconnecting different spheres of the social, reframing their boundaries and creating new networks of information and power. The traditional image of a top-down modality of surveillance, reduced to policing, was ineffective for understanding what was at work, and was even more unable to explain the acceptance of such forms of surveillance. The ideas of security assemblage, of simultaneously intimate and global surveillance have become widespread, and have focused more and more on technological possibilities.

This relation to technologies has been a drive as well as a limitation for surveillance studies. The focus on "new technologies" has sometimes created the impression of a brave "new" world where the term "new" has not been seriously discussed. Historians did not collaborate in the development of surveillance studies and it sometimes features a fetishism of technique and a depoliticization of the questions asked by early surveillance scholars in the mid-1970s. More specifically, political questions of surveillance have sometimes been reduced to public policy choices or a critique of its management, which is oblivious to the rationale of surveillance. Impact studies, especially those from the UK, are even keen to justify surveillance for the "good of citizen," returning to some very traditional visions of security in liberal societies.

A paradox has been that while one saw a critical dimension touching traditional security studies, a "normalization" of surveillance studies has taken place at the same time. The success of the "surveillance studies" affiliation has attracted more traditional criminologists, who tried to downplay the very first critical studies of CCTV (Norris, Moran, and Armstrong 1998), and to explain or justify the widespread use of CCTV, and then, after 2005, its usefulness against terrorism, organized crime and so on. Driven by funds from police organizations or private sector security firms, an uncritical managerial take is now also very present in surveillance studies.

Despite the widespread connections found in surveillance research—between local CCTV cameras and their political effects; the redistribution of authority and the surveillant gaze to new targets, and so on— relatively little discussion has connected surveillance, intelligence and military security. Surveillance studies has reframed criminology and the sociology of policing, but until recently it did not touch traditional security studies, and did not refer to what has recently emerged as critical security studies. Nevertheless some emblematic cases like Echelon, the EU-FBI agreements, the existence of Gladio and other transnational networks of clubs of intelligence analysts, specialized police meetings on terrorism, drugs, hooliganism, illegal migration, false documents, and so on, have required this gap to be bridged. The analysis of such cases has invoked discussions concerning the transnational logics of surveillance, as well as the blurring of the distinctions between internal and external forms of (in)security.

The entanglement between internal and external security and the blurring of their boundaries? Security and surveillance interconnectedness

The evolution of these two research groups, and the encounters between them, however, has very little to do with a natural evolution of the world towards a globalization of security through technologies. It is not the blurring of war and crime which explains the possible entanglement of security and surveillance. It is similarly very "naturalist" to reduce the explanation to an unfettered expansion of surveillance as part of a neoliberal capitalist global world; just as it is to reduce an historical process of struggle for civil liberties, freedom, security and protection to post-September 11 outcomes.

Instead, one of the key elements is to understand how a process of differentiation between the state's interior and exterior and how state forms of knowledge have been accepted as natural. Further it is important to understand how we have considered state thinking and categories (sovereignty, security, protection, reassurance) as "scientific categories," which may explain so-called state behavior. A genesis of the differentiation process and a longitudinal perspective are required to understand the contemporary practices of de-differentiation and the emergence of transnational guilds of (in)security experts who often share itineraries of carriers and social trajectories when they go beyond their national frontiers. Surveillance is not new, and is not always linked to technological gadgets, even if the interconnectedness permitted by recent technology changes the scale, reach and virtualities of surveillance. The connection between person and machine, technological capacity and the will to use it to its fullest extent, whether resisted or otherwise, has to be appreciated in relation to historical and political figurations.

Studies of surveillance which are historically reflexive often adopt materialist, neo Marxist perspectives. These studies focus on the role of material infrastructures and the interests of leading industries and risk managers, and often derive their understanding of security as if it was "a product of a cultural political economy" without discussing the meaning of security, for whom, how and why. They have the tendency to put the security market as one of the consequences of global capitalism, but cannot explain the relationship without referring to oppression, alienation, and merging sovereignty, discipline, security and surveillance into one "thing." They jump into what they call a critique in the name of "emancipation" from both security and capitalism. The boundary of the military-industrial complex expands to become a "security-surveillance-risk-management-industrial complex" so large that it is difficult to see who is excluded. Paradoxically, these studies often use the discourse of a global security regime and its inevitability. They oppose it, but do not discuss the truth regime of this governance, which is one of the key limitations of this literature.

Nevertheless, their insistence on materiality is more than welcome when contrasted with most critical security studies. In the name of constructivism, and opposition to the so-called realists of IR, the latter tend to neglect the material basis of the social construction of reality, and transform this notion into a "linguistic dimension" by quoting Wittgenstein, Austin, Searle and Derrida. The "securitization theory" developed by Ole Waever, Thomas Diez, or amended by Thierry Balzacq, to include the interaction or dialogical importance of the audience, is often at pains to explain the routines, the everyday practices of day-to-day surveillance and the technologies which accompany them. In contrast to the inclusive nature of materialist work on surveillance, securitization is seen as a process beyond the normal realm of politics, requiring exceptional measures. Nevertheless, for a group of researchers including Didier Bigo, Emmanuel Guittet, Tugba Basaran, Christian Olsson, Philippe Bonditti and, partly, Jef Huysmans and Ayse Ceyhan, the central aim is to deconstruct this linkage between securitization and politics of exception. The alternative to securitization is not to return to normal politics and desecuritization. Instead the process is one of (in)securitization which is grounded in everyday practices, the work of bureaucracies and the materiality of objects considered as security-objects. Professionals and experts in these everyday settings struggle to define "insecuritization" against a political backdrop, which asserts what it is to be securitized or not. These definitional struggles are never intellectual discussions (even if academics have a tendency to describe them as such). Instead they are molded into the professional habitus and routines of the professional activities they undertake. This habitus explains, through the structuration of the field and the objective power positions that the agents have in it, as well as their ascendant or descendant trajectories, their positionality in relation to security measures taken against specific threats, risk or vulnerabilities.

So, in contrast to the idealist constructivism discussed earlier, which treats ideas, norms and values as if they were organizing practices, it is important for an analysis to insist on materiality of conducts (and the conducts of conducts) of all the practices (including the discursive ones). One must go beyond the accumulated "capital" or "power" that agents have in an orthodox Bourdieusian sociology, as these agents are themselves embedded into situations where their actions are less dependent upon conscious or even sub-conscious strategies than they are on the socio-technical relationships into which they are embedded. These socio-technical power relations, which circulate inside and between the security professions and their associated bureaucracies, are more fluid than the gatekeepers of each field would like. So often, the "actant"—to use a terminology of Bruno Latour—is a human relation with a database. In the database, as software makes connections between different files, it appears as though the software mediates between the human and the database. The human behaves as if they were an intermediary attributing agency to the software, claiming "it's not me, it's the computer." What becomes enacted seems to depend less upon humans, their language, and their strategies than on the so-called "object": the networked computer system. This is not to revert to a technology-driven approach, as the dichotomy between human and object is exactly the boundary which needs to be discussed and deconstructed. Further, it is to foreground the materiality of this infrastructure, when activated by the man-machine relation, as this materiality is acting through humans as much as the historical trajectories and previous experiments of the human beings, and certainly more than their intellectual discussions about values. The field boundaries of the professional guilds of (in)security and their transnational dimensions as well as their penetration in many other domains of life, seem then to be correlated with this "infrastructure," the transversality of which so many studies of surveillance have explored. It has to be aligned with the so-called "security industrial complex" and to be considered as something which has transformed the field, and something which the interests of security professionals are obliged to negotiate and incorporate. Databases and software appear to be the material each agency uses and the symbolic capital they wish to accumulate. An agency (in the sense of an organization) has the authority to claim a performative discourse on security when it has succeeded in convincing other agencies that the database they possess is useful for them too. Managing (in)security through databases supports the belief that monitoring the future of human beings is possible, which has become the doxa of all security professionals obsessed with the "preventive dimension." This preventive dimension—as indicated through the emergence of surveillance studies—generates suspicion and discretion, destabilizes our notions of privacy, freedom and democracy as well as presumption of innocence. It is then central to analyze the transformation of democracy and freedom implied by a view of the future as a future already known, as a "future antérieur," as a future perfect. Our analysis must extend beyond surveillance and security, to an international political sociology of liberty.

The politics of (in)security: risk, suspicion and prevention—monitoring the future as future perfect

If an international political sociology of liberty asks "Whose (in)security?," is it not important for surveillance studies to ask "Whose surveillance?" as well as asking what "surveillance"—as an assignation—does, as opposed to what it means? To say that an object is surveillant perhaps has an impact upon the framing and construction of the social world. And surveillance scholars may have to take the dilemma exposed by Jef Huysmans seriously. In the context of a discussion about critical security studies, he states that the permanent enlargement of what can be considered "securitized" by those who critique security, can then result in their participation in its subsequent securitization.

What is going on with surveillance studies? Is it necessary to de-surveiller, to undo surveillance? Ole Waever proposed to "desecuritise" issues, when securitization was excluding them from normal politics and was justifying exception and arbitrary practices, so what about surveillance? What is the opposite of surveillance? Privacy, freedom, rule of law, care or love of surveillance? Certainly the discussion about the latter performative that McGrath explores is a central one, as it involves a politics, and a politics of the position of the researcher.

The tendency to avoid these questions has been to pool together security, insecurity, danger, surveillance and freedom under the category of risk, and to create a melting pot where every life event is a risk, both as an opportunity and as a danger. I will not develop a critique of this approach here, which transforms crime, social change and war into a risk which can be actuarialized and predicted. It is also a common concern for security and surveillance studies. If they wish to avoid becoming the adjunct of managerial techniques, they need to emphasize that monitoring the future and transforming it into a future perfect, a future already known, is impossible. Future always creates uncertainty and ambiguities, and the reduction of the former multiplies the latter. Liberty studies may be the other face of both security and surveillance studies, and it may be a way to understand better how they may join forces and to find ways to democratize not only (in)security and surveillance, but also freedom (Bigo *et al.* 2010).

References

Bigo, D., Carrera, S., Guild, E. and Walker, R. B. J. (2010). *Europe's 21st Century Challenge: Delivering Liberty and Security*, Aldershot: Ashgate.

Bigo, D. and Tsoukala, A. (eds). (2008). *Terror, Insecurity and Liberty. Illiberal Practices of Liberal Regimes after 9/11*, London and New York: Routledge.

Buzan, B. (1983). *People, States, and Fear: The National Security Problem in International Relations*, Chapel Hill: University of North Carolina Press.

C.A.S.E., COLLECTIVE. (2007). "Critical Approaches to Security in Europe: A Networked Manifesto," *Security Dialogue*, 37(4): 443–87.

Haggerty, K. D. and Ericson, R. V. (2000). "The Surveillant Assemblage," *British Journal of Sociology*, 51(4): 605–22.

Lyon, D. (2006). *Theorizing Surveillance: The Panopticon and Beyond*, Cullompton, Devon: Willan Publishing.

Marx, G. T. (1971). *Racial Conflict. Tension and Change in American Society*, Boston, MA: Little, Brown & Co.

Murakami Wood, D. (2009). "Situating Surveillance Studies," *Surveillance & Society*, 6(1): 52–61.

Norris, C., Moran, J. and Armstrong, G. (1998). *Surveillance, Closed Circuit Television and Social Control*, Aldershot: Ashgate.

Waever, O., Buzan, B., Kelstrup, M. and Lemaitre, P. (1993). *Identity, Migration and the New Security Agenda in Europe*, London: Pinter.

c. Surveillance and terrorism

Torin Monahan

Terrorism, or the threat of it, has been a remarkable catalyst for state surveillance. The attacks of 9/11 in particular galvanized a significant restructuring of the surveillance field, including legislation to facilitate state surveillance, reorganization of government agencies to prioritize national security, financial and political commitments to new surveillance programs and technologies, and exploration of various public-private partnerships for the provision of security.

However, state surveillance was not born out of the ashes of the collapsed World Trade Center towers, the smoldering Pentagon, or the burned wreckage of the hijacked airplane that crashed in Pennsylvania. In the United States, there is a rich history of surveillance operations. Two examples include the monumental Cold-War-era ECHELON system (still operational) that intercepts satellite and other communications to spy on enemies and allies alike, and the FBI and CIA's infamous COINTELPRO program that targeted civil-rights leaders and peaceful protestors of the war in Vietnam. These and other programs may have been reined-in by laws, but state surveillance practices persisted. The political climate after 9/11 simply encouraged politicians, state agents, and others to embrace surveillance programs, in a public way, once more.

While it is accurate to say that surveillance intensified after 2001, it is also true that it metamorphosed—it both adapted and contributed to a cultural ecology of insecurity. This ecology was characterized by media-provoked moral panics about individual vulnerability to terrorist attack; suspicion of others, especially Muslims; the declaration of a potentially endless "war on terror"; calls for American citizens to take responsibility for ensuring the safety of the country; and a bourgeoning private-sector security industry (Altheide 2006; Monahan 2010). Surveillance operations took on specific characteristics during this time. On one hand, federal efforts to ensure national security became more aggressive in form and invasive of civil liberties. On the other hand, individuals and private companies were enrolled in official and unofficial surveillance programs, while communities were charged with mitigating insecurities at the local level. These changes refashioned relationships among citizens, private companies, and the state. This chapter will review some of the more notable counterterrorism surveillance programs since 9/11 and assess their implications. Because other chapters in this handbook delve into the globalization of homeland security, the emphasis here will be on the United States.

The USA PATRIOT Act

A mere 45 days after the 9/11 attacks, US Congress enacted broad, far-reaching security legislation known as The USA PATRIOT Act of 2001 ("Uniting and Strengthening America by Providing Appropriate Tools

Required to Intercept and Obstruct Terrorism Act of 2001"). This legislation passed with close to unanimous support and almost no debate, afterwards opening the floodgates for law-enforcement surveillance and attenuating civil-liberties protections that had been in place for decades. According to surveillance-studies scholar Priscilla Regan: "The USA PATRIOT Act amends virtually every information privacy statute to facilitate access, increase data collection, and reduce the due process and privacy protections for record subjects" (Regan 2004: 482).

One controversial provision was for "national security letters" (NSLs), which were subpoenas that the Federal Bureau of Investigation (FBI) or other agencies could deliver to organizations, such as libraries, demanding information on patrons without needing to establish probable cause or submit to judicial oversight. There was also a gag order in place so that the recipient of an NSL could not disclose to anyone that she or he had received such a request, which effectively precluded access to legal counsel, stripping away this constitutionally guaranteed right. At least 192,499 NSLs were issued before the gag clause was struck down by the US District Court in 2007.

Another radical change brought about by the Patriot Act was the ability of law enforcement to collect electronic information on citizens. Many of the mechanisms by which this could take place were specified in the law, including the ability to serve administrative subpoenas to internet service providers, request records from cable companies, and access some banking and education records (Regan 2004). And while there were provisions in place for law enforcement to tap into routing information for internet traffic, domestic populations should have been protected from the wholesale surveillance of telecommunications content. They were not.

Starting with a *New York Times* story in December 2005 it gradually came to light that by an executive order signed by President George W. Bush, the National Security Agency (NSA) had been engaging in warrantless wiretaps of the phone calls, text messages, emails, and internet activity of citizens. This occurred in cooperation with telecommunications companies, such as AT&T, but in clear violation of the Foreign Intelligence Surveillance Act of 1978 (Monahan 2010). The authorities and telecommunications companies involved could have been charged for these crimes were it not for the rapid amendment of FISA in 2008, which granted *retroactive* immunity to the parties involved.

The Department of Homeland Security

On the heels of The USA PATRIOT Act came a massive government reorganization with the creation of the Department of Homeland Security (DHS) in 2002 (see Gates, this volume). This new department incorporated 22 different agencies, many of which previously had little to do with the provision of security, and yoked them to the mission of protecting the country (Monahan 2010). DHS is notorious for implementing a color-coded "Homeland Security Advisory System" to communicate threat levels to its agencies and the public. This graphic scale has become synonymous with an accepted, if manufactured, state of constant risk of terrorist attack; it is an emblem that represents the dominant ethos of post-9/11 insecurity. There have been some compelling critiques that this threat-level system has been used to maintain fear in the public and justify preemptive war in Iraq and state surveillance at home; it is further asserted that the scale has been manipulated for political purposes, with the threat level being increased unjustifiably close to the 2004 presidential election (Altheide 2006).

Probably the most visible incarnation of protective measures came in the form of airport security overseen by the Transportation Security Administration (TSA), which was an administration created in 2001 and moved into DHS in 2003. In an effort to prevent future acts of terrorism via airplanes or at airports, a panoply of screening systems were put in place, ranging from x-ray baggage screening to full-body scanners to behavioral monitoring to so-called random searches. Behind the scenes, counterterrorism dataveillance systems were phased in as well, such as "no-fly lists" that have been publicly criticized for apparent racial profiling and numerous "false positives"—both Nelson Mandela and the late Senator Edward Kennedy were included on no-fly lists, for instance. These systems of advance screening represent what Shoshana Magnet (2011) has insightfully called the "outsourcing of the border," which extends the scrutiny and filtering of travelers beyond physical borders to heterogeneous sites of data analysis. Additionally, most airport security systems lend themselves to unequal "social sorting" (Lyon 2003), where travelers are exposed to different degrees and types of surveillance based on their presumed risk levels (see Adey, Gates, this volume).

The creation of DHS helped normalize security operations in the USA. Whereas even the concept of "the homeland" would have sounded dangerously nationalistic before 9/11, by the end of George W. Bush's presidency in 2009 many Americans and the media used the term as a seemingly neutral description of the country in need of protection. On an organizational level, the fact that the agencies absorbed into DHS were given new missions that prioritize security over service provision means that the orientation of state agents to citizens and non-citizens has altered as well, arguably becoming more agonistic in the process. Finally, as elaborate surveillance rituals at airports and elsewhere have become commonplace, passive compliance is now the norm and anything else suspect.

DHS fusion centers

The Department of Homeland Security also founded counterterrorism organizations operating on local, tribal, state, and regional levels. These organizations, known as "fusion centers," engage in a mostly abstract form of surveillance: bringing together data from disparate public and private sources to aid in investigations of individuals, conduct threat assessments of events, identify patterns of criminal or terrorist activity, and, in conjunction with emergency operations centers, coordinate responses to disasters. As of 2010, there were 72 official fusion centers throughout the USA and a plethora of similar organizations performing "information analysis," including what appear to be private-sector versions of these entities that contract out to state and federal DHS offices. Most fusion centers are housed in local or state police departments and range from large-scale enterprises with futuristic video walls to smaller operations with just a few desktop computers. They are staffed by police, FBI, DHS and other analysts who constantly share information with representatives at other fusion centers and with federal agencies.

In some respects, the network of fusion centers is a decentralized version of the Defense Department's aborted "Total Information Awareness" (TIA) program. Whereas TIA was intended to engage in mass public surveillance without warrants for the purposes of identifying potential terrorists through data mining for pattern matches, fusion centers are allegedly conducting more focused surveillance on known or suspected threats. In practice, however, fusion centers have been involved in spying on peaceful anti-war protestors, interrogating individuals without appropriate jurisdiction, and compiling threat assessments encouraging racial profiling (Monahan 2011). Drawing upon "suspicious activity reports" and other documents, analysts at these centers construct profiles of threatening individuals and single those people out for further monitoring or preemptive intervention. This crime-prevention modality, known as "intelligence-led policing," apparently encourages the injection of cultural biases into police intelligence work and opens up opportunities for abuse (Monahan 2011).

Fusion centers are also increasingly connected to other advanced surveillance systems. In cities such as Boston and Chicago, for instance, fusion centers can control urban closed-circuit television (CCTV) cameras in real time. Some of these CCTV systems are equipped with algorithmic surveillance functions and audio systems, allowing "smart" cameras to automatically identify suspicious behavior, such as people congregating on a corner, or unique sound signatures, such as gunfire. And as unmanned aerial vehicles (UAVs), or drones, are deployed for purposes of domestic policing, fusion centers can access data from those devices as well, which is something that has occurred in Las Vegas and most likely in other cities too.

Additionally, it is important to note that fusion centers contribute to the general restructuring of the national security enterprise by partnering with, outsourcing to, or privileging the needs of the private sector (Monahan 2010). For starters, fusion centers purchase data from private-sector data aggregators, which are companies that hold billions of records on Americans, including credit information, consumer preferences, demographic and political profiles, and many other data points, some of which would be illegal for government agents to collect on their own. Next, fusion centers work to protect "critical infrastructure," be it publicly or privately owned—utilities, bridges, hotels, universities, and buildings can all count as critical infrastructure. To further this goal, fusion centers both collect information from these private entities and share information with them, and DHS is on record saying that fusion centers need to figure out ways to serve the private sector better. Finally, fusion centers employ private-sector analysts and invite representatives from large corporations to join them on-site, at the same time that members of the public or representatives from civil society groups are locked out. All of this is cause for concern because private contractors have significantly less accountability and fewer data-protection restrictions than government employees do and, more fundamentally, these arrangements obscure the fact that the interests of industry do not equate with the needs of society.

Citizen spies and discourses of preparedness

"We are all soldiers now," so the *Washington Post* declared the day after 9/11 (Monahan 2010: 8). The logic behind this and similar statements seemed to be that because terrorists refused to differentiate between civilians and soldiers, then everyone should adopt the subject position of combatant: on the lookout for threats and ready to fight. As the preceding sections illustrated, the legislation and the surveillance programs that were developed in the months following the attacks similarly stripped away traditional boundaries between citizens and government agents, and reduced civil-liberties protections to accommodate security imperatives.

The administration of George W. Bush was instrumental in developing a rubric of "preparedness" or "readiness" that has come to characterize a general relationship of citizens to the state (Andrejevic 2007). There are several noteworthy manifestations of this. First, government programs sought to enlist citizens to engage in surveillance, whether of suspicious individuals, packages, or critical infrastructure. Immediately following 9/11, for instance, the Justice Department attempted to implement a "Terrorism Information and Prevention System" (TIPS) program that would require service workers, such as postal carriers or cable technicians, to report anything they found to be suspicious in the houses they entered. A similar program called "Highway Watch," which was spearheaded by DHS, encouraged interstate truck drivers to call tip hotlines if they spotted anything unusual on the freeways or at rest stops. In a more mundane way, all public-relations campaigns to have everyday people participate in security-related surveillance fall into this category, such as the pervasive "if you see something, say something" slogans found in public transportation arenas.

A second version of preparedness thrusts responsibility upon individuals and communities for contending with human needs, especially in times of disaster. As with the attempted cultivation of citizen spies, disaster preparedness programs exploit a variety of media (pamphlets, websites, videos, reports, educational seminars) to communicate that the public must become the first line of defense against insecurities. So, people are advised to purchase products to help them cope with disasters, natural or otherwise: duct tape, bottled water, canned food, flashlights (torches), batteries, tissues, medical supplies, prescription drugs, plastic sheets, and so on. They are told to join or start community-preparedness and neighborhood-watch groups. And they are instructed to modify their behavior to minimize exposure to external risks, such as to influenza pandemics. Much of this becomes a form of self-surveillance, whereby people accept responsibility for their own well-being, while the state abdicates its own responsibility for ensuring human security, or freedom from fear or want. As the catastrophe caused by Hurricane Katrina in 2005 shows, this modality of preparedness can have deadly consequences. Messages of citizen responsibility coupled with the reorientation of government agencies to prioritize state—over human—security bring about conditions of heightened economic and environmental vulnerability for most members of society, especially the poorest.

Attempted terrorism and surveillance failures

Technological surveillance seems to have had very little success in stopping attempted terrorism since 9/11. Just as critical evaluations of CCTV have drawn attention to the lack of proven effectiveness of these systems for preventing crime (Monahan 2006), the same holds true for many of the surveillance and screening systems intended to interrupt terrorist plots. If anything, evidence points to the fact that older forms of intelligence gathering, such as people talking to people, is more likely to render useful information about potential terrorist attacks. There may be unpublicized cases where surveillance has prevented terrorism, but given that intelligence successes are frequently trumpeted by the respective agencies involved, it would be unusual for significant achievements to remain hidden for years.

A few prominent examples of known attempted terrorist attacks reveal the limitations of surveillance. In December 2001, Richard Reid, who has become known as "the shoe bomber," unsuccessfully attempted to ignite explosives in his shoes while traveling on an airplane flight from Paris to Miami. The recently revamped passenger-screening system failed to detect the explosives, although afterwards mandatory shoe screening was implemented at many airports. In December 2009, Umar Farouk Abdulmutallab similarly tried but failed to detonate explosives on a flight from Amsterdam to Detroit. He received serious burns for his efforts, because the explosives were in his underpants, but was, like Reid, ultimately subdued by passengers. While airport screening did not detect Abdulmutallab's explosives, it later became public that his father had reported him to the US Embassy in Nigeria as a potential threat, but that this intelligence was not communicated appropriately and therefore failed to result in Abdulmutallab being placed on a no-fly list.

In another example, from May 2010, Faisal Shahzad attempted to detonate a car bomb in Times Square in New York City. In spite of this site having a high concentration of CCTV cameras, it was a pair of street vendors who noticed smoke coming from the vehicle, heard popping sounds, and notified the police. Shahzad was apprehended after boarding an aircraft headed to Dubai. In this case, intelligence systems were used to locate the suspect, but the attack would have succeeded were it not for the faulty assembly of the explosives in the vehicle and the vigilance of the vendors. In one final example from October 2010, mail bombs originating in Yemen were sent in UPS packages being transported by airplanes to Chicago. Again, existing screening systems failed to detect the explosives. Instead, it was intelligence from an informant in Saudi Arabia, and a successful alert by Saudi security officials, that led agents in the United Arab Emirates and the United Kingdom to locate the bombs before they went off.

Obviously dangerous terrorist threats persist and need to be taken seriously. But these few examples call into question the efficacy of technological surveillance for preventing attacks. In the first three of these cases, the potential terrorists simply failed to detonate their explosives, most likely because of technical mistakes on their part, but also because of intervention by people who were not law-enforcement personnel. In the last case, human intelligence was successfully harnessed to inform others of the bombs, but only after existing systems for cargo screening failed spectacularly. Thus, faith in surveillance to mitigate terrorism is probably misplaced.

Conclusion and reflections on the field

This chapter explored the role of surveillance in post-9/11 institutional arrangements, legislation, policing practices, and public responses, with a focus on the USA. The USA PATRIOT Act brought about an intensification of surveillance through national security letters, tip hotlines, government spying on citizens and others, and illegal wiretaps. With the formation of the Department of Homeland Security, the missions of government agencies included in DHS were modified to prioritize national security over service provision and the public was conditioned to surveillance through airport screening and exposure to the color-coded Homeland Security Advisory System. Counterterrorism organizations known as fusion centers operate as decentralized organizations that model surveillance functions upon intelligence-led policing, preemptive risk management, and industry partnerships. Discourses of "preparedness" and "readiness" contribute to a paradigm of risk management (and self-surveillance) that stresses individual over institutional responsibility and may in turn aggravate conditions of human insecurity. Finally, several attempted terrorist attacks on the USA since 9/11 have failed largely due to errors on the part of would-be terrorists or the successful use of human intelligence, not technological surveillance, which calls into question the effectiveness of many of the developments in national security over the past decade.

The field of surveillance studies grew up in response to the changes wrought by 9/11. Just as state surveillance existed before these dramatic terrorist attacks, so did scholarship on surveillance, but it did not have the stability or coherence typically associated with well-established academic fields, such as having a dedicated journal, regular conferences, or academic degree programs. One of the first moves made by this rapidly maturing field was to correct the mistake of media and other commentators who perceived a simple cause-and-effect relationship between the 9/11 attacks and the unveiling of state surveillance programs and systems. Surveillance studies scholars drew attention instead to the "intensification" or "surge" of already present but largely hidden forms of systematic monitoring, tracking, analysis, and control by police and other state agents (Ball and Webster 2003; Lyon 2003; Wood et al. 2003). By the time of the terrorist bombings in London on 7 July 2005 the field was honed to analyze the surveillance failures and police responses with depth and sensitivity.

It is nonetheless the case that the field has privileged analysis of USA and UK surveillance practices. This observation holds true even for scholars who are not themselves located in these states. There are a few likely explanations for this. First, the media spectacle created by the attacks of 9/11 and 7/7 thrust these events into an international arena and captured public attention in a way that invited, or perhaps compelled, scholarly investigation. Related to this is the global dominance of Western media, which is predisposed to lend more airtime to matters pertaining to the USA and other English-speaking countries. Second, responses by the USA to terrorist threats have been extreme, as I have noted in this chapter, and provided ample content for study and theorization. Third, like all academic fields, surveillance studies has created a conversation around a set of primary interests, and members are encouraged, or normed, to participate in this ongoing dialogue. Engaging in this conversation advances the field, especially when academics acknowledge and then challenge current norms. Because the field grew so rapidly in response to security practices after 9/11, it makes sense that scholars would reproduce a focus on the West in general and the USA and UK in particular. But it is clearly time to expand the regions and topics of inquiry, which is exactly what is happening.

With regard to the topic of surveillance and terrorism, scholars in the field are now moving to document the emergence of a global security industry. Others are working to theorize national and cultural differences in deployments of security-based surveillance, including differences in the meanings attached to such systems. Still other researchers are exploring how surveillance systems may simultaneously function as security devices and consumer products that lend themselves to enjoyable uses. These are just a few of the important areas of research occurring in this burgeoning field. Government responses to terrorism have served as a foil for surveillance studies, and this continues to be the case, but many other avenues for research have opened up as well.

References

Andrejevic, M. (2007). *iSpy: Surveillance and Power in the Interactive Era*, Lawrence: University Press of Kansas.
Altheide, D. (2006). *Terrorism and the Politics of Fear*, Lanham, MD: Altamira Press.
Ball, K. and Webster, F. (eds). (2003). *The Intensification of Surveillance: Crime, Terrorism and Warfare in the Information Age*, Sterling, VA: Pluto Press.
Lyon, D. (2003). *Surveillance after September 11*, Malden, MA: Polity Press.

Magnet, S. (2011). *When Biometrics Fail: Gender, Race, and the Technology of Identity*, Durham, NC: Duke University Press.

Monahan, T. (2006). "Questioning Surveillance and Security," in T. Monahan (ed.), *Surveillance and Security: Technological Politics and Power in Everyday Life*, New York: Routledge.

——(2010). *Surveillance in the Time of Insecurity*, New Brunswick, NJ: Rutgers University Press.

——(2011). "The Future of Security? Surveillance Operations at Homeland Security Fusion Centers," *Social Justice*, 37(2–3): 84–98.

Regan, P. M. (2004). "Old Issues, New Context: Privacy, Information Collection and Homeland Security," *Government Information Quarterly*, 21: 481–97.

Wood, D., Konvitz, E. and Ball, K. (2003). "The Constant State of Emergency?: Surveillance after 9/11," in K. Ball and F. Webster (eds), *The Intensification of Surveillance: Crime, Terrorism and Warfare in the Information Age*, London: Pluto Press.

d. The globalization of homeland security

Kelly Gates

[H]homeland security must involve much more than protecting life and property within the borders of the United States. ... economic security must not now be seen as somehow incompatible with globalization. To the contrary, we seek to secure our homeland precisely so that we can enjoy the full benefits – economic and otherwise – of globalization. Homeland security and globalization are the flip sides of the same coin.

(Kenneth Juster, Austin, Texas, 13 February 2002)[1]

In his remarks at one of the many security conferences held in the United States in the wake of the September 11 terrorist attacks, Kenneth Juster, Under Secretary of Commerce for Export Administration, emphasized the integral relationship that would have to be forged between new "homeland security" programs and the forces of globalization. Juster's definition of "globalization" was instructive: "increased economic integration throughout the world—whether it be increased trade, increased flows of information and capital, increased foreign investment, or increased mobility of labor and the means of production." It was precisely this corporate-capitalist model of globalization that was under attack on September 11, according to Juster, and precisely what would need protection and bolstering. The terrorist attacks aimed to compel the nation "to abandon our global engagement," he explained. In response, homeland security would need to be forged on new security-centric public-private partnerships designed to guarantee that global capitalism could progress unabated. In addressing the need for intensified critical infrastructure protection in particular, Juster was emphatic that US security efforts would have to extend well beyond its borders, and that "only an unprecedented partnership between private industry and government will work."

Under Secretary Juster's comments are emblematic of the ways "homeland security" was conceptualized among neoliberal political elites from its earliest incarnations: a marriage of state agencies and private industry, with the primary aim of securing—physically and financially—the industries and infrastructures of global capitalism. The new levels of global insecurity inspired by the 9/11 terrorist attacks were seen as an unprecedented opportunity for growth in an already expanding global security industry. From its very beginnings, "homeland security" was conceived as a set of local, national, and transnational ventures aimed at maximum profitability, including proposals for massive investment in the development and deployment of new surveillance and security technologies. By the end of the decade, industry reports were estimating that the level of worldwide governmental spending on the products and services of this sector would be over $140 billion. (The reports themselves cost $2,500 or more.) According to promotional material for one such report, titled "Global Homeland Security 2009–19," "the high priority given to homeland security has made that market one of the few recession-resistant sectors of the defence industry."[2]

How have the priorities of "homeland security" in the post-9/11 era been mobilized to bolster an expanding global industry, and what are the consequences of this industry expansion on surveillance practices transnationally? It is the aim of this chapter to consider the *globalization of homeland security*. It examines the extent to which the US model of homeland security has been exported to other countries, and what the results have been for the spread of new surveillance practices across national borders. "Homeland security" is typically understood as a policy program instituted in the United States as a response to the 9/11 terrorist attacks. I argue that it is more adequately understood as a broader governmental rationality that reconfigures the US Cold War "national security" regime in ways more amenable to the post-Cold War context, and to the priorities of an emerging global security industry. In order to be promoted as a form of national identity, the US model of "homeland security" has been and must continue to be defined as uniquely "American." However, it is also being globalized in particular ways in order to serve as a powerful political and economic strategy in the "war on terror" (see also Hayes, this volume).

One focus of this strategy has been the USA-led effort to create a global surveillance apparatus, a dispersed system of monitoring and identification that aims to enact a USA-centric politics of inclusion and exclusion on a global scale. Not only the USA, but much of the world, is engaged in what Giorgio Agamben (2005) has called a permanent "state of exception." Here constitutional laws and human rights are suspended indefinitely, and individuals are continuously called upon to demonstrate their legitimate identity and right to exist. As the USA and its allies carry out the seemingly endless "war on terror," a heavily financed "security-industrial complex" has taken shape. Along with it has come a seemingly endless and increasingly integrated stream of new surveillance systems and practices.

What is "homeland security"?

In order to understand the extent and implications of the globalization of homeland security, it is first necessary to consider what the term encompasses. Although often used in ways that suggest that the meaning is self-evident, in fact "homeland security" is not a static or neutral concept. Precisely *how* it is conceptualized and operationalized, within and beyond the state, is a critical question that needs to be examined in order to make more adequate sense of its historical significance. A critical analysis of "homeland security" sheds light on the tension between, on the one hand, its status as a set of ideas, policies and practices central to US policy and national identity in the early twenty-first century, and on the other hand, efforts on the part of both the US security state and the private security industry to globalize it.

The concept of "security" that underpins the post-9/11 model of "homeland security" has important genealogical ties to the prevailing ways of conceptualizing state security that took shape during the Cold War. In fact, "homeland security" is not, as is often assumed, exclusively a post-9/11 invention. Terms like "homeland defense" and "homeland protection" appeared in US Congressional and military documents with some frequency in the 1990s (Beresford 2004: 4). The appearance of these terms in policy discussions *before* 9/11/01 suggests that state security actors were already beginning, out of perceived necessity, to reformulate the discourse of "national security" that defined the Cold War period. The emergence of the US national security state was indelibly tied to the battle to defeat communism worldwide, a conflict that was as much cultural as it was militaristic and policy-based. It was during this period that all of the major US federal security agencies were established, including the National Security Council (NSC), the National Security Agency (NSA), and the Central Intelligence Agency (CIA). This period also saw the coordination of the armed services, mandated by the National Security Act of 1947. While other countries formed national security programs of their own, the US paradigm of national security took on global and imperialistic proportions, exported to other countries in a variety of forms under the mantra of "international cooperation." In the USA, Cold War security discourse became firmly incorporated into national identity and notions of citizenship, at the core of a strategy of state legitimacy and social cohesion. The Soviet threat and anti-communist sentiment became foundational to American national and cultural identity in the post-WorldWar II period.

But as the well-known story goes, this vital source of US cultural identity and state legitimacy would begin to be called into question by the end of the twentieth century, as the Soviet Union disbanded and the threat of a communist takeover receded. From the perspective of state security actors, the prevailing paradigm of "security" would have to be reconfigured in this climate—both literally restructured and symbolically redefined—in order to continue to serve as an effective strategy of state legitimation and social mobilization. The 9/11 catastrophe provided an opportunity to catalyze new ways of thinking about the relationship between security and national identity better suited to the post-Cold War climate. Not only would homeland security replace Cold War security as a means of state legitimation and social mobilization, it would also provide a cohesive incentive, justification and promotion strategy for profitable new technology development, government outsourcing, and public-private institution building.

Without a doubt, "homeland security" became *the* defining term for US domestic policy in the post-9/11 context. Its distinctively American and post-9/11 connotations derive in part from the fact that it is the name given to a major US federal government agency formed in the months immediately following the 9/11 attacks: the Department of Homeland Security (DHS). Officially established by the Homeland Security Act and representing a major reorganization of federal government agencies, the DHS now encompasses a variety of agencies for airport security, border and immigration control, disaster response, and related areas: the Transportation and Security Administration (TSA), Customs and Border Inspection, Citizenship and Immigration Services, Immigrations and Customs Enforcement, the Secret Service, the Federal Emergency Management Agency, and the Coast Guard. The major topic areas listed at the DHS website suggest the kinds of programs for which the agency is primarily responsible: counterterrorism, border security, preparedness/response/recovery, immigration, and cybersecurity.

The agencies operating under the DHS umbrella do not encompass the entire range of actors formally charged with carrying out so-called homeland security policies and programs in the United States. The Federal Bureau of Investigation (FBI), which is not part of the DHS but the Department of Justice, has significant responsibilities considered central to homeland security, as do other agencies like the Department of Defense, the CIA, and the NSA. The Terrorist Screening Center, for example, charged with consolidating and managing a centralized watchlist database containing the identities of "terrorists," compiled from a variety of agency case files and intelligence gathering efforts worldwide, is part of the FBI. Outside of the federal government, state and local law enforcement agencies are also considered "homeland security" actors, responsible as they are for responding to incidents and identifying security threats at the community level. Some of these responsibilities are codified in federal statute. Under the Delegation of Immigration Authority Section 287(g) of the Immigration and Nationality Act, the Immigration and Customs Enforcement Agency (ICE) can formally and legally delegate authority for immigration enforcement to state and local law enforcement "partners." Once authority is designated, ICE conducts trainings and supervises all cross-designated police officers when they exercise their immigration authorities.

It is important to identify the range of official policies and programs that fall under the rubric homeland security, inside and outside of the authority of DHS agencies. However, it is also crucial to understand that "homeland security" can and does refer to an even broader range of political and governmental strategies that operate beyond these formal programs. Annette Beresford (2004) has argued that "homeland security" is best understood not as a neutral term that refers to a set of state policies and programs, but as an *American ideology*. By this she means a uniquely American system of beliefs that has functioned to support security programs and to provide the level of certainty required to sustain commitments and decision making in the post-9/11 US context (2004: 11). In her view, the purpose of establishing the DHS was not only to coordinate agencies, but also to create a tangible symbol of "homeland security" and to sustain it as a doctrine (2004: 13). As an ideology, homeland security carries with it a tendency to shut out alterative perspectives, according to Beresford, supporting the expansion of state security and military programs that do not necessarily lead to improvements in quality of life or other desirable ends.

Understanding "homeland security" as an ideology offers insight into how it becomes manifest in legal and institutional practice, public discourse, and daily life, and in turn, how it becomes an accepted, common-sense way of thinking about the world. It also helps highlight its historical and cultural specificity. Despite having origins in pre-9/11 policy discourse, "homeland security" has become inextricably tied to a set of ideas, strategies, and programs specific to the post-9/11 US context. "Homeland security" is distinctively American and distinctively post-9/11 in its political connotations and manifestations.

It is also important to understand that the "homeland security" paradigm codifies a heavily technocratic approach to government and security. Specifically, it has prioritized and provided legitimacy for the development and more widespread deployment of expensive new surveillance and identification technologies. These systems are designed to sort individuals according to risk and consumer-oriented categories of value. This represents an increasingly ubiquitous and data-intensive version of the "panoptic sort" that Oscar Gandy (1993) identified well before 9/11 as a powerful and largely invisible political-economic apparatus shaping human lives and life chances. As technical systems with a particular politics of inclusion and exclusion designed in, these new systems provide some measure of security for the access-privileged classes. Unfortunately they are not designed with the broader aim of providing more security for more people on the planet.

In fact, the "homeland security" paradigm depends fundamentally on a politics of inclusion and exclusion, a means of making determinations about who belongs to the "homeland" and who does not. Making this distinction has become the defining priority of a wide range of federal, state, and local agencies within and beyond the DHS. It is not only border and immigration control but law enforcement practice that is shot through with this politics of inclusion and exclusion. The police likewise are charged with sorting out who belongs to a community and who does not, who deserves protection as members of the community versus who poses a threat to the community. As the increasingly ubiquitous presence of identification systems suggests, the very definition of responsible citizenship now involves distinguishing oneself as non-threatening and civilized, proving one's legitimate legal identity on a constant basis (see Adey, Monahan, this volume).

This notion of responsible, always-identifiable citizenship points to another way of thinking about the meaning and implications of what is now called "homeland security," beyond its official state dimensions. For James Hay and Mark Andrejevic (2006), homeland security functions as a *governmental rationality* in the Foucauldian sense. It has become "an indispensable way of modernizing and rationalizing liberal government in these times," a way of mobilizing society around market-oriented models of risk management and self-securitization (2006: 331). In short, they see the US model of "homeland security" as "the new social security": a way of rethinking the state-centered social welfare programs of the New Deal period to bring them in line with the priorities of privatization. In this mode of governing, citizens are enjoined to take responsibility for their own security and risk management. Both the *National Strategy for Homeland Security* and the DHS "readiness" campaign emphasize the importance of self-reliance and self-help, positioning the state in more of a supportive role in providing security for citizens. As a governmental rationality, "homeland security" has been leveraged not only as an official policy orientation but also as a means of *government at a distance* from the official programs of the state.

Exporting "homeland security"

While "homeland security" is undeniably a US invention—a signifier of American national identity, territorial sovereignty, and governmental rationality in these times—it is also being exported beyond the territorial boundaries of the United States. As Under Secretary Juster's comments at the beginning of this chapter suggest, if the USA was going to continue to reap the benefits of its global economic dominance after 9/11, "homeland security" could not be conceived in narrowly protectionist or isolationist terms. From the earliest formation of homeland security strategy, US policy makers and political elites were explicit that it would require "international cooperation." Regardless of whether other countries saw the need to create their own "homeland security" agencies and programs, the global nature of security threats meant that the USA would need to enlist, or coerce if necessary, the assistance of other countries. Globalization itself—understood as the movement of people, goods, information and capital across national borders—meant that the new US security strategy, much like the old, would have to be a global endeavor.

Likewise for the security industry, a multinational approach to "homeland security" promised to invigorate new markets, but only if its US branding could be successfully navigated across national boundaries. Airport security, border control, passport policy, critical infrastructure protection, cybersecurity, and intelligence sharing were among the major areas that became sites for negotiating international cooperation and policy harmonization. They also became new profit centers for companies in the business of developing and deploying security technologies and services.

The coordination and cooperation of the European Union has been especially important to the global approach of US homeland security strategy. As a US Congressional Research Service Report noted in 2006, "in seeking to protect U.S. interests at home and abroad, many U.S. officials recognize that the actions or inactions of the European allies can affect U.S. domestic security" (Archick *et al.* 2006: 2). In some cases, the USA has successfully applied pressure to European countries to adopt new policies. For example, Belgium centralized its passport issuance process after the USA indicated that it might begin requiring visas for Belgians to enter the USA (ibid.: 5). USA-based defense and security think tanks have at times attempted to extend the concept of "homeland" outward to include other designated regions; for example, a 2006 report to NATO referred to "the transatlantic homeland" to encompass all of the USA, Canada and Europe.[3]

However, European countries have not always fallen in line with US homeland security proposals. In 2009, for example, the European Parliament rejected a proposal to mandate the use of whole-body scanners in all European airports. In addition, some European political elites have resisted the call to invest the level of attention and resources in counterterrorism that the USA has proposed. At a roundtable titled "Does Europe Need 'Homeland Security'?" hosted by a Belgium-based think tank in 2010, a representative from the UK's Royal Services Institute insisted that "terrorism is by no means the biggest threat to [critical infrastructure] and terrorism should by no means be the single biggest driver of [critical infrastructure protection]."[4] He pointed to severe weather conditions resulting from climate change as posing much greater threats to Europe's critical infrastructure. It is worthy of note that the International Civil Aviation Organization (ICAO) likewise, and surprisingly, has made environmental issues and climate change one of its most pressing "strategic objectives," on a par with airline security (see the ICAO's 2009 Annual Report[5] and its "Strategic Objectives" webpage). Despite the insistence on the part of many US policy makers that the "war on terror" be given top priority, a growing number of actors on the global stage are beginning to see a critical need to give greater priority to climate change and other manufactured environmental risks, as they likely pose an exponentially greater threat to the world's populations than terrorism.

However, there are considerable forces pressing European and other countries to invest major resources in security programs defined largely in terms of counterterrorism. Perhaps the greatest pressure on the EU to adopt a US-style "homeland security" strategy comes from efforts on the part of European countries to compete with the USA for a share of the security market. According to Ben Hayes, this competitive posturing has resulted in the rise of a "EU security-industrial complex." "Fuelled by a new politics of fear and insecurity," writes Hayes, "the corporate interest in selling security technology and the national security interest in buying security technology has converged at the EU level."[6]

The EU has been especially concerned about the competitive advantage of US security companies, and one avenue established to mitigate this advantage has been the formation of the European Security Research Programme (ESRP). The ESRP was formed on the recommendation of a group of security industry executives and EU politicians called the Group of Personalities (GoP). In their report, the GoP noted that, while the USA was taking a lead in the development of security technologies that could meet some of Europe's security needs, Europe should be cautious about adopting US technology. US dominance in this area would "progressively impose normative and operational standards worldwide," and put US companies "in a very strong competitive position" over European companies.[7] To remedy this problem, the group proposed that European security research be funded at a level similar to US levels. It called for a minimum of €1 billion per year in EU funds in order to "bridge the gap between civil and traditional defense research, foster the transformation of technologies across the civil, security and defense fields and improve the EU's industrial competitiveness" (ibid.).

Many countries have agreed to US demands for homeland security provisions in order to maintain good trade relationships with the largest consuming country in the world. As both major trading partners and bordering countries, Canada and Mexico have been under unique pressure to harmonize their border security policies with the USA. The cooperation of both countries has been pivotal to the successful deployment of biometrics and other surveillance technologies along US borders, and especially to the incremental implementation the US-VISIT automated entry-exit system.

These efforts on the part of other countries to maintain good relations with the USA on the one hand, or to bolster their own competitiveness in the global security market on the other, suggest that there have been significant economic drivers impacting the spread of "homeland security" programs on a global scale. Although other countries may not embrace the term itself or its unique connections to US identity, a significant proportion of the world's countries now place a premium on homeland security-oriented programs. Whether a response to political pressure from the USA, their own internal drivers, or some combination of these and other factors, countries are without a doubt moving toward globally harmonized security policies and programs. What is especially apparent is the global rollout of expensive new surveillance and identification technologies as part of the transition to so-called "smart borders."

The smart borders transition has been a transnational project, of necessity. "Smart borders are not just a matter of deploying hardware and software," as Rey Koslowski has noted; "they require international cooperation – and lots of it" (2005: 544). After 9/11, discussions between the USA and Canada initially considered the possibility of creating a "North American Perimeter" modeled on the European Union, lifting border controls between the countries and instead creating a common external border (Koslowski 2005). However, due in part to Canada's more extensive list of visitor visa exemptions, the North American Perimeter option was considered too ambitious a goal for policy harmonization. (The softening of internal border controls option was never seriously considered as an option between the USA and Mexico.) Subsequent discussions between the USA and Canada shifted toward "smart border agreements," focusing on pre-screening systems that would push US border security out beyond its borders (ibid.).

David Lyon (2003) has referred to the process of instituting stricter border security systems at points of departure beyond the territorial boundaries of states as the "delocalization of borders," what he calls "a prime example of globalized surveillance" (2003: 110). New "smart border" policies subject individuals and goods to inspection well before they arrive at a US border or airport. Without a doubt, the successful delocalization of borders requires considerable negotiation among participating countries, including the implementation of intensive systems of transnational information sharing. While there are certainly ways in which the 9/11 terrorist attacks slowed down the momentum of global flows of trade and migration, the attacks also stimulated certain globalizing processes, for example, by increasing flows of surveillance data across national borders (Lyon 2003).

The international airline system in particular now operates as a system of transnational surveillance, as does the global financial system. USA-based passenger screening operations, like the former CAPSS and

CAPSS-II and the more recent Secure Flight program, are powered by a new level of convergence among formerly discrete systems (ibid.). Authorities in the USA and the EU have been in ongoing negotiations over transnational transfers of passenger record name (PNR) data from Europe to the USA at least since 2006, when the European Court of Justice annulled a temporary data-transfer agreement based on a legal technicality. While US efforts to impose its own PNR data policies on Europe have met with some controversy, Europe has largely capitulated to US demands for PNR data. Throughout the dispute over PNR data transfers, writes one legal analyst, "the United States has been able to demand everything its legislation requires," without having to compromise in order to meet the legal requirements of the EU (Rasmussen 2008: 588). A similar scenario has played out over agreements concerning transnational transfers of financial data. In June 2006, three major US newspapers broke the story that the Belgian-based Society for Worldwide Interbank Financial Telecommunication (SWIFT) had been secretly sharing financial transaction data with the USA as part of the latter's Terrorist Finance Tracking Program (TFTP). Since then, the European Parliament has voted to end the agreement with the USA to share SWIFT data, determining it to be a violation of EU privacy law. Vocal opposition among European policy makers to US demands for airline, financial, and other transaction data clearly has made some difference. But whether in fact such transnational data-sharing programs have fully ceased to operate remains an open question, especially given the fact that they were secret and arguably illegal programs from the start.

Homeland security vs global security

Institutionalizing a globalized system of "smart borders," airline passenger screening, and financial data tracking not only requires harmonizing policies, integrating technologies, and sharing information transnationally. It also requires normalizing the governmental rationality of homeland security on a global scale. Part of this risk-management orientation to security involves the application (in theory if not realistically in practice) of a politics of inclusion and exclusion to the entirety of the world's population, treating every individual as a potential security threat who can be stripped of legal rights. While the ideology of homeland security posits this approach as common sense in the exceptional context of the "war on terror," in fact it is not hard to see how such a model slips easily into a scenario where the political order itself generates insecurity, with the state itself posing a threat to the well-being of excluded individuals. Some state systems seem to recognize this problem better than others. As Edna Keeble (2005) has argued, Canada's inclusionary orientation to immigrants, which views them as "citizens-in-waiting," is a more effective approach to creating a secure national community than the more exclusionary, or at best laissez faire, approach to immigration practiced in the USA. "Because the U.S. government's policies have undermined the sense of belonging of many ethnic communities," writes Keeble, "racial and ethnic cleavages are more evident there, and are more likely to be aggravated" (2005: 372). To the extent that the governmental rationality of "homeland security" depends at its core on determining who belongs to the homeland and who does not, who is entitled to security and who is a threat to that security, it remains at odds rather than commensurate with a truly global conceptualization of security and human rights.

What would a more global and human rights-oriented version of security look like? Is it possible for nation-states to view the planet in its entirety as the "homeland," and all of its inhabitants, whatever their differences, as belonging to it? In the face of climate change and global ecological crisis, the intensive focus on identification and border fortification during the first decade of the twenty-first century seems misguided. What use is the institutionalization of "smart borders" in the face of a planet being reconfigured by unsustainable practices of industrial production and consumption? To be sure, the fallout of climate change in the years ahead will likely exacerbate conditions of regional scarcity, prompting states to continue to fortify their borders and harshly delineate categories of belonging. To avoid such a dysfunctional and reactionary approach to the global crisis, a radical rethinking of global security is essential.

Some promising evidence is beginning to appear that members of the US security state are recognizing a critical need to reorient security policy around issues of global sustainability. *The New York Times* recently reported on a paper written by two military strategists (assistants to the chairman of the Joint Chiefs of Staff), in which they call on the United States "to see that it cannot continue to engage the world primarily with military force, but must do so as a nation powered by the strength of its educational system, social policies, international development, and diplomacy, and its commitment to sustainable practices in energy and agriculture" (Dwyer 2011: A20). One could be forgiven for being dismissive of the notion that the USA—which consumes a massively disproportionate share of the world's resources and has consistently undermined the international community's efforts to address climate change—is somehow a world leader in its commitment to sustainability. Nevertheless, the source and sentiment of the paper offers some hope that there may at least be a debate taking shape, within the state security community itself, over how security should be conceptualized and operationalized.

Notes

1 Remarks presented at *Critical Infrastructures: Working Together in a New World* at Austin, Texas, February 2002, www.bis.doc.gov/news/2002/communityactionimportantnhomelandsecurity.htm.
2 See ASD Reports at www.asdreports.com/shopexd.asp?ID=1442.
3 See report from the Center for Technology and National Security Policy, www.ndu.edu/CTNSP/docUploaded/Transatlantic Homeland Def.pdf.
4 See www.securitydefenceagenda.org/Portals/7/2010/Publications/Report_Homeland_Security.pdf.
5 See the International Civil Aviation Organization 2009 Annual Report at www.icao.int/icaonet/dcs/9921/9921_en.pdf.
6 See www.tni.org/report/neoconopticon, p. 6.
7 See http://database.statewatch.org/article.asp?aid=29438, p. 3.

References

Agamben, G. (2005). *State of Exception*, translated by Kevin Attell, Chicago, IL: University of Chicago Press.
Archick, K., Ek, C., Gallis, P., Miko, F. and Woehrel, S. (2006). *Congressional Report for Congress: European Approaches to Homeland Security and Counterterrorism*, RL33573, 24 July 2006.
Beresford, A. D. (2004). "Homeland Security as an American Ideology: Implications for U.S. Policy and Action," *Journal of Homeland Security and Emergency Management*, 1(3): 1–22.
Dwyer, J. (2011). "A National Security Strategy that Doesn't Focus on Threats," *The New York Times*, A20, 4 May 2011.
Gandy, O. (1993). *The Panoptic Sort: A Political Economy of Personal Information*, Boulder, CO: Westview Press.
Hay, J. and Andrejevic, M. (2006). "Toward an Analytic of Governmental Experiments in These Times: Homeland Security as the News Social Security," *Cultural Studies*, 20(4–5): 331–48.
Keeble, E. (2005). "Immigration, Civil Liberties, and National/Homeland Securities," *International Journal*, 60(2): 359–72.
Koslowski, R. (2005). "Smart Borders, Virtual Borders or No Borders: Homeland Security Choices for the United States and Canada," *Law and Business Review of the Americas*, 11(3–4): 527–45.
Lyon, D. (2003). *Surveillance After September 11*, Cambridge: Polity.
Rasmussen, D. R. (2008). "Is International Travel Per Se Suspicion of Terrorism? The Dispute Between the United States and Europe Over Passenger Name Record Data Transfers," *Wisconsin International Law Journal*, 28: 551–90.

Section 3.4.
Production, consumption, administration

a. Organization, employees and surveillance

Graham Sewell

Introduction

It may seem an obvious point but it is worth stating at the beginning of this chapter: any consideration of the purpose and consequences of workplace surveillance cannot meaningfully proceed without also considering our understanding of the nature of the employment relationship. As we shall see, although it is no doubt important, there is more to surveillance than developing the technical means to achieve specific practical ends (such as measuring and recording an individual's performance or maximizing organizational efficiency) and we should broaden discussion to include a consideration of the ethical, ideological, and political principles that are invoked to justify a broad range of disciplinary practices that we take for granted in today's organizations.

With this general objective in mind we can identify three main considerations that impinge on the operation of workplace surveillance. The first of these is the almost universal status of the contract-based employment relationship in modern capitalist economies. Unless they trust employees implicitly to fulfill their contractual obligations, employers need some way of knowing whether or not employees are doing what is expected of them. Second, there are the broad cultural expectations of fairness and reciprocity which mean that an individual employee's rewards, at least in part, ought to be proportional to their efforts—in other words, that they should get out of life what they put in. Finally, most organizations involve social relations based on some formal structure that includes supervisory and functional divisions of labor (usually established with reference to some idea of competence), combined with standardized notions of industrial or "factory" time. Taking these three considerations together, surveillance provides employers with absolute and relative data about conduct in the workplace in order to determine: (1) whether employees are fulfilling their contractual obligations; (2) how much reward those employees should receive based on their net contribution to the organization; and, (3) how their work efforts can be coordinated in time and space. Managing conduct, overseeing contracts, evaluating contributions, and ensuring coordination: these are the widely recognizable functions of workplace surveillance. As we shall see later, however, whether such narrowly defined purposes are legitimate or not will depend largely on whether the capitalist employment relationship is seen to be either a fair arrangement based on mutual obligation or an exploitative arrangement based on the subordination of employees. The former position implies that surveillance is essentially prophylactic in that it protects all parties from activities such as free-riding or wanton disruption. The latter position implies that surveillance is essentially coercive in that it is the principal instrument by which the interests of employees are subordinated to the interests of their employers. Before we consider such a fundamental ideological question though I wish to develop some ideas relating to the operation of surveillance in today's organizations.

How surveillance works at work: beyond the panopticon

Bentham, Foucault and Miller

My discussion of how workplace surveillance works—that is, how it is used to manage conduct, oversee contracts, evaluate contributions, and ensure coordination—begins, not with Michel Foucault's (1979) now ubiquitous treatment of Jeremy Bentham's Panopticon, but with a French contemporary who was also grappling with the challenge of understanding social order in modern societies. Jacques Alain-Miller (1987 [1975]) reminds us that there is more to surveillance than its panoptic qualities, although these are undoubtedly important. He does this by drawing attention to Jacque Lacan's distinction between *l'oeil* [the eye] and *le regard* [the gaze]. The former concerns subjective information gathered through physically embodied vision—quite literally, seeing is believing—while the latter is indeed panoptic in that it is concerned with gathering objective information via a disembodied system of rational scrutiny. Presently I will argue that, by considering the simultaneous operation of embodied vision and the disembodied gaze we can extend our understanding of workplace surveillance beyond a simple focus on the technological systems involved in the dyadic relationship between superiors and subordinates. This is, of course, not to discount the importance of Foucault's work to Surveillance Studies. On the contrary, in discussing the gaze in great detail Foucault reminds us not to underestimate the "epistemic" effects of surveillance that is principally aimed at classifying and differentiating human conduct. This epistemic gaze has, of course, important ramifications for employees who, at any one moment, are subjected to numerous forms of scrutiny and measurement that render them—in their own opinion and in the opinion of others—"good" or "bad," "compliant" or "recalcitrant," "effective" or "ineffective," etc. (or any combination of such qualities— Sewell 1998). In this limited sense, workplace surveillance *is* a specific example of the wider compulsion to rationalize and control associated with the modern state, manifested in techniques of disciplinary power that attempt to integrate individuals into a greater societal body. Historically, this involved a move toward preventing deviancy through a generalized process of "policing" and "normalization" where a supervisor (be they a schoolteacher, foreman, physician, psychiatrist, or prison warder) determined whether the conduct of a subordinate (be they a pupil, employee, patient, lunatic, or prisoner) was acceptable by reference to some norm of behavior. In the workplace, however, this kind of "vertical" surveillance (Sewell 1998) is only one response to the challenge of getting potentially unruly employees from diverse backgrounds and with varying abilities to become useful and productive members of the organization by compelling them to work at or close to their physical and cognitive limits. In addition there is the peer-to-peer scrutiny that subordinates perform against each other to ensure behavioral norms are observed—a form of "horizontal" surveillance (see also Bruno, this volume) that may or may not lead to behavior that is deemed to be organizationally appropriate conduct (Sewell 1998). Thus, conceptually we can identify two major dimensions of surveillance based on the direction of its operation: up and down and from side to side.

Building on this notion of directionality, à la Miller, we can then go on to consider the effects of subjective embodied vision in parallel with the operation of forms of the more commonly considered disembodied and apparently objective gaze. Finally, taking into account the subtleties of the capitalist employment relationship, we can distinguish between direct surveillance that is focused on the execution of work itself (i.e. the monitoring of an individual's actual work effort which can then be compared with explicit contractual performance expectations as well as with the relative performance of others performing similar roles) and the operation of indirect surveillance that is focused on revealing attitudes that are deemed to be important influences on an individual's work effort (e.g. whether they are "committed" or a "trouble maker"). Below, I explore how these six elements can be combined to build up a more conceptually integrated picture of workplace surveillance (see Table 3.4.1).

Table 3.4.1 The configurations of simple and complex workplace surveillance

		SIMPLE (Subjective & embodied)		COMPLEX (Objective & disembodied)
DIRECT	**Vertical:**	Embodied gaze of the overseer or supervisor ensured through a direct line of sight; gaze constrained by physical architecture of workplace; gaze may be extended by technological means (e.g. CCTV). Supervisors ensure discipline by using their own subjective assessments of an individual's performance.	**Vertical:**	Disembodied gaze of manager ensured through surveillance embedded in the technology of production; line of sight no longer necessary; gaze unconstrained by physical architecture of workplace. Managers ensure discipline by comparing objective individual performance data and enforcing standardized performance expectations.
	Horizontal:	Embodied mutual gaze of peers ensured through physical proximity to colleagues; mutual dependency reinforced by physical proximity. Peers ensure group discipline by using subjective assessments and value as well as everyone "pulls their weight."	**Horizontal:**	Surveillance embedded in the technology of production means that physical proximity to colleagues is no longer necessary to ensure peers' mutual gaze; mutual dependency reinforced by aggregation of individual performance measures or disaggregation of group performance measures. Peers ensure group discipline by drawing on measured individual performance to identify free-riders.
INDIRECT	**Vertical:**	Overseers or supervisors uses observations of subordinates' general attitudes and conduct to make moral judgments about their commitment to organizational norms and values. Supervisors ensure discipline through "moral" management.	**Vertical:**	Managers draw on standardized instruments (e.g. psychometric testing) to make moral judgments about an individual's commitment to organizational norms and values; augmented by other testing regimes (e.g. drugs, alcohol, genetic, etc.). Managers ensure discipline by trying to select ex ante people who will "fit in."
	Horizontal:	Peers use observations of each other's general attitudes and conduct to make moral judgments about an individual's commitment to group norms and values. Peers ensure group discipline by emphasizing mutual dependency and enforcing group norms and values.	**Horizontal:**	Peers take measured individual performance as a proxy for commitment to group and organizational norms and values. Peers ensure group discipline by emphasizing mutual dependency and enforcing group norms and values.

Workplace surveillance: vertical and horizontal; simple and complex; direct and indirect

Simple direct surveillance

This is analogous to Miller's *l'oeil* in the sense that it involves an individual collecting information about another's work effort using observation gathered through their own sensory experiences; primarily their eyes. It is subjective because the person collecting that information develops their own assessment of the other's performance without reference to standardized and obviously comparable measures of productivity. This means that, in its vertical form, supervisors may enforce discipline through rewards and sanctions based on an assessment of subordinates' performance that reflects the supervisor's personal prejudices or their unrealistic and potentially capricious expectations (although experienced supervisors are likely to develop a keen sense of who is and who is not performing at an "acceptable" level). Because it also literally involves embodied vision, it requires a direct line of sight between the supervisor and the subordinate, such as in a manufacturing workshop, traditional banking hall, or an open plan office, and is thus constrained by the architecture and layout of the workplace. Of course, the advent of CCTV surveillance means that some of these constraints have been relaxed but the intercession of technology does not change the embodied and subjective nature of the surveillance.

The horizontal form of simple direct surveillance is similarly subjective in that employees use their physical proximity to colleagues to "keep an eye on" each other. This proximity also reinforces a sense that "we are all in this together" by making the consequences of mutual dependency more obvious. For example, if a particular supermarket checkout operator or bank teller is much slower than their colleagues, then everyone is likely to experience longer queues and frustrated customers. Instances like this are likely to lead peers to discipline each other by invoking culturally familiar group norms such as the anticipation that everyone should be "pulling their weight," even if they don't know the exact circumstance under which a colleague fails to meet expectations (say because a barcode scanner or computer is malfunctioning). Again, the extension of the line of sight by technological means may loosen the constraints imposed by the need for physical proximity but its intercession still does not change the simple and direct nature of the surveillance.

Simple indirect surveillance

Although it is also analogous to Miller's *l'oeil*, simple indirect surveillance differs from its direct form in that monitoring is not aimed at an employee's work effort. Rather, it involves one individual developing a sense of another's more general disposition toward work by observing things such as what they say or how they comport themselves. It is subjective because a person has to rely on their own moral code to determine whether another lives up to expectations in terms of values and attitudes. Perhaps the best known example of this was Ford's notorious Sociology Department (operational between 1913 and 1921) which involved, among other things, the inspection of employees' homes to promote moral and physical hygiene. This kind of moralistic scrutiny introduces an arbitrary element into the relationship between superiors and subordinates or between peers that is not easily countered through formal checks and balances. Nevertheless, in its vertical form, simple indirect surveillance still exerts its disciplinary force through a superior's ability to subject subordinates to "moral management" when they are deemed not to have lived up to the normative standards of the organization. For example, a fast food restaurant employee or an airline cabin crew member who is regularly observed failing to smile in their encounters with customers may be deemed to have the "wrong attitude," requiring them to undergo some kind of retraining.

The horizontal form of simple indirect surveillance is also aimed at policing attitudes, which are compared with the normative framework established between peers themselves, rather than with the normative framework imposed by the organization (although these may well be in alignment). Again, it exerts its disciplinary force through "moral management," although this time employees direct their attention toward peers who have been subjectively deemed not to have lived up to the normative standards of the group. For example, a team member who is considered to be insufficiently committed to the team will be taken aside and reminded of their obligations to the group (Barker 1993).

Complex direct surveillance

This is analogous to Miller's *le regard* because it is no longer embodied and is thus freed from the constraints imposed by an architecture that ensures a direct line of sight through physical proximity. In this way complex direct surveillance is focused on an employee's productive work effort to generate measures of their individual work performance that can then be compared with others doing similar work. Familiar examples of this would be keystroke logging in data-entry work or audio monitoring in call centers but it can also be extended to occupations that have not traditionally been so closely monitored, such as home workers, senior managers, or professionals. When combined with the use of standardized performance targets it legitimates claims that complex direct surveillance is rational and objective, thereby contributing to the epistemic effect of such monitoring: individuals can be compared and differentiated down to the minutest levels of performance.

One of the most striking examples of complex direct surveillance in its vertical form to emerge in recent years is the imposition of performance standards on university professors by using measures such as the monetary value of research funding, the number and quality of research publications, or the number of individual citations. In bringing these measures together, university managers are convinced that the gaze can be used to determine the relative worth of their employees within and across traditional intellectual disciplines. In this way vertical complex direct surveillance is exerting a disciplinary force by enabling superiors to identify both those subordinates who are exceeding expectations and those who are not "up to scratch," even in occupations where there is notionally a high level of autonomy. Such judgments inform organizational decisions about reward and punishment and are difficult to counter given that they are legitimated by complex direct surveillance's claims to objectivity and rationality (Sewell and Barker 2006).

In its horizontal form, the impact of complex direct surveillance's apparent objectivity and rationality is also evident. In this case, however, employees use the data produced by such monitoring to identify free-riders or those who are "letting the side down," which leads them to discipline each other accordingly (Sewell 1998). For example, Barker (1993) observed that team members who had previously relied on subjective judgments of each other's work behavior began to create more formal standards of performance by resorting to information about things like attendance or punctuality, even when the reason for being absent or late involved important personal commitments outside the workplace.

Complex indirect surveillance

The emergence of psychometric instruments, drug or alcohol testing, and even genetic testing has extended the gaze of complex surveillance to the indirect arena—that is, tests are aimed at things that only indirectly contribute to an individual's work effort. In this way it is also analogous to Miller's *le regard*. Claims that such tests can identify an individual's temperament or "commitment," their predisposition to dissolute habits, or even their likelihood of contracting certain physical of psychological disorders offers a tantalizing prospect: if managers are really able to use objective and standardized means to identify a disruptive or poorly performing individual *ex ante*, then they also ought to be able to anticipate misconduct and prevent it from ever happening. Such claims have previously been confined to the realms of science fiction writers, although we are increasingly led to believe that the instruments involved in complex indirect surveillance are becoming more reliable and valid. Thus, in its vertical form, superiors use testing regimes to identify subordinates who do not "fit in" with the organization's norms, values, and behavioral expectations and are, therefore, unlikely to live up to their full work potential. Subordinates identified in this way can still be subjected to techniques of "moral management" but this time it is done in the name of objectivity or "science," rather than on the basis of a superior's hunch.

The difficulty of employees in gaining access to valid and reliable testing regimes means the prospects for creating a horizontal form of complex indirect surveillance are weaker. This is clearly an area where more detailed empirical research would be of great value but, at this stage, I wish to speculate on its operation. Thus, in the absence of rational and objective measures of individual temperament or attitudes, employees are likely to draw on a range of other indicators when they are passing judgment on their peers. For example, the output of complex direct surveillance can serve as a proxy for attitudinal data (that is, "poor performance" equals a "poor attitude") or that general conduct outside the workplace predicts performance in the workplace. Importantly, the line between the horizontal forms of simple and complex indirect surveillance is likely to be fuzzy and claims to objectivity may be quickly undermined on closer inspection. Nevertheless, the horizontal form of complex indirect surveillance is likely to be heavily dependent on the invocation of mutual dependency and the importance of group norms.

Analytical implications of the workplace surveillance typology

Having set out the typology of workplace surveillance summarized in Table 3.4.1 we can now reflect on its analytical implications. First of all, we should note that it is not exhaustive. The four ideal types (i.e. Simple Direct, Simple Indirect, Complex Direct, and Complex Indirect) are not meant to capture every possible form of surveillance, scrutiny, or monitoring that takes place in today's workplaces (for example, superiors may spy on their subordinates or employees may spy on their peers for purely prurient or nefarious reasons). Rather, they represent the main disciplinary techniques in play aimed at ensuring that an employee's actual labor approaches the limits set by their physical and mental capacities.

Second, we should also note that the four ideal types are not mutually exclusive. Indeed, it is highly likely for all forms of surveillance to be in operation simultaneously as superiors and subordinates or employees and their peers engage in vertical and horizontal surveillance respectively. This is not to say, however, that they are all continuous and of equal intensity or importance. Thus, there may be circumstances where the simple direct surveillance of peer-to-peer scrutiny gives way to its complex form or where the vertical form of complex direct surveillance is variously relaxed or intensified depending on whether superiors consider employees to have too little or too much autonomy. Here I simply want to warn against the tendency to think that the constant emergence of innovations in production technology or social organization mean that previous forms of workplace surveillance are automatically superseded: whether it is the state, the prison warder, or our employer who is watching us, we are also always watching each other and, in the process, we rely on numerous sources of information.

Finally, I would not like readers to take from this discussion that vertical surveillance—whether it be simple or complex—is an exclusively top-down affair. To be sure, by focusing on the desire of superiors to render their subordinates compliant and productive for the benefit of a greater entity such as an organization it appears that I am saying that workplace surveillance is effectively a technique associated with a distinctly pre-modern form of sovereign power. Such thinking would, of course, be at odds with Foucault's broader discussion of the exercise of power through the gaze (Caluya 2010). Thus, although managers may sometimes believe that they can indeed command fealty and utter obedience, we must recognize that this is nothing but hubris and that such would-be sovereign lords of the organization are themselves bound up in a web of power where the limits on their own acceptable conduct cannot stand outside their obligations as participants in a voluntary contractual arrangement (see also Gilliom and Monahan, this volume). This means that managers are always under observation by their subordinates as well as being subject to the epistemic gaze of their own superiors, although a detailed discussion of this is beyond the scope of this chapter (see Caluya 2010).

Concluding remarks and future directions

The time is ripe for a new metaphor for surveillance

An important theme of this chapter is that there is more to understanding workplace surveillance than merely pointing out its similarity to the panopticon. Having restated this caveat, however, it is also fair to say that continuing to consider the epistemic effects of complex direct surveillance—albeit in play with other forms—is still likely to yield important conceptual and empirical insights in the future (see Ball 2010). To be sure, many sociological discussions of surveillance in wider social settings have long warned against relying too heavily on Foucault's discussion of the panopticon (e.g. Haggerty 2006) but, in the limited conditions of a work situation governed by contract, the prospect of subjecting subordinates to the minutest vertical scrutiny is still seductive for those charged with maintaining order and maximizing employees' efforts. Nevertheless, if the metaphor of the panopticon does have its limitations when used in isolation—even in relation to workplace surveillance—then perhaps it is time to look for another more complete metaphor that adequately captures the interaction of the various forms of scrutiny that takes place between superiors and subordinates (that is, vertical surveillance) and between peers (that is, horizontal surveillance) in almost any organizational setting, whether these are founded on a subjective basis (à la Miller's *l'oeil*) or an objective basis (à la Miller's *le regard*).

In search of such a metaphor, it is helpful to go back to a time before Bentham developed his ideas of a perfectible surveillance machine to consider what a departure it was from ideas of social control that had operated in the Europe of the late Middle Ages. In the absence of any direct, immediate, and universal techniques of discipline, ensuring right conduct relied on the widespread promotion of a normative framework of acceptable behavior (Elias 1994). An obvious example of this was the attempt by religious organizations—most notable the centralized and hierarchical Roman Church—to counter the challenge to orthodoxy posed by local heresies that sprung up from time to time on the periphery of Christendom by commissioning allegorical devices that conveyed the basic principles of good conduct by which a Christian should live. Although these were widespread and were addressed to a largely illiterate population, one of the most famous renditions was Hieronymus Bosch's painting, *The Seven Deadly Sins*. The details of its composition, which it shares with other more vernacular versions, are instructive: seven sectors are arranged around a small circle. In each of the sectors one of the sins is depicted being practiced and the central circle clearly depicts the iris of an eye over which the motto *Cave, Cave, Deus Videt* (Beware, Beware, God is Watching) is superimposed. Although this fine version once hung in the bedchamber of King Phillip II of Spain, Figure 3.4.1 shows a sketch of a more rustic version of the same image from the knave wall of a rural English church.

The most obvious message conveyed by such images is powerful and unambiguous: God sees all and your sins shall find you out. There is, however, a more subtle message at play here. Thus, although the prospect of instantaneous divine retribution was considered a real threat and the prospect of spending time in purgatory was not particularly appealing, under Christian teaching the final judgment of sinners by God was actually to be delayed until one thousand years after the second coming of Christ (Cohn 1969). Your sins will find you out ... eventually. This posed a dilemma for someone of good conscience: even if they conducted themselves properly in accord with the teachings of Christ, what was to stop others from sinning if they were not to be judged immediately? The answer lies in the actual depiction of the sins for they are being practiced in full public view and the implication is clear: as members of a community it is incumbent on us to police each other's conduct on a day-to-day basis.

For me it is the peer scrutiny implied in *The Seven Deadly Sins* that marks out the pre-modern concept of surveillance in pursuit of social control as being different from Bentham's later utilitarian proto-modern version that was captured in his specifications for the panopticon. If we compare versions of *The Seven Deadly Sins* with the many plans and drawings Bentham produced of the panopticon, however, one is

Figure 3.4.1 A version of *The Seven Deadly Sins* uncovered in the nineteenth century

immediately struck by the formal similarities: replace the tableaux of the sins with prison cells and the central circle or iris of God's eye with the observation tower and you have the floor plan of the panopticon. Indeed, as an atheist and arch utilitarian, Bentham was intent on writing God out of the picture by replacing his numinous omnipresence with a completely rational form of direct vision. He clarified how this would be established by invoking the maxim, *nunquam minus solus cuam cum solus* (never less above than when alone). Thus, although the overseer would see a *multitude* he would not see a *crowd* as each inmate would be individually sequestered, alone with his conscience to work on his own reform through contemplation and penitence. The corollary of this is that the multitude could not make common cause and act as a crowd—that is, the disciplinary force of the panopticon would be purely psychological and solipsistic rather than social and intentional as inmates would be unable to interact with each other. The problem with this is obvious: in writing out the social it disregards the fact that, even under the most extreme forms of incarceration (let alone in the workplace), social contact is rarely lost completely. The upshot of this is that, with the best (or worst) of intentions, sequestration is never complete and the disciplinary force of socially enforced norms conveyed in the various versions of *The Seven Deadly Sins* must be considered. Thus, although we may have indeed replaced God's eye with the rational and epistemic surveillance of the human overseer, this will always interact with the peer scrutiny that stems from living in an essentially social world. The prospect of the juxtaposition of pre-modern normative scrutiny with modern rationalizing surveillance is intriguing.

Living with the contradictions of workplace surveillance

Having made a case for treating the operation of workplace surveillance in a more holistic manner I would like to devote my final comments to a reflection on a question I alluded to at the very beginning of this chapter: is workplace surveillance essentially prophylactic or is it essentially coercive? This is the normative judgment that lies at the heart of most debates about the legitimacy of workplace surveillance, especially in its complex direct form, and the position we take depends on whether we subscribe to one of two coherent ideological positions: (1) a "Liberal" point of view which sees the main purpose of surveillance to be the rationalization of human activity in a fair and efficient manner for the benefit of all; and (2) a "Radical" point of view that sees the main purpose of surveillance to be the organization of human activity in an equally rational manner but, in this instance, for the benefit of a few (Sewell and Barker 2006). Considering complex direct surveillance in this way, adopting a Radical perspective leads us to think of it as being irredeemably coercive; an extension of superordinate power aimed solely at extracting the very last ounce of effort out of the hapless employee by ensuring that they never waver from the standards imposed on them by their superiors. In line with this perspective, resisting the intrusion of surveillance is a perfectly rational response that is part of a game of cat and mouse underpinned by a grudging mutual respect: subordinates recognize superiors want them to work as hard as possible but, at the same time, superiors recognize the subordinates will do all they can to avoid this fate.

In contrast, the Liberal perspective leads us to think of complex direct surveillance as a neutral technology that is primarily aimed at improving efficiency (which ultimately benefits everyone in the organization) but also protects employees from being exploited by disruptive or free-riding co-workers. Under this rhetoric of mutuality and protection any opposition to the imposition of surveillance runs the risk of seeming irrational, for how could we possibly object to something that benefits us so much? Under these conditions, perhaps the most effective response would not be to oppose such surveillance at every turn but to test out its claims to be neutral and prophylactic. What we see here is a paradox of complex direct surveillance in that, up to a point, employees have to recognize its legitimacy in some circumstances in order to oppose it in others. Although this is at odds with a strategy of implacable opposition it does allow for negotiations to take place around specific practices of surveillance that can then make recourse to legal injunctions or cultural expectations such as privacy and mutual obligation. Attempts at striking a balance between the competing claims of employees and employers, however, demonstrate the tension at the heart of a strategy that sometimes involves accommodation and sometimes involves opposition. It depends on the assumption that agreement can actually be reached over those forms of surveillance that really are prophylactic (and are, therefore, acceptable by general agreement). Such localized debates will always take place around the operation of workplace surveillance and are likely to centre on the following matters: (1) Is the information it supplies recognized by superiors and subordinates alike to be accurate and objective (at least most of the time)?; (2) Are the ends to which it is directed also seen to be broadly legitimate by both parties?; and, (3) Do its intrusions fall within broadly accepted standards of privacy? The irony of this is that it is a case of applying the standards suggested by taking a liberal ideological position to determine whether workplace surveillance is or isn't coercive. It is, however, the kind of irony that all parties must live with in today's ever more intensely scrutinized workplaces.

References

Ball, K. (2010). "Workplace Surveillance: An Overview," *Labor History,* 51: 87–106.

Barker, J. R. (1993). "Tightening the Iron Cage: Concertive Control in Self Managing Teams," *Administrative Science Quarterly,* 38: 408–37.

Caluya, G. (2010). "The Post-panoptic Society? Reassessing Foucault in Surveillance Studies," *Social Identities,* 16: 621–33.

Cohn, N. (1969). *The Pursuit of the Millennium: Revolutionary Millenarians and Mystical Anarchists of the Middle Ages,* Oxford: Oxford University Press.

Elias, N. (1994). *The Civilizing Process*, Oxford: Blackwell.

Foucault, M. (1979). *Discipline and Punish: The Birth of the Prison*, London: Penguin.

Haggerty, K. D. (2006). "Tear Down the Walls: On Demolishing the Panopticon," in: *Theorising Surveillance: The Panopticon and Beyond,* edited by D. Lyon, Uffculme: Willan Publishing, pp. 23–45.

Miller, J-A. (1987 [1975]). "Jeremy Bentham's Panoptic Device," *October*, 41: 3–29.

Sewell, G. (1998). "The Discipline of Teams: The Control of Team-based Industrial Work through Electronic and Peer Surveillance," *Administrative Science Quarterly*, 43(2): 397–429.

Sewell, G. and Barker, J. R. (2006). "Coercion Versus Care: Using Irony to Make Sense of Organizational Surveillance," *Academy of Management Review,* 31: 934–61.

b. Public administration as surveillance

C. William R. Webster

Introduction

This chapter will explore the centrality of public administration to emergent surveillance societies. In particular, it will set out the role played by government and public services in assembling the apparatus of contemporary surveillance. The focus is the emergence of large public bureaucracies, the collection and processing of vast amounts of information about citizens, and the extension of these activities in order to make public services as effective and efficient as possible. The chapter will set out the emergence of these activities in the paper-based era and the evolution of these activities in the information age as new Information and Communication Technologies (ICTs) and "eGovernment" expands the surveillance possibilities and scope of public administration. These "modernization" processes are occurring in a number of countries, including those beyond North America and Europe.

Throughout the chapter there will be three underlying core themes. First, that public administration, because of its size, scope and function in society, is information-intensive. Consequently, it creates and maintains records and personal information in a range of service areas and for different purposes, from national security to taxation. In doing so, it can be seen to have a surveillance function. Second, and linked to the previous point is that public administration creates a platform for surveillance. Not only has it built a large bureaucratic machine to process information but it has also invested in the infrastructure to modernize surveillance through enhanced technological practices. In a drive to make government and public services more efficient and cost-effective, huge sums of money have been invested in electronic infrastructure, databases and eGovernment. In doing so, the rate of information exchange and the amount of information processed has expanded considerably. A third theme is that public administration normalizes surveillance by encouraging/requiring citizens to provide information in exchange for services. This is increasingly done through eGovernment. The crux of the chapter is that surveillance societies built around technologically mediated surveillance practices are to a large degree dependent upon the surveillance platform and apparatus created by public administration(s)—in terms of information/data processing, technological infrastructure and by making surveillance a normal part of everyday life. It is therefore important to see public administration not just as the administration of public services and policy but also *as* surveillance.

The chapter is organized around a number of themes which demonstrate the centrality of public administration to surveillance. They are: (1) public administration and the rise of bureaucracy; (2) public administration in the information age; (3) security and surveillance public policy and practice; (4) the regulation and governance of surveillance; and (5) public administration and the normalization of surveillance. Whilst the focus of the chapter is public administration as surveillance this emphasis is not intended to underplay the role of the commercial sector in emerging surveillance societies. The argument presented here is that public administration plays a crucial role in creating and sustaining surveillance societies, which happens in conjunction with the commercial sector and not separate from it. This point can be demonstrated by the blurring of the boundaries between the public and private sectors in service provision and the advent of privatization, consumerism and New Public Management. For example, the DVLA (Driver and Vehicle Licensing Agency) in the UK, the agency responsible for licensing drivers and vehicles, uses ICTs supplied and maintained by the commercial sector and exchanges information/data held in its databases for commercial purposes and financial gain. It sells personalized car registration plates and exchanges driver/vehicle information with ANPR systems operating in car parks and congestion charging systems. It is these administrative systems which provide the underlying rationale for creating systems and processes facilitating the emergence of surveillance societies. The role played by public policy and practice is therefore a critical underlying force which should be properly acknowledged.

Public administration and the rise of the bureaucracy

The term "public administration" can be understood to mean a variety of things, it can be: (1) the structure of government, including the institutional arrangements and decision-making mechanisms surrounding public policy making and service delivery; (2) the activities of those engaged in the provision of public policy and services; or (3) the study of 1 and 2 (Waldo 1955). Usually the term is closely associated with public services and with the formal institutions, organizational structures and implementation processes of government, as well as with decision-making mechanisms and the normative assumptions and principles underpinning the practice of public service provision. Whichever approach is taken, public administration can be seen to play a significant role in the emergence of societies where technologically mediated surveillance practices and technologies dominate. However, not only has public administration played a critical role in the emergence of contemporary surveillance societies, it can also be argued that public administration has always been concerned with surveillance, through the necessity of controlling access to scarce resources in society and in its role in ensuring accountability for resource use.

The roots of modern public administration lie in the aftermath of the Second World War and the desire by many societies to provide large-scale universal services to all eligible citizens, including services associated with healthcare, welfare, education and taxation. Large-scale rule-based hierarchical bureaucracies were perceived to be the only realistic organizational arrangement for delivering such services fairly to citizens. Public services were therefore traditionally organized according to bureaucratic principles associated with Weber's "ideal type" of bureaucracy (1947). They were large rational-legal hierarchical organizations with formal rules governing access to services. These bureaucracies created the apparatus for making decisions about the provision of public services and for implementing the actual delivery of service. This involved creating manual paper-based records, rule-based categorizations and paper-based personal identities. These were essential to check eligibility for services and for ensuring equity and fairness in large-scale service provision. Consequently, public administrations started to create personal information for citizens, such as unique passport and healthcare numbers, alongside the formation of large paper-based filing systems and vast quantities of records. A key task of public administration was therefore to create, manage and store records, to design protocols for accessing and sharing records and to determine the informational content of records.

The emergence of large bureaucracies utilized for the allocation and distribution of universal services can be seen as providing the "building blocks" of modern surveillance societies and demonstrates that surveillance has always been a feature of public administration. In this respect, "record keeping" and the processing of personal information have always been activities conducted by public administration. They are activities central to identifying individuals' rights of access to services, in categorizing levels of service and in maintaining records about services. Surveillance in this perspective refers to the manual creation of records and identities—the surveillance of citizens in order to control the provision of services. For example, in the UK in the paper-based era, the aforementioned DVLA created paper-based driving licenses, databases and administrative systems to implement and control eligibility to drive. These processes included the creation of personal driver identities (the "driver number") the categorization of different types of driving license (for motorbikes, cars, lorries and other types of vehicle) and a manual record of driving "entitlements" and "endorsements," the latter including a formal record of driving convictions and penalties. These entitlements and endorsements were cross-referenced with other administrative databases containing personal information about a driver's age, address, relevant medical conditions and car ownership.

Public administration in the information age

It is evident from the preceding section that public services have always been concerned with information. Public services are "information rich" because information collection and processing have always been a core part of their activities. The advent of the "information society" and the emergence of new ICTs have offered further opportunities to enhance the technical capabilities of traditional bureaucracies. Understanding the informational capabilities of information-age public services is vital to our appreciation of contemporary public administration and the perspective of public administration as surveillance. So, just as the technological capabilities offered by new ICTs offer the potential to transform public services, they also enhance the surveillance capacity of public administration.

The revolution in new ICTs is particularly relevant to public administration because these new technologies offer greater capacity and speed and because they emphasize information *and* its communication. The term "informatization" (Frissen and Snellen 1990) is intended to capture the intensification of the use of computers and information technology in public administration as well as the massive intensification in the uses and "flows" of information in and around the organizations of governance. In this respect, the ICT revolution has a number of important elements. First, developments in ICTs have enabled the computerization of the large databases and record-keeping systems created by public bureaucracies in the twentieth century. Here computerization via information systems allowed for greater capacity, speed of access and processing, and it is not surprising that public administrations are among the largest users of computers. Computers, however, are only one element of the ICT revolution; the second is telecommunications, which allow for the rapid communication of vast amounts of data and information between different locations. This has provided access to the data held in large databases from multiple and remote locations. The combination of these two elements means that ICTs are therefore convergent technologies—it is the combination of computers and telecommunications, in the form of networks, which makes the technologies so powerful. This convergence has occurred because both computers and telecommunications are now both digital technologies and therefore offer the possibility of electronic interaction. Consequently, in the information age, it has become possible to complete a number of service transactions online from service users' homes via home computers and the internet. In this way, service users can apply for a passport or a driving license online, they can pay for services online, such as "road tax," or they can update their personal records, for example, initiating a change of address in an electronic record, or extending the loan of a library book. All these electronic interactions rely on the existence of electronic record keeping, the computerization of large public databases, the ability to communicate electronically and to transfer information/data from these databases to multiple locations using a variety of digital platforms, including electronic kiosks, iDTV, the internet and mobile phones.

These changes to the provision and governance of public services have been captured by the "Information Polity" perspective (Taylor and Williams 1991). This perspective asserts that at the core of the contemporary polity are a set of relationships that are information intensive and that are profoundly amenable to exploitation through new ICTs, and that innovations in the use of new ICTs are interacting and evolving with traditional mechanisms and procedures within the polity. These evolving relationships include: internal relationships in the machinery of government, relations between service providers and service users embedded in electronic service delivery, new democratic relationships between governments and citizens, and new relationships between public service providers and commercial companies who provide the infrastructure and expertise for information-age services. The crux of this perspective is that the "informational" aspects of new ICTs are profoundly shaping relations within and around public administrations and that organizations in the information polity are increasingly dependent upon the informational infrastructure of the information society.

In the UK, the approach to the reorganization of public administration/services is captured by the "Modernising" and "Transformational" government agendas (Cabinet Office 1999; 2005). The approach is that public administration can utilize new ICTs in the delivery of public services *and* that the technologies can be harnessed to "transform" and reconfigure public administration around the informational capabilities offered by new ICTs. The central argument is that services can be more efficient and cheaper to deliver, that they can be more accessible, more convenient and provide greater choice, that they can be more effective and "joined-up," and that the culture and working practices of public administration can be transformed to become more business-like. New ICTs embedded in eGovernment are changing the machinery of government, relationships between citizens, service users and providers, and the culture, norms and institutional practices embedded within public administration (Bellamy and Taylor 1998).

A good example of how a "simple" online electronic service transaction involves the creation and exchange of electronic records and the computerization and networking of existing administrative systems is the UK's vehicle licensing system, and in particular the purchase of "Vehicle Excise Duty," a legal requirement for using a vehicle on UK roads. A "tax disc," which can be applied for online via the internet, has to be purchased and displayed in every vehicle eligible to be used on UK roads. The process of completing this online transaction involves electronic interaction between a number of public and private databases in order to check eligibility, identity, the categorization of tax type and electronic payment. The legally registered owner has to be verified by the DVLA, the "road worthiness" of the vehicle has to be checked against the "MOT"(Ministry of Transport) database, the existence of appropriate insurance is checked against the Motor Insurers' Bureau insurance database, and the financial credentials of the owner/driver are checked for electronic payment. In this example, the relevant information is stored in different records and in different databases that are networked together to provide a seamless online service with the data matching and sorting taking place "behind the scenes." In this way, the service becomes more convenient, in that it can be accessed at any time, and it provides new opportunities to deter uninsured vehicles from using the roads. Here there is a direct service enhancement realized by information flows embedded in new ICTs and which are being utilized to administer the service.

The practitioner and public policy view of public administration in the information age set out above focuses on the potential of new ICTs to deliver better services. The risk with this view is that the impacts of new ICTs are simplified to the extent whereby these technologies are seen as heralding a new unquestioned golden age—a "silver bullet" for improving public services and administration. The alternative view to this utopia is that these technologies will lead to an Orwellian nightmare where the very same technologies are used primarily for tracking and controlling citizens and that the surveillance function of public administration will be enriched by technological enhancements. This common polarization of views suggests that there are intrinsic characteristics embedded within new ICTs which lead automatically to certain outcomes. The technological determinism at the core of these visions is at odds with the empirical world where technologies are shaped by their social, political and institutional contexts. The reality is much more likely to be a messy incremental evolution of what has previously existed, in this case the evolution of large state bureaucracies at the heart of modern public administrations. Although the utopian-dystopian visions are at odds with reality they do highlight the significance surveillance potential of public administration and the surveillance logic embedded in the informatization of public administration.

Public administrations can therefore be seen as creating the apparatus and machinery for contemporary surveillance societies. The argument is not that all eGovernment services and related databases are automatically surveillance technologies, but that they have the potential to be utilized for surveillance purposes—because they are essentially about the processing of personal information—and that they are a necessary perquisite of contemporary surveillance societies. Without the creation of large state databases and without the development of appropriate communications infrastructure, technologically mediated surveillance societies are less likely to exist. This is not to suggest that public administration as surveillance is a dystopia, rather it is a perspective which suggests that new ICTs embody social power and institutional contexts and just as their informational qualities shape relationships in the polity, so do their surveillance qualities.

Security and surveillance public policy and practice

Whilst it can be argued that public administration creates the apparatus for surveillance via technological developments around eGovernment and the telecommunications infrastructure, the state also plays a pivotal role in developing technologies that are explicit surveillance technologies and which are more clearly used for surveillance purposes. Typically, the state does this in order to provide national, local, community and personal safety and security. This can be achieved by overtly or covertly monitoring individuals' behavior and communications, for example by monitoring the usage of mobile phones and the internet to observe communications, or the profiling of individuals through data matching and sorting. Interestingly, many of the technologies used for these purposes have been created as part of the eGovernment developments described in the previous section.

Much of the impetus for using new technology in this way derives from a general fear of crime and terrorism and a belief that new technologies can help catch and deter the perpetrators of crime. In this regard, surveillance technologies and practices are embedded in security public policy and practice. At the national level security systems based on new ICTs are used at border points, for checking ID and for profiling potential threats. Modern states create agencies and regulatory measures designed to ensure national security and local safety. At the EU level the Stockholm Programme (European Union 2010) recommends the development of an internal security strategy for the EU, with a view to improving the protection of citizens and the fight against organized crime and terrorism. This is partly to be achieved through the better use of personal information and the more effective exchange of information between European Union Member States. Interestingly, it is evident that, over time, surveillance technologies and practices deployed for national security and anti-terrorism purposes have filtered down into local settings and into practices associated with community safety. This is sometimes referred to as the domestification of military security or "surveillance creep." A good example is the diffusion of surveillance camera systems into public places for a variety of "security" and other purposes (Webster 2004). In this case, a technology which explicitly was installed for crime prevention and detection purposes is being utilized within communities to provide community safety and to deter undesirable behavior.

The argument is that there is a blurring between the use of technologies for public services and administration and for purposes more closely associated with security policy and practice. Clearly the two are interrelated and personal information created for one purpose can be equally valuable in another policy environment. This explains why techniques and practices developed for explicit surveillance have filtered down into the realm of public administration. This argument also reinforces the previous point about the "surveillance potential" of information-age technologies and the potential use to which these technologies could be put, if there was the political will to do so.

The regulation and governance of surveillance

Beyond creating the mechanisms and apparatus for surveillance the state plays a crucial role in the regulation and governance of surveillance and privacy. In Europe under the EU Data Protection Directive (Directive

95/46/EC) all Member States have a duty to create "instruments" (legislation, regulation and organizations) to govern the processing of personal information and to create appropriate agencies to oversee the implementation of these instruments. Under the Directive each Member State must set up a "supervisory authority"—an independent body that will monitor the data protection levels, give advice to the government about administrative measures and regulations, and start legal proceedings when data protection regulation has been violated. In the UK, the regulation of surveillance and data use is provided by statutory rules, common law decisions and codes of practice and guidelines issued by regulatory authorities, such as the Information Commissioners Office, and by public and private organizations. Beyond the UK and Europe, most countries have developed regulatory mechanisms to govern privacy, especially in relation to the transfer of personal information and developments associated with the internet (see Regan, this volume).

It is apparent that public administrations have two juxtaposed roles concerning the governance of surveillance and privacy. On the one hand they are creating the infrastructure and practices of surveillance, through eGovernment developments and security public policy, and on the other they have an important role in protecting individual privacy, and regulating surveillance and the exchange of personal information. So, at the same time as creating agencies responsible for establishing large databases of personal information, public administration creates other agencies to regulate and restrict the exchange of information emerging from other parts of the machinery of government. The argument is not to suggest that these two roles are mutually exclusive or incompatible, because they are not; rather that in the information age the flows of information around and within administrative bodies makes it increasingly difficult to judge the parameters of acceptability concerning access to and the exchange of personal information. Public services may increasingly need to process and exchange personal information in order to be efficient and effective, but they are also under increasing pressure to allow citizens and service users greater scope and control over their own personal identity and information. Reconciling these two competing demands is one of the conundrums of contemporary surveillance societies.

Public administration and the normalization of surveillance

From the arguments presented up until this point in the chapter it is evident that public administration plays an important role in providing a technological platform for, and the machinery of, surveillance. However, the role played by public administration goes much further. Not only does it create a technical environment amenable to the emergence of surveillance practices, it also makes surveillance—realized through new ICTs—a normal part of everyday life (Murakami Wood and Webster 2009). Surveillance then, as a set of practices and cultural norms, becomes something everybody is familiar with, something ordinary and normal and of which we are unafraid. There is a general acceptance of the need to provide a personal identity in order to access electronic public services, to travel by plane or cross international boundaries, or for public agencies to create surveillance systems in order to provide national and personal safety. Typically, these surveillance practices are unchallenged, and in this respect, we are very accepting of technologically mediated surveillance.

The normalization of surveillance takes place in a number of ways. First, it is normal for public administrations to create personal information and electronic identities, a necessary process for identifying citizens and for delivering electronic public services. Citizens and service users have become accustomed to the idea that their personal information is not created personally by them but by the administrative agencies of the state. Second, it has become normal for public agencies and other organizations to create and maintain large databases of records containing personal information and for administrators with administrative expertise to maintain and service these records. This is essential to realize economies of scale in service provision and to ensure probity of resource use. Third, it has become normal for citizens to exchange personal information in order to access public services, to travel and to undertake other transactions, such as opening a bank account, using a mobile phone, getting married or making online purchases. This makes surveillance normal for both the surveyor and the surveyed. In sum, it has become a normal "state of affairs" for public administrations to create, monitor and process large quantities of information so that citizens can participate in everyday life. Surveillance norms are therefore embedded in eGovernment and other administrative behaviors. In this perspective, not only is it "normal" to be the subject of surveillance, it is also normal to undertake surveillance and to monitor, process and exchange personal information. The latter point is important, not only because it means that we are accepting of the surveillance role played by public administration, but because it also means that there are a multitude of professional administrators engaged in mundane surveillance practices, including record keeping, which normalizes this behavior. The normalization of surveillance is therefore also about far more than just the proliferation of a range of surveillance artefacts and technologies, it is about how these are embedded in the norms and institutions of society and how they are reflective of other aspects of modern society (Murakami Wood and Webster 2009).

Whilst it is evident that public administration has a core surveillance function, which has been enhanced through new ICTs and which normalizes surveillance, these developments can be problematic and controversial for a number of reasons. One set of concerns relates to the handling of personal data by public agencies. For example, questions can be asked about the extent to which government agencies should be able to profit from the sale of personal data collected during the administration of traditional services. A similar question relates to the extent to which public services should be able to exchange personal data for the provision of service without the consent of service users. Similarly, another question would concern the extent to which public agencies should be able to create and store new forms of personal data, say for example new records about the DNA of children and the victims of crime (as opposed to the perpetrators of crime). There are also issues relating to the stewardship and security of personal information held on public service databases and the penalties attached to misuse or loss of this data, or for systems failure. A related issue would be the accuracy of personal information held on public databases and the processes undertaken to ensure accuracy or to correct data. A further set of concerns relate to the intensity of these surveillance practices and the degree to which they include or exclude individuals from participating in society. For example, the disproportionate use of surveillance cameras and ANPR in certain geographical areas implies the creation and maintenance of new electronic records about these communities and consequently heightened surveillance of their activities. Such practices may be resented and/or resisted and may create a divide between communities. Similarly, the profiling of citizens in order to target services to certain users, to identify fraudulent applications and to control immigration, all achieved via data-matching of existing databases, may result in access to services being denied for certain individuals. These issues and questions present a series of challenges for public administration, challenges which strike at the heart of citizen–state relations and the definition of certain citizen rights, such as the right to privacy and the right to freedom of movement.

Concluding comments

A core feature of emergent surveillance societies is the centrality of the role played by government and public administration. Information-intensive administrative activity has led to the development of large networked state databases, essential for the effective delivery of information-age democracy and public services. Further to this, public policy has played a central role in developing such systems in order to deliver internal and external security. Public administration and policy is therefore inherently intertwined with modern surveillance practices. It is the information intensity of our relations with the state, embedded in and reflected by the provision of new surveillance technologies, that determines and characterizes the nature of modern society and the extent to which society is dominated by surveillance relations.

This chapter argues that public administration can be seen as the "engine" of modern surveillance societies, primarily because it plays a central role in creating and sustaining surveillance apparatus, practices and norms. Public administration and administrators have a legitimate right to create personal identities/information, to collect and process vast quantities of personal information and to exchange this information. They do this in the national interest and in the provision of effective and efficient public services. By doing so, they also create the environment and apparatus necessary for surveillance practices to flourish and for surveillance norms to be embedded in citizen-state relationships. These developments present a series of significant challenges for public administration, challenges which relate to the accuracy and probity of record keeping and sharing, about the extent of information sharing and the creation of personal information and profiles. Debates about the legitimate boundaries of these activities are likely to be ongoing as technologically mediated surveillance practices proliferate.

Public administration has always been concerned with surveillance and the emergence of new ICTs has merely intensified traditional bureaucratic and administrative processes. Technological development is significant, not just for the evolution of the administrative function of the state, but because it provides a platform for the emergence of surveillance societies more generally. It is hard to imagine the emergence of technologically mediated surveillance practices without the infrastructure, databases and personal information created by the state—large electronic databases and networks which can be used for the rapid exchange of vast amounts of personal data. Whilst these processes are critical for the effective delivery of contemporary services so citizens can participate in everyday life, they also provide the basic "building blocks" for modern surveillance societies, where the same technical infrastructure and information can be used for monitoring and control. From this perspective it is easy to see *public administration as surveillance* and that surveillance as a concept and as a practice is inherently intertwined with public administration.

References

Bellamy, C. and Taylor, J. A. (1998). *Governing in the Information Age*, Buckingham: Open University Press.
Cabinet Office. (1999). *Modernising Government*, Cm. 4310, The Stationery Office.
——(2005). *Transformational Government: Enabled by Technology*, Cm. 6683, The Stationery Office.
European Union. (2010). *The Stockholm Programme—An Open and Secure Europe Serving and Protecting Citizens*, European Union: Official Journal C 115 of 4.5.2010.
Frissen, P. and Snellen, I. (1990). *Informatisation Strategies in Public Administration*, Amsterdam: Elsevier.
Murakami Wood, D. and Webster, C. W. R. (2009). "Living in Surveillance Societies: The Normalisation of Surveillance in Europe and the Threat of Britain's Bad Example," *Journal of Contemporary European Research*, 5(2): 259–73.
Taylor, J. and Williams, H. (1991). "Public Administration and the Information Polity," *Public Administration*, 69: 171–90.
Waldo, D. (1955). *The Study of Public Administration*, Garden City, NJ: Doubleday.
Weber, M. (1947). *The Theory of Social and Economic Organisations*, New York: Free Press.
Webster, C. W. R. (2004). "The Diffusion, Regulation and Governance of Closed-Circuit Television in the UK," *Surveillance & Society*, 2(2/3): 230–50.

c. Consumer surveillance

Context, perspectives and concerns in the personal information economy

Jason Pridmore

Introduction

Corporations are increasingly reliant upon the collection and analysis of data about the wants, needs and desires of consumers. This has become a crucial resource upon which business and marketing decisions are predicated, ranging from the services a corporation chooses to provide, to the locations in which they operate, to the "investments" made in particular "relationships" with consumers and more. Though the collection and use of consumer data are hemmed in to different extents by privacy regulations and data protection laws, the means by which consumers are surveiled is ever more innovative and enticing. Corporations are able to use the tools, processes and possibilities of new information and communication technologies, and employ rewards, discounts, entertainment, collaboration, special access, networking, recognition, better service and products, and coercion, amongst others, as mechanisms to produce detailed consumer-specific data. In addition, algorithmic processes can be used to extensively analyze this information, revealing associations and propensities between various sets of consumers that may be obvious or "non-obvious." In practice, these appear as "people who purchased this item also purchased ... " notifications on websites, loyalty programs targeting similar offerings to clusters of consumers who on the surface appear very different, as well as direct mail targeting based on geodemographic information systems.

The surveillance of both consumers and their associated consumption contributes to and is reliant upon the "personal information economy"—a context in which the use of personally identifiable data has become a primary resource and upon which many market economies are built. The personal information economy depends upon the gathering of data through surveillance systems and then analyses this data for patterns and associations deemed to be "of value," continually re-evaluating corporate practices and products based on these analyses. This circular process is directed towards obtaining the maximum current and potential profitability from differing sets of consumers. The results of these practices become evident in targeted advertisements, web site "cookies," tailored promotional materials, differing levels and promptness in customer service, social media feedback channels, viral marketing, diverse or tiered pricing structures, and others. In its most developed forms, consumer surveillance is used to influence, control and monitor consumer choices, guiding certain consumers toward products and practices that are of value to corporations and steering other less profitable consumers away. While a number of these practices are convenient, helpful and advantageous for certain sets of consumers, hidden assumptions and expectations embedded in consumer profiles limit the range of consumption possibilities for many and create significant disadvantages for others.

Research on the surveillance of consumers and consumption is multifaceted, particularly given the information and communication technology-rich context in which it takes place. In what follows, the text will focus on the context of consumer surveillance practices, the diversity of analytical approaches to these practices and the stakes (the concerns and implications) of such surveillance. To begin, the surveillance of consumers is now largely synonymous with marketing, a practice that has had—and continues to undergo—a significant transition since it emerged as a dominant tool of capitalism. Though surveillance-research approaches that critically analyze marketing practices often overlap, their differences create particular theoretical and empirical tensions. These differences in approach are pertinent to discussions about the stakes raised by such consumer surveillance practices, directing attention to different concerns, tools, and counter-strategies.

Context

At least on the surface, the surveillance of consumers and their consumption makes good business sense. Businesses are reliant upon knowledge regarding the marketplace, and information about individual consumers is increasingly seen as a crucial means for profit making. The ability to gather, store, retrieve and process information has become remarkably easier and less expensive, and this occurs against the backdrop of a world in which consumption has taken a more central role in the reproduction of culture and the development of personal identity. The digitized information available through these forms of surveillance has become the cornerstone for understanding consumers and their consumption along these same lines, as well as being a means for consumers' engagement and participation.

The practice of surveilling consumers and their consumption is intimately connected to contemporary marketing practices (see Pridmore and Zwick 2011). While market research in the West in the 1920s and 1930s seemed to view consumers as having a relatively stable, homogeneous, and immobile set of preferences that could be managed and controlled with mass advertising, the perspective of consumers as psycho-socially complex and a mutable collection of needs, wants, and desires emerged in the years following. The focus at this early stage in market research was on controlling consumers, reducing marketing complexities, and improving production efficiencies (see Arvidsson 2004). The intention was to align consumer preferences with products and brands already being produced.

This began to change during the 1950s and 1960s, when more psychologically inclined market researchers suggested that the primary challenge for the corporation lies in identifying and responding to consumers' changing needs and wants in the market. This led to production processes and marketing activities being geared toward satisfying consumers' needs and wants rather than controlling them for maximum sales. Simultaneously, the notion of "customer satisfaction" as a primary corporate objective became seen as a superior strategy for securing market share and maximizing profits. Taken together, the orientation of marketing and of corporations towards consumer needs and wants and their overall satisfaction bequeathed a new justification for intensified commercial consumer surveillance that dominates contemporary marketing discourse to this day. Market research is seen as central to knowing and providing what consumers want.

With conditions of increased competition, specifically with excess capacities of progressively more, and more alike, brands and products vying for the same consumer money, corporations have sought to collect massive amounts of detailed information about consumers. The ability to store, retrieve and process this information has become widely recognized as providing a key competitive advantage in contemporary information capitalism (Zwick and Denegri-Knott 2009). The shift to digitized information is perhaps the most important aspect for understanding the monitoring and measuring of consumers and their consumption practices as a form of surveillance. Specifically, the customer database has fundamentally changed the speed and degree to which companies are able to collect, sort and process information about consumers and thus construct an increasingly seamless surveillant assemblage (Haggerty and Ericson 2000).

The mundane, everyday practices of consumption have now taken on new meaning. They have become important building blocks for the performance of economies and become subject to both an increased amount of scrutiny and direction. Today, consumption is about more than buying stuff, about more than an expression of lifestyles, worldviews and identities. Consumption has become a proxy for proper citizenship, access to desirable socialities, and the possibility of connectedness to modern life and of cosmopolitanism. Corporations use consumption as a means for establishing long-term profitable relationships with consumers, aiding them with products and possibilities that fit their lifestyle and serve to solve their problems.

The shift towards "relationships" as the crucial metaphor for understanding producer-consumer interactions has helped ensure a business strategy focused on developing and nurturing long-term relationships with profitable consumers in order to create a sustainable competitive advantage. These relationships are seen to help retain loyal and more profitable customers, making opportunities for up-selling and cross-selling easier and more effective. This requires personal information to be actively sought and compiled about both current and potential clients in order to establish corporate-consumer relationships that go beyond a single commercial transaction, and are heavily reliant upon software to support Customer Relationship Management (CRM). At the heart of these systems is the attempt of marketers to learn from, understand and know their customers in order to "meet their needs."

The crucial element in the shift towards relationship marketing was the ability of corporations to make sense of and use personal information. Making sense of the data that was gathered, processing this into usable information, and distributing this information became central to the development of corporate analysis of consumers and the development of a "relationship" with them. Much of this information was built in part upon forms of classification already present like postal codes and government statistics. The distribution of this sort of information was dependent on large-scale systems of communication, that is, data processing and computer technologies. Databases were and are central to this, and they have been subject to a substantial amount of critique.

At present, concerns about databases have been superseded by the mechanisms and means by which these are connected. That is, the use of new technologies and protocols such as the internet, although reliant upon databases, has proved more significant than the databases themselves. The surveillance of consumers is interconnected with the use of the internet, from web stores to social networking sites to entertainment and media. In terms of consumer surveillance, the interconnections between databases creates an even stronger form of surveillance, perhaps most evident in behavioural advertising practices. These practices capture behaviours of internet use which are analyzed to provide further targeting and segmentation by marketers.

However, though the appeal for tracking consumption practices is high for producers, the appeal of the interactivity available in the use of the internet for both consumers and producers is significant. In fact, given the interactive nature of internet-based practices that have moved beyond the confines of social media, the differentiation between the consumer and the producer has become so blurred that some argue the distinctions make little sense. This perspective suggests rather a new world of "prosumption" with "prosumers" who are intimately involved in both the design and the production of consumer products. This is most readily apparent in online practices, specifically in participatory web cultures that flourish in social networking sites, wikis and blogs. Yet prosumption points to the ability of consumers to be involved in the crafting of the "products" they consume in other ways as well, with their feedback and their own creations becoming integrated into producer-consumer relationships in ways that were previously unseen. This presents a significant shift in the landscape and practices of consumer surveillance, and is increasingly central to conceptualizing how consumer surveillance occurs and its implications (see Bruno, this volume).

Approaches

The surveillance of consumers and their consumption has been critically examined in several different ways. These can be broadly described in five overlapping and often interconnected approaches, roughly categorized as "panoptic," "political economic," "modular," "contingent" and "normative." The concerns and issues raised about the surveillance of consumers in these approaches overlap significantly, in part because these theoretical conceptualizations themselves overlap.

Panoptic

In one of the earliest pieces to detail consumer surveillance practices, Oscar Gandy relied on Foucault's use of the panopticon to describe corporate practices. Gandy's text, *The Panoptic Sort*, hinges on mechanisms that act as "a kind of high-tech, cybernetic triage through which individuals and groups of people are being sorted according to their presumed economic or political value" (Gandy 1993). In his view, consumer data is gathered and analyzed in ways that serve to dictate corporate offerings to various categories and segmentations of clientele. This panoptic sorting draws upon past behavioural data to selectively narrow and limit options presented for future transactions, all of which are based on the identification, classification and assessments of current and potential customers. This rationalized marketing sorts out high-quality economic targets and discards others in its discriminatory wake, existing, Gandy argues, as an anti-democratic system of control.

These concerns are further expanded upon in Gandy's later work and the work of others by indicating that this type of sorting allows for the illusion of choice to be maintained against a backdrop of a continually narrowing range of options. In this perspective, the relationship between buyers and sellers has become an impersonal transaction controlled by cybernetic intelligence, using an increasingly automated collection of personal information that presumably allows for a form of personalized marketing. Central in this perspective is the role of the database through which sorting is made possible. Data-mining techniques are the primary basis for this processing and are argued to exclude classes of consumers from full participation in the market place, as these techniques serve to digitally discriminate consumers based on digitized characteristics that may or may not normally be seen as obvious.

The focus on databases is indicative of a perspective that sees these as operating, to paraphrase Mark Poster, like a market super-panopticon. However, the panoptic power of the customer database does not manifest itself in the individualization of identities, although this process is intrinsic to the recoding of consumer behaviour into discrete and virtual "data doubles" (Haggerty and Ericson 2000). Rather, this notion of panopticism is much more concerned with the collection of personal information to discriminate individuals into previously categorized consumer lifestyle groups or "profiles." The Foucauldian emphasis found in panoptic perspectives on consumer surveillance is extended further in the discussion below on modular approaches that draw heavily from conceptions of Deleuze and governmentality, however the focus here is specifically on the discriminatory sorting mechanisms provided through consumer surveillance.

Political economic

Gandy's argument in *The Panoptic Sort* relies not only on Foucault but also on critical political economy frames that utilize concepts derived from Karl Marx. That is, while the Foucauldian concerns about sorting practices are important and other theoretical influences such as Weberian rationality and Ellulian notions of technique are present, Marx's labor theory is essential in Gandy's analysis of consumer surveillance. This Marxian influence is increasingly present in other critical examinations of consumer surveillance, all of which at their basis hold that all labor and life is subsumed under capital. Consumer surveillance practices are seen as part and parcel of a contemporary "Informational Capitalism" that seeks to exploit consumers in line with objectives that benefit a system controlled and directed by those that already wield a substantial amount of (economic, material and political) wealth (see Arvidsson 2004).

From a political economic perspective, the growing automation of sorting practices inherent in systems of consumer surveillance leads to an increase in targeted messages and products that are meant to meet and fit personal lifestyles and choices. However, these practices are seen to create these very same lifestyle niches for consumers to inhabit, and the political economic perspective sees these as intended to maintain corporate capitalism as a desirable and inevitable way of life. Scholarly and activist critiques of consumer surveillance therefore require an understanding of the economic organization of marketing practices as they recursively maintain the validity of capitalist systems. This is perhaps most notable in recent discussions about the exploitative nature of interactive media. In this case, the prevalence of user-generated content is seen as a form of exploitation that seeks to manage and control consumer behaviour. It extracts unpaid, coerced, and alienated labor that serves to generate corporate profit through the conscious, intentional activity of users that is then transmitted back to consumer producers. This process produces surplus value for capital of which little is redistributed to consumers, yet is essential for new cycles of capital accumulation that occur through Web 2.0 platforms that depend upon consumer participation.

Political economic critiques of consumer surveillance demonstrate how consumer feedback and mechanisms of engagement with consumers produce additional economic value for capital as an essential component of its own continuation. Rather than a form of empowerment or possibility, consumer surveillance practices and the development of prosumption connected with new ICTs represent a continuation of imbalances of socioeconomic power first suggested by Marx two centuries ago. While in the panopticon Foucault produces a metaphor for understanding the mechanisms and methods of consumer sorting, the political economic perspective adds the dimension of socioeconomic interests of power that lie behind such practices.

Modular

Greg Elmer's (2004) conceptualization of electronic surveillance and database technologies fruitfully extends the influential Foucauldian analysis because it recognizes the need for database marketers to actively solicit consumers for information. Building upon the panoptic perspective, his work serves to conceptualize the development, mining, updating and distributing of the customer database as a systematic modulation of the consumer population (Zwick and Denegri-Knott 2009). While this is similar to the recursive perspective of political economy, it adds the idea that surveillance technologies perform a complex set of cultural, social and economic functions such as the spatial and temporal configuration of markets, the provision of various forms of knowledge and the flexible connection of consumption and production. It is a departure from Foucault's architectural and optical conception of disciplinary power focused on enclosures, molds and fixed castings (Deleuze 1992) that highlights the flexibility of capital in multiple forms. Drawing on Deleuze's notion of modulation, this perspective conceptualizes how control and power operate in and through techno-logical surveillance networks of contemporary information economies.

The shift in focus towards modulation and mechanisms of simulation still relies upon panoptic practices, as these provide the foundation for circular, recursive and self-reproducing strategies of power aimed at forecasting future positions "in an increasingly dispersed and automated infoscape" (Elmer 2004: 44). But it draws attention to the reflexive generation and projection onto consumers of market desires through the continuous configuration and reconfiguration of relationships and associations between always-changing data points. This perspective, which encompasses both notions of simulation and governmentality, emphasizes the feedback loop between data collection and analysis and the solicitation of consumers with more inquiries or with "more of the same" products. While maintaining an affinity with the political economic focus on the motivations of capital, the theory of information as modulation is seen to better explain how panoptic profiling machines operate to control and homogenize everyday consumption behaviour within contemporary capitalism.

Contingent

The emphasis on modulation and its co-existence with both panoptic and political economic framings of consumer surveillance maintains a particular focus on structures of power. In these structures, corporate informational power is always larger than the power afforded to consumers. Interestingly, the growing power of corporations in terms of consumer information occurs concurrently with a dominant ideology that suggests the consumer is "king" and that companies are dependent upon consumer choices and practices. However, though corporations may not fully be at the mercy of these consumers, they are reliant upon their continued collaboration in the development of current and new market offerings and strategies. Consumers often happily participate in the personal information economy and the surveillance practices that underpin it. They are keen to reap the rewards and benefits found in the "fun" of capitalism (see Thrift 2005), whatever the critiques of this system may be. This view sees that consumer surveillance serves to maintain consumer enticement and continues reflexive practices based on mechanisms of modulation, but argues that this engagement with consumers suggests a surveillance that is performative and highly contingent.

This contingent perspective on consumer surveillance holds that marketing has a role in performing and formatting the very phenomena it purports to describe (Pridmore forthcoming) and that this occurs in a recursive, cyclical format through which power can be seen as distributed throughout a network of corporate-consumer relations. This view of marketing practice, with its accompanying conceptions of segments, life-styles, life-stages, desires, and so on, is that which makes consumers tangible entities to be understood and engaged with. Yet taking its cues from Bruno Latour and Michel Callon, this performance-oriented understanding of marketing suggests that the notion of "consumers" is fully susceptible to change, and that the process of assembling and reassembling consumers is continual and indicative of a dynamic and iterative form of surveillance. Agency and power are distributed within the people, practices, systems and artefacts that comprise contemporary consumption and marketing. This demonstrates how contemporary practices of marketing are less of an "enclosure" in the panoptic sense but rather "configurations" of markets, created through the arrangement and ordering of marketing practice in ways that allow corporations to meet the needs of consumers that they "know" and define. These configurations determine corporate offerings and marketing strategies and allow for a continual adjustment and evolution of the market in ways that depend upon the collaboration and co-operation of consumers.

Normative

While the theoretical framings of consumer surveillance discussed above invariably maintain normative concerns both explicitly and implicitly, the discussion of these practices from business and marketing literature, media and legal studies, and policy evaluations, amongst others, often more fundamentally emphasizes the social, legal, political and ethical concerns raised by consumer surveillance in action. Rather than begin with a particular theoretical framework for understanding consumer surveillance, these texts are focused on its implications. While these (potential) implications are discussed in more detail below, the normative approach to consumer surveillance tends to emphasize the de-democratization of consumer surveillance techniques. Consumer surveillance, it is argued, creates "glass consumers" who are in many senses "ripe for manipulation" by informational systems that know more about consumers than consumers may know about themselves.

Again, this perspective is largely driven by the implications of such practices rather than a common theoretical frame that holds these together. There are however several similarities, which roughly can be summarized as follows:

Appropriateness of data use and collection: The utilization of data from multiple data sources is largely concealed from the view of the consumer and serves to create rich portraits or "biographies" of consumers. These biographies are often intimately detailed enough to conclude that a consumer would feel uncomfortable given the amount of information a corporation has on her.

Disproportionate corporate power: Though marketing has always been about persuasion and translation of customer data into actionable information, the increased knowledge that defines consumer segments, offerings and interactions gives large organizations even greater power. Using personal histories and affinities with other consumers, corporations have increased leverage in the marketplace which undermines the notion of consumer sovereignty.

The potential rigidity in merit based interactions: Consumer surveillance systems allow corporations the potential to evaluate what products and services should be offered to particular consumers based on the merits of their profile. Though the risks associated with digitized consumers may reflect already existing social stratification to some extent, the larger concern here is the degree to which the categories of merit begin to follow consumers in perpetuity, creating significant difficulties for consumers to change what previously defined them as high risk.

Consumer isolation: Several normative works suggest that new database marketing upends the democratization of commerce through practices of "mass customization." The use of new consumer surveillance technology to segment consumers allows for tailored advertising and product offerings to only specified consumers and actively discourages less profitable customers through practices of price discrimination. This can create a highly customized world of consumer goods, products and services, which, it is argued, can lead to the elimination of common culture and an increase in consumer anxiety and suspicion within an increasingly complex marketplace.

Each of these concerns is focused on the normative problems created by consumer surveillance—practices deemed unethical and unfair. This approach to critically assessing consumer surveillance is based on a conception of the marketplace as founded upon free and democratic principles. The problem with consumer surveillance practices is that these have significantly threatened this foundation, creating invasive systems of exclusion that afford tremendous power to corporations.

Stakes

The approaches discussed above highlight in different ways what is at stake in the personal information economy and the surveillance of consumption that underpins it. As well as other new or less predominant perspectives, these focus attention on specific issues and concerns raised by consumer surveillance practices. These also point to tools and counter-strategies that serve to minimize or eliminate the risks posed by this form of surveillance.

Perhaps the most obvious concern raised by the increased intensity and invasiveness in the surveillance of consumers, particularly by more normative approaches, is about personal privacy. The key question is whether or not current privacy regimes and their individualized focus on consumers act as an effective tool to limit corporate informational power over consumers. For instance, one question is whether or not the legal regulations regarding privacy can effectively be enforced given the complexity of database marketing and web-based tracking technologies. In addition, the effectiveness of privacy principles is called into question as these are focused on individual consumers in a context in which consumers are unwittingly associated with others based on predictive algorithms. Although privacy is seen as a tool to combat or resist the excesses of consumer surveillance, its ability to do so has drastically diminished with the speed of profiling systems, the prevalence of personal data and the pervasiveness of tracking tools and mechanisms. What is more, the perception of privacy advocates, which often becomes embedded in the language of data protection laws, often does not match the perceptions of consumers (see Coll 2010). To some extent, the means for protecting privacy paradoxically can produce the feeling of it being invaded, which makes it difficult to believe that consumers can or will actively pursue their own privacy protection.

The largest privacy issue is perhaps the inappropriate and improper sharing of personal information. Given the ability of literally hundreds of organizations and agencies to amass and aggregate both personally identifiable and non-personally identifiable data—data that can then be connected to and used to evaluate individual consumers—the ability of the consumer to maintain her privacy, that is to protect herself, control the flow of her data, or "be left alone," has become problematic. The concern about consumer surveillance is its contextual integrity in a context in which personal information is distributed on so many different systems for a variety of purposes. Whereas it may be beneficial and appropriate to share personal details, preferences, opinions, etc. in one context, this may not be the case in others. For instance, data derived from surveillance techniques and without consumer consent being provided to governmental agencies, healthcare providers, insurance agencies, and others, seriously infringes on people's expectations for privacy.

In addition to privacy, there is a lack of corporate transparency with regards to the amount of data held on customers and on corporate informational practices. Although some of these are outlined in privacy policies, most consumers remain uninformed about the extent and range of processing that occurs involving their own personal data. This data processing serves to dictate the range of opportunities and possibilities afforded by a corporation to a particular consumer, and the inability of consumers to know or understand the processes behind these automated decisions sets up and perpetuates an imbalance of informational power. This power imbalance renders the consumer open to the potential for or a continuation of exploitation.

The automated decision making of consumer surveillance systems can also be seen to recursively produce a world in which modes of being, in this case modes of consumption, become reiterated in the informatization of everyday practices. That is, the data drawn from consumers are projected back upon them in a way that anticipates their behaviours and regulates corporate interpretations of these practices. In the process, this reproduction of the same demonstrates that consumption patterns are no longer simply descriptive, but increasingly become prescriptive as well. The choices that are made in the consumer sphere may appear to be free, but in fact they are bound to cultural and corporate expectations that are embedded in continually adjusting informational systems.

Perhaps the most important concern connected to the automated decision making of consumer surveillance systems is the potential for cumulative disadvantage. In the context of consumption, although there is not an all-encompassing monolithic corporate view on consumers, the conglomeration of multiple partial views taken together may produce particular disadvantages for specific sets of consumers and groups. These consumers are deemed either unworthy of engagement or deemed high risk and incur significant economic disadvantages by virtue of their digital profile. While on a case-by-case basis this might appear reasonable, the accumulation of these disadvantages creates an undemocratic ghettoization of particular types of consumers that significantly affects their life chances and opportunities.

Conclusion

For all of the intentions inherent in the surveillance of consumers and their consumption, these practices are not always effective or effectively used. Nor are they always accepted. In many cases, both internal corporate resistance and external consumer advocacy groups significantly limit and undermine the monitoring and measuring of consumers. In addition, there is a wide gap between what is theoretically possible and desirable with the tools and techniques that are employed in marketing contexts. Empirical case studies of consumer surveillance in practice often make this abundantly evident. Yet this does not change what is fundamentally at stake given the increasing importance of consumption.

Consumer surveillance has begun to make even the most mundane consumption valuable as a form of information, value that can be re appropriated for the purposes of capital. This may be as simple as buying groceries, using the internet and sending text messages, much larger (and perhaps more significant) consumption choices. In the process, consumers are increasingly seen as digital composites of past and projected consumption, understood in terms of deciles, simulations and categories. The use of this information is mitigated by all sorts of factors, from consent to privacy regulations to consumer acceptance, though the concerns about the disproportionate informational power of corporations, the invasiveness of surveillance techniques, the accumulation of disadvantages, and others, remain. It is likely that these concerns will only become more pressing as consumption becomes more mobile (with the integration of mobile technologies in the marketplace), more ubiquitous (with the use of RFID, GPS tracking and the development of smart environments), and more participatory (with the rise of prosumption and Web 2.0 activities). The concern readily apparent in most critical analyses of consumer surveillance is that it will continue to perpetuate and amplify social divides and sorting that is antithetical to democratic principles.

References

Arvidsson, A. (2004). "On the '"Pre-History of the Panoptic Sort': Mobility in Market Research," *Surveillance & Society*, 1(4): 456–74.

Coll, S. (2010). *Consommation sous Surveillance: L'Exemple des Cartes de Fidélité*, Geneva: University of Geneva.

Deleuze, G. (1992). "Postscript on the Societies of Control," *October*, 59: 3–7.

Elmer, G. (2004). *Profiling Machines*, Cambridge, MA: MIT Press.

Gandy, O. H. (1993). *The Panoptic Sort: A Political Economy of Personal Information*, Boulder, CO: Westview.

Haggerty, K. D. and Ericson, R. V. (2000). "The Surveillant Assemblage," *British Journal of Sociology*, 51: 605–22.

Pridmore, J. (forthcoming). "Collaborative Surveillance: Configuring Contemporary Marketing Practice," in: *The Political Economy of Surveillance*, edited by L. Snider and K. Ball.

Pridmore, J. and Zwick, D. (2011). "Marketing and the Rise of Commercial Consumer Surveillance," *Surveillance & Society*, 8(3): 269–77.

Thrift, N. J. (2005). *Knowing Capitalism*, London: Sage Publications.

Zwick, D. and Denegri-Knott, J. (2009). "Manufacturing Customers: The Database as New Means of Production," *Journal of Consumer Culture*, 9: 221–47.

Section 3.5.
Digital spaces of surveillance

a. Globalization and surveillance

David Murakami Wood

Introduction

Some of the key questions for surveillance studies in the twenty-first century relate to the spatial extent of surveillance and the scale at which it operates. If the 1990s was the decade of economic globalization, the process of extension of a mode of neo liberal economic order beyond industrialized nations to the whole globe, then the post-9/11 world has made more explicit the globalization of security and surveillance. This has not necessarily been a process planned by any one organization. Whilst US sovereign power in particular has often been either employed or threatened to back the extension of the neoliberal economic mode, 9/11 also made for the globalization of a still emerging biopolitical governmental order, with distinctive surveillance norms, processes and technologies, that is not simply about military power projection (see Gates, this volume).

But what does it mean to argue that surveillance is globalizing? Globalization is a process of shifting scale, of rescaling. Whatever the thing being globalized, the process is always one of reconstructing something that had existed or had been taking place at smaller scales or in discrete places, at the larger scale of the entire globe. It is always a contested and often controversial process, which happens unevenly and unequally in both range and penetration. What is actually occurring is a series of globalizations (and simultaneous retreats from the global), and each process has its own history and socio-spatial relations.

Rescaling of a phenomenon often leads to definitional issues, and many forms of global surveillance are sometimes not considered as surveillance. But, as Foucault remarked, the analysis of governmentality should apply regardless of scale, from individuals to the "management of a whole social body" (Foucault 2008: 186). Surveillance is simply a mode of ordering. It is a response to a perceived problem of government, and is not linked fundamentally to a unique period of history or mode of production. However, it has been promoted as a mode of ordering at particular times, including the modern period in Western Europe, and its development at that time can be linked to our current period of increasing subordination of the art of government to the perceived demands of the "laws" of, first of all, the market (liberalism) and later, competition and entrepeurialism (neo liberalism) (Foucault 2008).

In considering the relationship between surveillance and the global, this chapter makes three main arguments. The first is that surveillance itself is one of the phenomena being rescaled and becoming global.

The second argument rests on the observation that surveillance, as a mode of ordering responding to a problem of government, is often not an end in itself, but is employed to facilitate the functioning of other activities and processes. While some governmental activities remain restricted in scope and scale, many are being globalized. In order to facilitate this rescaling and to enable these governmental functions to operate on a global level, there is what might be called a "surveillance of globalization" which entails monitoring the processes and practices which advance a distinctive form of neoliberal globalization. This is crucial, particularly for states and populations in the Global South.

The third argument is about outcomes. Although there is an identifiable emerging and perhaps potentially hegemonic form of global surveillance, there are still other more variable types of surveillance operating at the global level. Further, surveillance occurs in diverse ways and has radically different and uneven outcomes, in both social and spatial terms, depending on multiple interactions between global processes and national or local factors.

This chapter first outlines the recent historical origins of the globalization of surveillance in the post-Second World War world. It shows that the globalization of surveillance is an outcome of two parallel and interconnected processes: the Cold War and how it ended, and the transformation of capitalism from the 1970s onwards. It will then consider three examples of contemporary global surveillance: the economy, public goods and communications, before discussing the interaction of surveillance and global circuits of capital at the local level. Finally, I conclude with some thoughts on emerging possibilities for global surveillance politics.

Three Worlds of surveillance

The connection between surveillance and "the global" is not a smooth story of the spread of one form of surveillance from one place to all places. There is a long history of surveillance and there have also been previous waves of rescaling of government, in particular the origin of the modern nation-state, which involved characteristic forms of surveillance (see Weller, this volume).

Here, I start with the international order which emerged out of the economic depression, global conflicts and decolonization of the mid-twentieth century, through a critical reading of the contemporary "Three Worlds" theory, which divided up the globe into three parts in which very different norms and different forms of surveillance, prevailed.

In the "Second World," forms of totalitarian government persisted during this period, and indeed could be argued to have reached their apogee in the former East Germany. This totalitarian surveillance state was characterized by a very close, even paranoid, attention to personal lives by the internal security body, the Stasi, through detailed paper record-keeping, informers, and technical methods like postal interception and wire-tapping. However, the ongoing actual or supposed threat of totalitarianism became a resource for liberal democratic states, the "First World," which used it to justify imposing forms of surveillance on their own populations. While these never approached the intensity of the Stasi's practices, all of the same methods were used, although directed at a smaller subset of people, such as with the inquiries under Senator McCarthy in the 1950s, and the FBI/NSA investigations of "subversive" groups and individuals from the 1960s to 70s. New global webs of monitoring were also directed at those states deemed to be a threat. In many cases, with decolonization, liberal democratic states brought home the oppressive methods that such states had used outside of their own national borders (see e.g. McCoy 2009), but continued to export these methods under the cover of fighting "communism" and "insurgency" in the Global South (Mattelart 2008).

At the same time, the reconstruction of both national government in the First World, and emerging international governmental institutions, along neoliberal lines, produced a series of preconditions for economic and political globalization. The full outcomes of these processes were hidden at first because of the temporary resurgence of Keynesianism and more social democratic welfare states in the post-war period. These welfare states, in Europe in particular, also used surveillance in more intensive and broader ways to develop an extensive knowledge of their populations to facilitate the new universal health, education and social security systems.

As the sphere of government moved increasingly beyond the borders of nation-states, so too did problems of government, and thus the opportunity for surveillance to appear as one of a range of solutions at that scale. A wide assortment of governmental institutions was created after the Second World War, designed to enforce evolving neo liberal international norms. One stream of such activity is the legal-political as is apparent in international conventions, and the United Nations (UN), which was built on the ashes of the failed League of Nations. More recently these have been supplemented by organizations that extend criminal law co-operation, such as the international police agency, Interpol, and the International Criminal Court (ICC). Interpol, in particular, has helped to spread forms of police surveillance through transnational expertise and lesson-learning.

However other streams, in particular the economic, were more immediately influential. Several supranational bodies were created to regulate global flows of goods, services and finance capital, including the World Bank (for Reconstruction and Development) and the International Monetary Fund (IMF) after the Bretton Woods meetings of 1945, and, after many rounds of negotiations, the World Trade Organization (WTO) in 1999.

It was in the nascent post-colonial states, redefined as "Less Developed Countries" (LDCs) or the "Third World," that this influence was felt. The Development Studies literature has documented what happened to the autonomy of these states, as the IMF in particular began to develop systems to monitor their economies, and impose "structural adjustment" programs to bring them into line with the expectations of First World neoliberal governments. The IMF is rarely considered to be an agency of surveillance, yet economic surveillance is exactly what they name as one of their own core activities. Foucault made it clear in *The Birth of Biopolitics* that "political economy" as it evolved in the eighteenth century onwards was specifically related to how government should act towards the market, with the replacement of mercantilism by capitalism. As Lenin later observed in *Imperialism*, the "proper" role of government as it evolved both in the modern nation-state once capitalism had assumed its place as the "natural" economic order, and particularly when combined with colonial expansion, was to frame conditions for the easier penetration and exploitation of new markets by capital, and to provide a pacified and trained workforce. As the economy globalized, so these forms of industrial control both spread and rescaled, fostering a new global economic order that involves monitoring, information gathering and processing and consequent decisions made that affect whole populations.

Surveillance and contemporary globalization processes

The contemporary globalization of surveillance is multifaceted, and it would be impossible to deal with all aspects here (the only currently available broad survey is Mattelart 2010). However I will consider developments in three broad exemplary areas: the global economic system, emerging global public goods (particularly the environment), and global communications. These examples illustrate both that surveillance processes, practices and technologies are becoming increasingly global and, at the same time, that there are also significant surveillant mechanisms at work in ensuring the successful normalization of neoliberal economic globalization, what I earlier called "the surveillance of globalization."

Surveillance and global neoliberalism

Surveillance is used to enforce economic globalization and the norms of neoliberal global economic governance. Stephen Gill describes the use of surveillance in international government as the insititutionalization of panoptic practices and, using this simple framework, produces a critique of the discourse of international "transparency" demanded of LDCs by organizations like the IMF. These nations are required to be maximally open to scrutiny and "provide effective accounting techniques and data about fiscal and other economic policies partly as a means of ensuring that they finance their debts and obligations to foreign investors" (Gill 2008: 185). What is clear here is that, in a global neo liberal economy, it is the combination of the provision of credit and the subsequent monitoring of almost all aspect of a state's economy in order to facilitate not just repayment, but the continued compliance of the state with the norms of neo liberal competition, that provides the control mechanism.

This is not just analogous to the relationship of power/knowledge as operates between individuals and banks and other financial institutions, rather it is identical but simply rescaled. The same kinds of data-veillance and profiling operations take place on the "virtual nation" as on the "virtual body" of the consumer: both public and private information companies collect, collate and perform algorithmic operations on data relating to nation-states and profile these countries to assess their credit worthiness, and relative place in global markets.

As at the personal level, this surveillance is increasingly dominated by private companies. In addition to the IMF, the Organization for Economic Cooperation and Development (OECD) and other supranational governmental institutions, three major private global credit-rating agencies, Standard & Poor's,[1] Moody's[2] and Fitch Ratings,[3] derive their peculiar status from the US Securities and Exchange Commission selecting them as Nationally Recognized Statistical Rating Organizations (NRSROs) in 1975. For these bodies, nation-states hold no special status; they are simply a form of investment guarantee like any other guarantor of finance capital, and the economic surveillance of nation-states is a service for investors as much interested in "sovereign credit worthiness" as they are in the credit worthiness of companies or investment funds.

Recent work on global surveillance, even that accommodating or concentrating on the "Global South," does not deal with this form or scale of surveillance at all, concentrating instead on security at various scales as the defining feature of the current neo liberal era (Mattelart 2008) or on the urban scale within nation-states (Arteaga Botello 2009). But this process most certainly is surveillance as conventionally understood within Surveillance Studies and is perhaps the single most important form of surveillance operating in the world today at the global level. The reason lies in the outcomes of such profiles and ratings. If individual credit-scoring (re)produces comparative (dis)advantage and embeds poverty and class distinctions, then credit-scoring at the global scale can condemn whole national populations to economic marginality and set an inescapably negative context for individual and collective life chances. This is especially the case for those sections of national populations whose jobs, incomes and livelihoods are still tied into the national economy, as opposed to members of the increasingly footloose transnational ruling class. These ratings systems so affect economic decision making that even minor changes to the credit scores of governments can undermine national government policy, making states that have any substantial international debt—and that is almost every state in the world—ultimately responsible not to their electorates but to the demands of the rules of competition in finance capitalism.

The structural adjustment of LDCs in the 1970s prompted little concern except amongst advocates of what was then called "third world development;" however the "credit crunch" and global recession of the late 2000s onwards brought the global transformation home to neoliberal capitalist states, first Greece, then Ireland, Portugal, Spain, and more. At the time of writing the outcome remains uncertain, but with the Greek government still struggling to impose the austerity measures demanded by the IMF and the European Union in return for the multi-billion dollar emergency bail-out of its economy, and ongoing mass civil unrest, the importance of global economic surveillance might finally be realized by the people of the Global North as much as those of the Global South.

Surveillance and public goods

Another contemporary stream of global surveillance relates to "public goods." In recent years, there has been a substantial increase in data collection for a broad variety of reasons connected with the emergence of a "global polity," an imagined community with global concerns. These include mapping, meteorology, food and crops, and particularly, environmental management—for example, on carbon emissions or deforestation.

These forms of monitoring are not usually addressed as surveillance for several reasons additional to issues of scale. The first is the subject of monitoring which is, superficially at least, "non-human" and excluded by scholars for whom human subjects are a prerequisite for surveillance. The second is due to the fact that the protection of the environment often appears as an unquestioned good.

I do not want to argue here that all such monitoring is surveillance (see Donaldson, this volume), but I would like to argue that, regardless of the direct aim of such monitoring of public goods, such as global environmental management, the forms of monitoring employed are biopolitical and surveillant. This is because: first, they are conducted with the ultimate aim of changing the behavior of human subjects either individually or in populations; second, they often have multiple purposes, only some of which relate to their ostensible public benefits; and third, they also have other indirect and unintentional effects on humans.

One example here from the field of global environmental management, is the Systema de Vigilância de Amazonia (SIVAM), now known as CENSIPAM, a combined satellite and light aircraft monitoring system of the Amazon rainforest, set up by the Brazilian state with substantial funding and support from the USA, and based on technologies provided by Raytheon (Adey 2010). The politics of forest destruction and the conversion of primary forest to agricultural land are complex in every region where such forests are found. In Brazil, the issue touches on the ultranationalist sentiment that the United Nations is trying to take control of the Amazon away from Brazilian sovereign rule, as well as concerns that the USA is using SIVAM as a way to monitor Brazilian borders as part of its long-standing interventionist strategy in the region. With funding coming from US security budgets and the personal involvement of Donald Rumsfeld, not known for his environmental concern, this suggests that the latter explanation has some force.

US counter-insurgency surveillance strategy in Latin America through the "war on drugs" or "war on narco-terrorism" (another supposed global public good), particularly in Columbia, is one of a series on interventions that Armand Mattelart (2010) considers as crucial in the development of global surveillance broadly and more specifically in the globalization of counter-insurgency. This also connects the Brazilian SIVAM system to other areas of US imperial surveillance. For example, Alfred McCoy (2009) argues that, in the Philippines, the current form of security governance was the product of the culture of suspicion and intrigue fostered first by the US occupying forces and then by ongoing connections to US strategic concerns. He shows that the long US occupation of the Philippines meant that the Filipino state became irretrievably bound up with organized crime, yet in parallel also developed an insidious and powerful secret police system of spies and informers, and more recently the use of violence, surveillance, arbitrary imprisonment and intimidation by both the army and police under the cover of "anti-terrorism."

In global terms, the effects on the Philippines, Columbia and other nations subjected to such scrutiny seem to be of deeper and more immediately vital human and moral consequence than changes to domestic surveillance practices in the Global North. Such practices also connect to the markets: as the governance objects of the global polity, public goods—whether they be security, the environment or hunger and poverty—are becoming commodified through systems like tradable carbon credits and hedge funds betting on food futures. The monitoring of national resources and other global goods thus takes on the characteristics of the global economic surveillance outlined above: they become tools of global hegemony, or what Mattelart calls "*le nouvel ordre mondial de l'information*" ("new world order of information") (2008: 237).

Surveillance and global communications

Since the Second World War, the US military has been pursuing an increasingly systemic view of global surveillance, inspired by the work of Norbert Wiener's concept of cybernetics, that had come out of MIT-associated military funded laboratories, which aligned well with post-war Secretary of State, George Kennan's doctrine of containment (Gill 2008). Military power has been one form of control genuinely able to create encompassing systems of global surveillance. One example concerns the ongoing struggle for the control of orbital space. The generation of so-called "space power" evolved as an essential component of both Soviet and US strategy during the Cold War, and in the absence of its old enemy, the USA has very much "seized the high ground" since, and has de facto control of orbital space, as well as having reserved the strategic right to deny others its use.

Surveillance at this scale depends on already globalized (or globalizing) communications and technologies that allow for the automated sorting and categorization of vast amounts of data. The trajectories of global communications surveillance and US military strategic fantasies like the 1990s term, "full spectrum dominance" (see Wilson, this volume), have always been interrelated. The National Security Agency (NSA), in particular, has sought to build its priorities into global communications systems through its influence on network, hardware and software standards-setting bodies, as well as positioning its field interception stations in strategic locations where undersea communications cables make landfall, for example Morwenstow near Bude in Cornwall, UK. The US state has more generally tried to maintain its control over the governance of the internet, a system which itself originated from US military Advanced Projects Research Agency (ARPA) research and development in the 1960s, through the location and loyalty of ICANN, the body which assigns internet domain names.

The USA's attempts to control the internet are far from the only ones, nor the most restrictive. China, as one of the remaining and most effective totalitarian surveillance states, has a sophisticated system of censorship and monitoring, called the "Golden Shield," which is increasingly integrated with growing urban video surveillance systems, and both are particularly targeted at those seeking greater independence for Tibetan and Uighur peoples. Most technologically advanced states have proposed or passed laws that facilitate detailed monitoring, mandate the handing over of personal traffic and/or content data by Internet Service Providers (ISPs), and allow the removal of internet access from those contravening copyright and licensing regulations. Here the globalization of Intellectual Property (IP) rights meets the globalization of communications and computing, and the response of neo-liberal states has been to favor the smooth flow of acceptable and legally defined forms of content. In other words, state surveillance operates specifically to support competition between corporations against the interests of individuals.

Thus far, this globalization has occurred through industry standards-setting bodies, backroom agreements and secret handshakes, but at the time of writing some states were being more overt in suggesting internationally agreed laws between states to regulate the internet. At the "e-G8" meeting he hosted in 2011, and only months after the "Arab Spring" uprisings partly facilitated by internet-based social media such as Twitter, President Sarkozy of France suggested that the internet was unaccountable and uncivilized and needed to reflect the will of democratically elected governments. This was remarkably similar to how Michael McConnell, the ex-head of US intelligence, now working for the influential private contracting arm of the US government, Booz Allen Hamilton, has argued for the re-engineering of the internet.[4] He claims that the current openness of the internet means that terrorists and criminals can flourish in what some term an "open-source insurgency." This re-engineering would "make attribution, geo-location, intelligence analysis and impact assessment \ who did it, from where, why and what was the result \ more manageable." This is not much different from the "Golden Shield," just embedded within and justified by a discourse of civility, democracy and property.

While perhaps not as extreme, Sarkozy's view still reflects a less defined but growing anxiety about the "openness" of the internet from state representatives. And yet, the global spread of communications has at the same time offered new affordances for more geographically extensive and data-intensive surveillance both to states and corporations. The strategies of intelligence services in the era of open global networks rely increasingly on Open-Source Intelligence (OSINT) and gathering vast amounts of data from multiple sources into massive "Data Warehouses" or "Server Farms." In both, sophisticated software analytics attempt to sort, recognize and categorize not just the words and phrases of late twentieth-century automated wire-tapping like the NSA's ECHELON system, but increasingly also video images and data from many other media.

For state initiatives, like the US FBI's Investigative Data Warehouse (IDW), this includes attempts to accumulate as much of the feed from video surveillance cameras around the world as it can, and in the case of the US National Security Agency's new Utah facility and equivalents in the CIA, the image streams from multiple satellite systems as well as the increasing numbers of surveillance drones (Unmanned Aerial Vehicles or UAVs), which now operate not only in the skies over the warzone of the Afghanistan/Pakistan border, but also over the borders of the USA with Mexico and Canada, and even over individual cities (Adey 2010).

For global communications corporations like Microsoft, Apple, or Google, this has produced a concerted attempt to move the management of personal data away from the individual user's machines to "the cloud" (their networked servers). Facebook has been even more inventive with a deliberate strategy to replace privacy with "sharing" as an online social norm, but it is a sharing that essentially means signing over all personal data to the company to do with what it will, and this includes increasingly sophisticated facial recognition and location-tracking ("Places"), primarily to add marketing value to member profiles and their "social graphs" of interconnection.

Surveillance, security and global circuits of capital

These developments are clearly not just the product of state power and therefore cannot be simply attributed to the threat of, and war on, terrorism, in the aftermath of 9/11 and subsequent attacks on major Western cities. Global terrorism is undoubtedly being used, as with many other "threats," to justify an extension and intensification of particular forms of state control in the name of security, and this securitization extends military logic increasingly into a new normativity, what Armand Mattelart (2010) calls "*le paradigm techno-sécuritaire*" ("the techno-security paradigm"). However, one should not exaggerate the importance of 9/11 for two reasons.

First, many of these changes were visible before and can be seen both as part of longer-term military strategic agendas, a movement to governance based increasingly on risk, and the combination of the diffusion of technologies from a military-industrial complex looking to diversify into new markets in the climate of uncertainty at the end of the Cold War, as well as the globalization of the economy in the 1990s. This latter development generated major growth and globalization of technology and industrial sectors associated with surveillance and the emergence of significant global markets for inventory systems, security and crime control technology and personnel, and biometric systems for national and transnational governance (from identity cards to border controls). It also helps explain the increasing similarity of military and civilian security and surveillance technologies. It is not just that there is a movement from one to the other, but in many cases, the same security firms are producing platforms which can be adapted for multiple uses from combined "sensor-to-shooter" military systems to "less lethal" versions for domestic markets. Thus, for example, the same kinds of Radio-Frequency Identification (RFID)- and GPS (Global Positioning System)-based tracking technologies that are driving the integration of global logistics systems are also being used to track military "assets" on battlefields.

Second, many of these surveillance trends are no longer necessarily tied to a particular state agenda, and certainly not simply American (or any other) imperialism. They are the products of an orientation shared more or less, by almost all liberal democratic governments, and have their roots instead in the, as yet uneven, transformation of capitalism into a new neoliberal, global and technologically dependent form. This produces, indeed demands, what might be termed a technocratic global surveillant governmentality to support it.

Some of what I have discussed here may not be recognized as "surveillance," and I am not trying to extend "surveillance" to mean every kind of governmental or capitalist process. I began by observing that surveillance is both being globalized and at the same time is a mode of ordering which is being used to help ensure a particular series of other globalizations. There is a common purpose in controlling the flow and behavior of both people and things, particularly the free movement of goods, commodities and the new global entrepreneurial class, and to limit others, particularly the free movement of more "risky" people who do not fit the model of who is allowed to compete. This means that the capacity for surveillance is being reconstructed at many different scales. The same processes of data collection, categorization, classification and action operate here for companies and whole countries as for the surveillance processes involving individuals and groups with which we are more familiar.

But globalization does not mean homogeneity. There remains a complex and contingent "placedness" and temporality to surveillance (Murakami Wood 2009). First, nation-states and national cultures still matter. Different kinds of national surveillance societies are emerging with varied characteristics (see for example, the international comparative study conducted by Zureik *et al.* 2010). China is a living example that totalitarian forms of surveillance appear to be entirely compatible with voracious capitalist economic development, not just endogenous development but a deep engagement with the global neoliberal economy in which China is both the major manufacturer and increasingly a large consumer marketplace. There are also significant differences between liberal democratic states. Some European states, like Germany, have continued to resist a wholesale adoption of technocratic surveillant governmentality through the interpretation of constitutional rights. On the other hand, other European states have maintained greater transparency and accountability with higher levels of social surveillance and lower levels of privacy, for example Sweden. In many rapidly developing economies, such as Brazil and Mexico, the model of privately-provided surveillance for personal security continues to dominate (Arteaga Botello 2009).

However, the differentiations produced through the interaction of globalization and surveillance are not simply national. In fact, one could argue that the increasing adoption of surveillance powers by national governments are in part a reaction to the loss of control and the insecurity felt by national governments in an era of neoliberal globalism. The other major factor here is the demand for surveillance from populations, also feeling increasingly insecure, whether such feelings of insecurity are justified or not (Arteaga Botello 2009). But it is more than generalized global anxiety: there is a global reconstitution of social class (Gill 2008), which appears to be intimately involved in extending surveillance as part of neoliberal government. An overwhelming amount of work in surveillance studies has shown beyond doubt that surveillance is disproportionately targeted at the marginal, the "Other." However at the global level, surveillance is increasingly not simply targeted at the unwilling masses, but something embraced by the emerging global ruling class, for their own perceived safety in the spaces in which they live and work. The mobile global elite must have predictable experiences wherever they are in the world, and Global or World Cities provide them with familiar and secure spaces. Thus, divisions based on complex political economies of marketing combined with increasingly revanchist redevelopment are generating a number of clearly recognizable sociospatial forms that can be identified with neoliberal globalization, that come with surveillance "built in." These include Business Improvement Districts (BIDs), gated communities, enterprise zones, integrated logistics hubs and even the reconstruction of entire cities such as Singapore and Dubai (Davis and Monk 2007).

At the same time, globalization means a shift to more fragmented, uneven and dangerous spaces for many at the local level. There is an emerging geography of secure and surveiled enclaves (see Arteaga Botello 2009). And, because the emerging global ruling class has already embraced surveillance for itself, on this basis there is no social solidarity towards the marginal when surveillance is directed at them. This is not just a matter of policing the new class boundaries between the emerging global classes, but the globalization of a dominant idea of surveillance as a normal part of everyday social life. However, the ends to which surveillance are put, across different social classes, are entirely different: there is a spectrum from empowering to exclusionary surveillance that can be mapped onto a spectrum of class, or race, or other schema which chart political, social and economic centrality and marginality.

Conclusions and future directions

What links all of these phenomena is the rescaling of government towards a global level as the purpose of government has become increasingly identified with facilitating "free competition" (Foucault 2008). Thus, building mainly on Arteaga Botello (2009), Gill (2008) and Mattelart (2008), this chapter has briefly outlined a broad global political economy of surveillance, showing that surveillance is one of those phenomena being globalized in an era of neoliberal governmentality and, at the same time, is intimately involved in securing that form of economic and political globalization.

However, along with surveillance, resistance also frequently works through global networks. Responses to surveillance are generally constructed with recourse to the post-Second World War global governance framework, for example, Article 12 of the Universal Declaration on Human Rights, and the globalization of the Western/Northern concept of "privacy" (but see Bennett, this volume). Reactions to surveillance are nonetheless deeply embedded within existing social relations and culture, and that resistance is contingent and contextual, depending on histories of governance and state-citizen relations as well as specific national/local controversies and events that have generated active and informed campaigns. Resistance to surveillance has arisen in particular places and not just amongst the relatively privileged activists of the Global North (Arteaga Botello 2009; Wacquant 2009). Just as the globalization of surveillance interacts with place and culture, so too does resistance, which means that there is no single or "natural" reaction to surveillance for which researchers should be searching, nor a "normal" resistance, whose absence must be explained, even in an era when surveillance itself is becoming more globally homogenous.

As a result, there are many different possible directions for any emerging global politics of surveillance in the twenty-first century. The neoliberal vision is one of global society as a smoothly functioning marketplace, wherein surveillance works to ensure that all are able to compete but not challenge this framing of society as one defined by economic competition. This would see the complete normalization of surveillance in an increasingly globally homogenous culture, either as part of free-market personal information economies, or within several possible frameworks of regulation and rights that ostensibly offer means of redress for "excesses." However, the parallel and not always compatible logic of security implies the possibility of a renewed movement towards oppressive "security states" either as part of a reconstruction of national or local borders, or at a global scale. This could be seen as the "Chinese model" were it not that such totalitarianism is potential within any use of surveillance for security purposes, and there are many examples of actual totalitarian practice within liberal democratic nation-states. Another different set of possibilities derive from the movement towards openness and democratization, in which, rather than commodified or totalitarian surveillance, there is the development of a transparent society in which either surveillance is universal and universally accessible, or surveillance swallows itself and is felt to be unnecessary (or less necessary) because all life is lived (more) openly.

The multiple forms of reaction against surveillance from within and beyond neoliberal capitalism could also generate new and entirely different possibilities. What is clear is that, if the rescaling of society towards the global level continues, the globalization of surveillance needs to be met by a globalization of human values like autonomy and dignity, combined with global democracy and the transparency and accountability of states and corporations to people rather than the other way around. At present, this appears an unlikely direction.

Notes

1 Standard & Poor's: www.standardandpoors.com/home/en/us.
2 Moody's: www.moodys.com.
3 Fitch Ratings: www.fitchratings.com/index_fitchratings.cfm.
4 See Ryan Singel's "Cyberwar Hype Intended to Destroy the Open Internet" from *Wired Threat Level* blog, 1 March 2010, available at www.wired.com/threatlevel/2010/03/cyber-war-hype.

References

Adey, P. (2010). *Aerial Life: Spaces, Mobilities, Affects*, New York: Wiley and Sons.
Arteaga Botello, N. (2009). *Sociedad de la Vigilancia en el Sur-Global: Mirando América Latina*, Mexico: Miguel Angel Porrua.

Davis, M. and Monk, D. B. (2007). *Evil Paradises: Dreamworlds of Neoliberalism*, New York: New Press.

Foucault, M. (2008 [2004]). *The Birth of Biopolitics. Lectures at the College de France, 1979–1980*, New York: Picador.

Gill, S. (2008). *Power and Resistance in the New World Order*, 2nd edn, Basingstoke: Palgrave Macmillan.

Mattelart, A. (2008). *La Globalization de la Surveillance: Aux Origins de l'Ordre Sécuritaire*, Paris: La Decouverte.

McCoy, A. W. (2009). *Policing America's Empire: The United States, The Philippines and the Rise of the Surveillance State*, Madison: University of Wisconsin Press.

Murakami Wood, D. (2009). "The Surveillance Society: Questions of History, Place and Culture," *European Journal of Criminology*, 6(2): 179–94.

Wacquant, L. (2009). *Prisons of Poverty*, Minneapolis: Minnesota.

Zureik, E., Harling Stalker, L. L., Smith, E., Lyon, D. and Chan, Y. E. (eds). (2010). *Surveillance, Privacy, and the Globalization of Personal Information: International Comparisons*, Montreal: McGill-Queen's University Press.

b. Surveillance and participation on Web 2.0

Fernanda Bruno

The recent history of surveillance is very closely linked with information and communication technologies. With the convergence of information technology and telecommunications, distributed communications networks such as the internet have expanded significantly the possibilities for monitoring, collecting and classifying personal data. Day-to-day activities and social exchanges in cyberspace have become susceptible to tracking and constitute a valuable source of information and knowledge about individuals and groups. Curiously, the same technologies that provide more opportunities for broadcasting, accessing and distributing information have become potential surveillance and control instruments; the same technologies that allow anonymity in social and communicational relationships have proved to be efficient instruments of identification. In parallel with this, cyberspace is marked by expansion of the edges of visibility of what we used to understand by intimacy. Part of the sociability of the internet involves voluntary disclosure of personal traits, narratives and events from daily life.

Both these processes increased in intensity with the consolidation of the so-called Web 2.0, a term that refers broadly to a new generation of internet services and platforms whose content is produced or made available as a result of participation by users themselves: blogs, social networks (Facebook, MySpace, Twitter), sharing platforms (YouTube, Flickr), folksonomies (Del.icio.us, Technorati Tags), mashups (ChicagoCrime.org, Diggdot.us), etc. Participation has been understood as the defining principle of digital culture, having consolidated itself as one of the most important models for action, sociability, communication, and content production and distribution, especially on the internet.

This participatory impulse has had a variety of repercussions for surveillance processes. We can observe that the dynamics of surveillance on the internet are today intimately linked to the conflicts surrounding user participation. We use the term "conflicts" here to indicate that the meaning of participatory culture and the direction in which it is heading are the subject of dispute, as is its relationship with surveillance. User participation is today an engine of the internet as well as one of its most valuable assets and is the focus of interests and tensions in very different sectors, such as the entertainment, knowledge, marketing, politics, art and consumer sectors (see Pridmore, this volume). On the one hand, the participatory movement has developed alternatives to traditional models for producing and sharing information, knowledge and cultural assets (peer-to-peer platforms, free and open-source software, wiki websites and collaborative media production, etc.), as well as political counter-surveillance of and resistance to control systems (organizations geared towards the protection of personal data on digital networks, software that prevents users' browsing being traced and counter-surveillance groups, or watchers of the watchers). On the other hand, this same participation is being captured and capitalized on, whether it be to reinforce the logic of consumerism or feed surveillance processes.

We shall see how the intersections between surveillance and participation are the scene of conflicts and shall focus on three aspects of the internet as it is today. In the first section, we note how personal data disclosed on the internet is increasingly subject not only to police and corporate inspection, but also to monitoring and "lateral surveillance" (Andrejevic 2007) by family members, acquaintances and colleagues in a search for digital evidence supposedly intertwined in personal narratives circulating in participatory online environments (see Sewell, this volume). The following section analyzes how the production of content on Web 2.0 not only is subject to surveillance by others but also can itself place others under surveillance. Applications and platforms that encourage participation in the monitoring of urban spaces are analyzed in this section. Online maps of crimes in cities and websites that invite users to participate as video surveillance operators using their own PCs are some examples of how the so-called "produsers" (a deliberate neologism formed from combining 'producer' and 'user'. Proposed by Axel Bruns (2007).) of Web 2.0 are encouraged to undertake collaborative surveillance, thus supposedly guaranteeing participatory transparency. The third area of analysis concerns a less visible, but quite active, face of surveillance 2.0. We explore, underneath the huge flow of personal data in participatory platforms, the dataveillance, data-mining and data-profiling processes that monitor and classify this data, building knowledge that in turn supports proactive surveillance of individuals and populations (see Gandy, this volume).

The dynamics of surveillance in each of these areas is not uniform, but multifaceted and at times ambiguous. We shall explore this plurality and ambiguity, although not exhaustively, and shall highlight not only the main theoretical discussions about the issues in question, but also typical practices in terms of both surveillance and resistance to it in each area. Our approach is based on the definition of surveillance proposed by Lyon (2001): "any collection and processing of personal data, whether identifiable or not, for the purposes of influencing or managing those whose data have been garnered." We also note the distributed nature of contemporary surveillance, which is undertaken, particularly in the context of the participatory web, without stable hierarchies and with a variety of purposes and significations in very different sectors. The moving territories of distributed communications networks become confused with those of distributed surveillance; however, distributed surveillance is often a potential function or a secondary effect of mechanisms designed initially for other purposes, such as communication, marketing, entertainment and providing services. It is for this reason that any analysis of surveillance in these contexts must take into account its intersections with other processes circulating in the same sphere, such as sociability, visibility, entertainment, knowledge, security and consumption.

These intersections are examined in the following three sections, and the points at which surveillance and participation cross over are highlighted. In the conclusion to the chapter, we call attention to the main questions in each field in light of the notion of participatory surveillance and the conflicts that it embodies in the context of the internet.

Visibility, participation and surveillance

A recent study announced that according to technology experts and stakeholders, digital natives will lead society into a new world of personal disclosure and information-sharing using new media. The expression "digital natives" refers to the generation that grew up using digital technologies as a way of communicating, learning, playing, etc. (see Taylor, this volume). Some 67 percent of those interviewed agreed that this generation will continue to put personal data on networks and platforms using digital social technologies "in order to stay connected and take advantage of social, economic, and political opportunities."[1] Another study, on the other hand, showed that 71 percent of users of social networks between 18 and 29 years old reported that they had changed their privacy definitions on these networks to limit the amount of personal information shared online (see Steeves, this volume).[2]

It can be seen from these two small samples that there is neither definitive empirical results nor consensus regarding the attitudes of users of social networks to the disclosure and sharing of their personal data. Nevertheless, there is general agreement that details of people's daily lives, behavioral traits and subjective flows, such as tastes, beliefs and opinions, have never been so visible or so deliberately publicized. In a web in which the personal is social, we share our photographs on Flickr, our videos on YouTube, our professional data on Linkedin, books we have read on GoodReads, details of trips we have been to on Dopplr, places where we are on Foursquare, minisnapshots of our computer screens on Snoopon.me, all sorts of information on Twitter and Facebook, etc.

This disclosure of people's personal lives immediately raises questions related to surveillance. Among the many factors that contribute to this increased visibility of personal life, it is important to consider the meanings that the practices of seeing and being seen acquire for contemporary subjectivities. These subjectivities continue not only a disciplinary culture with panoptical principles (according to which a few see many in a normalizing hierarchy), but also the culture of the spectacle and the synoptical principles of the mass media (according to which many see a few, and individuals are stimulated as spectators of a common visual culture). Seeing and being seen do not just imply circuits of control for our subjectivities, but also circuits of pleasure, sociability, entertainment and care of oneself and others. Furthermore, a confessional, therapeutic culture has handed us down the idea that expressing our intimate feelings is the path to achieving an authentic self. These legacies come together and renew themselves in current visibility practices, multiplying the nuances of a subjectivity that is increasingly other-directed. From talk shows and reality shows to the recent social networks, seeing and being seen have acquired meanings linked to reputation, belonging, admiration, desire, protection and care, all of which have repercussions for the meanings that surveillance has acquired nowadays.

In these processes, surveillance practices take on their own shape, combining synoptical and panoptical features (Mathiesen 1997), or even taking the form of a "*palinopticon*" (to use the Greek root "*palin*," a two-way process), in which many are seen and placed under surveillance by many. Two sets of practices stand out in these contexts. The first consists of inspection by corporations and security organizations of this mass of personal data that is now permeable to the gaze of the other. The "old" surveillance agents enjoy a new source of data about their actual or potential targets. As far as corporations are concerned, although they usually limit the use of social networks at work, they also use these networks to find out about or recruit employees. A series of sites (such as fyiscreening; EmployeeScreenIQ; Abika) provide services that track personal data on social and other similar networks and provide companies with detailed dossiers on an individual's trail on the web. The practice has become so commonplace that law suits have already been started in Germany, for example, to limit the use of personal information from social networks as a criterion for hiring staff.

Some sectors responsible for public security also screen social networks and sharing sites as part of their investigations, whether as a source of data on suspects or as a platform for solving criminal cases. Documents analyzed by the Electronic Frontier Foundation show that agencies such as the Central Intelligence Agency (CIA), Federal Bureau of Investigation (FBI), Drug Enforcement Administration and Department of Justice have been using data from blogs, chat rooms and social networks for investigative purposes. Tools available on the web that can be used for this include MySpace Visualizer and YouTube Visualizer, which track connections between users on these networks, and MySpace Private Picture Viewer, a site that offers access to users' private information, infringing the MySpace Terms of Service. Recently, Ontario's Hamilton Police Service posted video surveillance pictures of a murder on YouTube to help them arrest the suspect. New Delhi traffic police created a page on Facebook to make it easier for the city's residents to see traffic violations.[3] Similar cases are springing up all around the world and in the media, showing how the visibility afforded by social networks can be placed at the service of police surveillance.

However, this monitoring of personal tracks is not restricted to the police or corporate universe. Countless "lateral surveillance" services (Andrejevic 2007) on the internet are designed with the family and affective domain in mind: sites that provide checks on an individual's background (Abika; peoplerecords), software that allows other people's e-mails and browsing history to be tracked (WinWhatWhere and TrueActive) and search engines that specialize in tracking personal information on the web (Spokeo, 123People). In Spokeo's own words: "Uncover personal photos, videos and secrets … Scan your email contacts to discover surprising facts about your friends." In parallel, and combined with this voyeuristic appeal, dates are preceded by information-checking procedures (CertifiedDates; DateSmart), and countless software packages offer services to monitor partners' and children's online activities (Catchacheat; Sentry Parental Controls), selling surveillance, suspicion and affection in the same package.

These procedures include some that reproduce unilateral police methods, while others exist in spheres that are more ambiguous, between care and control, desire and suspicion, love and distrust. They all, however, appear to have one thing in common: the assumption that this information has some degree of authenticity or power as evidence that encourages and excites not only police and corporate inspection, but also curiosity, voyeurism, distrust and watchfulness in affective and personal relationships. Furthermore, the assumption that such procedures give access to "digital evidence" satisfies a desire for transparency, security and risk prevention present both in public security policies and personal, corporate and social relationships. Such services offer the ideal of a democratized investigatory expertise (Andrejevic 2007) made possible by the increasingly less invasive, less ostensive means within everyone's reach.

Clearly, this ideal cannot be achieved without noise and resistance. This same disclosure of personal traits and narratives on the internet may be the very means of escaping from, subverting or resisting the surveillant gaze. The art of showing, far from being a totally transparent avenue, is known also to be a way of hiding or getting around the desire of others to see and know everything. Researchers insist that the disclosure of an individual's personal life on the internet, particularly by young people, does not indicate a careless attitude to privacy, but a certain wisdom when constructing a public and social face (boyd 2007). This wisdom implies modulating what is being shown according to the expected audience, and sometimes involves building small traps for the expected family, police or institutional inspections (ibid.). To give an example in the field of art, Hasan Elahi makes strategic use of visibility to disarm surveillance of his private life. Since he became suspected of terrorism by the FBI in 2002, the artist has made his whole life available continuously on the internet by means of photos, GPS and streaming. "The best way of protecting your private life is to make it public," says Elahi ironically, getting round the desire to see everything with the same excess of visibility. A similar tactic has been glimpsed by other authors (Bell 2009) in the exhibitionism, voyeurism and sexualization of surveillance in private webcams. Visibility in these cases is not a trap captured by the gaze of the other, but counter-surveillance achieved through the active construction of one's own image. Instead of the desire for objectivity and transparency implied by the surveillant gaze, these tactics show how much fiction, performance and acting there is in the practice of seeing and being seen.

However, while participation in this case produces a visibility that can be subject to surveillance or act as counter-surveillance, in a second set of practices it produces content that is itself surveillant.

The user as surveillant

A series of sites, applications and mashups on the internet invite users to monitor urban spaces so that they can report, or be informed about, incidents, crimes and suspicious situations or people. The user's participation, attention and perception are mobilized for surveillance purposes. Some of these initiatives are promoted by government bodies, such as the Texas Virtual Border Watch Program. This is a website that was established in 2008 by the US government in partnership with BlueServo. The site encourages people to help with video surveillance of the USA/Mexico border. From his or her own PC, anyone can register and access webcams and sensors that feed real-time videos on the website. If a suspect is detected, the volunteer surveillant can immediately send an alert to the border patrol.

There are also participatory surveillance projects run by businesses. Internet Eyes is a good example: this British site invites internet users to monitor video surveillance cameras installed on the premises of the site's clients in real time. If users witness a crime or see suspect scenes, they can send an alert, which is immediately sent to the owner of the cameras. To stimulate the internet users' surveillant eyes, there is a system of points and a cash prize, so that surveillance becomes a kind of game. Thus, Internet Eyes constitutes an "open circuit television" monitored by different collaborative eyes, combining surveillance, entertainment and business in one product.

The initiatives most commonly found and most typical of participatory surveillance on Web 2.0 are those developed by the "ordinary" internet user. A wide variety of examples can be found in map mash-ups, especially in crime maps made available on the internet, where crimes that happen "near you" can be reported and/or visualized. Wikicrimes is a map of Brazil produced collaboratively using reports from anyone who registers on the site. The site's slogan is "Share information about crimes. Find out which areas aren't safe!" A series of similar maps can be found on the internet, most of which are produced from publicly available data by individuals or groups who have no experience of cartography, surveillance or public security. In general, these maps allow people to visualize crimes in various locations. Some maps "specialize" in particular crimes, such as murders (Boston Crime) or sex abuse (Sex offenders register; Map sex offenders), whereas others are more comprehensive. Most give the type of crime, the scene of the crime and the time and date that the crime took place, while others make space available for more general reports (Citix; Wikicrimes), and some give information about the criminals, such as their name and a photograph (CriminalSearches; Family Watchdog). Reporting or looking at crimes and/or criminals is associated mostly with the exercising of citizenship—a surveillant citizenship, but one that can be used for personal ends and for a person's own safety. Armed with these maps, people can monitor the areas they pass through and make choices about safer routes, living accommodation, investments, etc. Some maps even offer personalized alerts and feeds that send warnings to users in the areas they have chosen: "Let us tell you when an offender moves in or out of your area!" (Familywatchdog).

Noticeable in all of these examples is the so-called "produser's" participation as surveillant. His or her attention, perception and even citizenship are directed towards the daily surveillance of urban spaces. This surveillance becomes distributed, is extended to "anyone" and, according to Koskela (2009), undergoes a reprivatization. It moves not just from the public sector to the private sector, but also to the private individual. Once again, the ideal of social transparency permeates these practices. The assumption behind this ideal of participatory transparency is that the gaze and surveillance of "ordinary" individuals, who have openly taken on the roles of "little brothers and sisters," will allow the state of the world, city and society to be seen in a "truer" more "authentic" light, as they are devoid of the filters and interests present in the gaze of the authorities, institutions or experts. It is worth noting, nevertheless, that instead of creating alternative processes of visibility, the transparency demanded by participatory surveillance ends up reiterating the principles that reproduce the logic of suspicion, accusation and fear prevailing in contemporary security discourses and policies, in this case extended to become the responsibility of the individual.

Different visibility regimes have been constructed using other forms of participation in cyberspace, some specifically for counter-surveillance purposes. From the tactics of *sousveillance* to cop-watching organizations (CopWatch.com) and other ways of placing surveillants under surveillance, there are a variety of practices which, although a minority, ensure that the relationship between surveillance and participation takes a different direction. Another type of case can be found in the disorderly, multifaceted field of amateur surveillance, where the participation of amateurs and anonymous individuals has been flooding social networks and sharing platforms on the internet with pictures of a surveillant, voyeuristic or counter-surveillant nature. Many of these images, which have a very wide variety of political, social and esthetic meanings, reproduce either a police/security logic or the voyeuristic logic of the paparazzi with different actors (Koskela 2009). Others, however, have a strong counter-surveillant effect, such as the images broadcast in 2002 of inmates held in the Abu Ghraib prison, Baghdad, being tortured by US soldiers, the images of the death of Ian Tomlinson during the G20 demonstrations in London in 2010, and those of the student Neda Agha-Soltan dying during the demonstrations in Iran in 2009. Such images have neither "an owner" nor, sometimes, a clearly defined objective, being the result of a random gaze and a fairly vague ethic, whose effects, nevertheless, create noise and cracks in the conventional channels of power and control.

Underneath participation: dataveillance, data mining and profiling

The previous sections emphasized the visible, exposed dimensions of the links between participation and surveillance. This section highlights procedures that make use of this disclosure but are themselves quite discrete and located *underneath* the participatory flow, although they have a significant influence on it. We analyze mechanisms used to collect, monitor, mine and classify huge volumes of personal data generated by Web 2.0 participatory platforms, the implications of which are decisive for the surveillance process.

The ease with which information can be stored and recovered by daily monitoring of individuals' actions is a common characteristic of information societies (Gandy 2002) and one which has become increasingly commonplace in the last 40 years. This bulimia involving personal data has become more severe with Web 2.0, where every content-creation platform is also potentially a content-capturing platform. Social, subjective and cultural processes thus become susceptible to daily monitoring. Data that was previously costly and difficult to access can be collected regularly, automatically and remotely. Behavioral, transactional, psychological, social and locational data are captured in real time without the traditional mediation of interviewers and questionnaires.

According to research carried out by AT&T Labs and the Worcester Polytechnic Institute, at the end of 2009 user-monitoring technologies were found in 80 percent of the 1,000 most popular internet sites, compared with 40 percent of these sites in 2005.[4] Monitoring methods range from tracking clicks and the time spent on each web page to automatically capturing what we type when we visit a site, for example. The aims of such monitoring vary, highlighting once again the distributed nature of surveillance processes, which here intersect with publicity, management, security and political strategies. In this complex landscape, we show how dataveillance on the internet is a means of acquiring knowledge of, classifying and intervening with individuals and groups. In other words, it acts like an apparatus that is at the same time epistemic, identitarian, taxonomic and performative.

All surveillance implies not only observation of individuals and populations, but also the production of knowledge that allows their behavior to be governed. In the cyberspace environment, this knowledge is produced primarily by analysis of the huge mass of personal data in circulation. Data mining is one of the preferred tools for doing this. It is a statistical technique involving the automatic processing of large volumes of data in order to extract patterns and generate knowledge. It is not by chance that this procedure is known as Knowledge Discovery in Databases (Gandy 2002 and Chapter 2.1.2 of this volume). Without it, the huge volume of personal data in information space would be just a chaotic flow of data that was difficult to visualize and understand. But what kind of knowledge is produced? The epistemic model is also a taxonomic model. Mining of this data flow produces classifications that constitute a taxonomy of cyberspace users and extracts patterns related to their habits, preferences and behaviors. Generally, the data is initially classified according to infra-individual categories (user of a certain service, site or platform, for example) and does not contain personal details that would identify the individuals who generated them (e.g. name, ID number). Patterns are then extracted using rule-generation mechanisms, the most common being associative ones (similarity, neighborhood and affinity) between at least two elements, which then differentiate between types of individuals or groups.

These types correspond to computer-generated profiles produced using a taxonomic technique known as profiling, which complements data mining. A profile is a pattern of occurrences of a factor (behavior, interest or a psychological trait) in a given set of variables. A simple example can be seen in Lotame, a marketing technology company that provides audience monitoring and planning. One of their audience-monitoring activities showed that "1 in 4 movie fans also express an interest in radio programming online. Video has not killed the radio star, or in this context, movie marketers may do well to consider online radio listeners as a reach extension to get butts in seats."[5] In addition: "Lotame Democrats are 3.6x more likely to express an interest in politics or political content online than Lotame Republicans."[6]

One can imagine the almost infinite number of taxonomies and profiles assembled from internet users' personal data. A specific production of identities is taking place, as the profile is not that of a particular individual but concerns the relationships between the traits of countless individuals and is more inter-personal than intrapersonal. The main aim is not to produce knowledge about an identifiable individual and his or her intrinsic characteristics, but to use a collection of personal characteristics to act on similar individuals, identifying patterns in tastes, interests, behaviors and abilities that will orient strategic measures aimed at individuals belonging to a category of commercial, marketing or security interest, among others. Note that the individual emerges as an *a posteriori* target, as the result of a surveillance process, instead of being present from the outset. The profiles thus represent a "pattern" and "knowledge," which, rather than being a reflection of a specific identity, are a projection of potential traits.

In this sense, the identities projected in the profiles constitute a series of proactive biographies. It is the future that is the focus of data mining (Gandy 2002) and profiling interventions, a future of an immediate nature, as it acts on the present, and one whose effect is performative and proactive, similar to that of an oracle. The power of the performative and oracular enunciation lies not in the ability to predict a necessary future but in the performative ability to turn into reality what was merely a potential. By being brought forward, the future becomes more "probable" or even effective. Would Oedipus have killed his father and married his mother if he hadn't consulted the oracle? Would I have wanted to buy a certain book or click on a particular link if Amazon.com and Google Instant, respectively, hadn't suggested that I do so? Such profiles seek to act on individuals' and groups' fields of possible actions and choices by offering them projections that should encourage or inhibit behaviors.

This discrete apparatus, acting underneath the participatory flow, exerts feedback on this same flow by offering opportunities for consumption, sociability, security, entertainment and knowledge that have an influence on participatory routes both on and off the web. It is in this performative and proactive power that the danger of data mining and profiling lies. The projection of behaviors, identities and personalities can "condemn" the present to the anticipated future in at least two major ways. On the one hand, pro-filing can give rise to social-sorting procedures that reinforce discriminatory mechanisms (Gandy 2002) or social inequalities. On the other, the potentially multiple dynamics of desires and actions circulating on the web can be limited to a taxonomy that favors the circuits of consumption or the logic of prevention and security.

The problematization of this little-seen face of data surveillance is decisive if its public, political and collective dimension is to be strengthened. Although debate on this subject has intensified in recent years, research has shown that internet users have a relatively low awareness of this type of monitoring. None-theless, measures continue to be taken by minority groups. These include the development of browsers that avoid our trails on the internet being tracked (Tor or Track-me-not) and political (governmental and non–governmental) action aimed at regulating or debating the social, subjective, economic and political implications of dataveillance, data mining and profiling.

Conclusion: participatory surveillance?

Throughout this chapter we have seen how the dynamics of surveillance on the internet are linked to the various faces of the participatory impulse that characterizes Web 2.0. In the three areas analyzed, we noted how user participation can give rise not only to control and surveillance processes but also to resistance processes. It can be seen that the direction in which these processes are heading is not yet defined and is, furthermore, the focus of many conflicts. Some of these conflicts can be glimpsed in the very notion of participatory surveillance, whose meaning is still the subject of dispute, as can be seen in recent communication and surveillance studies. Probably first used by Mark Poster (1990), the term "participatory surveillance" was proposed to show that with the new communication technologies we are not just disciplined but take active part in our own surveillance. At the time, the participatory culture had not yet become so central. Today the term has started to be used again and is attributed different meanings by three main groups. In the first, participatory surveillance is considered in a positive light, particularly in the context of social networks. According to this group, the mutual, voluntary and horizontal nature of surveillance in these networks ensures that users become empowered as they build their social relationships and their subjectivities (Albrechtslund 2008). A second group uses the term to designate sousveillance practices constituting a "participatory panopticon": a transparent society constantly watched and recorded not by states and large corporations but by the citizens themselves. According to Cascio (2005), "the participatory panopticon will be … a bottom-up version of the constantly watched society." Lastly, a third group uses the term to problematize the links between participation and surveillance in two main ways. The first consists of showing how the participatory injunction of interactive information networks can imply individualized reproduction of surveillance procedures historically linked to forms of police/state control (Andrejevic 2007). The second stresses the involvement of the participatory impulse, whether it be in the circuits of control or the logic of voyeurism and the spectacle, but also highlights the means by which participation brings about ruptures with these circuits and this logic. It also emphasizes the importance of rethinking traditional models and theories of surveillance in light of these new practices in the production, circulation and monitoring of personal data, narratives and images of oneself and others, as well as their social, ethical and political implications (Koskela 2009). These two approaches, which are in line with our thinking, allow the as yet unresolved issue of the direction in which participation and surveillance in cyberspace are heading to be brought into the collective arena. Taking part in this argument implies moving participatory and surveillance practices from the level of individual solutions to a level where policies for the visibility and production of data in cyberspace that problematize the existing means of surveillance and control can be collectively constructed instead of reiterating them.

Notes

1 Anderson, J. and Rainie, L. (2010). "Millennials Will Make Online Sharing in Networks a Lifelong Habit," *Pew Internet & American Life Project*, available at www.pewinternet.org/Reports/2010/Future-of-Millennials/Overview. aspx (accessed 20 October 2010).
2 See Madden, M. and Smith, A. (2010). "Reputation Management and Social Media," *Pew Internet & American Life Project*, available at www.pewinternet.org/Reports/2010/Reputation-Management.aspx (accessed 20 October 2010).
3 See Delhi Traffic Police (Facebook Page), available at www.facebook.com/pages/New-Delhi-India/Delhi-Traffic-Police/117817371573308 (accessed 20 October 2010).
4 See Angwin, J. (2010). "The Web's New Gold Mine: Your Secrets," *The Wall Street Journal*, 30 July 2010, available at http://online.wsj.com/article/SB10001424052748703940904575395073512989404.html (accessed 20 October 2010).
5 See www.lotame.com/2010/05/lotabytes-movie-fans-interests/ (accessed 20 October 2010).
6 See www.lotame.com/2010/06/lotabytes-democrats-interests-2/ (accessed 20 October 2010).

References

Albrechtslund, A. (2008). "Online Social Networking as Participatory Surveillance," *First Monday*, 13(3).
Andrejevic, M. (2007). *iSpy: Surveillance and Power in the Interactive Era*, Lawrence: University Press of Kansas.
Bell, D. (2009). "Surveillance is Sexy," *Surveillance & Society*, 6(3): 203–12.
boyd, d. (2007). "Why Youth (Heart) Social Network Sites: The Role of Networked Publics in Teenage Social Life," in D. Buckingham (ed.).—*MacArthur Foundation Series on Digital Learning—Youth, Identity, and Digital Media*, Cambridge, MA: MIT Press, pp. 119–42.

Cascio, J. (2005). "The Rise of the Participatory Panopticon," *The World Changing*, 4 May 2005.

Gandy, O. (2002). "Data Mining and Surveillance in the Post-9.11 Environment," paper presented at the Annual meeting of IAMCR, available at www.asc.upenn.edu/usr/ogandy/IAMCRdatamining.pdf (accessed 20 October 2010).

Koskela, H. (2009). "Hijacking Surveillance? The New Moral Landscapes of Amateur Photographing," in K. F. Aas, H. O. Gundhus and H. M. Lomell (eds), *Technologies of (In)security: The Surveillance of Everyday Life*, London: Routledge/Cavendish, pp. 147–67.

Lyon, D. (2001). *Surveillance Society: Monitoring Everyday Life*, London: Open University Press.

Mathiesen, T. (1997). "The Viewer Society: Michel Foucault's 'Panopticon' Revisited," *Theoretical Criminology,* 1(2): 215–34.

Poster, M. (1990). *The Mode of Information: Poststructuralism and Social Context*, Chicago, IL: University of Chicago Press.

c. Hide and seek

Surveillance of young people on the internet

Valerie Steeves

Disney's Club Penguin is a popular virtual community for pre-teen boys and girls, where children create their own penguins, decorate their igloos, play games and chat with friends. The children are encouraged to be creative and share their thoughts with others. For example, they can send their stories and drawings to the site so they can be viewed by others in the community. Parents are told that they can rest assured that their children are safe, because the site constantly monitors the children's chat and keeps a permanent record of their activities. Children can also help keep the site safe by volunteering to become "secret agents" who "spy" on other children who use bad words, reveal personal information or treat other children rudely (Marx and Steeves 2010). Any child breaking the rules will be banned from the site for "24 hours, 72 hours or forever, depending on the offence" (Disney.com 2011; Club Penguin: www.clubpenguin.com). Various testimonials from parents congratulate the company "for putting so much thought and care into such a wonderful and safe environment for our children." The site claims that parents "love the security of Club Penguin [because they] never worry about what [their] kids may happen upon while playing." As one parent testimonial concludes, "Your integrity as a company is inspiring."

As with other social networks, the business plan behind Club Penguin remains opaque. A careful perusal of the legal terms for the site indicates that the site collects personal and non-personal information for "various purposes related to our business" but those purposes are not enumerated. The primary function of the site, for children to play with branded content for hours on end to encourage both direct consumption of product and to embed the brand into the social world of the child (Steeves 2006; Grimes and Shade 2005), is hidden behind the statement that, "We do not allow third-party companies to solicit or advertise to our users. Our intention is to keep Club Penguin free from any of this sort of direct advertising" (Disney.com 2011).

This business of embedding brands into young people's online interactions is part of what Montgomery (2000) calls the new "children's digital media culture," a culture in which the blurring of the line between content and commerce is linked to a profound sense of intimacy between online marketers and the young people who play on corporate sites. Surveillance is expressly promoted on sites like Club Penguin as a way to protect children from online dangers, and parents are often co-opted into a joint surveillance project of care and control with benign corporate monitors. However, corporate surveillance also works to support the commodification of children's online activities. Everything a child does online, from the pages they visit, the conversations they have, the pictures they post, the games they play, is analyzed so that unique individuals—whether personally identified or not—can be parsed into categories based on the preferences, attitudes and relationships they share with others.

This sorting allows companies to do more than advertise to children online; companies can manipulate the online environment around those children to change the child's behavior and sense of self through behavioral targeting (BT). Marketer Rob Graham explains:

> To be effective in the new world, advertisers have to stop targeting 'us' and start targeting 'me.' The beauty of BT is that it allows publishers and advertisers to learn more about their customers not as group, but as individuals. Rather than sifting through mountains of data meant to encapsulate the buying patterns of groups of people ... [BT is] a way to look into the minds of a single, potential customer.
>
> *(Graham, cited in Estrin 2007: 1)*

The goal of looking is to change behavior: "the greatest benefit that rich media ads offer advertisers is the ability to help drive the consumer's behavior toward a specific marketing goal" (ibid.: 3). Graham sums it up: "There's no way to sugar coat this. In order to learn more about individual consumers, marketers have to resort to 'spying'" (1).

The complex interplay between children, parents and corporations in online spaces like Club Penguin illustrates many of the tensions found in the emerging surveillance society. Parental surveillance purports to protect the child from unknown dangers, in keeping with both moral panics related to children and technology, and with the neoliberal trend to download responsibility to individual parents and children. In this sense, online parental surveillance is a form of both care and control. Children are also co-opted as surveillance workers; they are encouraged to watch themselves as a form of self care and to watch other children who may pose dangers in and of themselves through transgressive behavior.

However, as the following discussion demonstrates, children first turned to the internet precisely because it was beyond the parental gaze. They continue to report that the visibility they enjoy online enables them to explore an adult world that is increasingly closed to them because of the risks and dangers it entails, and to deepen the social relationships that are so meaningful to them by watching—and being watched by—their peers. Accordingly, children have a complex relationship with online surveillance. Not only do young people turn to the internet to avoid the hyper-vigilant gaze of parents in physical spaces, but the ability to watch and be watched makes the internet an attractive medium for the type of identity play that is at the core of the work of childhood and adolescence. This work is complicated by how the online environment opens it up to the gaze of the corporations that own the sites young people use. At the same time, the reflexive nature of online surveillance creates spaces where young people can resist both care and control by refocusing the surveillant gaze on the watcher.

A brief history of online surveillance of children

Qualitative research on children's use of online media has created an interesting window into their lived experience with surveillance, and demonstrates how that experience has changed over time. While digital divide issues remain, a large proportion of children in developed countries have access to the net—more so than children in the global south. Children's access also reflects their socio-economic status, although there are indications that children in lower-income families in both developed and developing countries are increasingly getting access to the net through cell phones and other mobile devices.

One of the earliest research initiatives was conducted in 1999 by the Canadian non-governmental organization, the Media Awareness Network (2000), which held a series of focus group interviews with parents and children to explore children's use of the internet. Canada is an interesting exemplar because Canadian children were among the first to go online, and the vast majority enjoy relatively inexpensive high-speed access at home and school.

In the parents' groups, the mood was optimistic. The internet, it was believed, would expand children's educational opportunities and help them prepare to be the knowledge workers of tomorrow. Although there was some concern about children "wasting time" playing games online, things were pretty well under control. As with other forms of media, such as the television, parents kept a watchful, benign eye on their children's online actions, checking in on them from time to time. Almost all agreed that children needed their privacy. Although guidelines were important, rules were there to ensure that their children could learn from their mistakes, and more invasive forms of surveillance were thought to abrogate the trust that was essential to the parent–child relationship.

For their part, children in 1999 reported that not only were their online activities wholly unsupervised by their parents; parents could not watch them even if they wanted to because the internet was "uncontrollable." Children celebrated this new online space precisely because their real world environments were subjected to hyper-vigilant surveillance on the part of their parents. The internet was one place they could explore the adult world, try on new identities and connect with friends without being monitored. As such, a lack of parental surveillance was a defining element of both the space and the opportunities that children found there.

The one point of agreement between children and parents in 1999 was the need for children to be careful about releasing personal information to the strangers they would encounter in this new space. However children felt that online corporations were not strangers and could be trusted to provide age-appropriate content that would filter out some of the unwanted surprises children often found online. Accordingly, they reported a high level of comfort about providing personal information to corporations to win a prize, join a club or play a game.

A second set of qualitative interviews in 2004 told a very different story (Media Awareness Network 2004; see also Livingstone and Bober 2003). Parents expressed a deep frustration over the role of the internet in their children's lives. From their perspective, their children were merely wasting time playing and chatting endlessly; however, that playing and chatting exposed their children to multiplying risks and parents accordingly needed more control to protect them from the evils to which they were exposed online. Surveillance was seen as the solution. Monitoring would provide parents with a way to either find out exactly what their children were doing so they could intervene when needed, or to pre-emptively control their children's behavior in real time as they surfed so problems could be avoided. In this sense, surveillance would provide both care and control. Concerns about invading children's privacy and stunting their developmental need to develop resiliency by encountering and resolving difficult situations were no longer at the forefront.

Children in 2004 reported that this online surveillance was both patronizing and overly invasive. They argued that they were exposed to offensive content continuously across all forms of media, including the films, music videos and advertising they saw with their parents. From their perspective, pornography in particular was "everywhere" and they could not understand why their parents thought online pornography was any different (Media Awareness Network 2005: 11). Monitoring was especially problematic for them because the internet was where they achieved privacy from their parents. It was this ability to communicate outside of parental control that attracted children to the internet in the first place (ibid.: 12). Moreover, online surveillance put children in a difficult position. They felt that if monitoring software reported a pop-up ad with offensive content, for example, they would be unable to convince their parents or teachers that they did not seek out the material. This was particularly troublesome because they could lose access to the internet which would in turn cut them off from their circle of friends (ibid.: 11). Instead of surveillance, they called for more education so they could make their own informed choices about the sites they were comfortable visiting.

Interestingly, the one thing children and parents agreed on in 2004 was that branded online content was "safe"; a large company with a recognizable brand was "a friend, not a stranger" (Media Awareness Network 2004) and children could visit those sites safely. Both groups reported that corporations would not want to hurt them and could be trusted to act responsibly. The blurring line between content and advertising was largely unnoticed. Over three-quarters of children surveyed in a follow up quantitative study who played games with branded content said that they were "just games," not "mainly advertisements." Younger children were particularly prone to believe this: the percentage varied with age, from 81 percent of eight- and nine-year-olds, to 69 percent of 15- and 16-year-olds (Media Awareness Network 2005).

However, by 2007, this trust in corporations on the part of children was beginning to wane. Burkell, Steeves and Micheti (2007) report that many of the children they interviewed were uncomfortable with the amount of personal information corporations sought to collect from them. Young people likened corporate web sites to "stalkers" who were out to take advantage of them (ibid.: 15). As one 17-year-old boy put it, "Well, they're taking advantage of you, that your friends have a hotmail account, they're on Messenger, like you have to have Messenger … It's another way to control you" (ibid.). To protect themselves, many lied about their names when asked, but they were also concerned that corporations collected a great deal of information about them surreptitiously, such as their geographic location and their preferences. However, they felt that there was little they could do about this precisely because the internet was so central to their social interactions. And that centrality was rooted in the watching and being watched enabled by the space itself, which allowed them to try on new identities and deepen their social connections through their mediated communications.

Watching you watching me—the internet and the performance of identity

The emphasis on identity play is consistent with the developmental need to pursue what Livingstone calls "the social psychological task of adolescence—to construct, experiment with and present a reflexive project of the self in a social context" (Livingstone 2008: 396). From a Meadian perspective, this is an inherently social process: children perform various identities through their social interactions with others and their behavior is then mirrored back to them through intersubjective communication (Regan and Steeves 2010). In Livingstone's words, "the adolescent must develop and gain confidence in an ego identity that is simultaneously autonomous and socially valued, and that balances critical judgment and trust, inner unity and acceptance of societal expectations" (Livingstone 2008: 397). From this perspective, the ability to watch others, and be watched by them in turn, is an essential part of ego formation. It enables children to acquire the cultural capital they use to construct an identity, and then evaluate the authenticity of that identity by monitoring the reactions of peers to their own performance of it.

The internet is attractive to young people then at least in part because of its surveillant properties. Young people report that it is a relatively safe space to experiment with adult identities and try out social behaviors that they would not otherwise encounter. They can "lurk" on adult sites, "stalk" peers on Facebook and "flirt" in chat rooms, all while minimizing the social risk that face-to-face interaction entails (Livingstone and Bober 2003). They can also privately seek out information they might not want to ask their parents about. Ironically, what adults see as risks of online interaction children often embrace as opportunities (Livingstone 2008: 396).

Adults often also mistakenly assume that this desire to perform what was previously considered private behavior in a public space (ibid.: 404) means that children no longer value their privacy. Corporations in particular assert that this de-problematizes surveillance because being seen is an integral part of a narcissistic youth celebrity culture. Media headlines like, "Generation shock finds liberty online: the children of the internet age are ready to bare their bodies and souls in a way their parents never could" and "Kids today. They have no sense of shame. They have no sense of privacy" (cited in Livingstone 2008: 395) fail to appreciate the subtle ways in which young people negotiate whom to trust, and what to disclose, online (397).

One of Livingstone's most interesting insights is the distinction between the types of identities that children perform as they mature. Younger children typically construct an "elaborate, highly stylized statement of identity as display" (402) that appropriates highly coded cultural symbols, such as pink hearts for girls and fast cars for boys. The online projection of these identities provides an opportunity for children to be accepted and affirmed by their peers. However, as children grow older, they abandon this stylized presentation of the self in favor of a performance that privileges social connection with others. Hearts and cars are replaced by links to friends and photographs of social interactions with peers (ibid.). Both of these kinds of identities benefit from visibility: not only must they be seen, but the ability to see others provides an opportunity to learn about social conventions and ways of being, and to examine other people's location in their broader social network.

Negotiating self in this space necessitates careful and deliberate judgments about who sees what, as well as a familiarity with both the technical and social tools at one's disposal. And the process is highly gendered. For example, boys tend to make social networking profiles public, and girls tend to use privacy settings to restrict who can access what they post on their profiles. However, girls are much more likely to tell the truth about themselves, in contrast with boys who tend to lie and exaggerate. Girls also tend to use coded language to communicate with "insiders," posting song lyrics, for example, to tell intimate friends how they may be feeling about a relationship.

This skilful manipulation of public and private reflects the fact that young people seek both publicity and privacy online, in particular publicity with peers and privacy from parents. One research participant puts it this way:

> You don't mind [other] people reading it, but it's your parents, you don't really want your parents seeing it, because I don't really like my parents sort of looking through my room and stuff, because that's, like, my private space.

> *(quoted in Livingstone 2008: 405)*

This language resonates strongly with the views of parents expressed in 1999. Similar to those parents, children liken online parental surveillance to "having your pockets picked" (Livingstone and Bober 2003) and argue strongly that it is a breach of trust (Media Awareness Network 2004). However, this language is at odds with parental claims in 2004 that protection necessitates knowledge and control that can only be acquired through surveillance.

Surveillance as loving and responsible parenting

For their part, parents are under increasing pressure to monitor their children online. Part of this reflects a neoliberal regulatory regime that places the burden of protecting children on parents. Data protection legislation purports to give parents control by requiring web sites that target children to solicit parental consent before collecting, using and disclosing personal information from children (i.e. less than 13 to 18 years of age, depending on the legal jurisdiction). This in effect creates a binary switch: parents either consent or their children cannot participate in the online community. It also does little to push back against the commodification of children's online interactions, in effect legitimizing the site's surveillance practices through the contractual mechanism of informed consent.

In addition, online companies have been active promoters of media education initiatives that promote parental surveillance. Companies like Microsoft, Google and Verizon routinely sponsor public education sites that link parents directly to monitoring software and urge them to use online filters and other technical controls to protect their children. These controls enable parents to block "risky" sites, create a permanent log of their children's online activities, capture their children's online discussions in real time so they can "listen in" without their child knowing, and run their child's wall posts, profile information, instant messages, emails and posted comments through artificial intelligence software that will alert the parent by email or text when the software detects potential stalkers, bullying or suicide conversations (Marx and Steeves 2010: 13).

In spite of the fact that social science research repeatedly indicates that children are highly unlikely to be randomly subjected to these kinds of communications, marketers for parental control software expressly play up this construction of online risk. For example, PC Tattletale tells parents, "The Internet Is A Dangerous Place For Your Child … Studies have shown that one in five children have received some type of sexual (sic) related solicitation online. With an 87% growth rate of children online and not being monitored, now is the best time to begin a proactive stance in your children's lives to prevent your children from being witness to the virtually infinite number of dangers online." Not placing your child under surveillance "is just asking for trouble" because "No matter how much you trust your child to do the right thing, there are just too many peer pressures and other dangers lurking in cyberspace." With parental monitoring software, "you can relax knowing that you have a 'secret back door' that you can use to see exactly what they see, and what they are doing online. Do NOT risk your child becoming a potential victim. Take Control of Your Child's Online Experiences And Keep Them Safe" (quoted in Marx and Steeves 2010: 13).

Marx and Steeves argue that parental surveillance is presented "as an essential part of effective and loving parenting" (13), because parents cannot trust their children to talk to them about their online experiences. Again, PC Tattletale is illustrative: "Without Parental monitoring software you have no way of knowing what your kids do or where they go when they're online. And even if they are not supposed to, we all know that your child WILL go online unsupervised if they think that no one will find out!" (quoted in Marx and Steeves 2010: 14). From this perspective, early concerns about invading children's online privacy are superseded by the imperative to keep children safe from proliferating unknown and unknowable risks. Trust is replaced by monitoring, and the companies that own the sites children inhabit become well placed not only to provide surveillant tools to parents but also to actively monitor children on their sites to protect them from "inappropriate" content and communications. In this way, corporate surveillance is normalized and recedes into the background.

It's fantastic being plastic

It is in the background that corporate surveillance is the most powerful. Unlike the panoptic gaze of parental control software, which seeks to encourage the child to internalize the watcher, corporate surveillance seeks to invisibly manipulate the child's identity play to privilege behaviors and identities that conform to the needs of the marketplace.

As Grimes and Shade (2005) point out, children's social networking sites—like Club Penguin, Webkinz and Neopets—are modeled on a system of commerce that includes stores, a service industry, job opportunities and currency (including a banking system, a stock market and daily inflation reports, in the case of Neopets). Participating in this system of commerce is an essential part of participating in the virtual community. On Neopets, for example, children play games and get jobs to earn Neopoints so they can buy food and toys for their virtual pets. The Neopets Marketplace creates scarcity by selling limited quantities of virtual products for virtual currency over very short periods of time. Since goods sell out in seconds, children are encouraged to impulse shop. Moreover, this kind of "play" also reflects the "enormous focus placed on exchange and acquisition that pervades the game's activities and features. Thus a member's economic status can significantly limit or greatly enhance access and enjoyment of the site" (ibid.: 185). Since these virtual worlds are instructive, "teaching children models for being and experiencing the world," they encourage children to believe that the objective of play and social interaction is to acquire consumer goods.

Surveillance reinforces and deepens these lessons, by privileging certain kinds of identities. Early behavioral targeting involved directly collecting personal information from children and then using it to solicit product. For example, when "Jenna" filled out a personality survey on eMode in 2000, she was told that she was a politician. The site then directed her to a diet site (one of their corporate sponsors) so she could "prep her bod for success" (Steeves 2006: 175). However, with the advent of social networking, children are now encouraged to reveal personal details on an ongoing basis. That information is then analyzed and used not only to solicit product but to structure the child's online environment. I personally experienced one of the most powerful examples of this when I was doing research on a popular social networking site. Before I registered, I was served news items about world events. As soon as I registered as a 16-year old girl, the world news disappeared, and I was inundated with celebrity gossip and ads for plastic surgery and various diets (see also entries by Bruno and Pridmore, this volume).

Branded sites like Club Penguin, Webkinz and Barbie.com use the information they collect to create a personal relationship between the child and the brand by encouraging the child to interact with the brand as if it were a person. Girls playing on Barbie.com, for example, are asked to help surprise Ken by helping Barbie plan a special day for him. Barbie can also reach out from the screen and interact with the child in the physical world. For $1.99, Barbie will call a child to wish her Happy Birthday, read her a bedtime story or give her advice about how to get along with her siblings. The site tells girls, "Wow! You could get a call from your best friend—Barbie!" (ibid.: 178, emphasis added).

By interacting with a brand online, children learn to "trust" them and think of them as "friends." They also become "role models for children to emulate, in effect embedding the product right into the [child's] identity" (ibid.: 179). An interview with Hilary Duff posted on Barbie.com in 2005 illustrates this process well. Duff tells the girls, both in text and in audio:

> I was the biggest Barbie fan when I was younger, and I still admit I love Barbie. I just think that she's so pretty, and she's so motivated. She's had a lot of jobs. I think she's a really good, positive role model for young girls to look up to. … And I always looked up to Barbie when I was younger, and I think that she's such an inspiring, cool, hip, and trendy role model for girls to look up to, so I'm very excited. And she loves pink—just like me!
>
> *(Ibid.)*

However, as Livingstone (2008) points out, children's online experiences are shaped by both technical and social affordances. Technology and social practice are therefore coequal in that they mutually shape each other to frame potential acts of agency. This potential is evident in the move from wholesale acceptance of corporate surveillance on the part of children in 1999 to the distrust and resistance expressed by children in 2007. Again, Club Penguin is exemplary. In the process of research, I witnessed an impromptu "protest" in a Club Penguin village. As Grimes and Shade (2005) note above, the site emphasizes exchange and acquisition in ways that create varying levels of social capital between players. The differences are reinforced by the fact that only paying members can buy the "coolest" swag for their penguins from Club Penguin catalogues. It is not unusual to see a penguin waddling through the site wearing multiple hats, sun glasses, MP3 players and other paraphernalia. This has created animosity between non-members and members (who tend to be heavily burdened with goods). In spite of the fact that Club Penguin strictly limits what children can say and do in order to keep them "safe," children find ways to get around surveillant controls to express themselves and resist the constraints that are built into the site itself. For example, one member started a massive melee by yelling, "Throw snow balls at members!!" The penguins quickly took sides and non-members hurled insults at the members. Members responded by expressing anger and calling non-members names.

Regan and Steeves (2010) argue that the surveillance built into the online environment contains potential spaces of empowerment in which online users can turn the surveillant gaze aside, or turn it back on itself by reclaiming the publicity inherent in what appears to be a private space. They illustrate their point with an incident that occurred at George Washington University. Campus officials were monitoring students' Facebook pages to identify and prosecute under-aged drinkers. The students responded by posting a Facebook invitation to a "cake party." When the officials arrived to intervene, they found an empty room with a cake and no alcohol. Regan and Steeves conclude:

the top-down surveillance embedded in the site was reversed—the uni-directional gaze was transformed by a concerted resistive behaviour that unmasked both the watcher and the limits of the watcher's control. This indicates that top-down surveillance will be tolerated unless and until it disrupts the social interaction that is the primary reason young people participate in a [social networking site]. The site provides a private space in which they can deepen their social interactions, shape and present themselves, and experiment with social roles; and nodal surveillance is central to these forms of empowerment. However, the fact that they are also watched 'from above' provides an opportunity to publicize that private space and use it to 'talk back' to the institutional watcher who seeks to constrain and control their social interactions.

(161)

In sum, the ability to watch and be watched is central to young people's desire to use the net to explore their identities and try on a variety of social behaviors. At the same time, the net has opened up this previously private world of identity play and social interaction to the invisible gaze of corporations that seek to manipulate the online environment for their own purposes. For their part, many parents now employ invasive methods of surveillance that diminish both the trust between parent and child and the child's ability to develop resiliency by encountering risks and learning from mistakes. This surveillance is driven by moral panics about children and technology, as well as a neoliberal regulatory environment that seeks to maintain surveillance as a way to fuel the information marketplace. Children's experiences accordingly provide an excellent context in which to map the contradictory ways in which surveillance is implemented as an organizational principle within online spaces.

References

Burkell, J., Steeves, V. and Micheti, A. (2007). *Broken Doors: Strategies for Drafting Privacy Policies Kids can Understand*, Ottawa: Office of the Privacy Commissioner of Canada.

Disney.com. (2011). Club Penguin, available at www.clubpenguin.com/ (accessed 15 January 2011).

Grimes, S. and Shade, L. R. (2005). "Neopian Economics of Play: Children's Cyberpets and Online Communities as Immersive Advertising in Neopets.com," *International Journal of Media and Cultural Politics*, 1(2): 181–98.

Estrin, M. (2007). "Behavioural Marketing – Getting Ads to the Right Eyeballs," *iMedia Connection*, available at www.imediaconnection.com/content/14559.asp (accessed 15 January 2011).

Livingstone, S. (2008). "Taking Risky Opportunities in Youthful Content Creation: Teenagers' Use of Social Networking Sites for Intimacy, Privacy and Self-expression," *New Media & Society*, 10(30): 393–411.

Livingstone, S. and Bober, M. (2003). "UK Children Go Online: Listening to Young People'S Experiences," London: Economic and Social Research Council.

Marx, G. and Steeves, V. (2010). "From the Beginning: Children as Subjects and Agents of Surveillance," *Surveillance and Society*, 7(3): 6–45.

Media Awareness Network. (2000). Young Canadians in a Wired World: Parents and Youth Focus Groups in Toronto and Montreal.

——(2004) Young Canadians in a Wired World, Phase III: Focus Groups. Ottawa, Media Awareness Network.

——(2005) Young Canadians in a Wired World, Phase III: Trends and Recommendations.

Montgomery, K. (2000). "Digital kids: The New On-line Children's Consumer Culture," in D. G. Singer and J. Singers (eds), *Handbook of Children and the Media*, Thousand Oaks, CA: Sage Publications, pp. 635–50.

Regan, P. and Steeves, V. (2010). "Kids R Us: Online Social Networking and the Potential for Empowerment," *Surveillance & Society*, 8(2): 151–65.

Steeves, V. (2006). "It's Not Child'S Play: The Online Invasion of Children's Privacy," *University of Ottawa Law and Technology Journal*, 3(1): 169–88.

Part IV
Limiting surveillance

Introduction: Limiting surveillance

Introduction

Like studies of poverty or of violence, the analysis of surveillance demands that attention be paid to Lenin's question: "What is to be done?" And while few today would espouse the kinds of democratic centralism Lenin proposed, Lenin's acknowledgement of the complexity of seeking workable solutions to the problems confronting him at the turn of the twentieth century is worth bearing in mind. There are no easy answers.

Each author in this part of the book is acutely aware of the complexities involved in confronting surveillance, especially given its ambiguities and paradoxes, its increasingly technological cast, its political economy (where government and corporation work hand in glove), its global variations based on historical and cultural difference, its diffusion through numerous spheres of social life and the vastly varied opinions on whether, when the Pandora's box of personal data has been opened, it will ever be possible—or even desirable—to close the door again or even to stem the flow.

That said, each of the authors is deeply committed to the view that *something* should be done about the spread of surveillance. No complacency lurks in these lines. So this part begins by debating questions of ethics and of principle and by situating these debates in the context of what might be called "network societies." Beyond such necessary discussions, the second part looks at four kinds of approaches, based variously on institutional regulation, everyday resistance, social movements and human rights advocacy. They overlap and in some ways are mutually dependent. They acknowledge the use of legal remedies but also their inadequacy on their own. In short, they point to multi-faceted responses to today's surveillance challenges.

Although allusions are often made to the "ethics" of surveillance, not a lot of work has yet been done in this area. Exceptions, such as Helen Nissenbaum's *Privacy in Context* (2010) have made strides, along with some specific studies (often appearing in the journal *Ethics and Information Technology*), so Eric Stoddart's analysis here is welcome. Placing "rights-based" and "disclosive" ethics in tension, he argues that although the former frequently inform privacy and data protection law, they also have strict limits, especially in understanding what is actually happening. Surveillance studies itself, suggests Stoddart, thus appears wearing an ethical hat when it tries to plumb below surveillance surfaces. Stoddart's own perspective derives from a carefully crafted Christian ethics and this in turn is informed both by a reading of Foucault and of a feminist ethics of care.

One of the issues driving Stoddart's analysis is that technological change happens at such a dizzying pace, a problem that also enlivens Charles Rabb's interrogation of "principles." If mere rules tend to date quickly, can principles, developed for one new technical challenge, but then applied to another, analogous one, extend the scope of surveillance critique? While remaining a stalwart privacy advocate, Raab also asks what principles might refer to issues of fairness as well as privacy, and of possible group harms, rather than only individual ones. He discusses sympathetically Gary Marx's well-known "Ethics for the new surveillance" (1998) but concludes in the end that very human factors, "decisions and actions" and not just "technology" requires regulation.

Those rapid technological changes prompting Stoddart and Raab also feature in Ian Kerr and Jennifer Barrigar's exploration of privacy, anonymity and identity (the theme of a large-scale research project at the University of Ottawa). In a few short years the internet, once characterized by anonymity—famously, in the *New Yorker* cartoon caption: "On the internet, no one knows you're a dog"—now enjoys anything but. New identification technologies and the voluntary disclosure of personal details on social media have put a firm end to that. Their chapter poses a conundrum about the apparent unworkability of lofty notions of "informational self-determination" within the complexities of what they discuss as "network society." But confronting current realities is seen by these authors as part of the way forward.

While these difficulties, of ethics, principles and complexity, are accented by rapid technological change, some relief comes from a history of concrete activities in regulation. Priscilla Regan points out that, on an institutional level, there are several decades of technology regulation, frequently based on common principles, known as Fair Information Practices. These are guidelines that inform both attempts to obtain accountability of surveilors and to offer redress (through civil liberties pressure, for example) to the surveiled. An illuminating range of activity is presented, stretching from legal remedies to the efforts of commissions and report-writers, of self-regulation and of the codes of practice of professional bodies. None is simple and all are constantly in tension due to the liquid movement of new surveillance, but the fact of their existence and of their successes is a steadying one.

The same may be said for the usually less visible presence of what John Gilliom and Torin Monahan call "everyday resistance." Different from "opposition" (discussed by Bennett), such everyday resistance is best seen in cases like those brought to light by Gilliom himself in *Overseers of the Poor* (2001), where mothers on welfare evade notice, hold back some details and even collude with their case-workers to circumvent the technology-driven state welfare surveillance system. Or rather, they do this to help their families survive, which is an important point. Everyday resistance may well be carried out for some other value or purpose than seeing surveillance itself as a threat to be countered. The surveillance society predicated on a politics of visibility is defied by an alternative politics of invisibility.

So what might "opposition" to the spread of surveillance look like? This, in turn, is much more visible and indeed, it seeks publicity for the cause. "Privacy advocates," as they are commonly called, often operate collectively and champion human rights, civil liberties and consumer and digital freedom. Colin Bennett's analysis locates such collectivities within social movement theory, around the cluster of symbolic politics, accountability politics, leverage politics and information politics. They may have long-term goals, like Privacy International, or short-term ones, like the UK "NO2ID" campaign. They form a loose international network and have ties with both formal institutional–legal struggles against surveillance and also with organizations that may have agendas with little directly to do with surveillance.

Such liaisons are in part the subject of Yasmeen Abu-Laban's chapter on surveillance and human rights. She points out that those trying to limit surveillance may make strategic alliance with others who have little knowledge of surveillance as such, on the basis of human rights. After all, Article 12 of the *Universal Declaration of Human Rights* (1948) explicitly includes privacy. Indeed, making strategic alliances is part of Abu-Laban's agenda, in this chapter. Noting that surveillance studies has often been dominated by sociology, she proposes closer links with political studies. Recall that, for all the dispersal of surveillance through many social realms, the role of the state is still critically telling. But she also reminds us that, at the end of the day, human rights discourses are about shared humanness—needed because of the marginality of some—a theme that also resonates with the Abrahamic religions, Judaism, Christianity and Islam.

So what is to be done? No facile panaceas are found here. Rather, some probing analyses of the problems confronting those who would question the spread of surveillance along with some robust research on already-existing and emerging modes of regulating, opposition and resistance. Global variations and rapid technological change notwithstanding, these chapters show that human agency, collective action and shared principles are available to counter the "politics of visibility" in which surveillance studies is situated and with which it engages.

References

Gilliom, J. (2001). *Overseers of the Poor*, Chicago, IL: University of Chicago Press.
Marx, G. (1998). "Ethics for the New Surveillance," *The Information Society*, 14: 171–85.
Nissenbaum, H. (2010). *Privacy in Context: Technology, Policy and the Integrity of Social Life*, Stanford, CA: Stanford Law Books.

Section 4.1.
Ethics, law and policy

a. A surveillance of care

Evaluating surveillance ethically

Eric Stoddart

Approaches to evaluating surveillance ethically can be broadly categorized as either rights-based or discursive-disclosive. In the first, procedural guarantees by which rights can be protected, the recourse effected when these are breached, and grounds established by which public debate can be conducted are deemed to be vitally important but, as this chapter demonstrates, such an approach is, for many critics, inadequate. For such commentators, the primary objective of socio-technical systems is human flourishing and, therefore, substantive content to this vision and attention to what is being done, not merely what *ought* to be done, are both seen as necessary additional dimensions of an ethical critique. As a discourse that discloses what is being done to us, surveillance studies itself is, although at first not obviously so, a method of ethical enquiry. Foregrounding the ethics of surveillance is of singular importance given the threats to the boundaries of bodies (see van der Ploeg, this volume), from automation instead of human intervention, and the prospect of being "faded-out" as a person when viewed on a screen that epitomize the emerging issues in this field.

A rights-based approach

The technological sophistication of contemporary surveillance belies its continuity with the struggles of earlier societies to demand accountability of those with the power to watch. Turning today to a rights-based framework of ethical evaluation is to draw on often hard-won freedoms from the capricious acts of a sovereign. Although a notion of inalienable rights was known in antiquity and a higher, *natural* law to that of the ruler was treasured in the Middle Ages, it is the formulations of the closing decades of the eighteenth century that so significantly advanced the currency of a language of rights. The Virginia Declaration of Rights (1776) and the French Declaration of the Rights of Man and the Citizen (1789) propelled claims to self-determination and the limits on sovereign power that had already been advanced in the English Bill of Rights (1689) and would be developed in the twentieth century beyond national constitutions to aspirations and commitments enshrined with the Universal Declaration of Human Rights (1948) and, supra-nationally, in the European Convention of Human Rights (1950).

The political and cultural authority granted to such charters, against which surveillance strategies are weighed and often found wanting, relies on a fundamental assertion that the individual is not only a citizen but a *person*. Precise formulations of individual liberties *vis-à-vis* groups, customs or the state vary as do the extent to which a "free market" and the right to own property find concrete expression, but the state is widely held responsible for securing the conditions for the autonomy of the individual. National security, justice against oppression from one's fellow-citizens and the maintenance of the necessary public institutions are core elements of the broad constellation of notions of "liberal democracy."

This is the bedrock upon which current appeals are made in the face of surveillance tactics deemed to be eroding civil and human rights. A response that such surveillance is intended to *defend* those same rights lies, for many, at the core of disputes over cross-border exchange of travelers' personal information, identification card systems, scans and searches of persons and luggage at transport hubs, and many other data-collection exercises including flashpoints such as welfare support or health insurance. In some contexts, a surveillance practice might be legal yet deemed unethical when made accountable to claims of human rights; an outcome that befell the United Kingdom's Labour government in the 2008 ruling by the European Court of Human Rights over its policy of indefinitely retaining DNA data gathered from people charged but not convicted of a criminal offence. Two distinct, but inter-connected, routes are commonly adopted to defend our rights as both persons and citizens: the protection of personal data and of personal privacy (see also Raab, Regan and Kerr and barrigar, this volume).

Data protection

The United States has tended to develop data protection regulations on a sector-by-sector basis whilst other jurisdictions, most notably the European Union, have looked to comprehensive regulatory instruments. In exchanging data between agencies, organizations, and across internal and external national boundaries, a balancing is required of the right to privacy, economic interests and individuals' well-being. Surveillance will, in some form or other, involve flows of data that would come to an abrupt halt were privacy to be valorized to the exclusion of all other considerations. It is not difficult to imagine the effect of so protecting personal data that citizens might revel in their bolstered privacy but be without employment in an economy that is unable to function profitably. Similarly, commerce might lay unrestricted claim to data in an attempt to be the most competitive in a global market that relies upon such flows and aggregations of information. The result would be an affluent but naked consumer, laid bare before commercial interests. Even if data is protected in such a way that the human right to privacy is balanced with economic exigencies this is not to assume that individuals will flourish to become all they might. The right to privacy might be ensured at conceptual and legal levels but be of little consequence for those who have few alternatives but to surrender their data in circumstances of economic disadvantage.

It is to this nexus of interests that Gary T. Marx addressed his seminal "Ethics for the New Surveillance" (Marx 1998). He argued that broad principles of "fair information practice" (what is otherwise known as "data protection") are inadequate for the confluence and inter-weaving of new surveillance technologies that are rapidly appearing and the capacity of governments and commercial organizations to, in effect, compel the disclosure of personal data for subsequent aggregation, analysis and distribution. The necessarily generalized principles of an appeal to rights are further limited because, for Marx, they fail to appreciate that *more* data is not merely more *data* but also analysis, and that categorizing reveals a new reality. It may be all well and good to regulate for accountability in the storage and use of data, just as placing regulatory limits on its disclosure and retention is welcome within a regime of enforcing compliance. However, Marx argued, this does not probe the ethical question of whether a given means of collecting data is acceptable in the first place. Similarly, where increasing use is made of remote sensing, data is no longer limited to biographical information or details of commercial transactions entered manually by a human operator. Crucially, qualitative distinctions are required; urine samples and date of birth are not the same kind of data.

Marx in no way dismissed the importance of rights-based ethics for surveillance but brought his expertise as a social scientist to bear by developing such principles in order to take account of the factors that generate unease amongst many of the public when encountering new surveillance strategies. Through a list of 29 questions his attempt was directed at the tactics, the context of data collection and its goals. To sensitize surveillance practitioners Marx invited consideration of how harm, personal boundaries and relations of trust might be experienced by subjects. In an interesting adoption of the "Golden Rule" he asked those responsible for deploying and carrying out data collection to ponder whether or not they would be willing to be "subjects under the conditions in which they apply it to others." The symbolic meaning of the method was thereby brought to the surface whilst linking the specific goals of a given data practice to broader community aspirations (see also Raab, this volume).

Privacy

If attention to data is one facet of a rights-based evaluation of surveillance, then focusing on the individual's right to a life beyond the gaze and interference of unwanted intrusion is the other. It is immediately apparent that such an account suggests a normative understanding of privacy as a good to be guarded and is not merely neutrally descriptive of the situation in which one finds oneself when under surveillance. An ethical approach that draws upon privacy is situated firmly within a field where questions are asked about *which* instances of decreased—or, arguably just as importantly, increased—privacy are acceptable. The appeal to privacy seems to be the path taken by most people when they consider the ethics of monitoring and seek a bulwark against particular forms of surveillance. The pejorative connotations that persist around the term "surveillance" owe their origins and resilience in no small part to a discourse of privacy. To be in a position to avoid or be spared others' efforts to exercise control over one and to have the capacity so to resist such unwanted overtures is integral to conceptions of the person and, particularly, the right to self-determination.

To merely ask the question, "Does this surveillance tactic impinge upon someone's privacy?" offers little hope of a fruitful answer. Privacy is always a qualified, never an absolute, right. The state reserves to itself the right, even the duty, to place national security, the detection and prosecution of crime, public health and others' safety higher in priority. Such valuations are, of course, contestable and vigorously contested as in, for example, arguments over counter terrorist surveillance, national identification card schemes, or reporting particular communicable diseases. Legal precedence can be used to flesh out definitions of when, how, by whom and against whom privacy might not have been respected. Breaches of trust or confidentiality may be subject to compensation after the fact in contexts where illegitimate surveillance and distribution of associated data has occurred.

Adjectives qualifying surveillance are, in both popular and academic discourse, readily recognizable as, amongst others, "intrusive," "invasive," "interfering," "oppressive" or "violating." These are profoundly ethical designations derived from deeply-held notions of our right to make our own decisions, and our mistakes, without always being required to give an account of ourselves in public; the institutions of democratic polity depend to no small measure upon just such a space for us to undertake critical reflection. It is important that our reputations can be protected from harm through the disclosure of information that is distorted because it is partial. We value the semblance of a level-playing field that can be secured in the marketplace by legislation that constrains the flow of information about us and the benefit we accrue of privacy protecting us from being judged in one sphere, perhaps our workplace, with information gleaned from another, such as our sexual preferences. In these respects, and others, the value of privacy as a plumb line against which to test surveillance is inestimable.

Privacy, however, lacks sufficient traction over the slippery ground of new surveillance strategies. Helen Nissenbaum is representative of those who argue for a reconfiguring of privacy in order that it might be fit for purpose (Nissenbaum 2010). She finds it over-reliant upon, and reproducing of, the private/public dichotomy that focuses on a barrier between private individuals and government actors. Such a framework is limited in its usefulness in its rigid distinctions between political and domestic or personal realms. Furthermore, it leads to a preoccupation with protection of private information. In societies where surveillance is ubiquitous, large proportions of people claim that privacy is very important to them but when taking action choose convenience over principle. This might suggest that privacy fails to capture the limited alternatives that masquerade as "choice" for contemporary consumers. It also offers little help in what

Nissenbaum calls our "privacy in public." This is not simply the experience of being under surveillance in public or semi-public places (such as shopping malls) but the capability of technologies to gather, assemble, store and recategorize people. The ten or 20 of our actions that this number of strangers might have noticed become qualitatively different when viewed and analyzed by a surveillance system. The classification of information as "private" or "public" is becoming less useful. Nissenbaum's approach is to ask questions about the *appropriate* flow of personal information; to argue for data to be governed by its contextual integrity. In this way, ethical discussion coheres around the norms by which specific groups of people expect their information to be handled.

A rights-based approach to the ethics of surveillance is the most readily recognizable, but problematic for many analysts. The notion of *universal* claims is seen as a sleight-of-hand whereby the perspectives of those with the power to name norms are allowed to go unacknowledged by them in the mistaken belief that theirs need not be justified but all other particularist claims do. For example, the assertion that autonomy is vested in the individual is presented as self-evident when it can be understood as the vantage point of the independent-minded who fail to appreciate how autonomy is shared in relationships. These can be quite unequal in terms of capacities to function, such as in the shared-autonomy of parents and a cognitively disabled adult child. Furthermore, feminist theorists have challenged a method of ethical reasoning that prioritizes abstract principles over relationships between people. Although such principles must be highly abstract to have any saliency across the diverse domains of life, the decisions as to what is ethical, what is deemed "public" and what is "private" must be recognized as profoundly political and not assumed to be self-evident. Alternative approaches include those that challenge particular formulations of rights and the domains in which these are operative, but others claim to offer a radically different way of ethical inquiry.

A discursive approach

Rights-based approaches are built around principles of normative conduct; by contrast discursive ethics seek to disclose what is being done and the possibilities that might be available for alternative actions. The widespread use of Michel Foucault's account of the panopticon as an explanatory model for surveillance can belie its place within his broader ethical project. Foucault was concerned not with the normative questions of "What to do?" but with the subjective issue of "Who am I?" The answer, he contends, lies not in a substance but in the number of relationships that I have with myself through time and across a range of domains. I have been, and am being, formed by a constellation of structures, systems, symbols, traditions and relationships; the ethical task is to have concern for myself, to understand what is shaping me in order that I might identify scope for my agency.

In this way Foucault's genealogical research was an ethical act in breaking open the historical development of, in this case, disciplinary surveillance as a prelude to a second movement of identifying possibilities for more careful self-formation. This led Foucault to inquire into the practices, rather than only the processes, of liberation because it is necessary to define what one is seeking to be liberated into, not merely to repeat a call to liberty. Ethics is, "the considered form that freedom takes when it is informed by reflection" (Foucault 2000: 284). This concern, or care, for the self implies complex relationships with many others but does not place them first, before the self. Yet, he contended, this is not to disregard others for this ethic of freedom is also a way of caring for others (Foucault 2000: 287). A discursive approach discloses to both us and others what we did not previously know about our situations, the conditions under which we have been living and working and how we might be being exploited as, for example, in the extensive cross-referencing of personal data generated by people claiming social welfare benefit. Questions arise as to the techniques (such as discipline) that we have been encouraged or coerced into applying to our self-formation and how we are relating to the particular norms of conduct we are following. In many respects such an ethic invites us to question the sort of self that we have hitherto been seeking to become.

The output of ethical reasoning in this mode does not consist of principles (broad or specific) that can be applied as normative across various sites of surveillance. Codes of conduct are neither generated nor used as measures against which surveillance tactics can be evaluated for their congruence to accepted practice. In other words, ethics are not the outcome but the process itself. This requires a perceptual shift on the part of many who might not otherwise recognize many sociological treatises within surveillance studies as moments of ethical exploration. Within this discursive tradition two examples can help demonstrate its usefulness in more detail.

Nikolas Rose considers the new "public health" conception of crime control that does not seek to legitimate interventions in legal or rights language but in terms of the necessity of pre-emptive identification of those who pose a risk to the rest of society (Rose 2000). The unfolding context is not one where supposed biological factors are credited with a reductionist explanation, as in earlier eugenics arguments, for there is a confluence with a "new moralism" that emphasizes the moral culpability of offenders. Rose traces themes in the public discourse of science and culture from which a notion of the "risky individual" has emerged. In what he calls the "micropolitics of contemporary control practices" he locates the influence of biological criminology not so much upon convictions but in the subsequent determination of sentences. What emerges in Rose's study is a shift from mitigation of punishment to the socio-political impetus that demands the control, and if necessary, sequestration of those likely to endanger public safety. The sting in the tail that he discloses is the claim that, because *all* behavior has a biological basis, offenders are held morally accountable *irrespective* of any biological factors that may or not be identified or identifiable.

The search is on, therefore, not for those whose offending can be accounted for biologically but for those genetically "at risk" individuals who may be treated "as if they were certain to be affected in the severest fashion" (Rose 2000: 17). Surveillance thus takes two forms: data-gathering to understand the social conditions that may lead to such conduct and collection of biometric information (for example, genetic, neurochemical or hormonal) by which to construct markers for identifying risky individuals. Rose's approach is genealogical in the Foucauldian tradition as well as placing the current use of risk-management in this context under critical scrutiny. In disclosing the frames within which not only offenders but also the wider public are being variously enticed and coerced to construct a self, he offers us an ethic not *of* but *about* the new biological criminality.

Graham Sewell and James Barker provide us with a second example of a discursive ethic, this time regarding the workplace where they examine how power is invested in surveillance by talk, interaction and participation (Sewell and Barker 2001). Their "micro-ethics" arises as a model of scrutiny that asks questions about the meaning of surveillance; *why* it is deemed to be important in a particular workplace and *who says* that it is necessary. Such an enquiry unfolds into analytical issues of how surveillance becomes meaningful for this group of employers and employees: working back from the rules. Evaluation completes the model where it is not just a question of technical accuracy but an ethical appraisal that discloses who, why and how surveillance is to be used.

To reach disclosure Sewell and Barker first offer a genealogical account of privacy, particularly in its development from the supposed dichotomy of public-private. It becomes clear that these delineations are repeatedly contested and that such a process is itself integral to the fabric of liberal democratic communities. Nevertheless, the role of elites in setting normative criteria endures. This realization is not preparatory to ethical evaluation of surveillance in the contemporary workplace but is an integral dimension of such consideration. Exploring the construction, negotiation and contestation of the meaning of surveillance for both the one undertaking surveillance and its objects (the employees) is an ethical act. The outcome is not to declare surveillance in this workplace either good or bad but to understand how it is dangerous and where the dynamic of resistance-compliance by all parties might be more effectively practiced.

While a discursive approach does not seek to establish universalizable principles it is not without its own plurality of contextually normative contents. Whether these be Foucault's perspective on "freedom," Rose's appreciation of "justice" or Sewell and Barker's recognition of "self-determination," particular values and their sustaining narrative-communities are not expunged but exposed to critical assessment (itself a value). It is this transparency that creates space for tradition-conscious voices to make contributions to thinking ethically about surveillance. The most prominent of these is David Lyon who enriches his sociological analysis with allusions to the ancient wisdom of a Christian tradition in order to give substantive content to a vision of human flourishing.

To Lyon it is an instrumental attitude that is ousting moral orientations to surveillance; this is particularly obvious where data is used to categorize. Personal knowing is displaced by behavioral, biographical and biometric traces. In an obsession with the statistical norm, societies, he argues, betray their core ontology, namely of violence with its concomitants of competition and objectification. Little consideration is given, observes Lyon, to exploring an alternative ontology of peace which could offer possibilities for foregrounding care (Lyon 2001: 153). Herein is scope for the accumulated wisdom of ancient faith traditions that, when at their best, have challenged and demonstrated other ways of living.

Lyon unpacks the politics of surveillance strategies across many sites in which he questions the ethics of social categorization that results in material disadvantage in its logic of distribution. People, particularly the weakest and most marginalized, are the measure against which surveillance is to be continually evaluated. Personal freedom and dignity are rights to be respected but the impetus and sustaining motivation arises from an emphasis on the embodied person as the *image of God*. Social justice, for Lyon, is grounded in the prophetic tradition of the Hebrew Bible read through the hermeneutical lens of the Christian claim that God is incarnated in the particular, namely Jesus of Nazareth. The dominical parables convey an ethics of embrace of the stranger not through principles but stories that destabilize hearers' prevailing assumptions. Such an emphasis on a critical appraisal of attitudes and actions of one person to another, in embodied relationships is bolstered, for Lyon, in the phenomenological ethics of Emmanuel Levinas (to whom we return, below).

In an approach that lies more within the discursive-disclosive model and drawing on Christian understandings of relationality (largely from feminist and liberationist discussions) Stoddart offers a theological exploration of how an ethics of care generates challenges and affirmations to surveillance strategies. He interrogates the pillars of attempts to control the future that underpin a culture of risk to which surveillance is often a technological and existential response. Instead of an over-reliance upon privacy rights he encourages the development of the skill of (in)visibility; the skill, within constraints, of managing how we make ourselves visible, less visible or even invisible within social space. In contrast to the monarchical and domineering God who is easily parodied in Bentham's panopticon, Stoddart proposes that it is the figure of the crucified God—the Jesus who knew surveillance by his opponents and in whom mercy is embodied—who is the more salient in his solidarity with all who are disenfranchised by surveillance (Stoddart 2011).

Emerging issues

Almost every aspect of surveillance might be considered an "emerging issue" and it is *the person* who, in various ways, keeps coming to the foreground as the focus and agent of responsible action. The three most notable areas of concern are: the boundaries of bodies, the withdrawal of human intervention and mediation of relationships through screens. The *ways* in which these are addressed reveal not only particular challenges but also approaches to ethical decision-making.

Irma van der Ploeg contends that our ontology of the human body is of critical importance in the ethical moves we make with regard to biometric surveillance. The body is not unproblematic, extra-discursive and obviously "anatomical" but a historical construction that is not self-evident (van der Ploeg 2003). Our current moral and legal vocabularies are found wanting when it is far from clear where the boundary has been crossed between "the body itself" and the body beginning to be "information." This does not rest at issues of how people perceive their biometric data but unfolds into normative implications for the design as well as the use of scanning equipment in, for example, airport security, workplace monitoring or medical research and treatment. When surveillance takes the form of interpreting heart rates and temperature fluctuations, critical attention is required to the occluded ethical move wherein differences pertaining to particular socio-demographic characteristics are mistakenly presented as universal; the very politics of technology to which van der Ploeg draws our attention.

Scanning of the body's surface—say, at the airport—can be presented as not intrusive, with the result that questions of bodily integrity are set aside and the focus turned to the hitherto more common searches by security staff of clothing and sometimes bodies. Van der Ploeg takes a moment of ethical decision-making back to the point where the boundaries of a technology are stabilized because it is from there that the legitimating of particular surveillance strategies may, in effect, begin. To name a certain feature as a *property* of the technology under question is to conceal what is, in reality, a non-neutral shaping of the politics of technology. It is an ethical question when agency is attributed to a technological device or system rather than to people. This returns responsibility to us at multiple points when we are those who deploy technology as representatives of institutions, are involved in stages of design, are users of equipment, or, perhaps most significantly, are subjects of surveillance.

To withdraw human intervention from surveillance strategies is defended as an improvement on the limited capacity of human operators to process the complex and rapid streams of data that can be garnered from battle field, cityscape, medical centre or any other site we might care to mention. Human error is to be circumvented by software algorithms and the vulnerability of flight crews can be alleviated by remotely guided or autonomous drones gathering intelligence over hostile terrain. No algorithmic system of any useful complexity will deliver perfectly accurate results. A margin of error in identifying a specified marker can be calculated but the limits are strategic ethical decisions germane to particular contexts.

Calibrating sensor technology is not an ethically neutral act. Mis identifying innocent tourists as "terrorist threats" may be the result of limiting the number of false negatives because just one slipping through the security net would have catastrophic consequences. On the other hand, public acceptance of vetting and searching procedures relies on goodwill that would be sorely tried with too many false positives, especially if these hinder "normal" travelers. Similarly, battlefield threats might point to autonomous systems that are designed to limit the number of false negatives when identifying and neutralizing enemy combatants but be politically damaging when the consequences fall too frequently upon innocent bystanders.

In the domain of care for elderly people whose vulnerabilities need to be addressed with monitoring their actions in their home (e.g. using the stove) or for whom assistance with toileting or bathing might be required, developments in robotic "carers" pose ethical challenges (Sharkey and Sharkey 2010). Questions of reducing human contact (because the elderly person has a robot to "talk to") as well as significant issues of loss of control and privacy (when a robot could be gathering and relaying visual information back to a central point) and infantilization (encouraging people to view the robots as dolls) all come to the fore with considerable urgency. As Sharkey and Sharkey point out, such monitoring and supervising systems are being tested already in a variety of real-life contexts. As a preliminary step to traditional Value Sensitive Design approaches that explore how robots might be introduced into contexts without ethical problems, theirs includes an anticipatory disclosive dimension cognizant of "a pressing need to identify the likely effects of robot care before it becomes commonplace."

Although viewing someone on a screen may bring them closer as we bridge time and space, this manner of watching holds great potential for us to diminish if not neglect altogether our ethical responsibilities. Martin Brigham and Lucas Introna draw on Emmanuel Levinas's critique of ethics *following* philosophy, wherein we arise as ethical subjects in the moment of reason from which moral codes are subsequently developed. They question the propensity of computer-mediated encounters to require us to draw on categories to such an extent that we render another person as an object (Brigham and Introna 2007). Instead, the claim is that we are confronted, held hostage as it were, by the primordial sight of another's face. Such a face is uncontainable and makes an infinite call upon us before we have categorized and objectified it. Justice is born when we are exposed to our limitless responsibility for all others, just as we are a face to them. The very impossibility of such infinite responsibility continually disrupts our resort to settled codes and thematic representations.

The screen reveals the world according to the screen's own categories and is thereby an ethical-phenomenological problem; mere appearance displaces the moment of epiphanic encounter. This is not a counsel to dispose of computer-mediated relationships but a call to resist the fading out of the other. Neither ethics nor politics dominates but oscillate at both design and deployment stages so that assumed interpretations are exposed to being destabilized by the presence of otherwise faded-out people. Deliberate transparency in design processes is thus essential and to be actively secured.

Conclusion

Looking into the lens of a CCTV camera we see our reflection. The values, assumptions and norms of our society are embedded in the technologies designed, marketed and deployed, often explicitly in our name by our elected representatives but more widely still in the commercial field. In much the same way an "ethics of surveillance" faces us with the challenge not merely of what to do, but of who we want to become and the, largely neglected, notion of the virtues of discretion, modesty, and honesty that might be expected of practitioners and subjects of surveillance. Finding frameworks for evaluating surveillance ethically requires not looking in two directions but in two ways. A rights-based ethic offers principles which, even if these need to be abstract, can nonetheless generate regulatory frameworks to which specific people can be held accountable. Discursive-disclosive ethics have the potential to disrupt fatalistic or protected models of surveillance that foreclose possibilities for critical response. In this way, engagement in surveillance studies is a more profoundly ethical venture than its attention to explanatory models at first appears.

References

Brigham, M. and Introna, L. D. (2007). "Invoking Politics and Ethics in the Design of Information Technology: Undesigning the Design," *Ethics and Information Technology*, 9: 1–10.

Foucault, M. (2000). "The Ethics of the Concern for Self as a Practice of Freedom," in *Michel Foucault. Ethics: Subjectivity and Truth. The Essential Works of Foucault 1954–1984*, vol. 1, edited by R. Rabinow, London: Penguin Books, pp. 281–301.

Lyon, D. (2001). *Surveillance Society: Monitoring Everyday Life*, Buckingham: Open University Press.

Marx, G. T. (1998). "Ethics for the New Surveillance," *The Information Society*, 14(3): 171–85.

Nissenbaum, H. (2010). *Privacy in Context: Technology, Policy, and the Integrity of Social Life*, Stanford, CA: Stanford Law Books.

Rose, N. (2000). "The Biology of Culpability: Pathological Identity and Crime Control in a Biological Culture," *Theoretical Criminology*, 4(1): 5–34.

Sewell, G. and Barker, J. R. (2001). "Neither Good, Nor Bad, but Dangerous: Surveillance as an Ethical Paradox," *Ethics and Information Technology*, 3(3): 181–96.

Sharkey, A. and Sharkey, N. (2010). "Granny and the Robots: Ethical Issues in Robot Care for the Elderly," *Ethics and Information Technology*, Online First.

Stoddart, E. (2011). *Theological Perspectives on a Surveillance Society: Watching and being Watched*, Farnham: Ashgate.

van der Ploeg, I. (2003). "Biometrics and the Body as Information: Normative Issues of the Socio-technical Coding of the Body," in *Surveillance as Social Sorting: Privacy, Risk and Digital Discrimination*, edited by D. Lyon, London: Routledge, pp. 57–73.

b. Regulating surveillance

The importance of principles

Charles D. Raab

Introduction

As Regan's chapter in this book shows, over the last 40 years or more, arrangements have been put in place in a large number of countries, and at levels up to the global, to regulate personal information practices in the interest of protecting the privacy and other human rights of individuals. These regimes are intended to apply some generally accepted principles of data protection that can be seen as an application of ethical and human rights norms to the case of information processing. In the face of intense pressures in the commercial and governmental worlds to collect, analyze, and share personal data, the efficacy of these principles and the regulatory institutions to which they relate is far from certain. The relationship between—for example— national or international security, law enforcement, public-service provision, migration control, and business purposes on the one hand, and the protection of privacy and human rights, on the other, is tense and continually negotiated.

There are three overarching but related issues. One is the question of whether the regulatory principles that were shaped in terms of computerized databases can apply to the more complex globalized circumstances of today's technological surveillance. Information is now gathered and processed by highly sophisticated technologies for watching, listening, tracking movement, and detecting. The means of surveillance involve assemblages of technologies as well as the intensive analysis of data for profiling people and targeting action, and they involve worldwide flows of information. These tools are designed and deployed through decisions animated by powerful urges in the state, in international arenas, and in the private sector to know ever more about their citizens and customers.

Two further important questions will be discussed more briefly in this chapter. One of them arises because individuals are not stand-alone subjects of surveillance. Therefore, the question is how we should think about the consequences of privacy intrusion not only for individuals, but also for groups, categories, and the general fabric of society and the polity—which, as Solove (2008), Regan (1995) and others have argued, are also affected by intrusions on privacy, and which stand to benefit from its protection. The final question is related to this, but has to do with the effects of surveillance beyond its consequences for privacy, since surveillance may lead to discrimination and adverse decisions taken against individuals and groups in ways that cut across important values of fairness, equal treatment, and the rule of law, beyond any invasion of privacy itself. Chapters in Part II of this book contribute valuable perspectives on these processes. Whether the application of traditional regulatory principles to the issues raised by these questions is adequate is not at all certain.

The difference between individual and collective levels of information processing is reflected at the level of safeguards and discourse, as between individual data protection and the limitation of group surveillance. Data protection classically concerns intrusions on the privacy of an individual's personal data. Therefore the laws and systems that have been developed for protection and for redress operate within the orbit of individual human rights principles, assumptions, and rules. "Privacy" is of course, an indefinite concept that sprawls over conceptual territory within philosophy, psychology and other social sciences, law, and other realms of culture and thought. In a large and inconclusive literature, the concept has been seen within various theoretical frameworks. Depending upon the literature source, privacy either subsumes or is conducive to dignity, personality, selfhood, autonomy, social withdrawal, sociality, control over information, political engagement, liberty, and other values and interests pertaining to the conception in many societies and cultures of what it means to be a human being. This makes it difficult to say what should be protected when "privacy" is protected, and to what end(s) procedural principles should be oriented.

Solove (2008) considers that privacy is best seen as an umbrella term covering a variety of situations in which many different types of interest are affected. This approach recognizes that some kinds of personal information only become "private" owing to the circumstances in which they are collected or communicated, and that the context is crucial to an understanding of whether privacy values are engaged (Nissenbaum 2010). Complications proliferate if the reference is not only to information privacy, but to spatial, bodily, communications, and other dimensions of privacy as well. Nonetheless, uncertainty and disagreement about definitions and meanings do not vitiate practical attempts to protect privacy, and privacy is not the only human value or right that has been defined in various and often fuzzy ways (see also chapters by Kerr and barrigar, and Stoddart, this volume).

In terms of the regulatory issues, the first question is whether privacy or data protection is obsolete or still effective. Identity, identification, and the use of personal data are implicated in both the practice of privacy invasion and protection, and surveillance practices and their limitation. Regulatory policies, sometimes firmly grounded in human rights principles, are important in both. These policies have been developed in relation to privacy and data protection, and have been predicated upon notions of the "reasonable expectation of privacy" that have become part of privacy jurisprudence. The protective rules, assumptions, and institutional practices have embodied understandings of a generalized, abstract person whose privacy, or whose information, is to be protected.

Traditional privacy and data protection

Regulatory systems for information privacy have been built upon a traditional body of principles. These give rise to rules and guidelines for the fair collection and processing of personal data, somewhat heroically assuming that "personal data" is a reasonably clear concept. Although countries may differ in their numbering and wording of the principles, in various national interpretations there are requirements that the data should be:

- fairly and lawfully collected for a valid purpose;
- accurate, relevant, and up-to date; not excessive in relation to its purpose;
- not retained for longer than needed for the purpose;
- collected with the knowledge and consent of the individual or otherwise under statutory authority;
- not communicated to third parties except under specified conditions that might include consent;
- kept under secure conditions;
- accessible to the individual for amendment or challenge.

Moreover, organizations must be transparent about what they are doing, and accountable for their actions; these principles have become more strongly emphasized in recent years, establishing a closer link with "openness" dimensions of information policy.

Even with more specific guidance offered by regulatory agencies, consultants, and industry associations, these principles are very difficult to implement consistently within and across jurisdictions. This is especially so where the information processing involves law enforcement and national security purposes, for which there are normally exemptions, and where the flows of information cross national boundaries and come under different regulatory regimes. This is the case, for example, with data on airline passengers and international efforts to combat financial fraud, but principles are also difficult to apply in the more ordinary circumstances of international commerce, such as is conducted online for purchases and payments. A crucial point is how these or other principles relate to the new emphasis, in some fields, upon "principles-based regulation" (PBR) (Black 2008). PBR is considered to be part of a "new governance" approach in which broad principles take their place within a broader, more flexible regulatory strategy that involves more than law as such, rules, and their adjudication. There are advantages and disadvantages of PBR, and also paradoxes, perhaps the main one being that, while PBR fosters trust between regulators and the regulated, it also depends on trust (Black 2008: 35–36).

In any case, principles have to be seen as a type of rule operating alongside—or in the absence of—more detailed and specific rules. The relationship between principles' level of normative generality and the different forms and specificities of rules are analytical points that need deep analysis as well as application to the "case" of regulating surveillance, but these tasks must be set aside in this chapter. However, it is relevant to note that the Australian Law Reform Commission (ALRC 2008: Vol. 1) has favored PBR over "rules-based regulation." A reliance on principles provides flexibility in the midst of rapid technological change and growing threats to privacy, and aims at achievable outcomes rather than the strict enforcement of prescriptive rules. Although emphasizing principles, the ALRC's hybrid approach makes clear the importance of clear rules and sectoral regulation, in which the former are provided for sectors or fields needing clarity about how the principles should be put into practice, arguably by subordinate regulations supplemented by guidance. Many data protection systems around the world operate at both the level of broad principles and of more specific rules and guidance, while also using a wider range of instruments. These matters are germane to the current discussion, including the relationship to the institutional and instrumental complex through which privacy and surveillance may be regulated, and which is explored in other places in this book (see for example Rule, in this volume, and Regan, also in this volume).

Revising and extending principles

In various arenas, the role of principles has been re-thought in recent years in order to give them greater purchase on practice and to enlarge their significance for information rights. With reference to the UK, Pounder (2008) finds the existing system for data protection under the Data Protection Act (DPA) 1998 seriously deficient in terms of regulatory power and application. He argues that, with regard to the data protection principles, the legal tests relevant to interference with provisions of the Human Rights Act (HRA) 1998—which embodies the European Convention on Human Rights—only address how data processing takes place and not whether it should. He therefore proposes nine principles for assessing whether privacy is protected against state surveillance. In short form, they are:

Principle 1: The justification principle (requiring an assessment of surveillance to justify it in terms of pressing social needs and measurable outcomes);
Principle 2: The approval principle (requiring informed parliamentary scrutiny of legislation, and sometimes public debate);
Principle 3: The separation principle (requiring authorization of surveillance to be separated from carrying it out);
Principle 4: The adherence principle (requiring surveillance staff to be managed, audited, and trained in proper procedures);

Principle 5: The reporting principle (requiring the regulator to determine the keeping of surveillance records to ensure transparency and accountability);

Principle 6: The independent supervision principle (requiring supervision of surveillance to be independent of Government and empowered to investigate);

Principle 7: The privacy principle (requiring an enforceable right to privacy of personal data and a right, in certain cases, to object to data processing);

Principle 8: The compensation principle (requiring payment of compensation for unjustified damage, distress, or detriment);

Principle 9: The unacceptability principle (requiring cessation, steps towards compliance with principles, or parliamentary approval of non-compliance).

Principle 7 provides an important link between the DPA and the HRA with regard to the sixth of the classic data protection principles, which says: "Personal data shall be processed in accordance with the rights of data subjects under this Act." Pounder's Principle 7 makes the link by adding, "and, in particular, personal data shall not be processed in a way that does not respect the private and family life or correspondence of data subjects." Most of these principles are aimed at improving the UK institutional arrangements for assessing the necessity and proportionality of specific surveillance policy proposals. However, their spirit also seems applicable in other jurisdictions—probably most of those that exist—where data protection suffers from the same sources of inadequacy in its ability to challenge governments bent on surveillance.

A further development on the level of principles may be seen in the Madrid Resolution adopted by the International Conference of Data Protection and Privacy Commissioners (2009) in November, 2009. Although contained in a draft document promoting the wider adoption of uniform international "standards," the principles—as well as rights and obligations—include the usual data protection ones but seem to place emphasis on two that are perhaps less commonly discussed as principles: openness and accountability. Openness requires that:

> Every responsible person [any natural person or organization, public or private which, alone or jointly with others, decides on the processing] shall have transparent policies with regard to the processing of personal data.

The openness principle moves closer to rules in involving the publication of privacy policies, as well as the provision to the individual of information about the responsible person's identity, the intended purpose, the recipients of disclosures, how to exercise rights, and other further information necessary to guarantee fair processing.

The accountability principle, which is being promoted very heavily in current privacy and data protection discourse, links to the role of regulatory bodies described later in the Resolution and stipulates that principles must not only be observed but must be seen to be observed. The Madrid Resolution states:

> The responsible person shall:

> a. Take all the necessary measures to observe the principles and obligations … and

> b. have the necessary internal mechanisms in place for demonstrating such observance both to data subjects and to the supervisory authorities.

Paralleling, and probably influencing, this strengthening of accountability's presence in the international information privacy armory has been the work undertaken since 2009 through a deliberative process—the "Accountability Project"—involving a group of legal, business, and regulatory experts. They produced a discussion document that immediately preceded the Madrid Resolution and have developed it further since then (Centre for Information Policy Leadership 2010). In the context of global exchanges of personal information, the Project aims to provide a more reliable basis than the "adequacy" judgments made by the European Commission for assuring that transborder flows of personal data pass through jurisdictions whose information privacy safeguards conform to the standards expected by the European Union's 1995 Data Protection Directive 95/46/EC. However, this generic approach is not restricted to international activity. It provides a customized set of principled requirements to be adopted as "appropriate" in different contexts by different data processing organizations, which will have to demonstrate to external regulators their fulfillment of nine "fundamentals" regarding:

(1) Policies
(2) Executive oversight
(3) Staffing and delegation
(4) Education and awareness
(5) Ongoing risk assessment and mitigation
(6) Program risk assessment oversight and validation
(7) Event management and complaint handling
(8) Internal enforcement
(9) Redress.

In one sense, these requirements for accountability repackage much of the accumulated amalgam of legal compliance requirements, good practice, "soft law," and risk-reduction instruments that has evolved over the past 40 years or more of privacy protection and surveillance limitation. In another sense, however, the Project goes further in fleshing out the idea that, to implement fundamentally important requirements, privacy protection involves deep-seated organizational and cultural change beyond legal compliance, or even in the cause of demonstrating such compliance. On the other hand, too much leeway may be afforded to organizations to "do it their way," even if what they do is then subject to authoritative external evaluation.

There is a degree of political astuteness demonstrated within this process in putting accountability, along with transparency, squarely in the centre of the thinking of the world's privacy and data protection regulators, as witness the Madrid Resolution, the EU's Article 29 Data Protection Working Party[1] (comprised of Member States' regulatory agencies), and the promotion of an accountability approach for the EU's own organizations by the European Data Protection Supervisor (2010), who is their external regulator. However, skepticism about the clarity and adequacy of the accountability approach itself will be justified until the approach is instituted in practice following further Project iterations.

Although the future of such initiatives is not certain, given the international politics of data protection, this development—along with other initiatives aimed similarly at stock-taking and reform—focuses on principles and reorients them towards policy and practice. However, this is not the only show in town, and its closeness to corporate interests requires monitoring; nor does it address some of the deeper and darker aspects of surveillance that are probed by the questions asked earlier. Those aspects involve practices that are not centrally involved in processing personal data as such, and that engage not only individual privacy but also other important human values and rights, social and political relationships, and the fabric of society itself. Thus the movement towards accountability and transparency addresses, at most—albeit valuably—the first question posed earlier: whether the regulatory principles that were shaped in terms of computerized databases can apply to the more complex circumstances of today's surveillance, involving new technologies and globalization. A strong point is that it addresses it at international and global levels. However, it is not part of its province to address the second question: how we should think about the consequences of surveillance not only for individuals, but also for groups and categories, and for society generally. Nor does it tackle the third question, about non-privacy consequences. These too, benefit from a reconsideration of principles, as some contemporary scholars of surveillance and privacy have attempted to do in rethinking "privacy" outside the individual frame of reference (Regan 1995).

New surveillance ethics?

Further steps have meanwhile been taken along the path of ethical principles that should guide regulatory efforts. Gary T. Marx (1998) argues for the need to develop an ethics for the "new surveillance" in which personal information is collected by new technologies that threw into doubt the regulatory power of the established set of principles of data protection or fair information practice. A range of new surveillance technologies had already appeared, beyond those of the computer age in which principles and laws had been fashioned. These included DNA screening, location devices involving RFID chips, internet monitoring devices, intelligent transport systems, smart cards, satellites, and "smart homes" that transmit data about individuals. Today, we are accustomed to talking also about "ambient intelligence" or "ubiquitous computing," as well as unmanned flying drones, Google Earth, Facebook and social networking, deep packet inspection, body scanners, algorithms for analyzing huge aggregates of data and predicting behavior, and many more technologies. They pose even more sharply Marx's question about the ethics of data collection and use. They also pose the question of how traditional principles and means of regulation can effectively limit surveillance and keep it within bounds that preserve human rights and liberties.

According to Marx, the privacy or data protection principles and the way they are implemented are no longer sufficient, if they ever were. For one thing, ethical concerns—beyond procedural rules—have not tended to be raised about information collection or surveillance activities. He identifies three broad areas of importance. These concerns include: matters to do with the means by which the data are collected; the contexts in which these processes take place; and what the uses, purposes or goals are for which they are collected, or for which people are tracked, monitored, watched, overheard, or detected.

Addressing these three areas of concern, Marx asks 29 ethical questions about surveillance systems. Although some are ambiguous, taken together they are a good starting point for investigating these systems and for providing a principled framework that encompasses much of what is already in place in terms of data protection, although potentially going far beyond it. The questions touch on a wide range of important considerations about the effects of surveillance, and there are many overlaps. Their areas of concern include the means of surveillance, the data collection context, and the uses of surveillance. The complete inventory is too long to be discussed here, but among the most important issues are those that concern:

> The means of surveillance:
> do they cause physical or psychological harm?

> The data collection context:
> are individuals aware of who collects and why?
> do they consent?
> can people challenge results and provide alternative interpretations and data?
> is there redress and sanctions for unfairness and procedural violations?
> is there equality or inequality of availability and application of the means?

> The uses of surveillance:
> is there proportionality between ends and means?
> are the goals legitimate and appropriate?
> is there specificity or "creep" of purpose?
> is there harm or unfair disadvantage to the subject?

It is striking that, to one degree or another, the regulatory implications of a large number of Marx's questions have been addressed or anticipated by existing data protection laws and systems, with reference to individual privacy: so how new are the ethics for the "new surveillance"? Marx's list usefully reminds us of the work that remains to be done, and of the need to reconsider the application of old principles to new surveillance technologies and systems. But it is easier to ask questions about the new surveillance and the application of ethics than to answer them. One should therefore be cautious about assuming either that answers would not be disputed in terms of fact, or, even if there were consensus, that rules and mechanisms for regulation can be effectively applied to the surveillance systems involved: taking the ethical high ground is not likely, by itself, to make too much difference in practice (see also Stoddart, this volume).

Moreover, vigorous debate could be had about some of these ethical precepts, whether old or new. Space only permits one illustration of this, albeit a crucial one: the importance or necessity of consent, and how to apply it in practice. Following consultation, the ALRC (2008) thought that consent should not be a separate principle although it plays an important role in many other principles concerning international transfers of data and the collection and use of especially sensitive information. On the other hand, many insist on informed consent for any processing of personal data unless authorized by statute. But because instances of the latter are legion and for defensible causes, and because the gaining of truly informed consent is fraught with problems in many sectors, the principle of "informational self-determination" that consent exemplifies is likely to be more important as a touchstone than as a guide to clear rule-making, and not as a sine qua non for the legitimacy of surveillance. In any case, there needs to be a fundamental reconsideration of the role of consent, recognizing that the invocation of a right to privacy is shaped by individual and social expectations in specific contexts, as Nissenbaum (2010) has argued.

Even for those of Marx's questions that already seem to be covered by privacy law and regulation, there is not a particularly impressive or consistent record of protection for the individual, let alone the wider society. A likely consensus within and across countries would hold that the implementation of ethical principles and derivative rules has been generally weak and patchy in the limitation and regulation of surveillance. It would probably contend that—under current legal and institutional provisions, and under the global and "normalized" mood of fear and demands for security, safety and public order—the prospects are not bright for safeguarding people against adverse effects of fairly conventional means of personal data processing, and dimmer still with regard to likely future challenges. Nonetheless, these issues are now more firmly on policy agendas and in the public consciousness; some victories have been won and regulatory systems, including the courts, have played a valuable part.

Achievements in privacy protection under traditional principles have been hard won in the face of political, economic, and social opposition or indifference, and there is much unfinished business. Functions continue to creep, or perhaps even to gallop—for example, new uses for databases and video surveillance beyond their original rationale—and the legitimacy of surveillance goals as well as the proportionality of the means are heatedly contested by advocacy groups, in political debating chambers, and in the courts. The question of harm or unfair disadvantage has not been sufficiently debated, nor is there an agreed way of measuring harmful effects. Whether it is better to deal with privacy harms by preventative or remedial means is not yet clear, although techniques like Privacy Impact Assessment and Privacy by Design aim at a preventive strategy rather than either ignoring wrongs or righting them after they have been committed, and some of the Accountability Project "fundamentals" push further on the pedals of redress and risk analysis. In data collection, public awareness may have been improved, making it easier to realize this principle, but the extent to which challenges, alternative interpretations of data, and redress can be given effect is variable and tenuous.

Beyond privacy

As mentioned, a further, and pressing, matter for consideration is whether an updated configuration of principle, discourse, policy, and practice can be applied to the trans-individual consequences of information processing, and to the circumstances of contemporary surveillance practices. Many surveillance scholars doubt the efficacy of traditional or revised high-level principles of individual privacy protection as instruments for countering excessive surveillance and combating inequality between individuals, groups or categories of people, even where principles are embodied in legal regimes that specify rules. Privacy, they often argue, is not the main issue, or not even the issue at all: at best, a privacy focus is a lever for prying open a much broader set of issues concerning citizenship, human rights, and civil liberties. Accepting this argument, a great deal of work still remains to be done, not only in terms of describing and criticizing surveillance practices with reference to non-privacy criteria, but in terms of devising ways of challenging, overturning, limiting, or regulating practices by legal or other policy instruments.

As Marx hints, this may involve the formulation of a principle of equality or non-discrimination, or expanding one of privacy's meanings—that which concerns human dignity or self-worth—to embrace non-discrimination and equality of treatment as intrinsic to the dignity of the individual. However, the development of rules, principles, and practical machinery for controlling the broader group or societal effects of surveillance has not moved very far beyond those that exist for individual privacy or data protection. It has not been easy to address the issue of the protection of persons who come to the attention of the state or business, or who are dealt with, not so much on the basis of their information as individuals per se, but in terms of their self-asserted or imputed membership of categories and groups. The possibility of class action does not exist in many legal jurisdictions.

The concept of identity is germane to this, for identities and identification are central to many forms of surveillance. There is an important distinction between individual identity in the sense of uniqueness, and individual identity in the sense of membership of a group or a category. The two forms of identity—sometimes called ipse and idem—concern the identity of the self as a distinctive person or "self," and the identity or identities that an individual has through belonging to a class or category of others, whether one or many. Thus the questions canvassed in this chapter are not completely distinct from each other, because the outer limits of the applicability of current rules and systems of regulation may occur precisely at the point where surveillance and identification of the individual crosses the boundary into the surveillance of groups, and where who a person "is" becomes who a person "is like" in terms of shared characteristics and a shared fate. The "me," whose privacy surveillance may invade disproportionately, shades into the "us," whose social and political relationships are affected by surveillance—sometimes for the better, but in large part for the worse, or excessively.

It is not certain how far these protective systems can therefore deal with surveillance practices where targets are selected in terms of the categorical and collective entities with which persons self-identify or to which they are assigned in official administrative schemes, and where equality and inequality are implicated (see Jenkins, this volume). The "fairness" principle of data collection may not extend so far, and the applicability of the principles has not generally been tested outside the legal framework of the data subject and her individual rights. Information may be processed—collected, analyzed, and shared—to bring to light collective or group affiliations or characteristics, and to take some action accordingly, even if the basis for this is erroneous. This may affect the group as a whole, and perhaps to their disadvantage if they are subjected to surveillance on the basis of "categorical suspicion." It may also affect any individual who may identify herself or be identified as belonging to a certain ethnic, religious, or other group, and where the alleged characteristics of these groups—for example, their lack of trustworthiness or proneness to criminality— whether imputed by cultural stereotyping or by data analysis that arrives at average figures, may result in subjecting her to unwarranted surveillance. This subjection—in itself a possible infringement—may lead to substantive further disadvantage, even if she does not fit the description.

Conclusion

The community of scholars and practitioners in the field of surveillance studies may need to develop new forms of practice, and new questions—perhaps deriving from Marx's—to ask about surveillance in order to innovate the regulatory instruments, strategies, and institutions discussed elsewhere in this book. This repertory may be re-positioned or replaced, and its remit may be extended beyond the protection of privacy to embrace ways of keeping the broader and non-privacy implications of surveillance within bounds set by principles. Technological change toward more intensive, extensive, covert and ubiquitous ways of conducting surveillance plays a major role in prompting reform in regulation. But it would be insufficient to focus on technology as the cause, rather than as the facilitator or handmaiden, of surveillance, without taking account of the decisions made by individuals or on behalf of organizations that make use of technology to further their aims.

In that sense, it is not so much the regulation of technology that would be important, but the regulation of decision and action taken by human agents in specific practices or general policies. Better understanding is needed of this behavior: the motives, methods, values, ethics, and relationships that are found in situations where technology is invented or applied. Knowledge about these is the province of the human and social sciences; such knowledge is likely to help in seeing what can and should be regulated, and in what sense surveillance can also play a positive role in achieving desirable values for individuals, groups, and society, as well as in securing rights. It is also likely to contribute to the design of better and more effective regulatory institutions, instruments, and strategies that involve principles and their implementation, if only one knew how to measure effectiveness: an unresolved and political, rather than simply technical or administrative, issue in the study of surveillance.

Note

1 Article 29 Data Protection Working Party Opinion 3/2010 on the Principle of Accountability, 00062/10/EN, WP173, Brussels.

References

Australian Law Reform Commission (ALRC). (2008). *For Your Information – Australian Privacy Law and Practice*, Vol. 1, Report 108, Canberra: Australian Government, Australian Law Reform Commission.

Black, J. (2008). "Forms and Paradoxes of Principles Based Regulation," (September 23), LSE Legal Studies Working Paper No. 13/2008, available at http://ssrn.com/abstract=1267722 (accessed 15 November 2010).

Centre for Information Policy Leadership. (2010). "Demonstrating and Measuring Accountability – A Discussion Document, Accountability Phase II – The Paris Project," available at www.huntonfiles.com/files/webupload/CIPL_Accountability_Phase_II_Paris_Project.PDF (accessed 23 December 2010).

European Data Protection Supervisor. (2010). "Monitoring and Ensuring Compliance with Regulation (EC) 45/2001", Policy Paper, 13 December, Brussels: European Data Protection Supervisor.

International Conference of Data Protection and Privacy Commissioners. (2009). *International Standards on the Protection of Personal Data and Privacy – The Madrid Resolution.*

Marx, G. (1998). "An Ethics for the New Surveillance," *The Information Society*, 14(3): 171–86.

Nissenbaum, H. (2010). *Privacy in Context: Technology, Policy, and the Integrity of Social Life*, Stanford, CA: Stanford University Press.

Pounder, C. (2008). "Nine Principles for Assessing Whether Privacy is Protected in a Surveillance Society," *IDIS*, 1(1): 1–22.

Regan, P. (1995). *Legislating Privacy: Technology, Social Values, and Public Policy*, Chapel Hill, NC: University of North Carolina Press.

Solove, D. (2008). *Understanding Privacy*, Cambridge, MA: Harvard University Press.

c. Privacy, identity and anonymity

Ian Kerr and jennifer barrigar

A comprehensive understanding of surveillance requires an appreciation of its relationship to other core social constructs such as privacy, identity and anonymity.

The relationship between these concepts is uneasy and sometimes divisive among scholars of surveillance studies. Perhaps one reason for this is that surveillance and privacy are often misunderstood as binary opposites. The relationship is, in fact, more nuanced. As sociologist Stephen Nock observed in his study of the implications of an increasingly anonymous society of strangers, "A society of strangers is one of immense personal privacy. Surveillance is the cost of that privacy" (Nock 1993: 1). To the uninitiated, Nock's quote seems counterintuitive—after all, how can surveillance and privacy be anything but opposites? Does not more of one imply less of the other?

What appears at first blush to be a zero-sum game is in fact a set of interdependent relationships. For example, according to Nock, individuals actively participate in communities and are constantly monitored and assessed by other community members. From this assessment is derived a cumulative reputation about the individual, which in turn becomes its own key to future participation within that society. This leads to further communal assessment, a more in-depth reputational appraisal, future access and so on. Historically, these performances and assessments took place in the context of family and local community, where everyone (supposedly) knew everyone else. However, in a more geographically dispersed society, we are confronted with the absence of such easy community information sharing. Consequently, we have moved to the development of various proxies such as ordeals and credentials.

An ordeal is a form of integrity test—for example, a lie-detector or drug-test. In contrast, a credential is a token of trust such as a signature, a personal identification number or other "official" verifications in the forms of educational degrees or driver's licenses (Nock 1993: 11–16). Such proxies function as a crude form of authentication of the individual, but do not provide the extensive, detailed performance review that community knowledge can provide. Indeed, though such proxies can confirm the identity or (presumptive) truthfulness of an individual, they usually leave open the question of how to make an assessment of trustworthiness of the individual who has been identified.

Considered from another perspective, the relationship between information management and identity remains an integral one. Constructing an identity through the use of symbolic representations is a matter of information control. Successfully negotiating what information is attached to us, who knows what information, and how that information is protected from others becomes increasingly difficult in a technological environment where people can steal, distort, or delete your identity.

No matter what perspective is adopted, it seems that our ability to manage our privacy, including the power to identify oneself or not, to speak or act anonymously or without reference to one's "real" credentials, is not merely interrelated but perhaps even inextricably linked to the concept of surveillance. Just as our desire for functional privacy brings with it the necessity for surveillance, so too do the ever-growing collections of personal information and history, and their corresponding public availability make necessary the ability to separate some of our performances from that person of record.

The network society

The further migration of society to the realm of "cyberspace" (as today's technologically mediated relationships are colloquially understood) has exacerbated our reliance on credentials and other tokens of identification. The advent of the world wide web in the 1990s initially enabled everyone with access to a computer and modem to become unknown and in some cases invisible in public spaces—to communicate, emote, act and interact with relative anonymity. Indeed, since the impact of what one could say or do online was no longer limited by physical proximity or corporeality, it not only increased anonymity but also increased the range of connection/communication possible. The end-to-end architecture of the web's Transmission Control Protocol, for example, facilitated unidentified, one-to-many interactions at a distance. As the now famous cartoon framed the popular culture of the early 1990s, "On the internet, nobody knows you're a dog." Although this cartoon resonated deeply on various levels, at the level of architecture it reflected the simple fact that the internet's original protocols did not require people to identify themselves, enabling them to play with their identities, to represent themselves however they wished.

Network technologies fostered new social interactions of various sorts and provided unprecedented opportunities for individuals to share their thoughts and ideas en masse. Among other things, the internet permitted robust political speech in hostile environments. It allowed users to say and do things that they might never have dared to say or do in places where their identity was more rigidly constrained by the relationships of power that bracketed their experience of freedom. Anonymous browsers and messaging applications promoted frank discussion by employees in oppressive workplaces and created similar opportunities for others stifled by various forms of social stigma. Likewise, new cryptographic techniques promised to preserve personal privacy by empowering individuals to make careful and informed decisions about how, when and with whom they would share their thoughts or their personal information.

At the same time, many of these new information technologies created opportunities to disrupt and resist the legal framework that protects persons and property. Rather than embracing the freeing aspects of this technological change in mainstream ways, some instead began to exploit the network to defraud, defame and harass, to destroy property, to distribute harmful or illegal content, and to undermine national security.

In parallel with both of these developments, there has been a proliferation of various security measures in the public and private sectors designed to undermine the "ID-free" protocols of the original network. New methods of authentication, verification and surveillance have increasingly allowed persons and things to be digitally or biometrically identified, tagged, tracked and monitored in real-time and in formats that can be captured, archived and retrieved indefinitely. More recently, given the increasing popularity of social network sites and the pervasiveness of interactive media used to cultivate user-generated content, the ability of governments, not to mention the proliferating international data-brokerage industries that feed them, to collect, use and disclose personal information about everyone on the network is increasing logarithmically. This phenomenon is further exacerbated by corporate and government imperatives to create and maintain large-scale information infrastructures to generate profit and increase efficiencies.

In this new world of ubiquitous hand-held recording devices, personal webcams, interconnected surveillance cameras, RFID tags, smart cards, global satellite positioning systems, HTTP cookies, digital rights management systems, biometric scanners and DNA sequencers, the space for private, unidentified, or unauthenticated activity is rapidly shrinking. Many worry that the regulatory responses to real and perceived threats have already profoundly challenged our fundamental commitments to privacy, autonomy, equality, security of the person, free speech, free movement and free association. Add in the shifting emphasis in recent years towards public safety and national security, and network technologies appear to be evolving in a manner that is transforming the structures of our communications systems from architectures of freedom to architectures of control. We are shifting away from the original design of the network, from spaces where anonymity and privacy were once the default position to spaces where nearly every human transaction is subject to tracking, monitoring and the possibility of authentication and identification.

The effects of shifting social and technological architectures

These apparent shifts in our social and technological architectures raise a host of issues that occupy but also transcend the legal domain. The ability or inability to maintain privacy, construct our own identities, control the use of our identifiers, decide for ourselves what is known about us and, in some cases, disconnect our actions from our identifiers will ultimately have profound implications for individual and group behavior. It will affect the extent to which people, corporations and governments will choose to engage in global electronic commerce, social media and other important features of the network society. It will affect how we think of ourselves, the way that we choose to express ourselves, how we make moral decisions, and our willingness and ability to fully participate in political processes.

There is a fundamental tension mitigating our understanding of privacy, identity and anonymity. While privacy is usually understood as a fundamental human right, anonymity as a basic foundation of political free speech, and identity as something that must be self-directed and chosen, there is an increasing currency in the belief that information must be monitored, collected and stored with permanence, and assessed continuously in order to prevent significant social threats. These debates, and the perceived conflict between privacy and security, have become increasingly fraught since 9/11 and the attendant emergence of a security state, including a return to the "crypto-wars" of the 1970s/1980s in the recent government proposals requiring that telecommunications providers redesign their infrastructure in order to facilitate identifiability of users where required by the state.

Increases in the ability to identify users, as well as technological evolutions that allow for ever-greater storage and analysis of personal information, are also creating concerns around the public/private divide. This is happening in many different ways. States are seeking to regulate spam; keep records to allow identification of those who interact anonymously with users, especially youth; publicize data security breaches; and regulate directed/targeted advertising. Outside of state concern about private industries' collection, use, disclosure and retention/security of personal information, there is also a question of state access to that very information. Data protection legislation was originally directed at state personal information practices and, accordingly, places stringent rules on what information may be collected and by what means, as well as regulating its use, disclosure, etc. With the increase in private sector data collections, states are able to deputize private organizations, either formally or informally and thus gain access to these private databanks, which at least arguably may avoid some of the more stringent controls placed upon state organizations by data protection legislation. Finally, even where private organizations are not providing the state with access to their databanks, data is increasingly being collected, mined and used for a variety of profit-based activities.

The network society's shifting social and technological architectures further complicate the relationship between privacy, identity and anonymity, and their ultimate connection to surveillance. Each of these three concepts is briefly considered in turn.

Privacy

Larry Ellison is the CEO of Oracle Corporation and the 14th richest person alive. In the aftermath of September 11 2001, Ellison offered to donate to the US government software that would enable a national identification database, boldly stating in 2004 that "[t]he privacy you're concerned about is largely an illusion. All you have to give up is your illusions, not any of your privacy." Ellison was, in fact, merely reiterating a sentiment that had already been expressed some five years earlier by his counterpart at Sun Microsystems, Scott McNealy, who advised a group of journalists gathered to learn about Sun's data-sharing software, "You have zero privacy anyway. Get over it." More recently, we've seen Facebook founder Mark Zuckerberg opine that social norms have changed to favor public sharing of information instead of privacy. Indeed, many if not most contemporary discussions of privacy are about its erosion in the face of new and emerging technologies. One need only scan the media today to see this sentiment repeated in various ways, from the twitter hashtag #privacyisdead to op-eds and speeches from figures both public and private.

To judge whether privacy is dead (or dying) we must first understand it (see also Rule, Stoddart, this volume). Many academics have characterized privacy as a fundamental human right that goes to the core of preserving freedom and autonomy, and is essential to the workings of a healthy democracy. The judiciary has on many occasions shared this point of view. For example, Justice Gérard LaForest of the Supreme Court of Canada once opined that:

> grounded in man's physical and moral autonomy, privacy is essential for the well-being of the individual. For this reason alone it is worthy of constitutional protection, but it also has profound significance for the public order. The restraints imposed on government to pry into the lives of the citizen go to the essence of a democratic state

> *(R. v. Dyment* 1988: 427)

While the character of privacy has, without question, become more diverse in light of technologies of both the privacy-diminishing and privacy-preserving variety, the existence of privacy rights will not simply depend on whether our current technological infrastructure has re-shaped our privacy expectations in the descriptive sense. There has been significant academic attention to the shifting "reasonable expectation of privacy" standard used by courts and other decision-makers, and a general consensus remains that it is a normative rather than descriptive concept; contra Ellison and McNealy, it is not a like-it-or-lump-it proposition. However, recent work in the field relied upon by various courts, including the Supreme Court of Canada, suggests that our "reasonable expectations" must be understood in the context of a broader theoretical understanding of the manner in which information emanates from private spaces to public places (Kerr and McGill 2007: 392–432). Theories such as this also support a growing consensus that the meaning, importance, impact, and implementation of privacy may need to evolve alongside the emergence of new technologies.

How privacy ought to be understood—and fostered—in a network society certainly requires an appreciation of and reaction to new and emerging network technologies and their role in society. At the same time, an appropriate regulatory approach must be cautious to avoid threat- or issue-specific responses that neglect to articulate or reinforce the larger social value of privacy. One well-known example is the USA's Video Protection Privacy Act of 1988 enacted after Justice Robert Bork's video rental records were released to the news media during his confirmation hearing to the US Supreme Court. This is a perfect example of a law that is far too technology-specific. By narrowly focusing on a single technology, the Act had extremely limited application from the outset and is now, like the technology it sought to regulate, completely obsolete. This can be contrasted with a "technology-neutral" approach, such as the one adopted in the OECD Guidelines on the Protection of Privacy and Transborder Flows of Personal Data. The latter strategy involves the adoption of a set of "fair information practice" principles—regulating collection limitation, data quality, purpose specification, use limitation, security safeguards, openness and individual participation—which have subsequently been applied to an extremely broad range of emerging information technologies (OECD Guidelines: 23 September 1980). By providing concrete and well-grounded guidelines for the collection, use and disclosure of personal information, this approach alleviates the need to re-write privacy law each time a new privacy-implicating technology comes along.

Given that the currency of the network society is information, it is not totally surprising that these fair information practice principles were recharacterized in Germany and, subsequently, by a number of other courts as the means of ensuring "informational self-determination." Drawing on Alan Westin's classic definition of informational privacy as "the claim of individuals, groups, or institutions to determine for themselves when, how, and to what extent information about them is communicated to others" (Westin 1967: 7), many jurisdictions throughout Europe and around the globe have adopted the fair information principles mentioned above as the basis for data protection regimes. However, these principles and the laws that support them are not a panacea, as they have been developed and implemented on the basis of an unhappy compromise between those who view privacy as a fundamental human right and those who view it as an economic right. From one perspective, these laws are grounded in a human rights framework and aim to protect privacy, autonomy and dignity interests. From another, they are the lowest common denominator of fairness in the information trade. While some argue that data protection presumes the use and disclosure of personal information, creating (if anything) a limited right of control over what organizations do with one's personal information rather than "true" privacy. There is little or no acknowledgement that one might wish to prevent anything being done with the information or, indeed, the information being collected at all.

Identity

While lofty judicial conceptions of privacy such as "informational self-determination" set important normative standards, the traditional notion of a pure, disembodied and atomistic self, capable of making perfectly rational and isolated choices in order to assert complete control over personal information is not a particularly helpful fiction in a network society. Who we are in the world and how we are identified is, at best, a concession. Aspects of our identities are chosen, others assigned, and still others accidentally accrued. Sometimes they are concealed at our discretion, other times they are revealed against our will. Identity formation and disclosure are both complex social negotiations and, in the context of the network society, it is not usually the individual who holds the bargaining power.

Because the network society is to a large extent premised on mediated interaction, who we are—and who we say we are—are not self-authenticating propositions in the same way that they might be if we were close kin or even if we were merely standing in physical proximity of one another. Although we can be relatively certain that it is not a canine on the other end of an IM chat, the identity of the entity at the other end of a transaction may be entirely ambiguous. Is it a business partner, an imposter or an automated software bot? Indeed, it may be that we sometimes do not need to know (and in some cases might not care) whether our interlocutor has an authenticated identity. Other times—when dealing with finances or other extremely sensitive or personal information—it can be crucially important to ensure that access to this information is restricted to those with the proper authorization.

However, it is important to recognize that identification techniques can preserve or diminish privacy. Their basic function is to make at least some aspects of an unknown entity known by mapping it to a knowable attribute—essentially a new form of credentialing, intended to identify an entity as known or authorized. An identification technique is more likely to be privacy-preserving if it takes a minimalist approach with respect to those attributes that are to become known. For example, an automated highway toll system may need to authenticate certain attributes associated with a car or driver in order to appropriately debit an account for the cost of the toll. But to do so, it need not identify the car, the driver, the passengers or, for that matter, the ultimate destination of the vehicle. Instead, anonymous digital credentials could be assigned that would allow cryptographic tokens to be exchanged through a network in order to prove statements about them and their relationships with the relevant organization(s) without any need to identify the drivers or passengers themselves. Electronic voting systems can do the same thing.

Other strategies have focused not on collecting digital tokens from individuals themselves, but rather on the reputation an individual has achieved within her community. At its most basic, reputation is comprised of a record of interactions and past experiences. As Donath and boyd observe, "[m]ost of the qualities we are interested in about other people—is this person nice? Trustworthy? Can she do this job? Can he be relied on in an emergency? Would she be a good parent?—are not directly observable. Instead, we rely on signals, which are more or less reliably correlated with an underlying quality" (Donath and boyd 2004: 72). Reputation, while to some degree made up of signals, itself functions as a signal for such assessments. We assess these signals as we interact with others, and we refine and revisit our assessments with each interaction. As many scholars have noted, the role of reputation is inherently public—that is, while image is self-directed, reputation is by definition other-directed and derived. And it is derived for the purpose of functioning as a kind of social lubricant. As Nock has described, it facilitates relationships among strangers by reducing uncertainty and thus helping to create trust (Nock 1993: 124). Unsurprisingly, then, reputation has achieved ever greater importance and utility as the opportunities for uncertainty have increased.

An examination of the interaction of self and other in the construction of identity and the necessary connection between privacy/identity and broader discussions about power, gender, difference and discrimination therefore requires a deeper understanding of not only the interrelationship of these concepts but also how federated identity and/or reputation may function as forms of surveillance that come not only to authenticate an individual but also to police mainstream norms of presentation and performance (barrigar 2007). Identity formation and identification can be enabled or disabled by various technologies—data-mining, automation, ID cards, ubiquitous computing and human-implantable RFID—but each of these technologies too has potential narrowing effects, reducing who we are to how we can be counted, kept track of, or marketed to.

Anonymity

Anonymity allows for the creation of a new identity for many people owing to the fact that they have yet to have any signs ascribed to them, be they positive or negative. Anonymity allows for a public display of oneself (real or fantasy) in that anonymity means that there is no way to verify these claims.

Recently, Google CEO Eric Schmidt has suggested that:

> [p]rivacy is not the same thing as anonymity. It's very important that Google and everyone else respects people's privacy. People have a right to privacy; it's natural; it's normal. It's the right way to do things. But if you are trying to commit a terrible, evil crime, it's not obvious that you should be able to do so with complete anonymity. There are no systems in our society which allow you to do that. Judges insist on unmasking who the perpetrator was. So absolute anonymity could lead to some very difficult decisions for our governments and our society as a whole.
>
> *(Kirkpatrick 2010)*

Similarly, riffing on Andy Warhol's best-known turn of phrase, an internationally (un)known British street artist living under the pseudonym "Banksy" produced an installation with words on a retro-looking pink screen that say, "[i]n the future, everyone will have their 15 minutes of anonymity." Was this a comment on the erosion of privacy in light of future technology? Or, was it a reflection of Banksy's own experience regarding the challenges of living life under a pseudonym in a network society? While Warhol's "15 minutes of fame" recognized the fleeting nature of celebrity and public attention, Banksy's "15 minutes of anonymity" recognizes the long-lasting nature of information ubiquity and data retention. Indeed, anonymity may be the only way to guarantee privacy in a world where information is stored about us and easily shared.

Although privacy and anonymity are related concepts, it is important to realize that they are not the same thing. There are those who think that anonymity is the key to privacy. The intuition is that a privacy breach cannot occur unless the information collected, used or disclosed about an individual is associated with that individual's identity. Many anonymizing technologies exploit this notion, allowing people to control their personal information by obfuscating their identities. Interestingly, the same basic thinking underlies most data protection regimes, which one way or another link privacy protection to an identifiable individual. According to this approach, it does not matter if we collect, use or disclose information, attributes or events about people so long as the information cannot be (easily) associated with them. Of course, the notion that anonymization of information is a permanent solution is really only workable if technology ceases to evolve and change—as it is, the uncrackable of today will be the freely available of tomorrow. Similarly, a number of computer scientists have demonstrated various ways in which the ever-increasing amount of publicly available information allows anonymized information to be re-identified. Information that has been aggregated may also be put forward as "safe," but this too is uncertain and may depend on the amount of information made available, the size or specialization of particular pieces of information or locations, etc. The problem is that while actual identity information may have been stripped from the information, it becomes increasingly possible to re-identify that information because there are still parts of it that are identifiable in some way.

While anonymity enables privacy in some cases, it certainly does not guarantee it. As any recovering alcoholic knows all too well, even if Alcoholics Anonymous (AA) does not require you to show ID or use your real name, the meetings are anything but private. Anonymity in public is quite difficult to achieve. The fact that perceived anonymity in public became more easily achieved through the end-to-end architecture of the net is part of what has made the internet such a big deal. It created a renaissance in anonymity studies, not to mention new markets for the emerging field of identity management. The AA example illustrates another crucial point about anonymity. Although there is a relationship between anonymity and invisibility, they are not the same thing. As some leading academics have recently come to realize, visibility and exposure are also important elements in any discussion of privacy, identity and anonymity. Indeed, many argue that the power of the internet lies not in the ability to hide who we are, but in freeing some of us to expose ourselves and to make ourselves visible and/or heard on our own terms.

With the increase in avenues for comment and discussion via online spaces, we have seen a corresponding increase in legal actions where identification and identifiability are at the crux of the matter. Especially in areas such as cyber-bullying, cyber-harassment and cyber-stalking there is much speculation about how anonymity may enhance the abuser's power or even encourage behaviour that would not necessarily be performed were it visibly attached to an offline identity. Where currently US and Canadian courts facilitate identifiability upon commencement of suit, questions arise as to whether filing a full legal suit is necessary or appropriate where it is only this identification that is desired. Recognizing that identifiability often translates into accountability, James Grimmelman has posited (though he subsequently rejects) a system where complainants could trade their right to future legal remedies for reputation harm in exchange for learning the name of the person (or persons) responsible for a particular harmful posting or comment. Alternatively, Daniel Solove has proposed that people be able to sue without having their real names appear in the court record, thus allowing people to seek a remedy for the spread of information about them without having to increase the exposure of the information.

Given its potential ability to enhance privacy, on the one hand, and reduce accountability on the other, what is the proper scope of anonymity in a network society? A recent study of anonymity and the law in five European and North American jurisdictions suggests that the law's regard for anonymity is to some extent diminishing (Kerr et al. 2009: 437–538). Despite significant differences in the five legal systems and their underlying values and attitudes regarding privacy and identity, there seems to be a substantial overlap in how these legal systems have historically regarded anonymity—not generally as a right and certainly not as a foundational right. What seems an indisputable global trend is that anonymity is, once again, under fire. Interestingly, it appears that legal treatment of anonymity varies not from jurisdiction to jurisdiction as much as it does between subject matter. That is, in each jurisdiction reviewed, anonymity has been positioned as anything from a fundamental right to a fundamental non-right, depending on the subject matter of the complaint. Rather than explicitly recognized as a human or legal right, anonymity is instead found as an aspect of other concepts, and while it is highly valued and protected in the context of political speech, it does not receive the same treatment in other areas. To some degree, this accords with our own relationships with anonymity—although we speak of anonymity as integral to privacy and privacy as a fundamental human right, we must also recognize the extent to which identity is performed (and ascribed in response to performance) and interrogate whether true anonymity (and its resulting indistinguishability) is itself desired or whether it too becomes a (linguistic) proxy for privacy.

When one considers these emerging legal trends alongside the shifting technological landscape, it appears that the answer to our question posed at the outset is clear: the architecture of the network society seems to be shifting from one in which anonymity was the default to one where nearly every human transaction is subject to monitoring and the possibility of identity authentication. The implications of this are far-reaching, as the following case study suggests.

Case study

Diary of a London Call Girl is a site that debuted in 2003 and purported to relate the experiences of a young woman as she began and continued to work for a London Escort Agency. The author identified herself by the pseudonym "Belle de Jour." As the site became more popular and the franchise grew to include published books and a spin-off television series, there was much public speculation as to Belle's "real" identity. There are various explanations as to why this dual "self" came to an end—Dr Brooke Magnanti has suggested that an ex-boyfriend was on the verge of outing her, and an independent blogger has claimed to have noticed searches that suggested her identity was about to be reconciled and publicized. Accordingly, on November 15 2009, Dr Magnanti outed herself as Belle de Jour (Ungoed-Thomas 2009). Dr Magnanti is a research scientist at Bristol University in the UK, and has stated that she was employed by an escort agency for 14 months while completing her PhD thesis (Ungoed-Thomas 2009).

The use of the pseudonym "Belle de Jour" allowed Dr Magnanti to anonymously journal her experiences and commodify the popularity of her site while continuing her education and advancing her academic career. Interestingly, since the revelation, although each had investments in particular aspects of her "self," both the university and her publisher have been publicly supportive of the decision, with Bristol University stating that Dr Magnanti's past was irrelevant to her university position, and her publisher lauding her for the courage it had taken to come forward. The management of information and identity arguably enabled her to become established in both areas, such that the reconciliation was not destructive to either of her two identities.

An entry on her blog the day of the public revelation spoke about the importance of reconciling the different aspects of her personality, and denied that her offline self was any more "real" than her pseudonymous online self. Both in her decision to identify herself and in her subsequent comments, Dr Magnanti demonstrates many key aspects of the interrelationship between privacy, identity and anonymity. Choosing to control information about her via the use of a pseudonym allowed her the privacy and freedom to develop her selves without confusion or dissonance emerging between them. That is, the Belle de Jour (id) entity was able to expand her reach and brand without being accused of being fictitious or merely a product of Dr Magnanti's imagination, since few in the mainstream would comfortably accept that sex work would be performed by a well-known academic researcher. At the same time, Dr Magnanti was able to pursue a doctorate and then an academic career without worrying that Belle de Jour would compromise her opportunities or access to academic success. Dr Magnanti spoke explicitly in her journal entry about the revelation and about the power of anonymity to allow voices that might otherwise be silenced to be heard—in this situation, anonymity allowed not only her voice to be heard in dual spheres, but also permitted her to protect her privacy and develop those identities concurrently.

Conclusion

Dr Magnanti is not the first nor will she be the last to experience a loss of control over her personal information, pressure to identify herself and a diminishing ability to remain anonymous. As we migrate further and deeper into electronic environments, as our life chances and opportunities are further influenced by information intermediaries, social networks, ubiquitous computing, social sorting, actuarial justice and many other surveillant forces, it is suggested that the norms underlying privacy, identity and anonymity will continue to increase not only in their complexity but also in their broad social significance.

References

barrigar, j. (2007). "i want you to want me: the effect of reputation systems in online dating sites," On the Identity Trail, 13 February, available at www.anonequity.org/weblog/archives/2007/02/ (accessed 13 November 2010).

Donath, J. and boyd, d. (2004). "Public Displays of Connection," *BT Technology Journal*, 22(4): 71–82.

Kerr, I. and McGill, J. (2007). "Emanations, Snoop Dogs and Reasonable Expectation of Privacy," *Criminal Law Quarterly*, 53(2): 392–432.

Kerr, I., Steeves, V. and Lucock, C. (eds). (2009). *Lessons from the Identity Trail: Anonymity, Privacy and Identity in a Networked Society*, New York: Oxford University Press.

Kirkpatrick, M. (2010). "Google CEO Schmidt: 'People Aren't Ready for the Technology Revolution'," ReadWriteWeb, 4 August, available at www.readwriteweb.com/archives/google_ceo_schmidt_people_arent_ready_for_the_tech.php (accessed 7 November 2010).

Organization for Economic Co-Operation and Development. (1980). OECD Guidelines on the Protection of Privacy and Transborder Flows of Personal Data, available at www.oecd.org/document/18/0,3343,en_2649_34255_1815186_1_1_1_1,00.html (accessed 7 November 2010).

Nock, S. (1993). *The Costs of Privacy: Reputation and Surveillance in America*, New York: Aldine de Gruyter.

R. v. Dyment [1988] 2 S.C.R. 417.

Ungoed-Thomas, J. (2009). "Belle de Jour Revealed as Research Scientist Dr Brooke Magnanti," *The Sunday Times*, 15 November, available at http://entertainment.timesonline.co.uk/tol/arts_and_entertainment/books/article6917260.ece (accessed 13 November 2010).

Westin, A. (1967). *Privacy and Freedom*, New York: Atheneneum.

Section 4.2.
Regulation and resistance

a. Regulating surveillance technologies

Institutional arrangements

Priscilla M. Regan

Over the last 40 years there has been an ongoing debate about what type of government involvement and institutional arrangements should be employed to ensure that surveillance technologies are used in ways that are legally sanctioned, socially acceptable and practically effective. In order to achieve this outcome, such oversight during both the development of programs to use surveillance technologies and also the implementation of these programs is essential. A number of different models have been used to "regulate" surveillance technologies and practices, including regulation by national governments (executive, legislative, and judicial); extra-governmental organizations (watchdogs, ombudspersons and commissions); international agreements; and self-regulation by industry. Additionally, and often in conjunction with these models, governments have often instituted various study commissions to determine the scope and nature of policy problems resulting from surveillance technologies. This chapter will analyze the strengths and weaknesses of these different models as means to provide effective control over the use of surveillance technologies. The chapter provides empirical evidence from a number of countries.

Introduction

Elsewhere in this volume scholars analyze the development of what has become ubiquitous surveillance inserting into our everyday lives and account for the causes of this trend (see Andrejevic, this volume). This chapter instead focuses on the public and to a lesser extent, the private, sector responses to what is perceived as the over-reaching and unaccountability of surveillance technologies and practices. In virtually all countries and sectors, there is recognition that surveillance should not proceed unchecked by the laws, values, and institutional arrangements that govern other aspects of modern life. Surveillance should not get a "pass" simply because some argue that it is necessary for national security, or for law enforcement, or school safety, or an efficient consumer market—or whatever litany of goals might be achieved by more surveillance. Despite the general agreements regarding the need for oversight and accountability, it has not been easy for national and international bodies to construct institutional arrangements that meet with public approval and that are deemed effective.

Debates over policy approaches and types of institutional arrangements that might be politically possible and realistically likely to be successful in addressing the problems have been ongoing since the 1960s. In the late 1960s and early 1970s, government agencies and private sector organizations increasingly adopted computers to collect, retain, exchange and manipulate personally identifiable information. In all countries this innovation in record-keeping precipitated a concern with the rights of the individuals who were subjects of that data and with the responsibilities of the organizations processing the information (see Webster, this volume). Two models emerged during this time: some countries adopted a data protection approach and others a civil liberties approach (Flaherty 1989; Bennett 1992; Regan 1995). The data protection approach viewed the problem as one of accountability and responsibility on the part of the organizations collecting and using personally identifiable information. The solution then was framed in terms of placing procedural requirements for and oversight mechanisms on these organizations. The civil liberties approach viewed the problem as one of possible violation of rights of individuals in the context of their disclosure of information to organizations and the organizations' subsequent uses and elaborations on that information. The solution in this model was framed in terms of giving individuals legal rights by which they could find out what personally identifiable information was being collected and the uses and exchanges of such information, as well as grievance mechanisms by which they could challenge organizational practices and information quality.

At the core of both of these approaches was the framework of "fair information principles"; the two approaches differed mainly in whether these principles would be enforced by government oversight or by individual redress of grievances. David Flaherty conducted a detailed comparative study of the adoption and implementation of privacy and data protection laws in five countries—the Federal Republic of Germany, Sweden, France, Canada and the United States. His in-depth study of each country's politics and legal issues was based on both interviews with key participants and on government reports and documents. His analysis concluded with an emphasis of the critical role that an independent data protection agency plays in ensuring the effective implementation of laws designed to protect personally identifiable information. As he stated "it is not simply enough to pass a data protection law" (Flaherty1989: 381). Colin Bennett analyzed the policy processes resulting in privacy or data protection legislation in Sweden, the United States, West Germany and Britain in order to determine whether policy convergence or divergence was a result of technological determinism, emulation, elite networking, harmonization, or penetration. He concluded that pressures for convergence of policy in this area were likely to increase as the technology itself became more transnational, as insecurities about their effects intensified, and as international regimes promoted harmonization among laws (Bennett 1992: 251).

Although initial policy attention was on the surveillance issues raised by new information technologies, these information technologies also influenced new technological innovations and applications in communications and observation. Digital and wireless communication capabilities enabled faster transmissions, far greater capacities, and broader coverage at a much reduced cost. Miniaturization of recording and listening devices enabled unobstrusive capture of conversation. Similar changes occurred in video and photography technologies, enabling unseen yet detailed observation. All of these technological changes enhanced the ease of surveilling physical activities and movements, oral and written communications, and commercial and social transactions. As surveillance practices were used in more and more contexts, the need for regulating their use consistent with social norms and existing laws became a pressing policy issue. These new surveillance capabilities went beyond fair information practices and regulation of computerized information systems, and involved more generally the expansion of modern organizational power and social control.

The privacy and surveillance landscape and discourse changed dramatically throughout the world after the terrorist attacks in the United States on September 11, 2001. Concerns about privacy and civil liberties were trumped by concerns about security and identifying possible terrorists. Pew Research and Gallup public opinion polls in the United States conducted soon after 9/11 indicated support for sacrificing civil liberties, more extensive surveillance of communications and a national ID card. Forty-five days after the attacks, the United States Congress, with virtually no opposition, passed the USA PATRIOT Act of 2001 (Uniting and Strengthening America by Providing Appropriate Tools Required to Intercept and Obstruct Terrorism). Other countries passed similar measures. The Canadian Bill C-36 contained measures to enhance the government's ability to prevent and detect terrorist activity. The quick passage and over-reaching character of these initiatives provoked concerns, not only among human rights activists who saw these measures as conflicting with civil liberties and privacy protections, but also among conservative groups who viewed the measures as giving too much investigative power to law enforcement and intelligence officials without adequate judicial or legislative oversight.

Given this landscape of technological changes, organizational practices, and complex and conflicting pressures of modern life, there are a number of institutional arrangements to regulating surveillance technologies. The next sections will examine several of the most widely-used approaches, with particular attention as to why each might be selected and what its strengths and weaknesses are in effectively regulating surveillance technologies. In order to analyze these different arrangements, I will examine them in terms of several categories: regulation by national governments (executive, legislative and judicial); extra-governmental organizations (watchdogs, ombudspersons and commissions); international agreements; and self-regulation by industry.

National government regulatory arrangements

A number of institutional arrangements are available to national governments with variations in their power, scope and location. Some national institutions are strongly regulatory with some early models, such as in Sweden, providing for some form of licensing while others have more traditional regulatory authorities, and still others have largely advisory powers. The United States has long stood as an anomaly without having a national institution responsible for controlling surveillance. It is beyond the scope of this chapter to explore all the different models but other works have done so (Rule and Greenleaf 2008; and Bennett and Raab 2003), and have analyzed not only the effectiveness of different models but also how, and why, countries have changed their models. One impetus for change has been the European Union Directive, which required member countries to have some form of supervisory authority in the area of data protection, an area that in reality includes many surveillance activities. Such forces for more uniformity among national institutions, however, are tempered by national governmental structure and political history. France, for example, with its long history of centralized administration with enforcement through national bodies has adopted that approach in the area of data protection and surveillance. Germany, on the other hand, with its federal system has relied upon more decentralized administrative bodies and for data protection has employed federal, state and private sector efforts. Similarly Canada has both a federal Office of the Privacy Commissioner and also provincial Privacy Commissioners, as well as regulatory institutions with privacy and surveillance responsibilities for certain sectors such as the Canadian Radio-Television and Telecommunications Commission (CRTC). Australia, also a federal system, employs agencies at both levels.

The placement of these agencies within the national government also varies. Many observers, such as David Flaherty (1989), argue that because of the strong governmental interest in surveillance activities it is important that agencies be independent of the legislature and the executive. This has occurred in France where the CNIL (Commission nationale de l'informatique et des libertés), established in 1978, has not only enforced existing legislation but has also been active in recommending legislative modifications in response to new technological innovations. Although some have criticized the CNIL for working more through compromise rather than confrontation, it has become a respected institution with powers that generally have been further consolidated (see Vitalis in Rule and Greenleaf 2008). In Canada, the federal Privacy Commissioner is an officer of Parliament who is appointed by, and reports directly to, Parliament. In other countries, agencies are associated with the executive with less involvement by the legislature. For example, the Privacy Commissioner in Australia is by statute independent but appointed by the executive and dependent on the executive for its budget.

Additionally in most countries there is some appeal to the judiciary. Moreover the judiciary often serves as the first line of defense, dealing with cases involving uses of more innovative surveillance technologies before national laws have caught up to them and in this way charting the course for appropriate legislative approaches. The importance of the role of the judiciary is affected by the ability of other national institutions to address new surveillance technologies with more active judicial involvement in countries with weak or non-existent regulatory institutions, such as the United States. Interestingly, the judiciary in Hungary played a pivotal role in its 1991 ruling that the universal personal identification number could not constitutionally be used in an unrestricted manner; this ruling, during the early stages of policy deliberations, established an important legal standard and generated much public interest. But the courts can play a role in countries with rather strong regulatory institutions and thwart over-reaching efforts at surveillance (see Szekely in Rule and Greenleaf 2008). This occurred in Germany in 1983 when the Supreme Constitutional Court declared part of the Federal Census statute unconstitutional and again after September 11 when the Court overturned preventive uses of police surveillance techniques based upon the right to informational self-determination. In Canada, the Supreme Court declared unconstitutional a provision of the 2001 Anti-Terrorism Act which authorized the Attorney General to issue blanket certificates prohibiting the disclosure of any information for the purpose of protecting international relations, national defense, or security and thus permitting individuals to be detained based on secret information. In other countries, such as Australia, courts play a more minor role in part because statutes are more narrowly drawn to address specific data-gathering and surveillance activities rather than being broadly written and inviting more litigation (see Greenleaf in Rule and Greenleaf 2008).

The powers of regulatory institutions responsible for protecting privacy or personal data and overseeing surveillance activities vary among countries. Privacy International (www.privacyinternational.org) maintains country reports that provide a fairly up-to-date overview of the powers of institutions in each country. It is beyond the scope of this chapter to summarize them but a few illustrative examples follow. In Canada, the federal Office of the Privacy Commissioner receives complaints and conducts investigations for both the public and private sectors, including the power to subpoena witnesses and compel testimony, to enter premises in order to obtain documents and to conduct interviews. The Commissioner can issue findings and make recommendations but cannot issue orders or impose penalties. The Commissioner is also responsible for conducting periodic audits of both federal institutions and private organizations to determine their compliance with relevant legislation. In the United Kingdom, the Office of the Information Commissioner, which is responsible for enforcing the Data Protection and Freedom of Information Acts and the Privacy and Electronic Communication Regulations, has relatively limited powers, can only audit or "name and shame" violators with the permission of the controller and cannot impose fines for violations of data protection principles. The Swedish Data Inspection Board has somewhat more extensive powers in that it not only can investigate complaints but also requires that organizations notify, with some exceptions, the Board prior to automated data processing of personal information.

The abilities of traditional data protection or privacy institutions to expand their regulatory jurisdiction beyond traditional computerized information to new categories of information collection also vary. In Canada, for example, the federal Privacy Commissioner has taken the position that live and recorded video pictures of individuals constitute "personal information" and that, in a commercial context, video images can only be collected with consent of the individuals. It has also taken the position that public places should only be monitored for public safety reasons where a demonstrated need is shown and has issued guidelines for the use of video surveillance. In France, the CNIL first exercised jurisdiction over video surveillance but then lost it to prefects and departmental commissions. In the United Kingdom, oversight of surveillance activities has also been disaggregated with the Interception of Communications Commissioner having limited power over wiretapping, the Investigatory Powers Tribunal hearing complaints from individuals that they have been subject to illegal surveillance, and the Office of the Information Commissioner monitoring some collection of information under the Anti-terrorism, Crime and Security Act to ensure that information is not retained under the act for non-national security purposes. Similar overlaps occur in Australia for telecommunications privacy and surveillance with the Australian Communications and Media Authority, the Telecommunications Industry Ombudsman and the Privacy Commissioner having somewhat overlapping jurisdictions

Extra-governmental regulatory arrangements

Given that surveillance activities are a relatively modern development and do not fit neatly within existing regulatory regimes, many countries initially established study commissions to investigate what was occurring and with what implications and to make policy recommendations. The Privacy Protection Study Commission in the United States, established as a compromise in the 1974 Privacy Act, examined private sector information relationships with customers and clients, and issued policy recommendations for different sectors. In Britain, the Younger Committee in the early 1970s conducted similar investigations about the uses of personal information and made recommendations. The Australian Law Reform Commission, chaired in the late 1970s by Justice Michael Kirby, was instrumental in making recommendations on a range of privacy issues.

Such study commissions have also been established more recently as the landscape of surveillance has become more ubiquitous and hidden. For example, in 2006 the United Kingdom Information Commissioner contracted with the Surveillance Studies Network to analyze the scope and operations of surveillance activities and to make recommendations regarding regulatory challenges. Its thoughtful and well supported analysis points to several shortcomings, particularly fragmentation and weak coordination, in current regulatory frameworks. Its report is more comprehensive in its scope and recommendations than those of study commissions in other countries. In the United States, several federal agencies, most notably the Federal Trade Commission and the Department of Commerce, have conducted studies of various aspects of commercial uses of personal information and made a variety of recommendations. The National Academy of Sciences has also conducted similar examinations. In Canada, the Privacy Commissioner has been active in organizing study commissions on a range of privacy and surveillance issues.

Study commissions are not just established by individual countries but also by regional authorities. For example, the European Commission at various times has funded examinations of emerging privacy and surveillance issues or of the effectiveness of the implementation of existing regulatory schemes. Most recently (January 2011) the Commission funded a year-long study analyzing national privacy safeguards in 31 countries that was conducted by a number of civil society organizations including Privacy International, the Electronic Privacy Information Center in Washington, DC and the Center for Media and Communications Studies of the Central European University in Budapest.

International regulatory arrangements

Surveillance activities in the public and private sectors have also been directly and indirectly impacted by the rulings and policies of a number of international and regional bodies. These are not privacy or surveillance institutions per se but regulatory institutions, often tasked with trade or human rights, which have become involved in questions of surveillance. Internationally, the Organization for Economic Co-operation and Development (OECD) first considered privacy issues in the late 1970s with a number of studies on informatics and in 1980 issued "Guidelines Governing the Protection of Privacy and Transborder Flows of Personal Data." The OECD has continued to be active in the area of privacy and surveillance issuing guidelines on security (1992 and 2002), electronic commerce (1999) and global networks (1998). In 1990, the United Nations also issued "Guidelines Concerning Computerized Personal Data Files" which are based largely on the UN's human rights tradition.

More binding action has been taken by regional regulatory institutions (Schwartz 1995; Reidenberg 2000). The earliest body to act was the Council of Europe, which in 1981 issued the "Convention for the Protection of Individuals with regard to Automatic Processing of Personal Data." Although this technically only affects the member countries which have signed the Convention, its scope is broader as it impacts those who trade with member countries. It is similarly so with the European Union and European Community's "Directive on the Protection of Individuals with Regard to the Processing of Personal Data and on the Free Movement of Such Data" [hereafter referred to as EU Directive] in 1995. In analyzing the genesis for the EU Directive, Abraham Newman concludes that data protection regulators from individual European countries, particularly France and Germany, acted as "transgovernmental policy entrepreneurs" (2008: 11) and successfully advocated for their policy preferences at the regional level.

The EU Directive is only binding on member states but has had broader international consequences. The Directive requires member states to establish "supervisory authorities" to enforce national laws and for all states to provide "adequate protection," but also allows for exemptions for states to safeguard national and public security, law enforcement and important economic interests. The Directive establishes committees or working parties, which make recommendations and help set the agenda for new privacy and surveillance issues, such as the transfer of air passenger name records outside the EU. Perhaps most importantly the Directive requires that non-EU countries to which data are being transmitted provide "adequate protection" for that data. This has entailed the EU evaluating the data protection and/or information privacy policies in other countries. In order to provide a means by which organizations in the United States could comply with this requirement, the EU and the USA established a "safe harbor agreement."

More recently, the Asia-Pacific Economic Cooperation (APEC) adopted a "Privacy Framework" in 2005, which differs from the EU directive approach and is premised more on the importance of economic concerns and consumer confidence. Under this Framework, a cross-border privacy rules system is the means by which countries and economic actors can certify that a business's "privacy rules" are compliant with the Framework through a process of accreditation by an accountability agent, such as a trustmark, and the possibility of further enforcement by a government agency. Additionally, a Cross Border Privacy Enforcement Cooperation Arrangement has been established, currently administered by the US Federal Trade Commission, the Australian Information Commissioner, and the New Zealand Privacy Commissioner.

Self-regulatory arrangements

As private sector surveillance activities increase and are more intricately interwoven into normal business practices that are increasingly global in reach, several countries have recognized the need to work more cooperatively with the private sector. In France and Australia, for example, there have been efforts at co-regulation. In France, the *Forum des droits sur l'internet* (Rights on the Internet Forum) was established as a place where dialogue, resulting in policy recommendations, could occur among all stakeholders including public officials, private sector actors and civil society spokespersons. Similarly in Australia, initial efforts at self-regulation were not effective in controlling private sector activities and caused uncertainty and competition among private sector entities; self-regulation was replaced in 1999 with codes of conduct that were developed through co-regulatory mechanisms.

The United States has adopted the most aggressive self-regulatory approach (Schwartz and Reidenberg 1996; Gellman 2003; Regan in Rule and Greenleaf 2008). During the mid-1980s with the focus on electronic commerce and the global economy, the Clinton administration embraced the business community's predilection for self-regulation, in effect letting businesses respond to the market demands of consumers for their preferred level of privacy protection. The Safe Harbor agreement whereby US companies certified the adequacy of their data protection policies with the EU Directive similarly reflects a largely self-regulatory approach. Just recently (December 2010) the USA formally articulated what may be a slight shift in emphasis toward co-regulation in a Department of Commerce Green Paper that viewed the role of government as not a regulator but as a convener of stakeholders and coordinator of processes and which proposes establishing a Privacy Policy Office in the Department to work with the Federal Trade Commission in leading efforts to develop voluntary but enforceable privacy codes.

As organizations in both the public and private sectors increasingly moved transactions and services online, new privacy and surveillance issues emerged in a number of sectors, which generated policy discussions and actions outside of government institutions as well. Organizations such as the World Wide Web Consortium (W3C) and Institute of Electrical and Electronics Engineers (IEEE) served as forums for discussions of policy problems and solutions. W3C established a working group that developed principles for a Platform for Privacy Preferences (P3P) in 1998; P3P enabled websites to express their privacy practices in a standard format that could then be retrieved automatically and interpreted. The goal was both to convenience web users and also to enable users to integrate their ideal privacy standards into their web practices. Privacy protections were viewed as a key component in establishing trustworthy networked information systems and various groups, including the Computer Science and Telecommunications Board of the US National Research Council and the Rathenau Institute of the Royal Netherlands Academy of Sciences, held meetings of international technical and policy specialists and published various reports with policy and technical proposals.

Discussion

As the above summary of institutional arrangements demonstrates, there is no one model that fits all countries, surveillance practices, or time periods. The question of how to best regulate surveillance technologies so that they are used in ways that are legally sanctioned, socially acceptable and practically effective is one that is answered quite differently. The political culture and system of government are the two most crucial factors in explaining national variations and choices. But despite these differences in philosophy and approach, we can identify at least three common trends and challenges.

The symbolic language of privacy and surveillance is recast from time to time. Currently the focus of regulatory debates has shifted somewhat from individual rights, notice and choice to accountability, transparency and trust. Reports of various national, international and extra-governmental reports all include such modified emphasis in terminology. This shift in language reflects to some extent the social setting in which issues of privacy and surveillance occur, as well as the role of organizations and norms of social interactions in at least facilitating, if not regulating, the use of surveillance practices.

Institutional responses in all countries have evolved and continue to evolve. There is a widespread recognition and acceptance of the fact that this is an area of social and commercial life that requires flexibility of responses and institutional learning. Rigid practices rarely endure. Instead there is need for monitoring of the use of surveillance practices, of the public's reaction to those practices and re-evaluation of regulatory instruments and arrangements.

Related to such evolution is the need for sustained, active and sophisticated attention on the part of whatever institutional arrangement is used by a country, region or international body. Anticipating technological innovations and their potential uses in monitoring data, activities and conversations requires a robust set of skills and expertise, including legal, technological, administrative and cultural skills. The range of institutional regulatory arrangements, and the civil society groups that interact with regulatory bodies, provides a number of access points for information and opinions—both within one country and across countries.

References

Bennett, C. J. (1992). *Regulating Privacy: Data Protection and Public Policy in Europe and the United States*, Ithaca, NY: Cornell University Press.

Bennett, C. J. and Raab, C. D. (2003). *The Governance of Privacy: Policy Instruments in Global Perspective*, London: Ashgate (republished 2006 by Cambridge, MA: MIT Press).

Flaherty, D. H. (1989). *Protecting Privacy in Surveillance Societies*, Chapel Hill: University of North Carolina Press.

Gellman, R. (2003). "A Better Way to Approach Privacy Policy in the United States: Establish a Non-Regulatory Privacy Protection Board," *Hastings Law Journal*, 54: 1183–1226.

Newman, A. L. (2008). *Protectors of Privacy: Regulating Personal Data in the Global Economy*, Ithaca, NY: Cornell University Press.

Regan, P. M. (1995). *Legislating Privacy: Technology, Social Values, and Public Policy*, Chapel Hill: University of North Carolina Press.

Reidenberg, J. R. (2000). "Resolving Conflicting International Privacy Rules in Cyberspace," *Stanford Law Review*, 80(3): 471–96.

Rule, J. B. and Greenleaf, G. (2008). *Global Privacy: The First Generation*, Cheltenham: Edward Elgar.

Schwartz, P. M. (1995). "European Data Protection Law and Restrictions on International Data Flows," *Iowa Law Review*, 80(3): 471–96.

Schwartz, P. M. and Reidenberg, J. R. (1996). *Data Privacy Law*, Charlottesville, VA: Michie.

b. Everyday resistance

John Gilliom and Torin Monahan

Evasion of reporting requirements in the Greek tax system is so widespread that it was marked as a key factor in the 2010 economic crisis; an estimated $30 billion per year is lost to those who mask their wealth and income. Swimming pools, yachts, and income are widely hidden from the eyes of the state.

British factory workers foil management surveillance systems intended to micromanage the shop floor. Efforts at product inspection, quality control, and increased centralization of operations are undermined by "fiddles" and other practices that floor workers use to subvert surveillance procedures (see also Sewell, this volume).

Low-income Americans attempting to sell their blood serum to for-profit plasma firms over-hydrate in order to meet the weight requirement of the firms' donor surveillance systems. One underweight woman put rocks in her pockets and shoes: "It worked for a while, but then one day some rocks fell out of my pocket, and after that they 86'ed me from the plasma center" (Anderson and Snow 1995: 191).

"Lead-footed drivers" install radar and laser detectors to tip them off to the presence of patrol cars equipped with radar and laser equipment for apprehending highway speeders. Catalogs and websites hawk the newest products in an ongoing arms race over the technologies of surveillance and evasion.

These are all examples of people trying to beat a surveillance system. They are engaging in practices of *everyday resistance*. The central characteristics of everyday resistance practices are that they are unorganized, not explicitly tied to broader ideological critiques, and originate from direct concerns in daily life. Everyday resistance is a unique subset of resistance and opposition to surveillance: the category specifically excludes organized movements, traditional ideology, and public confrontations. Under this definition, opposition actions such as anti-surveillance protests by labor unions, organized uprisings against video camera installations, or litigation over privacy rights are *not* practices of everyday resistance. Lying, evading, masking, and cheating are some of the often invisible forms taken by everyday resistance to surveillance.

Nonetheless, resistance and opposition, as conceptual categories, lend each other clarity through comparison of differences. If opposition generally takes a more formal or public stance, such as civil-liberties organizations advocating for the protection of citizen's rights and filing lawsuits to achieve those ends, resistance is typically informal and hidden, such as people attempting to circumvent or quietly disrupt the surveillance systems to which they are exposed. It is important to note that, although resistance may not have explicit political objectives, in the traditional sense, it is still political in that it creates a tacit challenge and introduces symbolic friction to existing systems of domination or control.

This chapter offers a brief review of the concept and study of everyday resistance, examples of everyday resistance to surveillance, and a discussion of some of the key controversies surrounding its study. The latter include the extent to which academic attention to everyday resistance competes with, discounts, or weakens attention to more public and formal opposition to surveillance. It addresses whether everyday resistance marks an important dimension of anti-surveillance politics, and the politics behind cultural tendencies to view some patterns of everyday resistance benignly while others are subject to investigation and prosecution. Finally it questions whether the invisible spaces and subjective control typically necessary for resistance to occur will survive the increasingly dense webs of contemporary surveillance. To some observers, everyday resistance represents one of the most important dynamics in understanding the politics of surveillance in that widespread patterns of everyday resistance amount to a global anti-surveillance "movement" of staggering proportions (Gilliom 2001). To others, the focus on practices of everyday resistance glorifies petty acts of individualistic crime and deviance, and saps attention from the important work of more public and organized groups and movements (Handler 1992).

Theorizing everyday resistance

After close and sustained study of the politics at work in the relations between rich and poor in a small Malaysian village, the political scientist and anthropologist James Scott famously wrote:

> It seemed more important to understand what we might call everyday forms of peasant resistance—the prosaic but constant struggle between the peasantry and those who seek to extract labor, food, taxes, rents, and interest from them. Most of the forms this struggle takes stop well short of collective outright defiance. Here I have in mind the ordinary weapons of relatively powerless groups: foot dragging, dissimulation, false compliance, pilfering, feigned ignorance, slander, arson, sabotage, and so forth. The Brechtian forms of class struggle have certain features in common. They require little or no coordination or planning; they often represent a form of individual self-help; and they typically avoid symbolic confrontation with authority or with elite norms.
>
> *(Scott 1985: 29)*

> When a peasant hides part of his crop to avoid paying taxes, he is both filling his stomach and depriving the state of gain. … When such acts are rare and isolated, they are of little interest; but when they become a consistent pattern (even though uncoordinated, let alone organized) we are dealing with resistance. The intrinsic nature and, in one sense, the "beauty" of much peasant resistance is that it often confers immediate and concrete advantages, while at the same time denying resources to the appropriating classes, and that it requires little or no manifest organization.
>
> *(Scott 1985: 296)*

On the broader topic of everyday resistance as part of political struggle, Scott's observations and definitions are the most practicable and thoroughly developed perspectives from an intellectual dialogue that includes, in its most existential explorations of identity, authors such as Erving Goffman, Jean-Paul Sartre, Michel Foucault, and Gilles Deleuze. And while the focus here is on the more pragmatic and, appropriately, "everyday" manifestations and implications of everyday resistance to surveillance, this mode of inquiry is necessarily situated within a larger conversation about forms of knowledge engendered by resistance practices.

For instance, Michel Foucault, whose writings are a staple in Surveillance Studies, was keenly aware of the symbiotic relationship between forms of resistance and control. Foucault observed, "Where there is power, there is resistance, and yet, or rather consequently, this resistance is never in a position of exteriority in relation to power" (1978: 95). Instead of being in opposition to power, resistance is necessary and co-productive of the forms that power takes, including the control mechanisms through which power manifests and becomes visible (e.g. architecture, law, norms). Even so, resistance is subordinated in

Foucault's analyses of institutions, where the bulk of his observations are about pervasive constraints and their changing logics over time.

For a more nuanced theoretical treatment of resistance, Surveillance Studies would probably be better served by turning to the work of Michel de Certeau, which—with few exceptions—has been neglected in the field. In *The Practice of Everyday Life* de Certeau (1984) delves into the myriad ways that people operate within and poach upon structural constraints through a series of fluid, agential tactics. In explicit contradistinction to Foucault, de Certeau calls for scholarly attention to resistance and other tactics as an optimistic, affirmational response to the overdetermined construct of discipline. De Certeau (1984) writes:

> If it is true that the grid of "discipline" is everywhere becoming clearer and more extensive, it is all the more urgent to discover how an entire society resists being reduced to it, what popular procedures (also "miniscule" and quotidian) manipulate the mechanisms of discipline and conform to them only in order to evade them.
>
> *(xiv)*

For de Certeau, the task is not to discover how discipline works, but instead how people work within disciplinary structures to create and live—not as passive, "docile bodies," but as social actors and community members. He posits, "Perhaps in fact the system of discipline and control which took shape in the nineteenth century on the basis of earlier procedures, is today itself 'vampirized' by other procedures [such as resistance tactics]" (de Certeau 1984: 49).

One commonplace resistance tactic written about by de Certeau is that of *la perruque*, whereby one performs tasks for oneself during work hours and under the pretense, or guise, of official work responsibilities. Resistance of this sort is widespread, which today might include writing emails or surfing the web on company time, borrowing equipment for personal use, or running family errands when one is "on the clock." *La perruque* is not about absenteeism or theft in any usual sense; rather it is primarily about the appropriation of time and the corresponding practices of dissimulation to obscure that fact. Clearly, systems of workplace surveillance are designed to counter activities of this sort, and workers and managers engage in an ongoing dance of surveillance and resistance, which is something that has only intensified in the present post-industrial economy that pushes workers toward flextime or telecommuting.

Resistance is a cultural practice that lends meaning to everyday life, shapes relationships, and produces identities in conjunction with a host of other interactions and experiences. It is not simply a means by which hegemonic forms of discipline are tested and reinforced; nor is it merely a symbolic thorn in the side of totalizing systems of oppression and control. Instead, resistance is ultimately generative and frequently self-affirming. Through resistance, people test boundaries, build sociality, and achieve dignity, both within and between institutional structures and dominant cultural logics. Relationships of power are produced, in part, through the many invisible and half-seen, acknowledged or ignored, quotidian practices of resistance.

Surveillance and everyday resistance

The title of Gary Marx's (2003) "A Tack in the Shoe: Neutralizing and Resisting the New Surveillance" refers to the practice of tricking a lie-detector test by stepping on a thumbtack placed in one's shoe as questions are asked. The pain is believed to cause bodily responses which can mask those associated with the stress of misrepresentation. In his article, Marx catalogs 11 categories of tactics that individuals use in everyday struggles against surveillance. He identifies them as "discovery moves, avoidance moves, piggybacking moves, switching moves, distorting moves, blocking moves, masking moves, breaking moves, refusal moves, cooperative moves and counter-surveillance moves." *Discovery* moves attempt to discern whether or not a program of surveillance is under way. *Avoidance* moves simply shift the time and location of activities to an unsurveiled space. *Piggybacking* and *switching* involve beating certain types of surveillance by using non-surveiled or approved items or individuals to mask the presence of or change places with a subject of interest. *Distorting* moves attempt to foil the optics of surveillance by manipulating the data received by the system. *Blocking* and *masking* moves seek to prevent the submission of information to a surveillance system and, sometimes, to hide the act of prevention with the substitution of stand-in data. *Breaking* involves, well, breaking a surveillance device to render it inoperable. *Refusal* moves are when someone chooses *not* to participate in systems of voluntary surveillance. *Cooperative* moves entail working with sympathetic agents within the surveillance apparatus. Finally, *counter-surveillance* implies the use of surveillance to combat surveillance, such as turning personal cameras onto agents of the state.

In developing an ethnography of surveillance, Gilliom's 2001 book *Overseers of the Poor: Surveillance, Resistance, and the Limits of Privacy* identified widespread patterns of everyday resistance among the welfare poor in the chronically impoverished rural Appalachian United States. In a study originally designed to explore questions surrounding the vernacular terms with which people described and discussed surveillance initiatives, the research found that the women interviewed not only talked about surveillance in unexpected ways, but also worked to oppose surveillance in unconventional ways.

The surveillance program at the heart of the research was called CRIS-E, for Client Registry Information System—Enhanced. CRIS-E unified an entire state's welfare caseload into a single computer matrix that enabled online registration and management, automated benefits calculation, and automated fraud control sweeps including surveillance of banking practices, taxation data, Social Security information, and government programs and registries. In extensive anonymous interviews, women talked about how CRIS-E and the bureaucracy in which it worked were rude, degrading, and frightening. There were occasional references to the vaunted right to privacy, but most conversations centered on far more personal expressions of anger, shame, need, and fear. For the purposes at hand, it is most important to note that while none of the women interviewed took formal public action to oppose the new surveillance system, virtually all of them took personal, quiet action either to thwart or evade the program. By working or selling crafts for unreported cash, taking in boarders or daycare clients, accepting cash and food from neighbors and family, the women were able to hide small amounts of money and aid from a surveillance system designed to detect and prohibit.

The women's actions mobilized an effective politics of everyday resistance. They were able to evade detection by the surveillance system, carve out spaces of personal power and control, and effectively raise the monthly income of their families. Importantly, the research in *Overseers of the Poor* also showed that some members of the welfare agency staff assisted clients in besting the surveillance system. One example was the silent coaching of clients with head nods (yes) or shakes (no) as the client responded to questions during intake interviews that were logging data into the system.

On the basis of these findings, Gilliom argued that everyday resistance was an important and productive dimension of anti-surveillance politics. In an earlier writing about the attention to everyday resistance in the law and social movement literature, Handler (1992) argued that progressive scholars should focus on learning about potentials for strong, public, transformative movements and eschew the celebration of often petty, unthinking, and individualistic moments of everyday resistance. But Gilliom argued that the women studied in *Overseers of the Poor* actually achieved important ends, mobilized important values, and did so in a decidedly non-individualist manner. The ends, of course, were evading the system of surveillance in order to obtain the forbidden money and materials which they sought in order to meet their families' needs. The important values were found to reside in a widely shared "ethic of care" which centered their activities within a set of values related to their roles as parents. And, Gilliom argued, they were not authentically "individualistic." While the activities were necessarily secret and not formally organized, they were embedded in a cooperative context of family and friendship circles and were part of a large, silent, uncoordinated but ideologically coherent movement of those who resisted surveillance in order to meet the daily needs of their families. To discount these activities "fundamentally misconstrues the very basis of the economic and political struggle conducted daily by subordinate classes in repressive settings" (Scott 1985: 292).

When impoverished parents hide income from the state so that they can get more assistance for their children, they do not typically voice a detailed intellectual critique of the surveillance society. State surveillance is just one relatively minor part of their daily troubles and usually does not draw the sort of focused conceptual attention that would produce a developed ideological perspective. The surveillance system did, as noted, get attention as a burdensome, nosy system that degraded them and made it more difficult to survive, but the center of the women's attention was not on surveillance. They focused on the *need to survive and to care for their children*: welfare surveillance was understood as an obstacle to being a good mother.

These are not, of course, the frequently heard anti-surveillance protests about privacy rights and the like, but Gilliom argued that these practices of everyday resistance mobilized a trenchant critique of the compelled visibility of surveillance. Here, it is critically important to note that the system critiques embedded in practices of everyday resistance are frequently and necessarily tacit. The critique of surveillance is found in the actions of evasion; in the practices of trickery; in the tactics of masking—these actions simultaneously critique the goals and polices of the surveillance system and the practices and powers of surveillance itself.

People resist all kinds of surveillance, of course, not only surveillance operated by state agents. Workplaces probably represent the most common domain of resistance, especially as managers and others use electronic monitoring and tracking systems in efforts to optimize productivity and crack down on employees engaging in non-work activities (*la perruque*). A host of technologies, some old and others new, lend themselves to these purposes: time cards, keystroke tracking, performance evaluations, card keys, email and phone monitoring, radio-frequency identification (RFID) badges, global positioning systems (especially on company vehicles), routine audits or inspections, monitoring of social-networking sites, video surveillance, and so on.

Workers adapt resistance tactics to surveillance, inventing new ways of ensuring degrees of autonomy and satisfaction, or at least tolerance, in the face of expanding networks of control. For instance, in a large-scale study of employee-tracking systems in hospitals, Monahan and Fisher (2006) found that nurses would engage in a variety of improvised tactics to resist centralized technological systems of managerial scrutiny and intervention. When hospital administrators introduced RFID systems to track equipment, staff, and patients, some nurses interpreted this as an unwanted foray on their own territories and an attack on their existing systems of expertise, for instance concerning where to find a clean IV pump, from whom, and by the quickest means. Resistance included things like destroying RFID or misplacing RFID tags (e.g., in planters or down laundry chutes), forgetting or refusing to wear tags, unplugging detector equipment, cutting the wires on detector equipment, or hiding tagged equipment in hard-to-track locations (e.g., above ceiling tiles or in radiology rooms lined with lead, which would block radio waves).

For the present discussion of resistance, what is especially interesting about these examples is that they show how various forms of non-compliance draw upon existing material infrastructures, social norms and solidarity, and local tacit knowledge to create spaces (both symbolic and physical) that deflect or vitiate new forms of workplace surveillance. The organizational environment, in other words, becomes a resource for people engaging in resistance, and the better matched resistance tactics are to the environment, the more likely they are to succeed.

The politics of resistance

There is a substantial bias in how society looks upon different types of everyday resistance. On one end of the spectrum, the women studied in *Overseers of the Poor* faced the constant daily threat of apprehension and prosecution moving through worlds in which signs and posters decried "welfare fraud" and urged good citizens to call toll-free telephone numbers to report mothers who broke the rules. Somewhere in the middle, workplace employees avoiding managerial supervision, direction, and evaluation does not invoke comparable moral outrage, especially not when the public's safety is maintained. Then at the other end of the spectrum, in Greece, for example, there appears to be widespread tolerance, even celebration, of tax evasion and a well-used system for bribing tax collectors to look the other way. In one of the other examples from the epigraph to this chapter, fast drivers can turn to a variety of catalogs and websites to order the newest equipment for evading the police. And in the USA, when tax season rolls around, newspapers publish standard deduction rates for different income levels so that filers can figure out how much scamming they can do without raising a red flag and drawing the attention of the auditors. In an age-old pattern familiar to all students of society and politics, the more privileged are encouraged and even cajoled in their patterns of everyday resistance while the poor are hunted down and prosecuted.

Questions should be raised about whether the evasions of the more privileged should actually be defined as everyday resistances, since they are hardly the acts of a repressed peasantry. There are obvious and important differences between someone who resists surveillance in order to feed her children and someone who resists surveillance to drive quickly. While the risks and dangers associated with resistance may not be comparable, there are structural similarities across social and cultural contexts in relationships between surveillance forces and individual resistance. Everyone experiences a sense of fear and apprehension when the power of surveillance is turned upon an activity that is forbidden. At such moments, power inequalities are affirmed and viscerally embodied through the very acts that seek to circumvent or attenuate them. If we resist those powers, it may not be as noble as a mother feeding her children, but it is still a form of resistance to surveillance and a vital contribution to the ongoing development of power relationships.

Conclusion: everyday resistance and the (necessarily) implicit critique of surveillance

By its very nature, much everyday resistance is hidden—everyday resistance is the non-confrontational, below-the-radar means by which people quietly meet their needs. Scholarly failures to recognize these hidden patterns and transcripts have fueled important discussion about the historiography of class conflict and political struggle (Scott 1985: 292–97). But in the context of surveillance studies, the invisibility of everyday resistance takes on a different and greater meaning because surveillance counts on and develops a politics of visibility while everyday resistance counts on and develops a politics of invisibility. The secrets of everyday resistance are fundamentally contrary to the principles of surveillance in ways that more public and typical forms of opposition to surveillance cannot be. There is, therefore, a sense in which practices of everyday resistance against surveillance do more than merely trick the monitoring program in question. Because these acts of resistance are typically hidden, they also offer a broader ideological challenge to the forced visibility that is central to surveillance societies. Widespread patterns of everyday resistance carry with them a necessary challenge to the very organizing principles of the surveillance society and are, therefore, far more important than a simple, straight-on assessment of their political and social importance might suggest.

Along these lines, Kirstie Ball writes that "(w)e should seek to break circuits of knowledge, information, and threat by silencing ourselves—by not giving up information in an age where it is so valued as a commodity" (Ball 2010: 99). This is an apt recognition of the dynamic and imperative of everyday resistance, which, at the same time, points to the threat that resistance practices are becoming all the more difficult to sustain. That everyday resistance uses the shadows and blind spots and requires refusal and masking means that practices of resistance will become increasingly difficult to exercise as rhizomic patterns of surveillance create an increasingly dense, multi-perspective visibility and as people are effectively coerced into self-disclosure to participate in society. "Not giving up information" may simply become an unsustainable choice as institutions and actors increasingly demand it for the most mundane transactions and then record, share and compile it in ways that exclude the subject from any meaningful role. Thus, as the various nodes of surveillance are increasingly interwoven, the space necessary to perform everyday resistance will certainly become more restricted and tightly regulated.

All the same, as Fernandez and Huey (2009) remind us, "most forms of surveillance are, from their inception, already embedded in a power dynamic that could, with some help, lead to forms of resistance" (200). This insight, which resonates with Foucault's observation about power being necessarily inflected—and in some senses defined—by resistance, points to always-present latent possibilities for resistance to surveillance. Although surveillance systems are becoming more encompassing and totalizing, amassing data and manipulating people as objects, resistance remains one of the levers by which power relationships can be adjusted, in trivial or significant ways, within the machine of modern life.

References

Anderson, L. and Snow, D. (1995). "The Tainted Relationship: The Commercial Blood Plasma Industry and the Homeless in the United States," *Perspectives on Social Problems* 7: 181–202.

Ball, K. (2010). "Workplace Surveillance: An Overview," *Labor History* 51: 87–106.

de Certeau, M. (1984). *The Practice of Everyday Life*, Berkeley: University of California Press.

Foucault, M. (1978). *The History of Sexuality: An Introduction*, New York: Vintage.

Fernandez, L. A. and Huey, L. (2009). "Editorial: Is Resistance Futile? Thoughts on Resisting Surveillance," *Surveillance & Society*, 6(3): 198–202.

Gilliom, J. (2001). *Overseers of the Poor: Surveillance, Resistance, and the Limits of Privacy*, Chicago, IL: The University of Chicago Press.

Handler, J. (1992). "Postmodernism, Protest, and the New Social Movements," *Law and Society Review*, 26: 697–732.

Marx, G. T. (2003). "A Tack in the Shoe: Neutralizing and Resisting the New Surveillance," *Journal of Social Issues*, 59(2): 369–90.

Monahan, T. and Fisher, J. A. (2011) "Surveillance impediments: Recognising obduracy with the deployment of hospital information systems," *Surveillance & Society*, 9(1/2): 1–16.

Scott, J. (1985). *Weapons of the Weak: Everyday Forms of Peasant Resistance*, New Haven, CT: Yale University Press.

c. Privacy advocates, privacy advocacy and the surveillance society

Colin J. Bennett

Introduction

Every day numerous stories appear in the print and online media about the latest attempts by governments and businesses to capture and process personal information in the name of better risk management, service delivery or profit accumulation. Some of these practices emerge without much comment or concern; others are debated and tolerated; and others are resisted strenuously, widely and continuously.

The literature on how surveillance is challenged has tended to focus on two distinct processes. On the one hand, there is an enormous variety of work on the institutional and legal responses in the name of protecting privacy, or advancing the cause of personal data protection. This literature has focused on the content of law and the powers and responsibilities of privacy and data protection authorities and has drawn important lessons about what works and what does not. In recent years, it has become obvious that other non-legal policy instruments, of a self-regulatory and technological nature, are also necessary (Bennett and Raab 2006). A second set of responses resides at the individual level. Gary Marx has categorized the range of inventive strategies that individuals use in their day-to-day lives to subvert, distort, block and avoid surveillance (Marx 2003). John Gilliom documents similar techniques, often not conceived in traditional privacy terms, which poor people have used to resist intrusions by an over-bearing state (Gilliom 2001). These strategies have proliferated in the online environment as individuals surf, e-mail, blog and network anonymously or pseudonymously.

Between, or beyond, formal institutional responses on the one hand, and individual resistance on the other, there is of course the possibility of collective action through pressure groups, non-governmental organizations and/or social movements. Until recently, however, there has been little written about this form of response in any of the literature. The prevailing view is that privacy protection laws have generally arisen as a result of pressure and bargaining among elites, and has downplayed the role of civil society organizations in the larger story about the development of privacy rights in advanced industrial states. Some even regard the ragbag collection of privacy advocates that has emerged over the years as a marginal and disorganized irritant, more intent on grabbing headlines than effecting lasting social change. That general perception has led to skepticism about whether a broader "politics" of privacy protection would ever be possible.

The Privacy Advocates (Bennett 2008) attempted to fill a gap in the literature, and convince readers that this general perception is inaccurate and unfair. The more I looked, the more privacy advocates I found who, with courage, dedication, and ingenuity were pushing organizations to be more responsible and regulators to be more proactive. In every advanced industrial society, there exists one group or more whose self-defined mission is to advance the cause of personal privacy, and to campaign against excessively intrusive technologies and practices. Many privacy advocates work with few financial and human resources. At the same time, many of them have discovered creative ways to make a difference and to influence policy and practice.

Given the central importance of privacy protection, not only as a fundamental human right, but also as a prerequisite for securing citizen and consumer trust in international computer networks, the central role of privacy advocacy assumes a huge importance. Privacy advocates normally display a considerable technical sophistication and have therefore been prominent in the debates over the last decade about the future of the internet. In publicizing the problems associated with third-party cookies, spyware, key-escrow encryption schemes, or the personal information practices of a Microsoft, Google, or Facebook, their work has been important. The results of conflicts such as these have had significant implications for the future of digitally mediated communications (Bennett 2008: Ch. 5).

The Privacy Advocates was based on extensive documentary analysis and key informant interviews with some of the major privacy advocates in the world. The book allowed me to think through the same problems faced by advocates themselves, and thus to link my scholarship to their practical concerns. This entry updates and builds upon the analysis presented in that work. I begin by presenting a profile of the privacy advocacy network and suggesting a useful typology of both organizations and actors. Despite several dilemmas concerning the framing of the problem(s) in terms of "privacy," I contend that it matters deeply whether the issue is framed in terms of a civil liberty, a human right, a digital right, a consumer problem or in terms of a series of "single issues." These dilemmas are manifested in a deeper tension between the individualistic foundations of the right to privacy, and the collective prerequisites and grievances that tend to animate social movement politics. Nevertheless, while privacy may never mobilize a coherent social movement, it has certainly galvanized an important transnational activist network which engages in a combination of informational, symbolic, accountability and leverage politics (Keck and Sikkink 1998).

A profile of the privacy advocacy network

The opposition to excessive surveillance is generally framed in terms of "privacy advocacy", and those engaged in this critique and resistance are normally referred to as "privacy advocates" (Bennett 2008). The term is used widely, in the media and in the policy community. "Privacy" in the abstract is a cause that few people would wish to oppose, because we all have a subjective interest in the way our personal information is used. So there can be no self-declared counter-movement to the right for citizens to have control over their private space and their private information. There is no "anti-privacy" movement as there is an "anti-abortion" movement, for example.

In a broad sense, the term "privacy advocate" has emerged as shorthand to describe anybody that advances the cause in an official capacity, such as staff in data protection authorities, or chief privacy officers in government. However, there is also a sense that a privacy advocacy community exists as a relatively distinct network from those who are mandated to advance the cause within corporations or government agencies. There is a distinction between those who are paid to promote privacy protection, and those who emerge more spontaneously from civil society to promote the public interest, and act as the "gatekeepers" between a concerned but poorly informed citizenry and the organizations that process personal information. Governments and business also "reach out" to the privacy advocacy community by drawing them into consultative and advisory exercises (Bennett 2008: 169–97).

At an individual level, some self identify more as "activists" than advocates, focusing more on grassroots mobilization and a more uncompromising articulation of the value rather than a negotiation with competing social interests (Davies 1999). Activism tends to be rooted in the belief that real change can only come from below, by challenging the conditions that give rise to the perceived threats in the first place. Most privacy advocates have to engage in other activities—research and teaching, hardware and software development, journalism or various forms of artistic expression. Particularly controversial is the relationship between the role of advocate and that of the consultant. Some privacy advocates find it difficult to resist the temptation to take money for advice, public speaking, research, training or education. Most self-identified privacy advocates wear a number of hats, and juggle several responsibilities, some of which can entail significant conflicts of interest.

There are no easy generalizations about what motivates individuals to become interested in advocating for this cause. They are: men and women, black and white, gay and straight, young and old, rich and poor, and so on. Some are active churchgoers; most are not. Most have higher levels of education, though their educational backgrounds are extremely diverse—humanities, sciences, medicine, business, social sciences, law, librarianship, computer science and others. A few have personal experience of damaging privacy intrusions; most do not. They also come from every wing of the ideological spectrum. It is probably the case that most advocates share a somewhat centre-left, civil-libertarian political perspective. Others would find sympathies with an anti-capitalist or anti-globalization agenda (Webb 2007). Some spring from a libertarian philosophy of minimal governmental intervention (Harper 2006). Yet others find favor with those on the Christian right (Albrecht and McIntyre 2006). Privacy advocacy has no conventional ideology; it can be promoted and opposed by those from all political and partisan positions.

From any review of the universe of groups who agitate against surveillance (see www.privacyadvocates.ca), it is immediately obvious that the modern policy issue, defined as privacy in the United States and data protection in Europe, has sustained few advocacy groups whose sole interests are in these issues. There are exceptions, such as Privacy International, the Privacy Rights Clearinghouse, the Electronic Privacy Information Center (EPIC) or the Australian Privacy Foundation. But in most countries, the privacy advocacy role is inextricably linked to broader civil liberties, human rights, consumer or digital freedom questions. Most groups have arisen, therefore, for reasons beyond those of advocating for privacy rights.

It therefore matters profoundly how the issue is perceived and articulated through some broader framework. Some groups, for instance, advocate for privacy as a civil liberty and focus on intrusions by the instruments of the state and (most especially) by law enforcement agencies. The claims of civil liberties advocates tend to be made with reference to specific national constitutional guarantees, such as the Bill of Rights in the United States. Many would insist that privacy is fundamentally a human right, and claim that it is far broader than one among many civil liberties. Claims about privacy as a "human right" tend to be made in more universalistic terms and derive from certain inherent human rights by virtue of our humanity, rather than our citizenship. There is evidence that many groups in developing countries see the close relationship between surveillance and other forms of repression and have embraced a pro-privacy agenda, though they may not frame their agendas in those terms. Privacy issues are often brought to the fore as a result of the practical and inherent problems of campaigning for human rights in repressive regimes.

National and international consumer protection groups have a long involvement with privacy issues. For them, the illegitimate capture, collection, use and disclosure of personal information are all issues of deceptive trading. They have assisted individuals with complaints about consumer credit, direct-marketing, and identity theft as well as with the various consumer services on the internet. Virtually every group mentioned so far has been involved in internet privacy questions. Some, however, have emerged solely as a result of the internet and desires to create an open medium based on sound democratic principles. The notion of a separate set of "digital rights" which are an extension of more fundamental civil rights and liberties underpins the work of a number of national and international organizations, of which the Electronic Frontier Foundation (EFF) is the most prominent example. A final category embraces a sprawling number of single-issue groups which have decided for various reasons to concentrate their efforts on a particular technology or practice (such as RFID chips or video-surveillance), on a type of information (such as genetic information), on a set of vulnerable people (such as children) or on a particular business sector (such as direct marketing).

Traditional concepts do not adequately capture the dynamic, volatile, overlapping and fragmented nature of privacy advocacy. There is certainly no clear structure. Neither is there a social movement with an identifiable base. Perhaps the best label is the "advocacy network" which can be conceptualized as a series of concentric circles. At the centre are a number of privacy-centric groups, such as the Electronic Privacy Information Center (EPIC) in which other issues are peripheral and, if addressed, have to be entirely consistent with the core pro-privacy (or anti-surveillance) message. As we move out of the centre of the circle we encounter a number of privacy-explicit groups for whom privacy protection is one prominent goal among several; many of the civil liberties and digital rights organizations, such as the American Civil Liberties Union (ACLU) or the EFF fall into this category. Within the outer circle, there is an indefinite number of groups, for whom privacy is an implicit or potential goal. Their aims are defined in very different terms—such as defending the rights of women, gays and lesbians, the homeless, children, librarians, ethnic minorities, journalists and so on. Despite not explicitly focusing on privacy issues, the protection of personal information and the restriction of surveillance can be instrumental in promoting their chief aims. There is, therefore, a vast range of groups whose support could be mobilized given the right issue or correct case of intrusive governmental or corporate behavior (Bennett 2008: 57–61).

The privacy advocacy network therefore comprises multiple groups and individuals with varying commitment to the central value of privacy. It is non-hierarchical in the sense that no one group is considered more important than any other. There is no one person who can claim to speak for the network as a whole, any more than there is one group that is representative of the entire movement. It is an open network and has no defined limit, expanding and contracting depending on the issue and the opponent. The agents are consulted not as individuals, but as "privacy advocates" and are presumed to be articulating a public interest in this value. The term carries a significance and implication beyond the individual, and beyond the specific group to which he/she belongs, and often allows them to "punch beyond their weight."

Over the years, attempts to institutionalize that transnational cooperation have found expression in networks such as the European Digital Rights Initiative (EDRI), the Privacy Coalition or the Public Voice Coalition. These initiatives have been important. But the loose and open network of privacy-centric, privacy-explicit and privacy-marginal groups is apparent in many domestic contexts. Privacy advocacy springs from dedicated activists, but it also emerges out of existing civil libertarian, human rights, consumer and digital rights organizations. This pattern is evident in the United States, but in several other countries as well.

The politics of privacy advocacy

So what do privacy advocates do, exactly? The question is straightforward; the answer less so. Clearly any answer has to be framed in transnational terms. Surveillance is a global phenomenon; any challenge must be conceived similarly. In their study of advocacy politics in international politics, Margaret Keck and Katherine Sikkink (1998: 16) employ a fourfold typology of tactics used by international activist networks. Symbolic politics relates to the invocation of symbols, actions, narratives and other symbols to convey the implications and dangers of a particular practice within a particular culture. Accountability politics is about using legal and non-legal policy instruments to hold organizations responsible. Leverage politics implies that there is a threat or a sanction to non-compliance. Information politics relies on the ability to generate politically relevant information and to move it by the most effective means to the place where it will have the most impact.

Within the privacy advocacy network, there is plenty of symbolism on both sides of the debate. Verbal and non-verbal symbols generate attention and reduce the complexity of political problems for ordinary citizens. Over the years, this advocacy network has used the full range of written, audio and visual techniques to advance their arguments. They have always invoked the specter of "Big Brother" to warn of the slippery slopes toward total surveillance. They also engage in a certain amount of lampooning, such as with the annual Big Brother Awards, now organized in several countries. Symbolic interpretation is part of a process by which they can raise awareness, solidify their networks and expand the constituency of believers. But symbolic politics only is effective when it connects to a broader set of cultural understandings, such as when current programs are equated with poignant historical memories.

There are also many opportunities for the privacy advocacy network to call organizations to account. Privacy advocates have occasionally been the authors of high-profile complaints to privacy commissioners. Because of the lack of resources, they more rarely engage in litigation. In most countries, privacy obligations are enshrined within data protection laws, which cover both public and private sectors. Other rules are embodied within international agreements, or in a range of self-regulatory measures, such as codes of practice and privacy seals. Thus, even where legal rules do not exist, privacy advocates can still try to ensure that organizations "live up to their own rules." Once governments and corporations have publicly committed to privacy standards, advocates can use these positions to expose discrepancies between discourse and practice, and possible deception. When that occurs, they have a tendency to want to take immediate and widespread advantage. The revelation, for example, that Google was inadvertently collecting personal Wifi data through its Street View operation immediately provoked complaints to privacy commissioners in Canada, Australia and Europe and to the FTC in the United States.

Leverage politics assumes that the group has some power and that it can get what it wants from those in authority by threatening some cost if there is no change in practice. Possessing resources is the essence of this form of politics, which can be withdrawn if the advocates do not get the reforms they want. Like other public interest groups promoting a public good, their constituency is broad and diffuse. Unlike professional associations or labor unions, they have no ability to mobilize a membership and threaten the withdrawal of electoral or financial support for elected politicians. Thus the leverage politics of privacy advocacy is almost entirely about the loss of reputation or the "mobilization of shame." And privacy advocates have used subtle, and not so subtle, ways to name and shame organizations and individuals, from standard media campaigns to outright boycotts, to efforts to sway the investment decisions of shareholders.

Symbolic, accountability and leverage politics are important elements of privacy advocacy, but they are not the dominant way in which the network tries to advance the arguments. The major resource that privacy advocates possess is information—or, more specifically, expert information about the causes and consequences of surveillance mechanisms, and about the various remedies—legal, self-regulatory and technological.

There is a long tradition within social movement politics of inducing those in power to do something that they would not otherwise do through the constant reporting of facts and testimony about abuses of power and the resulting harms. With few exceptions, however, the information politics of privacy advocacy has generally not been about adopting a "human rights methodology" and about documenting facts relentlessly about actual harms to real people. For the privacy advocate, the politics of information tends to rely upon argumentation about potential consequences. Sometimes the social and individual risks require expert analysis and explanation, and might depend on the confluence of a complex set of institutional motivations and technological development. Information about privacy invasiveness sometimes has to rely on hypothesis rather than fact. It must draw together certain assumptions about what could happen to personally identifiable information if certain worse case scenarios materialized.

At one level, privacy advocates engage in a constant fight to influence the discourse at the earliest stages of system and program developments. This often involves a process of going back to square one and of explaining in philosophical terms the nature of the problem, and perhaps challenging the myth that "If you have nothing to hide, you have nothing to fear." At another level, the argumentation involves extrapolations from the experiences of surveillance systems in other times and places. Increasingly it involves considerable technical expertise, and sophisticated understandings of the operation of complex public and private organizations.

By and large, privacy advocates will try to enter the public debate about a particular practice earlier rather than later, and to generate relevant information about privacy implications in advance of the deployment of a product or service, or in anticipation of policy change. And they need to perform this role with respect to proposals which they support (such as a privacy protection bill), as well as those which they might oppose. Privacy advocates need to decide the appropriate institutional target given the constitutional framework and balance of institutional powers in individual countries. They also face vexing choices about whether to engage in sometimes perfunctory consultation exercises, and whether or not to sign non-disclosure agreements. Privacy advocates can, and do, spend enormous amounts of time injecting written and oral arguments into various stages of the policy cycle, and reacting to policy proposals developed by both executive and legislative agencies at the national level, as well as those by a myriad range of international organizations, including key technical standards bodies, such as the International Standardization Organization (ISO). Advocates have complained of a process of policy laundering, where national governments seek influence in international arenas to pursue controversial schemes, such as biometric passports, unattainable through domestic processes (www.policylaundering.org).

However, some are suspicious of the political process, or are not conveniently located to engage with decision-makers in the "corridors or power." They prefer to engage in public education. Others work well with reporters, are good at media interviews and have that ability to encapsulate the complex policy issue within the pithy one-liners that make good journalism. More rarely, other advocates will attempt to mobilize support on the streets. To the extent that this street-level politics has been encountered, it is entirely associated with high-profile governmental schemes in countries outside North America. In Germany, for instance, there were several early protests in the 1970s and 1980s against the national census, and more recent street activism against the data-retention directive mandating the surveillance of tele-communications traffic data. Identity card schemes have also sparked public protest, such as in Australia in the late 1980s, and more recently in the UK. When the Japanese government established its controversial "Juki Net" system, a national network of registration information on all Japanese residents, protestors shredded their identity cards on the steps of the Home Affairs Ministry.

The privacy advocacy network is therefore confronted with a series of choices and dilemmas within the frameworks of information, symbolic, accountability and leverage politics: whether to engage with governmental agencies and the private sector, to work out differences, establish compromises and advance pragmatic solutions, or to go public; whether to cast their net widely, and advocate for a broad range of privacy interests, or to focus on particular practices; whether to engage in broad and long-term research or to react more pragmatically to the events of the day; whether or not to build a broader constituency with a membership base; and whether or not to accept financial or other support from government and/or the private sector. As in any public interest advocacy network, these tensions create personal rivalries and jealousies, some of which have endured and cemented some entrenched and embittered views about who is true to the cause, and who has "sold out" (Bennett 2008: 129–32).

As an illustration, the recent introduction of "full-body scanners" into airports has been met with each of these forms of political activism. The symbolism of the naked scanned image has been reproduced many times to accentuate the level of intrusiveness. Privacy advocates have attempted to call governments to account by launching complaints to national privacy commissioners, or to the courts in the United States as an "unreasonable search and seizure" under the 4th Amendment. Analysis of the effectiveness and health risks of these scanners has been assembled and targeted to appropriate audiences. On 24 November 2010, activists planned a National Opt-Out Day to protest the use of full-body image scanners at American airports. The leverage stems from the choice of the day before Thanksgiving, and the hope that the consequent delays and line-ups could mobilize sufficient pressure against these new devices. Any contemporary privacy campaign ideally needs, therefore, a combination of information, accountability, leverage and symbolic politics—clear presentation of facts and analysis, ideally backed up by research; a media strategy which presents those facts with symbols that resonate with the wider culture; the skilful use of official avenues of redress, both domestically and internationally; and the judicious use of opportunities to name and shame.

Conclusion: the globalization of privacy advocacy

The Privacy Advocates concluded that the privacy advocacy network is increasing in visibility and significance, and is worth further scholarly research. Interactions within the network are becoming more regular and frequent. There is now a broader recognition that a diverse set of interests can be attracted to particular causes, thus making the network appear more politically significant than in the past. Privacy advocates might thus become more cohesive and institutionalized over time, and result in less pragmatic methods for setting priorities and engaging in campaigns. Any such realization will undoubtedly grow as more horizontal connections are made between privacy advocates internationally.

This process took a further important step with the agreement and publication of the Madrid Privacy Declaration. Coordinated through the Public Voice Coalition, this Declaration was launched at the international conference of Privacy and Data Commissioners in Madrid in October 2009. To date, the Declaration has been signed by over 100 organizations, and around 200 international experts, from many countries including several in the developing world. Among other things, the declaration reaffirms support for the "global framework of fair information practices," the data protection authorities, privacy-enhancing technologies and calls for a "new international framework for privacy protection." More controversially, the Declaration calls for a "moratorium on the development or implementation of new systems of mass surveillance, including facial recognition, whole body imaging, biometric identifiers, and embedded RFID tags, subject to a full and transparent evaluation by independent authorities and democratic debate" (http://thepublicvoice.org/madrid-declaration/).

It is instructive that this Declaration should be framed in terms of the language of "privacy," a concept that has been subject to so much criticism in the academic literature (Bennett 2011). "Privacy" and all that it entails is argued to be too narrow, too based on liberal assumptions about subjectivity, too implicated in rights-based theory and discourse, insufficiently sensitive to the discriminatory aspects of surveillance, culturally relative, overly embroiled in spatial metaphors about "invasion" and "intrusion," and ultimately practically ineffective. The essential difficulty, therefore, is about how to "frame" the issue in ways that define a sense of collective grievance following from excessive surveillance. Can that sense of shared grievance grow when the issue is invariably articulated through the conceptual lens of "privacy"? There is perhaps a fundamental dilemma in trying to energize collective action around an emotive and powerful concept that is derived from a very subjective and individualistic right.

Yet, the term has been remarkably resilient. It attaches to a huge array of policy questions, to a sprawling policy community, to a transnational advocacy network, to an academic literature and to a host of polemical and journalistic commentary. Despite the fact that nobody can supply a precise and commonly accepted definition, privacy maintains an enormous and global appeal, in the English-speaking world and beyond. Witness the fact that the Madrid Privacy Declaration was translated into ten different languages, and was supported by organizations and individuals in every region of the world. Furthermore, and as noted above, it is a term that spans the ideological divide. If one were to try to reframe the discourse in terms of a politics of "anti-surveillance" and to situate it within broader social antagonisms and struggles, these issues immediately become associated with a politics of the left. One can defeat an ID card, or a video-surveillance system, or a genetic database, or a health identifier, or a host of other surveillance measures, without engaging in a broader social "struggle." Perhaps one of the strengths of the contemporary privacy advocacy network, therefore, is that resistance can, and does, spring from a multitude of ideological sources at unpredictable moments.

This is not to say that the language of surveillance cannot be put to good use by the privacy advocacy network. But, with all its contradictions and vagueness, *privacy* is the concept around which this network has coalesced, and will probably evolve. It still carries a broad cultural and transnational appeal. For better or worse, "privacy advocates" have learned to live with it.

References

Albrecht, K. and McIntyre, L. (2006). *The Spychips Threat: Why Christians Should Resist RFID and Electronic Surveillance*, Nashville, TN: Nelson Current.

Bennett, C. J. (2008). *The Privacy Advocates: Resisting the Spread of Surveillance*, Cambridge, MA: MIT Press.

——(2011). "In Defence of Privacy: The Concept and the Regime," *Surveillance & Society*, 8(4): 485–96.

Bennett, C. J. and Raab, C. D. (2006). *The Governance of Privacy: Policy Instruments in Global Perspective*, Cambridge, MA: MIT Press.

Davies, S. (1999). "Spanners in the Works: How the Privacy Movement is Adapting to the Challenge of Big Brother," in C. J. Bennett and R. Grant (eds), *Visions of Privacy: Policy Choices for the Digital Age,* Toronto: University of Toronto Press.

Gilliom, J. (2001). *Overseers of the Poor: Surveillance, Resistance and the Limits of Privacy*, Chicago, IL: University of Chicago Press.

Harper, J. (2006). *Identity Crisis: How Identification is Over-Used and Misunderstood*, Washington, DC: Cato Institute.

Keck, M. E. and Sikkink, K. (1998). *Activists Beyond Borders: Advocacy Networks in International Politics*, Ithaca, NY: Cornell University Press.

Marx, G. (2003). "A Tack in the Shoe: Resisting and Neutralizing the New Surveillance," *Journal of Social Issues*, 59(2): 369–90.

Webb, M. (2007). *Illusions of Security: Global Surveillance and Democracy in the Post-9/11 World*, San Francisco, CA: City Lights.

d. The politics of surveillance

Civil liberties, human rights and ethics

Yasmeen Abu-Laban

Since the 1980s, increased scholarly attention to surveillance has underscored the ubiquity of "watching" historically and contemporaneously. Today, in the face of a growing and even dizzying array of new technologies that may be relied on for convenience, for fun, for personal safety, and for security, scholarly attention to surveillance may be expected to grow still further. It is the contention of this chapter that, as the multidisciplinary field of surveillance studies expands in the second decade of the twenty-first century, more explicit research attention to the politics of surveillance is especially critical. This is because overt attention to politics may fruitfully organize and shape the very questions that scholars ask, and as such contribute in distinctive ways to our collective understanding of the empirical implications of surveillance (what is), as well as the normative implications of surveillance (what ought to be).

To begin to cut into the idea of "politics"—itself an essentially contested concept—this chapter takes as its main focus the civil liberties and human rights dimensions evident in discussions of "surveillance" by scholars, as well as by state and non-state actors. A threefold approach structures the chapter. First, the relevance of civil liberties in surveillance studies work is established. Second, the opportunities (and limits) of a larger human rights framework for surveillance studies scholarship is explored. Finally, some consideration is given to possible reasons why human rights has not, to date, been a major component in surveillance studies scholarship.

I: Civil liberties versus surveillance

Civil liberties concerns the grouping of basic rights pertaining to free speech, due process/fair trial, assembly, voting, and privacy. Much work in surveillance studies has been squarely concerned with privacy rights (see e.g. Goold 2009 Volume II). The focus on privacy stems from several factors that grew in salience over the twentieth century. Privacy is enshrined as a right in most state constitutions (or at least treated as a constitutional principle) and internationally it has come to be viewed as a fundamental human right. A "fundamental" right is essential, in a way that other rights might not be. As well, privacy has been an issue that itself has expanded in significance over time as a result of shifting practices in state and non-state organizations, as well as new information technologies. Such shifts that have drawn the attention of surveillance specialists include the growth of state-issued national identification cards in both the global north and global south, the proliferation of credit cards issues by banks, and the advent of the internet. Additionally, states have variable privacy laws and internal oversight mechanisms (e.g., privacy offices and commissioners in many instances) which in themselves warrant thinking about privacy.

State surveillance projects are not new. Indeed, as argued by political scientist James C. Scott (1998: 2), a central preoccupation of all states is "legibility," that is, arranging the population in ways that simplify traditional state activities such as taxation, conscription, and thwarting civil unrest. However, since September 11 2001, scholarly and popular interest in civil liberties, including privacy, has also followed certain globalized shifts in the policies of states. For example, the intensification of surveillance in Europe and in North America in the context of "the war on terror" was made possible by new information technologies, and can involve data mining, and data sharing. Legislative changes, evident in many Western countries, have also facilitated intensified surveillance. As one instance, the 2001 *Uniting and Strengthening America by Providing Appropriate Tools Required to Intercept and Obstruct Terrorism Act* (hereafter the PATRIOT Act) expanded the authority of immigration officials to track, detain and deport non-citizens, and also eased the restrictions on law enforcement personnel searching communications (such as email and telephone communications) as well as financial and other records (including library records). The American Civil Liberties Union, among others, has repeatedly criticized the PATRIOT Act for infringing on the due process rights of non-citizens, and the privacy of innocent Americans. Yet, the possible challenges to civil liberties is even further amplified as technologies and surveillance policies from Western states may be exported to other countries, potentially losing even rudimentary protections in the process (United Nations 2009: 31). This has prompted the call, from within the United Nations, for a program to develop "global capacity building on privacy protection," seen to be especially needed to protect individual dignity in the context of anti-terrorism measures (United Nations 2009: 34).

Other trends and developments of the twenty-first century have also contributed to examining the relationship between surveillance and civil liberties. One is online social networking sites, as exemplified by two American-based services: Facebook (introduced in 2004) and Twitter (introduced in 2006). The implications of online social networking for the expansion or retraction of civil liberties have yet to be fully considered in comparative and international contexts. On the one hand, as these new forms of social networking have grown in popularity, they may be argued to represent an example of voluntary self-disclosure of personal information, feeding into a recreational form of surveillance which can allow access to information about others. Yet, even seemingly voluntarily given information may potentially carry risks to privacy and civil liberties. On the other hand, as part of an increasingly global cultural shift, social networking has also been relevant to civil society mobilization and fostering political expression, as exemplified by what has come to be referred to as the "Arab Spring"—the wave of democratizing movements that flourished in countries of the Middle East and North Africa in 2011. It is significant that just weeks prior to his resignation, in January 2011, Egyptian President Hosni Mubarak took the dramatic step of shutting down Egypt's internet and cell phone services in hopes of stemming the tide of political protest seen to be fuelled through communications on Facebook, Twitter and other sites.

Civil liberties are also of concern in light of other surveillance trends. These include the growing normalization of camera surveillance in public spaces (on the streets, in universities, in businesses), the use of digital face recognition cameras as well as body scanning in airports, a thriving "homeland security" industry post-September 11, and graphic and unprecedented examples of various levels of state agencies—and sometimes private agencies—collaborating in a securitized environment (what has been termed variously a fusion of security or integration of security). The bringing together of local and national security forces with private agencies, as well as American security forces, was exemplified in Canada in 2010 during the Winter Olympics in Vancouver. Likewise, the G8/G20 summit meeting held in Toronto the same year featured an integrated security unit. Both events led to accusations of breaches of privacy and civil liberties of citizens and non-citizens alike, with the Toronto G8/G20 being portrayed as an historically unprecedented peace-time violation of civil liberties by the province of Ontario's Ombudsman André Marin.

The evident and growing obsession with "security" at national and transnational levels cuts across many surveillance trends, and may involve both state and non-state actors. However, differentiating the implications of state breaches of privacy (and their relation to civil liberties) would benefit from consideration within a broader *human rights framework*. A human rights framework can also widen and deepen the questions that are asked, and be instrumental in encouraging greater thinking about the normative guideposts in which the *status quo* is defended, or alternatives are imagined. Given that surveillance is omnipresent, a human rights framework may also assist in illuminating the unequal impact of surveillance on specific collectivities.

II: Human rights as an empirical and normative framework

While surveillance studies specialists are often quick to point out that surveillance is not "new" (even if its particular growth, or intensification, or forms may be), students of human rights tend to be highly sensitized to the recentness of human rights as a discourse. The term "human rights" gained popular purchase only after the Second World War, and is widely seen to mark a response to the horrific atrocities committed by Nazi Germany. As such, the Preamble of the *Charter of the United Nations* holds that signatory states "reaffirm faith in fundamental human rights, in the dignity and worth of the individual person, in the equal rights of men and women and of nations large and small." As well, Article 1 stipulates that a major purpose of the United Nations lies "in promoting and encouraging respect for human rights and for fundamental freedoms for all without distinction as to race, sex, language or religion."

These commitments in the UN Charter were given further amplification by the United Nations General Assembly, which in 1948 passed the *Universal Declaration of Human Rights*. The Universal Declaration holds that "all human beings are born free and equal in dignity and rights" (Article 1) and that "everyone is entitled to all the rights and freedoms set forth in this Declaration, without distinction of any kind, such as race, colour, sex, language, religion, political or social opinion, national or social origin, property, birth or other status." The bulk of the Declaration's 30 articles concentrate on civil and political rights (Articles 3–21, with Article 12 specifically recognizing a right to privacy); to a lesser extent the Declaration also deals with economic, social and cultural rights (Articles 22–27). The 1948 Universal Declaration was significant for recognizing, for the first time at an international level, that human rights and freedoms were applicable to all people in all places. The *Universal Declaration of Human Rights*, in concert with the *International Covenant on Economic, Social and Cultural Rights* (1966) and the *International Covenant on Civil and Political Rights*, along with its *Optional Protocols* (1966; 1989), are collectively referred to as the "International Bill of Human Rights" and further enshrine as human rights principles both of self-determination and development.

The *Universal Declaration of Human Rights* is also significant for symbolically ushering in what has come to be referred to as "the human rights revolution." This might be seen as "revolutionary" from the stand point of 1948 since the UN was then composed of merely 58 countries precisely because so many of the peoples comprising the current 192 UN member states were under colonial rule, and colonized peoples were often viewed as inferior by colonizers. It may also be seen as "revolutionary" from the standpoint of the long history of social and political thought. Of course, arguably, elements of the idea that people are equal because of their shared humanness—or what liberals refer to as the principle of equal moral worth— can be found in earlier philosophical traditions as well as religious traditions (including Judaism, Christianity and Islam). However, it is the *popularization* of the idea of the equal worth of persons that is significant. This popularization is evident in how the Universal Declaration has been incorporated into the constitutions of many countries, and translated now in to close to 400 different languages. And this popularization is also evident in how claims have continued to be advanced in relation to rights, producing still more international UN conventions and declarations including on the rights of women (1979), children (1989) and indigenous peoples (2007).

As at the international level, at national levels human rights have incorporated individual and group claims. For instance, it is argued that, in Canada, the 1971 national policy of multiculturalism, and its constitutional enshrinement in the 1982 *Canadian Charter of Rights and Freedoms*, was a domestic response to the larger human rights revolution; and the subsequent post-Cold War embrace of multiculturalism within international organizations like the United Nations is also attributed to the human rights revolution (Kymlicka 2007). The European Union's *Charter of Fundamental Rights*, which came into force in 2009 through the Lisbon Treaty, also reflects the expanding scope of rights. The EU Charter variously recognizes the rights of children, the rights of the elderly, a right to fair and just working conditions, a right to collective bargaining and action, a right to social security, a right to health care, a right to environmental protection and, notably in light of the preceding discussion on privacy, a right to protection of personal data.

It can be anticipated that surveillance studies specialists will be compelled to focus on the possibilities and limits of data protection in the European Union, but it would be misleading to confine such a focus to privacy rights, or to neglect the continued relevance of national states in this international organization. This is because privacy is expressly seen to relate to other civil liberties, as well as state power. This is plainly stated in a document aimed at EU citizens spelling out "your rights as a data subject," in which it is noted, tellingly under "exceptions and limitations," that it is left to Member States to "establish exceptions" and "strike a balance in their data protection laws" since "the right to privacy may sometimes conflict with freedom of expression and in particular, freedom of the press and media."[1] Relatedly, breaches of privacy may impact other human rights, and this has been acknowledged in the United Nations. As noted by Martin Scheinin, the UN Human Rights Council Special Rapporteur on the Promotion and Protection of Human Rights and Fundamental Freedoms While Countering Terrorism:

> Surveillance regimes adopted as anti-terrorism measures have had a profound, chilling effect on other fundamental human rights. In addition to constituting a right in itself, privacy serves as a basis for other rights and without which the other rights would not be effectively enjoyed. Privacy is necessary to create zones to allow individuals and groups to be able to think and develop ideas and relationships. Other rights such as freedom of expression, association, and movement all require privacy to be able to develop effectively. Surveillance has also resulted in miscarriages of justice, leading to failures of due process and wrongful arrest.
>
> *(United Nations 2009: 19)*

Illustrating this point in and outside of liberal democratic contexts, Scheinin observes that in the United Kingdom, where surveillance cameras keep stored images now routinely taken from peaceful protests, a 2009 poll found fully one in three respondents were wary of engaging in any protest activity because of privacy concerns (United Nations 2009: 21). In the United States, Maryland State Police placed peaceful environmental protestors on "terrorist watch lists" (United Nations 2009: 21). And Iran was able to take advantage of the fact that lawful standards for intercepting communications requires communications companies to purposely design weaknesses in their technology. These intentional vulnerabilities have allowed the state to monitor the communications of protesters (United Nations 2009: 26).

David Lyon has introduced the useful concept of "social sorting" into the scholarly lexicon to capture the potential for surveillance to have disproportionate consequences on specific groups (an idea not captured in the more individualistic concept of "privacy"). In other words, rather than being neutral, or impacting seemingly random individuals, forms of surveillance may sustain or even create group-based harm, through for example, racial profiling (see Lyon 2003a). This insight has taken on renewed significance in the context of increased public debate in liberal-democratic countries over the legitimacy of ethnic/racial profiling by state officials in the "war on terrorism". Profiling in this context typically involves state security or immigration officials specifically targeting those who are (or are seen to be) Muslim and/or Arab. While not rejecting a focus on privacy, Lyon seeks to embolden the study of other surveillance consequences. As Lyon articulates it:

> Those who worry about privacy should not be discouraged from querying intensified surveillance. But they would also do well to move beyond the rampant individualism that perceives only 'snoops' to

consider the serious social consequences of the 'sorters' who categorize and profile, to assess and influence people's life chances.

(Lyon 2003b: 165)

Taking up a human rights framework, rather than simply privacy, or civil liberties, is one important avenue into a serious discussion about the potentially manifold effects of surveillance signaled in the important concept of "social sorting." More specifically, it may help to address the concern raised by Kevin Haggerty that, as the concept of "social sorting" has travelled from Lyon's own careful work, and come to be used by other scholars, they have not always attended to making explicit the "normative criteria" by which a specific instance of social sorting may reasonably be judged to be "unfair, unjust or inequitable" (Haggerty 2009: xvii).

If a human rights framework is considered, the consequences of surveillance in general, and under conditions of securitization post-9/11 in the global north in particular, may allow analysts to organize extant and emerging findings in a new way. Even the most cursory overview of the topics explored under the rubric of "surveillance" today reveals how variable are its sites and its targets. No doubt as the geography of surveillance differs (consider the contrast of home, schools, airports, borders, and skies), and the targets of surveillance differ (consider the contrast of the infant electronically monitored by loving parents with the racialized immigrant monitored by the state), this may encourage thinking about surveillance as ambiguous. And, it may indeed be difficult to make "definitive conclusions" about the implications across a range of what Haggerty refers to as "each discrete surveillant assemblage" (Haggerty 2009: xvii). However, a framework explicitly attuned to human rights—how they are enhanced, and how they are diminished—may assist in sharpening attention to the victims and beneficiaries across each.

In the post-9/11 period, publics in liberal-democratic countries of the global north have frequently encountered the argument, especially articulated in relation to the rapid passage of new anti-terrorism measures (like the PATRIOT Act in the United States or Canada's *Anti-Terrorism Act* of 2001), that "security" is being balanced against "freedom." In many ways the focus on privacy allows for a reification of this tension as the main (if not only) "trade off." A human rights framework however immediately signals to analysts a larger range of questions that might profitably be investigated since human rights have come to focus on both individual and group claims. From this vantage point it might be asked what does (intensified) surveillance mean for multicultural rights? What does (intensified) surveillance mean for indigenous rights? What does (intensified) surveillance mean for gender and racial equality? Not least, what does (intensified) surveillance mean for development? It is this last question that may be especially relevant to consider in light of the fact that surveillance studies emerged primarily in countries of the industrialized West (especially the United States and Britain) and is only now beginning to grapple with the similarities and differences in the global south, as well as conflict zones like the Occupied Palestinian Territories (see Zureik, Lyon and Abu-Laban 2011). A comparative frame of reference can generate a more comprehensive, as well as nuanced, understanding. For example, identification cards seem to carry very contextually specific meanings in relation to the expansion or contraction of human rights and citizenship rights for specific groups and in specific polities (Lyon 2009: 131–35). In light of the post-9/11 intensification of surveillance in the context of a global "war on terrorism," attention to a bigger range of world regions, their complex and varied histories, their place in the global political economy including in relation to surveillance industries, laws and practices, is especially warranted.

Since a human rights framework is not merely legal, but also expresses ongoing and evolving aspirational claims, it presents a normative vision in itself. It should be stressed therefore that the potential scholarly value of considering this framework for surveillance studies is not necessarily the same thing as advocating for its normative vision. In point of fact, while the theoretical/political/scholarly positions on human rights discourse are extremely divergent, they can be crudely divided into two camps. On one side, there are those who uphold the universal applicability and possibilities of human rights discourse. On the other side, there are those who argue that human rights discourse actually masks something more important: for some, it hides the continued relevance of national citizenship—and therefore the state—in actually protecting (or not protecting) rights; for others human rights conceals ethnocentric (Western) and/or secular values or interests; for still others human rights obscures the perpetuation of inequitable social relations including those of class and gender.

Liberal human rights, in short, can be legitimately criticized from a number of different perspectives and a range of alternative (including non-liberal) positions may be advanced. If the emphasis on the moral worth of persons is incomplete, to what should we attach moral worth? As just one example, a feminist care ethic approach would insist on the moral worth of relationships of care, and may attune us to other dimensions of human needs, and the kinds of institutions and practices that are necessary to meet these needs. Because a human rights framework inevitably provokes such normative debates, its explicit incorporation may complement the empirical findings that have emerged, and continue to emerge, in surveillance studies.

Already the importance of the normative dimension is recognized in certain scholarship in the field of surveillance studies. In his empirical examination of the qualitative shifts, and widening scope, of surveillance of the post-9/11 period and its specific social sorting (specifically "racial profiling") consequences for those defined, variously, as Arab/Middle Eastern/Muslim, Lyon devotes his concluding pages to underscoring still other normative issues. There are, he says, "questions that ought to be asked" not least of which is "What kind of world do we want to live in?" (2003b: 164). As Lyon avers:

> As I hinted at the start of this book, an appropriate ethic begins by hearing the voice of the Other. And social care starts with acceptance—not suspicion of the Other. Such an ethic does not exist in a cultural vacuum, however. It grows like green shoots in the soil of shared visions of desired worlds. But such visions seem in short supply today, when history is downplayed by mass media and securing the present preoccupies politicians.
>
> *(2003b: 166)*

It is precisely this kind of articulation that suggests the value of a greater conversation about ethics in surveillance. The human rights framework may assist in this, because whether it is normatively advanced or even rejected, it focuses attention on ethics.

To summarize then, the human rights framework—present in law and in the constitutions of many states—may sensitize us to some of the empirical implications of surveillance in a way that is cognizant of differential outcomes for specific social groups. In other words, it offers a more comprehensive approach than simply a focus on privacy or civil liberties. The human rights framework may assist in suggesting responses to surveillance, since state forms of surveillance may carry especially injurious consequences for specific collectivities. Not least, the human rights framework, because it is debatable on normative grounds, may also serve as an entry point into numerous other normative analyses (feminist care ethics, etc., see Stoddart, this volume) that may enable a larger conversation about human needs in relation to surveillance.

III: Surveillance studies: Foucault, the state and society

Given the above points about privacy, civil liberties, and human rights, it can be asked why a human rights framework has not been a strong feature of extant surveillance studies scholarship? In a nutshell, the answer may be seen to lie in how a human rights framework still brings with it a strong emphasis on the state, or formal politics. At a domestic level, human rights discourse draws attention to the relationship between the state (and its laws and constitution) and the citizen. And, even though there has been a "human rights revolution" which has made human rights part of an international discourse, the ongoing debate about whether the state is still central to rights protection, also tends to draw attention to formal politics. The case of refugees is instructive here. Writing prior to the Second World War, Hannah Arendt famously highlighted how a person's "right to have rights" was contingent on membership in a state. Following the Second World War, despite the growth of a strong discourse, backed by international agreements around human rights, including the rights of refugees, many scholars emphasize the power of states in receiving and in granting (or not) rights to refugees and other migrants.

Three observations can be made about the field of surveillance studies which may provide clues into why the formal politics of the state (and by extension a human rights framework) has not been a major feature. The first relates to the influence of the work of Michel Foucault in surveillance studies. Foucault's concepts of "disciplinary power" and "panopticon" as well as "biopower" grace the pages of much work in surveillance studies until now. The continued popularity and utility of a concept like "panopticon" has been questioned by specialists (see Haggerty 2009). However, Foucault's work also defines in very distinct ways the idea of government, and this understanding is different from much of the work attuned to the state (whether from Marxist, feminist or the dominant Weberian perspective). In particular, Foucault sees government as not merely concerning the legal-formal institutions and practices of the state, but rather that government involves *all* endeavors which shape the conduct of others.

Second, while there are certainly examples of works in which surveillance and state power were linked—from novelist George Orwell's classic on totalitarianism *1984* to journalist David Burnham's treatment of America in *The Rise of the Computer State* (1983) which addressed rapidly evolving digital technologies—overall the intellectual climate of the 1980s encouraged reconsideration of the centrality of "the state" in the social sciences. This is relevant insofar as surveillance studies as an academic field took flight during the 1980s. Yet, at the exact same time, across different disciplines of the social sciences, analysts also began to grapple with the portent of the flows—of people, of information, of capital—associated with contemporary forms of globalization. With growing force by the late 1990s, there was a challenge to the rigid methodological nationalism that had structured much post-Second World War social science in its portrayal of national states (or national societies) as the "natural" form of the modern world. This in turn opened the way for greater consideration of larger forces beyond the national "state"/"society" context, even if these two concepts remain embedded in the lexicon of the social sciences.

Third, for reasons of distinctive disciplinary tradition, and the breadth of possible sociological inquiry, sociologists have been at the forefront of contributing to the multidisciplinary area of surveillance studies. This may also be why the surveillance studies literature strongly retains a traditional orienting concept of the discipline of sociology: society. This is exemplified in the frequent references, growing theorization, and growing popular purchase of the concept of "surveillance society." By way of contrast, the language/concept of a "surveillance state" is less featured in the current literature, perhaps because practitioners in disciplines for which the state has been a central orienting concept (especially political science, as well as law and philosophy) have been relatively slower in reflecting on, or contributing to, extant findings in surveillance studies. Not incidentally, it is also practitioners in the disciplines of political science, law and philosophy (especially political philosophy) who are frequently attuned to the "stuff" of human rights: constitutions, laws, conventions/agreements, and ethics.

Quite apart from human rights, the state is also relevant to consider in relation to agency and power. The recent work of political scientist Colin Bennett (2008) on privacy advocates in the United States, Canada, Australia and countries of Europe, points to the scholarly neglect of questions such as who mobilizes against surveillance, how, and with what effect? (2008: x). Although Bennett is careful to nuance his discussion of the state in relation to globalization, his findings, based on personal interviews with civil society activists, are instructive as concerns the continued relevance of the state in one critical strategy for advancing privacy protection. As Bennett describes it:

> Much of their activity involves generating politically relevant information about privacy protection and moving it to where it will have the most impact. Thus many privacy advocates perform a range of fairly traditional advocacy functions in relation to the official agencies of the state. They give

testimony. They comment on legislative and administrative proposals for new uses of personal information. They generate research and analysis.

(2008: xiv)

In considering the foregoing discussion, surveillance studies practitioners have clearly made extensive contributions in the past three decades, and it can be expected that the area will continue to grow in the decade to come, building on this scholarly legacy. Greater cross-disciplinary engagement would be beneficial to bringing the findings of surveillance studies to bear more closely across all disciplines of the human sciences, and greater participation from specialists in such disciplines as political science, philosophy and law may help in further advancing the empirical and ethical dimensions of surveillance studies. As a starting point, moving from an emphasis on privacy and/or civil liberties to a human rights framework may be catalytic in potentiating the politics of surveillance.

Note

1 See the European Union *Data Protection in the European Union* guide, available at http://ec.europa.eu/justice/policies/privacy/docs/guide/guide-ukingdom_en.pdf.

References

Bennett, C. J. (2008). *The Privacy Advocates: Resisting the Spread of Surveillance*, Cambridge, MA and London: MIT Press.

Burnham, D. (1983). *The Rise of the Computer State*, New York: Random House.

Goold, B. J. (ed.) (2009). *Surveillance: Critical Concepts in Criminology* (Volumes I-IV), London and New York: Routledge.

Haggerty, K. D. (2009). "Foreword," in *Surveillance: Power, Problems, and Politics,* Vancouver: UBC Press, pp. ix-xviii.

Kymlicka, W. (2007). *Multicultural Odysseys: Navigating the New International Politics of Diversity*, Oxford: Oxford University Press.

Lyon, D. (ed.). (2003a). *Surveillance as Social Sorting: Privacy, Risk and Digital Discrimination*, London: Routledge.

Lyon, D. (2003b). *Surveillance After September 11*, Cambridge: Polity Press.

Lyon, D. (2009). *Identifying Citizens: ID Cards and Surveillance*, Cambridge: Polity Press.

Scott, J. C. (1998). *Seeing Like a State: How Certain Schemes to Improve the Human Condition Have Failed*, New Haven, CT and London: Yale University Press.

United Nations. Human Rights Council. (2009). *Promotion and Protection of All Human Rights, Civil, Political, Economic, Social, and Cultural Rights, Including the Right to Development* (Report of the Special Rapporteur on the Promotion and Protection of Human Rights and Fundamental Freedoms while Countering Terrorism, Martin Scheinin), A/HRC/13/37 (28 December).

Zureik, E., Lyon, D. and Abu-Laban, Y. (eds). (2011). *Surveillance and Control in Israel/Palestine: Population, Territory and Power*, London: Routledge.

Index